CONTENTS

ACKNOWLEDGEMENTS

We wish to acknowledge the valuable contributions of the following who have submitted information and provided photographs which have greatly enhanced this edition.

Richard Abdy *(The British Museum)*
Tony Abramson
Dr Martin Allen *(Fitzwilliam Museum)*
Dr Mark Blackburn *(Fitzwilliam Museum)*
Joe Bispham
Nigel Clark
Chris Comber
Barrie Cook *(The British Museum)*
Geoff Cope
Simon Cope
Jonathan Cope
Dave Craddock
Joe Cribb *(The British Museum)*
Mike Cuddeford
Paul Davies
Paul Dawson
Tim Everson
David Fletcher
Glen Gittoes
Megan Gooch
David Guest
Dr John Hulett
Peter Jackson
Richard Kelleher *(The British Museum)*
Geoff Kitchen
Ian Leins *(The British Museum)*
Joe Linzalone
Mark Rasmussen
The Schneider Family
Dr Irving Schneider
May Sinclair
Peter D Spencer
Andrew Wayne
Tim Webb-Ware
Walter Wilkinson
Barry Williams
Gareth Williams *(The British Museum)*
Paul & Bente R. Withers
Peter Woodhead

Museums/Institutions
The Trustees of the British Museum, London
The Fitzwilliam Museum, Cambridge

Photography
Richard Hodges
Paul & Bente R. Withers
Andrew Williams

PREFACE

Thank you for buying the new 43rd edition of Coins of England, still the most comprehensive and accurate single-volume reference work featuring market values for every major coin type from ancient Celtic Britain to the present day.

It was always tradition for this book to appear on the shelves during September; however, with last year's edition appearing later than usual in November due to the changeover to full colour printing it allowed us to also incorporate much more up-to-date pricing information based on the busy 'Coinex' week of auctions in London. We therefore feel that a November release date makes this catalogue more relevant, taking in statistics from the entire year in the coin trade.

'Coinex' week this year proved that the market was as buoyant as ever for English coins, our own auction at Spink on 27 September realising a staggering total of £1,914,747 with several items selling for as much as twenty times their estimates!

The highlight of the sale was our featured cover coin for this year's Coins of England, the Charles II 'Petition' Crown by Thomas Simon which sold for an astounding £207,100. This numismatic masterpiece is the creation of the great engraver, Thomas Simon. Following the Restoration of the Monarchy Charles II ordered trials for a milled coinage from the Royal Mint. Simon, aggrieved that he had not been given the commission, was determined to win the King over and be chosen as the official designer with his clever concepts.

Thomas Simon engraved the dies for this Crown featuring a bust of Charles II on the obverse with "Simon" engraved just below the King's clothed neckline. The "Petition" is two hundred raised letters in two lines around the coin's rim which is only 35mm in depth and reads:

THOMAS SIMON MOST HVMBLY PRAYS YOVR MAJESTY TO COMARE THIS HIS TRYALL PIECE WITH THE DVTCH AND IF MORE TRVLY DRAWN & EMBOSS'D MORE GRACE; FVLLY ORDER'D AND MORE ACCURATELY ENGRAVEN TO RELIEVE HIM

The "Petition" Crown was presented at the King's court, an incident recorded by Samuel Pepys in his diary. Simon's engraving was greatly admired and won him a position at the Royal Mint as one of the Chief Engravers. Whilst it is a 'Pattern' piece and not issued for circulation it is nevertheless one of the finest English coins ever struck.

Work is always in progress to improve this book but errors do creep in and many of those which found their way in to last year's edition have been picked up by the keen eyes of collectors and specialists. Thank you to everyone who took the time to write to us with comments, both positive and negative, it all helps to upgrade, with you, the user in mind. We encourage more feedback but do stress that the book is intended to be a guide to the standard types of English coinage and not a specialised work and many of the suggestions that we receive simply are not practical to include in this book. If you are looking for more detailed information about your coins then we refer you to the bibliography in Appendix I, most of the titles quoted there are available from the Book Department at Spink where we stock thousands of titles on coins.

Don't forget that as well as holding auctions of coins, Spink are active dealers in coins, medals, banknotes and stamps and we would be pleased to hear from you if you are looking for that elusive item for your collection or if you are thinking of selling, please feel free to contact one of our specialists.

If you are in London, why not call in to meet with us at our newly refurbished showroom in central London where you always will find a warm welcome and expert advice on hand.

Happy collecting, until next year.

Philip Skingley
Editor, Coins of England

MARKET TRENDS

The market for British coins remains very strong indeed. Prices continue to grow though the emphasis is more than ever on higher grade rarities especially those which carry a weighty provenance. At this top end of the market the conditions remain where a limited supply is met with a growing demand. The past year has seen the arrival in the market of new buyers attracted to coins by the relative affordability vis-à-vis other collectables.

On average we see a rise of 15% in the values for the top quoted grade of very fine in the hammered series against only a 6% overall rise in prices in the fine grade. In the early milled series values given for coins in extremely fine condition have on average risen some 11% against a rise of only 4% for specimens in very fine condition. The later milled, the bread and butter of much of the numismatic business, remains vibrant with rare dates continuing to rise; on average around 10%.

Certain series have performed particularly well. At a memorable sale in Copenhagen in December of 2006 an extremely fine London monogram type portrait penny of Alfred the Great fetched £13,000 - more than double the previous record for this popular coin. Such prices are indicative of the growth of interest in the Saxon series, in particular portrait Pennies from the middle period, and collectors now appreciate the rarity of this series in the higher grades. Common late Saxon pennies are selling strongly and frequently attract multiple orders when listed in the Numismatic Circular.

Medieval hammered silver remains a popular series though it would be interesting to see how prices would respond should a quality collection of choice specimens appear for sale. The large but mixed grade Ivan Buck collection sold by Spink in November 2005 was readily absorbed by the market but there has been no comparable offering since. Handsome medieval gold type coins are selling particularly well.

The demand for quality Tudor and Stuart remains insatiable. The attraction for selling in the current conditions is obvious though many established collectors continue to hold clearly confident in future market growth. Formed over the last 25 years the Dr Ferrari collection of Crowns was sold by Spink in June 2007, and clearly demonstrated how impressive the returns could be with extremely fine hammered Crowns realising double the level they were making in the Van Roekel sale in 2001.

The Spink Coinex week sale on the 27th of September 2007 continued the tradition of producing record prices. The highlight was the 'Glenister' Petition Crown of Charles II which made an astonishing £207,000 the first British silver coin to break the £200,000 level. The previous record was also held by a Petition Crown, the Slaney specimen sold by Spink in 2003 for £138,000.

In addition to the Glenister collection this sale also offered an excellent selection of English silver and gold coins. Four Tudor Sovereigns all sold well above high estimate and a very rare Commonwealth Unite dated 1660 with mint mark anchor grossed £32,300, the same coin sold for £4840 in 1988. The strength of the milled series in top grade was clear with some big prices for large gold in extremely fine or better; a choice George II Five Guineas dated 1738 making £21,950.

The large Gregory collection of copper and bronze coins dispersed via auction by Baldwin over the past 18 months has been a considerable test for the market in this series.

Generally speaking prices were strong as collectors and dealers seized on the opportunity to acquire key date rarities in superb condition. Choice bun head pennies sold very well, an 1860 beaded border / toothed border mule making £3400 hammer while high prices were paid for truly uncirculated 18th Century copper pieces retaining their full original lustre.

Concurrent with the marked rise in the price of gold bullion over the past two years is the increased number of new collectors and specialist dealers of modern gold Sovereigns. As with any sharp increase in collecting activity, exciting new discoveries are made and the series becomes more complex. Pre 1860's Sovereigns have now become quite scarce as a large amount of material has been absorbed by collectors. The values for this denomination have risen sharply to reflect this buoyant market.

As always in a strong market it is important to inject an element of caution as grading standards can become more elastic but given this proviso we are confident the existing trends show no signs of abating.

SOME NUMISMATIC TERMS EXPLAINED

Obverse	That side of the coin which normally shows the monarch's head or name.
Reverse	The side opposite to the obverse, the 'Tails'.
Blank	The coin as a blank piece of metal, i.e. before it is struck.
Flan	The whole piece of metal after striking.
Type	The main, central design.
Legend	The inscription. Coins lacking a legend are called 'mute' or anepigraphic.
Field	That flat part of the coin between the main design and the inscription or edge.
Exergue	That part of the coin below the main design, usually separated by a horizontal line, and normally occupied by the date.
Die	The block of metal, with design cut into it, which actually impresses the coin blank with the design.
Die variety	Coin showing slight variation of design.
Mule	A coin with the current type on one side and the previous (and usually obsolete) type on the other side, or a piece struck from two dies that are not normally used together.
Graining or reeding	The crenellations around the edge of the coin, commonly known as 'milling'.
Proof	Carefully struck coin from special dies with a mirror-like or matt surface. (In this country 'Proof' is not a term used to describe the state of preservation, but the method of striking.)
Hammered	Refers to the old craft method of striking a coin between dies hammered by hand.
Milled	Coins struck by dies worked in a coining press. The presses were hand powered from 1560-1800, powered by steam from 1790 and by electricity from 1895.

INTRODUCTION

Arrangement

The arrangement of this catalogue is not completely uniform, but generally it is divided into metals (gold, silver, copper, etc) under each reign, then into coinages, denominations and varieties. In the Celtic section the uninscribed coins are listed before the dynastic coins; under Charles II all the hammered coins precede the milled coinage; the reign of George III is divided into coins issued up to 1816 and the new coinage from 1816 to the end of the reign; and under Elizabeth II the decimal issues are separated from the pre-decimal *(£.s.d.)* coinages.

Every major coin type is listed though not every variety. We have endeavoured to give rather more coverage to the varieties of relatively common coins, such as the pennies of Edward I, II and III, than to the very much rarer coins of, for instance, King Offa of Mercia.

Values

The values given represent the range of retail prices at which coins are being offered for sale at the time of going to press and **not** the price which a dealer will pay for those coins. These prices are based on our knowledge of the numismatic market, the current demand for particular coins, recent auction sale prices and, in those cases where certain coins have not appeared for sale for some years, our estimation of what they would be likely to sell at today, bearing in mind their rarity and appeal in relation to somewhat similar coins where a current value is known. Values are given for two grades of preservation from the Celtic period onwards and three to four grades of preservation for coins of the 17th to the 20th century.

Collectors normally require coins in the best condition they can afford and, except in the case of a really rare coin, a piece that is considerably worn is not wanted and has little value. The values given in the catalogue are for the exact state of preservation stated at the head of each column and bearing in mind that a score of identical coins in varying states of wear could be lined up in descending order from mint condition (FDC, *fleur de coin*), through very fine (VF) to *poor* state. It will be realized that only in certain instances will the values given apply to particular coins. A 'fine' (F) coin may be worth anything between one quarter and a half of the price quoted for a 'very fine' (VF); on the other hand, a piece in really mint condition will be valued substantially higher than the price quoted for 'extremely fine' (EF). The designation BV has been adopted for coins whose value on the market has yet to exceed its bullion value. Purchasing sovereigns, catalogued as BV, will attract a dealers' premium.

We emphasize again that the purpose of this catalogue is to give a general value for a particular class of coin in a specified state of preservation, and also to give the collector an idea of the range and value of coins in the English series. The value of any particular piece depends on three things:

Its exact design, legend, mintmark or date.

Its exact state of preservation; this is of prime importance.

The demand for it in the market at any given time.

Some minor varieties are much scarcer than others and, as the number of coins issued varies considerably from year to year, coins of certain dates and mintmarks are rarer and of more value than other pieces of similar type. The prices given for any type are for the commonest variety, mintmark or date of that type.

The Scope

Coin collecting, numismatics, is a fascinating hobby. It requires very little physical exertion and only as much mental effort as one wishes or is able to put into it at any time. There is vast scope and boundless ramifications and byways encompassing not only things historical and geographical, but also touching on economics, metallurgy, heraldry, literature, the fine arts, politics, military history and many other disciplines. This catalogue is solely concerned with British coinage from its earliest times right up to date. From the start the beginner should appreciate that the coinage of our own nation may be seen as a small but very important part of the whole story of world currency.

The first coins, made of electrum, a natural alloy of gold and silver, were issued in western Asia Minor (Lydia) in the later seventh century B.C. Over the next century or so coinage of gold and silver spread across the Aegean to mainland Greece, southwards to the eastern Mediterranean lands and eventually westward to the Greek colonies in southern Italy, Sicily (Magna Graecia) and beyond. The coins of the Greeks are noted for their beautiful, sometimes exquisite craftsmanship, with many of the coin types depicting the patron deities of their cities. Coins of Philip II of Macedon (359-336 B.C.), father of Alexander the Great, circulated amongst the Celtic peoples of the Danubian Basin and were widely copied through central Europe and by the Gauls in France. Gold Gaulish staters were reaching Britain around the beginning of the first century B.C. and the earliest gold to be struck in the island must have been produced shortly afterwards. Although their types and designs copy the Apollo head and racing charioteer of Philip II's gold coins, they are stylistically much removed from the original representation and very individually Celtic in concept.

The coins of the Romans cover some seven centuries and include an enormous number of different types that were current throughout a major part of the civilized world from Spain to Syria and from the Rhine in the north to the Sudan in the south. The Roman province of Britain was part of this vast empire for four hundred years from AD 43 until the early fifth century. Innumerable Roman coins have been recovered from sites in this country, most being made of brass or bronze. Many of these are quite inexpensive and very collectable. In recent years many hoards of gold and silver coins have been found, usually by use of metal detectors.

Following the revival of commerce after the Dark Ages, coinage in Western Europe was virtually restricted to silver until the thirteenth century, though gold was still being minted in Byzantium and in the Islamic world. In the Middle Ages many European cities had their own distinctive coinage and money was issued not only by the kings but also by nobles, bishops and abbots. From the time of the later Crusades gold returned to the West, and the artistic developments of the Renaissance in the fifteenth century brought improved portraiture and new minting techniques.

Large silver crown-size thalers were first minted at Joachimsthal in Bohemia early in the sixteenth century. The substantial shipments of silver coming to Europe from the mines of Spanish America over the next couple of centuries led to a fine series of larger coins being issued by the European states and cities. The larger size allowed greater artistic freedom in the designs and the portraits on the coins.

Both Germany and Italy became unified nation states during the later nineteenth century, thereby substantially reducing the number of mints and coin types. Balancing the reduction in European minting authorities were the new coins that were issued by the independent states of South and Central America. Since the 1950s many new nations have established their independence and their coinage provides a large field for the collector of modern coins.

It can be seen that the scope for the collector is truly vast, but besides the general run of official coinage there is also the large series of token coins—small change unofficially produced to supplement the inadequate supply of authorized currency. These tokens were issued by merchants, innkeepers and manufacturers in many towns and villages in the seventeenth, eighteenth and nineteenth centuries and many collectors specialize in their local issues.

Some coins have designs of a commemorative nature; an example being the Royal Wedding crown of 1981, but there are also large numbers of commemorative medals which, though never intended for use as coinage, are sometimes confused with coins because they are metal objects of a similar shape and sometimes a similar size to coins. This is another interesting field for collectors as these medals often have excellent portraits of famous men or women, or they may commemorate important events or scientific discoveries. Other metallic objects of coin-like appearance that can be confusing for the beginner are reckoning counters, advertising tickets, various other tickets and passes, and items such as brass coin weights.

Minting processes

From the time of the earliest Greek coins in the late seventh century BC to about the middle of the sixteenth century AD, coins were made by hand. The method of manufacture was simple. The obverse and reverse designs were engraved or punched into the prepared ends of two bars of bronze or iron, shaped or tapered to the diameter of the required coin. The obverse die, known as the *pile*, was usually spiked so that it could be anchored firmly into a block of wood or metal. The reverse die, the *trussel*, was held by hand or grasped by tongs.

The coin was struck by placing a metal blank between the two dies and striking the trussel with a hammer. Thus, all coinage struck by this method is known as 'hammered'. Some dies are known to have been hinged so there would be an exact register between the upper and lower die. Usually a 'pair of dies' consisted of one obverse die (normally the more difficult to make because it had the finer detail, such as the ruler's portrait) and two reverse dies. This was because the shaft of iron bearing the reverse design eventually split under the constant hammering; two reverse dies were usually needed to last out the life of the obverse die.

Some time toward the middle of the sixteenth century, experiments, first in Germany and later in France, resulted in the manufacture of coins by machinery.

The term 'milled', which is applied to all machine-made coins, comes from the type of machinery used – the mill and screw press. With this machinery the obverse die was fixed as the lower die and the reverse die brought down into contact with the blank by heavy vertical pressure applied by a screw or worm-drive connected to a cross bar with heavy weights at each end. These weights usually had long leather thongs attached which allowed a more powerful force to be applied by the operators who revolved the arms of the press. New blanks were placed on the lower die and the struck coins were removed by hand. The screw press brought more pressure to bear on the blanks and this pressure was evenly applied, producing a far better and sharper coin.

Various attempts were made during the reigns of Elizabeth I and Charles I to introduce this type of machinery with its vastly superior products. Unfortunately problems associated with the manufacture of blanks to a uniform weight greatly reduced the rate of striking and the hand manufacture of coins continued until the Restoration in 1660, when Charles II brought to London from Holland the Roettiers brothers and their improved screw press.

The first English coins made for circulation by this new method were the silver crowns of 1662, which bore an inscription on the edge, DECVS ET TVTAMEN, 'an ornament and a safeguard', a reference to the fact that the new coins could not be clipped, a crime made easy by the thin and often badly struck hammered coins.

The mill and screw press was used until new steam-powered machinery made by Boulton and Watt was installed in the new mint on Tower Hill in London. This machinery had been used most successfully by Boulton to strike the large 'cartwheel' two- and one- penny pieces of 1797 and other coins, including 'overstriking' Spanish *eight-reale* pieces into Bank of England 'dollars' since the old Mint presses were not able to exert sufficient power to do this. This new machinery was first used at the Mint to strike the 'new coinage' halfcrowns of 1816, and it operated at a far greater speed than the old type of mill and screw presses and achieved a greater sharpness of design.

The very latest coining presses now operating at the Royal Mint at Llantrisant in South Wales, are capable of striking at a rate of up to 800 coins a minute.

Condition

One of the more difficult problems for the beginner is to assess accurately the condition of a coin. A common fault among collectors is to overgrade and, consequently, to overvalue their coins.

Most dealers will gladly spare a few minutes to help new collectors. Many dealers issue price lists with illustrations, enabling collectors to see exactly what the coins look like and how they have been graded.

Coins cannot always be graded according to precise rules. Hammered coins often look weak or worn on the high parts of the portrait and the tops of the letters; this can be due to weak striking or worn dies and is not always attributable to wear through long use in circulation. Milled coins usually leave the Mint sharply struck so that genuine wear is easier to detect. However a x5 or x10 magnifying glass is essential, especially when grading coins of Edward VII and George V where the relief is very low on the portraits and some skill is required to distinguish between an uncirculated coin and one in EF condition.

The condition or grade of preservation of a coin is usually of greater importance than its rarity. By this we mean that a common coin in superb condition is often more desirable and more highly priced than a rarity in poor condition. Coins that have been pierced or mounted as a piece of jewellery generally have little interest to collectors.

One must also be on the lookout for coins that have been 'plugged', i.e. that have been pierced at some time and have had the hole filled in, sometimes with the missing design or letters re-engraved.

Badly cleaned coins will often display a complexity of fine interlaced lines and such coins have a greatly reduced value. It is also known for coins to be tooled or re-engraved on the high parts of the hair, in order to 'increase' the grade of coin and its value. In general it is better to have a slightly more worn coin than a better example with such damage.

Cleaning coins

Speaking generally, *do not* clean coins. More coins are ruined by injudicious cleaning than through any other cause, and a badly cleaned coin loses much of its value. A nicely toned piece is usually considered desirable. Really dirty gold and silver can, however, be carefully washed in soap and water. Copper coins should never be cleaned or washed, they may be lightly brushed with a brush that is not too harsh.

Buying and selling coins

Exchanging coins with other collectors, searching around the antique shops, telling your relatives and friends that you are interested in coins, or even trying to find your own with a metal detector, are all ways of adding to your collection. However, the time will come when the serious collector needs to acquire specific coins or requires advice on the authenticity or value of a coin.

At this point an expert is needed, and the services of a reputable coin dealer are necessary. There are now a large number of coin dealers in the UK, many of whom belong to the B.N.T.A. (The British Numismatic Trade Association) or the I.A.P.N. (The International Association of Professional Numismatists) and a glance through the 'yellow pages' under 'coin dealer' or 'numismatist' will often provide local information. Many dealers publish their own lists of coins. Studying these lists is a good way for a collector to learn about coins and to classify and catalogue their own collections.

The Standard Catalogue of Coins of England and the UK has been published since 1929. It serves as a price guide for all coin collectors. Spink also publish books on many aspects of English, Greek, Roman and Byzantine coins and on British tokens which serve as a valuable source of information for coin collectors. Our books are available directly from Spink or through reputable booksellers. Many branches of W. H. Smith, and other High Street booksellers, stock copies of *The Standard Catalogue*.

Numismatic Clubs and Societies

There are well over one hundred numismatic societies and clubs in the British Isles. For details of how to contact them see page 531. Joining one is the best way to meet fellow enthusiasts, learn about your coins and other series and acquire coins in a friendly and informative way.

Useful suggestions

Security and insurance. The careful collector should not keep valuable coins at home unless they are insured and have adequate protection. Local police and insurance companies will give advice on what precautions may be necessary.

Most insurance companies will accept a valuation based on *The Standard Catalogue*. It is usually possible to have the amount added to a householder's contents policy but particularly valuable individual coins may have to be separately listed. A 'Fire, Burglary and Theft' policy will cover loss only from the insured's address, but an 'All Risks' policy will usually cover accidental damage and loss anywhere within the U.K.

For coins deposited with a bank or placed in a safe-deposit box a lower insurance premium is usually payable.

Keeping a record. All collectors are advised to have an up-to-date record of their collection and, if possible, photographs of the more important and more easily identifiable coins. This should be kept in a separate place from the collection so that a list and photographs can be given to the police should loss occur. Note the price paid, from whom purchased, the date of acquisition and the condition of the coin.

Storage and handling. New collectors should get into the habit of handling coins by the edge. This is especially important as far as highly polished proof coins are concerned.

Collectors may initially keep their coins in paper or plastic envelopes housed in boxes, albums or special containers. Many collectors will eventually wish to own a hardwood coin cabinet in which the collection can be properly arranged and displayed. If a home-made cabinet is being constructed avoid using oak and cedar wood; mahogany, walnut and rosewood are ideal. It is important that coins are not kept in a humid atmosphere; especial care must be taken with copper and bronze coins which are very susceptible to damp or condensation which may result in a green verdigris forming on them.

From beginner to numismatist
The new collector can best advance to becoming an experienced numismatist by examining as many coins as possible, noting their distinctive features and by learning to use the many books of reference that are available. It will be an advantage to join a local numismatic society, as this will provide an opportunity for meeting other enthusiasts and obtaining advice from more experienced collectors. Most societies have a varied programme of lectures, exhibitions and occasional auctions of members' duplicates.

Those who become members of one or both of the national societies, the Royal Numismatic Society and the British Numismatic Society, receive an annual journal containing authoritative papers and have access to the societies' library and programme of lectures.

Many museums have coin collections available for study, although they may not always be displayed, and a number of museum curators are qualified numismatists.

ABBREVIATIONS

Archb.	Archbishop	laur.	laureate
Æ	bronze	mm.	mintmark
Ʀ	silver	mon.	monogram
Aʋ	gold	O., obv.	obverse
Bp.	Bishop	p.	new penny, pence
BV	bullion value	pl	plume
cuir.	cuirassed	quat.	quatrefoil
d.	penny, pence	qtr.	quarter
diad.	diademed	rad.	radiate
dr.	draped	R., rev.	reverse
ex.	exergue	r.	right
grs.	grains	s.	shillings
hd.	head	stg.	standing
i.c.	inner circle	trun.	truncation
illus.	illustration	var.	variety
l.	left	wt.	weight

CELTIC COINAGE

The Celtic or Ancient British issues are amongst the most interesting and varied of all British coins. They are our earliest coins and are the product of a society that left no historical sources of its own. It is therefore often difficult to be specific about for whom, when or where they were produced. Despite only being used for approximately a hundred and fifty years they do provide a rich variety of designs and types in gold, silver and bronze. Collectors looking for a theme to concentrate on may find the coins of one tribe, an individual ruler or a particular phase in the coinage interesting.

Grading Celtic Coins

The majority of Celtic coins were struck by hand, sometimes resulting in a loss of definition through weak striking. In addition, the design on the dies was often bigger than the blank flan employed, resulting in the loss of some of the design. Coins with full legends are generally more valuable than examples with incomplete legends. Bronze coins in good condition (VF or better) and especially toned examples attract a premium. Factors that detract from a coin's value are chips, scratches and verdigris on bronze coins. It is important to take into account these factors as well as the amount of wear on a coin when assessing its grade.

Cunobelin Bronze Unit   Epaticcus Silver Unit   Cunobelin Gold Stater

Fine

Very Fine

Plated Coins

Plated gold staters, quarter staters and silver units are recorded for many known types. They vary considerably in the quality of their production and are usually priced at around a quarter of the substantive types value. Their exact purpose or relation to the type they copy is not fully understood.

References and Select Bibliography.

M   Mack, R.P. (1975) 3rd edition, The Coinage of Ancient Britain.
V   Van Arsdell, R.D. (1989), Celtic Coinage of Britain.
BMC   Hobbs, R. (1996), British Iron Age Coins in the British Museum.

de Jersey, P. (1996), Celtic Coinage in Britain. *A good general introduction to the series.*
Nash, D. (1987), Coinage in the Celtic World. *Sets the coinage in its social context.*

The layout of the following list is derived from the standard works by Mack, Van Arsdell and the British Museum Catalogue by Richard Hobbs. References are made to these works where possible, in the case of the last work it should be noted that the British Museum collection is not exhaustive, and therefore should not be used to assess the rarity of a coin. More detailed information than that given here can be gained from these works.

IMPORTED COINAGE

The earliest coins to circulate in Britain were made in northern Gaul (Belgica) and imported into the south-east of England from around 150 B.C. onwards. They were principally the product of two tribal groups in this region, the Ambiani and Suessiones. In Britain these types are known as Gallo-Belgic A to F. The first type Gallo-Belgic A is ultimately derived from the Macedonian gold staters (M) of Philip II (359-336 B.C.)

The reasons why they were imported are not fully understood. However, the context for their importation is one of close social, political and economic ties between Britain and Gaul. Within this cross-channel relationship they undoubtedly had various functions, such as payment for military service or mercenaries, in exchanges between the elite of each society: in cementing alliances for example, or as gifts in a system of exchange.

Numbers in brackets following each entry refer to numbers employed in previous editions of this catalogue.

GALLO-BELGIC ISSUES

	2	4	5	7		
					F	VF
					£	£

From c.150 B.C. – c.50 B.C.

		F	VF
1	**Gold Stater.** Gallo-Belgic A. (Ambiani). Good copy of Macedonian stater, large flan. Laureate head of Apollo r. R. Horse l. *M. 1; V. 10. (1)*	1050	4000
2	Similar, but head and horse l. *M. 3; V. 12. (1)*	850	2750
3	B. (Ambiani). Somewhat similar to 1, but small flan and 'defaced' *obv.* die. R. Horse r. *M. 5; V. 30. (3)*	425	1200
4	— Similar, but with lyre between horse's legs. *M. 7; V. 33. (3)*	475	1450
5	C. (Ambiani), *Stater.* Disintegrated Apollo head. R. horse. *M. 26; V. 44. (5)*	240	700
6	**Gold Quarter Stater.** Gallo-Belgic A. Similar to 1. *M. 2; V .15. (2)*	275	850
7	— Similar to 2. *M. 4; V. 20. (2)*	240	700
8	B. Similar to 3. *M. 6; V. 35. (4)*	225	525
9	— Similar. R. Two horses l. with lyre between legs. *M. 8; V. 37. (4)*	150	350
10	D. Portions of Apollo head R. A mixture of stars, crescents, pellets, zig-zag lines; often referred to as 'Geometric' types,(See also British 'O', S. 46.). *M. 37, 39, 41, 41a, 42; V. 65/7/9/146. (6)*	75	160

From c.50 B.C.

11

		F £	VF £
11	**Gold Stater.** Gallo-Belgic E. (Ambiani). Blank obv. ℞. Disjointed curved horse r., pellet below, zig-zag in exergue. *M. 27; V. 52, 54. (7)*	150	275
12	F. (Suessiones). Devolved Apollo head r. ℞. Disjointed horse r. With triple-tail. *M. 34a; V. 85. (8)*	325	900
13	Xc. Blank except for VE monogram at edge of coin, ℞. S below horse r. *M. 82; V. 87-1. (9)*	240	750

Armorican (Channel Islands and N.W. Gaul, c.75-50 B.C.)

14	**Billon Stater.** Class I. Head r. ℞. Horse, boar below, remains of driver with Victory above, lash ends in or two loops, or 'gate'. *(12)*	35	125
15	— Class II. Head r. ℞. Horse, boar below, remains of Victory only, lash ends in small cross of four pellets. *(13)*	30	120
16	— Class III. Head r., anchor-shaped nose. ℞. Somewhat similar to Class I. *(14)*	30	120
17	— Class IV. Head r. ℞. Horse with reins, lyre shape below, driver holds vertical pole, lash ends in three prongs. *(15)*	35	125
18	— Class V. Head r. ℞. Similar to last, lash ends in long cross with four pellets. *(16)*	40	160
19	— Class VI. Head r. ℞. Horse, boar below, lash ends in 'ladder' *(17)*	45	175
20	**Billon Quarter Stater.** Similar types to above. *(18)*	45	160

CELTIC COINS STRUCK IN BRITAIN

Coin production in Britain began at the very end of the second century B.C. with the cast potin coinage of Kent (Nos 62-64). Inspired by Gaulish issues and ultimately derived from the potin coins of Massalia (Marseilles) in southern Gaul, the precise function and period of use of this coinage is not fully understood. The domestic production of gold coins started around 70 B.C., these issues are traditionally known as British A-P and are derived from imported Gallo-Belgic issues. Broadly contemporary with these issues are quarter staters, silver units, and bronze units. Recent work by John Sills has further enhanced our understanding of this crucial early period with the identification of two new British staters (Insular Belgic C or Kentish A and the Ingoldisthorpe type) and their related quarters and a Westerham quarter stater. The Insular Belgic C or Kentish A type derived from Gallo-Belgic C now becomes the first British stater.

EARLY UNINSCRIBED COINAGE

20A   20B

		F £	VF £
20A	**Gold Stater.** Insuler Belgic C/Kentish A type. Devolved Apollo head r. R. Disjointed horse r, a rosette behind or in front, or both. *M. —; V. —; BMC —*	450	1350
20B	Ingoldisthorpe type. Similar to last, as illustration. *M.—; V.—; BMC—..*	375	1250

21   22   23   24

21	British A. Westerham type. Devolved Apollo head r. R. Disjointed horse l. large pellet below. *M. 28, 29; V. 200, 202; BMC 1-32 (19)*	200	475
22	B. Chute type. Similar to 9 but crab-like object below horse. *M. 32; V. 1205; BMC 35-76. (20)*	150	300
23	C. Yarmouth type. Similar to 9 but star-like object in front of horse. *M. 31; V. 1220; BMC 78-85. (21)*	575	1600
24	D. Cheriton type. Similar to Chute type but with large crescent face. *M. 33; V. 1215; BMC 86-128. (22)*	225	650
25	E. Waldingfield type. Annulet and pellet below horse. *M. 48; V. 1462; BMC — —. (23)*	675	2250

26   27

		F	VF
		£	£
26	F. Clacton type 1. Similar to Westerham type but rosette below horse. M. 47; V. 1458; BMC 137-44. (24)	325	950
27	G. Clacton type 2. Similar but horse r., with pellet, or pellet with two curved lines below. M. 46, 46a; V. 30, 1455; BMC 145-79. (25)	300	875

28   30

28	H. North-East Coast type. Variety of 9, pellet or rosette below horse to r. M. 50, 50a, 51, 51a; V. 800; BMC 182-191. (26)	190	450
29	I. — Similar, horse l., pellet, rosette or star with curved rays below. M. 52-57; V. 804, 805, 807; BMC 193-211. (27)	190	450
30	J. Norfolk Wolf type. R. Crude wolf to r. M. 49; V. 610-1; BMC 212-16. (28)	250	725
31	— Similar but wolf to l. Usually base gold. M. 49a/b; V. 610-2/3; BMC 217-78. (28A).	150	450

32   36

32	L. Whaddon Chase type. R. Spirited horse r. of new style, various symbols below. M. 133-138a, 139a; V. 1470-6; 1485/7/9/93; BMC 279-343. (31)	175	475
33	— Plain. R. Horse r. With ring ornament below or behind. M. 140-143; V. 1498-1505; BMC 344-46. (32)	225	650
33A	— Climping type. Similar to Whaddon Chase type but horse left, bird-like object above, pellet in ring and crescent below. M.-;V.-; BMC-	475	1350
34	Lx. NorthThames group. Blank apart from reversed SS. R. Similar to last. M. 146; V. 1509; BMC 350. (33)	825	2500
35	Lz. Weald group. Blank with some traces of Apollo head. R. Horse r., large wheel ornament below. M. 144-145; V. 1507; BMC 347-49. (36)	500	1450
36	Ma. Wonersh type. Crossed wreath design with crescents back to back in centre. R. Spiral above horse, wheel below. M. 148; V. 1520; BMC 351-56. (37)	300	825

37   38

		F £	VF £

37   Mb. Savernake Forest type. Similar but *obv.* plain or almost blank. *M. 62; V. 1526; BMC 361-64*.. **185**   **525**

38   Qa. British 'Remic' type. Crude laureate head. R. Triple-tailed horse, wheel below. *M. 58, 60, 61; V. 210-124; BMC 445-58. (41)*................... **225**   **575**

39   Qb. — Similar, but *obv.* blank. *M. 59; V. 216; BMC 461-76. (42)*.......... **175**   **400**

39A   **Gold Quarter Stater.** Insuler Belgic C/Kentish A type. Similar to Gallo-Belgic D, but with rosette in field on obverse. *M. —; V.—; BMC—* **225**   **725**

39B   Ingoldisthorpe type. Similar to last but with sperm-like objects in field. *M.—; V.—; BMC—* **235**   **750**

39C   British A. Westerham type. Similar to last but of cruder style, or with L-shapes in field on rev. *M.—; V.—; BMC—*.. **185**   **575**

40   British D. Cheriton type. Similar to Stater, large crescent face. R. Cross motif with pellets. *M. —; V. 143 var; BMC 129-136* **180**   **525**

41   F/G. Clacton type. Plain, traces of pattern. R. Ornamental cross with pellets. *M. 35; V. 1460; BMC 180-1. (43A)*.. **175**   **500**

42   H. Crescent design and pellets. R. Horse r. *M. —; V. —; BMC 192*........ **175**   **500**

43   44   45

43   Lx. N.Thames group. Floral pattern on wreath. R. Horse l. or r. *M. 76; V. 234; BMC 365-370. (44)*.. **165**   **450**

44   Ly. N.Kent group. Blank. R. Horse l. or r. *M. 78; V. 158; BMC 371-3. (45)* **140**   **350**

45   Lz. Weald group. Spiral design on wreath. R. Horse l. or r. *M. 77; V. 250; BMC 548-50. (46)*.. **140**   **350**

46   47   48

46   O. Geometric type. Unintelligible patterns (some blank on obv.). *M. 40, 43-45; V. 143, 1225/27/29; BMC 410-32. (49)* **65**   **150**

47   P. Trophy type. Blank. R. Trophy design. *M. 36, 38; V. 145-7; BMC 435-44. (50)*.. **125**   **300**

48   Qc. British 'Remic' type. Head or wreath pattern. R. Triple-tailed horse, l. or r. *M. 63-67; 69-75; V. 220-32, 36, 42-6, 56; BMC 478-546. (51)*..... **130**   **325**

49   Xd. Head l. of good style, horned serpent behind ear. R. Horse l. *M. 79; V. 78; BMC 571-575. (11)*.. **250**   **750**

50   53

		F £	VF £
50	**Silver Unit** Lx. Head l.or r. R. Horse l. or r. *M. 280, 435, 436, 438, 441; V. 80, 1546, 1549, 1555; BMC 376-382. (53)*	70	225
51	— Head l. R. Stag r. with long horns. *M. 437; V. 1552; BMC 383-7. (54)*	90	350
52	— **Silver Half Unit.** Two horses or two beasts. *M. 272, 442, 443, 445; V. 474, 1626, 1643, 1948; BMC 389-400. (55)*..	85	325
53	Lz. Danebury group. Head r. with hair of long curves. R. Horse l., flower above. *M. 88; V. 262; BMC 580-82*	80	285

54   54A

54	— Helmeted head r. R. Horse r. wheel below. *M. 89; V. 264; BMC 583 -592. (58)*	90	335
54A	Cruciform pattern with ornaments in angles. R. Horse l., ear of corn between legs, crescents and pellets above, *M.—; V.—; BMC—*	75	275
55	— **Silver Quarter Unit.** As last. *M. 90; V. 268; BMC 642-43. (59)*.......	45	150

56   61

56	— Head r. R. Horse r. star above, wheel below. *M. –; V. 280; BMC 595-601*	70	240
57	— Head l., pellet in ring in front. R. Horse l. or r. *M. –; V. 284; BMC 610-630*	50	165
58	— Serpent looking back. R. Horse l. *M. –; V. 286; BMC 631-33*	70	240
59	— **Silver Quarter Unit.** Cross pattern. R. Two-tailed horse. *M. 119; V. 482; BMC 654-56. (56C). (Formerly attributed to Verica)*	35	125
60	**Bronze Unit.** Lx. Winged horse l. R. Winged horse l. *M. 446; V. 1629; BMC 401 (78)*	80	325
61	Chichester Cock type. Head r. R. Head r. surmounted by cock. *M. –; V. – BMC 657-59*	75	275

POTIN
(Cast Copper/Tin alloy)

62

		F £	VF £
62	**Unit.** Thurrock type.Head l. R. Bull butting l. or r. *M. —; V. 1402-42;* *BMC 660-666. (84A)*	25	85

63   64

63	Class I type. Crude head. R. Lines representing bull *(Allen types A-L.)* *M. 9-22a; V. 104, 106, 108, 112, 114, 115, 117, 119, 120, 122, 123, 125,* *127, 129, 131, 133; BMC 667-714. (83)*	20	60
64	Class II type. Smaller flan, large central pellet. *(Allen types M-P.)* *M. 23-25; V. 135-39; BMC 715-23. (84)*	20	55

CELTIC DYNASTIC AND LATER UNINSCRIBED COINAGE

From Julius Caesar's expeditions to Britain in 55/54 B.C. and his conquest of Gaul in 52 B.C. to the Claudian invasion in 43 A.D., southern Britain was increasingly drawn into the orbit of the Roman world. This process is reflected not only in the coins but also in what we know about their issuers and the tribes they ruled. Latin legends begin to appear for the first time and increasingly accompany objects and designs drawn from the classical world. A lot of what we know about the Celtic tribes and their rulers, beyond just their names on coins, is drawn from contemporary and slightly later Roman historical sources. A great deal however is still uncertain and almost all attributions to either tribes or historically attested individuals have to be seen as tentative.

The coin producing tribes of Britain can be divided into two groups, those of the core and those of the periphery. The tribes of the core, the Atrebates/Regni, Trinovantes/Catuvellauni and Cantii, by virtue of their geographical location controlled contact with the Roman world. Unlike the tribes of the periphery they widely employed Latin legends, classical designs and used bronze coinage in addition to gold and silver.

Following the Roman invasion of 43 A.D. it is likely that some coinage continued to be produced for a short time. However in 61 A.D. with the death of King Prasutagus and the suppression of the Boudiccan revolt that followed, it is likely that Celtic coinage came to an end.

TRIBAL/MINT MAP

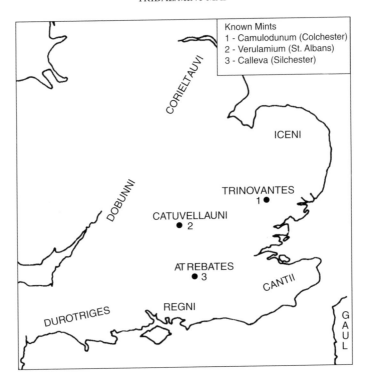

Known Mints
1 - Camulodunum (Colchester)
2 - Verulamium (St. Albans)
3 - Calleva (Silchester)

ATREBATES AND REGNI

The joint tribal area of these two groups corresponds roughly with Berkshire and Sussex and parts of northern and eastern Hampshire. The Atrebatic portion being in the north of this region with its main centre at Calleva (Silchester). The Regni occupying the southern part of the region centred around Chichester.

COMMIUS
(Mid to Late 1st Century B.C.)

The first inscribed staters to appear in Britain, closely resemble British Q staters (no.38) and are inscribed 'COMMIOS'. Staters and silver units with an inscribed 'E' are also thought to be related. Traditionally this Commius was thought to be the Gaulish chieftain who Caesar refers to in De Bello Gallico, as firstly serving him in his expeditions to Britain and finally fleeing to Britain c.50 B.C. This attribution does however present chronological problems, and the appearance of a few early staters reading 'COM COMMIOS' suggests that the Commius who issued coins is more likely to have been the son of Caesar's Commius.

65

		F £	VF £
65	**Gold Stater.** Devolved Apollo head r. R. COMMIOS around triple tailed horse r., wheel below. *M. 92; V. 350; BMC 724-29. (85)*	275	800

66   67

66	Similar, but 'E' symbol above horse instead of legend. *M. —;V. 352. BMC 730*	300	850
67	**Gold Quarter Stater.** Blank except for digamma. R. Horse l. *M. 83; V. 353-5; BMC —. (10)*	125	275

69

69	**Silver Unit.** Head l. R. Horse l. Mostly with 'E' symbol above. *M. —;V. 355; BMC 731-58. (57)*	40	145

70

70	**Silver Minim.** Similar to Unit. *M. —; V. 358-5; BMC 759-60*	40	130

TINCOMARUS or TINCOMMIUS

(Late 1st Century B.C. – Early 1st Century A.D.)

Successor to Commius and on his coins styled as 'COM.F' (son of Commius). Early coins of the reign like his predecessors are very obiviously Celtic in their style. However later coins exhibit an increasing tendancy towards Roman designs. Indeed Tincommius is recorded as a supliant king of the Roman emperor Augustus (Res Gestae, xxxii), finally fleeing to Rome in the early 1st century A.D. The discovery of the Alton Hoard in 1996 brought to light gold staters with the new legend TINCOMARVS.

72   73

		F £	VF £
71	**Gold Stater.** *Celtic style.* Devolved Apollo head r. R. TINC COMM. F. around horse. *M. 93; V. 362; BMC —. (86)*	425	1350
72	Similar but legend reads TINCOMARVS. *M. 94; V. 363; BMC 761-765. (86)*	350	950
73	**Gold Quarter Stater.** Spiral with pellet centre. R. Horse r. T above. *M. 81; V. 366; BMC 781-797. (46)*	115	250

74   75

74	TINCOM, zig-zag ornament below. R. Horse l. *M. 95; V. 365; BMC 798-810. (87)*	125	350
75	**Gold Stater.** *Classical style.* TINC(O) on a sunk tablet. R. Horseman with javelin r. often with CF in field. *M. 96-98; V. 375-76; BMC 765-769. (88)*	325	850

76   77

76	COM.(F). on a sunk tablet. R. Horseman with javelin r. TIN in field *M. 100; V. 385; BMC 770-774. (88)*	275	675
77	**Gold Quarter Stater.** TINC on a tablet, C above, A or B below. R. Winged head (Medusa?) facing. *M. 97; V. 378; BMC 811-826. (89)*	175	475
78	TIN on tablet. R. Boar l. *M. 99; V. 379; BMC 827-837. (90)*	110	250

79

83

		F £	VF £
79	COMF on tablet. R. Horse r. TIN around. *M. 101; V. 387; BMC 838-841. (90)*	115	260
80	— R. Horse l. TIC around. *M. 102; V. 388; BMC 842-851. (90)*	115	260
81	COM on tablet. R. Horse l. T above. *M. 103; V. 389; BMC 852-3. (90)*	120	275
82	COMF on tablet. R. Horse r. TINC around. *M. 104; V. 390; BMC 854-879. (90)*	115	260
83	**Silver Unit.** Laureate head r. TINCOM in front, V behind. R. Eagle stg. on snake. *M. 105; V. 397; BMC 880-905. (91)*	45	160
84	Laureate head l. R. Bull l. TINC around. *M. 106; V. 396; BMC 906-910. (91A)*	50	175
85	Laureate head r. R. Bull r. TIN(C) around. *M. —; V. 381; BMC 911-925. (92B)*	40	135
86	Facing head. R. Bull l. TINC around. *M. —; V. 370; BMC 926-29 (92)*	50	185

87

91

87	TINC in angles of cross, R. Lion l. *M. —; V. 372; BMC 930-45. (93B)*	40	140
88	Star. R. Boy riding dolphin r. TINC in field. *M. —; V. 371; BMC 946-977. (93C)*	35	120
89	TINC around pellet. R. Lion l. *M. 106a; V. 382; BMC 978-80. (93)*	45	160
90	Head l. TINCOMMIVS in front. R. Horse l. lyre above. *M. 131b; V. 473; BMC —. (92C) (Formerly attributed to Verica)*	50	175
91	**Silver Minim.** CF within two interlinked squares. R. Boar? r. TINC. *M. 118; V. 383-1; BMC 981-82. (94)*	35	110
92	As above but CO. R. Bull r. TI. *M. —; V. 383-5; BMC —-*	40	120
93	C inside box, box above and below. R. Bull r. TIN. *M. —; V. 383-7; BMC 983*	40	125
94	Cross, T? in angles. R. uncertain object. *M. 120; V. 483; BMC 984-85. (Formerly attributed to Verica)*	35	110

EPPILLUS

(Later 1st Century B.C. – Early 1st Century A.D.)

His reign is likely to have coincided with that of Tincommius's, who also claimed to be a son of Commius. Two coinages appear in his name, one for Kent and one minted at Calleva (Silchester, Hants.) in the northern part of the territory of the Atrebates and Regni. The coins of Calleva conform to the southern denominational structure of gold and silver with fractions of each, whilst the Kentish series is distinctly tri-metallic, replacing the silver minim with bronze. A joint coinage was issued by Eppillus and Verica. It is not understood if Eppillus held both territories simultaneously.

COINAGE STRUCK AT CALLEVA

		F	VF
		£	£

95   96

| 95 | **Gold Stater.** Devolved Apollo head r. R. EPPI COMMI F around horse. M. –; V. 405; BMC – | 975 | 3500 |
| 96 | **Gold Quarter Stater.** CALLEV, star above and below. R. Hound r. EPPI. M. 107; V. 407-08; BMC 986-1005. (95) | 110 | 275 |

97   98

| 97 | COMM F EPPILV, around crescent. R. Horse r. M. –; V. 409; BMC 1006-1009. (95A) | 115 | 285 |
| 98 | EPPI COMF in two lines. R. Winged horse r. M. 302; V. 435; BMC 1010-15. (129) | 110 | 275 |

99   100

99	**Silver Unit.** Crescent REX CALLE above and below. R. Eagle r. EPP. M. 108; V .415. BMC 1016-1060. (96)	40	140
100	Bearded hd. r. in wreath. R. Boar r. EPPI(L) F CO(M). M. –; V. 416; BMC 1061-87. (96A)	40	150
101	Bearded hd. in pellet border. R. Lion r. EPP COMF. M. 305; V. 417; BMC 1088-1115. (131)	40	150
102	**Silver Minim.** Floral cross. R. Eagle r. EPPI. M. –; V. 420; BMC 1116-17	40	140
103	Spiral and pellets. R. Ram r. EPP. M. –; V. 421; BMC 1118-20. (96C)	40	150
104	Bulls head facing. R. Ram r. EPP. M. –; V. 422; BMC 1121-24. (96D)	50	165
105	Wreath pattern. R. Boar r. EPP. M. –; V. 423; BMC –-	50	175
106	Crescent cross. R. Hand holding trident. M. –; V. 487; BMC –. (111C)	50	175

KENTISH TYPES

107

		F	VF
		£	£

107 **Gold Stater.** COMF within wreath. R. Horseman l. EPPILLVS above.
M. 300; V. 430; BMC 1125-26. (127) ... 1000 3500

108 Victory holding wreath l., within wreath. R. Horseman r. holding
carnyx, F EPPI COM below. M. 301; V. 431; BMC 1127-28. (128) ... 1350 4750

109 **Gold Quarter Stater.** Crossed wreaths, EPPI in angles. R. Horse l. M. 303;
V. 436; BMC 1129. (130) ... 325 950

110 COMF in pellet border. R. Horse r. EPPI. M. 304; V. 437;
BMC 1130-31. (130) ... 300 800

111 **Silver Unit.** Head l. EPPIL in field. R. Horseman holding carnyx, EPPILL.
M. 306; V. 441; BMC 1132. (131) ... 185 625

112 **Bronze Unit.** Bow cross, EPPI COMF around. R. Eagle facing. M. 309;
V. 450; BMC 1137-38. (134) ... 50 250

113 Bull r., EPPI COF around. R. eagle facing. M. 310; V. 451;
BMC 1139-41. (134) ... 50 250

114 Head l., EPPI in front. R. Victory l. holding wreath and standard.
M. 311; V. 452; BMC 1142. (133) ... 60 300

115 Bearded hd. r., EPPI CF. R. Biga r. CF. M. 312; V. 453; BMC — ... 65 350

JOINT TYPES OF EPPILUS AND VERICA

116 **Silver Unit.** Head l. CO VIR in front. R. Victory, EP. M. 307; V. 442;
BMC 1133-34. (132) ... 250 775

117

117 Head r. VIR CO in front. R. Capricorn l. EPPI COMF. M. 308/a; V. 443;
BMC 1135-36. (132) ... 165 500

VERICA

(c.10.-c.40 A.D.)

The exact details of Verica's succession and relationship to Eppillus and Tincommius are not fully understood. However by c.10 A.D. it seems likely that Verica was the sole ruler of the southern region. His close contact with Rome, both political and economic, seen in the increasing use of classical designs on his coins, culminated in his flight to Rome in c.42 A.D. to seek assistance from Claudius.

		F £	VF £
118	**Gold Stater.** COM:F on tablet. R. Horseman r. holding spear, VIR below. *M. 109; V. 460; BMC 1143-44. (97)*	275	750
119	COM.F. on tablet, pellet in ring ornament above and below. R. Similar to last. *M.121; 461; BMC 1146-53. (97)*	275	750

120   121

120	COM.F on tablet. R. Horseman r. holding spear, VIR above, REX below. *M. 121 var; V. 500; BMC 1155-58. (98)*	235	575
121	Vine-leaf dividing VI RI. R. Horseman r. with shield and spear. COF in field. *M. 125; V. 520-1; BMC 1159-73. (99)*	250	650
122	Similar, reads VE RI. *M. 125; V. 520-5/7; BMC 1174-76. (99)*	265	675
123	**Gold Quarter Stater.** COMF on tablet. R. Horse l. VIR. *M. 111; V. 465; BMC 1177-78. (100)*	125	325

124

124	COMF on tablet, pellet in ring ornament above and below R. Horse r. VI. *M. 112; V. 466; BMC 1179-1206. (100)*	120	250
125	COMF on tablet, pellet border. R. Horse r. VI above. *M. 113; V. 467; BMC 1207-16. (100)*	120	250

126   128

126	COM FILI. in two lines, scroll in between. R. Horse r. VIR(I) above. *M. 114; V. 468; BMC 1217-22. (100)*	120	275
127	VERI COMF, crescent above, star below. R. Horse r. REX below. *M. 122; V. 501; BMC 1223-36. (101)*	120	275
128	VERI beneath vine-leaf. R. Horseman r. with sword and shield, FRX in field. *M. 124; V. 525; BMC 1237-38. (102)*	185	675
129	COM, horseman r. R. Seated figure, VERICA around. *M. 126; V. 526; BMC 1239. (103)*	300	1050
130	Similar to last. R. Laureate bust r., VIRI in front. *M. 127; V. 527; BMC 1240. (103)*	275	975

		F	VF
		£	£

131   **Silver Unit.** COMF, crescent and or pellet in ring above and below. R. Boar r.
VI(RI) below. *M. 115; V. 470/72; BMC 1241-1331. (104)* 40 135

132   133

132   VERICA COMMI F around pellet in ring. R. Lion r. REX below.
M. 123; V. 505; BMC 1332-1359. (105) 50 175
133   COMMI F, horseman with shield r. R. VERI CA, mounted warrior with
spear r. *M. 128; V. 530; BMC 1360-92. (106)* 50 180

134   137

134   Two cornucopiae, COMMI F. R. Figure seated r. VERICA. *M. 129;
V. 531; BMC 1393-1419. (107)* 40 140
135   Bust r. VIRI. R. Figure seated l. *M. 130; V. 532; BMC 1420. (108)* 85 325
136   Naked figure l. R. Laureate bust r., COMMI F. *M. 131; V. 533;
BMC 1421-49. (108)* 40 140
137   VERICA REX, bull r. R. Figure stg. l., COMMI F. *M. —; V. 506;
BMC 1450-84. (108B)* 40 140
138   COMF, in tablet and scroll. R. Eagle facing, VI RI. *M. —; V. 471;
BMC 1485-1505. (104A)* 40 140
139   VIRIC across field, ornaments above and below. R. Pegasus r., star
design below. *M. —; V. —; BMC —. (104B)* 75 275
140   Head r. Verica. R. COMMI F., eagle l. *M. 131A; V. 534; BMC —. (108A)* 85 350
141   **Silver Minim.** COF in tablet, R. Facing head (Medusa?), VE below. *M. —;
V. 384; BMC 1506.(94A). (Formerly attributed to Tincommius)* 40 150
142   Head r. R. Horse r., VIRICO. *M. 116; V. 480; BMC —. (109)* 40 150
143   Pellet and ring pattern. R. Lion r. VIR. *M. 120a/c; V. 484;
BMC 1514-17. (109)* 35 120
144   VIRIC reversed. R. Boar r. *M. —; V. 485; BMC 1518* 35 120
145   Cross. R. Trident. *M. —; V. 486-1; BMC —-* 45 160
146   Uncertain. R. Boar r. *M. 120b; V. 510-1; BMC —. (109)* 30 110
147   Crescent cross. R. Boar r. *M. —; V. 510-5; BMC 1521-23. (109)* 40 135
148   VIR VAR in tablets. R. Winged horse r. CO. *M. 120d; V. 511;
BMC 1507-12. (109)* 35 135

149   150

149   Vine-leaf, CFO. R. Horse r. VERI CA. *M. —; V. 550; BMC 1524-25* 35 135
150   CF in torc. R. Head r. VERIC. *M. 132; V. 551; BMC 1526-33. (111A)* 30 125

	F £	VF £
151 Altar, CF, R. Bulls head facing, VERICA. *M. 120e; V. 552; BMC 1534-37. (109)*	45	175
152 Temple, CF. R. Bull r, VER REX. *M. —; V. 553; BMC 1538-41*	30	110

153   154

153 Cornucopia, VER COM. R. Lion r. *M. —; V. 554; BMC 1542*	35	135
154 Two cornucopiae. R. Eagle l. *M. —; V. 555; BMC 1543-58*	30	100
155 Floral pattern, CF. R. Lion r. *M.—; V. 556; BMC 1559-63. (111E)*	35	135
156 Sphinx r., CF, R. dog curled up, VERI. *M. —; V. 557; BMC 1564-68. (109B)*	30	120
157 VERI. R. Urn, COMMI F. *M. —; V. 559; BMC —-*	40	150
158 A in star. R. Bird r. *M. 316; V. 561; BMC 1569-71*	45	160
159 Urn, Rex. R. Eagle r., VERRICA COMMI F. *M. —; V. 563; BMC 1572-78. (109C)*	30	110
160 VIR inside tablet. R. Boars head r. *M. 117; V. 564; BMC 1579-81. (109A)*	30	120
161 Cross. R. bull l. *M. —; V. —; BMC 1582*	35	140
162 Boars head r., CF, R. Eagle, VE. *M. —; V. —; BMC 1583-86*	30	110
163 Head r, COMM IF., R. Sphinx, R VE. *M. —; V. —; BMC 1587-89*	35	140
164 A in tablet. R. Boar r. VI CO. *M. —; V. —; BMC 1590*	45	170
The two following coins are possibly issues of Epatticus.		
165 Bull r. R. Eagle with snake l. *M. —; V. 512; BMC 2366-70*	35	140
166 Bust r. R. dog r. *M. —; V. 558; BMC 2371-74*	40	150

CANTII

The Cantii, who gave their name to Kent, occupied a similar area to that of the modern county. Caesar considered this the most civilised part of Britain and the early production of potin units in Kent can be seen as indicative of this. A number of Kentish rulers for whom we have coins, appear to be dynasts from the two neighbouring kingdoms, who were involved in struggles to acquire territory. Eppillus (see Atrebates and Regni) produced coins specifically for circulation in Kent and like those of Cunobelin they circulated widely.

EARLY UNINSCRIBED

167 **Gold Stater.** Ly. Blank. R. Horse l. numerous ring ornaments in field. *M. 293; V. 142; BMC 2472. (34)*	375	1350
168 Blank. R. Horse r. numerous ornaments in field. *M. 294; V. 157; BMC— (34)*	375	1350

169   170

169 Lz. Blank. R. Horse l., box with cross hatching below. *M. 84, 292; V. 150, 144; BMC 2466-68. (35)*	450	1500
170 **Gold Quarter Stater.** Ly. Blank. R. Horse r., pentagram below. *M. 285; V. 163; BMC 2473-74. (45)*	125	250

171   173   176

		F	VF
		£	£
171	Blank. ℞. Horse r., 'V' shape above. *M. 284; V. 170; BMC 2475-77. (45)*	125	240
172	Lz. Blank. ℞. Horse l., 'V' shape above. *M. 85; V. 151; BMC 2469-70. (47)*	125	250
173	**Silver Unit.** Curved star. ℞. Horse r. Pentagram below. *M. 272a; V. 164; BMC—. (56)*	125	400
174	Serpent torc. ℞. Horse r., box with cross hatching below. *cf Mossop 8; BMC 2478*	175	650
175	**Silver Half Unit.** Spiral of three arms. ℞. Horse l. *M. —; V. —; BMC 2479*	70	275
176	**Bronze Unit.** Various animal types, ℞. Various animal types. *M. 295-96, 316a-d; V. 154/167; BMC 2480-91. (80/141-44)*	50	225

DUBNOVELLAUNUS
(Late 1st Century B.C.)

Likely to be the same Dubnovellaunus recorded on coins in Essex (see Trinovantes / Catuvellauni). The two coinages share the same denominational structure and have some stylistic similarities. It has been suggested that Dubnovellaunus is the British king of that name mentioned along with Tincommius as a client king in the Res Gestae of the Roman emperor Augustus.

177   180

177	**Gold Stater.** Blank. ℞. Horse r., bucranium above, serpent like object below, DUBNOV[ELLAUNUS] or similar around. *M. 282; V. 169; BMC 2492-96. (118)*	250	600
178	— ℞. Horse r., but without bucranium and with wheel below. *M. 283; V. 176; BMC 2497-98. (118)*	300	875
179	**Silver Unit.** Winged animal r. ℞. Horse l., DVBNO. *M. 286; V. 171; BMC 2499-2501. (119)*	110	325
180	Winged animal l. ℞. Seated fig. l., holding hammer, DVBNO. *M. 287; V. 178; BMC 2502-03. (119)*	120	350
181	**Bronze Unit.** Horse r. ℞. Lion l., DVBN. *M. 290; V. 166; BMC 2504-06. (122).*	70	275
182	Boar l., DVBNO. ℞. Horseman r. *M. 291; V. 181; BMC 2507-08. (121).*	70	275
183	Boar r., DVBNO. ℞. Eagle facing. *M. 289; V. 180; BMC 2509-10. (121)*	65	260

VOSENOS
(Late 1st Century B.C./ Early 1st Century A.D.)
Little is known of this ruler who issued coins in a characteristically Kentish style similar to those of Dubnovellaunus.

	F £	VF £
184 **Gold Stater.** Blank. R. Horse l., bucranium above, serpent like object below., [VOSE]NOS. *M. 297; V. 184; BMC 2511-12. (123)*	1350	4000

185

185 **Gold Quarter Stater.** Blank. R. Horse r., VOSI below. *M. 298; V. 185; BMC 2514-15. (124)*	450	1350
186 **Silver Unit.** Horse and griffin. R. Horse r., retrograde legend. *M. 299a; V. 186; BMC —. (125)*	175	650

"SA" or "SAM"
(Late 1st Century B.C./ Early 1st Century A.D.)
An historically unattested individual whose coins are stylistically associated with those of Dubnovellaunus and Vosenos. His coins have been predominantly found in north Kent

187 **Silver Unit.** Head l., R. Horse l., SA below. *M. —; V. —; BMC —*	240	800
187A **Bronze Unit.** Boar l., R. Horse l., SA below. *M. 299; V. 187; BMC 2516-19. (126)*	110	375

187B

187B Horse l., SAM below. R. Horse l., SAM below. *M. —; V. —; BMC —*	120	400

AMMINUS
(Early 1st Century A.D.)
Issued a coinage stylistically distinct from other Kentish types and with strong affinities to those of Cunobelin. Indeed it has been suggested that he is the Adminius recorded by Suetonius, as a son of Cunobelin. The enigmatic legend DVN or DVNO may be an unknown mint site.

188

188 **Silver Unit.** Plant, AMMINUS around. R. Winged horse r., DVN. *M. 313; V. 192; BMC 2522-23. (136)*	85	300
189 (Last year 190). A in wreath. R. Capricorn r., S AM (I). *M. 314; V. 194; BMC 2520-21. (137)*	85	300
190 **Bronze Unit.** (Last year 189). AM in wreath. R. Horse r., DVNO. *M. —; V. 193; BMC ——*	65	275
191 Head r. R. Hippocamp r., AM. *M. 315; V. 195; BMC 2524. (139)*	75	325

TRINOVANTES AND CATUVELLAUNI

Occupying the broad area of Essex, southern Suffolk, Bedfordshire, Buckinghamshire, Hertfordshire, parts of Oxfordshire, Cambridgeshire and Northamptonshire, they are likely to have been two separate tribes for most of their history. The Trinovantes were originally located in the eastern half of this area, with their main centre at Camulodunum (Colchester). The original Catuvellauni heartland was further west, with their main centre at Verulamium (St.Albans). The whole area eventually came under the control of Cunobelin at the end of the period.

TRINOVANTES

ADDEDOMAROS
(Late 1st Century B.C.)

Unknown to history, he appears to have been a contemporary of Tasciovanus. The design of his staters is based on the Whaddon Chase type (No.32) which circulated widely in this region.

200

		F £	VF £
200	**Gold Stater.** Crossed wreath. R. Horse r., wheel below, AθθIIDOM above. *M. 266; V. 1605; BMC 2390-94. (148)*	275	625

201   202

		F £	VF £
201	Six armed spiral. R. Horse r., cornucopia below, AθθIIDOM above. *M. 267; V. 1620; BMC 2396-2404. (148)*	240	525
202	Two opposed crescents. R. Horse r., branch below, spiral or wheel above, AθθDIIDOM. *M. 268; V. 1635; BMC 2405-2415. (149)*	275	675
203	**Gold Quarter Stater.** Circular flower pattern. R. Horse r. *M. 271; V. 1608; BMC 2416. (44)*	145	400
204	Cross shaped flower pattern. R. Horse r. *M. 270; V. 1623; BMC 2417-21. (44)*	135	325
205	Two opposed crescents. R. Horse r., AθθDIIDOM around. *M. 269; V. 1638; BMC 2422-24. (150)*	175	500
206	**Bronze Unit.** Head l. R. Horse l. *M. 274; V. 1615/46 BMC 2450-60. (77)*	30	110

DUBNOVELLAUNUS

(Late 1st Century B.C./ Early 1st Century A.D.)

Dubnovellaunus is likely to have been the successor to Addedomaros, with whom his coins are stylistically related. It is not clear if he was the same Dubnovellaunus who also issued coins in Kent (see Cantii) or if he is the same Dumnobeallaunos mentioned in the Res Gestae of the emperor Augustus c.AD14.

207   208

		F £	VF £
207	**Gold Stater.** Two crescents on wreath. R. Horse l., leaf below, pellet in ring, DVBNOVAIIAVNOS above. *M. 275; V. 1650; BMC 2425-40. (152)*.....	275	700
208	**Gold Quarter Stater.** Similar. *M. 276; V. 1660; BMC 2442. (153)*........	135	325

209   210

209	**Silver Unit.** Head l., DVBNO. R. Winged horse r., lattice box below. *M. 288; V. 165; BMC 2443-44. (120)*..	120	350
210	Head l., legend ?, R. Horse l. DVB[NOV]. *M. 278; V. 1667; BMC 2445. (154)*..	110	300
211	**Bronze Unit.** Head l., R. Horse l., DVBNO above. *M. 281; V. 1669; BMC 2446-48. (154)*..	60	200
212	Head r., R. Horse l. *M. 277; V. 1665; BMC 2461-65. (154)*....................	50	175

DIRAS

(Late 1st Century B.C./ Early 1st Century A.D.)

An historically unattested ruler, responsible for a gold stater related stylistically to Dubnovellaunus's.

| 213 | **Gold Stater.** Blank. R. Horse r., DIRAS? above, yoke like object above. *M. 279; V. 162; BMC 2449. (151)* .... | 1350 | 4250 |

CATUVELLAUNI

TASCIOVANUS
(Late 1st Century B.C./ Early 1st Century A.D.)

The early gold coins of Tasciovanus, like those of his contemporary Addedomaros, are based on the Whaddon Chase stater. Verulamium (St.Albans) appears to have been his principal mint, appearing as VER or VERL on the coinage. Staters and quarter staters inscribed CAM (Camulodunum/ Colchester) are known and perhaps suggest brief or weak control of the territory to the east. The later coins of Tasciovanus use increasingly Romanised designs. The adoption of the title RICON, perhaps a Celtic equivalent to the Latin REX (King), can be seen as a parallel move to that of his contemporary Tincommius to the south.

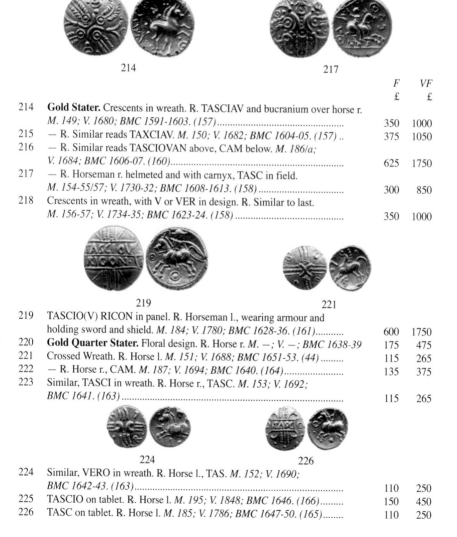

		214		217		

		F	VF
		£	£
214	**Gold Stater.** Crescents in wreath. R. TASCIAV and bucranium over horse r. *M. 149; V. 1680; BMC 1591-1603. (157)*	350	1000
215	— R. Similar reads TAXCIAV. *M. 150; V. 1682; BMC 1604-05. (157)*	375	1050
216	— R. Similar reads TASCIOVAN above, CAM below. *M. 186/a; V. 1684; BMC 1606-07. (160)*	625	1750
217	— R. Horseman r. helmeted and with carnyx, TASC in field. *M. 154-55/57; V. 1730-32; BMC 1608-1613. (158)*	300	850
218	Crescents in wreath, with V or VER in design. R. Similar to last. *M. 156-57; V. 1734-35; BMC 1623-24. (158)*	350	1000

		219		221		

219	TASCIO(V) RICON in panel. R. Horseman l., wearing armour and holding sword and shield. *M. 184; V. 1780; BMC 1628-36. (161)*	600	1750
220	**Gold Quarter Stater.** Floral design. R. Horse r. *M. —; V. —; BMC 1638-39*	175	475
221	Crossed Wreath. R. Horse l. *M. 151; V. 1688; BMC 1651-53. (44)*	115	265
222	— R. Horse r., CAM. *M. 187; V. 1694; BMC 1640. (164)*	135	375
223	Similar, TASCI in wreath. R. Horse r., TASC. *M. 153; V. 1692; BMC 1641. (163)*	115	265

		224		226		

224	Similar, VERO in wreath. R. Horse l., TAS. *M. 152; V. 1690; BMC 1642-43. (163)*	110	250
225	TASCIO on tablet. R. Horse l. *M. 195; V. 1848; BMC 1646. (166)*	150	450
226	TASC on tablet. R. Horse l. *M. 185; V. 1786; BMC 1647-50. (165)*	110	250

		F £	VF £
227	**Silver Unit.** Head l. R. Horse r. *M. —; V. 1698; BMC 1654*....................	65	200
228	Cross and box. R. Horse r., VER in front. *M. —; V. —; BMC 1655*........	65	225
229	Cross and crescent. R. Horse l., TASCI. *M. —; V. —; BMC 1665-57*......	65	200
230	Bearded head l. R. Horseman r., TASCIO. *M. 158; V. 1745; BMC 1667-68. (167)*....................	75	300
231	Winged horse l., TAS. R. Griffin r., within circle of pellets. *M. 159; V. 1790; BMC 1660. (168)*....................	70	250
232	Eagle stg. l., TASCIA. R. Griffin r. *M. 160; V. 1792; BMC 1658-59. (169)*	75	300
233	VER in beaded circle. R. Horse r., TASCIA. *M. 161; V. 1699; BMC 1670-73. (170)*....................	70	275
234	— R. Naked horseman. *M. 162; V. 1747; BMC 1674-76. (171)*..............	70	275

235   238

235	Laureate hd. r., TASCIA. R. Bull l. *M. 163; V. 1794; BMC 1681-82. (172)*	70	275
236	Cross and box, VERL. R. Boar r. TAS. *M. 164; V. 1796; BMC 1661-62. (173)*....................	75	275
237	TASC in panel. R. Winged horse l. *M. 165; V. 1798; BMC 1664-65. (174)*	65	200
238	— R. Horseman l., carrying long shield. *M. 166; V. 1800; BMC 1677-79. (174)*....................	60	185
239	Two crescents. R. Winged griffin, VIR. *M. —; V. —; BMC 1666*............	85	325
240	Head r., TAS?. R. Horseman r. *M. —; V. —; BMC 1669*........................	75	300

241

| 241 | **Bronze Double Unit.** Head r., TASCIA, VA. R. Horseman r. *M. 178; V. 1818; BMC 1685-87. (190)*.................... | 175 | 625 |

242

242	**Bronze Unit.** Two heads in profile, one bearded. R. Ram l., TASC. *M. 167; V. 1705; BMC 1711-13. (178)*....................	50	175
243	Bearded head r. VER(L). R. Horse l., VIIR or VER. *M. 168; V. 1707; BMC 1714-21. (179)*....................	45	165
244	Bearded head r. R. Horse l., TAS. *M. 169; V. 1709; BMC 1722-23. (179)*	50	175
245	Head r., TASC. R. Winged horse l., VER. *M. 170; V. 1711; BMC 1688-89. (180)*....................	45	165
246	— R. Horseman r., holding carnyx, VIR. *M. 171; V. 1750; BMC 1724-27. (182)*....................	45	165

247

		F £	VF £
247	VERLAMIO between rays of star. R. Bull l. *M. 172; V. 1808; BMC 1745-51. (183)*	40	145
248	Similar without legend. R. Bull r. *M. 174; V. 1810; BMC 1752-55. (185)*	50	175
249	Similar. R. Horse l., TASCI. *M. 175; V. 1812; BMC 1709-10. (186)*	50	175
250	Head r., TASCIO. R. Lion r., TA SCI. *M. 176; V. 1814; BMC 1736-38. (188)*	40	165
251	Head r. R. Figure std. l., VER below. *M. 177; V. 1816; BMC 1739-44. (189)*	50	175
252	Cross and Crescents. R. Boar r., VER. *M. 179; V. 1713; BMC 1702-05. (191)*	45	165
253	Laureate head r. R. Horse l., VIR. *M. 180; V. 1820; BMC 1706-08. (192)*	45	165
254	Raised band across centre, VER or VERL below. R. Horse grazing r. *M. 183a; V. 1717; BMC —. (193)*	60	225
255	**Bronze Fractional Unit.** Animal r. R. Sphinx l. *M. 181; V. 1824; BMC 1760-61. (198)*	35	150
256	Head l., VER. R. Goat r. *M. 182; V. 1715; BMC 1765-68. (199)*	30	135
257	Head r. R. Boar r, *M. 183; V. 1826; BMC 1762-64. (199)*	30	135
258	Head l. R. Animal with curved tail. *M. 183b, c; V. 1822; BMC 1759. (200)*	35	150

ASSOCIATES OF TASCIOVANUS
(Early 1st Century A.D.)

Towards the end of his reign, a number of joint issues bearing his name and the name of either Sego or Dias appear. In addition coins similar in style to those of Tasciovanus appear with either the name Andoco or Rues. It has been suggested that these issues belong to a period of struggle following the death of Tasciovanus and are all rival contestants for the throne. Another theory is that they are associates or sub-kings of Tasciovanus responsible for areas within the wider territory.

SEGO

259

259	**Gold Stater.** TASCIO in tablet, annulets above. R. Horseman with carnyx r., SEGO. *M. 194; V. 1845; BMC 1625-27. (162)*	1350	3750

260

		F £	VF £

260 **Silver Unit.** SEGO on panel. R. Horseman r. *M. 196; V. 1851;*
BMC 1684. (176) 325 900

261 **Bronze Unit.** Star shaped pattern. R. Winged sphinx l., SEGO. *M. 173; V. 1855;*
BMC 1690. (184) 125 400

ANDOCO

262

262 **Gold Stater.** Crescents in wreath. R. Bucranium over horse r., AND below.
M. 197; V. 1860; BMC 2011-14. (202) 475 1350
263 **Gold Quarter Stater.** Crossed wreaths, ANDO in angles. R. Horse l. *M. 198;*
V. 1863; BMC 2015-17. (203) 135 425

264

264 **Silver Unit.** Bearded head l. R. Winged horse l., ANDOC. *M. 199; V. 1868;*
BMC 2018. (204) 110 350

265

265 **Bronze Unit.** Head r., ANDOCO. R. Horse r., ANDOCO. *M. 200; V. 1871;*
BMC 2019-20. (205) 55 185
266 Head r., TAS ANDO. R. Horse r. *M. 175a; V. 1873; BMC −. (187)* 70 250

DIAS

267   268

267 **Silver Unit.** Saltire over cross within square. R. Boar r., TASC DIAS.
M. −; V. −; BMC 1663. (173A) 100 325
268 DIAS CO, in star. R. Horse l., VIR. *M. 188; V. 1877; BMC 1683. (177).* 110 350

269

	F £	VF £

269 **Bronze Unit.** Bearded head r., DIAS TASC. R. Centaur r., playing pan pipes.
M. 192; V. 1882; BMC 1728-35. (197) 70 300

RUES

270 **Bronze Unit.** Lion r., RVII. R. Eagle. M. 189; V. 1890; BMC 1691. (194) 60 250
271 — R. Similar reads RVE. M. 189; V. 1890-3; BMC 1692. (194) 55 235

272 273

272 Bearded head r., RVIIS. R. Horseman r., VIR. M. 190; V. 1892;
BMC 1698-1701. (195) 60 250
273 RVIIS on tablet. R. Winged sphinx l. M. 191; V. 1895;
BMC 1693-97. (196) 55 235
274 **Bronze Fractional Unit.** Annulet within square with curved sides. R.
Eagle l.,RVII. M. 193; V. 1903; BMC 1756-58. (201) 60 250

CUNOBELIN
(Early 1st Century A.D. to c.40 A.D.)

Styled as son of Tasciovanus on some of his coins, Cunobelin appears to have ruled over the unified territories of the Trinovantes and Catuvellauni, with additional territory in Kent. His aggressive policy of expansion that involved members of family eventually lead to Roman concern over the extent of his power. Following his death just prior to 43 AD, the emperor Claudius took the decision to invade Britain.

During his long reign an extensive issue of gold, silver and bronze coins used ever increasingly Romanised designs. It has been estimated from a study of known dies that around one million of his gold corn ear staters were produced. His main centre and mint was at Camulodunum (Colchester) appearing as the mint signature CAMV. The names SOLIDV and AGR appear on a few coins associated with Cunobelin and are likely to represent personal names.

280 281

280 **Gold Stater.** Biga type. CAMVL on panel. R. Two horses l., wheel below,
CVNOBELIN. M. 201; V. 1910; BMC 1769-71. (207) 625 1750
281 Linear type. Corn ear dividing CA MV. R. Horse r., branch above,
CVN. M. 210; V. 1925; BMC 1772-76. (208) 250 550

		F	VF
		£	£

282 — Similar, privy mark 'x' above a letter in *obv.* legend. *M. 210a;*
VA 1925-3/5; BMC 1777-81. (208).. 300 850

283   285

283 Wild type. Corn ear dividing CA MV. R. Horse r., branch above.,
CVN(O). *M. 211/2; V. 1931/33; BMC 1784-92/1804-08. (208)*.............. 260 550
284 — Similar, heart shaped object between horses forelegs. *M. 211 var;*
V. 1931-3; BMC 1793. (208).. 325 950
285 — Similar, privy mark pellet or pellet triangle above a letter(s) in *obv.*
legend. *M. —; V. 1931-5/7/9; BMC 1797-1803. (208)* 275 650

286   288

286 Plastic type. Corn ear dividing CA MV. R. Horse r., branch above.,
CVNO. *M. 203/13; V. 2010-1/3/5; BMC 1809-11/15-23. (208)*.............. 265 575
287 — Similar, 'B' in front of horse. *M. —; V. 2010-7; BMC 1813. (208)*..... 325 875

289   290

288 Classic type. Corn ear dividing CA MV. R. Horse r., branch above.,
CVNO. *V. 206-07; V. 2025/27; BMC 1827-31/33. (208)*...................... 275 675
289 — Similar, horse l., lis like object above. *M. 208; V. 2029;*
BMC 1834-35. (209).. 575 1500
290 **Gold Quarter Stater.** Biga type. Similar to 280. *M. 202; V. 1913;*
BMC 1836/A. (210)... 200 475

292   296

292 Linear type. Similar to 281. *M. 209; V. 1927; BMC 1837-42. (211)*........ 135 300
293 Wild type. Similar to 283. *M. —; V. 1935; BMC 1843-44. (211)*............ 135 275
294 Plastic type. Similar to 286. *M. 204; V. 2015; BMC 1846-48. (211)*........ 120 250
295 — Similar but corn ear dividing CAM CVN. *M. 205; V. 2017;*
BMC 1845. (212) 135 300
296 Classic type. Similar to 288. *M. —; V. 2038; BMC —. (211)* 175 450

299

		F £	VF £
299	**Silver Unit.** Two bull headed serpents, inter twined. R. Horse l., CVNO. *M. 214; V. 1947; BMC 1856. (213)*	100	375
300	Curled serpent inside wheel. R. Winged horse l., CVN. *M. —; V. —; BMC 1857*	100	375
301	CVN on panel R. Horse l., (C)M. *M. 255; V. 1949; BMC 1858-59. (228)*	75	225
302	CVNO BELI on two panels. R. CVN below horseman r. *M. 216/7; V. 1951/53; BMC 1862. (215)*	80	250
303	Head l., CAMVL. R. CVNO beneath Victory std. r. *M. 215; V. 2045; BMV 1863-65. (214)*	85	275

304   305

304	Two leaves dividing CVN. R. Horseman r., CAM. *M. 218; V. 2047; BMC 1866-67. (216)*	75	250
305	Flower dividing CAMV. R. CVNO below horse r. *M. 219; V. 2049; BMC1867A. (217)*	90	350
306	CVNO on panel. R. CAMV on panel below griffin. *M. 234; V. 2051; BMC 1868-69. (218)*	85	325
307	CAMVL on panel. R. CVNO below centaur l. carrying palm. *M. 234a; V. 1918; BMC —. (219)*	90	350
308	CAMVL on panel. R. Figure seated l. holding wine amphora, CVNOBE. *M. —; V. —; BMC —. (219A)*	75	250
309	Plant, CVNOBELINVS. R. Figure stg. r. holding club and thunderbolt dividing CA MV. *M. —; V .—; BMC 1897. (219B)*	90	350
310	Laur. hd. r., CVNOBELINVS. R. Winged horse springing l., CAMV below. *M. —; V. —; BMC —. (219C)*	90	325
311	CVNO on panel, wreath around. R. Winged horse r., TASC F. *M. 235; V. 2053; BMC 1870. (220)*	90	325

312   313

312	Head r., CVNOBELINI. R. Horse r., TASCIO. *M. 236; V. 2055; BMC 1871-73. (221)*	70	225
313	Winged bust r., CVNO. R. Sphinx std. l., TASCIO. *M. 237; V. 2057; BMC 1874-78. (222)*	50	150

314   316

			F £	VF £
314		Draped female fig. r., TASCIIOVAN. Ɍ. Figure std. r. playing lyre, tree behind. *M. 238; V. 2059; BMC 1879-82. (223)*	75	250
315		Figure stg. l., holding club and lionskin., CVNO. Ɍ. Female rider r., TASCIOVA. *M. 239; V. 2061; BMC 1884-85. (224)*	70	235
316		Female head r., CVNOBELINVS. Ɍ. Victory r., TASCIO(VAN). *M. —; V. —; BMC 1883. (224A)*	70	235
317		Fig. r. carrying dead animal, CVNOBELINVS. Ɍ. Fig. stg. holding bow, dog at side, TASCIIOVANI. *M. 240; V. 2063; BMC 1886-88. (225)*	75	250

318

		F £	VF £
318	CVNO on panel, horn above, dolphin below. Ɍ. Fig. stg. r. altar behind. *M. 241/41a; V. 2065; BMC 1889-90. (226)*	80	300
319	CVN on panel. Ɍ. Fig. holding club walking r., CVN. *M. 254; V. 2067; BMC 1891-92. (227)*	80	300
320	CVN in wreath. Ɍ. CAM, dog? trampling on serpent r. *M. 256; V. 2069; BMC 1893. (229)*	90	350
321	Winged horse l., CVN. Ɍ. Std. fig. r. *M. 258; V. 2071; BMC 1896. (230)*	80	300
322	CVNO in angles of cross. Ɍ. Capricorn r., CVNO. *M. —; V. —; BMC 1898*	80	300

BRONZE

		F £	VF £
323	Head l., CVNO. Ɍ. Boar l., branch above. *M. 220; V. 1969; BMC—. (232)*	45	175
324	CVNOB ELINI in two panels. Ɍ. Victory std. l., TASC. *M. 221; V. 1971; BMC 1921-27. (233)*	40	135
325	Winged horse l., CAM. Ɍ. Winged Victory stg l., CVN. *M. 222; V. 1973; BMC 1938-43. (234)*	40	150

326

		F £	VF £
326	Bearded head facing Ɍ. Boar l., CVN. *M.223; V.1963; BMC 1904-05. (235)*	45	160
327	Ram-headed animal coiled up in double ornamental circle. Ɍ. Animal l., CAM. *M. 224; V. 1965; BMC —. (236)*	45	175
328	Griffin r., CAMV. Ɍ. Horse r., CVN. *M. 225; V. 2081; BMC 1909-12. (237)*	40	150
329	Bearded head l., CAMV. Ɍ. CVN or CVNO below horse l. *M. 226, 229; V. 2085/2131; BMC 1900-01. (238)*	40	150
330	Laureate head r., CVNO. Ɍ. CVN below bull butting l. *M. 227; V. 2083; BMC 1902-03. (239)*	40	160
331	Crude head r., CVN. Ɍ. Figure stg. l., CVN. *M. 228; V. 2135; BMC —. (240)*	45	180

332

	F	VF
	£	£

332 CAMVL / ODVNO in two panels. R. CVNO beneath sphinx crouching
l. *M. 230; V. 1977; BMC 1928-30. (241)*.. 40 150

333 Winged horse l., CAMV. R. Victory stg. r. divides CV NO. *M. 231;*
V. 1979; BMC 1931-34. (242).. 40 150

334 Victory walking r. R. CVN below, horseman r. *M. 232; V. 1981;*
BMC 1935. (243) 50 180

335 Head l., CAM. R. CVNO below eagle. *M. 233; V. 2087; BMC −. (244)* 50 180

336   337

336 Head l., CVNOBELINI. R. Centaur r., TASCIOVANI.F. *M. 242;*
V. 2089; BMC 1968-71. (245).. 35 125

337 Helmeted bust r. R. TASCIIOVANII above, sow stg. r., F below.
M. 243; V. 2091; BMC 1956-60. (246).. 35 125

338 Horseman galloping r. holding dart and shield, CVNOB. R. Warrior stg.
l., TASCIIOVANTIS. *M. 244; V. 2093; BMC 1961-67. (247)* 35 110

339   340

339 Helmeted bust l., CVOBELINVS REX. R. TASC FIL below boar l.,
std. on haunches. *M. 245; V. 1983; BMC 1952-55. (248)* 40 150

340 Bare head r., CVNOBELINVS REX. R. TASC below bull butting r.
M. 246; V. 2095; BMC 1944-51. (249).. 35 135

341 Bare head l., CVNO. R. TASC below bull stg. r. *M. 247; V. 1985;*
BMC −. (250)... 40 160

342   343

342 Head l., CVNOBELIN. R. Metal worker std. r. holding hammer, working
on a vase, TASCIO. *M. 248; V. 2097; BMC 1972-83. (251)*.................... 40 150

343 Winged horse r., CVNO. R. Victory r. sacrificing bull, TASCI. *M. 249;*
V. 2099; BMC 1913-19. (252).. 30 110

344 CVNO on panel within wreath. R. CAMV below horse, prancing r.
M. 250; V. 2101; BMC 1987-90. (253).. 40 150

345   346

	F £	VF £
345 Bearded head of Jupiter Ammon l., CVNOBELIN. R. CAM below horseman galloping r. *M. 251; V. 2103; BMC 1984-86. (254)*	40	150
346 Janus head, CVNO below. R. CAMV on panel below, sow std. r. beneath a tree. *M. 252; V. 2105; BMC 1998-2003. (255)*	40	150

347

347 Bearded head of Jupiter Ammon r., CVNOB. R. CAM on panel below lion crouched r. *M. 253; V. 2107; BMC 1991-97. (256)*	35	140
348 Sphinx r., CVNO. R. Fig stg. l. divides CA M. *M. 260; V. 2109; BMC 2004-09. (257)*	40	150
349 Horse r. R. CVN below horseman r. *M. 261; V. 1987; BMC 1936-47. (258)*	45	160
350 Animal l. looking back. R. CVN below horse l. *M. 233a; V. 1967; BMC—. (259)*	40	160
350A Ship, CVN below. R. Fig. r. dividing S E. *M. —; V. 1989; BMC 2010.*	125	575

"SOLIDV"

351

351 **Silver Unit.** SOLIDV in centre of looped circle. R, Stg. fig. l., CVNO. *M. 259; V. 2073; BMC 1894-95. (231)*	300	1000

"AGR"

352   353

352 **Gold Quarter Stater.** Corn ear dividing CAM CVN. R. Horse r., branch above., AGR below *M. —; V. —; BMC 1854*	325	900
353 — R. Horse r., branch above., cross and A below. *M. —; V. —; BMC 1855*	325	900

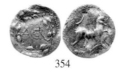

354

	F	VF
	£	£

354   **Silver Unit.** AGR inside wreath. R. Female dog r., AGR below. *M. —; V. —;*
       BMC 1899   275   750

EPATICCUS
(1st Half 1st Century A.D.)

Epaticcus, styled as a son of Tasciovanus on his coins, was most probably a brother of Cunobelin.
The corn ear employed on his staters is similar to that of his brother's produced at Colchester. His
coins appear in northern Atrebatic territory and conform to the area's denominational structure.
It seems likely that Epaticcus's coinage reflects an incursion into Atrebatic territory by the
Trinovantian/Catuvellaunian dynasty.

355

355   **Gold Stater.** Corn ear dividing TAS CIF. R. Horseman r., with spear and
       shield. EPATI. *M. 262; V. 575; BMC 2021-23. (112)*   725   2250

356   357
356   **Silver Unit.** Head of Hercules r., EPAT(I). R. Eagle stg. on snake.
       M. 263/a; V. 580; BMC 2024-2268/2270-76. (113)   30   85
357   Victory seated r. TASCIOV. R. Boar r., EPAT. *M. 263; V. 581;*
       BMC 2294-2328. (114)   35   135

358
358   Bearded head l., TASCIO. R. EPATI below lion r. *M. —; V. 582;*
       BMC 2329   110   350
359   EPATI inside panel. R. Lion r. *M. —; V. 583; BMC 2330. (114A)*   100   325

360   361
360   **Silver Minim.** EPATI. R. Boars head r., TA. *M. 264; V. 585; BMC 2331-46.*
       (115)   35   110
361   TA inside star. R. Winged horse r., EPA below. *M. —; V. 560;*
       BMC 2351-57. (116)   30   100
362   Helmeted head r. R. Horse r., E below. *M. —; V. —; BMC 2358-63*   30   100
363   EPATI. R. Winged horse r., cross below. *M. —; V .—; BMC 2365*   40   150

CARATACUS
(1st Half 1st Century A.D.)

Coins inscribed CARA have been traditionally associated with the historically attested son of Cunobelin, Caratacus the leader of British resistance against Rome. His coins appear in the same area as those of Epaticcus and he may have been his successor.

364   364A

	F £	VF £
364 **Silver Unit.** Head of Hercules r., CARA. ℞. Eagle stg. on snake. *M. 265; V. 593; BMC 2376-84. (117)*..	90	300
364A **Silver Minim.** CARA around pellet in ring. ℞. Winged horse r. *M. —; V. 595; BMC 2385-89. (117A)*...	75	200

DUROTRIGES
(Mid 1st Century B.C. to Mid 1st Century A.D.)

The Durotriges inhabited West Hampshire, Dorset and adjoining parts of Somerset and Wiltshire. Their coinage is one of the most distinctive in Britain due to its rapid debasement. The disappearance of precious metals from the coinage should perhaps be linked to the declining trade between the south-west and western Gaul, following the Roman conquest of the Gaul. Hengistbury Head is the probable mint site of the cast bronzes. Coins inscribed CRAB have been traditionally associated with the tribe.

UNINSCRIBED

365	**Silver Stater.** White Gold type. Derived from Westerham stater (no. 21). *M. 317; V. 1235, 52, 54, 55; BMC 2525-2731. (60)*..............................	95	300

366   368

366	Silver type. Similar. *M. 317; V. 1235, 52, 54, 55; BMC 2525-2731. (60)*	35	110
367	Billon type. Similar. *M. 317; V. 1235, 52, 54, 55; BMC 2525-2731. (60)*	25	55
368	**Silver Quarter Stater.** Geometric type. Crescent design. ℞. Zig-zag pattern. *M. 319; V. 1242/29; BMC 2734-79. (61). Quality of metal varies, obv. almost blank on later issues*..	25	70

369 371

		F	VF
		£	£

369 Starfish type. Spiral. R. Zig-zag pattern. *M. 320; V. 1270; BMC 2780-81 (61A)* 50 200

Hampshire Thin Flan type. Crude head of lines and pellets. R. Stylised horse l. *M. 321; V. 1280; BMC 2782-87. (62)* 50 200

371 **Bronze Stater.** Struck Bronze type. Similar to No.365-67. *M. 318; V. 1290; BMC 2790-2859. (81)* 20 50

372

372 Cast Bronze type. Many varities, as illustration. *M. 322-70; V. 1322-70; BMC 2860-2936. (82)* 25 115

"CRAB"

373

373 **Silver Unit.** CRAB in angles of cross. R. Eagle. *M. 371; V. 1285; BMC 2788. (145)* 250 800

373A **Silver Minim.** CRAB on tablet. R. Star shape. *M. 372; V. 1286; BMC 2789. (146)* 125 375

DOBUNNI
(Mid 1st Century B.C. to Mid 1st Century A.D.)

Dobunnic territory stretched over Gloucestershire, Hereford and Worcester and into parts of Somerset, Wiltshire and Gwent. The earliest Dobunnic coins are developed from the British Q stater, and have the distinctive tree-like motif of the tribe on the obverse. The inscribed coinage is difficult to arrange chronologically and it may be that some of the rulers named held different parts of the territory simultaneously.

UNINSCRIBED

374
374 (variant)

375

		F £	VF £
374	**Gold Stater.** Plain except for tree-like object. R. Three tailed horse r., wheel below. *M. 374; V. 1005; BMC 2937-40. (43)*	300	900
375	**Gold Quarter Stater.** Plain with traces of wreath pattern. R. Horse r. *M. 68; V. 1010-3; BMC 2942-46. (52)*	135	325
376	Wreath pattern. R. Horse l., pellet in ring motifs in field. *M. 74; V. 1015; BMC 2949. (51)*	135	325

377

378

377	**Silver Unit.** Allen types A-F/I-J. Regular series. Head r. R. Triple-tailed horse l. or r. *M. 374a, b/75/76, 378a-384; V. 1020/45/49/74/78/95/1135/1137; BMC 2950-3011. (63-64). Style becomes progressively more abstract, from-*	25	90
378	Allen types L-O. Irregular series. Similar to last. *M. 377-384d; V. 1170-85; BMC 3012-22. (63-64)*	30	125

INSCRIBED
The following types are not arranged chronologically.

ANTED

379

379	**Gold Stater.** Dobunnic emblem. R. ANTED or ANTEDRIG over triple tailed horse r., wheel below. *M. 385-86; V. 1062-69; BMC 3023-3031. (260)*	475	1350

		F £	VF £

380 **Silver Unit.** Crude head r. R. ANTED over horse. *M. 387; V. 1082; BMC 3032-38. (261)* 30 110

EISV

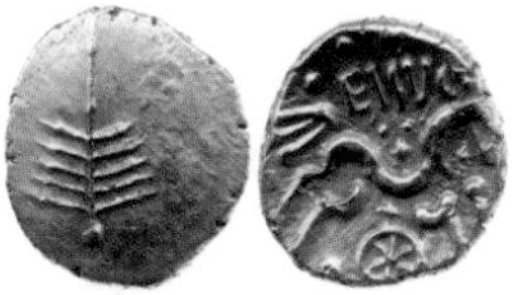

381 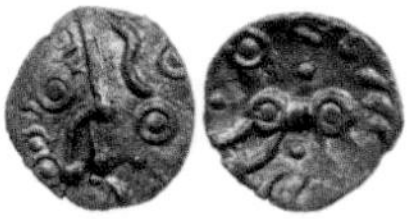 382

381 **Gold Stater.** Dobunnic emblem. R. EISV or EISVRIG over triple tailed horse r., wheel below. *M. 388; V. 1105; BMC 3039-42. (262)* 525 1500

382 **Silver Unit.** Crude head r. R. Horse l., EISV. *M. 389; V. 1110; BMC 3043-55. (263)* 25 95

INAM or INARA

383 **Gold Stater.** Dobunnic emblem. R. INAM or INARA over triple tailed horse r., wheel below. *M. 390; V. 1140; BMC 3056. (264)* 850 3000

CATTI

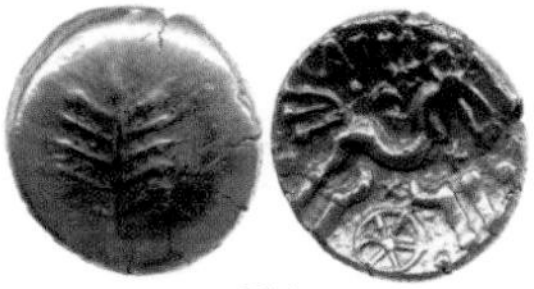

384

384 **Gold Stater.** Dobunnic emblem. R. CATTI over triple tailed horse r., wheel below. *M. 391; V. 1130; BMC 3057-60. (265)* 425 1250

COMUX

385 **Gold Stater.** Dobunnic emblem. R. COMVX retrograde, over triple tailed horse r., wheel below. *M. 392; V. 1092; BMC 3061-63. (266)* 750 2500

CORIO

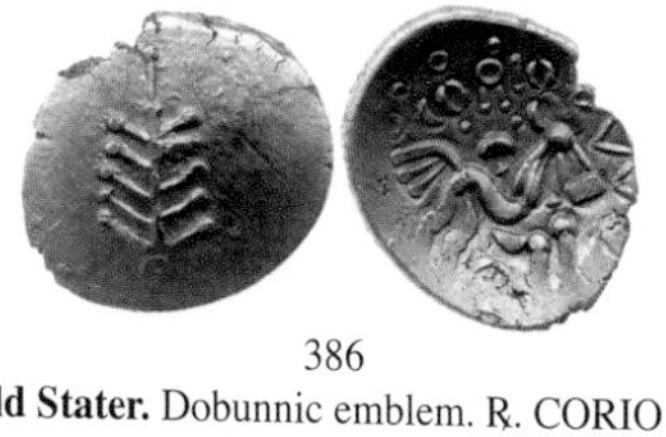

386 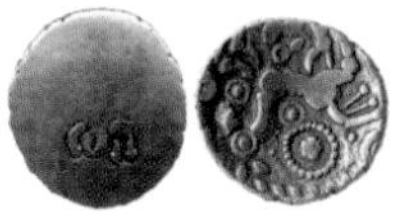 387

386 **Gold Stater.** Dobunnic emblem. R. CORIO over triple tailed horse r., wheel below. *M. 393; V. 1035; BMC 3064-3133. (267)* 425 1250

387 **Gold Quarter Stater.** COR in centre. R. Horse r., without legend. *M. 394; V. 1039; BMC 3134. (268)* 375 1000

BODVOC

388   389

		F £	VF £
388	**Gold Stater.** BODVOC across field. R. Horse r., without legend. *M. 395; V. 1052; BMC 3135-42. (269)*	725	2000
389	**Silver Unit.** Head l., BODVOC. R. Horse r., without legend. *M. 396; V. 1057; BMC 3143-45. (270)*	125	375

CORIELTAUVI

The Corieltauvi, formerly known as the Coritani, occupied Lincolnshire and adjoining parts of Yorkshire, Northamptonshire, Leicestershire and Nottinghamshire. The earliest staters, the South Ferriby type, are developed from Gallo-Belgic C staters, and are associated with the silver Boar/ Horse types. The distinctive dish shaped scyphate coinages have no parallels in Britain and stand apart from the main series. The later inscribed issues present a complex system of inscriptions. It has been suggested that some of the later inscriptions refer to pairs of names, possibly joint rulers or moneyers and rulers.

EARLY UNINSCRIBED
(Mid to Late 1st Century B.C.)

390   393

390	**Gold Stater.** South Ferriby type. Crude laureate head. R. Disjointed horse l., rosette or star below, anchor shape and pellets above. *M. 449-50; V. 809-815/19; BMC 3146-3179. (30)*	150	350
391	Wheel type. Similar, but wheel below horse. *M. 449c; V. 817; BMC 3180*	325	850
392	Kite type. Similar to 390, but diamond shape containing pellets above, spiral below horse. *M. 447; V. 825; BMC 3181-84. (29)*	200	550
393	Domino type. Similar to last, but with rectangle containing pellets. *M. 448; V. 829; BMC 3185-86. (29)*	190	500

394   395

	F £	VF £
394 Trefoil type. Trefoil with central rosette of seven pellets. R. Similar to 390. *M. 450a; V. 821; BMC —. (30A)*	1350	4500
395 North Lincolnshire Scyphate type. Stylised boar r. or l. R. Large S symbol with pellets and rings in field. *M. —; V. —; BMC 3187-93*	225	525

* chipped or cracked specimens are often encountered and are worth less

396

396 **Silver Unit.** Boar/Horse type I. Boar r., large pellet and ring motif above, reversed S below. R. Horse l. or r., pellet in ring above. *M. 405-06, 451; V. 855-60, 864, 867; BMC 3194-3214. (66)*	40	140
397 Boar Horse type II. Vestiges of boar on obv. R. Horse l. or r. *M. 410, 452-53; V. 875-877; BMC 3214-27. (68)*	25	95

398   399

398 Boar Horse type III. Blank. R. Horse l. or r. *M. 453-54; V. 884-77; BMC 3228-35. (69)*	20	75
399 **Silver Fractional Unit.** Similar to 396-97. *M. 406a, 451a; V. 862/66; BMC 3236-3250. (67)*	25	90
400 Similar to 398. *M. —; V. 877-81; BMC 3251-55. (70/71)*	20	70
401 Pattern/Horse. Flower pattern. R. Horse l. *M. —; V. —; BMC 3256-57...*	50	200

INSCRIBED

(Early to Mid 1st Century A.D.)
The following types are not arranged chronologically.

AVN COST

402   403

		F	VF
		£	£

402 **Gold Stater.** Crude wreath design. R. Disjointed horse l., AVN COST.
M. 457;V. 910; BMC 3258. (286) 475 1350

403 **Silver Unit.** Remains of wreath or blank. R. AVN COST, horse l. M. 458;
V. 914; BMC 3261-66. (287)... 30 95
404 **Silver Fractional Unit.** Similar. M. —; l V. 918; BMC 3267-68. (288) .. 25 75

ESVP RASV

405

405 **Gold Stater.** Crude wreath design. R. Disjointed horse l., IISVP RASV.
M. 456b; V. 920; BMC 3269. (289) 325 850

406 **Silver Unit.** Similar. M. 456c; V. 924; BMC 3272-73. (290) 70 225

VEP

407

407 **Gold Stater.** Blank or with traces of wreath. R. Disjointed horse l., VEP.
M. —; V. 905; BMC 3274-75. (296) 350 900

408 **Silver Unit.** Blank or with traces of wreath. R. VEP, horse r. M. —; V. 963;
BMC 3277-82. (297)... 35 110
409 **Silver Half Unit.** Similar. M. 464b; V. 967; BMC 3283-3295. (298) 25 80

VEP CORF

410

412

		F £	VF £

410 **Gold Stater.** Crude wreath design. R. Disjointed horse l., VEP CORF. *M. 459, 460; V. 930/40/60; BMC 3296-3304. (291)* ... 325 800

411 **Silver Unit.** Similar. *M. 460b/464; V. 934/50; BMC 3305-14. (292)* ... 30 90

412 Similar but VEPOC (M)ES, pellet in ring below horse. *M. —; V. 955; BMC —. (294)* ... 40 135

413 **Silver Half Unit.** Similar. *M. 464a; V. 938/58; BMC 3316-24. (293/95)* 30 90

DVMNO TIGIR SENO

414

415

414 **Gold Stater.** DVMN(OC) across wreath. R. Horse l., TIGIR SENO. *M. 461; V. 972; BMC 3325-27. (299)* ... 475 1350

415 **Silver Unit.** DVMNOC in two lines. R. Horse r., TIGIR SENO. *M. 462; V. 974; BMC 3328-29. (300)* ... 120 425

VOLISIOS DVMNOCOVEROS

416

416 **Gold Stater.** VOLISIOS between three lines in wreath. R. Horse r. or l., DVMNOCOVEROS. *M. 463/a; V. 978-80; BMC 3330-3336. (301)* ... 350 900

417 **Silver Unit.** Similar. R. Horse r., DVMNOCO. *M. 463a; V. 980; BMC 3339. (302)* ... 135 500

418 **Silver Half Unit.** Similar. *M. 465; V. 984; BMC 3340-41. (303)* ... 55 185

VOLISIOS DVMNOVELLAUNOS

419

		F £	VF £

419 **Gold Stater.** VOLISIOS between three lines in wreath. R. Horse r. or l., DVMNOVELAVNOS. *M. 466; V .988; BMC 3342-43. (304)* 625 1750

420 **Silver Half Unit.** As last but DVMNOVE. *M. 467; V. 992; BMC 3344-46. (305).* 110 375

VOLISIOS CARTIVEL

421 **Silver Half Unit.** VOLISIOS between three lines in wreath. R. Horse r., CARTILEV. *M. 468; V. 994; BMC 3347-48. (306)* 200 675

IAT ISO E

422 **Silver Unit.** IAT ISO (retrograde)on tablet, rosettes above and below. R. Horse r., E above. *M. 416; V. 998; BMC 3349-51. (284)* 125 375

CAT

422A **Silver Unit.** Boar r., pellet ring above, CAT above. R. Horse r. *M. —; V. —;* *BMC 3352* 175 625

LAT ISON

423

423 **Gold Stater.** LAT ISO(N) in two lines retrograde. R. Horse r., ISO in box above, N below. *M. —; V. —; BMC —. Only recorded as an AE/AV plated core, as illustrated.* .... *Extremely rare*

ICENI

The Iceni, centered on Norfolk but also occupying neighbouring parts of Suffolk and Cambridgeshire, are well attested in the post conquest period as the tribe who under Boudicca revolted against Roman rule. Their earliest coins are likely to have been the British J staters, Norfolk Wolf type (no.30/31), replaced around the mid first century B.C. by the Snettisham, Freckenham and Irstead type gold staters and quarter staters. Contemporary with these are silver Boar/Horse and Face/Horse units and fractions. The introduction of legends around the beginning of the millennia led to the adoption of a new obverse design of back to back crescents. The continuation of the coinage after the Roman invasion is attested by the coins of King Prasutagus. Some of the Face/Horse units (no.434) have been attributed to Queen Boudicca.

EARLY UNINSCRIBED
(Mid to Late 1st Century B.C.)

424

		F	VF
		£	£
424	**Gold Stater.** Snettisham type. Blank or with traces of pellet cross. R. Horse r., serpent like pellet in ring motif above. *M. —; V .—; BMC 3353-59....*	300	850
425	Similar. Blank or with 3 short curved lines. R. Horse r., symbol above more degraded. *M. —; V. —; BMC 3360-83*	275	725

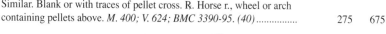

426   427

426	Freckenham type. Two opposed crescents with stars or pellets in field. R. Horse r., various symbols in field. *M. 397/99; V. 620; BMC 3384-89. (38)*	250	650
427	Similar. Blank or with traces of pellet cross. R. Horse r., wheel or arch containing pellets above. *M. 400; V. 624; BMC 3390-95. (40)*	275	675

428

| 428 | Similar. Trefoil on cross design. R. Similar. *M. 401-03; V. 626; BMC 3396-3419. (39)* | 250 | 650 |

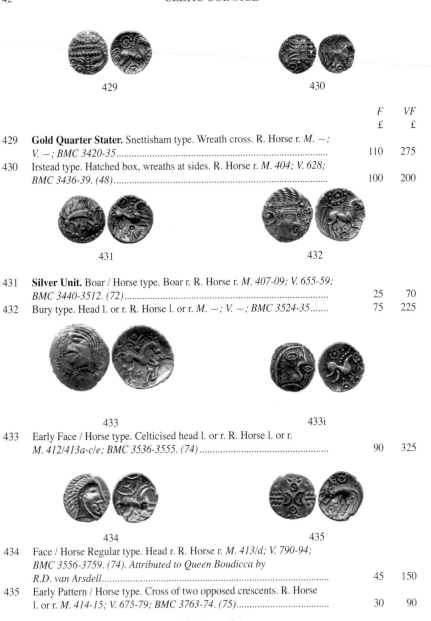

429

430

		F £	VF £
429	**Gold Quarter Stater.** Snettisham type. Wreath cross. R. Horse r. *M. —; V. —; BMC 3420-35*	110	275
430	Irstead type. Hatched box, wreaths at sides. R. Horse r. *M. 404; V. 628; BMC 3436-39. (48)*	100	200

431

432

| 431 | **Silver Unit.** Boar / Horse type. Boar r. R. Horse r. *M. 407-09; V. 655-59; BMC 3440-3512. (72)* | 25 | 70 |
| 432 | Bury type. Head l. or r. R. Horse l. or r. *M. —; V. —; BMC 3524-35* | 75 | 225 |

433

433i

| 433 | Early Face / Horse type. Celticised head l. or r. R. Horse l. or r. *M. 412/413a-c/e; BMC 3536-3555. (74)* | 90 | 325 |

434

435

| 434 | Face / Horse Regular type. Head r. Ꞧ. Horse r. *M. 413/d; V. 790-94; BMC 3556-3759. (74). Attributed to Queen Boudicca by R.D. van Arsdell* | 45 | 150 |
| 435 | Early Pattern / Horse type. Cross of two opposed crescents. Ꞧ. Horse l. or r. *M. 414-15; V. 675-79; BMC 3763-74. (75)* | 30 | 90 |

436

| 436 | ECEN symbol type. Two opposed crescents. Ꞧ. Horse r. *M. 429; V. 752; BMC 4297-4325* | 20 | 50 |

	F	VF
	£	£

437 **Silver Half Unit.** Boar / Horse type. Similar to 431. *M. 411; V. 661;*
BMC 3513-20. (73) 20 50

438 **Silver Fractional Unit.** Early Pattern / Horse type. Similar to 435. *M. 417/a;*
V. 681-83; BMC 3775-89. (76/A) 20 50

INSCRIBED
(Early to Mid 1st Century A.D.)
The following types are not arranged chronologically.

CAN DVRO

439

439 **Silver Unit.** Boar. R. Horse r., CAN(S) above, DVRO below. *M. 434; V. 663;*
BMC 3521-23. (271) 85 275

ANTED

440

440 **Gold Stater.** Triple crescent design. R. Horse r., ANTED monongram below.
M. 418; V. 705; BMC 3790. (272) 475 1250

441

441 **Silver Unit.** Two opposed crescents. R. Horse r., ANTED. *M. 419-21;*
V. 710-11/15; BMC 3791-4025. (273) 25 60

442 **Silver Fractional Unit.** Similar to last. *M. 422; V. 720; BMC 4028-31. (274)* 25 80

ECEN

443

		F £	VF £

443 **Gold Stater.** Triple crescent design. R. Horse r., ECEN below. *M. —; V. 725; BMC 4032.* 850 2500

443A **Silver Unit.** Two opposed crescents. R, Horse r., ECEN. *M. 424; V. 730; BMC 4033-4215. (275)* 20 55

443B **Silver Half Unit.** Similar to last. *M. 431; V. 736; BMC 4216-17. (276)* . 20 50

EDN

444 **Silver Unit.** Two opposed crescents. R, Horse r., ED, E, EI or EDN. *M. 423, 425b; V. 734/40; BMC 4219-81. (277)* 20 55

ECE

444A **Gold Stater** Triple crescent design R. Horse r., ECE. *M. — ; V. — ;* 975 3000

445

445 **Silver Unit.** Two opposed crescents. R, Horse r., ECE. *M. 425-28; V. 761-66; BMC 4348-4538. (278-80)* 25 60

SAENU

446 **Silver Unit.** Two opposed crescents. R. Horse r., SAENV. *M. 433; V. 770; BMC 4540-57. (281)* 35 110

AESU

447

447 **Silver Unit.** Two opposed crescents. R. Horse r., AESV. *M. 432; V. 775; BMC 4558-72. (282)* 35 110

ALE SCA

448 **Silver Unit.** Boar r., ALE. R. Horse r., SCA. *M. 469; V. 996; BMC 4576* 100 300

AEDIC SIA

	F	VF
	£	£

449   **Silver Unit.** AEDIC in two lines. R. Horse r., SIA? below. *M.—; V.—;*
BMC 4581   175   575

PRASUTAGUS

450

450   **Silver Unit.** Romanised head l., SUB RII PRASTO. R. Rearing horse r.,
ESICO FECIT. *M. 434a; V. 780; BMC 4577-80. (283)*   475   1650
*This legend translates as "Under King Prasto, Esico made me", giving the name of both
King and moneyer.*

The systematic conquest of Britain by the Romans began in A.D. 43 when the Emperor Claudius (41-54), anxious to enhance his military reputation, authorized an invasion in which he personally participated, albeit in a purely symbolic role. The initial military contact between the two cultures had taken place almost a century before when Julius Caesar, during the course of his conquest of Celtic Gaul, led expeditions to the island in 55 and 54 B.C. Although no actual Roman occupation of Britain resulted from Caesar's reconnoitring campaigns, commercial intercourse was certainly accelerated, as evidenced by the 'Romanization' of the British Celtic coinage in the final decades of its production.

The Claudian conquest, commencing in A.D. 43, brought about a complete change in the nature of the currency circulating in Britain and ushered in a period lasting more than three and a half centuries during which Roman coinage was the only official medium of exchange. Local copies of the money brought with them by the four legions of the invasion army began to appear at a very early stage, the most popular type for imitation being the well-known Claudian copper as with reverse type fighting Minerva. Some of these copies are well-executed and of a style not much inferior to the prototype, suggesting that their local minting may have been officially sanctioned by the Roman government in order to make good a shortage of currency in the newly-conquered territory. Other examples are of much poorer style and execution and are frequently well below the normal weight of a Claudian as (usually between 10 and 11 grams). These copies must have been issued unofficially and provide evidence of the huge demand for this type of currency in a population which had never before experienced the benefits of having base metal coins available for small everyday transactions.

In the decades that followed, the boundaries of the Roman province of Britannia were continually pushed further north and west until, under the celebrated Flavian governor Gnaeus Julius Agricola, the Roman army even penetrated to northern Scotland (A.D. 83/4). A few years later, under Trajan, the northern frontier was established along the Tyne-Solway line, a barrier made permanent by the construction of Hadrian's Wall following the emperor's visit to the province in 122. For a brief period in the mid-2nd century the frontier was temporarily advanced to the Forth-Clyde line with the building of the Antonine Wall, though this seems to have been abandoned early in the reign of Marcus Aurelius (ca. 163) when the Hadrianic barrier was re-commissioned and became the permanent frontier. The security thus provided to the now-peaceful province in the south facilitated urban expansion and the development of commerce. The new prosperity brought a flood of Roman coinage into the island-province and it was no longer necessary for shortages to be made good by large scale local imitation.

Until the mid-3rd century the production of Roman coinage remained the prerogative of the mint in the capital, with only occasional issues from provincial centres to serve short-term local needs. But with the deepening political and economic crisis in the third quarter of the century there was a dramatic decentralization of minting operations, with permanent establishments being set up in many important cities in the western as well as the eastern provinces. Britain, however, still remained without an official mint at this time and in the dark days of the 270s, when the separatist Gallic Empire to which Britain belonged was close to collapse, large scale production of imitative antoniniani (commonly called 'barbarous radiates') occurred in the province. The integrity and prestige of the Empire was, to some extent, restored by a rapid succession of Illyrian 'soldier emperors', until the situation was finally stabilized by Diocletian (A.D. 284-305) who established the tetrarchy system under which governmental responsibility was shared by four rulers. By the end of the 3rd century Britain had been reorganized into a civil diocese of four provinces: it had already been subdivided into Britannia Superior and Britannia Inferior almost a hundred years before, under Septimius Severus or Caracalla.

It was left to the colourful and enigmatic usurper Carausius (A.D. 287-293) to establish mints in Britain. It was, of course, vital for him to do so as his dominion was mostly confined to the island-province. Londinium (London) was his principal mint, with a secondary establishment at a place usually signing itself 'C' (probably Camulodunum, modern Colchester). After the downfall of Carausius' murderer and successor Allectus (293-296) Britain was restored to the central government, an event commemorated by the celebrated gold medallion of Constantius I showing the Caesar riding alongside the Thames approaching the gateway of the city of Londinium. At this point the mysterious 'C' mint disappears from the picture. Londinium, on the other hand, retained its status as an official mint under Diocletian's tetrarchy and its successors down to A.D. 325, when it was closed by Constantine the Great who regarded it as superfluous to his needs. In nearly four decades of existence as a Roman mint Londinium had produced a varied and extensive coinage in the names of almost all the emperors, empresses and Caesars of the period. It was destined never again to be active during Roman times, unless the extremely rare gold and silver issues of the late 4th century usurper Magnus Maximus, signed AVG, AVGOB and AVGPS, are correctly attributed to Londinium under its late Roman name of Augusta.

The termination of Roman rule in the British provinces is traditionally dated to A.D. 410 when the emperor Honorius, in response to an appeal for aid from his British subjects, told them to arrange for their own defence as best they might ('Rescript of Honorius'). In reality, the end probably came quite gradually. As the machinery of government ground to a halt and the soldiers stopped receiving their pay there would have been a steady drift of population away from the semi-ruinous cities and military installations to the countryside, where they could better provide for themselves through farming. Under these conditions the need for coinage would have been drastically reduced, as a primitive economy based on barter would largely have replaced the complex monetary economy of the late Roman period. In any case the supply of coinage from the Continent would now have dried up. The few monetary transactions which still took place were made with worn-out coins from earlier periods augmented by local imitations, production of which in Britain had resumed in the mid-4th century. Such was the pitiful end of the long tradition of Roman coinage in the remote island-province of Britannia. More than two centuries of 'Dark Ages' were to elapse before England's new rulers, the Anglo-Saxons, commenced the issue of gold thrymsas, the designs of many of which were based on late Roman types.

As Rome's Imperial coinage provided the currency needs of this country over a period of almost four centuries no representative collection of British coins is complete without some examples of these important issues. The following listing is divided into four categories: 1. Regular Roman issues, all of which would have been legal tender in Britain after A.D. 43; 2. Issues with types referring specifically to the province of Britannia, usually in commemoration of military campaigns in the north; 3. Official Roman coinage struck in Britain; 4. Imitations of Roman coins produced in Britain, all but possibly some of the earliest being of unofficial origin. The reference 'R.R.C.' is to the listing of the type in Michael Crawford's *Roman Republican Coinage* (Cambridge, 1974); and 'R.I.C.' to *The Roman Imperial Coinage* (London, 1923-1994, in ten volumes).

For more detailed collectors' information on Roman coinage, including a more comprehensive listing of types, the reader is referred to *Roman Coins and their Values Volumes 1, 2 and 3* by David R. Sear. A complete catalogue of silver issues may be found in the 5 volumes of *Roman Silver Coins* (H.A. Seaby and C.E. King) which provides a quick and convenient reference and is especially aimed at the collector. Gilbert Askew's *The Coinage of Roman Britain* (2nd edition) concentrates on those issues which are particularly associated with the Roman province of Britannia, but does not provide valuations. More recent works on this subject include R. Reece's *Coinage in Roman Britain* and *The Coinage of Roman Britain*, and also David R. Sear's *The History and Coinage of the Roman Imperators, 49-27 BC* which is devoted to the vital two decades of transition from Republic to Empire.

The standard works on the coinages of the Roman Republic and the Roman Empire have already been mentioned *(Roman Republican Coinage and Roman Imperial Coinage)*. These monumental publications are essential to the advanced collector and student and their importance cannot be overstated. The British Museum Catalogues (3 volumes of Republican, 6 volumes of Imperial recently reprinted by SPINK) are also vital. They contain superb interpretive material in their introductions and are very fully illustrated. A similar work is Anne S. Robertson's *Roman Imperial Coins in the Hunter Coin Cabinet,* in 5 volumes (volume 4 is especially important for the later 3rd century coinage). For more general reading we may recommend J.P.C. Kent and M. & A. Hirmer's *Roman Coins,* undoubtedly the most lavishly illustrated book on the subject; C.H.V. Sutherland's *Roman Coins;* and R.A.G. Carson's *Coins of the Roman Empire.* Finally, for a most useful single-volume work on interpretation and background information, we would suggest A *Dictionary of Ancient Roman Coins* by John Melville Jones.

1. REGULAR ROMAN ISSUES

A token selection of the types of Roman coins which might be found on Romano-British archaeological sites. Many of the rarer emperors and empresses have been omitted and the types listed often represent only one of hundreds of variant forms which might be encountered.

		F £	VF £
451	**THE REPUBLIC: P. Aelius Paetus** (moneyer), 138 B.C. Æ *denarius*. Helmeted hd. of Roma r. Rev. The Dioscuri galloping r. R.R.C. 233/1 ... *Although dating from long before the Roman conquest many Republican coins circulated well into the Imperial period and found their way to Britain where they are often represented in early hoards.*	20	60
452	**L. Thorius Balbus** (moneyer), 105 B.C. Æ denarius. Hd. of Juno Sospita r., clad in goat's skin. Rev. Bull charging r. *R.R.C. 316/1.*	25	70
453	**Q. Antonius Balbus** (moneyer), 83-82 B.C. Æ *denarius*. Laur. hd. of Jupiter r. Rev. Victory in quadriga r. *R.R.C. 364/1.*	25	70

454   456

		F £	VF £
454	**C. Calpurnius Piso** (moneyer), 67 B.C. Æ *denarius*. Laur. hd. of Apollo r. Rev. Horseman galloping r., holding palm-branch. *R.R.C. 408/1a.*	30	70
455	**Mn. Acilius Glabrio** (moneyer), 49 B.C. Æ *denarius*. Laur. hd. of Salus r. Rev. Valetudo stg. l., holding snake and resting on column. *R.R.C. 442/1.*	20	60
456	**Julius Caesar** (dictator), visited Britain 55 and 54 B.C., died 44 B.C. Æ *denarius*. CAESAR. Elephant r. Rev. Priestly emblems. *R.R.C. 443/1....*	75	175
456A	— Wreathed hd. of Caesar r. Rev. P. SEPVLLIVS MACER. Venus stg. l., holding Victory and sceptre. *R.R.C. 480/9.*	300	800
457	**Mark Antony** (triumvir), died 30 B.C. Æ *denarius*. Galley r. Rev. LEG. II. Legionary eagle between two standards. *R.R.C. 544/14.*	50	125

458   459

		F £	VF £
458	**Octavian** (triumvir), named Augustus 27 B.C. Æ *denarius*. Bare hd. of Octavian r. Rev. IMP. CAESAR. Trophy set on prow. *R.I.C. 265a.*	90	200
459	**THE EMPIRE: Augustus,** 27 B.C.-A.D. 14. Æ *denarius*. Rev. C. L. CAESARES AVGVSTI F COS DESIG PRINC IVVENT. The emperor's grandsons, Gaius and Lucius, stg. facing, with spears and shields. *R.I.C. 207.* *Almost all the coins in the Roman Imperial series have a head or bust of the emperor, empress or prince as their obverse type. Therefore, in most instances only the reverses will be described in the following listings.*	60	140

	F	VF
	£	£
460 Æ as. ROM. ET AVG. The altar of Lugdunum. *R.I.C. 230.*	50	125
460A Æ quadrans. Obv. Anvil. Rev. Moneyers' inscription around large S. C. *R.I.C. 443.*	15	35
461 **Augustus and Agrippa,** general and designated heir of Augustus, died 12 B.C. Æ *dupondius.* Obv. Their hds. back to back. Rev. COL. NEM. Crocodile r., chained to palm-branch. *R.I.C. 159.* .... *See also no. 468.*	60	150
462 **Divus Augustus,** deified A.D. 14. Æ as. PROVIDENT S. C. Large altar. *R.I.C. 81.*	60	150
463 **Tiberius,** A.D. 14-37. *N aureus.* PONTIF MAXIM. Livia (?) seated r., holding sceptre and branch. *R.I.C. 29.*	400	1100

464   467

464 *R* denarius. Similar. *R.I.C. 30.* .... *This type is commonly referred to as the 'Tribute Penny' of the Bible (Matthew 22, 17-21).*	80	175
464A Æ *as.* Inscription around large S. C. *R.I.C. 44.*	55	140
465 **Livia,** wife of Augustus, mother of Tiberius. Æ *dupondius.* Obv. Veiled bust of Livia as Pietas r. Rev. Inscription of Drusus Caesar around large S. C. *R.I.C. 43.*	150	375
466 **Drusus,** son of Tiberius. Æ *as.* Inscription around large S. C. *R.I.C. 45.*	65	175
467 **Caligula,** A.D. 37-41. Æ *as.* VESTA S. C. Vesta seated l. *R.I.C. 38.*	85	240

468

468 **Agrippa,** grandfather of Caligula, died 12 B.C. Æ *as.* S. C. Neptune stg. l., holding dolphin and trident. *R.I.C. 58.* .... *See also no. 461 and under Category 4.*	60	180
469 **Germanicus,** father of Caligula, brother of Claudius, died A.D. 19. Æ *as.* Inscription of Caligula around large S. C. *R.I.C. 35.*	75	175
470 **Agrippina Senior,** mother of Caligula, died A.D. 33. Æ *sestertius.* S.P.Q.R. MEMORIAE AGRIPPINAE. Carpentum drawn l. by two mules. *R.I.C. 55.*	250	850

471   474

		F	VF
		£	£
471	**Claudius,** A.D. 41-54, initiated the conquest of Britain by his invasion in A.D. 43. Æ *as*. LIBERTAS AVGVSTA S. C. Libertas stg. r., holding pileus. *R.I.C. 113.*	65	175
471A	Æ *quadrans*. Obv. Hand holding scales. Rev. Inscription around large S. C. *R.I.C. 85.*	15	35
	See also under Categories 2 and 4.		
472	**Nero Claudius Drusus,** father of Claudius, died 9 B.C. Æ *sestertius*. TI. CLAVDIVS CAESAR AVG. P. M. TR .P. IMP. P. P. S. C. Claudius seated l. on curule chair amidst arms. *R.I.C. 109.*	130	450
	See also under Category 4.		
473	**Antonia,** mother of Claudius, died A.D. 37. Æ *dupondius*. TI. CLAVDIVS CAESAR AVG P.M. TR. P. IMP. S. C. Claudius stg. l., holding simpulum. *R.I.C. 92.*	100	275
	See also under Category 4.		
474	**Nero,** 54-68, emperor at the time of Queen Boudicca's rebellion in Britain. *N aureus*. SALVS. Salus seated l. *R.I.C. 66.*	550	1300
475	*R denarius*. IVPPITER CVSTOS. Jupiter seated l. *R.I.C. 53.*	85	275
476	Æ *sestertius*. ROMA S. C. Roma seated l., holding Victory and parazonium. *R.I.C. 274.*	150	475
476A	Æ as. S. C. Victory hovering l., holding shield inscribed S. P. Q. R. *R.I.C. 312.*	60	160
477	**Galba,** 68-69. *R denarius*. S.P.Q.R. / OB / C.S. within oak-wreath. *R.I.C. 167.*	100	275
478	**Otho,** 69. *R denarius*. SECVRITAS P. R. Securitas stg. l. *R.I.C. 10.*	200	550
479	**Vitellius,** 69. *R denarius*. CONCORDIA P. R. Concordia seated l. *R.I.C. 90.*	100	250
480	**Vespasian,** 69-79, commanded Legio II in the Claudian invasion of Britain (43) and appointed Agricola to governorship of the province in 77/8. *N aureus*. ANNONA AVG. Annona seated l. *R.I.C. 131a*	500	1200

481

481	*R denarius*. VICTORIA AVGVSTI. Victory advancing r., crowning standard. *R.I.C. 52.*	30	80
481A	Æ *dupondius*. FELICITAS PVBLICA S. C. Felicitas stg. l. *R.I.C. 554...*	40	110
482	**Titus,** 79-81 (Caesar 69-79). *R denarius*. TR. P. IX. IMP. XV. COS. VIII. P. P. Thunderbolt on throne. *R.I.C. 23a.*	50	140

483   485

	F	VF
	£	£

483 **Domitian,** 81-96 (Caesar 69-81), recalled Agricola in 83/4 and abandoned the conquest of northern Scotland (ca. 87). Æ *denarius.* IMP. XIX. COS. XIIII. CENS. P. P. P. Minerva stg. l., resting on spear. *R.I.C. 140* 25 75

484 Æ *dupondius.* VIRTVTI AVGVSTI S. C. Virtus stg. r. *R.I.C. 393* 35 85

484A Æ *as.* MONETA AVGVSTI S. C. Moneta stg. l. *R.I.C. 354b.* 35 85

485 **Nerva,** 96-98. Æ *denarius.* AEQVITAS AVGVST. Aequitas stg. l. *R.I.C. 13.* 50 120

485A Æ *as.* LIBERTAS PVBLICA S. C. Libertas stg. l. *R.I.C. 86.* 55 140

486 **Trajan,** 98-117, established the northern frontier in Britain along the Tyne-Solway line (ca. 100). Æ *aureus.* P. M. TR. P. COS. VI. P. P. S. P. Q. R. Genius stg. l., holding patera and corn-ears. *R.I.C. 347.* 450 1100

487   489

487 Æ *denarius.* COS. V. P. P. S. P. Q. R. OPTIMO PRINC. Military trophy. *R.I.C. 147* 25 75

488 Æ *sestertius.* S. P. Q. R. OPTIMO PRINCIPI S. C. Spes walking l., holding flower. *R.I.C. 519.* 50 175

488A Æ *dupondius.* SENATVS POPVLVSQVE ROMANVS S. C. Emperor advancing between two trophies. *R.I.C. 676.* 50 100

489 **Hadrian,** 117-138, visited Britain in 122 and initiated the construction of a fortified frontier line (Hadrian's Wall). Æ *aureus.* HISPANIA. Hispania reclining l. *R.I.C. 305.* 500 1200

490 Æ *denarius.* P. M. TR. P. COS. III. Roma stg. l., holding Victory and spear. *R.I.C. 76.* 30 85

491 Æ *sestertius.* COS. III. S. C. Neptune stg. r., holding dolphin and trident, foot on prow. *R.I.C. 632.* 50 175

491A Æ *as.* FELICITATI AVG COS. III. P. P. S. C. Galley travelling l. over waves. *R.I.C. 719.* 40 120

See also under Category 2.

492 **Sabina,** wife of Hadrian. Æ *denarius.* IVNONI REGINAE. Juno stg. l. *R.I.C. 395a.* 40 120

493 **Aelius Caesar,** heir of Hadrian, 136-138. Æ *denarius.* CONCORD. TR. POT. COS. II. Concordia seated l. *R.I.C. 436.* 75 200

493A Æ *as.* TR. POT. COS. II. S. C. Spes walking l., holding flower. *R.I.C. 1067.* 50 130

		F £	VF £

494 **Antoninus Pius,** 138-161, ordered the expansion of the Roman province
to include southern Scotland and constructed the Antonine Wall on the
Forth-Clyde line (beginning ca. 143). An uprising in northern Britain in the
150s results in a permanent withdrawal to the Hadrianic frontier early in
the next reign. *N aureus.* COS. IIII. Togate emperor stg. l., holding globe.
R.I.C. 233b. 400 900

495 *R denarius.* PIETATI AVG. COS. IIII. Pietas stg. l. between two children,
holding two more in her arms. *R.I.C. 313c.* 25 70

496

496 *Æ sestertius.* SALVS AVG. S. C. Salus stg. l. at altar, feeding snake.
R.I.C. 635. .... 40 160

496A *Æ dupondius.* TR. POT. XX. COS. IIII. S. C. Providentia stg. l., pointing
at globe at her feet and holding sceptre. *R.I.C. 2025.* 25 60
See also under Categories 2 and 3.

497 **Antoninus Pius and Marcus Aurelius Caesar**. *R denarius.* Obv. Laur.
hd. of Antoninus Pius r. Rev. AVRELIVS CAESAR AVG PII F. COS. Bare
hd. of young Marcus Aurelius r. *R.I.C. 417a.* 50 130

498   501

498 **Divus Antoninus Pius,** deified 161. *R denarius.* CONSECRATIO.
Four-storeyed crematorium of Antoninus Pius. *R.I.C. 436.* 25 75

499 **Diva Faustina Senior,** wife of Antoninus Pius, deified 141. *R denarius.*
AETERNITAS. Aeternitas stg. l., holding globe and billowing veil. *R.I.C. 351.* 25 75

499A *Æ sestertius.* AVGVSTA S. C. Ceres stg. l., holding two torches. *R.I.C. 1120.* 30 110

500 **Marcus Aurelius,** 161-180 (Caesar 139-161), re-established Hadrian's Wall
as the permanent northern frontier of the province, ca. 163. *N aureus.*
PROV. DEOR. TR. P. XV. COS. III. Providentia stg. l., holding globe and
cornucopiae. *R.I.C. 19.* 450 950

501 *R denarius.* PIETAS AVG. Priestly emblems. *R.I.C. 424a.* 25 75

501A — SALVTI AVG. COS. III. Salus stg. l. at altar, feeding snake. *R.I.C. 222.* 20 70

502 *Æ sestertius.* CONCORD. AVGVSTOR. TR. P. XVI. COS. III. S. C. Marcus
Aurelius and Lucius Verus stg. face to face, clasping hands. *R.I.C. 826.*. 40 160

502A *Æ as.* HONOS TR. POT. II. COS. II. S. C. Honos stg. r. *R.I.C. 1271a.* .. 30 75

	F £	VF £

503 **Divus Marcus Aurelius,** deified 180. Æ *denarius*. CONSECRATIO.
Eagle stg. r. on altar. *R.I.C. 272.* 25 70

504 506A

504 **Faustina Junior,** daughter of Antoninus Pius, wife of Marcus Aurelius.
Æ *denarius*. FECVNDITAS. Fecunditas stg. r., holding sceptre and child.
R.I.C. 677. .... 25 60

504A Æ *sestertius*. HILARITAS S. C. Hilaritas stg. l. *R.I.C. 1642.* 35 120

505 **Diva Faustina Junior,** deified 175. Æ *as*. S. C. Crescent and seven stars.
R.I.C. 1714. .... 35 80

506 **Lucius Verus,** 161-169. Æ denarius. PAX TR. P. VI. IMP. IIII. COS. II.
Pax stg. l. *R.I.C. 561.* 30 80

506A Æ *dupondius*. TR. P. IIII. IMP. II. COS. II. S. C. Mars stg. r., resting on
spear and shield. *R.I.C. 1387.* 35 95

507 **Lucilla,** daughter of Marcus Aurelius, wife of Lucius Verus. Æ *denarius*.
IVNONI LVCINAE. Juno stg. l., holding child in swaddling clothes.
R.I.C. 771. .... 30 75

507A Æ *sestertius*. PIETAS S. C. Pietas stg. l., altar at feet. *R.I.C. 1756.* 35 120

508 **Commodus,** 177-192 (Caesar 175-177), major warfare on the British
frontier early in the reign; situation restored by Ulpius Marcellus in 184/5,
followed by unrest in the British legions. Æ *denarius*. LIB. AVG. IIII. TR.
P. VI. IMP. IIII. COS. III. P. P. Liberalitas stg. l. *R.I.C. 22.* 30 80

509 511

509 Æ *sestertius*. IOVI VICTORI IMP. III. COS. II. P. P. S. C. Jupiter seated l.
R.I.C. 1612. .... 40 140

509A Æ *as*. ANN. AVG. TR. P. VII. IMP. IIII. COS. III. P. P. S. C. Annona stg. l.,
modius at feet. *R.I.C. 339.* 25 70
See also under Category 2.

510 **Crispina,** wife of Commodus. Æ *denarius*. CONCORDIA. Clasped hands.
R.I.C. 279. .... 30 75

511 **Pertinax,** January-March 193, formerly governor of Britain, ca. 185-7. Æ
denarius. PROVID. DEOR. COS. II. Providentia stg l., reaching up to star.
R.I.C. 11a. 250 600

512   513

		F	VF
		£	£

512   **Didius Julianus,** March-June 193. Æ *denarius.* CONCORD MILIT.
       Concordia Militum stg. l., holding standards. *R.I.C. 1.* 375   850
513   **Clodius Albinus,** 195-197 (Caesar 193-195), governor of Britain (from
       191/2) at the time of his imperial proclamation by his troops. Æ *denarius.*
       MINER. PACIF. COS. II. Minerva stg. l. *R.I.C. 7.* 60   140
513A   — FIDES LEGION. COS. II. Clasped hands holding legionary eagle.
       R.I.C. 20b. 75   175

514A   516

514   **Septimius Severus,** 193-211, restored the frontier forts in northern Britain
       following the downfall of Clodius Albinus; later repaired Hadrian's Wall,
       and spent the years 208-11 in Britain campaigning in Scotland; divided
       Britannia into two provinces, Superior and Inferior; died at York, February
       211. Æ *denarius.* VIRT AVGG. Roma stg. l., holding Victory, spear and
       shield. *R.I.C. 171a.* 20   50
514A   — P.M. TR. P. XVIII. COS. III. P. P. Jupiter stg. l. between two children.
       R.I.C. 240. 20   50
       See also under Category 2.
515   **Julia Domna,** wife of Septimius Severus, mother of Caracalla and Geta,
       accompanied her husband and sons on the British expedition, 208-211, and
       probably resided in London during the northern campaigns. Æ *denarius.*
       VENERI VICTR. Venus stg. r., resting on column. *R.I.C. 536.* 15   45
515A   — VESTA. Vesta stg. l., holding palladium and sceptre. *R.I.C. 390.* 15   45
516   **Caracalla,** 198-217 (Caesar 196-198), accompanied his father and brother
       on the British expedition, 208-211, and led the final campaign in Scotland
       in 210 during Severus' illness; made frontier dispositions before returning
       to Rome and finalized his father's arrangements for the division of Britain
       into two provinces. Æ *antoninianus (double denarius,* introduced in 215).
       VENVS VICTRIX. Venus stg. l., holding Victory and resting on shield.
       R.I.C. 311c. 30   75
517   Æ *denarius.* PART. MAX. PONT. TR. P. IIII. Trophy with two captives at
       base. *R.I.C. 54b.* 15   50
517A   — P. M. TR. P. XV. COS. III. P. P. Hercules stg. l., holding olive-branch
       and club. *R.I.C. 192.* 15   50
       See also under Category 2.

	F	*VF*
	£	£

518 **Plautilla,** wife of Caracalla. Ρ *denarius.* PROPAGO IMPERI. Caracalla
and Plautilla clasping hands. *R.I.C. 362.* 25 75

519 522

519 **Geta,** 209-212 (Caesar 198-209), accompanied his father and brother on
the British expedition, 208-211, and took charge of the civil administration
in London during the northern campaigns. Ρ *denarius.* PRINC. IVVENTVTIS.
Prince stg. l. beside trophy, holding branch and spear. *R.I.C. 18.* 20 50
519A — FORT RED TR. P. III. COS. II. Fortuna seated l. *R.I.C. 75.* 25 65
See also under Category 2.
520 **Macrinus,** 217-218. Ρ *denarius.* PROVIDENTIA DEORVM. Providentia
stg. l., globe at feet. *R.I.C. 80.* 35 110
521 **Diadumenian,** 218 (Caesar 217-218). Ρ *denarius.* PRINC. IVVENTVTIS.
Prince stg. l., two standards behind. *R.I.C. 109.* 70 175
522 **Elagabalus,** 218-222. Ρ *antoninianus.* MARS VICTOR. Mars advancing r.
R.I.C. 122. .... 22 55
522A Ρ *denarius.* P. M. TR. P. III. COS. III. P. P. Jupiter seated l., eagle at feet
R.I.C. 27. .... 20 40
523 **Julia Paula,** first wife of Elagabalus. Ρ *denarius.* CONCORDIA.
Concordia seated l. *R.I.C. 211.* 40 100
524 **Aquilia Severa,** second wife of Elagabalus. Ρ *denarius.* CONCORDIA.
Concordia stg. l., altar at feet. *R.I.C. 226.* 60 150
525 **Julia Soaemias,** mother of Elagabalus. Ρ *denarius.* VENVS CAELESTIS.
Venus seated l., child at feet. *R.I.C. 243.* 30 75
526 **Julia Maesa,** grandmother of Elagabalus and Severus Alexander. Ρ
denarius. SAECVLI FELICITAS. Felicitas stg. l., altar at feet. *R.I.C. 271.* 25 60
527 **Severus Alexander,** 222-235 (Caesar 221-222). Ρ *denarius.*
PAX AETERNA AVG. Pax stg. l. *R.I.C. 165.* 15 40
527A — P. M. TR. P. XIII. COS. III. P. P. Sol advancing l., holding whip. *R.I.C. 123.* 15 40

528

528 Æ *sestertius.* MARS VLTOR S. C. Mars advancing r., with spear and shield.
R.I.C. 635. .... 30 85

		F £	VF £

529 **Orbiana,** wife of Severus Alexander. Æ *denarius.* CONCORDIA AVGG.
Concordia seated l. *R.I.C. 319.* 70 175

530 **Julia Mamaea,** mother of Severus Alexander. Æ *denarius.* VESTA.
Vesta stg. l. *R.I.C. 362.* 20 50

530A Æ *sestertius.* FELICITAS PVBLICA S. C. Felicitas stg. facing, hd. l.,
resting on column. *R.I.C. 676.* 30 85

531A

531 **Maximinus I,** 235-238. Æ *denarius.* PAX AVGVSTI. Pax stg. l. *R.I.C. 12.* 20 50

531A Æ *sestertius.* SALVS AVGVSTI S. C. Salus seated l., feeding snake arising
from altar. *R.I.C. 85.* 30 85

532 **Maximus Caesar,** son of Maximinus I. Æ *denarius.* PRINC IVVENTVTIS.
Prince stg. l., two standards behind. *R.I.C. 3.* 50 175

533 **Gordian I Africanus,** March-April 238, governor of Britannia Inferior
late in the reign of Caracalla. Æ *denarius.* P. M. TR. P. COS. P. P. Togate
emperor stg. l. *R.I.C. 1.* 250 650

534 **Gordian II Africanus,** March-April 238. Æ *denarius.* VIRTVS AVGG.
Virtus stg. l., with shield and spear. *R.I.C. 3.* 250 650

535 **Balbinus,** April-July 238. Æ *antoninianus.* FIDES MVTVA AVGG.
Clasped hands. *R.I.C. 11.* 75 175

535A Æ *denarius.* PROVIDENTIA DEORVM. Providentia stg. l., globe at feet.
R.I.C. 7. .... 50 140

536 **Pupienus,** April-July 238. Æ *antoninianus.* AMOR MVTVVS AVGG.
Clasped hands. *R.I.C. 9a.* 75 175

536A Æ *denarius.* PAX PVBLICA. Pax seated l. *R.I.C. 4.* 50 140

537

537 **Gordian III,** 238-244 (Caesar 238). Æ *antoninianus.* LAETITIA AVG. N.
Laetitia stg. l. *R.I.C. 86.* 15 30

538 Æ *denarius.* DIANA LVCIFERA. Diana stg. r., holding torch. *R.I.C. 127.* 15 30

538A Æ *sestertius.* AETERNITATI AVG. S.C. Sol stg. l., holding globe. *R.I.C. 297a.* 22 65

539

	F	VF
	£	£

539 **Philip I,** 244-249. Æ *antoninianus.* ROMAE AETERNAE. Roma seated l.
R.I.C. 65. .... | 12 | 30

539A Æ *sestertius.* SECVRIT. ORBIS S. C. Securitas seated l. *R.I.C. 190.* ..... | 25 | 75

540 **Otacilia Severa,** wife of Philip I. Æ *antoninianus.* PIETAS AVGVSTAE.
Pietas stg. l. *R.I.C. 125c.* .... | 15 | 40

540A Æ *sestertius.* CONCORDIA AVGG. S. C. Concordia seated l. *R.I.C. 203a.* | 25 | 75

541 **Philip II,** 247-249 (Caesar 244-247). Æ *antoninianus.* PRINCIPI IVVENT.
Prince stg. l., holding globe and spear. *R.I.C. 218d.* .... | 20 | 50

541A Æ *sestertius.* PAX AETERNA S. C. Pax stg. l. *R.I.C. 268c.* .... | 25 | 80

542   543

542 **Trajan Decius,** 249-251. Æ *antoninianus.* DACIA. Dacia stg. l., holding
staff with ass's hd. *R.I.C. 12b.* .... | 15 | 35

542A Æ *sestertius.* PANNONIAE S. C. The two Pannoniae stg., each holding
standard. *R.I.C. 124a.* .... | 25 | 75

543 **Herennia Etruscilla,** wife of Trajan Decius. Æ *antoninianus.* PVDICITIA
AVG. Pudicitia stg. l. *R.I.C. 58b.* .... | 15 | 35

544 **Herennius Etruscus,** 251 (Caesar 250-251). Æ *antoninianus.* PIETAS
AVGG. Mercury stg. l., holding purse and caduceus. *R.I.C. 142b.* .... | 25 | 65

545 **Hostilian,** 251 (Caesar 251). Æ *antoninianus.* PRINCIPI IVVENTVTIS.
Apollo seated l., holding branch. *R.I.C. 180.* .... | 35 | 85

546 **Trebonianus Gallus,** 251-253. Æ *antoninianus.* FELICITAS PVBLICA.
Felicitas stg. l., resting on column. *R.I.C. 34A.* .... | 12 | 30

546A Æ *sestertius.* SALVS AVGG S. C. Salus stg. r., feeding snake held in her
arms. *R.I.C. 121a.* .... | 25 | 75

547 **Volusian,** 251-253 (Caesar 251). Æ *antoninianus.* VIRTVS AVGG.
Virtus stg. l. *R.I.C. 186.* .... | 12 | 30

548 **Aemilian,** 253. Æ *antoninianus.* PACI AVG. Pax stg. l., resting on column.
R.I.C. 8. .... | 50 | 120

549 **Valerian,** 253-260. Billon antoninianus. FIDES MILITVM. Fides stg. r.,
holding two standards. *R.I.C. 241.* .... | 8 | 20

550 **Diva Mariniana,** wife of Valerian, deified 253. Billon *antoninianus.*
CONSECRATIO. Empress seated on peacock flying r. *R.I.C. 6.* .... | 45 | 110

		F	VF
		£	£
551	**Gallienus,** 253-268, during whose reign Rome temporarily lost control over Britain when Postumus rebelled and established the independent Gallic Empire in 260. Billon *antoninianus*. VIRT GALLIENI AVG. Emperor advancing r., captive at feet. *R.I.C. 54.*	10	25

552

552	— DIANAE CONS. AVG. Doe l. *R.I.C. 176.*	8	20
552A	— SOLI INVICTO. Sol stg. l., holding globe. *R.I.C. 658.*	8	18
553	**Salonina,** wife of Gallienus. Billon *antoninianus*. VENVS FELIX. Venus seated l., child at feet. *R.I.C. 7.*	8	20
553A	— IVNONI CONS. AVG. Doe l. *R.I.C. 16.*	8	20
554	**Valerian Junior,** son of Gallienus, Caesar 256-258. Billon *antoninianus*. IOVI CRESCENTI. Infant Jupiter seated on goat r. *R.I.C. 13.*	15	35
555	**Divus Valerian Junior,** deified 258. Billon *antoninianus*. CONSECRATIO. Large altar. *R.I.C. 24.*	12	30
556	**Saloninus,** 260 (Caesar 258-260). Billon *antoninianus*. PIETAS AVG. Priestly emblems. *R.I.C. 9.*	12	30
557	**Macrianus,** usurper in the East, 260-261. Billon *antoninianus*. SOL. INVICTO. Sol stg. l., holding globe. *R.I.C. 12.*	35	85
558	**Quietus,** usurper in the East, 260-261. Billon *antoninianus*. INDVLGENTIAE AVG. Indulgentia seated l. *R.I.C. 5.*	35	85

559

559	**Postumus,** usurper in the West, 260-268, founder of the 'Gallic Empire' which temporarily detached Britain from the rule of the central government, a state of affairs which continued until Aurelian's defeat of Tetricus in 273. Billon *antoninianus*. HERC. DEVSONIENSI. Hercules stg. r. *R.I.C. 64.*	12	30
560	— MONETA AVG. Moneta stg. l. *R.I.C. 75.*	10	25
560A	Æ *sestertius*. FIDES MILITVM. Fides stg. l., holding two standards. *R.I.C. 128.*	50	140
561	**Laelianus,** usurper in the West, 268. Billon *antoninianus*. VICTORIA AVG. Victory advancing r. *R.I.C. 9.*	110	275
562	**Marius,** usurper in the West, 268. Billon *antoninianus*. CONCORDIA MILITVM. Clasped hands. *R.I.C. 7.*	35	85
563	**Victorinus,** usurper in the West, 268-270. Billon *antoninianus*. INVICTVS. Sol advancing l. *R.I.C. 114.*	8	20

	F	*VF*
	£	£

564 **Tetricus,** usurper in the West, 270-273, defeated by Aurelian, thus ending the 'Gallic Empire' and the isolation of Britain from the authority of Rome. Billon *antoninianus*. LAETITIA AVGG. Laetitia stg. l. *R.I.C. 87.* 8 25
    See also under Category 4.

565 **Tetricus Junior,** son of Tetricus, Caesar 270-273. Billon *antoninianus*. SPES PVBLICA. Spes walking l., holding flower *R.I.C. 272.* 8 20
    See also under Category 4.

566 **Claudius II Gothicus,** 268-270. Billon *antoninianus*. IOVI STATORI. Jupiter stg. r. *R.I.C. 52.* 8 20

567 **Divus Claudius II,** deified 270. Billon *antoninianus*. CONSECRATIO. Large altar. *R.I.C. 261.* 8 20
    See also under Category 4.

568 **Quintillus,** 270. Billon *antoninianus*. DIANA LVCIF. Diana stg. r., holding torch. *R.I.C. 49.* 18 45

569 **Aurelian,** 270-275, restored Britain to the rule of the central government through his defeat of Tetricus in 273; possibly began construction of the chain of 'Saxon Shore' forts on the eastern and southern coastlines. Billon *antoninianus*. ORIENS AVG. Sol stg. l. between two captives. *R.I.C. 63.* 10 25

569A — RESTITVT. ORBIS. Female stg. r., presenting wreath to emperor stg. l. *R.I.C. 399.* 10 25

570 **Aurelian and Vabalathus,** ruler of Palmyra 267-272 and usurper in the East from 271. Billon *antoninianus*. Obv. Laur. bust of Vabalathus r. Rev. Rad. bust of Aurelian r. *R.I.C. 381.* 25 70

571   574A

571 **Severina,** wife of Aurelian. Billon *antoninianus*. PROVIDEN. DEOR. Concordia (or Fides) Militum stg. r., facing Sol stg. l. *R.I.C. 9.* 18 45

572 **Tacitus,** 275-276. Billon *antoninianus*. SECVRIT. PERP. Securitas stg. l., leaning on column. *R.I.C. 163.* 15 35

573 **Florian,** 276. Billon *antoninianus*. LAETITIA FVND. Laetitia stg. l. *R.I.C. 34.* 30 75

574 **Probus,** 276-282, suppressed governor's revolt in Britain and lifted restrictions on viticulture in Britain and Gaul. Billon *antoninianus*. ADVENTVS PROBI AVG. Emperor on horseback l., captive seated before. *R.I.C. 160.* 10 25

574A — VICTORIA GERM. Trophy between two captives. *R.I.C. 222.* 15 40

575 **Carus,** 282-283. Billon *antoninianus*. PAX EXERCITI. Pax stg. l., holding olive-branch and standard. *R.I.C. 75.* 15 40

576 **Divus Carus,** deified 283. Billon *antoninianus*. CONSECRATIO. Eagle facing, hd. l. *R.I.C. 28.* 18 45

577 **Carinus,** 283-285 (Caesar 282-283). Billon *antoninianus*. SAECVLI FELICITAS. Emperor stg. r. *R.I.C. 214.* 12 35

		F £	*VF* £

578 **Magnia Urbica,** wife of Carinus. Billon *antoninianus.* VENVS VICTRIX.
    Venus stg. l., holding helmet, shield at feet. *R.I.C. 343* 60 150

579 **Numerian,** 283-284 (Caesar 282-283). Billon *antoninianus.* CLEMENTIA
    TEMP. Emperor stg. r., receiving globe from Jupiter stg. l. *R.I.C. 463....* 15 40

580 **Diocletian,** 284-305. Æ *argenteus.* VIRTVS MILITVM. The four tetrarchs
    sacrificing before gateway of military camp. *R.I.C. 27a (Rome).* 100 200

581 Billon *antoninianus.* IOVI CONSERVAT AVGG. Jupiter stg. l. *R.I.C. 162.* 10 25

582 Æ *follis.* GENIO POPVLI ROMANI. Genius stg. l. R.I.C. 14a *(Alexandria).* 10 30

582A — (post-abdication coinage, after 305). PROVIDENTIA DEORVM QVIES
    AVGG. Quies and Providentia stg. facing each other. *R.I.C. 676a (Treveri).* 22 65
    See also under Category 3.

583 **Maximian,** 286-305 and 306-308, failed in his attempts to suppress the
    usurpation of Carausius in Britain. Æ *argenteus.* VICTORIA SARMAT. The
    four tetrarchs sacrificing before gateway of military camp. *R.I.C. 37b (Rome).* 100 200

584

584 Billon *antoninianus.* SALVS AVGG. Salus stg. r., feeding snake held in
    her arms. *R.I.C. 417.* 8 20

585 Æ *follis.* SAC. MON. VRB. AVGG. ET CAESS. NN. Moneta stg. l.
    R.I.C. 105b (Rome). 12 35

585A — (second reign). CONSERVATORES VRB SVAE. Roma seated in
    hexastyle temple. *R.I.C. 84b (Ticinum).* 12 35
    See also under Category 3.
    *[For coins of the usurpers **Carausius** and **Allectus** see under Category 3]*

586 **Constantius I,** 305-306 (Caesar 293-305), invaded Britain 296 and defeated
    the usurper Allectus, thus restoring the island to the rule of the central
    government; Britain now divided into four provinces and the northern
    frontier defences reconstructed; died at York, July 306. Æ *argenteus.*
    PROVIDENTIA AVGG. The four tetrarchs sacrificing before gateway
    of military camp. *R.I.C. 11a (Rome).* 110 220

587

587 Æ *follis.* GENIO POPVLI ROMANI. Genius stg. l. *R.I.C. 26a (Aquileia).* 12 35

587A — SALVIS AVGG. ET CAESS. FEL. KART. Carthage stg. l., holding
    fruits. *R.I.C. 30a (Carthage)* 15 40
    See also under Category 3.

588

	F £	VF £
588 **Galerius,** 305-311 (Caesar 293-305). Æ argenteus. VIRTVS MILITVM. The four tetrarchs sacrificing before gateway of military camp. *R.I.C. 15b (Ticinum).*	100	200
588A — XC / VI in wreath. *R.I.C. 16b (Carthage).*	150	350
589 *Æ follis.* GENIO AVGG ET CAESARVM NN. Genius stg. l. *R.I.C. 11b* *(Cyzicus).*	12	35
589A — GENIO IMPERATORIS. Genius stg. l. *R.I.C. 101a (Alexandria)......* *See also under Category 3.*	8	25
590 **Galeria Valeria,** wife of Galerius. *Æ follis.* VENERI VICTRICI. Venus stg. l. *R.I.C. 110 (Alexandria).*	35	85
591 **Severus II,** 306-307 (Caesar 305-306). *Æ follis.* FIDES MILITVM. Fides seated l. *R.I.C. 73 (Ticinum).* *See also under Category 3.*	35	85
592 **Maximinus II,** 310-313 (Caesar 305-310). *Æ follis.* GENIO CAESARIS. Genius stg. l. *R.I.C. 64 (Alexandria).*	8	25
592A — GENIO POP. ROM. Genius stg. l. *R.I.C. 845a (Treveri).* *See also under Category 3.*	8	20

593

593 **Maxentius,** 306-312 (Caesar 306). *Æ follis.* CONSERV. VRB. SVAE. Roma seated in hexastyle temple. *R.I.C. 210 (Rome).*	10	30
594 **Romulus,** son of Maxentius, deified 309. *Æ quarter follis.* AETERNAE MEMORIAE. Temple with domed roof. *R.I.C. 58 (Ostia).*	35	85
595 **Licinius,** 308-324. *Æ follis.* GENIO AVGVSTI. Genius stg. l. *R.I.C. 198b* *(Siscia).*	8	20
595A Æ 3. IOVI CONSERVATORI AVGG. Jupiter stg. l. *R.I.C. 24 (Nicomedia).* *See also under Category 3.*	8	20
596 **Licinius Junior,** son of Licinius, Caesar 317-324. Æ 3. CAESARVM NOSTRORVM around wreath containing VOT. / V. *R.I.C. 92 (Thessalonica).*	8	22
597 **Constantine I, the Great,** 307-337 (Caesar 306-307), campaigned with his father Constantius I against the Picts in northern Britain, summer 306, and proclaimed emperor by the legions at York on Constantius' death in July; closed the London mint early in 325 ending almost four decades of operation. *Æ follis.* GENIO POP ROM. Genius stg. l. *R.I.C. 719b (Treveri).*	12	35
598 — SOLI INVICTO COMITI. Sol stg. l. *R.I.C. 307 (Lugdunum).*	6	18
598A Æ 3. PROVIDENTIAE AVGG. Gateway of military camp. *R.I.C. 153* *(Thessalonica).*	5	15

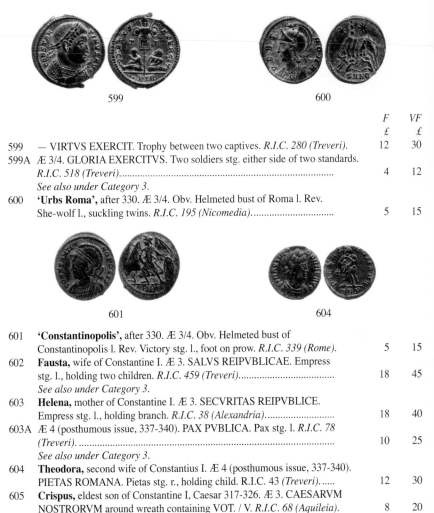

599 600

	F £	VF £

599 — VIRTVS EXERCIT. Trophy between two captives. *R.I.C. 280 (Treveri)*. 12 30

599A Æ 3/4. GLORIA EXERCITVS. Two soldiers stg. either side of two standards.
R.I.C. 518 (Treveri).. 4 12
See also under Category 3.

600 **'Urbs Roma',** after 330. Æ 3/4. Obv. Helmeted bust of Roma l. Rev.
She-wolf l., suckling twins. *R.I.C. 195 (Nicomedia).*............................... 5 15

601 604

601 **'Constantinopolis',** after 330. Æ 3/4. Obv. Helmeted bust of
Constantinopolis l. Rev. Victory stg. l., foot on prow. *R.I.C. 339 (Rome)*. 5 15

602 **Fausta,** wife of Constantine I. Æ 3. SALVS REIPVBLICAE. Empress
stg. l., holding two children. *R.I.C. 459 (Treveri)*.................................... 18 45
See also under Category 3.

603 **Helena,** mother of Constantine I. Æ 3. SECVRITAS REIPVBLICE.
Empress stg. l., holding branch. *R.I.C. 38 (Alexandria)*........................... 18 40

603A Æ 4 (posthumous issue, 337-340). PAX PVBLICA. Pax stg. l. *R.I.C. 78
(Treveri).* 10 25
See also under Category 3.

604 **Theodora,** second wife of Constantius I. Æ 4 (posthumous issue, 337-340).
PIETAS ROMANA. Pietas stg. r., holding child. R.I.C. 43 *(Treveri)*...... 12 30

605 **Crispus,** eldest son of Constantine I, Caesar 317-326. Æ 3. CAESARVM
NOSTRORVM around wreath containing VOT. / V. *R.I.C. 68 (Aquileia)*. 8 20
See also under Category 3.

606 **Delmatius,** nephew of Constantine I, Caesar 335-337. Æ 3/4. GLORIA
EXERCITVS. Two soldiers stg. either side of two standards. *R.I.C. 90
(Antioch).* 18 45

607 **Hanniballianus,** nephew of Constantine I, Rex 335-337. Æ 4. SECVRITAS
PVBLICA. River-god Euphrates reclining r. *R.I.C. 147 (Constantinople)*. 100 225

608 **Constantine II,** 337-340 (Caesar 317-337). Æ 3. BEATA
TRANQVILLITAS. Altar inscribed VOT / IS / XX. *R.I.C. 312 (Treveri)*. 8 20

608A Æ 3/4. GLORIA EXERCITVS. Two soldiers stg. either side of standard.
R.I.C. 392 (Rome). 4 10
See also under Category 3.

609 **Constans,** 337-350 (Caesar 333-337), visited Britain in 343, the last
reigning emperor to do so. Æ 2. FEL. TEMP. REPARATIO. Soldier r.,
dragging barbarian from hut beneath tree. *R.I.C. 103 (Aquileia)*............ 10 30

609A
611B

	F £	VF £
609A — FEL. TEMP. REPARATIO. Emperor stg. l. on galley steered by Victory. *R.I.C. 219 (Treveri)*............................	10	30
609B Æ 4. VICTORIAE DD. AVGG. Q. NN. Two Victories stg. face to face. *R.I.C. 195 (Treveri)*............................	5	10
610 **Constantius II,** 337-361 (Caesar 324-337). Æ 3/4. GLORIA EXERCITVS. Two soldiers stg. either side of two standards. *R.I.C. 85 (Cyzicus)*..........	5	12
611 Æ *siliqua.* VOTIS / XXX. / MVLTIS / XXXX. in wreath. *R.I.C. 207 (Arelate).*	25	70
611A Æ 2. FEL. TEMP. REPARATIO. Emperor stg. l. on galley. *R.I.C. 218* *(Treveri).*	10	30
611B Æ 3. FEL. TEMP. REPARATIO. Soldier advancing l., spearing fallen horseman. *R.I.C. 189 (Lugdunum).*	5	15

See also under Categories 3 and 4.

612
616

612 **Magnentius,** usurper in the West, 350-353, temporarily detached Britain from the rule of the legitimate Constantinian dynasty. Æ 1. SALVS DD. NN. AVG. ET CAES. *Chi-Rho* Christian monogram between Alpha and Omega. *R.I.C. 34 (Ambianum)*............................	75	175
612A Æ 2. FELICITAS REIPVBLICE. Emperor stg. l., holding Victory and labarum. *R.I.C. 264 (Treveri)*............................	15	40
See also under Category 4.		
613 **Decentius,** brother of Magnentius, Caesar 351-353. Æ 2. VICTORIAE DD. NN. AVG. ET CAE. Two Victories supporting between them shield inscribed VOT. / V. / MVLT. / X. *R.I.C. 146 (Lugdunum).*	20	50
See also under Category 4.		
614 **Vetranio,** 'usurper' in the Balkans, 350. Æ 2. CONCORDIA MILITVM. Emperor stg. l., holding two labara. *R.I.C. 281 (Siscia)*............	50	125
615 **Constantius Gallus,** Caesar under Constantius II, 351-354. Æ 2. FEL. TEMP. REPARATIO. Soldier advancing l., spearing fallen horseman. *R.I.C. 94 (Cyzicus)*............................	15	40
616 **Julian II,** 360-363 (Caesar 355-360). Æ *siliqua.* VOT. / X. / MVLT. / XX. in wreath. *R.I.C. 309 (Arelate)*............................	25	70

	F	VF
	£	£
617 Æ 1. SECVRITAS REIPVB. Bull stg. r. *R.I.C. 411 (Siscia)*.	45	140
617A Æ 3. VOT. / X. / MVLT. / XX. in wreath. *R.I.C. 108 (Sirmium)*	8	25
618 **Jovian,** 363-364. Æ 3. VOT. / V. / MVLT. / X. in wreath. *R.I.C. 426 (Siscia)*.	12	35

619

619   **Valentinian I,** 364-375 (in the West), during whose reign the Roman province of Britannia was devastated by the simultaneous attack of hordes of invaders on several fronts (the 'Barbarian Conspiracy'); order eventually restored by Count Theodosius, father of the future emperor . *N solidus.* RESTITVTOR REIPVBLICAE. Emperor stg. r., holding standard and Victory. *R.I.C. 2b (Antioch)*.   120   275

619A   Æ 3. GLORIA ROMANORVM. Emperor advancing r., dragging barbarian and holding labarum. *R.I.C. 14a (Siscia)*.   5   15

619B   — SECVRITAS REIPVBLICAE. Victory advancing l. *R.I.C. 32a (Treveri)*.   5   15

620   **Valens,** 364-378 (in the East). Æ *siliqua.* VRBS ROMA. Roma seated l. *R.I.C. 27e (Treveri)*.   25   70

620A   Æ 3. SECVRITAS REIPVBLICAE. Victory advancing l. *R.I.C. 42b (Constantinople)*.   5   15

621   **Procopius,** usurper in the East, 365-366. Æ 3. REPARATIO FEL. TEMP. Emperor stg. r., holding standard and shield. *R.I.C. 17a (Constantinople)*.   50   125

622   **Gratian,** 367-383 (in the West), overthrown by Magnus Maximus who had been proclaimed emperor by the army in Britain. Æ *siliqua.* VRBS ROMA. Roma seated l. *R.I.C. 27f (Treveri)*.   30   75

623   **Valentinian II,** 375-392 (in the West). Æ 2. REPARATIO REIPVB. Emperor stg. l., raising kneeling female figure. *R.I.C. 20c (Arelate)*.   10   30

623A   Æ 4. SALVS REIPVBLICAE. Victory advancing l., dragging barbarian. *R.I.C. 20a (Alexandria)*.   5   12

624   **Theodosius I,** the Great, 379-395 (in the East), son of the Count Theodosius who had cleared Britain of barbarian invaders in the reign of Valentinian I; the Emperor Theodosiua twice restored Britain to the rule of the central government, by his defeat of the usurpers Magnus Maximus (in 388) and Eugenius (in 394). Æ *siliqua.* CONCORDIA AVGGG. Constantinopolis enthroned facing, foot on prow. *R.I.C. 55a (Treveri)*.   30   75

624A

624A — VIRTVS ROMANORVM. Roma enthroned facing. *R.I.C. (Aquileia) 28d*.	30	75
624B Æ 2. VIRTVS EXERCIT. Emperor stg. r., foot on captive, holding labarum and globe. *R.I.C. 24b (Heraclea)*	12	35

	F	VF
	£	£

625 **Aelia Flaccilla,** wife of Theodosius I. Æ 2. SALVS REIPVBLICAE.
Victory seated r., inscribing Christian monogram on shield set on cippus.
R.I.C. 81 (Constantinople).. 25 65

626 627

626 **Magnus Maximus,** usurper in the West, 383-388, proclaimed emperor
by the army in Britain, invaded Gaul, and overthrew the legitimate western
emperor Gratian; possibly reopened the London mint for a brief issue of
precious metal coinage (Rudyard Kipling presented a rather fanciful
version of his career in "Puck of Pook's Hill"). Æ *siliqua*. VIRTVS
ROMANORVM. Roma enthroned facing. *R.I.C. 84b (Treveri)*.............. 35 95
See also under Category 3.

627 **Flavius Victor,** son of Magnus Maximus, co-emperor 387-388. Æ 4.
SPES ROMANORVM. Gateway of military camp. *RIC 55b (Aquileia)*. 40 100

628 **Eugenius,** usurper in the West, 392-394, recognized in Britain until his
defeat by Theodosius the Great. Æ *siliqua*. VIRTVS ROMANORVM.
Roma seated l. on cuirass. *R.I.C. 106d (Treveri)*. 120 275

629 631

629 **Arcadius,** 395-408 (in the East, co-emperor with his father Theodosius I
from 383). Æ *solidus*. VICTORIA AVGGG. Emperor stg. r., foot on
captive, holding standard and Victory. *R.I.C. 1205 (Milan).* 100 250

629A Æ 2. GLORIA ROMANORVM. Emperor stg. l., holding standard and
shield, captive at feet. *R.I.C. 41 (Antioch)*... 15 40

630 **Honorius,** 395-423 (in the West, co-emperor with his father Theodosius I
and brother Arcadius from 393), this reign saw the end of Roman rule in
Britain following a succession of usurpations in the province, culminating
in that of Constantine III against whom the Britons rebelled in 409;
Honorius' celebrated 'Rescript' of the following year instructed the
provincials to look to their own defence as he was no longer able to assist
them. Æ *solidus*. VICTORIA AVGGG. Emperor stg. r., foot on captive,
holding standard and Victory. *R.I.C. 1287 (Ravenna).* 100 250

630A Æ *siliqua*. VIRTVS ROMANORVM. Roma seated l. on cuirass.
R.I.C. 1228 (Milan)... 35 85

631 **Constantine III,** usurper in the West, 407-411, proclaimed emperor by the
army in Britain, but his authority rejected by the Romano-Britons two years
later, thus effectively ending 366 years of Roman rule in Britain. Æ *siliqua*.
VICTORIA AVGGG. Roma enthroned l. *R.I.C. 1532 (Treveri)*............... 150 325

| | F | VF |
| | £ | £ |

632   **Valentinian III,** 425-455 (in the West), during whose reign the Saxon
      conquest of the former Roman province commenced, following the final
      unsuccessful appeal of the Romano-Britons for help addressed to the general
      Aetius in 446. *N solidus.* VICTORIA AVGGG. Emperor stg. facing, foot
      on human-headed serpent. *R.I.C. 2010 (Ravenna).* .... 125 | 300

632A Æ 4. VOT. PVB. Gateway of military camp. *R.I.C. 2123 (Rome).* .... 25 | 75

2. ISSUES WITH TYPES REFERRING SPECIFICALLY
TO THE PROVINCE OF BRITANNIA

Struck in Rome, unless otherwise indicated. These usually commemorate military operations in the
northern frontier region of the province or beyond.

633   635

| | F | VF |
| | £ | £ |

633   **Claudius,** A.D. 41-54. AV aureus, celebrating the early stages of the
      Roman conquest of Britain which commenced in A.D. 43. DE BRITANN
      on architrave of triumphal arch. *R.I.C. 33.* .... 1000 | 2500

634   *R denarius.* Similar. *R.I.C. 34.* .... 300 | 750

634A *R didrachm* of Caesarea in Cappadocia. DE BRITANNIS. Emperor in
      triumphal quadriga r. *R.I.C. 122.* .... 300 | 750

635   **Hadrian,** 117-138. Æ as, commemorating the restoration of order in the
      province following a serious uprising (or invasion) in the north, probably
      early in the governorship of Q. Pompeius Falco (118-122). BRITANNIA
      PONT. MAX. TR. POT. COS. III. S. C. Britannia seated facing on rock.
      R.I.C. 577a. .... 175 | 450

636   *Æ sestertius,* commemorating Hadrian's visit to the province in 122, when
      he planned and initiated the construction of the northern frontier system
      which bears his name. ADVENTVI AVG. BRITANNIAE S.C. Emperor
      and Britannia stg. either side of altar. *R.I.C. 882.* .... *Extremely rare*

637
637   — BRITANNIA S. C. Britannia seated facing, foot resting on rock.
      R.I.C. 845. .... *Extremely rare*

	F	VF
	£	£

637A   Æ *dupondius* or as. *Similar. R.I.C. 846*..   *Extremely rare*

638   Æ *sestertius,* commemorating Hadrian's attention to the legionary garrison strength of the province, principally his transfer of *VI Victrix* from Germany in 122. EXERC. BRITANNICVS S. C. Emperor on horseback r., addressing gathering of troops. *R.I.C. 912.* ....   *Extremely rare*

638A   — EXERC. BRITANNICVS S.C. Emperor stg. r. on tribunal, addressing gathering of troops. *R.I.C. 913.* ....   *Extremely rare*

639   **Antoninus Pius,** 138-161. *N aureus,* commemorating the conquests in Scotland by the governor Q. Lollius Urbicus (138/9-142/3) at which time construction of the Antonine Wall was begun. BRITAN. IMPERATOR II. Victory stg. l. on globe. *R.I.C. 113.*   800   2000

640

640   Æ *sestertius.* BRITANNIA S. C. Britannia seated l. on rock, holding standard. *R.I.C. 742.*   550   1400

641   — BRITAN. IMPERATOR II. S. C. Helmeted Britannia seated l., foot on rock. *R.I.C. 743*.................   550   1450

642   — BRITAN. IMPERATOR II. S. C. Britannia seated l. on globe above waves, holding standard. *R.I.C. 744.*   650   1700

643   — BRITAN. IMPERATOR II. S. C. Victory stg. l. on globe. *R.I.C. 719.*   200   500

643A   — BRITANNIA IMPERATOR II. S. C. Britannia seated l. on rock, holding standard. *R.I.C. 745.*   550   1400

644   Æ *as.* IMPERATOR II. S. C. Victory hovering l., holding shield inscribed BRI / TAN. *R.I.C. 732.*   90   225

645   Æ *dupondius,* commemorating the quelling of a serious uprising in the north, ca. 154/5, necessitating the evacuation of the recently constructed Antonine Wall in Scotland. BRITANNIA COS. IIII. S. C. Britannia seated l. on rock, shield and vexillum in background. *R.I.C. 930.*   80   200

| | | F | VF |
| | | £ | £ |

646 Æ as. Similar. *R.I.C. 934.*   75   185

Many specimens of this type are carelessly struck on inadequate flans.
Moreover, they have been found in significant quantities on Romano-British
sites, notably in Coventina's Well at Carrawburgh fort on Hadrian's Wall,
raising the interesting possibility that they may have been issued from a
temporary mint in Britain. The style of the engraving is quite regular,
indicating that even if locally produced these coins would have been struck
from normal Roman dies brought to Britain especially for this purpose.
See under Category 3.

647 **Commodus,** 177-192. Æ *sestertius,* commemorating the victories in
Scotland of the governor Ulpius Marcellus in 184/5. These were in
retribution for a major barbarian invasion several years earlier resulting
in serious damage to Hadrian's Wall, which had been temporarily overrun,
and the defeat and death of an unknown governor. BRITT. P. M. TR. P.
VIIII. IMP. VII. COS. IIII. P. P. S. C. Britannia stg. l., holding curved
sword and helmet. *R.I.C. 437.* ....   *Extremely rare*

648

648 — VICT. BRIT. P. M. TR. P. VIIII. (or X.) IMP. VII. COS. IIII. P. P. S. C.
Victory seated r., about to inscribe shield. *R.I.C. 440, 452.*   120   300

649

649 **Septimius Severus,** 193-211. *N aureus,* commemorating the success of
the punitive Roman campaigns in Scotland during 209 and 210 culminating
in the illness and death of Severus at York in Feb. 211. VICTORIAE BRIT.
Victory advancing l. *R.I.C. 334.*   1200   3000

650 — VICTORIAE BRIT. Victory advancing r., leading child by hand.
R.I.C. 302.   1500   3500

651 Æ *denarius.* VICTORIAE BRIT. Victory advancing r. *R.I.C. 332.*   40   90

651A — VICTORIAE BRIT. Victory stg. facing beside palm-tree with shield
attached. *R.I.C. 336.*   40   90

651B — VICTORIAE BRIT. Victory stg. l. *R.I.C. 333.*   40   90

651C — VICTORIAE BRIT. Victory seated l., holding shield. *R.I.C. 335.*   40   85

652

		F £	VF £
652	Æ *sestertius*. VICTORIAE BRITTANNICAE S. C. Two Victories placing shield on palm-tree with captives at base. *R.I.C. 818.*	300	875
653	— P. M. TR. P. XVIII. COS. III. P. P. S. C. Similar. *R.I.C. 796.*	175	400
654	Æ *dupondius*. VICT. BRIT. P. M. TR. P. XIX. COS. III. P. P. S. C. Victory stg. r. between two captives, holding vexillum. *R.I.C. 809.*	100	275
655	Æ *as*. VICTORIAE BRITTANNICAE S. C. Similar. *R.I.C. 837a.*	100	275
656	Billon *tetradrachm* of Alexandria in Egypt. NEIKH KATA BRET. Nike flying l. *Milne 2726.*	*Extremely rare*	
657	**Caracalla,** 198-217. *N aureus,* commemorating the victories achieved by the Romans in Scotland during the campaigns led jointly by Severus and Caracalla in 209, and by Caracalla alone the following year during his father's illness. VICTORIAE BRIT. Victory seated l., holding shield. *R.I.C. 174.*	1200	3000

658   659A

		F	VF
658	Æ *denarius*. VICTORIAE BRIT. Victory advancing l. *R.I.C. 231.*	40	85
658A	— VICTORIAE BRIT. Victory advancing r., holding trophy. *R.I.C. 231A.*	40	85
659	Æ *sestertius*. VICTORIAE BRITTANNICAE S. C. Victory stg. r., erecting trophy to r. of which Britannia stands facing, captive at feet. *R.I.C. 464.*	250	675
659A	— VICT. BRIT. TR. P. XIIII. COS. III. S.C. Similar. *Cf. R.I.C. 483c.*	225	600
660	Æ *dupondius*. VICTORIAE BRITTANNICAE S. C. Victory stg. r., inscribing shield set on palm-tree. *R.I.C. 467*	100	275
661	Æ *as*. VICT. BRIT. TR. P. XIIII. COS. III. S. C. Similar. *R.I.C. 490.*	100	250
662	**Geta,** 209-212. Æ *denarius,* commemorating the victories achieved by his father and brother in Scotland in 209-10 while he and his mother were resident in London. VICTORIAE BRIT. Victory stg. l. *R.I.C. 92*	40	85
662A	— VICTORIAE BRIT. Victory advancing r. *R.I.C. 91.*	40	85

663

		F	VF
		£	£
663	Æ *sestertius*. VICTORIAE BRITTANNICAE S. C. Victory seated r., inscribing shield set on knee. *R.I.C. 166.*	300	750
663A	— VICT. BRIT. TR. P. III. COS. II. S. C. Similar. *R.I.C. 172b.*	250	600
664	Æ *as*. VICTORIAE BRITTANNICAE S. C. Victory seated l., balancing shield on knee. *R.I.C. 191a*	100	275
665	Billon *tetradrachm* of Alexandria in Egypt. NEIKH KATA BRETAN. Nike advancing l. *B.M.C. (Alexandria) 1481.*	*Extremely rare*	

3. OFFICIAL ROMAN COINAGE STRUCK IN BRITAIN

The London mint, and the associated 'C' mint (possibly Colchester), were created by the usurper Carausius soon after his seizure of Britain in 287. Prior to this, in the mid-2nd century, there may have been minting of 'Britannia' asses of Antoninus Pius in the province using dies brought from Rome, though this has not been firmly established. After the downfall of the rebel British regime in 296 the minting establishment in London (though not the subsidiary mint) was retained by the tetrarchal government and the succeeding Constantinian administration. Early in 325, however, Constantine the Great closed the London mint after almost four decades of operation. A possible brief revival under the usurper Magnus Maximus has been postulated for gold and silver coins marked 'AVG', 'AVGOB' and 'AVGPS', though the attribution has not received universal acceptance.

		F	VF
		£	£
666	**Antoninus Pius,** 138-161. Æ *as,* struck in northern Britain (?) in 155. BRITANNIA COS. IIII. S. C. Britannia seated l. on rock, shield and vexillum in background. *R.I.C. 930*	75	185

Many poorly struck examples of this type have been found on Romano-British sites, notably at Brocolitia (Carrawburgh) fort on Hadrian's Wall in Northumberland, where no fewer than 327 specimens were discovered in the great votive deposit in the well which formed part of the shrine of the water-nymph Coventina. There appears to be a very real possibility that many of these 'Britannia' asses had been issued from a temporary mint in Britain, most likely situated in the north. The dies, however, are quite regular, and would thus have been brought from Rome to the island province for the express purpose of supplementing the money supply at a time of crisis.

		F	VF
667	**Carausius,** usurper in Britain and northwestern Gaul, A.D. 287-293. *A aureus,* London. CONSERVAT. AVG. Jupiter stg. l., eagle at feet, ML in ex. *R.I.C. 1*	5000	12500
668	Æ *denarius,* London. EXPECTATE VENI. Britannia stg. r. and emperor l., clasping hands, RSR in ex. *R.I.C. 555*	450	1200

669 672A

		F	VF
		£	£
669	— RENOVAT. ROMANO. She-wolf r., suckling twins, RSR in ex. *R.I.C. 571.*	350	900
670	Billon *antoninianus,* London. COMES AVG. Victory stg. l., S—P in field, ML in ex. *R.I.C. 14.*	45	110
670A	— HILARITAS AVG. Hilaritas stg. l., B—E in field, MLXXI in ex. *R.I.C. 41.*	30	80
671	— LAETITIA AVG. Laetitia stg. l., F—O in field, ML in ex. *R.I.C. 50..*	30	80
671A	— LEG. II. AVG. Capricorn l., ML in ex. *R.I.C. 58*	80	195
	Legio II Augusta was stationed at Isca (Caerleon in South Wales).		
672	— LEG. XX. V. V. Boar stg. r. *R.I.C. 82.*	80	195
	Legio XX Valeria Victrix was stationed at Deva (Chester in the northwest Midlands).		
672A	— PAX AVG. Pax stg. l., F—O in field, ML in ex. *R.I.C. 101.*	25	70
673	— Similar, but without mint mark. *R.I.C. 880.*	25	65
673A	— PROVIDENT. AVG. Providentia stg. l., B—E in field, MLXXI in ex. *R.I.C. 149.*	30	80
674	— SALVS AVGGG. Salus stg. r., feeding snake held in her arms, S—P in field, ML in ex. *R.I.C. 164.*	30	80
	The reverse legends with triple-ending (AVGGG.) presumably are subsequent to Carausius' recognition by Diocletian and Maximian in 289 following the failure of the latter's attempt to dislodge the usurper from his island stronghold.		
674A	— TEMPORVM FELICITAS. Felicitas stg. l., B—E in field, ML in ex. *R.I.C. 172.*	25	70
675	— VIRTVS AVGGG. Mars (or Virtus) stg. r., holding spear and shield, S—P in field, MLXXI in ex. *R.I.C. 183.*	30	80
676	Billon *antoninianus,* Colchester (?). CONCORDIA MILIT. Emperor stg. r. and Concordia l., clasping hands, C in ex. *R.I.C. 205.*	55	130
676A	— EXPECTATE VENI. Britannia stg. r. and emperor l., clasping hands, MSC in ex. *R.I.C. 216.*	100	250
677	— FELICITAS AVG. Galley with mast and rowers, CXXI in ex. *R.I.C. 221.*	80	200
677A	— FORTVNA RAEDVX. Fortuna seated l., SPC in ex. *R.I.C. 237.*	40	100
678	— LAETITIA AVG. Laetitia stg. l., globe at feet, S—P in field, C in ex. *R.I.C. 255.*	30	80
678A	—-MONETA AVG. Moneta stg. l., CXXI in ex. *R.I.C. 287.*	30	80
679	— ORIENS AVG. Sol stg. l., C in ex. *R.I.C. 293.*	35	85
679A	— PAX AVGGG. Pax stg. l., S—P in field, MC in ex. *R.I.C. 335.*	30	70

680

		F	VF
		£	£
680	— PROVID. AVG. Providentia stg. l., S—P in field, C in ex. *R.I.C. 353.*	30	80
680A	— SALVS AVG. Salus stg. l. at altar, feeding snake, S—C in field, C in ex. *R.I.C. 396.*	30	80
681	— SPES PVBLICA. Spes walking l., holding flower, S—P in field, C in ex. *R.I.C. 413.*	30	80
681A	— VICTORIA AVG. Victory advancing l., captive at feet, MC in ex. *R.I.C. 429.*	35	85
682	**Carausius, Diocletian and Maximian,** after 289. Billon *antoninianus,* Colchester (?). Obv. CARAVSIVS ET FRATRES SVI. Conjoined busts of the three emperors l. Rev. PAX AVGGG. Pax stg. l., S—P in field, C in ex. *R.I.C. 1.*	800	2000

682A   684A

682A	— MONETA AVGGG. Moneta stg. l., S—P in field, C in ex. *R.I.C. —..* *See also nos. 693-4 and 698-700 as well as regular Carausian types with the triple-ending 'AVGGG.' on reverse.*	1000	2500
683	**Allectus,** usurper in Britain, 293-296. *N aureus,* London. ORIENS AVG. Sol stg. l. between two captives, ML in ex. *R.I.C. 4*	7000	17500
684	Æ *antoninianus,* London. LAETITIA AVG. Laetitia stg. l., S—A in field, MSL in ex. *R.I.C. 22.*	30	80
684A	— PAX AVG. Pax stg. l., S—A in field, ML in ex. *R.I.C. 28.*	35	80
685	— PROVID. AVG. Providentia stg. l., holding globe and cornucopiae, S—P in field, ML in ex. *R.I.C. 36.*	35	85
685A	— SALVS AVG. Salus stg. r., feeding snake held in her arms, S—A in field, MSL in ex. *R.I.C. 42*	30	80
686	— TEMPOR. FELICITAS. Felicitas stg. l., S—A in field, ML in ex. *R.I.C. 47.*	30	80
686A	— VICTORIA AVG. Victory advancing l., S—P in field, ML in ex. *R.I.C. 48.*	30	80
687	Æ *antoninianus,* Colchester (?). AEQVITAS AVG. Aequitas stg. l., S—P in field, C in ex. *R.I.C. 63.*	30	80
687A	— FIDES MILITVM. Fides stg. l., holding two standards, S—P in field, C in ex. *R.I.C. 69.*	30	80

688A

		F	VF
		£	£
688	— LAETITIA AVG. Laetitia stg. l., S—P in field, CL in ex. *R.I.C. 79.*...	40	100
	This form of mint mark has given rise to the alternative identification of		
	this mint as Clausentum (Bitterne, Hants.)		
688A	— MONETA AVG. Moneta stg. l., S—P in field, C in ex. *R.I.C. 82.*......	40	95
689	— PAX AVG. Pax stg. l., S—P in field, C in ex. *R.I.C. 86.*	35	80
689A	— PROVIDENTIA AVG. Providentia stg. l., globe at feet, S—P in field,		
	C in ex. *R.I.C. 111.*..	30	80
690	— TEMPORVM FELIC. Felicitas stg. l., S—P in field, CL in ex. *R.I.C. 117.*	40	100
690A	— VIRTVS AVG. Mars stg. r., holding spear and shield, S—P in field,		
	C in ex. *R.I.C. 121.*	30	80
691	Æ *'quinarius'*, London. VIRTVS AVG. Galley l., QL in ex. *R.I.C. 55.*...	30	85
	An experimental denomination issued only during this reign, the types of		
	the so-called 'quinarius' would seem to indicate that it was in some way		
	associated with the operations of the fleet upon which the survival of the		
	rebel regime in Britain was totally dependent.		

692 693

692	Æ *'quinarius'*, Colchester (?). LAETITIA AVG. Galley r., QC in ex.		
	R.I.C. 124...	35	85
692A	— VIRTVS AVG. Galley l., QC in ex. *R.I.C. 128.*..................................	35	85
693	**Diocletian,** 284-305. Billon *antoninianus* of London, struck by Carausius		
	between 289 and 293. PAX AVGGG. Pax stg. l., S—P in field, MLXXI		
	in ex. *R.I.C. 9.*	35	85
694	Billon *antoninianus* of Colchester (?), same date. PROVID AVGGG.		
	Providentia stg. l., globe at feet, S—P in field, C in ex. *R.I.C. 22*............	35	85

695

	F	VF
	£	£

695 Æ *follis*, London. GENIO POPVLI ROMANI. Genius stg. l., LON in ex.
R.I.C. 1a.. 125 275
*By the time the central government had recovered control of Britain in 296
the antoninianus had been replaced by the larger follis under Diocletian's
sweeping currency reform. London was retained as an official imperial
mint, but the secondary British establishment (at Colchester?) was now
abandoned. Except for its initial issue in 297 (marked 'LON') the London
mint under the tetrarchic government produced only unsigned folles
throughout its first decade of operation. Perhaps Constantius did not
wish to draw attention to his employment of a mint which had been the
creation of a rebel regime.*

696 — Similar, but without mint mark. R.I.C. 6a. 15 35

697 — (post-abdication coinage, after 305). PROVIDENTIA DEORVM
QVIES AVGG. Quies and Providentia stg. facing each other (no mint mark).
R.I.C. 77a.. 30 65

697A

697A — QVIES AVGG. Quies stg. l., holding branch and sceptre, PLN in ex.
R.I.C. 98... 20 50

698 **Maximian,** 286-305 and 306-308. *N aureus* of London, struck by
Carausius between 289 and 293. SALVS AVGGG. Salus stg. r., feeding
snake held in her arms, ML in ex. R.I.C. 32. .... *Extremely rare*

699 Billon *antoninianus* of London, same date. PROVIDENTIA AVGGG.
Providentia stg. l., S—P in field, MLXXI in ex. R.I.C. 37...................... 35 85

700 Billon *antoninianus* of Colchester (?), same date. PAX AVGGG. Pax stg.
l., S—P in field, C in ex. R.I.C. 42. .... 35 85

701 Æ *follis*, London. GENIO POPVLI ROMANI. Genius stg. l., LON in ex.
R.I.C. 2... 100 250

702 — Similar, but without mint mark. R.I.C. 23b. 15 35

703 — (post-abdication coinage, after 305). PROVIDENTIA DEORVM
QVIES AVGG. Quies and Providentia stg. facing each other (no mint mark).
R.I.C. 77b.. 30 65

704

		F	VF
		£	£
704	— (second reign). GENIO POP. ROM. Genius stg. l., PLN in ex. *R.I.C. 90.*	20	40
704A	— HERCVLI CONSERVATORI. Hercules stg. l., resting on club, PLN in ex. *R.I.C. 91.*	30	75
705	**Constantius I,** 305-306 (Caesar 293-305). Æ *follis,* London (as Caesar). GENIO POPVLI ROMANI. Genius stg. l., LON in ex. *R.I.C. 4a.*	110	275

706

706	— Similar, but without mint mark. *R.I.C. 30.*	15	35
707	— (as Augustus). Similar. *R.I.C. 52a.*	20	45
708	**Divus Constantius I,** deified 306. Æ *follis,* London. MEMORIA FELIX. Altar flanked by eagles, PLN in ex. *R.I.C. 110.*	20	50
709	**Galerius,** 305-311 (Caesar 293-305). Æ *follis,* London (as Caesar). GENIO POPVLI ROMANI. Genius stg. l., LON in ex. *R.I.C. 4b.*	110	275
710	— Similar, but without mint mark. *R.I.C. 15.*	10	25
711	— (as Augustus). Similar. *R.I.C. 42.*	12	30
711A	— GENIO POP. ROM. Genius stg. l., PLN in ex. *R.I.C. 86.*	18	45
712	**Severus II,** 306-307 (Caesar 305-306). Æ *follis,* London (as Caesar). GENIO POPVLI ROMANI. Genius stg. l. (no mint mark). *R.I.C. 58a* ...	35	85
713	— (as Augustus). Similar. *R.I.C. 52c*	35	85
714	**Maximinus II,** 310-313 (Caesar 305-310). Æ *follis,* London (as Caesar). GENIO POPVLI ROMANI. Genius stg. l. (no mint mark). *R.I.C. 57*	15	40
715	—-GENIO POP. ROM. Genius stg. l., PLN in ex. *R.I.C. 89a.*	15	40
716	— (as Augustus). Similar, but with star in r. field. *R.I.C. 209b*	12	30
717	**Licinius,** 308-324. Æ *follis,* London. GENIO POP. ROM. Genius stg. l., star in r. field, PLN in ex. *R.I.C. 209c.*	12	30
717A	— Similar, but with S—F in field. *R.I.C. 3.*	8	20
718	— SOLI INVICTO COMITI. Sol stg. l., holding globe, S—P in field, MSL in ex. *R.I.C. 79.*	10	25
719	**Constantine I, the Great,** 307-337 (Caesar 306-307). Æ *follis,* London (as Caesar). GENIO POPVLI ROMANI. Genius stg. l. (no mint mark). *R.I.C. 72*	25	65
719A	— GENIO POP. ROM. Genius stg. l., PLN in ex. *R.I.C. 88b*	15	35

		F £	*VF* £
720	— PRINCIPI IVVENTVTIS. Prince stg. l., holding standards, PLN in ex. *R.I.C. 97*..	25	60
721	— (as Augustus). ADVENTVS AVG. Emperor on horseback l., captive on ground before, star in r. field, PLN in ex. *R.I.C. 133*...........................	22	55
722	— COMITI AVGG. NN. Sol stg. l., holding globe and whip, same mint mark. *R.I.C. 155*..	18	45
723	— CONCORD. MILIT. Concordia stg. l., holding standards, same mint mark. *R.I.C. 195*..	15	40
724	— MARTI CONSERVATORI. Mars. stg. r., holding spear and shield, star in l. field, PLN in ex. *R.I.C. 254.*...	15	35
724A	— SOLI INVICTO COMITI. Sol stg. l., holding globe, S—F in field, MLL in ex. *R.I.C. 27*...	10	25
725	Æ 3, London. VICTORIAE LAETAE PRINC. PERP. Two Victories supporting shield, inscribed VOT. / P. R., over altar, PLN in ex. *R.I.C. 159.*	10	25

726

726	— VIRTVS EXERCIT. Vexillum, inscribed VOT. / XX., between two captives, PLN in ex. R.I.C. 191.	10	25
727	— BEAT. TRANQLITAS. Altar, inscribed VOT / IS / XX., surmounted by globe and three stars, PLON in ex. *R.I.C. 267*....................................	10	25
727A	— SARMATIA DEVICTA. Victory advancing r., trampling captive, PLON and crescent in ex. *R.I.C. 289*..	20	45
728	— PROVIDENTIAE AVGG. Gateway of military camp, PLON in ex. *R.I.C. 293*..	10	25
729	**Fausta,** wife of Constantine I. Æ 3, London. SALVS REIPVBLICAE. Empress stg. l., holding two children, PLON in ex. *R.I.C. 300*................	60	150
730	**Helena,** mother of Constantine I. Æ 3, London. SECVRITAS REIPVBLICE. Empress stg. l., holding branch, PLON in ex. *R.I.C. 299*........................	60	150
731	**Crispus,** eldest son of Constantine I, Caesar 317-326. Æ 3, London. SOLI INVICTO COMITI. Sol stg. l., holding globe, crescent in l. field, PLN in ex. *R.I.C. 144.*	12	30
731A	— VIRTVS EXERCIT. Vexillum, inscribed VOT. / XX., between two captives, PLN in ex. *R.I.C. 194.*	12	30
732	— BEATA TRANQVILLITAS. Altar, inscribed VOT / IS / XX., surmounted by globe and three stars, P—A in field, PLON in ex. *R.I.C. 211.*	12	30
733	— CAESARVM NOSTRORVM around wreath containing VOT. / X., PLON and crescent in ex. *R.I.C. 291*..	12	30

734   737A

		F	VF
		£	£
734	— PROVIDENTIAE CAESS. Gateway of military camp, PLON in ex. *R.I.C. 295*.	10	25
735	**Constantine II,** 337-340 (Caesar 317-337). Æ 3, London (as Caesar). CLARITAS REIPVBLICAE. Sol stg. l., holding globe, crescent in l. field, PLN in ex. *R.I.C. 131.*	12	30
736	— VICTORIAE LAETAE PRINC. PERP. Two Victories supporting shield, inscribed VOT. / P. R., over altar ornamented with wreath, PLN in ex. *R.I.C. 182.*	12	30
737	— VIRTVS EXERCIT. Vexillum, inscribed VOT. / XX., between two captives, PLON in ex. *R.I.C. 190.*	12	30
737A	— BEATA TRANQVILLITAS. Altar, inscribed VOT / IS / XX., surmounted by globe and three stars, PLON in ex. *R.I.C. 236.*	10	25
738	— CAESARVM NOSTRORVM around wreath containing VOT. / X., PLON and crescent in ex. *R.I.C. 292.*	10	25
738A	— PROVIDENTIAE CAESS. Gateway of military camp, PLON in ex. *R.I.C. 296.*	10	25
739	**Constantius II,** 337-361 (Caesar 324-337). Æ 3, London (as Caesar). PROVIDENTIAE CAESS. Gateway of military camp, PLON in ex. *R.I.C. 298.*	25	60
740	**Magnus Maximus,** usurper in the West, 383-388. *N* solidus, London (?). RESTITVTOR REIPVBLICAE. Emperor stg. r., holding labarum and Victory, AVG in ex. *R.I.C. 1.*		*Unique*

The attribution to London of this rare series has not been firmly established, though Maximus was certainly proclaimed emperor in Britain and it is well attested that the principal city of the British provinces bore the name 'Augusta' in the late Roman period (Ammianus Marcellinus XXVII, 8, 7; XXVIII, 3, 7).

741

741	— VICTORIA AVGG. Two emperors enthroned facing, Victory hovering in background between them, AVGOB in ex. *R.I.C. 2b.*	5000	10000

Maximus appears to have struck a similar type in the name of the eastern emperor Theodosius I (cf. R.I.C. 2a), though it is presently known only from a silver-gilt specimen preserved in the British Museum.

742	Æ *siliqua,* London (?). VOT. / V. / MVLT. / X. within wreath, AVG below. *R.I.C. 4.*	850	2000
742A	— VICTORIA AVGG. Victory advancing l., AVGPS in ex. *R.I.C. 3.*	750	1750

4. IMITATIONS OF ROMAN COINS PRODUCED IN BRITAIN

At certain periods during the three and a half centuries of its occupation Roman Britain seems to have been the source of much local imitation of the official imported coinage. This began soon after the Claudian invasion in A.D. 43 when significant quantities of sestertii, dupondii and asses (especially the last) were produced in the newly conquered territory, as evidenced by the frequency of their occurrence in archaeological finds. The technical excellence of many of these 'copies', together with the surprising extent of their minting, would seem to indicate that some, at least, of these coins were produced with official sanction in order to make good an unexpected deficiency in the currency supply. Others are much poorer and well below weight, representing the 'unofficial' branch of this operation, some of it probably emanating from territory as yet unconquered. As conditions in the new province settled down rapid Romanization and urbanization of British society brought a general increase in wealth, and with it a much greater volume of currency flowing into the country. Local imitation now virtually ceased, except for the occasional activities of criminal counterfeiters, and this state of affairs lasted down to the great political crisis and financial collapse of the second half of the 3rd century. At this point large scale minting of imitations of the debased antoniniani of the late 260s and early 270s began in Britain and in the other northwestern provinces, all of which had been serioulsy affected by the political dislocation of this turbulent era. This class of imitations is usually referred to as 'barbarous radiates', the emperor's spiky crown being a constant and conspicuous feature of the obverses. Most frequently copied were the antoniniani of the Gallic rulers Tetricus Senior and Tetricus Junior (ca. 270-273) and the posthumous issues of Claudius Gothicus (died 270). The quality of the 'barbarous radiates' is variable in the extreme, some exhibiting what appears to be a revival of Celtic art forms, others so tiny that it is virtually impossible to see anything of the design. Their production appears to have ended abruptly with Aurelian's reconquest of the western provinces in 273. A similar phenomenon, though on a lesser scale, occurred in the middle decades of the following century when normal life in Britain was again disrupted, not only by usurpation but additionally by foreign invasion. With supplies of currency from the Continent temporarily disrupted local imitation, particularly of the 'Æ 2' and 'Æ 3' issues of Constantius II and the usurper Magnentius, began in earnest. How long this continued is difficult to determine as life in the island province was now subject to increasingly frequent episodes of dislocation. By now urban life in Britain was in serious decline and when Roman rule ended early in the 5th century, bringing a total cessation of currency supplies, the catastrophic decline in monetary commerce in the former provinces rendered it no longer necessary for the deficiency to be made good.

		F	VF
		£	£
743	**Agrippa,** died 12 B.C. Æ as, of irregular British mintage, imitating the		
	Roman issue made under Agrippa's grandson Caligula, A.D. 37-41.		
	S. C. Neptune stg. l., holding dolphin and trident.	40	100
	The large official issue of Agrippa asses was made shortly before the		
	Claudian invasion of Britain in A.D. 43 and would thus have comprised		
	a significant proportion of the 'aes' in circulation at this time. In		
	consequence, it would soon have become familiar to the new provincials		
	providing an ideal prototype for imitation.		
744	**Claudius,** 41-54. Æ sestertius, of irregular British mintage. SPES		
	AVGVSTA S. C. Spes walking l., holding flower.	75	250
745	Æ dupondius, of irregular British mintage. CERES AVGVSTA S. C.		
	Ceres enthroned l., holding corn- ears and torch.....................................	35	100

746

	F	VF
	£	£

746   Æ *as*, of irregular British mintage. S. C. Minerva advancing r., brandishing
spear and holding shield.   30   85
*This is by far the commonest of the Claudian imitations and the prototypes
must have represented the bulk of the aes coinage carried by the legions at
the time of the invasion. The martial type may well have been specially
selected as a suitable theme for the initial import of coinage into the newly
conquered territory.*

747   **Nero Claudius Drusus,** father of Claudius, died 9 B.C. Æ *sestertius,* of
irregular British mintage. TI. CLAVDIVS CAESAR AVG. P. M. TR .P.
IMP. S. C. Claudius seated l. on curule chair amidst arms   85   300
*This type was issued by Claudius half a century after his father's death and
would thus have been prominently represented in the initial wave of coinage
imported into the new province.*

748   **Antonia,** mother of Claudius, died A.D. 37. Æ *dupondius,* of irregular British
mintage. TI. CLAVDIVS CAESAR AVG P.M. TR. P. IMP. P. P. S. C. Claudius
stg. l., holding simpulum.   60   175
*Another Claudian issue for a deceased parent, this represents one of only
two dupondius types struck during this reign and would have entered
Britain in significant quantities at the time of the invasion in A.D. 43.*

749A   749B

749C

749   **'Barbarous radiates',** ca. 270-273. British and Continental imitations of
billon *antoniniani,* principally of Divus Claudius II (A), Tetricus Senior
(B) and Tetricus Junior (C). The inscriptions are usually blundered and
the types sometimes unrecognizable. British mintage can only be
established by provenance.   5   10

750   **Barbarous 4th century,** mostly of the second half of the century, and principally
imitated from 'Æ 2' and 'Æ 3' issues of the later Constantinian period, notably those
of Constantius II ('soldier spearing fallen horseman' type), and the usurpers
Magnentius and Decentius ('two Victories' type). The copies, especially those of
Magnentius and Decentius, are often of excellent style and execution, though the
legends frequently contain small errors. Those of Constantius II are sometimes very
barbarous and poorly struck, occasionally over regular issues of the earlier
Constantinian period. Again, the likelihood of British mintage can only be established
by provenance.   5-8   10-15

Grading of Hammered Coins

As the name suggests, hammered coins were struck by hand with a hammer. This can lead to the coin being struck off centre, double struck, weak in the design, suffer cracks or flan defects. It is important to take these factors into account when assessing the grade of this series. Value is considerably reduced if the coin is holed, pierced, plugged or mounted.

Extremely Fine	**Very Fine**	**Fine**
Design and legends sharp and clear.	Design and legends still clear but with slight evidence of wear and/or minor damage.	Showing quite a lot of wear but still with design and legends distinguishable.

William I PAXS type penny

Henry VIII 1st coinage gold Angel

Edward VI silver shilling

EARLY & MIDDLE ANGLO-SAXON KINGDOMS & MINTS (C.650-973)

EARLY ANGLO-SAXON PERIOD, *c.* 600-*c.* 775

The withdrawal of Roman forces from Britain early in the 5th century A.D. and the gradual decline of central administration resulted in a rapid deterioration of the money supply. The arrival of Teutonic raiders and settlers hastened the decay of urban commercial life and it was probably not until late in the 6th century that renewed political, cultural and commercial links with the kingdom of the Merovingian Franks led to the appearance of small quantities of Merovingian gold *tremisses* (one-third solidus) in England. A purse containing such pieces was found in the Sutton Hoo ship-burial. Native Anglo-Saxon gold *thrymsas* were minted from about the 630s, initially in the style of their continental prototypes or copied from obsolete Roman coinage and later being made in pure Anglo-Saxon style. By the middle of the 7th century the gold coinage was being increasingly debased with silver, and gold had been superseded entirely by about 675.

These silver coins, contemporary with the *deniers or denarii* of the Merovingian Franks, are the first English pennies, though they are commonly known today as *sceattas* (a term more correctly translated as 'treasure' or 'wealth'). They provide important material for the student of Anglo-Saxon art.

Though the earliest sceattas are a transition from the gold thrymsa coinage, coins of new style were soon developed which were also copied by the Frisians of the Low Countries. Early coins appear to have a standard weight of 20 grains (1.29 gms) and are of good silver content, though the quality deteriorates early in the 8th century. These coins exist in a large number of varied types, and as well as the official issues there are mules and other varieties which are probably contemporary imitations. Many of the sceattas were issued during the reign of Aethelbald of Mercia, but as few bear inscriptions it is only in recent years that research has permitted their correct dating and the attribution of certain types to specific areas. Some silver sceattas of groups II and III and most types of groups IV to X were issued during the period (A.D. 716-757) when Aethelbald, King of Mercia, was overlord of the southern English. Though a definitive classification has not yet been developed, the arrangement given below follows the latest work on the series: this list is not exhaustive.

This section has been catalogued in line with research published by Dr D. M. Metcalf. Wherever possible the catalogue number previously in use has been retained. Where it has been necessary to allocate a new and different number, the 'old' S. number is listed, in brackets, at the end of the entry. New entries are given a new number. The primary sceattas are followed by the secondary sceattas and, finally, the continental sceattas. This is not chronologically correct but has been adopted for ease of reference and identification. The reference 'B.M.C.' is to the type given in *British Museum Catalogue: Anglo-Saxon Coins*. Other works of reference include:

North, J. J. *English Hammered Coinage*, Vol. 1, *c.* 650-1272 (1994).
Metcalf, D. M. *Thrymsas and Sceattas in the Ashmolean Museum*, Vols I-III.
Rigold, S. E. *'The two primary series of sceattas'*, B.N.J., xxx (1960).
Sutherland, C. H. V. *Anglo-Saxon Gold Coinage in the light of the Crondall Hoard* (1948).
Gannon, A. *The Iconography of Early Anglo-Saxon Coinage* (2003)
Abramson, T. *Sceattas, An Illustrated Guide* (2006)
Op den Velde, W. & Klassen, C. J. F. *Sceattas and Merovingian Deniers from Domburg and Westenschovwen.* (2004)

ᚠᚾᚦᛖᚱᚲ·ᚷᛈᚾᚻᛁ ᛢᛋᚳᚣᛡᛏᛒᛗᚻᚱᚷᚻᛢᚠᚪᛡᚾ

f u th o r k z w h n i j jh p x s t b e m l ng d oe a Æ ea y

Early Anglo-Saxon Runes

GOLD

752

A.   Early pieces, of uncertain monetary status

751	Thrymsa. Name and portrait of Bishop Leudard (chaplain to Queen Bertha of Kent). R. Cross.	*Extremely rare*
752	Solidus. Imitating solidi of Roman rulers. Blundered legends, some with runes.	*Extremely rare*

753   754   758

	F £	VF £

B.   **Crondall types, *c.*620 – *c.*645**

Twelve different types, which are almost certainly English, were found in the Crondall hoard of 1828. All are thrysmas, containing 70-40% gold.

753	'Witmen' type. Bust r. with trident. R. Cross. Legend normally blundered. *M. 1-21*	750	1750
754	London-derived type. Head r. with pseudo-legend. R. Cross. Pseudo-legend. *M. 22-32*	850	2250
755	'Licius' type. Elegant imitation of Roman triens. Bust l. R. VOT XX. *M. 33-41*	950	2750
756	'LEMC' type. Head l. R. Maltese cross with letters L, E, M, C in angles, or cross on steps. *M. 42-9*	850	2250
757	'LONDINIV' type. Facing bust, crosslets l. and r. R. Tall cross, LONDVNIV and pseudo-legend around. *M. 51-7*	1100	3250
758	Eabald of Kent (616-40) London. Bust r. AVDVARLD REGES. R. Cross on globule, LONDENVS. Usually garbled. *M. 50*	1000	3000
758A	— Canterbury. As 758 but DOROVERNVS M. *M-*	1500	3750
759	Other crude types, usually with head or bust, R. Cross. *M. 58-72*	625	1450

C.   **Ultra-Crondall types, *c.*620 – 655?**

Thrymsas not represented in the Crondall hoard, but probably of the same date range.

760   761   762

760	'Benutigo' type. Bust r., blundered legend. R. Cross on steps, runic legend (Benutigoii?)	900	2500
761	'Wuneetton' type. Bust r., cross before. R. Cross. Blundered legend (WVNEETON or similar). *M. 77*	750	2000
762	'York' type. Stylised face, crosslets to l. and r., squared pattern beneath. R. Cross. Blundered legend. *M. 76*	1100	3250
762A	— similar, but rev. with four 'faces' around central square. *M. p.51*	1000	3000

D.   **Post-Crondall types, *c.*655 – *c.*675**

Pale gold types, visibly debased and sometimes almost silvery, containing 35-10% gold.

764   765

764	'Crispus' type. Helmeted bust, r. CRISPUS NOB CAES. R. Cross and XX in wreath, runic legend Desaiona. *N.7*	1100	3250
764A	'Daisy and annulet-cross' type. Flower pattern. R. annulet Latin cross in pseudo wreath.	1500	3750
765	'Concordia' type. Radiate bust r. R. Clasped hands. *N.5*	1100	3250
766	'Oath-taking' type. Bust r. or l. with hand placed against cross. R. Lyre-shaped object, or eight-rayed symbol. *N.6*	850	2350

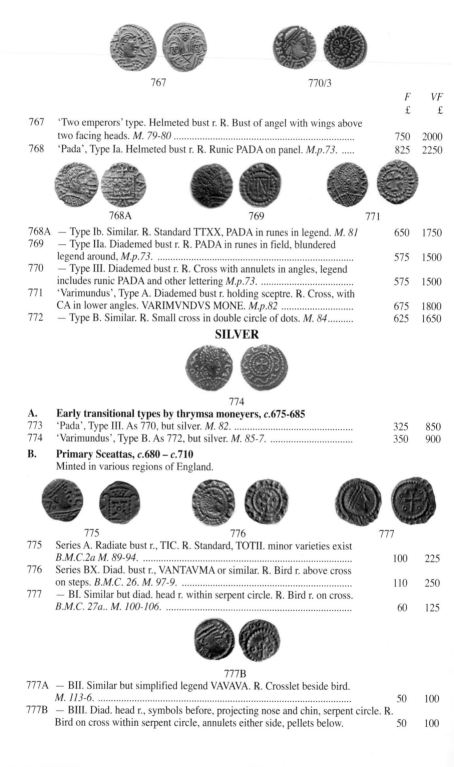

767   770/3

		F £	VF £

767 'Two emperors' type. Helmeted bust r. R. Bust of angel with wings above two facing heads. *M. 79-80* 750 2000

768 'Pada', Type Ia. Helmeted bust r. R. Runic PADA on panel. *M.p.73.* 825 2250

768A   769   771

768A — Type Ib. Similar. R. Standard TTXX, PADA in runes in legend. *M. 81* 650 1750

769 — Type IIa. Diademed bust r. R. PADA in runes in field, blundered legend around, *M.p.73.* 575 1500

770 — Type III. Diademed bust r. R. Cross with annulets in angles, legend includes runic PADA and other lettering *M.p.73.* 575 1500

771 'Varimundus', Type A. Diademed bust r. holding sceptre. R. Cross, with CA in lower angles. VARIMVNDVS MONE. *M.p.82* 675 1800

772 — Type B. Similar. R. Small cross in double circle of dots. *M. 84*.......... 625 1650

SILVER

774

A.   Early transitional types by thrymsa moneyers, *c.*675-685

773 'Pada', Type III. As 770, but silver. *M. 82.* 325 850

774 'Varimundus', Type B. As 772, but silver. *M. 85-7.* 350 900

B.   Primary Sceattas, *c.*680 – *c.*710
Minted in various regions of England.

775   776   777

775 Series A. Radiate bust r., TIC. R. Standard, TOTII. minor varieties exist *B.M.C.2a M. 89-94.* 100 225

776 Series BX. Diad. bust r., VANTAVMA or similar. R. Bird r. above cross on steps. *B.M.C. 26. M. 97-9.* 110 250

777 — BI. Similar but diad. head r. within serpent circle. R. Bird r. on cross. *B.M.C. 27a.. M. 100-106.* 60 125

777B

777A — BII. Similar but simplified legend VAVAVA. R. Crosslet beside bird. *M. 113-6.* 50 100

777B — BIII. Diad. head r., symbols before, projecting nose and chin, serpent circle. R. Bird on cross within serpent circle, annulets either side, pellets below. 50 100

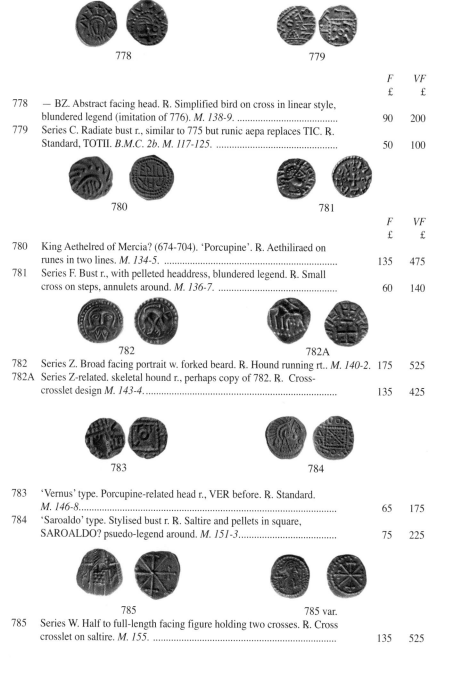

		F £	VF £
778	— BZ. Abstract facing head. R. Simplified bird on cross in linear style, blundered legend (imitation of 776). *M. 138-9.*	90	200
779	Series C. Radiate bust r., similar to 775 but runic aepa replaces TIC. R. Standard, TOTII. *B.M.C. 2b. M. 117-125.*	50	100

		F £	VF £
780	King Aethelred of Mercia? (674-704). 'Porcupine'. R. Aethiliraed on runes in two lines. *M. 134-5.*	135	475
781	Series F. Bust r., with pelleted headdress, blundered legend. R. Small cross on steps, annulets around. *M. 136-7.*	60	140

782	Series Z. Broad facing portrait w. forked beard. R. Hound running rt.. *M. 140-2.*	175	525
782A	Series Z-related. skeletal hound r., perhaps copy of 782. R. Cross-crosslet design *M. 143-4.*	135	425

783	'Vernus' type. Porcupine-related head r., VER before. R. Standard. *M. 146-8.*	65	175
784	'Saroaldo' type. Stylised bust r. R. Saltire and pellets in square, SAROALDO? psuedo-legend around. *M. 151-3.*	75	225

| 785 | Series W. Half to full-length facing figure holding two crosses. R. Cross crosslet on saltire. *M. 155.* .... | 135 | 525 |

D.   Secondary Sceattas, c.710-760

Minted in all the main regions of southern and eastern England, but especially in the south-east and the Thames basin.

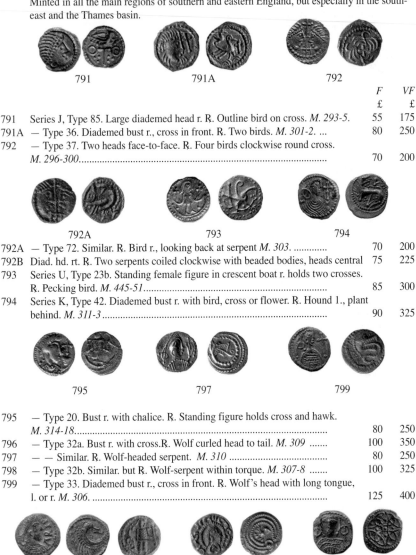

791   791A   792

		F	VF
		£	£
791	Series J, Type 85. Large diademed head r. Ɍ. Outline bird on cross. *M. 293-5.*	55	175
791A	— Type 36. Diademed bust r., cross in front. Ɍ. Two birds. *M. 301-2.* ...	80	250
792	— Type 37. Two heads face-to-face. Ɍ. Four birds clockwise round cross. *M. 296-300*	70	200

792A   793   794

792A	— Type 72. Similar. Ɍ. Bird r., looking back at serpent *M. 303.*	70	200
792B	Diad. hd. rt. Ɍ. Two serpents coiled clockwise with beaded bodies, heads central	75	225
793	Series U, Type 23b. Standing female figure in crescent boat r. holds two crosses. Ɍ. Pecking bird. *M. 445-51*	85	300
794	Series K, Type 42. Diademed bust r. with bird, cross or flower. Ɍ. Hound l., plant behind. *M. 311-3*	90	325

795   797   799

795	— Type 20. Bust r. with chalice. Ɍ. Standing figure holds cross and hawk. *M. 314-18*	80	250
796	— Type 32a. Bust r. with cross.Ɍ. Wolf curled head to tail. *M. 309*	100	350
797	— — Similar. Ɍ. Wolf-headed serpent. *M. 310*	80	250
798	— Type 32b. Similar. but Ɍ. Wolf-serpent within torque. *M. 307-8*	100	325
799	— Type 33. Diademed bust r., cross in front. Ɍ. Wolf's head with long tongue, l. or r. *M. 306.*	125	400

801 rev1/rev2   802   804

800	'Archer' type. Kneeling archer r. Ɍ. Bird on branch r., head turned back. *M. 349.*	425	1350
801	'Carip' group. Bust r., CARIP. Ɍ. include pecking bird, wolf-serpent, or standing figure. *M. 336-40.*	150	525
802	Series O, Type 38. Bust r. in cable border. Ɍ. Bird r. in torque. *M. 373-5.*	85	275
803	— Type 21. Similar, but peg-nosed bust l. Ɍ. Standing figure with two crosses. *M. 376*	135	475

		F £	VF £
804	'Triquetras' type. Facing bust, man and crosses, winged figure, or bird and branch. ℞. Interlace pattern. *M.p.425.*	125	425

805   806   807

805	Series H, Type 39. Pecking bird. ℞. Round shield with bosses. *M. 283-4.*	85	250
806	— Type 49. 'Wodan' head, bosses around. ℞. Pecking bird. *M. 285-8.*	95	300
807	— Type 48. Whorl of 3 wolf heads. ℞. Round shield with bosses. *M. 289-92*	80	240

808   809A   810

808	Series G. Diademed bust r., cross before. ℞. Standard with 3 or 4 saltires. *M. 267-70.*	65	185
809	— crude copies, some with bird or bird on cross. *M. 271-4*	35	110
809A	Series M. Sinuous animal r. ℞. Spiral vine. *M. 363-6.*	90	325
810	Series N. Type 41. Two standing figures. ℞. Monster looking back r. or l. *M. 368-72*	70	200

811   813   815

811	Series O, Type 40. Standing figure holds two crosses. ℞. Monster looking back, foreleg raised. *M. 379-81.*	85	240
812	— Type 43. ℞. Interlace cross. *M.p.482.*	115	375
813	— Type 57. Peg-nosed bust r. in cable border. ℞. Monster looking back l. *M. 377.*	110	350
814	'Animal mask' group. Facing animal (lion?) mask. ℞. Bird, figure, monster or cross. *M. 354-6.*	275	800
815	Series V. Wolf and twins. ℞. Bird in vine. *M. 453.*	175	575

816   818

816	Series T. Diad. bust r., +LEL. ℞. 'Porcupine' l or r. *M. 442-4.*	110	325
818	Series L, Type 12. Bust r., LVNDONIA. ℞. Standing figure in crescent boat holds two crosses. *M. 319-22.*	135	425
820	— Type 13. Similar. ℞. Seated figure holds hawk and cross. *M.p.409.*	225	675
821	— Type 14. Similar, but bust l. ℞. Celtic cross. *M.p.427.*	135	425

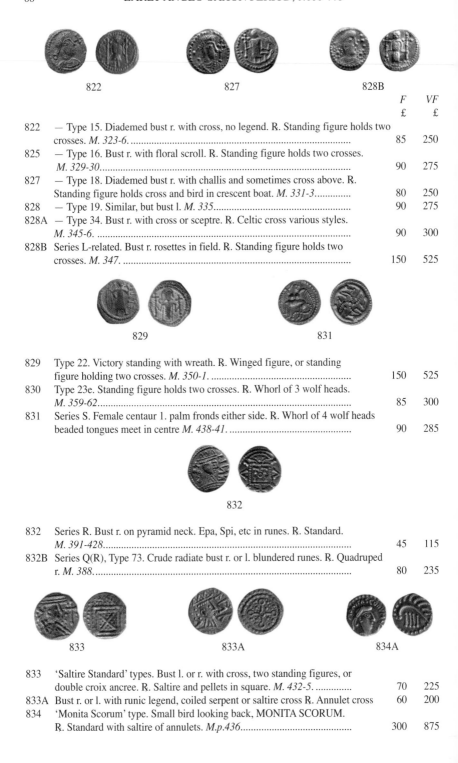

822　　　　　　　　　827　　　　　　　828B

	F £	VF £
822	— Type 15. Diademed bust r. with cross, no legend. R. Standing figure holds two crosses. *M. 323-6.*	85	250
825	— Type 16. Bust r. with floral scroll. R. Standing figure holds two crosses. *M. 329-30.*	90	275
827	— Type 18. Diademed bust r. with challis and sometimes cross above. R. Standing figure holds cross and bird in crescent boat. *M. 331-3*	80	250
828	— Type 19. Similar, but bust l. *M. 335*	90	275
828A	— Type 34. Bust r. with cross or sceptre. R. Celtic cross various styles. *M. 345-6.*	90	300
828B	Series L-related. Bust r. rosettes in field. R. Standing figure holds two crosses. *M. 347.*	150	525

829　　　　　　　　　831

829	Type 22. Victory standing with wreath. R. Winged figure, or standing figure holding two crosses. *M. 350-1.*	150	525
830	Type 23e. Standing figure holds two crosses. R. Whorl of 3 wolf heads. *M. 359-62*	85	300
831	Series S. Female centaur l. palm fronds either side. R. Whorl of 4 wolf heads beaded tongues meet in centre *M. 438-41.*	90	285

832

832	Series R. Bust r. on pyramid neck. Epa, Spi, etc in runes. R. Standard. *M. 391-428.*	45	115
832B	Series Q(R), Type 73. Crude radiate bust r. or l. blundered runes. R. Quadruped r. *M. 388.*	80	235

833　　　　　　　833A　　　　　　834A

833	'Saltire Standard' types. Bust l. or r. with cross, two standing figures, or double croix ancree. R. Saltire and pellets in square. *M. 432-5.*	70	225
833A	Bust r. or l. with runic legend, coiled serpent or saltire cross R. Annulet cross	60	200
834	'Monita Scorum' type. Small bird looking back, MONITA SCORUM. R. Standard with saltire of annulets. *M.p.436*	300	875

			F £	VF £
834A	— Bust r., MONITA SCORUM. R. 'porcupine' l., figure with two crosses, or triquetra. *M. 348.*		350	975

835    836C    836D

835	Type 70. Saltire-standard. R. Standard. *M. 436-7.*	40	125
836	Series Q, Types QII-IVd Bird l. or r. R. Quadruped l. or r. *M. 386-7.*	115	325
836A	— Type QIVe Quadruped both sides. *M.p.501*	120	375
836B	— Type QIe Bust r. with cross. R. Walking bird l. *M. 383.*	135	425
836C	— Type QIf Standing figure with two crosses. R. Walking bird l., pellets in field. *M. 384.*	165	575
836D	— Type QIg Facing head. R. Long-legged quadruped looking back. *M.p.492.*	225	675

844    844A

844	Type 30. Facing 'Wodan' head various styles. R. Two standing figures, or standard. *M. 429-31*	150	475
844A	— Type 53. 'Porcupine', similar to 787. R. Stepped cross, annulet at centre. *M. 258-62*	65	170

C.   Continental Sceattas, *c.695-c.*740
Most are from the Rhine area, or Frisia

786    786A

786	Series D. Porcupine-like figure incoporating various geometric figures. R Standard w. TOTII design	30	80
786A	Series E. Porcupine-like figure, body with annulet at lower end, triangle head w. pellet eye. R. 'Standard' with four pellets around central annulet. *Dorestad.* *M. 209-11.* (786)	30	80

787   788   789

		F	VF
		£	£
787	— Similar, with triangular fore-leg. R. 'Standard' with four lines and central annulet. *M. 200-5.*	30	75
788	— Similar, with parallel lines in curve of body. R. 'Standard' with VICO. *M. 194-8.*	30	75
789	— Figure developed into plumed bird. R. Standard with a variety of geometric symbols. *M. 190-3.*	40	125
790	Later issues.'Porcupine'. Innumerable varieties. R. 'Standard'. *M. 214-53.*	30	75

832A   838   839

832A	Type 10. Bust r., AEPA or APA. R. Porcupine modified into profile face. *Mint? M.p.248.*	150	375
838	'Porcupine' R. Small cross, S E D E in angles. *Mint? M. 263.*	200	650
839	Series D, Type 2c. Bust r., APA. R. Plain cross with pellets in angles. Letters around. *M. 158-80.*	40	95

840   841   842

840	— Type 8. Crude Standard with angular symbols. R. As 839. *M. 183-6.*	30	80
841	'Maastricht' Type. Crude head l. R. Quatrefoil interlaced cross. *M. 265-6*	150	450
842	'Hexagon' Type. Seal of Solomon enclosing central cross. R. Unbalanced radial arrangement, cross near centre and above. *M. 325-8*	150	450

843

843	Series X. Facing 'Wodan' head. R. Monster l. or r. *Ribe, Jutland, M. 275-81.*	115	325
843A	— cruder copies. *English, M. 282.*	125	375

KINGS OF NORTHUMBRIA AND BISHOPS OF YORK

The issues associated with pre-Viking Northumbria encompass a late seventh-century emission of gold, the following series of silver sceattas and the subsequent styca coinage. On the fringe of the later are two special issues, Eanred's penny and Wigmund's *solidus,* for neither of which is there yet evidence of use within the kingdom.

The Stycas developed in two phases, becoming a robust currency of small-denomination coins which seem to have been of great practical use. Production must have ceased early in Osberht's reign, although the old money may have continued in circulation until the Viking capture of York in 867. The official styca coinage, however, does appear to have been overwhelmed by irregular issues, which may reflect a period of civil war during the years *c.* 843 to *c.* 855.

The separation of kings and archbishops is no longer regarded as appropriate and the classification is chronological. In the spelling of names *U* for *W* would be appropriate in the Northumbrian context. *W* is based on West Saxon practice, but is used here on grounds of familiarity.

		F	VF
		£	£
762	**AV thrymsa,** *temp.* Kite-shaped shield enclosing cross, crosslets to l. and r., squared pattern beneath. R. Cross. Blundered (runic?) legend. *M. 76 (see also under Early Anglo-Saxon Period, Ultra-Crondall types)*	1100	3250

846   852

ℛ sceattas (a). Regal issues

846	**Aldfrith** (685-705). ALFRIDVS in semi-uncial lettering around central boss. R. Lion(?) l. triple tail above	275	750
847	**Eadberht** (737-758). Small cross (mainly). R. Stylized stag, to l. or r.	90	265
848	**Aethelwald Moll** (759-765). (A possible, though disputed, issue is known)	*Extremely rare*	

849

849	**Alchred** (765-774). Small cross. R. Stylized stag to l. or r.	225	650
850	**Aethelred I** (first reign, 774-779/80). R. Stylized stag to l. or r.	325	950
851	**Aelfwald I** (779/80-788). R. Stylized stag to l. or r.	250	700

ℛ sceattas (b). Joint issues, by kings and archbishops

852	**Eadberht** with **Abp. Ecgberht** (737-758). Small cross. R. Mitred figure holding two crosses	165	400
853	**Aethelwald Moll** with **Abp. Ecgberht** (759-765). Cross each side	675	1750
854	**Alchred** with **Abp. Ecgberht** (765-766). Cross each side	275	800
855	**Aethelred I,** with **Abp. Eanbald I** (*c.* 779-780). Various motifs.	200	600

Stycas Phase Ia. Issues in base silver, for kings and archbishop separately, c. 790-830, with moneyers named

856	**Aethelred I** (second reign, 789-796). R. CUDHEARD, or others	85	200
857	– R. 'Shrine', CUDCILS	275	850

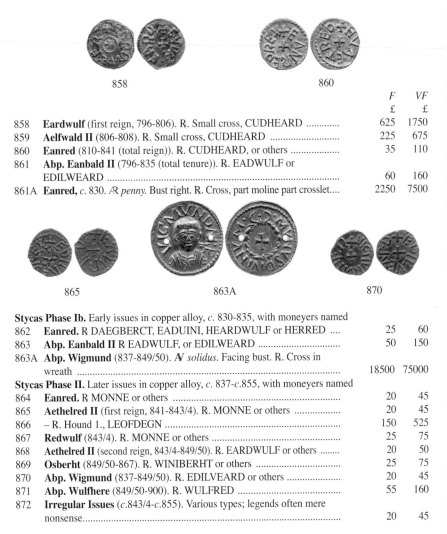

858   860

		F £	*VF* £
858	**Eardwulf** (first reign, 796-806). R. Small cross, CUDHEARD	625	1750
859	**Aelfwald II** (806-808). R. Small cross, CUDHEARD	225	675
860	**Eanred** (810-841 (total reign)). R. CUDHEARD, or others	35	110
861	**Abp. Eanbald II** (796-835 (total tenure)). R. EADWULF or EDILWEARD	60	160
861A	**Eanred,** *c*. 830. Æ *penny*. Bust right. R. Cross, part moline part crosslet....	2250	7500

865   863A   870

Stycas Phase Ib. Early issues in copper alloy, *c*. 830-835, with moneyers named

862	**Eanred.** R DAEGBERCT, EADUINI, HEARDWULF or HERRED	25	60
863	**Abp. Eanbald II** R EADWULF, or EDILWEARD	50	150
863A	**Abp. Wigmund** (837-849/50). Æ *solidus*. Facing bust. R. Cross in wreath	18500	75000

Stycas Phase II. Later issues in copper alloy, *c*. 837-*c*.855, with moneyers named

864	**Eanred.** R MONNE or others	20	45
865	**Aethelred II** (first reign, 841-843/4). R. MONNE or others	20	45
866	– R. Hound 1., LEOFDEGN	150	525
867	**Redwulf** (843/4). R. MONNE or others	25	75
868	**Aethelred II** (second reign, 843/4-849/50). R. EARDWULF or others	20	50
869	**Osberht** (849/50-867). R. WINIBERHT or others	25	75
870	**Abp. Wigmund** (837-849/50). R. EDILVEARD or others	20	45
871	**Abp. Wulfhere** (849/50-900). R. WULFRED	55	160
872	**Irregular Issues** (*c*.843/4-*c*.855). Various types; legends often mere nonsense..	20	45

Pirie E.J.E. Coins of the Kingdom of Northumbria c.700-867. 1996

In the kingdom of the Franks a reformed coinage of good quality *deniers* struck on broad flans had been introduced by Pepin in 755 and continued by his son Charlemagne and his descendants. A new coinage of *pennies* of similar size and weighing about 20 grains (1.3 gms) was introduced into England, probably by Offa, the powerful king of Mercia, about 755/780, though early pennies also exist of two little known kings of Kent, Heaberht and Ecgberht, of about the same period.

The silver penny (*Lat.* 'denarius', hence the *d.* of our *£ s. d.*) remained virtually the sole denomination of English coinage for almost five centuries, with the rare exception of occasional gold coins and somewhat less rare silver halfpence. The penny reached a weight of 24 grains, i.e., a 'pennyweight' during the reign of Alfred the Great. Silver pennies of this period normally bear the ruler's name, though not always his portrait, and the name of the moneyer responsible for their manufacture.

Pennies were issued by various rulers of the Heptarchy for the kingdoms of Kent, Mercia, East Anglia and Wessex by the Danish settlers in the Danelaw and the Hiberno-Norse kings of York, and also by the Archbishops of Canterbury and a Bishop of London. Under Eadgar, who became the sole ruler of England, a uniform coinage was instituted throughout the country, and it was he who set the pattern for the 'reformed' coinage of the later Anglo-Saxon and Norman period.

Halfpence were issued by most rulers from Alfred to Eadgar between 871-973 for S. England, and although all are rare today, it is probable that reasonable quantities were made.

Nos. 873-1387 are all silver pennies except where stated.

NB. Many pennies of the early part of this period have chipped flans and prices should be reduced accordingly.

KINGS OF KENT

		F	VF
		£	£
873	**Heaberht** (*c.* 765). Monogram for REX. R. Five annulets, each containing a pellet, joined to form a cross	3250	8500
874	**Ecgberht** (*c.* 780). Similar. R. Varied	850	2750

875   877

875	**Eadberht Praen.** Type 1. (796-798). As illustration. R. Varied	950	3000
875A	— Type 2. (*c.* 798). His name around, ⵍ in centre, R. Moneyer's name in angles of a tribrach	925	3000
876	**Cuthred** (798-807). *Canterbury.* Various types without portrait	650	1850
877	— — Portrait. R. Cross and wedges or A	625	1750

878   881

878	**Anonymous** (*c.* 822-823). *Canterbury.* As illustration or 'Baldred' style head	675	2250
879	**Baldred** (*c.* 823-825). *Canterbury.* diademed head r. R. DRUR CITS within inner circle	900	3000
880	— Cross each side	650	1850
881	*Rochester.* Bust r. R. Cross moline or wheel design	825	2750

883

		F £	VF £

881A **Jaenberht** (765-792). New type (early). Under Ecgberht II of Kent (?). (before *c.* 780 ?) His name around small cross of pellets in centre. R. PONTIFEX in three lines 975 3250

882 Under Offa of Mercia (*c.* 780-792) His name around central ornament or cross and wedges. R. OFFA REX in two lines 850 2400

883 — His name in three lines. R. OFFA or OFFA REX between the limbs of Celtic cross 900 2750

884 **Aethelheard** (el. 792, cons. 793, d. 805). With Offa as overlord. First issue (792-?), with title *Pontifex* 800 2400

885   887

885 — Second issue (?-796), with title *Archiepiscopus* 725 2250

885A — Third issue (*c.* 796-798), with title *Archiepiscopus*. His name and AR around EP in centre. R. Moneyer's name, EADGAR or CIOLHARD..... 850 2750

886 — With Coenwulf as overlord. (798-800 ?) Fourth Issue. As last. R. King's name in the angles of a tribrach 800 2400

886A — Fifth issue (*c.* 798-805?). As last R. Coenwulf's name around Ⓜ in centre 725 2250

887 **Wulfred** (805-832). group I (805-*c.* 810). As illustration. R. Crosslet, alpha-omega.. 675 2350

888 — Group II (*c.* 810). As last. R. DOROVERNIA C monogram 625 2000

889 — Group III (pre- 823). Bust extends to edge of coin. R. As last........... 600 1850

890 — Groups IV and V (*c.* 822-823). Anonymous under Ecgberht. Moneyer's name in place of the Archbishop's. R. DOROBERNIA CIVITAS in three or five lines 625 2000

891 — Group VI (*c.* 823-825). Baldred type. Crude portrait. R. DRVR CITS in two lines.. 850 3000

892 — Group VII (*c.* 832). Second monogram (Ecgberht) type. Crude portrait r., PLFRED. R. DORIB C. Monogram as 1035 .... 800 2750

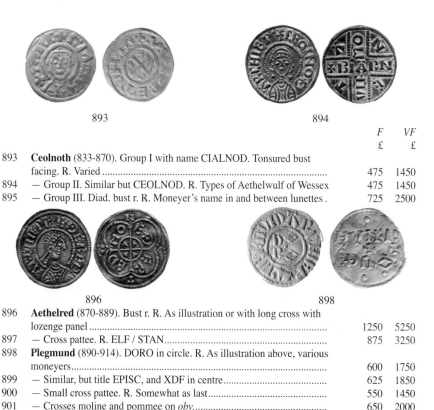

893 894

	F	VF
	£	£

893 **Ceolnoth** (833-870). Group I with name CIALNOD. Tonsured bust
facing. R. Varied 475 1450

894 — Group II. Similar but CEOLNOD. R. Types of Aethelwulf of Wessex 475 1450

895 — Group III. Diad. bust r. R. Moneyer's name in and between lunettes . 725 2500

896 898

896 **Aethelred** (870-889). Bust r. R. As illustration or with long cross with
lozenge panel 1250 5250

897 — Cross pattee. R. ELF / STAN.. 875 3250

898 **Plegmund** (890-914). DORO in circle. R. As illustration above, various
moneyers.. 600 1750

899 — Similar, but title EPISC, and XDF in centre...................................... 625 1850

900 — Small cross pattee. R. Somewhat as last.. 550 1450

901 — Crosses moline and pommee on *obv.*... 650 2000

901A — Halfpenny. As 900 .... 875 3500

KINGS OF MERCIA

Until 825 Canterbury was the principal mint of the Kings of Mercia and some moneyers also struck
coins for the Kings of Kent and Archbishops of Canterbury.

GOLD

902 903

902 **Offa** (757-796). Gold *dinar*. Copy of Arabic dinar of Caliph Al Mansur,
dated 157 A.H. (A.D. 774), with OFFA REX added on *rev.*...................... 85000 325000

903 Gold *penny*. Bust r., moneyer's name. R. Standing figure, moneyer's name 17500 67500

*A copy of a solidus with a diademed bust appears to read CIOLHEARD and is probably Mercian of
this or the following reign.*

SILVER

904   905

		F	VF
		£	£
904	Light Coinage. (*c.* 780?-792) *London and Canterbury.* Various types without portraits. Small flans	475	1250
905	— (*c.* 780?-792) *London and Canterbury.* Various types with portraits. Small flans.	750	2650
906	— East Anglia. Various types with portraits. R. Some with runic letters, small flans	825	2750

908   909

907	— — Various types without portraits. R. often with runic letters, small flans	575	1500
908	Heavy Coinage. (*c.* 792-796) *London, Canterbury and East Anglia.* Various types without portraits, large flans.	525	1350
909	**Cynethryth** (wife of Offa). Coins as light coinage of Offa. As illustration	1750	6500
910	— *O. As rev.* of last. R. EOBA on leaves of quatrefoil	875	3000
911	**Eadberht** (Bishop of London, died 787/789). EADBERHT EP in three lines or ADBERHT in two lines within a beaded rectangle, EP below. R. Name of Offa	925	3250

912

912	**Coenwulf, King of Mercia** (796-821). Gold *penny* or *Mancus* of 30 pence. London, diademed bust of Coenwulf right, finely drawn with four horizontal lines on the shoulders	37500	165000
912A	Penny. Group I (796-805). *London.* Without portrait. His name in three lines. R. Varied	575	1750
913	— *Canterbury.* Name around as illus. below. R. Moneyer's name in two lines	625	1850

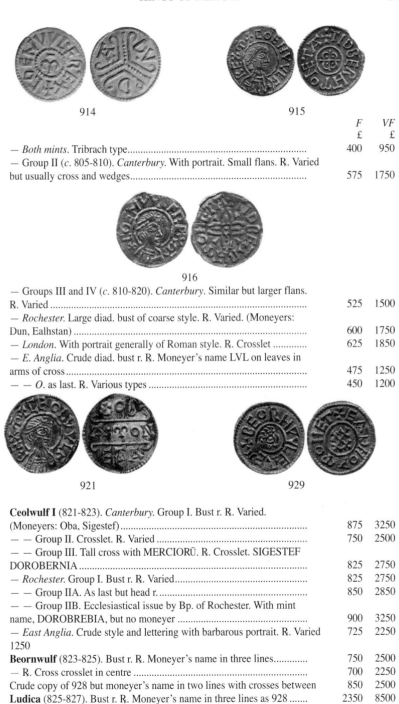

914 915

		F £	VF £
914	— *Both mints.* Tribrach type..	400	950
915	— Group II (*c.* 805-810). *Canterbury.* With portrait. Small flans. R. Varied but usually cross and wedges..	575	1750

916

916	— Groups III and IV (*c.* 810-820). *Canterbury.* Similar but larger flans. R. Varied	525	1500
917	— *Rochester.* Large diad. bust of coarse style. R. Varied. (Moneyers: Dun, Ealhstan)	600	1750
918	— *London.* With portrait generally of Roman style. R. Crosslet	625	1850
919	— *E. Anglia.* Crude diad. bust r. R. Moneyer's name LVL on leaves in arms of cross...	475	1250
920	— — *O.* as last. R. Various types	450	1200

921 929

921	**Ceolwulf I** (821-823). *Canterbury.* Group I. Bust r. R. Varied. (Moneyers: Oba, Sigestef)..	875	3250
922	— — Group II. Crosslet. R. Varied	750	2500
923	— — Group III. Tall cross with MERCIORŪ. R. Crosslet. SIGESTEF DOROBERNIA	825	2750
924	— *Rochester.* Group I. Bust r. R. Varied...	825	2750
925	— — Group IIA. As last but head r.	850	2850
926	— — Group IIB. Ecclesiastical issue by Bp. of Rochester. With mint name, DOROBREBIA, but no moneyer	900	3250
927	— *East Anglia.* Crude style and lettering with barbarous portrait. R. Varied 1250	725	2250
928	**Beornwulf** (823-825). Bust r. R. Moneyer's name in three lines.............	750	2500
929	— R. Cross crosslet in centre	700	2250
930	Crude copy of 928 but moneyer's name in two lines with crosses between	850	2500
931	**Ludica** (825-827). Bust r. R. Moneyer's name in three lines as 928	2350	8500

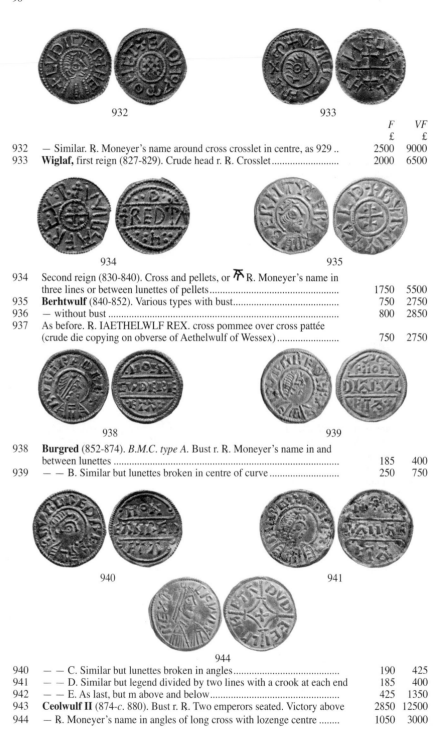

932

933

		F £	VF £

932   — Similar. Ŗ. Moneyer's name around cross crosslet in centre, as 929 ..   2500   9000

933   **Wiglaf,** first reign (827-829). Crude head r. Ŗ. Crosslet   2000   6500

934

935

934   Second reign (830-840). Cross and pellets, or ᛉ Ŗ. Moneyer's name in three lines or between lunettes of pellets   1750   5500

935   **Berhtwulf** (840-852). Various types with bust   750   2750

936   — without bust   800   2850

937   As before. Ŗ. IAETHELWLF REX. cross pommee over cross pattée (crude die copying on obverse of Aethelwulf of Wessex)   750   2750

938

939

938   **Burgred** (852-874). *B.M.C. type A.* Bust r. Ŗ. Moneyer's name in and between lunettes   185   400

939   — — B. Similar but lunettes broken in centre of curve   250   750

940

941

944

940   — — C. Similar but lunettes broken in angles   190   425

941   — — D. Similar but legend divided by two lines with a crook at each end   185   400

942   — — E. As last, but m above and below   425   1350

943   **Ceolwulf II** (874-*c.* 880). Bust r. Ŗ. Two emperors seated. Victory above   2850   12500

944   — Ŗ. Moneyer's name in angles of long cross with lozenge centre   1050   3000

KINGS OF EAST ANGLIA

945

		F	VF
		£	£
945	**Beonna,** King of East Anglia, *c*. 758. Æ sceat. Pellet in centre, Runic inscription. R. EFE in Roman characters around saltire cross	525	1350
945A	— Similar. R. WILRED in runic around pellet or cross.........................	575	1500
945B	— Similar. R. Interlace pattern (large flans)..	850	3000
945C	**Alberht** (749-?). Pellet in centre, AETHELBERT (runic) around R. Rosette in circle, TIAELRED (runic) around......................................	1350	4500
946	**Aethelberht** (d. 794). bust r. R. wolf and twins....................................	3750	16500
947	**Eadwald** (*c*. 798). King's name in three lines. R. Moneyer's name in quatrefoil or around cross	825	2750
947A	— King's name around cross or Ⓜ in centre. R. Moneyer's name in quartrefoil	850	2850

948   951

948	**Aethelstan I** (*c*. 825-840). Bust r. or l. R. Crosslet or star	750	2500
949	Bust r. R. Moneyer's name in three or four lines....................................	750	2500
950	Alpha or A. R. Varied	300	900
951	*O*. and *rev*. Cross with or without wedges or pellets in angles	325	950
952	— Similar, with king's name both sides	350	975
952A	Name around ship in centre. R. Moneyer Eadgar, around cross of pellets or in two lines (Possibly the earliest of his coins.)	1750	6500

953   954

953	**Aethelweard** (*c*. 840-*c*. 855), A, Omega or cross and crescents. R. Cross with pellets or wedges	450	1350
954	**Edmund** (855-870). Alpha or A. R. Cross with pellets or wedges	240	675
955	— *O*. Varied. R. Similar..	240	675

For the St. Edmund coins and the Danish issues struck in East Anglia bearing the name of Aethelred I, see Danish East Anglia.

		F	VF
		£	£

Danish East Anglia, _c_. 885-915

956	**Aethelstan II** (878-890), originally named Guthrum? Cross pattee. ℞. Moneyer's name in two lines	850	2850
957	**Oswald** (unknown except from his coins). Alpha or A. ℞. Cross pattee..	1250	4000
958	— Copy of Carolinigian 'temple' type. ℞ Cross and pellets	1350	4500
959	**Aethelred I.** (_c_.870) As last, with name of Aethelred I. ℞. As last, or cross-crosslet	1000	3500
959A	— As 954	825	2750

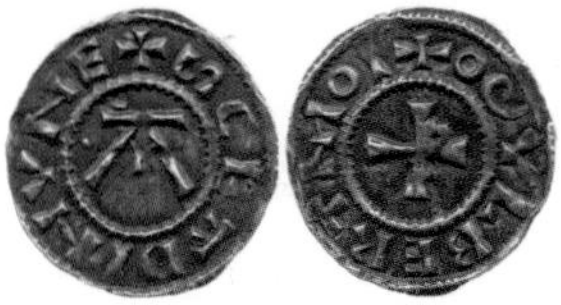

960 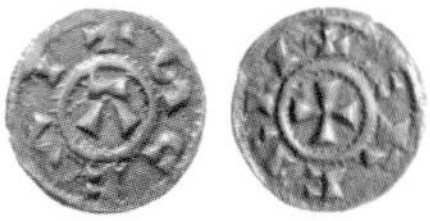   962

960	**St. Edmund,** memorial coinage, Æ _penny_, type as illus. below, various legends of good style	125	275
961	— Similar, but barbarous or semi-barbarous legends	120	265
962	_Halfpenny._ Similar	375	1050
963	**St. Martin of Lincoln.** As illustration	1650	6000
964	**Alfred.** (Viking imitations, usually of very barbarous workmanship.) Bust r. ℞. _Londonia_ monogram	775	3000

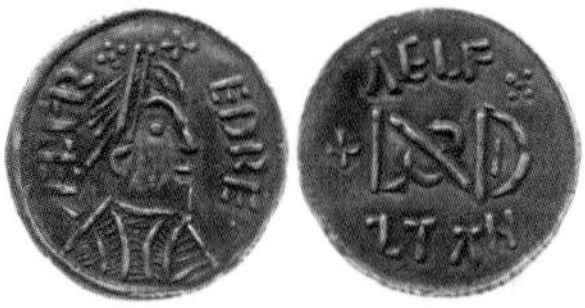

965

965	— Similar, with moneyer's name added	950	3500
966	— Small cross, as Alfred group II (_Br. 6),_ various legends, some read REX DORO	300	700
967	— Similar. ℞. 'St. Edmund type' A in centre	425	950
968	— Two emperors seated. ℞. As 964. (Previously attributed to Halfdene.)	1750	6000
969	_Halfpenny._ As 964 and 965	425	1050

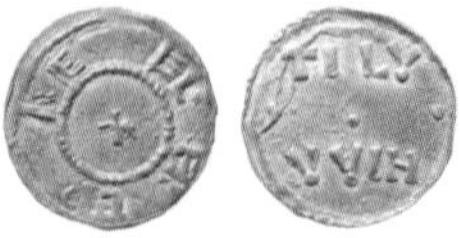

970

| 970 | — As 966 | 350 | 800 |

DANELAW, *c.* 898-915

971

975

		F	VF
		£	£
971	**Alfred** (Imitations). ELFRED between ORSNA and FORDA. ℞. Moneyer's name in two lines (occasionally divided by horizontal long cross)	475	1050
972	— *Halfpenny.* Similar, of very crude appearance	525	1250
973	**Alfred/Plegmund.** *Obv.* ELFRED REX PLEGN	575	1650
974	**Plegmund.** Danish copy of 900	425	975
975	**Earl Sihtric.** Type as 971. SCELDFOR between GVNDI BERTVS. ℞ SITRIC COMES in two lines	1850	6250

Viking Coinage of York?

References are to 'The Classification of Northumbrian Viking Coins in the Cuerdale hoard', by C. S. S. Lyon and B. H. I. H. Stewart, in Numismatic Chronicle, 1964, p. 281 ff.

975A	**Guthfrith.** GU DE F. RE Small cross. ℞. Moneyer's name in two lines.	1350	5250
976	**Siefred.** C. SIEFRE DIIS REX in two lines. ℞. EBRAICE CIVITAS (or contractions), small cross. *L. & S. Ia, Ie, Ii*	275	725
977	— Cross on steps between. ℞. As last. *L. & S. If, Ij*	350	900
978	— Long cross. ℞. As last. *L. & S. Ik*	300	800
979	SIEFREDVS REX, cross crosslet within legend. ℞. As last. *L. & S. Ih* ..	185	450

980

984

980	SIEVERT REX, cross crosslet to edge of coin. ℞. As last. *L. & S. Ic, Ig, Im*	225	575
981	— Cross on steps between. ℞. As last. *L. & S. Il*	350	925
982	— Patriarchal cross. ℞. DNS DS REX, small cross. *L. & S. Va*	300	750
983	— — ℞. MIRABILIA FECIT, small cross. *L. & S. VIb*	325	850
984	REX, at ends of cross crosslet. ℞. SIEFREDVS, small cross. *L. & S. IIIa, b*	225	575
985	— Long cross. ℞. As last. *L. & S. IIIc*	215	550
986	*Halfpenny.* Types as 977, *L. & S. Ib; 980, Ic; and 983, VIb*	525	1350
987	**Cnut.** CNVT REX, cross crosslet to edge of coin. ℞. EBRAICE CIVITAS, small cross. *L. & S. Io, Iq*	210	525
988	— — ℞. CVNNETTI, small cross. *L. & S. IIc*	200	500
989	— Long cross. ℞. EBRAICE CIVITAS, small cross. *L. & S. Id, In, Ir*	145	300
990	— — ℞. CVNNETTI, small cross. *L. & S. IIa, IId*	140	285
991	— Patriarchal cross. ℞. EBRAICE CIVITAS, small cross. *L. & S. Ip, Is*	135	275
992	— — ℞.— *Karolus* monogram in centre. *L. & S . It*	650	1850

993   995

	F £	VF £
993 — — ℞. CVNNETTI, small cross. *L. & S. IIb, IIe*	125	250
994 *Halfpenny.* Types as 987, *L. & S. Iq; 989, Id; 991, Is; 992, Iu; 993,* *IIb and e*	400	950
995 As 992, but CVNNETTI around *Karolus* monogram. *L. & S. IIf*	375	900
996 **Cnut and/or Siefred.** CNVT REX, patriarchal cross. ℞. SIEFREDVS, small cross. *L. & S. IIId*	250	650
997 — — ℞. DNS DS REX, small cross. *L. & S. Vc.*	300	800

998

998 — — ℞. MIRABILIA FECIT. *L. & S. VId*	180	425
999 EBRAICE C, patriarchal cross. ℞. DNS DS REX, small cross. *L. & S. Vb*	275	750

1000   1002

1000 — — ℞. MIRABILIA FECIT. *L. & S. VIc*	185	450
1001 DNS DS REX in two lines. ℞. ALVALDVS, small cross. *L. & S. IVa*	675	2250
1002 DNS DS O REX, similar. ℞. MIRABILIA FECIT. *L. & S. VIa*	300	800
1003 *Halfpenny.* As last. *L. & S. VIa*	475	1350
1004 **'Cnut'.** Name blundered around cross pattée with extended limbs. ℞. QVENTOVICI around small cross. *L. & S. VII*	375	1050
1005 *Halfpenny.* Similar. *L. & S. VII*	475	1350

York, early tenth century issues

1006

1009

		F £	VF £
1006	**St. Peter coinage.** Swordless type. Early issues. SCI PETRI MO in two lines. ℞. Cross pattee	235	575
1007	— similar. ℞. 'Karolus' monogram	750	2500
1008	*Halfpenny*. Similar. ℞. Cross pattee	600	1350
1009	**Regnald** (blundered types). RAIENALT, head to l. or r. ℞. EARICE CT, 'Karolus' monogram	1650	6000

1010

1010	— Open hand. ℞. Similar	1350	4500
1011	— Hammer. ℞. Bow and arrow	1500	5750
1012	Anonymous ℞. Sword	1350	4250

ENGLISH COINS OF THE HIBERNO-NORSE VIKINGS

Early period, *c.* 919-925

1013	**Sihtric** (921-927). SITRIC REX, sword. ℞. Cross, hammer or T	1650	5500
1014	**St. Peter coinage.** Sword type. Late issues SCI PETRI MO, sword and hammer. ℞. EBORACEI, cross and pellets	675	1750

1015

1016

1015	— Similar. ℞. Voided hammer	625	1600
1016	— Similar. ℞. Solid hammer	675	1750
	St. Peter coins with blundered legends are rather cheaper.		

| | F | VF |
| | £ | £ |

Later period, 939-954 (after the battle of Brunanburh). Mostly struck at York.

1017	**Anlaf Guthfrithsson,** 939-941. Flower type. Small cross, ANLAF REX TO D. ℞. Flower above moneyer's name	1650	6500
1018	— Circumscription type, with small cross each side, ANLAF CVNVNC, M in field on reverse *(Derby)*	1500	5000
1018A	— Two line type. ONLAF REX. Large letter both sides *(Lincoln?)*	1500	5000

1019

1019	— Raven type. As illustration, ANLAF CVNVNC	1350	4750
1020	**Olaf Sihtricsson,** first reign, 941-944. Triquetra type. As illus., CVNVNC. ℞. Danish standard	1600	5750
1021	— Circumscription type (a). Small cross each side, CVNVNC	1350	4750
1022	— Cross moline type, CVNVN C. ℞. Small cross	1450	5000
1023	— Two line type. Small cross. ℞. ONLAF REX. ℞. Name in two lines	1350	4750
1024	**Regnald Guthfrithsson,** 943-944. Triquetra type. As 1020. REGNALD CVNVNC	1500	5500
1025	— Cross moline type. As 1022, but REGNALD CVNVNC	1500	5500
1026	**Sihtric Sihtricsson,** *c.* 942. Triquetra type. As 1020, SITRIC CVNVNC	1500	5250
1027	— Circumscription type. Small cross each side	1350	4750
1027A	**Anonymous?** Two line type. Small cross ELTANGERHT. ℞. RERNART in two lines	1100	3250
1028	**Eric Blood-axe,** first reign, 948. Two line type. Small cross, ERICVC REX A; ERIC REX AL; or ERIC REX EFOR. ℞. Name in two lines	2250	7000
1029	**Olaf Sihtricsson,** second reign, 948-952. Circumscription type (b). Small cross each side. ONLAF REX	1450	4750
1029A	— Flower type. small cross ANLAF REX ℞. Flower above moneyer's name	1600	5750
1029B	— Two line type. Small cross, ONLAF REX. ℞. Moneyer's name in two lines	1350	4750
1030	**Eric Blood-axe,** second reign, 952-954. Sword type. ERIC REX in two lines, sword between. ℞. Small cross	2350	7500

Later, KINGS OF ALL ENGLAND FROM 959
All are silver pennies unless otherwise stated

BEORHTRIC, 786-802
Beorhtric was dependent on Offa of Mercia and married a daughter of Offa.

1031

		F	VF
		£	£
1031	As illustration	2750	9500
1032	Alpha and omega in centre. R. Omega in centre	2500	9000

ECGBERHT, 802-839
King of Wessex only, 802-825; then also of Kent, Sussex, Surrey, Essex and East Anglia, 825-839, and of Mercia also, 829-830.

| 1033 | *Canterbury.* Group I. Diad. hd. r. within inner circle. R. Various .... | 850 | 2650 |
| 1034 | — II. Non-portrait types. R. Various .... | 675 | 2000 |

1035

1035	— III. Bust r. breaking inner circle. R. DORIB C	825	2500
1036	*London.* Cross potent. R. LVN / DONIA / CIVIT	1350	4500
1037	— — R. REDMVND MONE around TA..	850	2650
1038	*Rochester,* royal mint. Non-portrait types with king's name ECGBEO RHT	725	2250
1039	— — Portrait types, ECGBEORHT...	875	2750
1040	*Rochester,* bishop's mint. Bust r. R. SCS ANDREAS (APOSTOLVS)....	950	3500
1041	*Winchester.* SAXON monogram or SAXONIORVM in three lines. R. Cross	725	2250

Son of Ecgberht; sub-King of Essex, Kent, Surrey and Sussex, 825-839; King of all southern
England, 839-855; King of Essex, Kent and Sussex only, 855-858. No coins are known of his son
Aethelbald who ruled over Wessex proper, 855-860.

1043   1045

		F	VF
		£	£
1042	*Canterbury.* Phase I (839-c. 843). Head within inner circle. R. Various. *Br. 3*	425	1350
1043	— — Larger bust breaking inner circle. R. A. *Br. 1 and 2*	475	1500
1044	— — Cross and wedges. R. SAXONIORVM in three lines in centre. *Br. 10*	325	950
1045	— — Similar, but OCCINDENTALIVM in place of moneyer. *Br. 11*	350	1050
1046	— Phase II (*c.* 843-848?). Cross and wedges. R. Various, but chiefly a form of cross or a large A. *Br. 4*	350	1050
1047	— — New portrait, somewhat as 1043. R. As last. *Br. 7*	450	1450
1048	— — Smaller portrait. R. As last, with *Chi/Rho* monogram. *Br. 7*	450	1500

1049   1051

1049	— Phase III (*c.* 848/851-*c.* 855). DORIB in centre. R. CANT mon. *Br. 5*	325	975
1050	— — CANT mon. R. CAN M in angles of cross. *Br. 6*	425	1350
1051	— Phase IV (*c.* 855-859). Type as Aethelberht. New neat style bust R. Large voided long cross. *Br. 8*	375	1250
1052	*Winchester.* SAXON mon. R. Cross and wedges. *Br. 9*	425	1350

Son of Aethelwulf; sub-King of Kent, Essex and Sussex, 858-860; King of all southern England, 860-865/6.

1053

	F	VF
	£	£
1053 As illustration above..	350	1100
1054 *O*. Similar, R. Cross fleury over quatrefoil...	575	1850

AETHELRED I, 865/866-871

Son of Aethelwulf; succeeded his brother Aethelberht.

1055

1055 As illustration..	375	1150
1056 Similar, but moneyer's name in four lines..	625	2000

For another coin with the name Aethelred see 959 under Viking coinages.

Brother and successor to Aethelred, Alfred had to contend with invading Danish armies for much of his reign. In 878 he and Guthrum the Dane divided the country, with Alfred holding all England south and west of Watling Street. Alfred occupied London in 886.

Types with portraits

1057

1058

	F £	VF £
1057 Bust r. R. As Aethelred I. *Br. 1* (*name often* AELBRED)	475	1350
1058 — R. Long cross with lozenge centre, as 944, *Br. 5*	1050	3750
1059 — R. Two seated figures, as 943. *Br. 2*	4500	17500
1060 — R. As Archbp. Aethered; cross within large quatrefoil. *Br. 3*	1350	5250

1061

1061 *London*. Bust. r. R. LONDONIA monogram	1100	3500
Copies made of tin at the Wembley Exhibition are common		
1062 — R. Similar, but with moneyer's name (Tilewine) added	1200	3750
1063 — *Halfpenny*. Bust r. or rarely l. R. LONDONIA monogram as 1061	475	1350
1064 *Gloucester*. R. Æ GLEAPA in angles of three limbed cross	2750	9000

Types without portraits

1065 King's name on limbs of cross, trefoils in angles. R. Moneyer's name in quatrefoil. *Br. 4.*	2250	6750

1066   1069

1066 Cross pattée. R. Moneyer's name in two lines. *Br. 6*	375	850
1067 — As last, but neater style, as Edw, the Elder	385	875
1068 — *Halfpenny*. As 1066	350	800
1069 *Canterbury*. As last but DORO added on *obv. Br. 6a*	400	950
1070 *Exeter?* King name in four lines. R. EXA vertical	2350	8500
1071 *Winchester?* Similar to last, but PIN	2350	8500
1071A *Oxford*. Elfred between OHSNA and FORDA. R. Moneyer's name in two lines (much commoner as a Viking Imitation - see 971)	725	2250
1072 'Offering penny'. Very large and heavy. AELFRED REX SAXORVM in four lines. R. ELIMO in two lines i.e. (*Elimosina*, alms)	6750	27500

For other pieces bearing the name of Alfred see under the Viking coinages.

Edward, the son of Alfred, aided by his sister Aethelflaed 'Lady of the Mericians', annexed all England south of the Humber and built many new fortified boroughs to protect the kingdom.

Rare types

1074

1078

		F	VF
		£	£
1073	*Br. 1. Bath?* R. BA	1250	4500
1074	— 2. *Canterbury.* Cross moline in pommee. R. Moneyer's name	975	3250
1075	— 3. *Chester?* Small cross. R. Minster	1250	4250
1076	— 4. — Small cross. R. Moneyer's name in single line	750	2000
1077	— 5. — R. Two stars	875	3000
1078	— 6. — R. Flower above central line, name below	1250	4000

1079

1081

1079	— 7. — R. Floral design with name across field	1250	4000
1080	— 8. — R. Bird holding twig	1750	6750
1081	— 9. — R. Hand of Providence, several varieties	1350	4500
1082	— 10. — R. City gate of Roman style	1250	4250

1083

1083	— 11. — R. Anglo-Saxon burg	975	3500

Ordinary types

1084

1087

1084	*Br. 12.* Bust l. R. Moneyer's name in two lines	725	2250
1086	— 12a. Similar, but bust r. of crude style	750	2400
1087	— 13. Small cross. R. Similar (to 1084)	200	525
1087A	— — As last, but in *gold*	20000	67500
1088	**Halfpenny.** Similar to last	675	1850
1088A	— — R. Hand of Providence	975	3250

Aethelstan, the eldest son of Eadward, decreed that money should be coined only in a borough, that every borough should have one moneyer and that some of the more important boroughs should have more than one moneyer.

1089

		F	VF
		£	£
1089	**Main issues.** Small cross. R̶. Moneyer's name in two lines..............	240	675
1090	Diad. bust r. R̶. As last	750	2500
1091	— R̶. Small cross	700	2000
1092	Small cross both sides...	285	825

1093

1095

1093	— Similar, but mint name added..	300	825
1094	Crowned bust r. As illustration. R̶. Small cross	625	1850
1095	— Similar, but mint name added..	650	1850
1096	**Local Issues.** *N. Mercian mints.* Star between two pellets. R̶. As 1089...	825	2250
1097	— Small cross. R̶. Floral ornaments above and below moneyer's name .	925	3000
1098	— Rosette of pellets each side...................................	325	900
1099	— Small cross one side, rosette on the other side	350	950

1100

1104

1100	*N.E. mints.* Small cross. R̶. Tower over moneyer's name..............	975	3500
1101	Similar, but mint name added....................................	1000	3750
1102	— Bust in high relief r. or l. R̶. Small cross	750	2500
1103	— Bust r. in high relief. R̶. Cross-crosslet....................	725	2500
1104	'Helmeted' bust or head r. R̶. As last or small cross.............	775	2650
1104A	**Halfpenny,** small cross. R̶. Moneyer's name in two lines	675	1850

Eadmund, the brother of Aethelstan, extended his realm over the Norse kingdom of York.

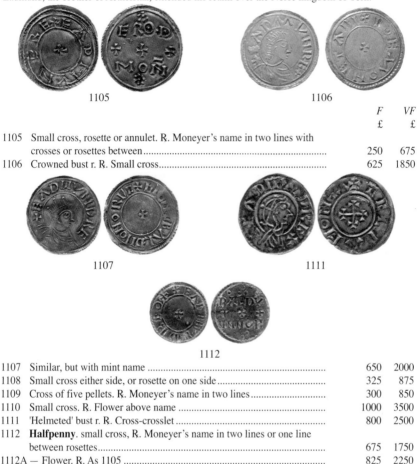

		F £	VF £
1105	Small cross, rosette or annulet. R. Moneyer's name in two lines with crosses or rosettes between	250	675
1106	Crowned bust r. R. Small cross	625	1850

1107	Similar, but with mint name	650	2000
1108	Small cross either side, or rosette on one side	325	875
1109	Cross of five pellets. R. Moneyer's name in two lines	300	850
1110	Small cross. R. Flower above name	1000	3500
1111	'Helmeted' bust r. R. Cross-crosslet	800	2500
1112	**Halfpenny**. small cross, R. Moneyer's name in two lines or one line between rosettes	675	1750
1112A	— Flower. R. As 1105	825	2250

EADRED, 946-955

Eadred was another of the sons of Eadward. He lost the kingdom of York to Eric Bloodaxe.

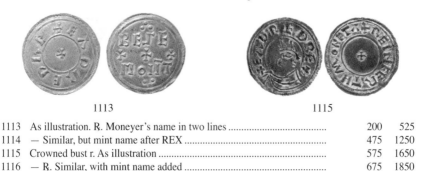

1113	As illustration. R. Moneyer's name in two lines	200	525
1114	— Similar, but mint name after REX	475	1250
1115	Crowned bust r. As illustration	575	1650
1116	— R. Similar, with mint name added	675	1850

	F	VF
	£	£
1117 Rosette. R. As 1113...	300	775
1118 Small cross. R. Rosette	300	775
1119 — R. Flower enclosing moneyer's name. *B.M.C. II*	1000	3500
1120 **Halfpenny**. Similar to 1113..	575	1350

HOWEL DDA, d. 949/950

Grandson of Rhodri Mawr, Howel succeeded to the kingdom of Dyfed *c.* 904, to Seisyllog *c.* 920 and became King of Gwynedd and all Wales, 942.

1121

1121 HOPÆL REX, small cross or rosette. R. Moneyer's name in two lines .	7500	28500

EADWIG, 955-959

Elder son of Eadmund, Eadwig lost Mercia and Northumbria to his brother Eadgar in 957.

1122   1123

1122 *Br. 1*. Type as illustration	375	950
1123 — — Similar, but mint name in place of crosses	575	1500
1124 — 2. As 1122, but moneyer's name in one line.......................	825	2500
1125 — 3. Similar. R. Floral design	1250	4000
1126 — 4. Similar. R. Rosette or small cross...............................	525	1350
1127 — 5. Bust r. R. Small cross	2250	8500

1128

1128 **Halfpenny**. Small cross. R. Flower above moneyer's name....................	875	2750
1128A — Similar. R. PIN (Winchester) across field...........................	975	3500
1128B — Star. R. Moneyer's name in two lines.................................	825	2250

King in Mercia and Northumbria from 957; King of all England 959-975.

It is now possible on the basis of the lettering to divide up the majority of Eadgar's coins into issues from the following regions: N.E. England, N.W. England, York, East Anglia, Midlands, S.E. England, Southern England, and S.W. England. (See 'Anglo-Saxon Coins', ed. R. H. M. Dolley.)

1129   1135

1136

	F £	VF £
1129 *Br 1.* Small cross. R. Moneyer's name in two lines, crosses between, trefoils top and bottom	175	375
1130 — — R. Similar, but rosettes top and bottom (a N.W. variety)	185	450
1131 — — R. Similar, but annulets between	200	475
1132 — — R. Similar, but mint name between (a late N.W. type)	275	750
1133 — 2. — R. Floral design	950	3000
1134 — 4. Small cross either side	175	400
1135 — — Similar, with mint name	275	750
1136 — — Rosette either side	225	600
1137 — — Similar, with mint name	300	875
1138 — 5. Large bust to r. R. Small cross	700	2000
1139 — — Similar, with mint name	750	2250
1140 **Halfpenny.** (8.5 grains.) *Br. 3.* Small cross. R. Flower above name	825	2500
1140A — — R. Mint name around cross (Chichester)	975	3500
1140B — Bust r. R. 'Londonia' monogram	750	2250

For Eadgar 'reform' issues see next page.

In 973 Eadgar introduced a new coinage. A royal portrait now became a regular feature and the reverses normally have a cruciform pattern with the name of the mint in addition to that of the moneyer. Most fortified towns of burghal status were allowed a mint, the number of moneyers varying according to their size and importance: some royal manors also had a mint and some moneyers were allowed to certain ecclesiastical authorities. In all some seventy mints were active about the middle of the 11th century (see list of mints pp. 124-128).

The control of the currency was retained firmly in the hands of the central government, unlike the situation in France and the Empire where feudal barons and bishops controlled their own coinage. Coinage types were changed at intervals to enable the Exchequer to raise revenue from new dies and periodic demonetization of old coin types helped to maintain the currency in a good state. No halfpence were minted during this period. During the latter part of this era, full pennies were sheared into 'halfpennies' and 'farthings'. They are far rarer than later 'cut' coins.

Further Reading: On the initial reform of the coinage under Eadgar see K. Jonsson, *The NewEra: The Reformation of the Late Anglo-Saxon Coinage* (London: 1987). The nature and purpose of frequent periodic recoinages is explored by I. Stewart, '*Coinage and recoinage after Edgar's reform*', in *Studies in Late Anglo-Saxon Coinage*, ed. K. Jonsson (Stockholm: 1990), 455-85. References to individual types for mints and moneyers for much of the first half of the period may be found in K. Jonsson, *Viking Age Hoards and Late Anglo-Saxon Coins* (Stockholm: 1986).

Eadgar, 959-975 *(continued)*

1141

	F	VF
	£	£
1141 **Penny**. Reform Small Cross type. Small diademed bust left. King's name 'Eadgar'. R. Small cross, name of moneyer and mint.............................	750	2250

EDWARD THE MARTYR, 975-978

The son of Eadgar by his first wife, Æthelflaed, Edward was murdered at Corfe in Dorset.

1142

| 1142   Sole type. As 1141, but reading 'Eadward'. .... | 900 | 2750 |

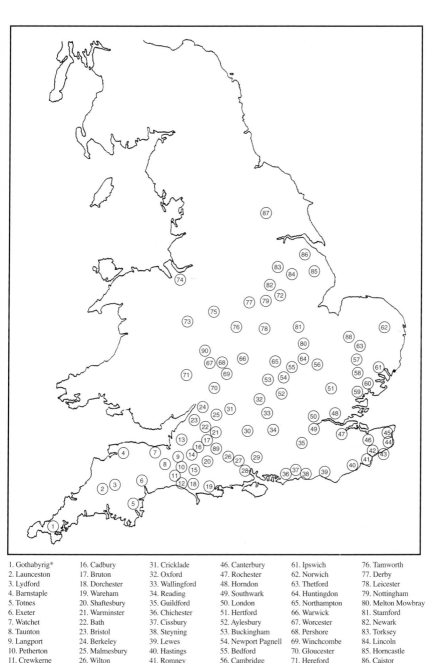

1. Gothabyrig*	16. Cadbury	31. Cricklade	46. Canterbury	61. Ipswich	76. Tamworth
2. Launceston	17. Bruton	32. Oxford	47. Rochester	62. Norwich	77. Derby
3. Lydford	18. Dorchester	33. Wallingford	48. Horndon	63. Thetford	78. Leicester
4. Barnstaple	19. Wareham	34. Reading	49. Southwark	64. Huntingdon	79. Nottingham
5. Totnes	20. Shaftesbury	35. Guildford	50. London	65. Northampton	80. Melton Mowbray
6. Exeter	21. Warminster	36. Chichester	51. Hertford	66. Warwick	81. Stamford
7. Watchet	22. Bath	37. Cissbury	52. Aylesbury	67. Worcester	82. Newark
8. Taunton	23. Bristol	38. Steyning	53. Buckingham	68. Pershore	83. Torksey
9. Langport	24. Berkeley	39. Lewes	54. Newport Pagnell	69. Winchcombe	84. Lincoln
10. Petherton	25. Malmesbury	40. Hastings	55. Bedford	70. Hereford	85. Horncastle
11. Crewkerne	26. Wilton	41. Romney	56. Cambridge	71. Hereford	86. Caistor
12. Bridport	27. Salisbury	42. Lympne	57. Bury St Edmunds	72. Grantham*	87. York
13. Ilchester	28. Southampton	43. Hythe	58. Sudbury	73. Shrewsbury	88. Wilton. Norfolk*
14. Ilchester	29. Winchester	44. Dover	59. Maldon	74. Chester	89. Frome
15. Miborne Port	30. Bedwyn	45. Sandwich	60. Colchester	75. Stafford	90. Droitwich

*Possible location of uncertain mint

Son of Eadgar by his second wife Ælfthryth, Æthelred ascended the throne on the murder of his half-brother. He is known to posterity as 'The Unready' from 'Unrede', meaning 'without counsel', an epithet gained from the weakness of his royal government.During this reign England was subjected to Viking raids of increasing frequency and strength, and a large amount of tribute was paid in order to secure peace. Large hoards have been found in Scandinavia and the Baltic region and coins are often found peck-marked. There is a high degree of regional variation in the style of dies, particularly in Last Small Cross type, for which readers are advised to consult the following paper: C.S.S. Lyon, 'Die cutting styles in the Last Small Cross issue of c.1009-1017…', *BNJ* 68 (1998), 21-41.

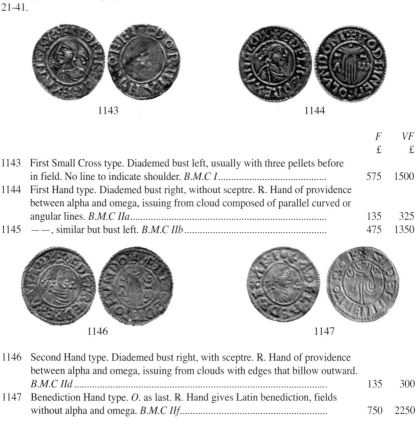

1143   1144

		F £	VF £
1143	First Small Cross type. Diademed bust left, usually with three pellets before in field. No line to indicate shoulder. *B.M.C I*	575	1500
1144	First Hand type. Diademed bust right, without sceptre. R. Hand of providence between alpha and omega, issuing from cloud composed of parallel curved or angular lines. *B.M.C IIa*	135	325
1145	— —, similar but bust left. *B.M.C IIb*	475	1350

1146   1147

1146	Second Hand type. Diademed bust right, with sceptre. R. Hand of providence between alpha and omega, issuing from clouds with edges that billow outward. *B.M.C IId*	135	300
1147	Benediction Hand type. *O.* as last. R. Hand gives Latin benediction, fields without alpha and omega. *B.M.C IIf*	750	2250

1148   1150

1148	Crux type. Bare-headed bust left, with sceptre. R. Voided short cross with letters C, R, V, X, in angles. *B.M.C IIIa*	120	240
1149	Small Crux type. Reduced weight, small flans, sceptre inclined to bust such that the base penetrates drapery.	125	250
1150	Intermediate Small Cross type. RX at end of legend separate letters. *B.M.C I*	750	2000

1151

1152

		F	VF
		£	£
1151	Long Cross type. Bare-headed bust left. R. Voided long cross. *B.M.C IVa*	125	250
1152	Helmet type. Armoured bust left in radiate helmet. *B.M.C VIII*...............	130	275
1153	As last but struck in gold.	23500	85000

1154

1156

1154	Last Small Cross type. Diademed bust left, RX at end of legend ligated together as one letter-form. *B.M.C I*	110	225
1154A	— —, similar but bust right.	225	675
1155	— —, similar but bust to edge of coin.	375	1000
1156	Angus Dei type. As illustration. *B.M.C X*..	4250	15000

Son of King Swein Forkbeard of Denmark, Cnut was acclaimed king by the Danish fleet in England in 1014 but was forced to leave; Cnut returned and harried Wessex in 1015. Æthelred II died in 1016 and resistance to the Danes was continued by his son Eadmund Ironside, for whom no coins are known, but upon the latter's death in 1016 Cnut became undisputed king. The following year Cnut consolidated his position by marrying Emma of Normandy, the widow of Æthelred II.

There is a high degree of regional variation in the style of dies, particularly in Quatrefoil type, for which readers are advised to consult the following paper: M.A.S. Blackburn and C.S.S. Lyon, 'Regional die production in Cnut's Quatrefoil issue' in *Anglo-Saxon Monetary History*, ed. M.A.S. Blackburn (Leicester: 1986), 223-72. There is considerable weight fluctuation within and between the types.

Substantive types

1157   1158

1159

		F	VF
		£	£
1157	Quatrefoil type (c.1017-23). Crowned bust left. *B.M.C VIII*	100	200
1158	Pointed Helmet type (1024-1030). *B.M.C XIV*	95	185
1159	Short Cross type (c.1029-1035/6). *B.M.C XVI*	90	175
1159A	— —, similar but sceptre replaced with a banner	575	1500

Posthumous type

1160	Jewel Cross type. BMC XX..	450	1200

Type considered to have been struck under the auspices of his widow, Queen Emma of Normandy.

Harold was the illegitimate son of Cnut by Ælfgifu of Northampton and was appointed regent on behalf of his half-brother Harthacnut. Queen Emma of Normandy initially held Wessex for her son, Harthacnut, but by 1137 she had been driven from the country and Harold had been recognised as king throughout England. The principal issue was the Jewel Cross type which is also found in the name of Cnut and Harthacnut, cf. nos. 1160 and 1166.

1165

		F	VF
		£	£
1162	Short Cross type (Autumn 1035). As 1159, but in the name of Harold. B.M.C. IIIa	750	2250
1163	Jewel Cross type (c.1036-38). B.M.C. I	250	625
1164	Fleur-de-Lis type (1038-40). Armoured and diademed bust left. R. Voided long cross, trefoil of pellets in each angle. B.M.C. V	250	625
1165	— —, similar but fleur-de-lis between two pellets in each angle. B.M.C. V	240	600

HARTHACNUT, 1035-1042

Although Harthacnut was the only legitimate son of Cnut and his legitimate heir, the political situation in Denmark prevented him from leaving for England until 1040, by which time Harold had secured the kingdom. Harold's death allowed Harthacnut to reclaim England without bloodshed, but he himself died after two years of sole rule. The main variety of Harthacnut is Arm and Sceptre type from his sole reign. The Jewel Cross type from the early period is also found in the name of Cnut and Harold I, cf. nos. 1160 and 1163.

Early period (during regency) 1035–7

1166	Jewel Cross type. As 1163, but in the name of Harthacnut. Diademed bust left. B.M.C. I	875	2750

1167   1168

1167	— —, similar but bust right. B.M.C I	825	2500

Sole reign 1040–42

1168	Arm and Sceptre type. King's name given as 'Harthacnut'. Diademed bust left with sceptre in left hand, forearm visible across bust B.M.C. II	725	2000

1169   1170

1169	— —, Similar but king's name given as 'Cnut'.	425	950
1170	**Danish types.** Types exist in the name of Harthacnut other than those listed above and are Scandinavian in origin.	250	550

EDWARD THE CONFESSOR, 1042-1066

Son of Æthelred II and Emma of Normandy, Edward spent twenty-five years in Normandy before he was adopted into the household of his half-brother Harthacnut in 1040. On the death of Harthacnut, Edward was acclaimed king. He is known by the title 'The Confessor' owing to his piety and he was canonised after his death. There is considerable weight fluctuation within and between the types, which is often unaffected by the smallness of the flan, rather the coin might be thicker to compensate.

Further reading: P. Seaby, 'The sequence of Anglo-Saxon types 1030–1050', *BNJ* 28 (1955-7), 111–46; T. Talvio, 'The design of Edward the Confessor's coins', in *Studies in Late Anglo-Saxon Coinage*, ed. K. Jonsson (Stockholm: 1990), 489–99.

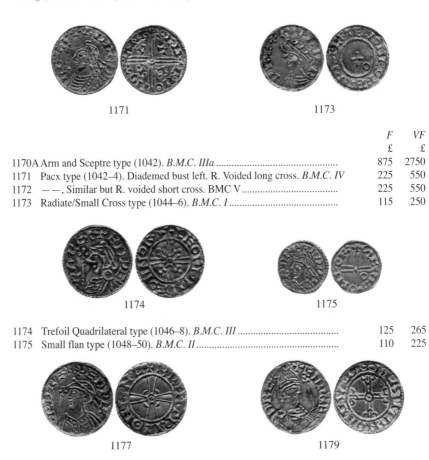

1171   1173

		F	*VF*
		£	£
1170A	Arm and Sceptre type (1042). *B.M.C. IIIa*	875	2750
1171	Pacx type (1042–4). Diademed bust left. R. Voided long cross. *B.M.C. IV*	225	550
1172	— —. Similar but R. voided short cross. BMC V	225	550
1173	Radiate/Small Cross type (1044–6). *B.M.C. I*	115	250

1174   1175

1174	Trefoil Quadrilateral type (1046–8). *B.M.C. III*	125	265
1175	Small flan type (1048–50). *B.M.C. II*	110	225

1177   1179

1176	Expanding Cross type (1050–53). Light issue, small flans; weight approx. 1.16g. *B.M.C. V*	135	300
1177	— —. Heavy issue, large flans; weight approx. 1.74g. *B.M.C. V*	135	300
1178	— —, Similar but struck in gold	25000	85000
1179	Pointed Helmet type (1053–6). Bearded bust right in pointed helmet. *B.M.C. VII*	130	285
1180	— —, Similar but bust left.	575	1750

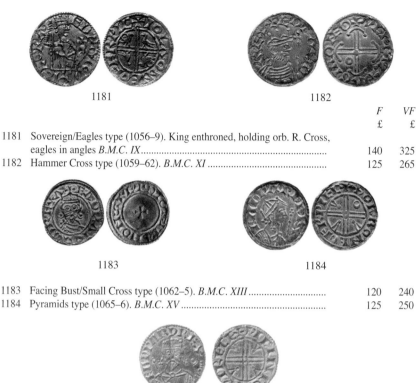

1181 1182

		F £	VF £

1181 Sovereign/Eagles type (1056–9). King enthroned, holding orb. R. Cross, eagles in angles *B.M.C. IX*.. 140 325

1182 Hammer Cross type (1059–62). *B.M.C. XI* 125 265

1183 1184

1183 Facing Bust/Small Cross type (1062–5). *B.M.C. XIII* 120 240

1184 Pyramids type (1065–6). *B.M.C. XV* 125 250

1185

1185 Transitional Pyramids type (c.1065). *B.M.C. XIV* 1250 3500

Most York coins of this reign have an annulet in one quarter of the reverse.

HAROLD II, 1066

Harold was the son of Earl Godwine of Wessex, who had dominated the royal court, and was brother-in-law to Edward the Confessor. Harold successfully repulsed an invasion of Harald Hardrada of Norway, but was himself killed in the Battle of Hastings after a reign of ten months.

Further reading: H. Pagan, 'The coinage of Harold II', in Studies in Late Anglo-Saxon Coinage, ed. K. Jonsson (Stockholm: 1990), 177–205.

1186 1187

1186 Pax type. Crowned head left with sceptre. R. PAX across field. *B.M.C. I* 675 1450

1187 — —, Similar but without sceptre. *B.M.C. Ia* 700 1500

1188 — —, Similar but head right. *B.M.C. Ib* 1250 3500

In late Anglo-Saxon and Norman times coins were struck in the King's name at a large number of mints distributed in centres of population, and in times of emergency in places of refuge, across England and Wales. During the 10th century the use of a mint signature was sporadic but from the Reform type of Edgar the mint name is almost invariably given, usually in conjunction with that of the moneyer responsible, e.g. EDGAR ON BERCLE. At the peak, 71 mints struck the quatrefoil type of Cnut and 65 the PAXS type of William I and they provide a valuable insight into the economic and social structures of the period.

The output of the mints varied enormously and a dozen are exceptionally rare. Approximately 100,000 pennies survive, half of which emanate from the great centres of London, Canterbury, Lincoln, Winchester and York. At the other end of the scale a mint such as Rochester is known from about 500 coins, Derby from around 250, Guildford 100, Bedwyn 25, Horncastle 4 and Pershore 1. Many of these coins, particularly those from the great Scandinavian hoards, are in museum collections and are published in the Sylloge of Coins of the British Isles (SCBI) series.

There are too many type for mint combinations, over 1500 Saxon and 1000 Norman, to price each individually and our aim is to give an indication of value for the commonest Saxon and Norman type, in VF condition, for each of the 102 attested mints (excluding Baronial of Stephen's reign), and for a further 10 mints whose location or attribution is uncertain. The threshold VF price for a Norman coin (H1 B.M.C.15 £400) exceeds that for a Saxon coin (Cnut short cross £175) accounting for the difference in starting level. Prices for coins in lower grade would be less and there is a premium for the rarer types for each mint, but for many types, e.g. in the reigns of Harthacnut or Henry I, the value of the type itself far exceeds that of many of the constituent mints and a scarce mint is only worth a modest premium over a common one.

We also give the most characteristic mint signatures (often found abbreviated) and the reigns for which the mint is known. There are many pitfalls in identifying mints, not least that Saxon and Norman spelling is no more reliable than that of other ages and that late Saxon coins were widely imitated in Scandinavia. There is extensive literature and the specialist in this fascinating series can, for further details, consult J J North, English Hammered Coinage Vol.1.

Alf	—	Alfred the Great	Hd1	—	Harold I
EdE	—	Edward the Elder	HCn	—	Harthacnut
A'stn	—	Aethelstan	EdC	—	Edward the Confessor
Edm	—	Edmund	Hd2	—	Harold II
Edw	—	Edwig	W1	—	William I
Edg	—	Edgar	W2	—	William II
EdM	—	Edward the Martyr	H1	—	Henry I
Ae2	—	Aethelred	St	—	Stephen
Cn	—	Cnut			

Berkeley   Hastings

	SAXON	NORMAN
	VF	VF
	£	£
Axbridge (AXAN, ACXEPO) Edg, Ae2, Cn, HCn	2250	—
Aylesbury (AEGEL, AEEL), Ae2, Cn, EdC	2000	—
Barnstable (BARD, BEARDA) Edw, Edg, Ae2-Hd1, EdC, W1, H1	850	1250
Bath (BADAN) EdE-A'stn, Edw-EdC, W1-St	350	650
Bedford (BEDAN, BEDEFOR) Edw-St	300	600
Bedwyn (BEDEPIN) EdC, W1	1200	2500
Berkeley (BEORC, BERCLE) EdC	6500	—
Bramber (BRAN) St	—	2750
Bridport (BRYDI, BRIPVT) A'stn, Ae2, Cn, HCn, EdC-W1	900	900
Bristol (BRICSTO, BRVCSTO) Ae2-St	300	600
Bruton (BRIVT) Ae2, Cn, HCn, EdC	1500	—
Buckingham (BVCIN) Edg, EdM-Hd1, HCn, EdC	2000	—
Bury St.Edmunds (EDMVN, S.EDM) EdC, W1, H1, St	750	550
Cadbury (CADANBY) Ae2, Cn	3500	—
Caistor (CASTR, CESTR) EdM, Ae2, Cn	3500	—
Cambridge (GRANTE) Edg-St	225	650
Canterbury (DORO, CAENTPA, CNTL) Alf, A'stn, Edr, Edg-St	175	400
Cardiff (CIVRDI, CAIERDI) W1, H1, St, Mat	—	900
Carlisle (CARD, EDEN) H1, St	—	1250
Castle Rising (RISINGE) St (type II-VII)	—	1250
Chester (LEIGE, LEGECE, CESTRE) A'stn, Edm, Edg-St	325	600
Chichester (CISSAN, CICEST) A'stn, Edg, Ae2-St	250	500
Christchurch (orig. Twynham) (TVEHAM, TPIN) W1, H1	—	2000
Cissbury (SIDESTEB, SIDMES) Ae2, Cn	1500	—
Colchester (COLN, COLECES) Ae2-St	250	500
Crewkerne (CRVCERN) Ae2, Cn, Hd1	2500	—
Cricklade (CROCGL, CRECCELAD, CRIC) Ae2-W2	900	800
Derby (DEORBY, DERBI) A'stn, Edm, Edg-St	650	750
Dorchester (DORCE, DORECES) Ae2-H1	650	750
Dover (DOFERA, DOFRN) A'stn, Edg, Ae2-St	200	500
Droitwich (PICC, PICNEH) EdC, Hd2	3000	—
Dunwich (DVNE) St	—	1350
Durham (DVNE, DVRHAM, DVNHO) W1-St	—	1750
Exeter (EAXA, EAXCESTRE, IEXECE) Alf, A'stn, Edw-St	225	500
Frome (FRO) Cn, HCn, EdC	3000	—
Gloucester (GLEAP, GLEPECE, GLOPEC) Alf, A'stn, Edg-St	350	600
Grantham (GRANTHA, GRE) Ae2	3500	—
Guildford (GYLD, GILDEFRI) EdM-W2	900	2000
Hastings (HAESTINGPOR, AESTI) Ae2-St	250	600
Hedon (HEDVN) St	—	5000
Hereford (HEREFOR, HRFRD) A'stn, Edg, Ae2-St	400	600
Hertford (HEORTF, HRTFI, RET) A'stn, Edw-EdC, W1-H1	300	1000
Horncastle (HORN) EdM, Ae2	5000	—
Horndon (HORNIDVNE) EdC	5000	—
Huntingdon (HVNTEN, HVTD) Edg, Ae2-St	250	800
Hythe (HIÐEN, HIDI) EdC, W1, W2	2500	1000
Ilchester (GIFELCST, GIVELC, IVELCS) Edg, Ae2-St	600	1000
Ipswich (GIPESWIC, GYPES) Edg-St	250	500
Langport (LANCPORT, LAGEPOR) A'stn, Cn-EdC	2000	—
Launceston (LANSTF, LANSA, SANCTI STEFANI) Ae2, W1-H1	3000	1500
Leicester (LIHER, LEHRE, LEREC) A'stn, Edg, Ae2-St	300	600
Lewes (LAEPES, LEPEEI, LAPA) A'stn, Edg-St	250	600
Lincoln (LINCOLN, NICOLE) Edr, Edg-St	175	400
London (LVNDO, LVNDENE) Alf, A'stn, Edw-St	175	400
Lydford (LYDANFOR) Edg-EdC	350	—
Lympne (LIMENE, LIMNA) A'stn, Edg-Cn	850	—
Maldon (MAELDVN, MIEL) A'stn, Edg, Ae2-Hd1, EdC-W2	350	800
Malmesbury (MALD, MEALDMES, MELME) Edg, Ae2-W2	800	1250
Marlborough (MAERLEBI) W1, W2	—	3000
Melton Mowbray (MEDELTV) Ae2, Cn	5000	—
Milborne Port (MYLE) Ae2, Cn	5000	—

	SAXON VF £	NORMAN VF £
Newark (NEWIR, NIWOR) Edg-Cn	3000	—
Newcastle (CAST) St	—	1500
Newport (NIPANPO, NIPEPORT) Edw, Edg, EdC	3000	—
Northampton (HAMTVN, HMTI, NORHAM) Edw, Edg-St	300	500
Norwich (NORDPIC) A'stn-Edr, Edg-St	175	400
Nottingham (SNOTING) A'stn, Ae2-St	750	1000
Oxford (OXNA, OCXEN, OXENFO) Alf, A'stn, Edr-St	300	500
Pembroke (PEI, PAN, PAIN) H1, St	—	2500
Pershore (PERESC) EdC	6500	—
Petherton (PEDR, PEDI) Cn, EdC	4000	—
Pevensey (PEFNESE, PEVEN) W1-St	—	1750
Reading (READIN, REDN) EdC	4000	—
Rhuddlan (RVDILI) W1	—	3000
Rochester (ROFEC, ROFSC) A'stn, Edg-H1	350	1000
Romney (RVMED, RVMNE) Ae2-H1	350	700
Rye (RIE) St	—	3000
Salisbury (SEREB, SEARB, SALEB) Ae2-EdC, W1-St	300	500
Sandwich (SANDPI) EdC, W1-St	350	600
Shaftesbury (SCEFTESB, CEFT, SAFTE) A'stn, Edg-St	350	600
Shrewsbury (SCROB, SCRVBS, SALOP) A'stn, Edg, Ae2-St	400	650
Southampton (HAMPIC, HAMTVN) A'stn, Edw-Cn	500	—
Southwark (SVDBY, SVDGE, SVDPERC) Ae2-St	175	400
Stafford (STAFFO, STAEF) A'stn, Edg, Ae2-Hd1, EdC, W1-St	400	750
Stamford (STANFORD) Edg-St	175	400
Steyning (STAENIG, STENIC) Cn-W2, St	250	500
Sudbury (SVDBI, SVBR) Ae2, Cn, EdC, W1-St	400	600
Swansea (SVENSEI) St	—	2500
Tamworth (TOMPEARÐ, TAMPRÐ) A'stn, Edg-Hd1, EdC, W1-St	1000	800
Taunton (TANTVNE) Ae2-St	600	700
Thetford (ÐEOTFOR, DTF, TETFOR) Edg-St	175	400
Torksey (TVRC, TORC) EdM-Cn	2500	—
Totnes (DARENT, TOTANES, TOTNES) A'stn, Edw-HCn, W2, H1	350	1250
Wallingford (PELINGA, PALLIG) A'stn, Edm, Edg, Ae2-H1	350	650
Wareham (PERHAM, PERI) A'stn, Edg-St	400	650
Warminster (PORIME) Ae2-Hd1, EdC	2000	—
Warwick (PAERINC, PERPIC, PAR) A'stn (?), Edg-St	500	750
Watchet (PECED, PICEDI, WACET) Ae2-EdC, W1-St	1000	1250
Wilton (PILTVNE) Edg-St	250	500
Winchcombe (WENCLES, PINCEL, PINCL) Edg, Ae2, Cn, HCn-W1	900	1000
Winchester (PINTONIA, PINCEST) Alf, A'stn, Edw-St	175	400
Worcester (PIGER, PIHREC, PIREC) EdM, Ae2-St	450	600
York (EBORACI, EFORPIC, EVERWIC) A'stn, Edm, Edg-St	175	500

Mints of uncertain identification or location

	SAXON VF £	NORMAN VF £
"Brygin" (BRYGIN) Ae2	3000	—
"Dyr/Dernt" (DYR, DERNE, DERNT) EdC	1250	—
"Weardburh" (PEARDBV) A'stn, Edg	2500	—
Abergavenny (?) (FVNI) W1	—	2000
Gothabyrig (GEODA, GODABYRI, IODA) Ae2-HCn	2500	—
Eye (?) (EI, EIE) St	—	1500
Peterborough (?) (BVRI) W1, St	—	3000
Richmond, Yorks (?) (R1), St (type 1)	—	1750
St Davids (?) (DEVITVN) W1	—	1750
Wilton, Norfolk (?) (PILTV) Ae2 (LSC)	2000	—
Bamborough (BCI, CIB, OBCI) Henry of Northumberland	—	4250
Corbridge (COREB) Henry of Northumberland	—	4250

Aylesbury

Barnstaple

Cricklade

Dunwich

Exeter

Frome

Guildford

Horncastle

Ilchester

London

Milborne Port

Newark

Oxford

Pevensey

Rochester

Stafford

Torksey

Winchcombe

York

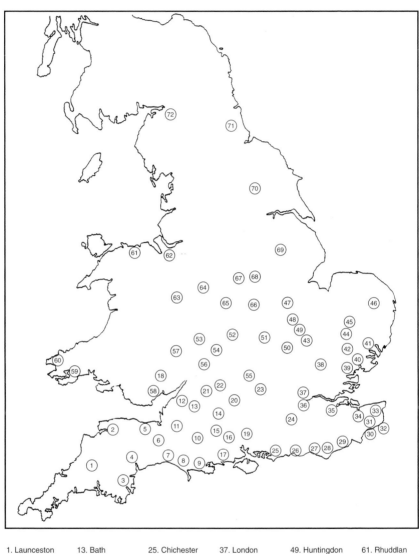

1. Launceston	13. Bath	25. Chichester	37. London	49. Huntingdon	61. Rhuddlan
2. Barnstaple	14. Marlborough	26. Steyning	38. Hertford	50. Bedford	62. Chester
3. Totnes	15. Wilton	27. Lewes	39. Maldon	51. Northampton	63. Shrewsbury
4. Exeter	16. Salisbury	28. Pevensey	40. Colchester	52. Warwick	64. Stafford
5. Watchet	17. Christchurch	29. Hastings	41. Ipswich	53. Worcester	65. Tamworth
6. Taunton	18. Abergavenny*	30. Romney	42. Sudbury	54. Winchcombe	66. Leicester
7. Bridport	19. Winchester	31. Hythe	43. Cambridge	55. Gloucester	67. Derby
8. Dorchester	20. Bedwyn	32. Dover	44. Bury	56. Gloucester	68. Nottingham
9. Wareham	21. Malmesbury	33. Sandwich	45. Thetford	57. Hereford	69. Lincoln
10. Shaftesbury	22. Cricklade	34. Canterbury	46. Norwich	58. Pembroke	70. York
11. Ilchester	23. Wallingford	35. Rochester	47. Stamford	59. Pembroke	71. Durham
12. Bristol	24. Guildford	36. Southwark	48. Peterborough	60. St Davids*	72. Carlisle

* *Possible location of uncertain mint*

William I maintained the Anglo-Saxon mint system and the practice of conducting frequent periodic recoinages by change of coin type. However, the twelfth-century witnessed a gradual transition from regional to centralised minting. Nearly seventy towns had moneyers operating under William I, but only thirty mint towns took part in the recoinage initiated by the Cross-and-Crosslets ('Tealby') coinage in 1158. Cut halfpennies and cut farthings were made during this period, but are scarce for all types up to BMC 13 of Henry I; cut coins are more frequently encountered for subsequent types.

Further reading: G.C. Brooke, *Catalogue of English Coins in the British Museum. The Norman Kings*, 2 volumes (London, 1916). (Abbr. BMC Norman Kings). I. Stewart, 'The English and Norman mints, c.600–1158', in *A New History of the Royal Mint*, ed. C.E. Challis (Cambridge, 1992), pp. 1–82.

WILLIAM I, 1066-1087

Duke William of Normandy claimed the throne of England on the death of his cousin Edward the Confessor. An important monetary reform occurred towards the close of the reign with the introduction of the *geld de moneta* assessed on boroughs. This may be seen as part of the raft of administrative reforms initiated by William I, which included the compilation of Domesday Book in 1086.

The date of the Paxs type is central to the absolute chronology of this and the subsequent reign. Currently evidence is equivocal on the matter. In BMC Norman Kings (London, 1916) it was designated the last type of the reign, an attribution maintained here, but some students regard it as having continued into the reign of William II or begun by him.

Further reading: D.M. Metcalf, 'Notes on the "PAXS" type of William I', *Yorkshire Numismatist* 1 (1988), 13–26. P.Grierson, 'Domesday Book, the geld de moneta and monetagium: a forgotten minting reform' *British Numismatic Journal* 55 (1985), 84–94.

1250   1251

		F	VF
		£	£
1250	**Penny**. *B.M.C.* 1: Profile left type.	275	725

1252   1253

1251	*B.M.C.* 2: Bonnet type.	200	475
1252	*B.M.C.* 3: Canopy type	300	850

1254   1255

1253	*B.M.C.* 4: Two sceptres type.	250	675
1254	*B.M.C.* 5: Two stars type.	225	500
1255	*B.M.C.* 6: Sword type.	300	750

1256   1257

	F	*VF*
	£	£
1256 *B.M.C.* 7: Profile right type	350	950
1257 *B.M.C.* 8: Paxs type	200	450

WILLIAM II, 1087-1100

Second son of William I was killed while hunting in the New Forest. Five of the thirteen coin types in the name of 'William' have been assigned to the reign of William II, although it remains uncertain whether the Paxs type of his father continued into his reign.

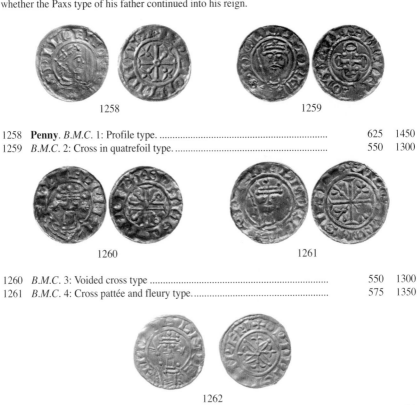

1258   1259

| 1258 **Penny**. *B.M.C.* 1: Profile type. .... | 625 | 1450 |
| 1259 *B.M.C.* 2: Cross in quatrefoil type. .... | 550 | 1300 |

1260   1261

| 1260 *B.M.C.* 3: Voided cross type .... | 550 | 1300 |
| 1261 *B.M.C.* 4: Cross pattée and fleury type. .... | 575 | 1350 |

1262

| 1262 *B.M.C.* 5: Cross fleury and piles type. .... | 625 | 1500 |

Henry was the third son of William I. Administrative reforms and military action to secure Normandy dominated the king's work. After the death of his son in 1120 Henry sought to guarantee the throne for his daughter Matilda, widow of German Emperor Henry V.

The coin types continue to be numbered according to BMC Norman Kings (London, 1916), but the order 1, 2, 3, 4, 5, 6, 9, 7, 8, 11, 10, 12, 13, 14, 15 is now accepted as a working hypothesis for the reign. Greater uncertainty pertains to the chronology of the coin types. The reign coincided with a period of monetary crisis. Scepticism concerning the quality of coinage led to the testing of coins by the public, hindering their acceptance in circulation. In response the government ordered all coins mutilated at issue to force the acceptance of damaged coins. Thus, a few coins of type 6 and all of those of types 7–14 have an official edge incision or 'snick'. Round halfpennies were produced and as some are found snicked they can be dated to the period when official mutilation of the coinage was ordered. In 1124 there was a general purge of moneyers in England as the royal government attempted to restore confidence in the coinage.

Further reading: M.A.S. Blackburn, 'Coinage and currency under Henry I; A review', *Anglo-Norman Studies* 13 (1991), 49–81. M.M. Archibald and W.J. Conte, 'Five round halfpennies of Henry I. A further case for reappraisal of the chronology of types', *Spink's Numismatic Circular* 98 (1990), 232–6.

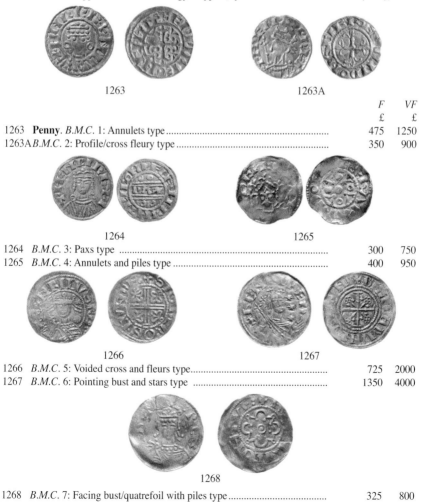

		F	VF
		£	£
1263	**Penny**. *B.M.C.* 1: Annulets type	475	1250
1263A	*B.M.C.* 2: Profile/cross fleury type	350	900
1264	*B.M.C.* 3: Paxs type	300	750
1265	*B.M.C.* 4: Annulets and piles type	400	950
1266	*B.M.C.* 5: Voided cross and fleurs type	725	2000
1267	*B.M.C.* 6: Pointing bust and stars type	1350	4000
1268	*B.M.C.* 7: Facing bust/quatrefoil with piles type	325	800

1269   1270

		F	VF
		£	£

| 1269 | *B.M.C.* 8: Large profile/cross and annulets type .... | 1500 | 4500 |
| 1270 | *B.M.C.* 9: Facing bust/cross in quatrefoil type .... | 675 | 1750 |

1271   1272

| 1271 | *B.M.C.* 10: Facing bust/cross fleury type .... | 225 | 625 |
| 1272 | *B.M.C.* 11: Double inscription type .... | 575 | 1450 |

1273   1274

| 1273 | *B.M.C.* 12: Small profile/cross and annulets type .... | 475 | 1250 |
| 1274 | *B.M.C.* 13: Star in lozenge fleury type .... | 450 | 1200 |

1275   1276

| 1275 | *B.M.C.* 14: Pellets in quatrefoil type .... | 225 | 525 |
| 1276 | *B.M.C.* 15: Quadrilateral on cross fleury type .... | 150 | 400 |

1277   1277A

| 1277 | *Round halfpenny*. Facing head. R. Cross potent with pellets in angles.... | 1500 | 3500 |
| 1277A | — —, As last but reverse from penny die of type 9. .... | 2250 | 5500 |

Stephen of Blois seized the English throne on the death of his uncle, Henry I, despite his oath to support Matilda, with whom he contended for power during his reign.

Substantive types BMC 1 and BMC 7 were the only nation-wide issues, the latter introduced after the conclusion of the final political settlement in 1153. The other substantive types, BMC 2 and BMC 6, were confined to areas in the east of England under royal control. In western England coinage was issued by or on behalf of the Angevin party (q.v. below). In areas without access to new dies from London, coinage was produced from locally made dies and initially based on the designs of regular coins of BMC 1. Particular local types were produced in the midlands and the north, associated with prominent magnates, in the king's name or occasionally in the name of barons. Entries contain references to the article by Mack (M).

Further reading: R.P. Mack, 'Stephen and the Anarchy 1135-54', *British Numismatic Journal* 35 (1966), 38–112. M.A.S. Blackburn, 'Coinage and currency', in *The Anarchy of King Stephen's Reign*, ed. E. King (Oxford, 1994), 145–205.

Substantive royal issues

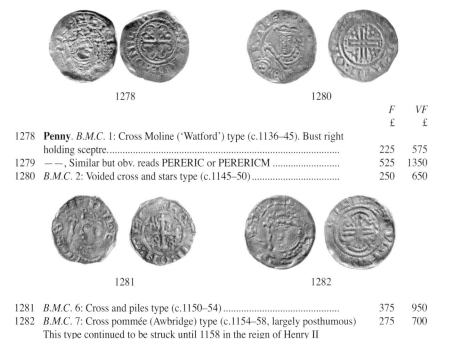

	1278		1280		

			F	*VF*
			£	£
1278	**Penny**. *B.M.C.* 1: Cross Moline ('Watford') type (c.1136–45). Bust right holding sceptre..		225	575
1279	— —, Similar but obv. reads PERERIC or PERERICM		525	1350
1280	*B.M.C.* 2: Voided cross and stars type (c.1145–50).................................		250	650

	1281		1282	

1281	*B.M.C.* 6: Cross and piles type (c.1150–54)...	375	950
1282	*B.M.C.* 7: Cross pommée (Awbridge) type (c.1154–58, largely posthumous)	275	700
	This type continued to be struck until 1158 in the reign of Henry II		

The types designated BMC 3, 4 and 5 are non-substantive, listed as 1300–1302.

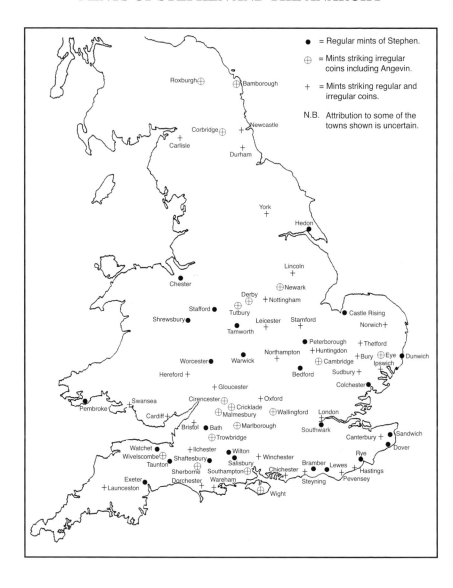

LOCAL AND IRREGULAR ISSUES OF THE CIVIL WAR

Coins struck from erased dies late 1130's to c.1145

The association of these coins with the Interdict of 1148 is erroneous. Some of the marks that disfigured the dies were probably cancellation marks, but the exigencies of the civil war required the re-employed of the dies. Other defacements may well be an overtly political statement.

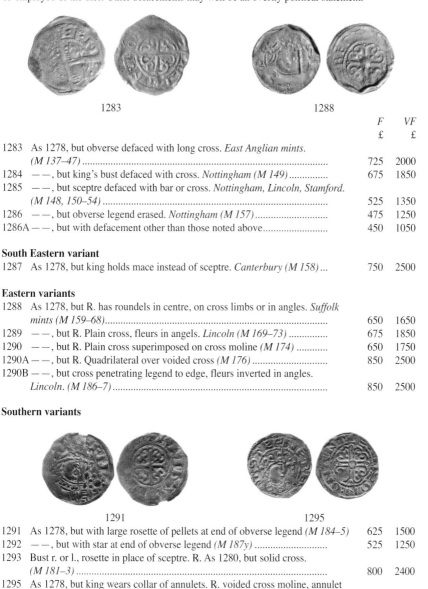

1283   1288

	F	VF
	£	£
1283 As 1278, but obverse defaced with long cross. *East Anglian mints.*		
(M 137–47)	725	2000
1284 — —, but king's bust defaced with cross. *Nottingham (M 149)*	675	1850
1285 — —, but sceptre defaced with bar or cross. *Nottingham, Lincoln, Stamford.*		
(M 148, 150–54)	525	1350
1286 — —, but obverse legend erased. *Nottingham (M 157)*	475	1250
1286A — —, but with defacement other than those noted above	450	1050

South Eastern variant

1287 As 1278, but king holds mace instead of sceptre. *Canterbury (M 158)* ...	750	2500

Eastern variants

1288 As 1278, but R. has roundels in centre, on cross limbs or in angles. *Suffolk*		
mints (M 159–68)	650	1650
1289 — —, but R. Plain cross, fleurs in angels. *Lincoln (M 169–73)*	675	1850
1290 — —, but R. Plain cross superimposed on cross moline *(M 174)*	650	1750
1290A — —, but R. Quadrilateral over voided cross *(M 176)*	850	2500
1290B — —, but cross penetrating legend to edge, fleurs inverted in angles.		
Lincoln. (M 186–7)	850	2500

Southern variants

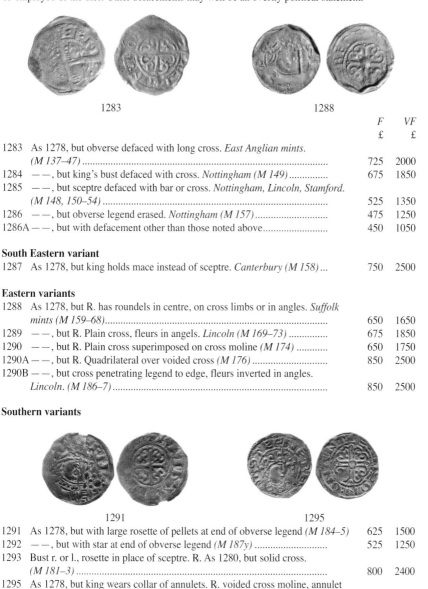

1291   1295

1291 As 1278, but with large rosette of pellets at end of obverse legend *(M 184–5)*	625	1500
1292 — —, but with star at end of obverse legend *(M 187y)*	525	1250
1293 Bust r. or l., rosette in place of sceptre. R. As 1280, but solid cross.		
(M 181–3)	800	2400
1295 As 1278, but king wears collar of annulets. R. voided cross moline, annulet		
at centre. *Southampton. (M 207–212)*	275	850

		F	*VF*
		£	£
1296	As 1278, but reverse cross penetrates legend with fleur-de-lis tips. Leicester *(M 177–8)*...	725	1850
1297	— —, but crude work. R. Voided cross, lis outward in angles. *Tutbury (M 179)*...	750	2000

1298   1300

1298	— —, but crude work. R. Voided cross with martlets in angles. *Derby (M 175)*...	1500	4500
1299	— —, but R. plain cross with T-cross in each angle *(M 180)*....................	850	2500
1300	*B.M.C.* 3: Facing bust. R. Cross pattée, fleurs inwards. *Northampton and Huntingdon (?) (M 67–71)*	975	3250

1301   1302

1301	*B.M.C.* 4: Lozenge fleury type. *Lincoln or Nottingham (M 72–5)*...........	525	1250
1302	*B.M.C.* 5: Bust half-right. R. Lozenge in Cross Moline with fleurs. *Leicester (M 76)*...	875	2500
1303	As 1280, but obverse legend ROBERTVS. *(M 269)*.................................	1750	6500

North-Eastern and Scottish Border variants

1304	As 1278, but star before sceptre. R. Anullets at tips of fleurs *(M 188)*	675	1750
1305	— —, but voided cross penetrating legend to edge *(M 189–92)*...............	725	2000
1306	— —, but crude style *(M 276–9, 281–2)*..	575	1500
1307	— —, but R. Cross with cross pattée and crescent in angles *(M 288)*	1350	4250

King David I of Scotland

| 1308 | As 1305, but obverse legend DAVID REX *(M 280)* .... | 1500 | 4000 |

Earl Henry of Northumberland (son of King David I of Scotland)

1309	As 1278, but legend hENRIC ERL *(M 283–5)*	1500	4250
1310	— —, Similar but reverse cross fleury *(M 286–7)*	1750	5250
1311	As 1307, but obverse legend NENCI:COM *(M 289)*	1650	4500

York Issues: The Ornamented Group attributed to York (*c.*1150)
King Stephen

| 1312 | As 1278, but obverse inscription NSEPEFETI or NSEPINEI. R. letters (sometimes retrograde) and ornaments in legend *(M 215–6, 227)* .... | 1350 | 4250 |

1313   1315

	F £	VF £

1313 Flag type. As 1278, but lance with pennant before face, star right. R. As
      1278, letters and four ornaments in legend *(M 217)*.................................. 850 | 2250

1313A — —, Similar but with eight ornaments in reverse legend. *(M 217)* .... | 875 | 2500

1314 As 1278, but legend STEIN and pellet lozenge for sceptre-head *(M 218)* | 1050 | 3000

1314A King standing facing, holding sceptre and standard with triple pennon. R. Cross pattée,
      crescents and quatrefoils in angles, ornaments in legend. .... | 1750 | 5500

King Stephen and Queen Matilda

1315 Two full-length standing figures holding sceptre. R. Legend of ornaments.
      (M 220) .... | 1850 | 6500

1317   1320

Eustace fitz John

1316 EVSTACIVS, knight standing with sword. R. Cross in quatrefoil,
      EBORACI EDTS or EBORACI TDEFL *(M 221-222)* .... | 1500 | 4750

1317 — —, Similar but reverse legend ThOMHS FILIUS VLF *(M 223)* .... | 1500 | 4750

1318 — —, Similar but reverse legend of ornaments and letters. *(M 224)*........ | 1350 | 4250

1319 [EVSTA]CII. FII. IOANIS, lion passant right. R. Cross moline, ornaments in
      legend *(M 225)*.. | 1650 | 5250

1320 EISTAOhIVS, lion rampant right. R. Cross fleury, ornaments in legend
      (M 226) .... | 1500 | 5000

1322

Rodbert III de Stuteville

1321 ROBERTVS IESTV, knight holding sword on horse right. R. as 1314.
      (M 228) .... | 2750 | 9000

1321A Type copying 1278, but obverse legend RODBDS[T DE?] *(M 227)*....... | 2500 | 8500

Henry Murdac, Archbishop of York

1322 HENRICVS EPC, crowned bust, crosier and star before. R. similar to 1314
      but legend STEPHANVS REX *(M 229)* .... | 2350 | 7500

Uncertain issues

		F	VF
		£	£
1323	Obv. as 1278. R. Cross pattée with annulets in angles *(M 272)*	650	1350
1324	Obv. as 1275 (Henry I, *B.M.C.* 14), but reverse as last *(M 274 extr)*	850	2500
1325	Other miscellaneous types/varieties	650	1350

THE ANGEVIN PARTY

Matilda was the daughter of Henry I and widow of German Emperor Henry V (d.1125) and had been designated heir to the English throne by her father. Matilda was Countess of Anjou by right of her second husband Geoffrey of Anjou. Matilda arrived in England in pursuit of her inheritance in 1139 and established an Angevin court at Bristol and controlled most of south-western England. Matilda's cause was championed by her half-brother, Henry I's illegitimate son, Robert, Earl of Gloucester.

The initial phase of coinage in Matilda's name copied the designs of Stephen's BMC 1 and are dated to the early 1140s. The second type was only discovered in Coed-y-Wenallt hoard (1980). A group of coins invokes the names of past Norman kings 'William' and 'Henry' and the designs of Stephen BMC 1 and Henry I BMC 15. These coins were formally and erroneously attributed to Earl William of Gloucester and Duke Henry of Normandy. Coins of Earl William, and his father Earl Robert, of the Lion type are now known thanks to the discovery of the Box, Wiltshire hoard (1994). In addition to these great magnates a few minor barons placed their names on the coinage.

Further Reading: G. Boon, *Welsh Hoards 1979–81* (Cardiff, 1986). M.M. Archibald, 'The lion coinage of Robert Earl of Gloucester and William Earl of Gloucester', *British Numismatic Journal* 71 (2001), 71–86.

1326

Matilda (in England 1139–48)

1326	As 1278, but cruder style, legend MATILDI IMP or variant (M 230–40) *Bristol, Cardiff, Oxford and Wareham.*	975	3000
1326A	— —, legend MATILDI IMP or IM.HE.MA. R. Cross pattée over fleury (Coed-y-Wenallt hoard) *Bristol and Cardiff.*	975	3000
1326B	— —, as last but triple pellets at cross ends (Coed-y-Wenallt hoard). *Bristol and Cardiff.*	1100	3500

Henry de Neubourg

1326C	Similar type to 1326A but legend hENRICI dE NOVOB (Coed-y-Wenallt hoard) *Swansea.*	1650	5000

Anonymous issues in the name 'King Henry' and 'King William'

1327	As 1278, but obverse legend hENRICVS or HENRICVS REX *(M 241–5)*	1250	3750
1327A	As 1295, but legend hENRIC *(M 246)*	1350	4000
1327B	As 1326A, but hENNENNVS	1350	4250
1328	Obv. as 1278. R. Cross crosslet in quatrefoil *(M 254)*	1650	5000
1329	— —, R. Quadrilateral on cross fleury *(M 248–53)*	1350	4250

1330   1331

	F	VF
	£	£
1330 Facing bust and stars. R. Quadrilateral on cross botonnée *(M 255–8)*	1650	5000
1331 — —, Quadrilateral on voided cross botonnée *(M 259–61)*	1650	5000
1332 As 1329, but legend WILLEMVS or variant *(M 262)*	1500	4500
1333 As 1330, but legend WILLEMVS or variant *(M 263)*	1650	5000
1334 As 1331, but legend WILLEMVS or variant *(M 264–8)*	1650	5000

Earl Robert of Gloucester (1121/22–1147)

1331A +ROB' COM' GLOC' (or variant), lion passant right. R. Cross fleury (Box hoard)	1500	4250

Earl William of Gloucester (1147-1183)

1332A +WILLEMVS, lion passant right. R. Cross fleury (Box hoard)	1500	4250

Brian Fitzcount, Lord of Wallingford (?)

1335 As 1330, but legend B.R:C.I.T.B.R *(M 270)*	2750	8500

1336

Earl Patrick of Salisbury (?)

1336 Helmeted bust r. with sword, star behind. R. As 1329. *(M 271)*	2750	8500

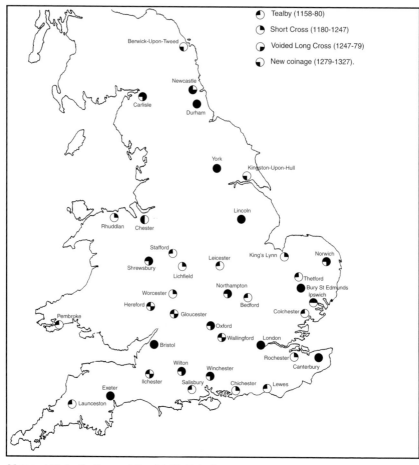

Moneyer table for the Cross and Crosslets (Tealby) coinage

London: Accard (CD), Alwin (ABCDF), Edmund (ACDE), Geffrei (ACE), Godefrei (ACDEF),	*From F £*
Godwin (BDE), Hunfrei (AC), Iohan (ACDEF), Lefwine (BCEF), Martin (ABC), Pieres (ACEF),	
Pieres Mer. (ABD), Pieres Sal. (AEF), Ricard (ABCD), Rodbert (AC), Swetman (ABC), Wid (A),	90
Canterbury: Alferg (A), Goldhavoc (ABCDEF), Goldeep (C), Lambrin (F), Raul (CDEF),	
Ricard (ABCDEF), Ricard Mr. (ABCDE), Rogier (ABCDEF), Rogier F. (A), Willem (C),	
Wiulf (ABCDEF),	90
Bedford: Arfin (A),	*Extremely Rare*
Bristol: Elaf (ACF), Rogier (ADEF), Tancard (ABD),	200
Bury St Edmunds: Henri (BDE), Raul (F), Willem (A),	120
Carlisle: Willem (ACDEF),	120
Chester: Andreu (A), Willem (AD),	185
Colchester: Alwin (AC), Pieres (CE),	200
Durham: Cristien (C), Iohan (B), Walter (A),	150
Exeter: Edwid (AC), Guncelin (AC), Rainir (BC), Ricard (A), Rogier (AD),	185
Gloucester: Godwin (A), Nicol (A), Rodbert (A), Sawulf (A),	230
Hereford: Driu (AC), Osburn (A), Stefne (A), [—]ward (A),	200
Ilchester: Adam (CDF), Reinard (A), Ricard (A), Rocelin (A),	185
Ipswich: Nicole (BCDEF), Robert (CEF), Turstain (CF),	90
Launceston: Willem (A),	*Extremely Rare*
Leicester: Ricard (A), Robert (A),	200
Lewes: uncertain (F),	*Extremely Rare*
Lincoln: Andreu (ABCDE), Godric (ABCD), Lanfram (ABCDF), Raulf (ABCDEF),	
Raven (ACF), Swein (ACD),	120
Newcastle: Willem (ACDEF),	130
Northampton: Ingeram (AC), Iosep (A), Pieres (A), Reimund (AC), Stefne (A), Waltier (AC),	
Warnier (AC),	150

HENRY II, 1154-1189

Cross-and-crosslets ('Tealby') Coinage, 1158-1180

Coins of Stephen's last type continued to be minted until 1158. Then a new coinage bearing Henry's name replaced the currency of the previous reign which contained a high proportion of irregular and sub-standard pennies. The new Cross and Crosslets issue is more commonly referred to as the 'Tealby' coinage, as over 6000 of these pennies were discovered at Tealby, Lincolnshire, in 1807. Twenty nine mints were employed in this re-coinage, but once the re-minting had been completed not more than a dozen mints were kept open. The issue remained virtually unchanged for twenty-two years apart from minor variations in the king's portrait. The coins tend to be poorly struck on irregular flans.

Cut coins occur with varying degrees of frequency during this issue, according to the type and local area. Further reading: *A Catalogue of English Coins in the British Museum. The Cross-and-Crosslet ("Tealby") Type of Henry II.* (London: 1951) by D.F. Allen.

	1337	1338	1339

		F £	VF £
1337	Class A (1158-c.1163). No hair, no collar. Mantle falls from chin as two parallel lines between which is a line of pellets.	95	250
1338	Class B (c.1162-c.1163). Similar, but mantle of two folds which meet at chin (various compositions)	100	275
1339	Class C (c.1163-c.1167). Curl of hair at temple. Jewelled collar, mantle of many folds, field between sometimes jewelled, as is cuff.	95	250

	1340	1341	1342

1340	Class D (c.1167-c.1170). Jewelled collar continues down shoulder unbroken. Single curl of hair at temple, folds of mantle horizontal	90	250
1341	Class E (c.1170-c.1174). Similar to 1340. Jewelled collar only. Folds of mantle rise from hand to top of shoulder.	100	275
1342	Class F (c.1174-c.1180). Similar to 1341, but hair falls in long ringlets from temple.	90	250

Moneyer table for the Cross and Crosslets (Tealby) coinage (cont.)

	From F £
Norwich: Gilebert (ABF), Herbert (ACD), Herbert R (A)., Hugo (ACF), Nicol (AC),	150
Picot (ABC), Reiner (AD), Ricard (A),	185
Oxford: Adam (ADE), Aschetil (A), Rogier (A),	*Extremely Rare*
Pembroke: Walter (A),	185
Salisbury: Daniel (A), Levric (A),	*Extremely Rare*
Shrewsbury: Warin (A),	230
Stafford: Colbrand (AC), Willem (C),	120
Thetford: Siwate (ACD), Turstain (ACD), Willem (ACDF), Willem Ma (A), Willem De (A),	*Extremely Rare*
Wallingford: Fulke (A),	185
Wilton: Anschetil (A), Lantier (A), Willem (A),	120
Winchester: Herbert (AC), Hosbert (ACD), Ricard (AE), Willem (AC),	
York: Cudbert (A), Gerrard (A), Godwin (AD), Griffin (AD), Herbert (ACD), Hervi (A),	
Iordan (A), Norman (A), Willem (A), Wulfsi (A),	120

Letters in brackets after mint name indicate Class known to exist for the mint and moneyer combination

The publishers would like to thank the late Prof. Jeffrey Mass for re-organising and updating the short cross series.

'Short Cross' coinage of Henry II (1180-1189)

In 1180 a coinage of new type, known as the Short Cross coinage, replaced the Tealby issue. The new coinage is remarkable in that it covers not only the latter part of the reign of Henry II, but also the reigns of his sons Richard and John and on into the reign of his grandson Henry III, and the entire issue bears the name 'hENRICVS'. There are no English coins with the names of Richard or John. The Short Cross coins can be divided chronologically into various classes: ten mints were operating under Henry II and tables of mints, moneyers and classes are given for each reign.

1343   1344

1345

		F	VF
		£	£
1343	Class 1a^1 - 1a^3. Small face, square E, and/or C, and/or round M, irregular number of curls	135	375
1343A	Class 1a^4 and 1a^5. Small face, seriffed X, round E and C, square M, irregular number of curls	75	175
1344	1b. Fine portrait, curls 2 left and 5 right, stop before REX on most coins	60	150
1345	1c. Portrait less finely shaped, irregular number of curls, normally no stop before REX	50	145

RICHARD I, 1189-1199

Pennies of Short Cross type continued to be issued throughout the reign, all bearing the name hENRICVS. The coins of class 4, which have very crude portraits, continued to be issued in the early years of the next reign. The only coins bearing Richard's name are from his territories of Aquitaine and Poitou in western France.

1346   1347   1348A   1348C

1346	2. Chin whiskers made of small curls, no side whiskers, almost always 5 pearls to crown, frequently no collar, sometimes RE/X	95	275
1347	3. Large or small face, normally 7 pearls to crown, chin and side whiskers made up of small curls	75	200

1348A 4a. Normally 7 pearls to crown, chin and side whiskers made up of small
pellets, hair consisting of 2 or more non-parallel crescents left and right 65 175
1348B 4a* Same as last, but with reverse colon stops (instead of single pellets) 80 250
1348C 4b Normally 7 pearls to crown, chin and side whiskers made up of small
pellets, single (or parallel) crescents as hair left and right, frequent
malformed letters 60 150

JOHN, 1199-1216

'Short Cross' coinage *continued.* All with name hЄNRICVS
The Short Cross coins of class 4 continued during the early years of John's reign, but in 1205 a re-coinage was initiated and new Short Cross coins of better style replaced the older issues. Coins of classes 5a and 5b were issued in the re-coinage in which sixteen mints were employed. Only ten of these mints were still working by the end of class 5. The only coins to bear John's name are the pennies, halfpence and farthings issues for Ireland.

1349   1350A   1350B

1351   1352   1353   1354

| | F | VF |
	£	£
1349 4c. Reversed S, square face at bottom, 5 pearls to crown, normally single crescents as hair left and right	85	275
1350A 5a1 Reversed or regular S, irregular curved lines as hair (or circular curls containing no pellets), cross pattée as initial mark on reverse, *London and Canterbury* only	135	425
1350B 5a2 Reversed S, circular curls left and right (2 or 3 each side) containing single pellets, cross pommée as initial mark on reverse	75	225
1350C 5a/5b or 5b/5a	60	165
1351 5b. Regular S, circular pelleted curls, cross pattée as initial mark on reverse	50	140
1352 5c. Slightly rounder portrait, letter X in the form of a St. Andrew's cross	50	135
1353 6a. Smaller portrait, with smaller letter X composed of thin strokes or, later, short wedges	55	140
1354 6b. Very tall lettering and long rectangular face	45	100

For further reading and an extensive listing of the English Short Cross Coinage see:
Sylloge of Coins of the British Isles. *The J. P. Mass Collection of English Short Cross Coins 1180-1247*

'Short Cross' coinage *continued* (1216-47)

The Short Cross coinage continued for a further thirty years during which time the style of portraiture and workmanship deteriorated. By the 1220s minting had been concentrated at London and Canterbury, one exception being the mint of the Abbot of Bury St. Edmunds.

Halfpenny and farthing dies are recorded early in this issue; a few halfpennies and now farthings have been discovered. See nos 1357 D-E.

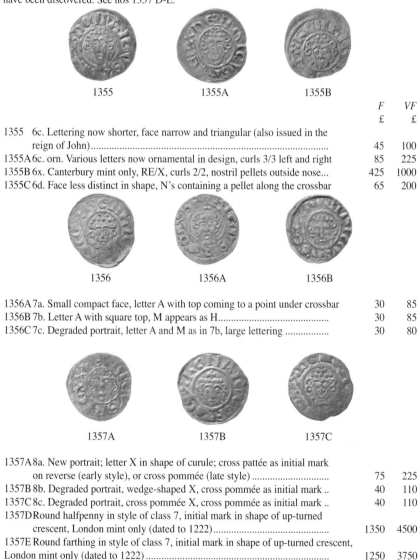

| | 1355 | 1355A | 1355B |

	F	*VF*
	£	£
1355 6c. Lettering now shorter, face narrow and triangular (also issued in the reign of John)	45	100
1355A 6c. orn. Various letters now ornamental in design, curls 3/3 left and right	85	225
1355B 6x. Canterbury mint only, RE/X, curls 2/2, nostril pellets outside nose...	425	1000
1355C 6d. Face less distinct in shape, N's containing a pellet along the crossbar	65	200

| | 1356 | 1356A | 1356B |

1356A 7a. Small compact face, letter A with top coming to a point under crossbar	30	85
1356B 7b. Letter A with square top, M appears as H	30	85
1356C 7c. Degraded portrait, letter A and M as in 7b, large lettering	30	80

| | 1357A | 1357B | 1357C |

1357A 8a. New portrait; letter X in shape of curule; cross pattée as initial mark on reverse (early style), or cross pommée (late style)	75	225
1357B 8b. Degraded portrait, wedge-shaped X, cross pommée as initial mark ..	40	110
1357C 8c. Degraded portrait, cross pommée X, cross pommée as initial mark ..	40	110
1357D Round halfpenny in style of class 7, initial mark in shape of up-turned crescent, London mint only (dated to 1222)	1350	4500
1357E Round farthing in style of class 7, initial mark in shape of up-turned crescent, London mint only (dated to 1222)	1250	3750

Moneyer tables for the short cross coinage

Fine

Henry II:
London: Aimer (1a-b), Alain (1a-b), Alain V (1a-b), Alward (1b), Davi (1b-c),
Fil Aimer (1a-b), Gefrei (1c), Gilebert (1c), Godard (1b), Henri (1a-b),
Henri Pi (1a), Iefrei (1a-b), Iohan (1a-b), Osber (1b), Pieres (1a-c),
Pieres M (1a-b), Randvl (1a-b), Ravl (1b-c), Reinald (1a-b), Willelm (1a-b)   50
Carlisle: Alain (1b-c)   85
Exeter: Asketil (1a-b), Iordan (1a-b), Osber (1a-b), Ravl (1b), Ricard (1b-c),
Roger (1a-c)   75
Lincoln: Edmvnd (1b-c), Girard (1b), Hvgo (1b), Lefwine (1b-c), Rodbert (1b),
Walter (1b), Will. D.F. (1b), Willelm (1b-c)   65
Northampton: Filip (1a-b), Hvgo (1a-b), Ravl (1a-c), Reinald (1a-c), Simvn (1b),
Walter (1a-c), Willelm (1a-b)   50
Oxford: Asketil (1b), Iefrei (1b), Owein (1b-c), Ricard (1b-c), Rodbert (1b),
Rodbt. F. B. (1b), Sagar (1b)   70
Wilton: Osber (1a-b), Rodbert (1a-b), Iohan (1a)   75
Winchester: Adam (1a-c), Clement (1a-b), Gocelm (1a-c), Henri (1a),
Osber (1a-b), Reinier (1b), Rodbert (1a-b)   50
Worcester: Edrich (1b), Godwine (1b-c), Osber (1b-c), Oslac (1b)   75
York: Alain (1a-b), Efrard (1a-c), Gerard (1a-b), Hvgo (1a-c), Hunfrei (1a-b),
Isac (1a-b), Tvrkil (1a-c), Willelm (1a-b)   50

Richard I
London: Aimer (2-4a), Fvlke (4a-b), Henri (4a-b), Ravl (2), Ricard (2-4b),
Stivene (2-4b), Willelm (2-4b)   60
Canterbury: Goldwine (3-4b), Hernavd (4b), Hve (4b), Ioan (4b), Meinir (2-4b),
Reinald/Reinavd (2-4b), Roberd (2-4b), Samvel (4b), Simon (4b), Vlard (2-4b)   60
Carlisle: Alein (3-4b)   125
Durham: Adam (4a), Alein (4a-b), Pires (4b)   150
Exeter: Ricard (3)   135
Lichfield: Ioan (2)   2500
Lincoln: Edmvnd (2), Lefwine (2), Willelm (2)   100
Northampton: Giferei (4a), Roberd (3), Waltir (3)   110
Northampton or Norwich: Randvl (4a-b), Willelm (4a-b)   100
Shrewsbury: Ive (4a-b), Reinald/Reinavd (4a-b), Willem (4a)   175
Winchester: Adam (3), Gocelm (3), Osbern (3-4a), Pires (4a), Willelm (3-4a)   65
Worcester: Osbern (2)   250
York: Davi (4a-b), Efrard/Everard (2-4b), Hvgo/Hve (2-4a), Nicole (4a-b),
Tvrkil (2-4a)   60

John
London: Abel (5c-6b), Adam (5b-c), Beneit (5b-c), Fvlke (4c-5b), Henri (4c-5b/5a),
Ilger (5b-6b), Ravf (5c-6b), Rener (5a/b-5c), Ricard (4c-5b), Ricard B (5b-c),
Ricard T (5a/b-5b), Walter (5c-6b), Willelm (4c-5b), Willelm B (5a/b-5c),
Willelm L (5b-c), Willelm T (5b-c)   45
Canterbury: Goldwine (4c-5c), Hernavd/Arnavd (4c-5c), Hve (4c-5c), Iohan (4c-5c),
Iohan B (5b-c), Iohan M (5b-c), Roberd (4c-5c), Samvel (4c-5c), Simon (4c-5c)   45
Bury St Edmunds: Fvlke (5b-c)   90
Carlisle: Tomas (5b)   110
Chichester: Pieres (5b/a-5b), Ravf (5b/a-5b), Simon (5b/a-5b), Willelm (5b)   80
Durham: Pieres (5a-6a)   90
Exeter: Gileberd (5a-b), Iohan (5a-b), Ricard (5a-b)   75

Ipswich: Alisandre (5b-c), Iohan (5b-c)   60
Kings Lynn: Iohan (5b), Nicole (5b), Willelm (5b)   125
Lincoln: Alain (5a), Andrev (5a-5c), Hve (5a/b-5c), Iohan (5a), Ravf (5a/b-5b),
Ricard (5a-5b/a), Tomas (5a/b-5b)   45
Northampton: Adam (5b-c), Roberd (5b), Roberd T (5b)   60
Northampton or Norwich: Randvl (4c)   80
Norwich: Gifrei (5a/b-5c), Iohan (5a-c), Renald/Renavd (5a-c)   60
Oxford: Ailwine (5b), Henri (5b), Miles (5b)   70
Rochester: Alisandre (5b), Hvnfrei (5b)   90
Winchester: Adam (5a-c), Andrev (5b-c), Bartelme (5b-c), Henri (5a), Iohan (5a-c),
Lvkas (5b-c), Miles (5a-c), Ravf (5b-c), Ricard (5a-b)   45
York: Davi (4c-5b), Nicole (4c-5c), Renavd (5b), Tomas (5a/b-5b)   45

Henry III

London: Abel (6c-7a), Adam (7b-c), Elis (7a-b), Giffrei (7b-c), Ilger (6c-7b),
Ledvlf (7b-c), Nichole (7c-8c), Ravf (6c-7b), Ricard (7b), Terri (7a-b),
Walter (6b-c)   30
Canterbury: Arnold (6c/6x, 6x), Henri (6c-6c/d, 7a-c), Hivn/Ivn (6c-7b),
Iohan (6c-7c, 8b-c), Ioan Chic (7b-c), Ioan F. R. (7b-c), Nichole (7c, 8b-c),
Osmvnd (7b-c), Robert (6c, 7b-c), Robert Vi (7c), Roger (6c-7b),
Roger of R (7a-b), Salemvn (6x, 7a-b), Samvel (6c-d, 7a), Simon (6c-d, 7a-b),
Tomas (6d, 7a-b), Walter (6c-7a), Willem (7b-c, 8b-c), Willem Ta (7b-c)   30
Bury St Edmunds: Iohan (7c-8c), Norman (7a-b), Ravf (6c-d, 7a), Simvnd (7b-c),
Willelm (7a)   35
Durham: Pieres (7a)   80
Winchester: Henri (6c)   125
York: Iohan (6c), Peres (6c), Tomas (6c), Wilam (6c)   125

Irregular Local Issue
Rhuddlan (in chronological order)   95
Group I (c. 1180 – pre 1205) Halli, Tomas, Simond
Group II (c.1205 – 1215) Simond, Henricus

Rhuddlan

'Long Cross' coinage (1247-72)

By the middle of Henry's reign the coinage in circulation was in a poor state, being worn and clipped. In 1247 a fresh coinage was ordered, the new pennies having the reverse cross extended to the edge of the coin to help safeguard the coins against clipping. The earliest of these coins have no mint or moneyers' names. A number of provincial mints were opened for producing sufficient of the Long Cross coins, but these were closed again in 1250, only the royal mints of London and Canterbury and the ecclesiastical mints of Durham and Bury St. Edmunds remained open.

In 1257, following the introduction of new gold coinages by the Italian cities of Brindisi (1232), Florence (1252) and Genoa (1253), Henry III issued a gold coinage in England. This was a gold 'Penny' valued at 20 silver pence and twice the weight of the silver penny. The coinage was not a success, being undervalued, and it ceased to be minted after a few years; few coins have survived.

Cut halfpennies and farthings are common for this period, with a greater concentration in the early part. They are up to 100 times commoner than in late Anglo-Saxon times.

Without sceptre

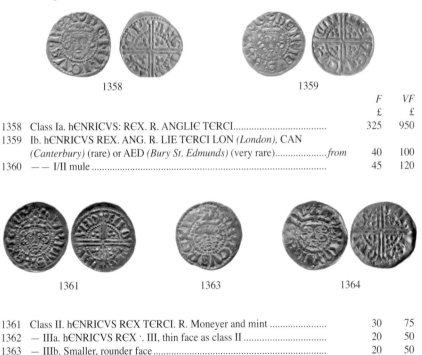

1358   1359

		F	VF
		£	£
1358	Class Ia. hENRICVS: REX. R. ANGLIE TERCI....................................	325	950
1359	Ib. hENRICVS REX. ANG. R. LIE TERCI LON *(London)*, CAN *(Canterbury)* (rare) or AED *(Bury St. Edmunds)* (very rare)...................*from*	40	100
1360	— — I/II mule	45	120

1361   1363   1364

1361	Class II. hENRICVS REX TERCI. R. Moneyer and mint	30	75
1362	— IIIa. hENRICVS REX ·. III, thin face as class II	20	50
1363	— IIIb. Smaller, rounder face..	20	50
1364	— IIIc. Face with pointed chin, neck indicated by two lines, often a pellet between curls, usually REX: III	20	50

With sceptre

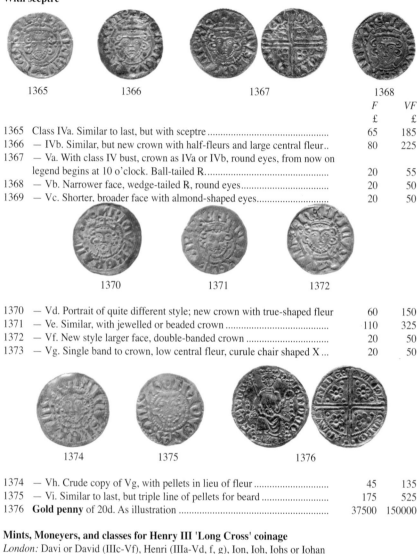

1365   1366   1367   1368

		F	VF
		£	£
1365	Class IVa. Similar to last, but with sceptre	65	185
1366	— IVb. Similar, but new crown with half-fleurs and large central fleur..	80	225
1367	— Va. With class IV bust, crown as IVa or IVb, round eyes, from now on legend begins at 10 o'clock. Ball-tailed R.	20	55
1368	— Vb. Narrower face, wedge-tailed R, round eyes..................................	20	50
1369	— Vc. Shorter, broader face with almond-shaped eyes...........................	20	50

1370   1371   1372

1370	— Vd. Portrait of quite different style; new crown with true-shaped fleur	60	150
1371	— Ve. Similar, with jewelled or beaded crown	110	325
1372	— Vf. New style larger face, double-banded crown	20	50
1373	— Vg. Single band to crown, low central fleur, curule chair shaped X ...	20	50

1374   1375   1376

1374	— Vh. Crude copy of Vg, with pellets in lieu of fleur	45	135
1375	— Vi. Similar to last, but triple line of pellets for beard	175	525
1376	**Gold penny** of 20d. As illustration	37500	150000

Mints, Moneyers, and classes for Henry III 'Long Cross' coinage

	Fine
London: Davi or David (IIIc-Vf), Henri (IIIa-Vd, f, g), Ion, Ioh, Iohs or Iohan (Vc-g), Nicole (Ib/II mule, II-Vc), Renaud (Vg-i), Ricard (IIIc-Vg), Robert (Vg), Thomas (Vg), Walter (Vc-g), Willem (Vc-g and gold penny).............................	20
Bristol: Elis (IIIa, b, c), Henri (IIIb) , Iacob (IIIa, b, c), Roger (IIIa, b, c), Walter (IIIb, c)...	25
Bury St. Edmunds: Ion or Iohs (II-Va, Vg, h, i), Randulf (Va-f), Renaud (Vg), Stephane (Vg)	25

Fine

Canterbury: Alein (Vg, h), Ambroci (Vg), Gilbert (II-Vd/c mule, Vf, g), Ion, Ioh, Iohs, or Iohanes (IIIc-Vd, f, g), Nicole or Nichole (Ib/II mule, II-Vh), Ricard (Vg, h), Robert (Vc-h), Roger (Vh), Walter (Vc-h), Willem or Willeme (Ib/II mule, II-Vd, f, g)... 20

Carlisle: Adam (IIIa, b), Ion (IIIa, b), Robert (IIIa, b), Willem (IIIa, b)............. 50
Durham: Philip (IIIb), Ricard (V, b, c), Roger (Vg), Willem (Vg)...................... 70
Exeter: Ion (II-IIIc), Philip (II-IIIc), Robert (II-IIIc), Walter (II-IIIb)................. 30
Gloucester: Ion (II-IIIc), Lucas (II-IIIc), Ricard (II-IIIc), Roger (II-IIIc)........... 35
Hereford: Henri (IIIa, b), Ricard (IIIa, b, c), Roger (IIIa, b, c), Walter (IIIa, b, c) 40
Ilchester: Huge (IIIa, b, c), Ierveis (IIIa, b, c), Randulf (IIIa, b, c), Stephe (IIIa, b, c) 70
Lincoln: Ion (II-IIIc), Ricard (II-IIIc), Walter (II-IIIc), Willem (II-IIIc)............. 25
Newcastle: Adam (IIIa, b), Henri (IIIa, b, c), Ion (IIIa, b, c), Roger (IIIa, b, c).. 25
Northampton: Lucas (II-IIIb), Philip (II-IIIc), Tomas (II-IIIc), Willem (II-IIIc) 25
Norwich: Huge (II-IIIc), Iacob (II-IIIc), Ion (II-IIIc), Willem (II-IIIc).............. 30
Oxford: Adam (II-IIIc), Gefrei (II-IIIc), Henri (II-IIIc), Willem (II-IIIc)........... 35
Shrewsbury: Lorens (IIIa, b, c), Nicole (IIIa, b, c), Peris (IIIa, b, c), Ricard (IIIa, b, c) 45
Wallingford: Alisandre (IIIa, b), Clement (IIIa, b), Ricard (IIIa, b), Robert (IIIa, b) 60
Wilton: Huge (IIIb, c), Ion (IIIa, b, c), Willem (IIIa, b, c) 35
Winchester: Huge (II-IIIc), Iordan (II-IIIc), Nicole (II-IIIc), Willem (II-IIIc) 25
York: Alain (II-IIIb), Ieremie (II-IIIb), Ion (II-IIIc), Rener (II-IIIc), Tomas (IIIb, c) 25

EDWARD I, 1272-1307

'Long Cross' coinage (1272-78). With name hЄNRICVS

The earliest group of Edward's Long Cross coins are of very crude style and known only of Durham and Bury St. Edmunds. Then, for the last class of the type, pennies of much improved style were issued at London, Durham and Bury, but in 1279 the Long Cross coinage was abandoned and a completely new coinage substituted.

Cut halfpennies and farthings also occur for this issue, and within this context are not especially rare.

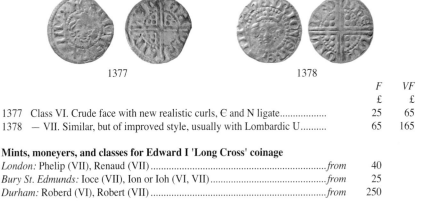

1377   1378

	F	VF
	£	£
1377 Class VI. Crude face with new realistic curls, Є and N ligate..................	25	65
1378 — VII. Similar, but of improved style, usually with Lombardic U..........	65	165

Mints, moneyers, and classes for Edward I 'Long Cross' coinage

London: Phelip (VII), Renaud (VII) ....*from*	40	
Bury St. Edmunds: Ioce (VII), Ion or Ioh (VI, VII) ....*from*	25	
Durham: Roberd (VI), Robert (VII) ....*from*	250	

New Coinage (from 1279).

A major re-coinage was embarked upon in 1279 which introduced new denominations. In addition to the penny, halfpence and farthings were also minted and, for the first time, a fourpenny piece called a 'Groat', wt. 89 grs., (from the French *Gros*).

The groats, though ultimately unsuccessful, were struck from more than thirty obverse dies and form an extensive series with affinities to the pence of classes 1c to 3g. The chronology of this series has now been definitively established (see Allen, M. The Durham Mint, pp. 172-179).

As mint administration was now very much centralized, the practice of including the moneyer's name in the coinage was abandoned (except for a few years at Bury St. Edmunds). Several provincial mints assisted with the re-coinage during 1279-81, then minting was again restricted to London, Canterbury, Durham and Bury.

The provincial mints were again employed for a subsidiary re-coinage in 1300 in order to remint lightweight coins and the many illegal *esterlings* (foreign copies of the English pennies, mainly from the Low Countries), which were usually of poorer quality than the English coins.

1379A   1379E

	F	VF
	£	£
1379A **Groat**. *London*. Variety a. (Fox 5). Small crowned bust within a quatrefoil of three lines, flowers in spandrels. Flat crown with pellet ornaments, drapery of two wedges with rosette below..	2000	6000
1379B — b. (Fox 6). Larger face with flat hair. Unusual crescent crown carrying pearl ornaments, drapery with rosette in centre..	1850	5750
1379C — c. (Fox 3). Similar face with bushy hair. Crown with plain band and pearl ornaments, drapery is foreshortened circle with rosette in centre ...	2250	6250
1379D — d. (Fox 7). New portrait with smaller pointed face, trefoils in spandrels. Crown with spearhead ornaments, drapery is segment of a circle with rosette in centre..	2250	6250
1379E — e. (Fox 4). Larger oval face with bushy hair, flowers in spandrels. Crown with spearhead ornaments, thick curved drapery without rosette.............	1850	5750
1379F — f. (Fox 1). Broader face and shorter hair. Crown with spread side fleurs, drapery of two wedges, trefoil of pellets below	2500	6500
1379G — — (Fox 2). Quatrefoil of two lines. Drapery of two wedges, trefoil of pellets below	2250	6250
1379H — g. (Fox -). Quatrefoil of two lines. Crown with bifoliate side fleurs, drapery of two wedges with annulet (?) on breast, two annulets after ANG.........	2500	6500

Edward I groats were often mounted as brooches and gilt. Such specimens are worth considerably less

1382   1383

		F £	*VF* £
1380	**Penny.** *London.* Class 1a. Crown with plain band, ЄDW RЄX; Lombardic Ꞑ on *obv;* pellet 'barred' S on rev. A with sloping top	175	525
1381	— 1b. — ЄD RЄX; no drapery on bust, Roman N	725	2500
1382	— 1c. — ЄDW RЄX; Roman N, normal or reversed; small lettering	25	75
1383	— 1d. — ЄDW R;—; large lettering and face	25	70

1384   1385   1386

1384	— — — Annulet below bust	85	275
1385	— 2a. Crown with band shaped to ornaments; usually broken left petal to central fleur portrait as 1d. N usually reversed	20	50
1386	— 2b. — tall bust; long neck; N reversed	20	50

1388

1387	— 3a. Crescent-shaped contraction marks; pearls in crown, drapery is foreshortened circle with hook ends	25	70
1388	— 3b. — — drapery is segment of a circle, pearls in crown	20	60
1389	— 3c. — normal crown; drapery in one piece, hollowed in centre	20	50

1391   1392   1394

1390	— 3d. — — drapery in two pieces, broad face	20	50
1391	— 3e. — long narrow face (Northern mints)	20	55
1392	— 3f. — broad face, large nose, rougher work, late S first used	25	75
1393	— 3g. — Spread crown small neat bust, narrow face	20	45
1394	— 4a. Comma-shaped contraction mark, late S always used, C and Є open	20	50

1395   1396   1397   1398

		F £	VF £
1395	— 4b. Similar, but face and hair shorter	20	45
1396	— 4c. Larger face with more copious hair; nick to band of crown	25	60
1397	— 4d. Pellet at beginning of *obv.* and *rev.* legend	20	45
1398	— 4e. Three pellets on breast, ropy hair, pellet in *rev.* legend (no pellets on Bury or Durham)	20	55

1399   1400

1399	— 5a. Well spread coins, pellet on breast, face as 1398, A normally unbarred	25	75
1400	— 5b. Coins more spread, tall lettering, long narrow face, pellet on breast	25	75

1401   1402   1403

1401	— 6a. Smaller coins, smaller lettering with closed E (from now on) initial cross almost plain, crown with wide fleurs, crude appearance	65	200
1402	— 6b. Initial cross pattée	40	120
1403	— 7a. Rose on breast (except Bury), short hair; almond-shaped eyes, double barred N	30	85

1404   1406   1406A

1404	— 7b. Rose on breast (London only) longer hair, new crown	35	100
1405	— 8a. Crown resembling 7b with central fleur usually broken	25	60
1406	— 8b. Similar to 1405 with wider drapery, top-tilted S	25	60
1406A	— 8c — — Crown with very arched band	30	85

1408   1409A

		F £	VF £
1407	— 9a. Drapery of two wedges, pellet eyes, crown of 8a-b or new flatter one; often star on breast......	20	45
1408	— 9b. Small coins; Roman N, normal, un-barred, or usually of pot-hook form; often star or (very rarely) pellet on breast. Some Durham coins are from locally made dies..........	20	45
1408A	– 9c. Larger crude lettering with barred A and abbreviation marks. (only found in combination with dies of 9b or 10ab, except Bury).......	30	90

1409 - 10ab   1409B - 10b

		F	VF
1409	— 10ab. ЄDWARD. Bifoliate crown (converted 9b or new taller one). Narrow incurved lettering..........	20	45
1409A	— 10ab. Similar with annulet on breast or a pellet each side of head and on breast..........	60	175
1409B	— 10ab. ЄDWAR (rarely ЄDWR). Similar to 1409. A few early coins have the trifoliate crown of 9b..........	20	45

1410   1411

| Crown 1 | Crown 2 | Crown 3 | Crown 4 | Crown 5 |

		F	VF
1410	— 10cf1. Crown 1 (Axe-shaped central fleur, wedge-shaped petals). ЄDWA from now on. Stub-tailed. R......	20	45
1411	— 10cf2. Crown 2 (Well-shaped central lis, no spearheads). Spreading hair.	20	45

1413   1414

	F £	VF £
1412 — 10cf3. Crown 3 (Left-hand arrowhead inclines to right). Early coins have the broken lettering of 10cf2; later have new lettering with .... round-backed Є..................	20	45
1413 — 10cf4. Crown 4 (Neat with hooked petal to right-hand side fleur)......	25	75
1414 — 10cf5. Crown 5 (taller and more spread, right-hand ornament inclines to left). Later coins are on smaller flans.	20	50

Some of the coins of class 10cf3 (c.1307-9), and all of the coins of classes 10cf4 and 10cf5 (c.1309-10), were struck in the reign of Edward II.
For a more detailed classification of Class 10, see 'Sylloge of British Coins, 39, The J. J. North Collection, Edwardian English Silver Coins 1279-1351', The Classification of Class 10, c. 1301-10, by C. Wood.

Prices are for full flan, well struck coins.
The prices for the above types are for London. For coins of the other mints see following pages; types are in brackets, prices are for the commonest type of each mint.

Berwick Type 1   Type II   Type III   Type IV

1415	*Berwick-on-Tweed.* (Blunt types I-IV) Local dies................	20	55
1416	*Bristol.* (2; 3b; c, d; 3f, g; 9b)................	20	50
1417	*Bury St. Edmunds.* Robert de Hadelie (3c, d, g; 4a, b, c)........	45	120
1418	— Villa Sci Edmundi (4e; 5b; 6b; 7a; 8ab, 9a – 10 cf 5)........	20	50
1419	*Canterbury.* (2; 3b-g; 4; 5; 7a; 7b; 9;10)................	20	45
1420	*Chester.* (3g; 9b)................	30	80
1421	*Durham.* Plain cross mm (9b; 10ab; 10cf 2-3; 10cf 5)........	20	50
1422	— Bishop de Insula (2; 3b, c, e, g; 4a)................	20	50
1423	— Bishop Bec (4b-e; 5b; 6b; 7b; 9a, 9b, 10) with *mm.* cross moline......	20	50
1424	— — (4b) cross moline in one angle of *rev.*................	100	325
1425	*Exeter.* (9b)................	25	70
1426	*Kingston-upon-Hull.* (9b)	30	85
1427	*Lincoln.* (3c, d, f, g)	20	45
1428	*Newcastle-upon-Tyne.* (3e; 9b; 10ab)................	20	45
1429	*York.* Royal mint (2; 3b, c, d, e, f; 9b)................	20	45
1430	— Archbishop's mint (3e, f; 9b). R. Quatrefoil in centre........	20	45
1431	**Halfpenny,** *London.* Class 3b. ЄDWR ANGL DNS hYB, drapery composed of curved line with wedges above........	35	110
1432	— 3c Drapery composed of two wedges................	20	65

1434A

	F	VF
	£	£
1433 — 3g. New wide crown, thick-waisted S, drapery as 3b..........................	20	65
1433A — — 4c. Narrower crown, drapery of two unequal wedges..................	30	90
1433B — — Similar, pellet before LON	40	120
1434 — 4e. Single-piece collar with (usually) three pellets on breast.............	45	135
1434A — 6. Small face with short hair, large coarse crown, closed Є	45	140
1435 — 7. Larger face with square jaw, open Є, usually double-barred N.......	35	110
1436 — 8. Similar, new crown with straight sides.......................................	40	125
1437 — 10. ЄDWAR R ANGL DNS hYB, bifoliate or trifoliate crown, new waisted letters	30	90

The above prices are for London; halfpence of the mints given below were also struck.

1438 *Berwick-on-Tweed.* (Blunt types I, II and III)...	50	135
1439 *Bristol.* Class 3c, 3g, 4c	30	90
1440 *Lincoln.* Class 3c...	35	100
1441 *Newcastle.* Class 3e, single pellet in each angle of *rev.*	50	135
1442 *York.* Class 3c-e..	35	100

1443A   1445

1443 **Farthing,** *London.* Class 1a. Base silver issue (6.65 grains), ЄDWARDVS REX. bifoliate crown with no intermediate jewels, inner circle. R. LONDONIЄNSIS, (rarely LONDRIЄNSIS), ...	45	165
1443A — 1c. Similar trifoliate crown..	30	110
1444 — 2. Smaller face, trifoliate crown with intermediate jewels	30	90
1445 — 3c. New tapering face, wide at top, crown with curved band.............	30	90
1445A — 3de. Sterling silver issue (5.51 grains.) Є R ANGLIЄ bust (usually) to bottom of coin, no inner circle. R. LONDONIЄNSIS	35	100
1446 — 3g. Similar, new wide crown with curving side fleurs.	25	80
1446A — 4de. Similar to 3de. R. CIVITAS LONDON.....................................	40	135
1446B — 5. Similar, crude wide crown.	40	135
1447 — 6-7. New large face with wide cheeks, pellet or almond eyes.............	35	125
1448 — 8. Similar, small rounded face, tall crude crown	35	125
1449 — 9a. Є R ANGL DN, small tapering face, (a variety has the face of class 6-7)..	40	135
1449A — 9b. Small ugly face, usually wide crown with outwards-sloping sides..	35	125
1450 — 10 ЄDWARDVS REX (-, A, AN or ANG,) large bust within inner circle.	20	60
Type 1450 often appears on oval flans.		

It is now thought that the order of London Farthings is class 4de, 6-7, 5, 9a, 8, 9b

1446	1452

	F	VF
	£	£
1451 *Berwick-on-Tweed*. (Blunt type I, IIIb)	110	350
1452 *Bristol*. Class 2, 3c, 3de	35	100
1453 *Lincoln*. Class 3de	35	110
1453A*Newcastle*. Class 3de, ꞦNOVI CASTRI	225	725
1454 *York*. Class 2, 3c, 3de	40	125

For further information see Farthings and Halfpennies, Edward I and II, Paul and Bente R Withers, 2001

EDWARD II, 1307-27

The coinage of this reign differs only in minor details from that of Edward I. No groats were issued in the years *c*. 1282-1351.

1458 (12a)	1459 (13)	1460 (14)
1461 (15a)	1462 (15b)	1463 (15c)

		F	VF
1455	**Penny,** *London*. Class 11a. Broken spear-head or pearl on l. side of crown; long narrow face, straight-sided N; round back to C and Є	20	50
1456	— 11b. — Є with angular back (till 15b), N with well-marked serifs (late)	20	50
1457	— 11c. — — A of special form	40	110
1458	— 12a. Central fleur of crown formed of three wedges; thick cross mm	25	70
1458A	— 12b — Crown with diamond-shaped petals and cruciform central fleur; cross of four wedges mm	45	150
1458B	— 12c — Crown with heart-shaped petals; cross pattée mm	65	200
1459	— 13. Central fleur of crown as Greek double axe	25	65
1460	— 14. Crown with tall central fleur; large smiling face with leering eyes	20	50
1461	— 15a. Small flat crown with both spear-heads usually bent to l.; face of 14	25	65
1462	— 15b. — very similar, but smaller face	20	60
1463	— 15c. — large face, large Є	25	60

| Berwick Type V | Type VI | Type VII |

	F	*VF*
	£	£
1464 *Berwick-on-Tweed*. (Blunt types V, VI and VII) Local dies except V......	25	75
1465 *Bury St. Edmunds*. (11; 12; 13; 14; 15)...	20	50
1466 *Canterbury*. (11; 12a; 13; 14; 15)	20	50
1467 *Durham*. King's Receiver (11a), *mm.* plain cross....................................	20	55
1468 — Bishop Bec. (11a), *mm.* cross moline	20	55
1469 — Bishop Kellawe (11; 12a; 13), crozier on *rev.*	20	55
1470 — Bishop Beaumont (13; 14; 15), *mm.* lion with lis..............................	25	85
1471 *mm.* plain cross (11a, 14, 15c)	60	150

1472

1472 **Halfpenny**, *London*. Class 10-11, ЄDWARDVS REX (-, A, AN, ANG, ANGL or ANGLI,) bifoliate or trifoliate crown......................................	45	135
1473 — *Berwick-on-Tweed*. (Blunt type V)...	85	250

1474

1474 **Farthing**, *London*. Class 11, 13, ЄDWARDVS RЄX (-, A, AN, or AG), face with pellet eyes..	30	100
1475 — *Berwick-on-Tweed*. (Blunt type V)...	100	375

During Edward's early years small quantities of silver coin were minted following the standard of the previous two reigns, but in 1335 halfpence and farthings were produced which were well below the .925 Sterling silver standard. In 1344 an impressive gold coinage was introduced comprising the Double Florin or Double Leopard valued at six shillings, and its half and quarter, the Leopard and the Helm. The design of the Florin was based on the contemporary gold of Philip de Valois of France.

The first gold coinage was not successful and it was replaced later the same year by a heavier coinage, the Noble, valued at 6s. 8d, i.e., 80 pence, half a mark or one third of a pound together with its fractions. The Noble was lowered in weight in two stages over the next few years, being stabilized at 120 grains in 1351. With the signing of the Treaty of Bretigni in 1360 Edward's title to the Kingdom of France was omitted from the coinage, but it was resumed again in 1369.

In 1344 the silver coinage had been re-established at the old sterling standard, but the penny was reduced in weight to just over 20 grains and in 1351 to 18 grains. Groats were minted again in 1351 and were issued regularly henceforth until the reign of Elizabeth.

Subsequent to the treaty with France which gave England a cross-channel trading base at Calais, a mint was opened there in 1363 for minting gold and silver coins of English type. In addition to coins of the regular English mints, the Abbot of Reading also minted silver pence, halfpence and farthings with a scallop shell in one quarter of the reverse while coins from Berwick display one or two boar's or bear's heads.

There is evidence of re-use of dies at later periods, e.g. 3rd coinage halfpennies.

For further study of the English Hammered Gold Coinage see: Sylloge of Coins of the British Isles, 47, the Herbert Schneider Collection Volume One, by Peter Woodhead. 1996.

Mintmarks

| 6 | 1 | 2 | 3 | 74 | 4 | 5 | 7a |

1334-51	Cross pattée (6)	1356	Crown (74)
1351-2	Cross 1 (1)	1356-61	Cross 3 (4)
1351-7	Crozier on cross end (76a, *Durham*)	1361-9	Cross potent (5)
1352-3	Cross 1 broken (2)	1369-77	Cross pattée (6)
1354-5	Cross 2 (3)		Plain cross (7a)

The figures in brackets refer to the plate of mintmarks in Appendix III.

GOLD

Third coinage, 1344-51, First period, 1344

			1476		1477	1478

		F	VF
		£	£

1476	**Double-florin (Double Leopard).** (=6s.; wt. 108 grs.). King enthroned beneath canopy; crowned leopard's head each side. R. Cross in quatrefoil	52500	225000
1477	**Florin.** Leopard sejant with banner l. R. Somewhat as last	13500	52500
1478	**Half-florin .** Helmet on fleured field. R. Floriate cross	6750	25000

Second period, 1344-46

1479	**Noble** (=6s. 8d., wt. 138.46 grs.). King stg. facing in ship with sword and shield. R. L in centre of royal cross in tressure	6500	24000
1479A	**Half-noble.** Similar	3500	12000
1480	**Quarter-noble.** Shield in tressure. R. As last	975	3000

1481

1482

Third period, 1346-51

1481	**Noble** (wt. 128.59 grs.). As 1479, but Є in centre; large letters	1050	3250
1482	**Half-noble.** Similar	975	3500
1483	**Quarter-noble.** As 1480, but Є in centre	325	850

Fourth coinage, 1351-77
Reference: L. A. Lawrence, *The Coinage of Edward III from 1351.*
Pre-treaty period, 1351-61. With French title.

		F	VF
		£	£
1484	**Noble** (wt. 120 grs.), series B (1351). Open Є and C, Roman M; *mm.* cross 1 (1)	725	2000
1485	− − *rev.* of series A (1351). Round lettering, Lombardic M and N; closed inverted Є in centre	750	2250
1486	C (1351-1352). Closed Є and C, Lombardic M; *mm.* cross 1 (1)	575	1450
1487	D (1352-1353). *O.* of series C. R. *Mm.* cross 1 broken (2)	1250	3750

1490   1498

1488	E (1354-1355). Broken letters, V often has a nick in r. limb; *mm.* cross 2 (3)	575	1450
1489	F (1356). *Mm.* crown (74)	725	2250
1490	G (1356-1361). *Mm.* cross 3 (4). Many varieties	550	1350
1491	**Half-noble,** B. As noble with *rev.* of series A, but closed Є in centre not inverted	525	1350
1492	C. *O.* as noble. *Rev.* as last	550	1450
1493	E. As noble	675	2000
1494	G. As noble. Many varieties	425	1050
1495	**Quarter-noble,** B. Pellet below shield. R. Closed Є in centre	275	675
1496	C. *O.* of series B. *Rev.* details as noble	325	850
1497	E. *O.* as last. *Rev.* details as noble, pellet in centre	300	750
1498	G. *Mm.* cross 3 (4). Many varieties	225	525

Transitional treaty period, 1361. French title omitted, replaced by that of Aquitaine on the noble and (rarely) on the half-noble, but not on the quarter-noble; irregular sized letters; *mm.* cross potent (5).

1499
1499	**Noble.** Ŗ. Pellets or annulets at corners of central panel	575	1650

1504

	F £	VF £

1500 **Half-noble.** Similar 325 850
1501 **Quarter-noble.** Similar. Many varieties. Pellet and rarely Є in centre.... 200 425

Treaty period, 1361-69. Omits FRANC, new letters, usually curule-shaped X; *mm.* cross potent(5).
1502 **Noble.** *London.* Saltire or nothing before ЄDWARD 600 1350
1503 — Annulet before ЄDWARD (with, rarely, crescent on forecastle)......... 575 1300
1504 *Calais.* C in centre of *rev.,* flag at stern of ship 625 1400
1505 — — without flag.. 625 1450

1506   1508

1506 **Half-noble.** *London.* Saltire before ЄDWARD...................................... 325 875
1507 — Annulet before ЄDWARD 350 925
1508 *Calais.* C in centre of *rev.,* flag at stern of ship 650 1600
1509 — — without flag.. 750 2000
1510 **Quarter-noble.** *London.* As 1498. R. Lis in centre............................. 210 450
1511 — — annulet before ЄDWARD.. 210 450
1512 *Calais.* R. Annulet in centre.. 225 525
1513 — — cross in circle over shield 250 600
1514 — R. Quatrefoil in centre; cross over shield 275 675
1515 — — crescent over shield.. 325 750

Post-treaty period, 1369-1377. French title resumed.
1516 **Noble.** *London.* Annulet before ЄD. R. Treaty period die...................... 750 2250
1517 — — — crescent on forecastle.. 625 1650
1518 — — — post-treaty letters. R. Є and pellet in centre............................. 600 1500
1519 — — — — R. Є and saltire in centre.. 675 1750
1520 *Calais.* Flag at stern. R. Є in centre.. 675 1750

1521

	F £	VF £
1521 — — *Rev.* as 1518, with Є and pellet in centre	625	1500
1522 — As 1520, but without flag. R. Є in centre	650	1650
1523 **Half-noble.** *London. O.* Treaty die. *Rev.* as 1518	900	2750
1524 *Calais.* Without AQT, flag at stern. R. Є in centre	800	2250
1525 — — R. Treaty die with C in centre	875	2500

SILVER

First coinage, 1327-35 (0.925 fineness)

1526   1530

1526 **Penny.** *London.* As Edw. II; class XVd with Lombardic n's	275	850
1527 *Bury St. Edmunds.* Similar	350	1000
1528 *Canterbury; mm.* cross pattée with pellet centre	200	525
1529 — — three extra pellets in one quarter	175	500
1530 *Durham.* R. Small crown in centre	525	1500
1530A *Reading.* R. Escallop in 2nd quarter	625	1750
1531 *York.* As 1526, but quatrefoil in centre of *rev;* three extra pellets in TAS quarter	165	450
1532 — — — pellet in each quarter of *mm.*	165	450

1535   1537   1539

1534 — — — Roman N's on *obv.*	165	450
1535 *Berwick* (1333-1342, Blunt type VIII). Bear's head in one quarter of *rev.*	475	1500
1536 **Halfpenny.** *London.* Indistinguishable from EDWARD II (cf. 1472)	45	135
1537 *Berwick* (Bl. VIII). Bear's head in one or two quarters	65	185
1538 **Farthing.** *London.* Indistinguishable from those of EDWARD II (cf. 1474)	30	90
1539 *Berwick* (Bl. VIII). As 1537	50	150

1540   1542

| | F | VF |
| | £ | £ |

Second coinage, 1335-43 (0.833 fineness)

1540	**Halfpenny.** *London.* ЄDWARDVS RЄX AN(G). Six-pointed star after AN and before LON. Bifoliate or trifoliate crown.	20	60
1540A	— — New tall crown. Star of eight or six points after ANG and DON and before CIVI or none on rev.	20	60
1541	*Reading.* Escallop in one quarter, star before or after mint	200	650
1542	**Farthing.** *London.* A (N), six-pointed star after A (rarely omitted) and before LON, flat crown.	25	70
1542A	— ANG, star after ANG and before LON or after DON, tall crown	25	75

Third or florin coinage, 1344-51. Bust with bushy hair. (0.925 fine, 20 grs.)

1543   1544

Reverses: I. Lombardic ᴨ II. Roman N. III. Reversed N. IV. Reversed Double-barred N.

1543	**Penny.** *London.* Class 1. ЄDW, Lombardic N. Rev. I.	20	75
1544	— — Class 2, ЄDWA, Lombardic N. Rev. I, II.	20	70
1545	— — Class 3. ЄDW. Roman N. Rev. I, II, III.	20	70
1546	— — Class 4. ЄDW. Reversed N. Rev. I, II, III, IV (doubtful)	20	70
1546A	— Unusual types designated A to E.	35	110
1547	— Canterbury. Class 2. as 1544. Rev. I.	50	150
1548	— — Class 4. as 1546 Rev. I.	45	140
1549	*Durham,* Sede Vacante (possibly 1345 issues of Bishop Richard de Bury or Bishop Hatfield). A, ЄDWR rev. No marks	35	100
1550	— — B, similar, ЄDWAR R.	40	125
1551	— Bp. Hatfield. C, similar, but pellet in centre of *rev.*	35	110
1552	— — — Crozier on *rev.*	40	110
1553	— — — — with pellet in centre of *rev.*	45	125
1554	— — D, ЄDWARDVS RЄX Aᴨ, crozier on *rev.*	65	200

1555

1555	*Reading. obv.* as 1546. ℞. Escallop in one quarter	150	525
1555A	— — ЄDWARDVS RЄX AᴨG. Rev. as 1555.	165	550
1556	*York. obv.* as 1546. ℞. Quatrefoil in centre	20	60

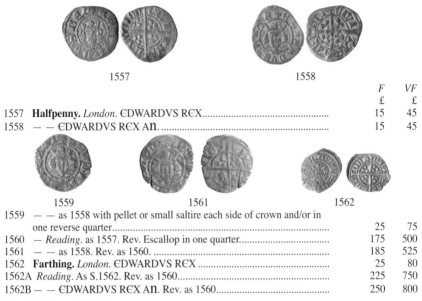

1557   1558

		F	VF
		£	£
1557	**Halfpenny.** *London.* ЄDWARDVS RЄX..	15	45
1558	— — ЄDWARDVS RЄX AП.	15	45

1559   1561   1562

1559	— — as 1558 with pellet or small saltire each side of crown and/or in one reverse quarter..	25	75
1560	— *Reading.* as 1557. Rev. Escallop in one quarter...................................	175	500
1561	— — as 1558. Rev. as 1560.	185	525
1562	**Farthing.** *London.* ЄDWARDVS RЄX	25	80
1562A	*Reading.* As S.1562. Rev. as 1560..	225	750
1562B	— — ЄDWARDVS RЄX AП. Rev. as 1560...	250	800

Fourth coinage, 1351-77

Reference: L. A. Lawrence, *The Coinage of Edward III from 1351.*
A large variety of mules exist between styles and issue.
Pre-treaty period, 1351-61. With French title.

1563   1565

1567

1563	**Groat** (=4d., 72 grs.). *London,* series B (1351). Roman M, open C and Є; *mm.* cross 1	175	575
1564	— — — crown in each quarter..	1500	6000
1565	— C (1351-2). Lombardic m, closed C and Є, R with wedge-shaped tail; *mm.* cross 1	50	180
1566	— D (1352-3). R with normal tail; *mm.* cross 1 or cross 1 broken (2).....	60	240
1567	— E (1354-5). Broken letters, V often with nick in r. limb; *mm.* cross 2 (3)	45	175

		F £	VF £
1568	− − − lis on breast..	50	225
1569	− F (1356). *Mm.* crown (74)	60	200

1570

1572

1570	− G (1356-61). Usually with annulet in one quarter and sometimes under bust, *mm.* cross 3 (4). Many varieties	50	175
1571	*York*, series D. As London	175	500
1572	− E. As London	65	200

1573

1581

1573	**Halfgroat.** *London*, series B. As groat	95	300
1574	− C. As groat	35	110
1575	− D. As groat	40	125
1576	− E. As groat	35	120
1577	− F. As groat	40	125
1578	− G. As groat	35	120
1579	− − − annulet below bust	40	125
1580	*York,* series D. As groat...	75	250
1581	− E. As groat	45	150
1582	− − − lis on breast..	60	200
1583	**Penny.** *London.* Series A (1351). Round letters, Lombardic m and n, annulet in each quarter; *mm.* cross pattee	65	250

1584

1585

1591

1584	− C. Details as groat, but annulet in each quarter	20	75
1585	− D. Details as groat, but annulet in each quarter	25	85
1586	− E. Sometimes annulet in each quarter..............................	20	75
1587	− F. Details as groat	25	85
1588	− G. Details as groat	20	70

	F	VF
	£	£
1589 — — — annulet below bust	20	70
1590 — — — saltire in one quarter	35	125
1591 *Durham,* Bp. Hatfield. Series A. As 1583, but extra pellet in each quarter, VIL LA crozier DVRRЄM	65	250
1592 — C. Details as groat. R. Crozier, CIVITAS DVNЄLMIЄ	20	75
1593 — D — — —	25	85
1594 — E — — —.	30	90
1595 — F — R. Crozier, CIVITAS DVRЄMЄ	25	85
1596 — G — — —	25	80
1597 — — — — — annulet below bust	25	85
1598 — — — — — saltire in one quarter	35	120
1599 — — — — — annulet on each shoulder	30	100
1600 — — — — — trefoil of pellets on breast	30	100
1601 — — — R. Crozier, CIVITAS DVRЄLMIЄ	40	135
1602 *York,* Royal Mint. Series D	25	85
1603 — — E	20	75
1604 — Archb. Thoresby. Series D. R. Quatrefoil in centre	25	90
1605 — — G —	20	70
1606 — — — annulet or saltire on breast	25	85

	1607	1609	1609A		
1607 **Halfpenny.** *London.* Series E. ЄDWARDVS RЄX Aη				70	225
1608 — G, but with *obv.* of F (*mm.* crown). Annulet in one quarter				100	350
1609 **Farthing.** *London.* Series E. ЄDWARDVS RЄX				75	250
1609A — — Series G. Annulet in one quarter				80	275

Transitional treaty period, 1361. French title omitted, irregular sized letters; *mm.* cross potent (5).

1610 **Groat.** *London.* Annulet each side of crown	375	1200

	1611	1612	1615		
1611 **Halfgroat.** Similar, but only seven arches to tressure				125	375
1612 **Penny,** *London.* Omits RЄX, annulet in two upper qtrs. of *mm*				75	225
1613 *York,* Archb. Thoresby. Similar, but quatrefoil enclosing pellet in centre of *rev.*				50	150
1614 *Durham.* Bp. Hatfield. Similar. R. Crozier, CIVITAS DORЄLMЄ				60	175
1615 **Halfpenny.** Two pellets over *mm.,* ЄDWARDVS RЄX Aη				75	275

Treaty period, 1361-69. French title omitted, new letters, usually 'Treaty' X, rarely curule chair X *mm.* cross potent (5).

		F	VF
		£	£
1616	**Groat,** *London.* Many varieties	75	225
1617	— Annulet before ЄDWARD	75	225
1618	— Annulet on breast	110	375

1617

1618

1619	*Calais.* As last	125	400

1620

1620	**Halfgroat,** *London.* As groat	40	135
1621	— — Annulet before ЄDWARDVS	40	135
1622	— — Annulet on breast	45	160
1623	*Calais.* As last	80	275
1624	**Penny,** *London.* ЄDWARD AΠGL R, etc	30	100
1625	— — — pellet before ЄDWARD	35	120
1626	*Calais.* R. VILLA CALЄSIE	115	350
1627	*Durham.* R. CIVITAS DVΠЄLMIS	45	150
1628	— R. Crozier, CIVITAS DVRЄMЄ	35	125
1629	*York,* Archb. Thoresby. Quatrefoil in centre of *rev.,* ЄDWARDVS DЄI G RЄX AΠ	35	125
1630	— — — ЄDWARDVS RЄX AΠGLI	25	90
1631	— — — — quatrefoil before ЄD and on breast	30	100
1632	— — — — annulet before ЄD	30	100
1633	— — — ЄDWARD AΠGL R DΠS HYB	35	125
1634	**Halfpenny.** ЄDWARDVS RЄX AΠ, pellet stops	25	90

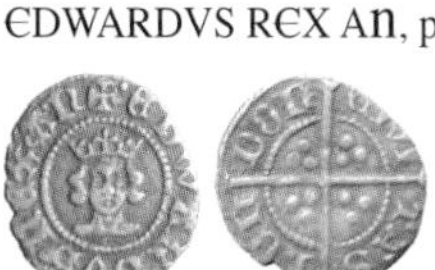

1635

1636

1635	— Pellet before ЄD, annulet stops	25	90
1636	**Farthing.** ЄDWARDVS RЄX, pellet or no stops	85	275

Post-treaty period, 1369-77. French title resumed, X like St. Andrew's cross; *mm.* 5, 6, 7a.

1637   1639

		F	VF
		£	£
1637	**Groat.** Various readings, *mm.* cross pattee	100	350
1638	— — row of pellets across breast (chain mail)	375	1350
1639	— row of annulets below bust (chain mail); *mm.* cross potent with four pellets	425	1500
1640	**Halfgroat.** Various readings	120	350

1641

1640A	— Thin portrait of Richard II	135	475
1641	— row of pellets one side of breast (chain mail)	175	650
1642	**Penny,** *London.* No marks on breast	35	135
1643	— Pellet or annulet on breast	40	135
1644	— Cross or quatrefoil on breast	30	110
1645	*Durham,* Bp. Hatfield. *Mm.* 7a, CIVITAS DVnOLM, crozier	35	130
1646	— — — — annulet on breast	40	135
1647	— — — — lis on breast	35	130
1648	*York.* Archb. Thoresby or Neville. R. Quatrefoil in centre	25	95
1649	— — — lis on breast	30	100
1650	— — — annulet on breast	30	100
1651	— — — cross on breast	35	120

1652

1652	**Farthing.** EDWARD REX ANGL, large head without neck	125	450

For further reading see:
Halfpennies and Farthings of Edward III and Richard II. *Paul and Bente R. Withers, 2002.*

There was no change in the weight standard of the coinage during this reign and the coins evolve from early issues resembling those of Edward III to late issues similar to those of Henry IV.

There is no overall, systematic classification of the coins of Richard II but a coherent scheme for the gold coinage has been worked out and is published in the Schneider Sylloge (SCBI 47). This classification has been adopted here.

Reference: *Silver coinages of Richard II, Henry IV and V.* (B.N.J. 1959-60 and 1963).

Mintmark: cross pattée (6)

GOLD

	F	VF
	£	£
1653 **Noble**, *London*. Style of Edw. III. IA. Lis over sail	850	2250

1654   1658

1654	— IB. Annulet over sail..	725	1650
1655	French title omitted. IIA. Crude style, saltire over sail. IIB. Fine style, trefoil over sail. IIC. Porcine style, no mark over sail	750	1800
1656	French title resumed. IIIA. Fine style, no marks.....................................	750	1750
1657	— IIIB. Lis on rudder. IIIC. Trefoil by shield	850	2250
1658	Henry IV style. IVA. Escallop on rudder. IVB. Crescent on rudder.........	875	2500
1659	*Calais*. Style of Edw. III, IA, Edw. III lettering..	1200	3500
1660	Style of Edw. III. IB. New lettering. Voided quatrefoil over sail	825	1850

1661   1662

1661	French title omitted. IIA. Crude style, no marks. IIB. Fine style, trefoil over sail. IIC. Porcine style, no marks..	725	1650
1662	French title resumed. IIIA. Fine style, no marks	750	1850
1663	— IIIB. Lion on rudder. IIIC. Two pellets by shield	950	2500

	F	*VF*
	£	£
1664 **Half-noble,** *London.* With altered *obv.* of Edw. III. Usually muled with *rev.* or altered *rev.* of Edw. III	850	2750

1665   1673

1665	Style of Edw. III. IB. No marks or saltire over sail	825	2500
1666	French title omitted. IIA. New style, no marks	875	2750
1667	French title resumed. IIIA. No marks. IIIB. Lion on rudder	900	2750
1668	Henry IV style. IVB. Crescent on rudder	1050	3000
1669	*Calais.* Mule with *obv.* or *rev.* of Edw. III	1200	3500
1670	Style of Edw. III. IB. Quatrefoil over sail	1200	3500
1671	Late style. French title. IIIA. No marks. IIIB. Saltire by rudder	1050	3250
1672	**Quarter-noble,** *London.* IA. R in centre of *rev.*	450	900
1673	IB Lis in centre of *rev.*	375	825
1674	— lis or cross over shield	400	900

1675   1677

1675	IIIA. Pellet in centre of *rev.*	350	800
1676	IIIB. Trefoil of annulets over shield or trefoils in spandrels	450	950
1677	IVA. Escallop over shield	425	900

SILVER

1680

1678	**Groat.** I. Style of Edw. III, F *(i.e. et)* before FRANC, etc.	475	1500
1679	II. New lettering, retrograde Z before FRANC, etc.	400	1350
1680	III. Bust with bushy hair, 'fishtail' serifs to letters	475	1500
1681	IV. New style bust and crown, crescent on breast	1250	4500

1682

		F £	VF £
1682	**Halfgroat.** II. New lettering; with or without French title	225	750
1683	III. As 1680	275	850
1684	– – with *obv.* die of Edw. III (1640A)...	375	1250
1685	IV. As 1681, but no crescent	625	2250
1686	**Penny,** *London*. I Lettering as 1678, RICARDVS REX ANGLIE	150	475
1688	– II. As 1679, Z FRANC lis on breast	165	500

1688   1692

1689	– III. As 1680, RICARD REX AnGLIE, fish-tail letters	175	575
1690	*York*. I. Early style, usually with cross or lis on breast, quatrefoil in centre of *rev*	45	185
1691	– II. New bust and letters, no marks on breast.......................................	45	185
1692	– Local dies. Pellet above each shoulder, cross on breast, REX ANGLIE or ANGILIE	45	225
1693	– – – REX DNS EB..	90	375
1694	– – – REX ANG FRANC	85	350
1695	– III. As 1680, REX ANGL Z FRANC (scallop after TAS)...................	65	250
1696	– IV. Very bushy hair, new letters, R. R in centre of quatrefoil..............	135	500
1697	*Durham*. Cross or lis on breast, DVNOLM..	110	375

1698   1699   1701   1704A

1698	**Halfpenny.** Early style. LONDON, saltire or annulet (rare) on breast	45	150
1699	Intermediate style. LONDON, no marks on breast	35	95
1700	Type III. Late style. Similar, but fishtail letters	35	100
1700A	Type IV. Short, stubby lettering..	40	120
1701	**Farthing.** Small bust and letters..	95	300
1703	Similar but no neck	90	300
1704	Rose in each angle of *rev.* instead of pellets	135	450
1704A	Large head with broad face as Henry IV	135	450

For further reading see:
Halfpennies and Farthings of Edward III and Richard II. *Paul and Bente R. Withers, 2002.*

HENRY IV, 1399-1413

In 1412 the standard weights of the coinage were reduced, the noble by 12 grains and the penny by 3 grains, partly because there was a scarcity of bullion and partly to provide revenue for the king, as Parliament had not renewed the royal subsidies. As in France, the royal arms were altered, three fleur-de-lis taking the place of the four or more lis previously displayed.

Mintmark: cross pattée (6)

GOLD

Heavy coinage, 1399-1412

1706   1707

		F	*VF*
		£	£
1705	**Noble** (120 grs.), *London.* Old arms with four lis in French quarters; crescent or annulet on rudder...	4000	13500
1706	— New arms with three lis; crescent, pellet or no marks on rudder	3750	13000
1707	*Calais.* Flag at stern, old arms; crown on or to l. of rudder......................	4500	15000

1709

1708	— — new arms; crown or saltire on rudder	4250	14500
1709	**Half-noble,** *London.* Old arms..	3250	10000
1710	— new arms..	3000	9500
1711	*Calais.* New arms	4250	12500
1712	**Quarter-noble,** *London.* Crescent over old arms....................................	950	3000
1713	— — — new arms..	900	2750
1714	*Calais.* New arms. R. *Mm.* crown..	1000	3500

1715

	F	VF
	£	£

Light coinage, 1412-13

1715 **Noble** (108 grs.). Trefoil, or trefoil and annulet, on side of ship. R. Trefoil
in one quarter 1350 3750

1716 **Half-noble.** Similar, but always with annulet 1750 5250

1717

1717 **Quarter-noble.** Trefoils, or trefoils and annulets beside shield, lis above. R.
Lis in centre 525 1250

SILVER

Heavy coinage, 1399-1412

1718 **Halfgroat** (36 grs.). Star on breast 1050 3500

1718A — Muled with Edw. III (1640A) *obv.*... 750 2250

1719 **Penny,** *London.* Similar, early bust with long neck............................... 625 1750

1720 — later bust with shorter neck, no star... 625 1750

1722   1723   1725

1722 *York* Bust with broad face, round chin.. 450 1200

1723 **Halfpenny.** Early small bust 175 500

1724 — later large bust, with rounded shoulders,.. 175 500

1725 **Farthing.** Face without neck.. 625 1650

Light coinage, 1412-13

1726   1732

		F	VF
		£	£
1726	**Groat** (60 grs.). I. Pellet to l., annulet to r. of crown; altered die of Richard II	2500	6500
1727	New dies; II. Annulet to l., pellet to r. of crown, 8 or 10 arches to tressure	1850	5750
1728	— III. Similar but 9 arches to tressure	1750	5250
1729	**Halfgroat.** Pellet to l., annulet to r. of crown	750	2000
1730	Annulet to l., pellet to r. of crown	675	1750
1731	**Penny,** *London.* Annulet and pellet by crown; trefoil on breast and before CIVI	525	1500
1732	— — annulet or slipped trefoil before LON	625	1650
1733	— Pellet and annulet by crown	525	1500
1734	*York.* Annulet on breast. R̲. Quatrefoil in centre	300	800
1735	*Durham.* Trefoil on breast, DVnOLM	275	750

1737   1738

		F	VF
1737	**Halfpenny.** New dies; annulets by crown or neck, or no marks	175	575
1738	**Farthing.** Face, no bust; trefoil after RЄX	575	1500

For further information see:
Halfpennies and Farthings of Henry IV, V and VI. *Paul and Bente R. Withers, 2003.*

There was no change of importance in the coinage of this reign. There was, however, a considerable development in the use of privy marks which distinguished various issues, except for the last issue of the reign when most marks were removed. The Calais mint, which had closed in 1411, did not re-open until just before the end of the reign. There is now some uncertainty as to whether types A and B of Henry V should be given to Henry IV.

Mintmarks

Cross pattee (4)   Pierced cross with   Pierced cross (18).
                       pellet centre (20)

GOLD

		F £	VF £
1739	**Noble.** A. Quatrefoil over sail and in second quarter of *rev.* Short broad letters, no other marks	1350	4000
1740	— B. Ordinary letters; similar, or with annulet on rudder	875	2250
1741	— C. Mullet by sword arm, annulet on rudder	725	1750

1742   1744

1742	— — — broken annulet on side of ship	700	1650
1743	—D. Mullet and annulet by sword arm, trefoil by shield, broken annulet on ship	750	1800
1744	— E. Mullet, or mullet and annulet by sword arm, trefoil by shield, pellet by sword point and in one quarter, annulet on side of ship	725	1750
1745	— — Similar, but trefoil on ship instead of by shield	800	1850
1746	— F. Similar, but no pellet at sword point, trefoil in one quarter	800	1850
1747	— G. No marks; annulet stops, except for mullet after first word	900	2250
1748	**Half Noble.** B. As noble; Hen. IV *rev.* die	1350	4500
1749	— C. Broken annulet on ship, quatrefoil below sail	675	1650
1750	— — Mullet over shield, broken annulet on *rev.*	625	1450
1751	— F. Similar, but no annulet on ship, usually trefoil by shield	825	2500
1752	— F/E. As last, but pellet in 1st and annulet in 2nd quarter	800	2500

1753   1756

		F £	VF £
1753	— G. As noble, but quatrefoil over sail, mullet sometimes omitted after first word of *rev.*	700	1850
1754	**Quarter Noble.** A. Lis over shield and in centre of *rev.* Short broad letters; quatrefoil and annulet beside shield, stars at corners of centre on *rev.*	650	1650
1755	— C. Ordinary letters; quatrefoil to l., quat. and mullet to r. of shield	350	825
1756	— — — annulet to l., mullet to r. of shield	275	600
1757	— F. Ordinary letters; trefoil to l., mullet to r. of shield	300	700
1758	— G. — no marks, except mullet after first word	300	700

SILVER

1759

1759	**Groat.** A. Short broad letters; 'emaciated' bust	950	3250
1760	— — muled with Hen. IV *obv*	975	3750
1761	— — muled with Hen. IV *rev*	950	3250

1762   1767

1762	B. Ordinary letters; 'scowling' bust	375	1100
1762A	— — mullet in centre of breast	450	1250
1762B	— — mullet to r. of breast	475	1350
1763	— — muled with Hen. IV	650	1750
1764	C. Normal bust	275	800
1765	— — mullet on r. shoulder	135	400
1766	— — R muled with Hen. IV	575	1650
1767	G. Normal bust; no marks	325	950
1768	**Halfgroat.** A. As groat, but usually with annulet and pellet by crown	525	1350

		F	VF
		£	£
1769	B. Ordinary letters; no marks	325	900
1770	— — muled with Hen. IV *obv.*..................................	650	1750
1771	C. Tall neck, broken annulet to l. of crown............................	115	350
1772	— — — mullet on r. shoulder	125	375

1774   1775   1788

		F	VF
1773	— — — mullet in centre of breast	110	325
1774	F. Annulet and trefoil by crown, mullet on breast	115	350
1775	G. New neat bust: no marks...	125	375
1776	**Penny.** *London.* A. Letters, bust and marks as 1768	225	700
1777	— Altered Hen. IV *obv.* with mullet added to l. of crown......................	475	1250
1778	— C. Tall neck, mullet and broken annulet by crown	30	125
1779	— D. Similar, but whole annulet	30	130
1780	— F. Mullet and trefoil by crown	35	135
1781	— G. New neat bust, no marks, DI GRA	40	145
1782	*Durham.* C. As 1778 but quatrefoil at end of legend.....................	35	135
1783	— D. As 1779	35	135
1784	— G. Similar, but new bust. Ŗ. Annulet in one qtr.	40	150
1785	*York.* C. As 1778, but quatrefoil in centre of *rev.*	25	100
1786	— D. Similar, but whole annulet by crown	25	100
1787	— E. As last, but pellet above mullet	40	150
1788	— F. Mullet and trefoil by crown	25	100
1789	— — Trefoil over mullet to l., annulet to r. of crown	35	125
1790	— G. Mullet and trefoil by crown (London dies)...................................	35	135

1791   1796   1798

		F	VF
1791	— — Mullet and lis by crown, annulet in one qtr. (usually local dies)....	30	125
1792	**Halfpenny.** A. Emaciated bust, annulets by crown..............................	135	450
1793	— altered dies of Hen. IV..	175	575
1794	C. Ordinary bust, broken annulets by crown	25	80
1795	D. Annulets, sometimes broken, by hair.................................	25	80
1796	F. Annulet and trefoil by crown	25	80
1797	G. New bust; no marks, (usually muled with Henry VI annulet *rev.*)	35	135
1797A	**Farthing.** *London.* B. Very large head	325	900
1798	— G. Small face with neck...	225	575
1798A	*Calais.* G. as 1798, VILLA CALIS	375	1250

For further information see:
Halfpennies and Farthings of Henry IV, V and VI. *Paul and Bente R. Withers, 2003.*

The supply of gold began to dwindle early in the reign, which accounts for the rarity of gold after 1426. The Calais mint had reopened just before the death of Henry V and for some years a large amount of coin was struck there. It soon stopped minting gold; the mint was finally closed in 1440. A royal mint at York was opened for a short time in 1423/4.

Marks used to denote various issues become more prominent in this reign and can be used to date coins to within a year or so.

Reference: C. A. Whitton Heavy Coinage of Henry VI. (B.N.J. 1938-41).

Mintmarks

9 15 136 7a 105 18 133 8

1422-7	Incurved pierced cross (136)	1422-34	Cross pommée (133)
1422-3	Lis (105, York)	1427-34	Cross patonce (8)
1422-60	Plain cross (7a, intermittently		Cross fleury (9)
	Lis (105, on gold)	1434-35	Voided cross (15)
1422-27	Pierced cross (18)	1435-60	Cross fleury (9)
1460	Lis (105, on rev. of some groats)		

For Restoration mintmarks see page 198.

GOLD

1799

		F £	*VF* £
Annulet issue, 1422-c.1430			
1799	**Noble.** *London.* Annulet by sword arm, and in one spandrel on *rev.;* trefoil stops on *obv.* with lis after hЄnRIC, annulets on *rev.,* with mullet after IhC	575	1400
1800	— Similar, but *obv.* from Henry V die	950	3000
1801	— As 1799, but Flemish imitative coinage	375	950

1802

1802	*Calais.* As 1799, but flag at stern and C in centre of *rev*	725	2250

	F £	VF £
1803 — — with h in centre of *rev.*	675	1750
1804 *York*. As London, but with lis over stern	750	2250

1805

1805 **Half-noble.** *London*. As 1799	475	1250
1806 — Similar, but *obv.* from Henry V die	750	2250
1807 *Calais*. As noble, with C in centre of *rev.*	825	2400
1808 — — with h in centre of *rev.*	800	2250
1809 *York*. As noble	850	2500
1810 **Quarter-noble.** *London*. Lis over shield; *mm.* large lis	200	525
1811 — — — trefoil below shield	225	575
1812 — — — pellet below shield	225	575
1813 *Calais*. Three lis over shield; *mm.* large lis	325	750

1814   1819

1814 — Similar but three lis around shield	275	650
1815 — As 1810, but much smaller *mm.*	225	550
1816 *York*. Two lis over shield	275	650

Rosette-mascle issue, c.1430-31

1817 **Noble.** *London*. Lis by sword arm and in *rev.* field; stops, rosettes, or rosettes and mascles	1100	3000
1818 *Calais*. Similar, with flag at stern	1350	4000
1819 **Half-noble.** *London*. Lis in *rev.* field; stops, rosettes and mascles	1500	4500
1820 *Calais*. Similar, flag at stern; stops, rosettes	1600	4750
1821 **Quarter-noble.** *London*. As 1810; stops, as noble	600	1350
1822 — without lis over shield	650	1500
1823 *Calais*. Lis over shield, rosettes r. and l., and rosette stops	700	1750

Pinecone-mascle issue, c.1431-2/3

1824

		F £	VF £
1824	**Noble.** Stops, pinecones and mascles	1100	3000
1825	**Half-noble.** *O*. Rosette-mascle die. R. As last	2250	6500
1826	**Quarter-noble.** As 1810, but pinecone and mascle stops	750	1850

1828

Leaf-mascle issue, c.1432/3-6

1827	**Noble.** Leaf in waves; stops, saltires with two mascles and one leaf	2250	6500
1828	**Half-noble.** (Fishpool hoard and Reigate hoard)	2000	6000
1829	**Quarter-noble.** As 1810; stops, saltire and mascle; leaf on inner circle of *rev*.	750	1850

Leaf-trefoil issue, c.1436-8

1830	**Noble.** Stops, leaves and trefoils	2000	6000
1830A	**Half-noble.**	2250	6500
1831	**Quarter-noble.** Similar	800	2000

Trefoil issue, 1438-43

1832	**Noble.** Trefoil to left of shield and in *rev*. legend	2000	5750

Leaf-pellet issue, 1445-54

1833	**Noble.** Annulet, lis and leaf below shield	2250	6750

Cross-pellet issue, 1454-61

1834	**Noble.** Mascle at end of *obv*. legend	2500	8000

Muling exists in Henry VI coins spanning two or three issues. Full flan coins in the smaller denominations are difficult to find.

SILVER

Annulet issue, 1422-30

1835

1836

		F	VF
		£	£
1835	**Groat.** *London.* Annulet in two quarters of *rev.*	55	135
1836	*Calais.* Annulets at neck. R. Similar	45	120
1837	— — no annulets on *rev.*	70	225

1838

1838	*York.* Lis either side of neck. R. As 1835	975	3000
1839	**Halfgroat.** *London.* As groat	40	125

1840

1843

1840	*Calais.* As 1836	35	90
1841	— — no annulets on *rev.*	45	135
1843	*York.* As groat	675	1750

1845

1844	**Penny.** *London.* Annulets in two qtrs.	30	90
1845	*Calais.* Annulets at neck. R. As above	25	80

		F	VF
		£	£
1846	— — only one annulet on *rev.*	35	125
1847	*York*. As London, but lis at neck	650	1750
1848	**Halfpenny.** *London*. As penny	20	50
1849	*Calais*. Similar, but annulets at neck	20	50

1850

1852

		F	VF
1850	*York*. Similar, but lis at neck	275	850
1851	**Farthing.** *London*. As penny, but *mm*. cross pommée	90	225
1852	*Calais*. Similar, but annulets at neck	125	375
1852A	*York*. Similar, but lis at neck	525	1350

Annulet-trefoil sub-issue

1854

1855

		F	VF
1854	**Groat.** *Calais,* as 1836 but trefoil to l. of crown.	75	225
1855	**Halfgroat.** *Calais,* similar, only known as a mule with annulet issue (both ways) or with rosette mascle rev.	65	200
1856	**Penny.** *Calais*. Similar, only one annulet on *rev*	65	200

Rosette-mascle issue, 1430-31. All with rosettes (early) or rosettes and mascles somewhere in the legends.

		F	VF
1858	**Groat.** *London.*	65	200

1859

1861

		F	VF
1859	*Calais*	50	135
1860	— mascle in two spandrels	65	175
1861	**Halfgroat.** *London.*	90	350

		1862		1870		1872

		F	VF
		£	£
1862	*Calais*	35	110
1863	— mascle in two spandrels	40	125
1864	**Penny.** *London*	175	450
1865	*Calais*	35	110
1866	*York.* Archb. Kemp. Crosses by hair, no rosette	30	110
1867	— — Saltires by hair, no rosette	35	125
1868	— — Mullets by crown	30	120
1869	*Durham,* Bp. Langley. Large star to l. of crown, no rosette, DVnOLMI	45	140
1870	**Halfpenny,** *London*	20	60
1871	*Calais*	20	60
1872	**Farthing,** *London*	125	375
1873	*Calais. Mm.* cross pommée	135	450

Pinecone-mascle issue, 1431-32/3. All with pinecones and mascles in legends.

		1874		1876		

1874	**Groat,** London	50	130
1875	*Calais*	45	125
1876	**Halfgroat,** *London*	55	150
1877	*Calais*	50	135
1878	**Penny,** *London*	40	120
1879	*Calais*	35	110
1880	*York,* Archb. Kemp. Mullet by crown, quatrefoil in centre of *rev.*	35	120
1881	— — rosette on breast, no quatrefoil	35	120
1882	— — mullet on breast, no quatrefoil	35	125
1883	*Durham,* Bp. Langley. DVnOLMI	45	150

1884   1886

		F £	VF £
1884	**Halfpenny,** *London*	20	60
1885	*Calais*	25	65
1886	**Farthing,** *London*	125	.350
1887	*Calais. Mm.* cross pommée	135	425

Leaf-mascle issue, 1432/3-6. Usually with a mascle in the legend and a leaf somewhere in the design.

1888	**Groat.** *London*. Leaf below bust, all appear to read DOnDOn	175	675
1889	— — *rev.* of last or next coinage	135	425

1890

1890	*Calais.* Leaf below bust, and usually below MЄVM	125	350
1891	**Halfgroat.** *London*. Leaf under bust, pellet under TAS and DON...........	110	325
1892	*Calais.* Leaf below bust, and sometimes on *rev.*	110	325

1897

1893	**Penny.** *London*. Leaf on breast, no stops on *rev.*......................................	65	175
1894	*Calais.* Leaf on breast and below SIЄ	70	185
1895	**Halfpenny.** *London*. Leaf on breast and on *rev.*......................................	30	80
1896	*Calais.* Leaf on breast and below SIЄ	65	175

Leaf-trefoil issue, 1436-8. Mostly with leaves and trefoil of pellets in the legends.

1897	**Groat.** *London*. Leaf on breast	75	200
1898	— without leaf on breast	70	200

	F	VF
	£	£
1899 *Calais*. Leaf on breast..	475	1350
1900 **Halfgroat.** *London.* Leaf on breast; *mm.* plain cross	65	185
1901 — *O. mm.* cross fleury; leaf on breast	55	165
1902 — — without leaf on breast	60	185
1902A *Calais*. leaf on breast, mule with leaf mascle *rev.*	140	475
1903 **Penny.** *London.* Leaf on breast...	60	185
1903A *Calais*. Similar..	275	700
1904 *Durham,* Bp. Neville. Leaf on breast. R. Rings in centre, no stops, DVnOLM	110	275

1905   1907

1905 **Halfpenny.** *London.* Leaf on breast	20	55
1906 — without leaf on breast	20	60
1906A *Calais*. leaf on breast, mule with leaf mascle rev.	90	275
1907 **Farthing.** *London.* Leaf on breast; stops, trefoil and saltire on *obv.*.........	110	325

Trefoil issue, 1438-43. Trefoil of pellets either side of neck and in legend, leaf on breast.

1910

1908 **Groat.** *London.* Sometimes a leaf before LON......................	75	225
1909 — Fleurs in spandrels, sometimes extra pellet in two qtrs.	90	275
1910 — Trefoils in place of fleurs at shoulders, none by neck, sometimes extra pellets..	85	250
1911 *Calais*..	275	850

1911A   1912A

1911A **Halfgroat,** *London* Similar, but trefoil after DEUM and sometimes after POSUI Mule only with leaf trefoil *obv.*......................	135	415
1911B — *Calais Obv.* Similar to 1911, mule with leaf mascle *rev.*......................	275	800
1912 **Halfpenny,** *London*	20	70
1912A **Farthing,** *London*..	135	375

Trefoil pellet issue, 1443-5

1913

		F	VF
		£	£
1913	**Groat.** Trefoils by neck, pellets by crown, small leaf on breast; sometimes extra pellet in two quarters	135	450

1915   1917

Leaf-pellet issue, 1445-54. Leaf on breast, pellet each side of crown, except where stated.

1914	**Groat.** ANGL; extra pellet in two quarters	65	200
1915	*Similar,* but ANGLI	60	190
1916	− − trefoil in *obv.* legend	75	225
1917	Leaf on neck, fleur on breast, often extra pellet in two quarters	60	185
1918	As last, but two extra pellets by hair	175	575
1919	**Halfgroat.** As 1914 *mm.* Cross patonce	65	185
1920	Similar, but *mm.* plain cross, some times no leaf on breast, no stops	60	175
1921	**Penny.** *London.* Usually extra pellets in two quarters	45	135
1922	− − pellets by crown omitted	45	135
1923	− − trefoil in legend	50	150
1924	*York,* Archb. Booth. R. Quatrefoil and pellet in centre	40	110
1925	− − two extra pellets by hair (local dies)	40	110
1926	*Durham,* Bp. Neville. Trefoil in *obv.* legend. R. Two rings in centre of cross	60	160

1928   1930

1927	− − Similar, but without trefoil	65	160
1928	**Halfpenny.** Usually extra pellet in two quarters	20	60
1929	− *mm.* plain cross	20	60
1930	**Farthing.** As last	125	350

Unmarked issue, 1453-4

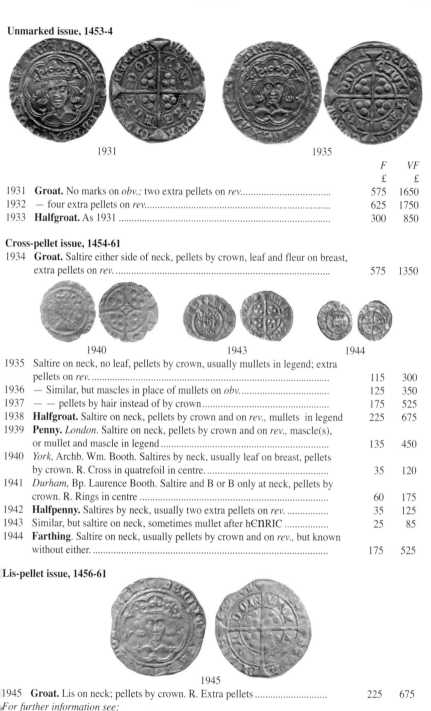

1931   1935

		F	VF
		£	£
1931	**Groat.** No marks on *obv.;* two extra pellets on *rev.*	575	1650
1932	— four extra pellets on *rev.*	625	1750
1933	**Halfgroat.** As 1931	300	850

Cross-pellet issue, 1454-61

1934	**Groat.** Saltire either side of neck, pellets by crown, leaf and fleur on breast, extra pellets on *rev.*	575	1350

1940   1943   1944

1935	Saltire on neck, no leaf, pellets by crown, usually mullets in legend; extra pellets on *rev.*	115	300
1936	— Similar, but mascles in place of mullets on *obv.*	125	350
1937	— — pellets by hair instead of by crown	175	525
1938	**Halfgroat.** Saltire on neck, pellets by crown and on *rev.*, mullets in legend	225	675
1939	**Penny.** *London.* Saltire on neck, pellets by crown and on *rev.*, mascle(s), or mullet and mascle in legend	135	450
1940	*York,* Archb. Wm. Booth. Saltires by neck, usually leaf on breast, pellets by crown. R. Cross in quatrefoil in centre.	35	120
1941	*Durham,* Bp. Laurence Booth. Saltire and B or B only at neck, pellets by crown. R. Rings in centre	60	175
1942	**Halfpenny.** Saltires by neck, usually two extra pellets on *rev.*	35	125
1943	Similar, but saltire on neck, sometimes mullet after hЄnRIC	25	85
1944	**Farthing.** Saltire on neck, usually pellets by crown and on *rev.*, but known without either.	175	525

Lis-pellet issue, 1456-61

1945

1945	**Groat.** Lis on neck; pellets by crown. R. Extra pellets	225	675

For further information see:
Halfpennies and Farthings of Henry IV, V and VI. *Paul and Bente R. Withers, 2003.*

THE HOUSE OF YORK, 1461-1485

EDWARD IV, First Reign, 1461-70

In order to increase the supply of bullion to the mint the weight of the penny was reduced to 12 grains in 1464, and the current value of the noble was raised to 8s. 4d. Later, in 1465, a new gold coin was issued, the Ryal or 'Rose Noble', weighing 120 grains and having a value of 10s. However, as 6s. 8d. had become the standard professional fee the old noble was missed, and a new coin was issued to take its place, the Angel of 80 grains.

Royal mints were set up in Bristol, Coventry, Norwich and York to help with the recoinage. The Coventry and Norwich mints were not open for long, but the York and Bristol mints remained open until 1471 and 1472 respectively.

Reference: C. E. Blunt and C. A Whitton, *The Coinage of Edward IV and Henry VI (Restored)*, B.N.J. 1945-7.

Mintmarks

105	9	7a	33	99	28	74	11

1461-4	Lis (105)	1467-70	Lis (105, *York*)	
	Cross fleury (9)	1467-8	Crown (74)	(often
	Plain cross (7a)		Sun (28)	combined)
1464-5	Rose (33 and 34)	1468-9	Crown (74)	(sometimes
1464-7	Pall (99, *Canterbury*)		Rose (33)	combined)
1465-6	Sun (28)	1469-70	Long cross	
1466-7	Crown (74)		fitchee (l.c.f) (11)	(often
			Sun (28)	combined)

GOLD

Heavy coinage, 1461-4

	F	VF
	£	£

1946

1946	**Noble** (=6s. 8d., wt. 108 grs.). Normal type, but *obv.* legend commences at top left, lis below shield; *mm.*-/lis (Spink's sale May 1993)	2400	7500
1947	— Quatrefoil below sword arm; *mm.* rose/lis	2650	8500
1948	— R. Roses in two spandrels; *mm.* rose	2850	10000
1949	**Quarter-noble**	1500	4250

1950

| | *F* | *VF* |
| | £ | £ |

Light coinage, 1464-70

1950 **Ryal** or rose-noble (=10s., wt. 120 grs.), *London*. As illustration. Large
    fleurs in spandrels; *mm.* 33-74...   575   1375

1951 — — Small trefoils in spandrels; *mm.* 74-11   575   1375

1952

			F	*VF*
1952	— Flemish imitative coinage (mostly 16th cent. on a large flan)		425	900
1953	*Bristol*. B in waves, large fleurs; *mm*. sun, crown		750	2000
1954	— — small fleurs in spandrels; *mm*. sun, crown		775	2100
1955	*Coventry*. C in waves; *mm*. sun		1500	4000
1956	*Norwich*. Π in waves; *mm*. sun, rose		1600	4250
1957	*York*. Є in waves, large fleurs in spandrels, *mm*. sun, lis		725	1850
1958	— — small fleurs, *mm*. sun. lis		750	2000
1959	**Half-ryal.** *London*. As 1950		525	1300
1960	*Bristol*. B in waves; *mm*. sun, sun/crown		825	2250
1961	*Coventry*. C in waves; *mm*. sun		2750	9000
1962	*Norwich*. Π in waves; *mm*. rose		2650	8500

1963   1965

	F	VF
	£	£
1963 *York.* Є in waves; *mm.* 28, 105, 33/105	625	1500
1963A Similar but lis instead of Є in waves (probably York).............................	675	1750
1964 **Quarter-ryal.** Shield in tressure of eight arcs, rose above. R. Somewhat as half ryal; *mm.* sun/rose	750	2000
1965 Shield in quatrefoil. Є above, rose on l., sun on r.; *mm.* 33/28-74/33	275	800
1966 — — sun on l., rose on r.; *mm.* 74-11...	300	825

1967

1967 **Angel** (=6s. 8d., wt. 80 grs.). St. Michael spearing dragon. R. Ship, rays of sun at masthead, large rose and sun beside mast; *mm.*-/33........................	4250	14000
1968 — — small rose and sun at mast; *mm.*-/74..	4500	15000

SILVER

1969   1972

Heavy coinage, 1461-4

1969 **Groat** (60 grs.). Group I, lis on neck, pellets by crown; *mm.* 9, 7a, 105, 9/105	165	475
1970 — Lis on breast, no pellets; *mm.* plain cross, 7a/105	175	525
1971 — — with pellets at crown; *mm.* plain cross....................................	175	525
1972 II, quatrefoils by neck, crescent on breast; *mm.* rose................................	165	475
1973 III, similar but trefoil on breast; *mm.* rose	150	425

1974

1979

		F	VF
		£	£
1974	− − − eye in *rev.* inner legend, *mm.* rose	135	400
1975	− Similar, but no quatrefoils by bust	200	675
1976	− − Similar, but no trefoil on breast	175	575
1977	IV, annulets by neck, eye after TAS; *mm.* rose	375	1250
1978	**Halfgroat.** I, lis on breast, pellets by crown and extra pellets in two qtrs.; *mm.* 9, 7a	325	1000
1979	II, quatrefoils at neck, crescent on breast; *mm.* rose	275	675
1980	III, similar, but trefoil on breast, eye on rev.; *mm.* rose	225	550
1981	− Similar, but no mark on breast	225	550
1982	IV, annulets by neck, sometimes eye on *rev.; mm.* rose	275	675
1983	**Penny** (15 grs.), *London.* I, marks as 1978, but mascle after RЄX; *mm.* plain cross	225	675
1984	II, quatrefoils by neck; *mm.* rose	185	500

1985   1991   1994

1985	III, similar, but eye after TAS; *mm.* rose	175	475
1986	IV, annulets by neck; *mm.* rose	200	525
1987	*York,* Archb. Booth. Quatrefoils by bust, voided quatrefoil in centre of *rev.; mm.* rose	110	275
1988	*Durham. O.* of Hen. VI. R. DVΠOLIΠ	125	300
1988A	King's Receiver (1462-4). Local dies, mostly with rose in centre of rev.; *mm.* 7a, 33	25	75
1989	**Halfpenny.** I, as 1983, but no mascle	65	175
1990	II, quatrefoils by bust; *mm.* rose	40	110
1991	− saltires by bust; *mm.* rose	35	100
1992	III, no marks by bust; *mm.* rose	35	100
1992A	− saltires by bust, eye after TAS, *mm.* rose	75	225
1993	IV, annulets by bust; *mm.* rose	40	110
1994	**Farthing.** I, pellets by crown, extra pellets on rev., with or without lis on breast	175	500
1994A	II. saltires by bust; *mm.* rose	185	525
1994B	III, no marks by bust; *mm.* rose	150	475

Light coinage, 1464-70. There is a great variety of groats and we give only a selection. Some have pellets in one quarter of the reverse, or trefoils over the crown; early coins have fleurs on the cusps of the tressure, then trefoils or no marks on the cusps, while the late coins have only trefoils.

		F	VF
		£	£
1995	**Groat** (48 grs.), *London*. Annulets at neck, eye after TAS; *mm*. 33 (struck from heavy dies, IV)	125	400
1996	— — — Similar, but new dies, eye after TAS or DOn	135	450
1997	— Quatrefoils at neck, eye; rose (heavy dies, III)	100	300
1998	— — — Similar, but new dies, eye in *rev*. legend	100	300
1999	— No marks at neck, eye; *mm* rose	175	575

	2000		2002	
2000	— Quatrefoils at neck, no eye; *mm*. 33, 74, 28, 74/28, 74/33, 11/28		45	140
2001	— — — rose or quatrefoil on breast; *mm*. 33, 74/28		50	165
2002	— No marks at neck; *mm*. 28, 74, 11/28, 11		55	200
2003	— Trefoils or crosses at neck; *mm*. 11/33, 11/28, 11		50	175
2004	*Bristol*. B on breast, quatrefoils at neck; *mm*. 28/33, 28, 28/74, 74, 74/28		60	200
2005	— — trefoils at neck; *mm*. sun		85	275
2006	— — no marks at neck; *mm*. sun		135	475
2007	— Without B, quatrefoils at neck; *mm*. sun		135	475

Bristol is variously rendered as BRESTOLL, BRISTOLL, BRESTOW, BRISTOW.

2008	*Coventry*. C on breast, quatrefoils at neck, COVETRE; *mm*. 28/33, 28...	150	450
2009	— — Local dies, similar; *mm*. rose	150	475
2010	— — — as last, but no C or quatrefoils	150	475
2011	Norwich. n on breast, quatrefoils at neck, nORWIC or nORVIC, *mm*. 28/33, 28	130	350
2012	*York*. Є on breast, quatrefoils at neck, ЄBORACI; *mm*. 28, 105/74, 105, 105/28	60	185
2013	— Similar, but without Є on breast, *mm*. lis	75	250
2014	— Є on breast, trefoils at neck; *mm*. 105/28, 105	65	200
2015	**Halfgroat.** *London*. Annulets by neck (heavy dies); *mm*. 33	200	575

2016

2016	— Quatrefoils by neck; *mm*. 33/-, 28/-, 74, 74/28	50	150
2017	— Saltires by neck; *mm*. 74, 74/28	60	180
2018	— Trefoils by neck; *mm*. 74, 74/28, 11/28	60	180
2019	— No marks by neck; *mm*. 11/28	90	275

		F	VF
		£	£
2020	*Bristol.* Saltires or crosses by neck; *mm.* 33/28, 28, 74, 74/-	135	400
2021	— Quatrefoils by neck; *mm.* 28/-, 74, 74/-	125	350
2022	— Trefoils by neck; *mm.* crown	135	400
2023	— No marks by neck; *mm.* 74/28	150	450
2024	*Canterbury,* Archb. Bourchier (1464-7). Knot below bust; quatrefoils by neck; *mm.* 99/-, 99, 99/33, 99/28	40	135
2025	— — — quatrefoils omitted *mm.* 99	35	125
2026	— — — saltires by neck; *mm.* 99/-, 99/28	40	135
2026A	— — — trefoils by neck; *mm.* 99	45	150
2027	— — — wedges by hair and/or neck; *mm.* 99, 99/–, 99/33, 99/28	40	135
2028	— — As 2024 or 2025, but no knot	40	135
2029	— (1467-9). Quatrefoils by neck; *mm.* 74, 74/-	40	130
2030	— — Saltires by neck; *mm.* 74/-, 74	40	130
2031	— — Trefoils by neck; *mm.* 74, 74/-, 74/28, 33	35	125
2032	— No marks by neck; *mm.* sun	65	200
2033	*Coventry.* Crosses by neck; *mm.* sun	475	1250
2034	*Norwich.* Quatrefoils or saltires by neck; *mm.* sun	450	1250

2035   2063

2035	*York.* Quatrefoils by neck; *mm.* sun, lis, lis/-	60	175
2036	— Saltires by neck; *mm.* lis	60	170
2037	— Trefoils by neck; *mm.* lis, lis/-	65	185
2038	— Є on breast, quatrefoils by neck; *mm.* lis/-	65	185
2039	**Penny** (12 grs.), *London.* Annulets by neck (heavy dies); *mm.* rose	150	450
2040	— Quatrefoils by neck; *mm.* 74, sun. crown	45	125
2041	— Trefoil and quatrefoil by neck; *mm.* crown	45	125
2042	— Saltires by neck; *mm.* crown	45	125
2043	— Trefoils by neck; *mm.* crown, long cross fitchée	50	140
2044	— No marks by neck; *mm.* long cross fitchée	100	325
2045	*Bristol.* Crosses, quatrefoils or saltires by neck, BRISTOW; *mm.* crown	125	375
2046	— Quatrefoils by neck; BRI(trefoil)STOLL	125	375
2047	— Trefoil to r. of neck BRISTOLL	135	400
2048	*Canterbury,* Archb. Bourchier. Quatrefoils or saltires by neck, knot on breast; *mm.* pall	60	160
2049	— — Similar, but no marks by neck	60	160
2050	— — As 2048, but no knot	65	175
2051	— — Crosses by neck, no knot	65	175
2052	— Quatrefoils by neck; *mm.* crown	125	375
2053	— King's Receiver (1462-4). Local dies, mostly with rose in centre of rev.; *mm.* 7a, 33	25	75
2054	— *Durham,* Bp. Lawrence Booth (1465-70). B and D by neck, B on *rev.; mm.* 33	35	125
2055	— — Quatrefoil and B by neck; *mm.* sun	30	110
2056	— — B and quatrefoil by neck; *mm.* crown	35	125
2057	— — D and quatrefoil by neck; *mm.* crown	35	125
2058	— — Quatrefoils by neck; *mm.* crown	30	110
2059	— — Trefoils by neck; *mm.* crown	30	110
2060	— Lis by neck; *mm.* crown	30	110

		F	VF
		£	£
2061	*York,* Sede Vacante (1464-5). Quatrefoils at neck, no quatrefoil in centre of *rev.; mm.* sun, rose	35	135
2062	— Archb. Neville (1465-70). Local dies, G and key by neck, quatrefoil on *rev.; mm.* sun, plain cross	25	100
2063	— — London-made dies, similar; *mm.* 28, 105, 11	30	135
2064	— — Similar, but no marks by neck; *mm.* large lis	35	135
2065	— — — Quatrefoils by neck; *mm.* large lis	35	135
2066	— — — Trefoils by neck; *mm.* large lis	30	125

2068   2077

		F	VF
2067	**Halfpenny,** *London.* Saltires by neck; *mm.* 34, 28, 74	25	85
2068	— Trefoils by neck; *mm.* 28, 74, 11	25	85
2069	— No marks by neck; *mm.* 11	30	115
2070	*Bristol.* Crosses by neck; *mm.* crown	85	250
2071	— Trefoils by neck; *mm.* crown	75	225
2072	*Canterbury.* Archb. Bourchier. No marks; *mm.* pall	60	150
2072A	— — — Trefoils by neck, *mm.* pall	60	150
2073	— Saltires by neck; *mm.* crown	55	135
2074	— — Trefoils by neck; *mm.* crown	50	130
2074A	*Norwich.* Quatrefoils by neck., *mm.* Sun	225	600
2075	*York.* Royal mint. Saltires by neck; *mm.* lis/-, sun/-	45	125
2076	— — Trefoils by neck; *mm.* lis/-	40	110
2077	**Farthing,** *London.* ЄDWARD DI GRA RЄX, trefoils by neck, *mm.* crown	225	675

Full flan coins are difficult to find in the smaller denominations.

For further information see:
Halfpennies and Farthings of Edward IV to Henry VII. *Paul and Bente R. Withers, 2004.*

The coinage of this short restoration follows closely that of the previous reign. Only angel gold was issued, the ryal being discontinued. Many of the coins have the king's name reading hЄnRICV – another distinguishing feature is an R that looks like a B.

Mintmarks

Cross pattée (6)   Rose (33, Bristol)
Restoration cross (13)   Lis (105)
Trefoil (44 and 45)   Short cross fitchée (12)

GOLD

2078

		F	VF
		£	£
2078	**Angel**, *London*. As illus. but no B; *mm*. -/6, 13, -/105, none	1250	3000
2079	*Bristol*. B in waves; *mm*. -/13, none	1500	4750
2080	**Half-angel**, *London*. As 2078; *mm*. -/6, -/13, -/105	1500	5000
2081	*Bristol*. B in waves; *mm*. -/13	2250	6750

SILVER

2082   2084

2082	**Groat**, *London*. Usual type; *mm*. 6, 6/13, 6/105, 13, 13/6, 13/105, 13 /12	165	475
2083	*Bristol*. B on breast; *mm*. 13, 13/33, 13/44, 44, 44/13, 44/33, 44/12	325	900
2084	*York*. Є on breast; *mm*. lis, lis/sun	175	525
2085	**Halfgroat**, *London*. As 2082; *mm*. 13, 13/-	225	650
2086	*York*. Є on breast; *mm*. lis	275	750
2087	**Penny**, *London*. Usual type; *mm*. 6, 13, 12	175	575
2087A	*Bristol*. Similar; *mm*. 12	325	900
2088	*York*. G and key by neck; *mm*. lis	175	525
2089	**Halfpenny**, *London*. As 2087; *mm*. 12, 13,	125	325
2090	*Bristol*. Similar; *mm*. cross	200	575

The Angel and its half were the only gold denominations issued during this reign. The main types and weight standards remained the same as those of the light coinage of Edward's first reign. The use of the 'initial mark' as a mintmark to denote the date of issue was now firmly established.

Mintmarks

| 33 | 105 | 12 | 55 | 44 | 55 | 28 | 56 | 17 |

| 30 | 37 | 6 | 18 | 19 | 20 | 31 | 11 | 38 |

1471-83	Rose (33, *York & Durham*)	1473-7	Cross pattée (6)
	Lis (105, *York*)		Pierced cross 1 (18)
1471	Short cross fitchee (12)	1477-80	Pierced cross and
1471-2	Annulet (large, 55)		pellet (19)
	Trefoil (44)		Pierced cross 2 (18)
	Rose (33, *Bristol*)		Pierced cross, central
1471-3	Pansy (30, *Durham*)		pellet (20)
1472-3	Annulet (small, 55)		Rose (33, *Canterbury*)
	Sun (28, *Bristol*)	1480-3	Heraldic cinquefoil (31)
1473-7	Pellet in annulet (56)		Long cross fitchee
	Cross and four pellets (17)		(11, *Canterbury*)
	Cross in circle (37)	1483	Halved sun and rose (38)
			(Listed under Ed. IV/V.)

GOLD

2091   2093

		F	VF
		£	£
2091	**Angel.** *London*. Type as illus.; *mm.* 12, 55, 56, 17, 18, 19, 31	525	1250
2092	*Bristol*. B in waves; *mm.* small annulet	1750	5000
2093	**Half-angel.** As illus.; *mm.* 55, cross in circle, 19, 20/19, 31	525	1200
2094	King's name and title on rev.; *mm.* 12/-	575	1350
2095	King's name and the title both sides; *mm.* 55/-	625	1500

SILVER

2097

		F	VF
		£	£
2096	**Groat,** *London.* Trefoils on cusps, no marks by bust; *mm.* 12-37	60	175
2097	— — roses by bust; *mm.* pellet in annulet..................................	90	325
2098	— Fleurs on cusps; no marks by bust; *mm.* 18-20..............................	60	175
2099	— — pellets by bust; *mm.* pierced cross	85	275
2100	— — rose on breast; *mm.* 31	60	175

2101   2107

2101	*Bristol.* B on breast no marks by bust; *mm.* 33, 33/55, 28/55, 55, 55/-, 28	175	475
2102	*York.* Є on breast no marks by bust; *mm.* lis...	135	375
2103	**Halfgroat,** *London.* As 2096; *mm.* 12-31	45	135
2104	*Bristol.* B on breast; *mm.* 33/12	200	625
2105	*Canterbury.* Archb. Bourchier. As 2103; *mm.* 33, 11, 11/31, 31	40	135
2106	— C on breast; *mm.* rose	35	125
2107	— — R. C in centre; *mm.* rose	35	125
2108	— — R. Rose in centre; *mm.* rose	35	125
2109	*York.* No. Є on breast; *mm.* lis	100	275
2110	**Penny,** *London.* No marks by bust; *mm.* 12-31	35	125
2111	*Bristol.* Similar; *mm.* rose	150	475
2112	*Canterbury.* Archb. Bourchier. Similar; *mm.* 33, 11	45	150
2113	— C on breast; *mm.* rose	70	200
2114	*Durham,* Bp. Booth (1471-6). No marks by neck; *mm.* 12, 44	25	95

2115   2116

2115	— — D in centre of *rev.;* B and trefoil by neck; *mm.* 44, 33, 56..............	25	100
2116	— — — two lis at neck; *mm.* rose	30	110
2117	— — — crosses over crown, and on breast; *mm.* rose...............................	30	100
2118	— — — crosses over crown, V under CIVI; *mm.* rose, pansy....................	30	100
2119	— — — B to l. of crown, V on breast and under CIVI............................	25	95

		F £	VF £
2120	— — — As last but crosses at shoulders	25	100
2121	— — R. D in centre; *mm.* rose	30	110
2122	— Bp. Dudley (1476-83). V to r. of neck; as last	30	100

2123   2125   2131

2123	— — D and V by neck; as last, but *mm.* 31	25	95

Nos. 2117-2123 are from locally-made dies.

2124	*York,* Archb. Neville (1471-2). Quatrefoils by neck. R. Quatrefoil; *mm.* 12 (over lis)	40	125
2125	— — Similar, but G and key by neck; *mm.* 12 (over lis)	25	90
2126	— Neville suspended (1472-5). As last, but no quatrefoil in centre of *rev.*	35	110
2126A	— — no marks by bust, similar; *mm.* annulet	40	125
2127	— — No marks by neck, quatrefoil on *rev.; mm.* 55, cross in circle, 33..	25	85
2128	— — Similar but Є and rose by neck; *mm.* rose	25	85
2129	— Archb. Neville restored (1475-6). As last, but G and rose	30	100
2130	— — Similar, but G and key by bust	25	85
2131	— Sede Vacante (1476). As 2127, but rose on breast; *mm.* rose	30	100
2132	— Archb. Lawrence Booth (1476-80). B and key by bust, quatrefoil on *rev.; mm.* 33, 31	25	85
2133	— Sede Vacante (1480). Similar, but no quatrefoil on rev.; *mm.* rose	30	100

2134   2140

2134	— Archb. Rotherham (1480-3). T and slanting key by neck, quatrefoil on *rev.; mm.* 33	25	90
2135	— — — Similar, but star on breast	40	100
2136	— — — Star on breast and to r. of crown	45	125
2137	**Halfpenny,** *London.* No marks by neck; *mm.* 12-31	30	90
2138	— Pellets at neck; *mm.* pierced cross	35	100
2139	*Canterbury* (Archbishop Bourchier). C on breast and in centre of *rev.; mm.* rose	65	175
2140	— C on breast only; *mm.* rose	60	160
2141	— Without C either side; *mm.* 11	60	160
2142	*Durham,* Bp. Booth. No marks by neck. R. DЄRA̅ M, D in centre; *mm.* rose	135	375
2142A	— — Lis either side of neck. R. with or without D in centre	140	400
2142B	— — B to l. of crown, crosses at shoulders. R. with or withoutD. in centre; *mm.* rose	140	400
2143	— — — Bp. Dudley V to l. of neck; as last	135	375

Full flan coins are very difficult to find in the small denominations.

On 12th February, 1483, the prolific cinquefoil coinage of Edward IV came to an end and an indenture between the king and the new master of the mint, Bartholomew Reed, saw the introduction of the sun and rose mintmark.

Edward IV died on 9th April, 1483, but the sun and rose coinage continued, essentially unaltered, through the short reign of Edward V and into the reign of Richard III, ending with the indenture of 20th July, 1483, with Robert Brackenbury, who had been Richard's ducal treasurer, and the introduction of the boar's head mintmark.

New dies prepared after the accession of Richard III on 26th June, 1483, bear his name but coins of the sun and rose coinage struck under Edward IV and Edward V can only be distinguished by arranging the dies in sequence. This is possible for the angels (Schneider Sylloge, SCBI 47, p.41) but has not yet been achieved for the silver coinage.

Mintmark: Halved sun and rose.

GOLD

2144A

		F	*VF*
		£	£
2144	**Angel.** Type As 2091, reading EDWARD DEI GRA (Edward IV).........	2250	6250
2144A	— Similar but reading EDWARD DI GRA (Edward V)........................	6500	18500
2145	**Half-angel.** As 2093 (probably Edward IV)	2500	6750

SILVER

2146   2146A

2146	**Groat.** *London,* pellet below bust, reading EDWARD or EDVARD.......	800	2500
2146A	— — No pellet below, reading EDWARD or EDWRD..........................	750	2400
2147	**Penny.** *London* As 2110	900	3250
2148	**Halfpenny.** *London* As 2137..	225	575

Richard's ruthless seizure of the crown left a core of bitter opposition which coalesced around Henry Tudor, earl of Richmond who had found asylum in Brittany. At Bosworth on 22 August, 1485, Richard was killed on the battlefield and the War of the Roses ended.

Richard's coinage follows the pattern of previous reigns. The portrait on the silver denominations remains stylised, though increasingly distinctive. It can be divided into three types according to mintmark. Type 1, the first sun and rose coinage, lasted 24 days to 20th July 1483. Type 2, the boar's head coinage, was issued until about June 1484. Type 3, the second sun and rose coinage, was struck until the end of the reign (Schneider Sylloge, SCBI 47, pp. 41-2).

It is evident that coin dies were stored in a 'loose-box' system which led to extensive muling between types. As an interim measure, after the indenture of 20th July, 1483, at least eleven existing sun and rose obverse dies, both gold and silver, were overpunched with the boar's head mark. The seven overpunched groat dies included four Edward IV/V dies, then still in use, and three dies of Richard III type 1.

Mintmarks

SR1   BH1   BH2   SR2   SR3   105   33

Halved sun and rose, 1, 2 and 3.
Boar's head, 1 (62) 2 (63).
Lis (105, *Durham*)
Rose only (33).

GOLD

![2150 and 2152 gold coins]

2150   2152

		F	VF
		£	£
2149	**Angel.** 1. Reading RICARD. R. R and rose by mast; *mm.* sun and rose 1	2250	6250
2150	— 2a. Reading EDWARD. R. E and rose or R and rose by mast; *mm.* boar's head 1 over sun and rose 1/sun and rose 1	5250	13500
2151	— 2b. Reading RICARD. R. R and rose by mast; mm. boar's head 1 over sun and rose 1/sun and rose 1, boar's head 1, boar's head 2 (often muled)	1850	5250
2152	— 3. Reading RICARD or RICAD; *mm.* sun and rose 2	1750	5000

2153

2153	**Half-angel.** 2b. R. R and rose by mast; *mm.* boar's head 1	3500	10500

SILVER

2154   2155

		F £	VF £
2154	**Groat.** *London.* Reading RICARD 1. *mm.* sun and rose 1	550	1450
2155	— 2a. Reading EDWARD; *mm.* boar's head 1 over sun and rose 1/sun and rose 1	1350	3250

2156 - BH2   2158 - SR3

2156	— 2b. Reading RICARD; *mm.* boar's head 1 over sun and rose 1/sun and rose 1, boar's head 1, boar's head 2 (often muled)	625	1650
2157	— 3. *mm.* sun and rose 2, sun and rose 3	550	1450
2158	— — Pellet below bust, *mm.* sun and rose 2, sun and rose 3	575	1500
2159	*York.* 3. *mm.* sun and rose 2/-	1250	3250

2161   2164   2166

2160	**Halfgroat.** *London.* 2a. Reading EDWARD; *mm.* boar's head 1 over sun and rose 1/- (the *mm.* is indistinct)	1750	5250
2161	— 2b. Reading RICARD; *mm.* boar's head 2/-	1500	4500
2162	— 3. *mm.* sun and rose 2, sun and rose 2/-	875	2500
2163	— — Pellet below bust; *mm.* sun and rose 2..	925	2650
2164	**Penny.** *London.* 2a. Reading EDWARD; *mm.* boar's head 1 over sun and rose 1/-	1250	3500
2165	— 2b. Reading RICARD; *mm.* boar's head 1/-.......................................	1100	3250
2166	*York.* Archb. Rotherham. T and upright key at neck. R. Quatrefoil in centre; *mm.* boar's head 1/-	275	800
2167	— — *mm.* rose/-	250	750
2168	— No marks at neck; *mm.* sun and rose 2/-	275	800

2169   2171

2169	*Durham.* Bp. Sherwood. S on breast. R. D in centre; *mm.* lis/-...............	225	600
2170	**Halfpenny.** *London.* 2b. No marks by neck; *mm.* boar's head 1/-	225	675
2171	— 3. *mm.* sun and rose 2/-	200	575
2171A	**Farthing.** *London.* 3. *mm.* sun and rose 2/-...	950	2500

THE HOUSE OF TUDOR, 1485-1603

HENRY VII, 1485-1509

For the first four years of his reign Henry's coins differ only in name and mintmark from those of his predecessors, but from 1489 radical changes were made in the coinage. On the Groat and subsequently on the lesser denominations the tradional open crown was replaced with an arched imperial crown. Though the pound sterling had been a denomination of account for centuries, a pound coin had never been minted. Now a magnificent gold pound was issued, and, from the design of the king enthroned in majesty, was called a 'Sovereign'. A small simplified version of the Sovereign portrait was at the same time introduced on the silver pence. The reverse of the gold 'Sovereign' had the royal arms set in the centre of a Tudor rose. A few years later the angel was restyled and St. Michael, who is depicted about to thrust Satan into the Pit with a cross-topped lance, is no longer a feathered figure but is clad in armour of Renaissance style. A gold ryal of ten shillings was also minted again for a brief period.

The other major innovation was the introduction of the shilling in the opening years of the 16th century. It is remarkable for the very fine profile portrait of the king which replaces the representational image of a monarch that had served on the coinage for the past couple of centuries. This new portrait was also used on groats and halfgroats but not on the smaller denominations.

Mintmarks

| 39 | 41 | 40 | 42 | 33 | 11 | 7a | 123 |

| 105 | 76b | 31 | 78 | 30 | 91 | 43 | 57 |

| 85 | 94 | 118 | 21 | 33 | 53 |

1485-7	Halved sun and rose (39)	1495-8	Pansy (30)
	Lis upon sun and rose (41)		Tun (123, *Canterbury*)
	Lis upon half rose (40)		Lis (105, York)
	Lis-rose dimidiated (42)	1498-9	Crowned leopard's head (91)
	Rose (33, *York*)		Lis issuant from rose (43)
1487	Lis (105)		Tun (123, *Canterbury*)
	Cross fitchée (11)	1499-1502	Anchor (57)
1487-8	Rose (33)	1502-4	Greyhound's head (85)
	Plain cross (7a, *Durham*)		Lis (105, profile issue only)
1488-9	No marks		Martlet (94, *York*)
1489-93	Cinquefoil (31)	1504-5	Cross-crosslet (21)
	Crozier (76b, *Durham*)	1504-9	Martlet (94, (*York, Canterbury*)
1492	Cross fitchée (11, gold only)		Rose (33, *York* and
1493-5	Escallop (78)		*Canterbury*)
	Dragon (118, gold only)	1505-9	Pheon (53)
	Lis (105, *Canterbury and York*		
	Tun (123, *Canterbury*)		

GOLD

	F £	VF £
2172 **Sovereign** (20s; wt. 240 gr.). Group I. Large figure of king sitting on backless throne. R. Large shield crowned on large Tudor rose. *mm*. 31 ..	42500	150000
2173 — Group II. Somewhat similar but throne has narrow back, lis in background. R. Large Tudor rose bearing small shield. *mm*. -/11	27500	92500

2174

2174 — III. King on high-backed very ornamental throne, with greyhound and dragon on side pillars. R. Shield on Tudor rose; *mm*. dragon	16500	52500
2175 — IV. Similar but throne with high canopy breaking legend and broad seat, *mm*. 105/118, (also with no *obv*. i.c. *mm*. 105/118, very rare)	15000	45000
2176 — Narrow throne with a portcullis below the king's feet (like Henry VIII); *mm*. 105/21, 105/53	13500	40000
2177 **Double-sovereign** and **Treble-sovereign** from same dies as 2176. These piedforts were probably intended as presentation pieces *mm*. 105/21, 105/53	52500	185000

2178

2178 **Ryal** (10s.). As illustration: *mm*. -/11	13500	45000
2179 **Angel** (6s. 8d). I. Angel of old type with one foot on dragon. R. PЄR CRVCЄM. etc., *mm*. 39, 40, (also muled both ways)	1250	3250
2179A — With Irish title, and legend over angel head. *mm*. 33/-	1350	3500
2180 — — Name altered from RICARD? and h on *rev*. from R. *mm*. 41/39, 41/40, 41/-, 39/?	1500	3750

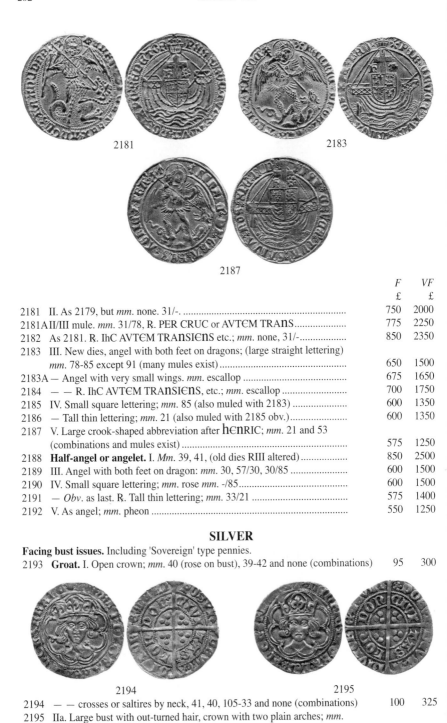

2181   2183

2187

		F	VF
		£	£
2181	II. As 2179, but *mm.* none. 31/-.	750	2000
2181A	II/III mule. *mm.* 31/78, R. PER CRUC or AVTEM TRANS	775	2250
2182	As 2181. R. IhC AVTEM TRANSIENS etc.; *mm.* none, 31/-	850	2350
2183	III. New dies, angel with both feet on dragons; (large straight lettering) *mm.* 78-85 except 91 (many mules exist)	650	1500
2183A	— Angel with very small wings. *mm.* escallop	675	1650
2184	— — R. IhC AVTEM TRANSIENS, etc.; *mm.* escallop	700	1750
2185	IV. Small square lettering; *mm.* 85 (also muled with 2183)	600	1350
2186	— Tall thin lettering; *mm.* 21 (also muled with 2185 obv.)	600	1350
2187	V. Large crook-shaped abbreviation after hENRIC; *mm.* 21 and 53 (combinations and mules exist)	575	1250
2188	**Half-angel or angelet.** I. *Mm.* 39, 41, (old dies RIII altered)	850	2500
2189	III. Angel with both feet on dragon: *mm.* 30, 57/30, 30/85	600	1500
2190	IV. Small square lettering; *mm.* rose *mm.* -/85	600	1500
2191	— *Obv.* as last. R. Tall thin lettering; *mm.* 33/21	575	1400
2192	V. As angel; *mm.* pheon	550	1250

SILVER

Facing bust issues. Including 'Sovereign' type pennies.

2193	**Groat.** I. Open crown; *mm.* 40 (rose on bust), 39-42 and none (combinations)	95	300

2194   2195

2194	— — crosses or saltires by neck, 41, 40, 105-33 and none (combinations)	100	325
2195	IIa. Large bust with out-turned hair, crown with two plain arches; *mm.* none, 31, 31/-, 31/78	75	225

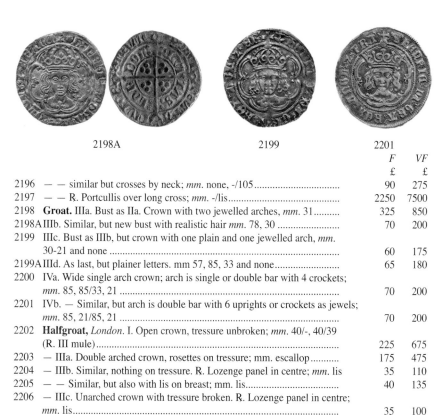

	2198A	2199	2201	

		F	VF
		£	£
2196	— — similar but crosses by neck; *mm.* none, -/105...............................	90	275
2197	— — R. Portcullis over long cross; *mm.* -/lis..	2250	7500
2198	**Groat.** IIIa. Bust as IIa. Crown with two jewelled arches, *mm.* 31..........	325	850
2198A	IIIb. Similar, but new bust with realistic hair *mm.* 78, 30	70	200
2199	IIIc. Bust as IIIb, but crown with one plain and one jewelled arch, *mm.* 30-21 and none	60	175
2199A	IIId. As last, but plainer letters. mm 57, 85, 33 and none......................	65	180
2200	IVa. Wide single arch crown; arch is single or double bar with 4 crockets; *mm.* 85, 85/33, 21	70	200
2201	IVb. — Similar, but arch is double bar with 6 uprights or crockets as jewels; *mm.* 85, 21/85, 21	70	200
2202	**Halfgroat,** *London.* I. Open crown, tressure unbroken; *mm.* 40/-, 40/39 (R. III mule)..	225	675
2203	— IIIa. Double arched crown, rosettes on tressure; mm. escallop...........	175	475
2204	— IIIb. Similar, nothing on tressure. R. Lozenge panel in centre; *mm.* lis	35	110
2205	— — Similar, but also with lis on breast; mm. lis....................................	40	135
2206	— IIIc. Unarched crown with tressure broken. R. Lozenge panel in centre; *mm.* lis..	35	100
2206A	— — — Similar but smaller dies and much smaller lettering	35	110

2211

2207	*Canterbury,* Archb. Morton. I. Open crown, crosses by neck. R. M in centre; *mm.* tun/-..	40	135
2208	— — II. Similar, but double-arched crown; no *mm.*	40	135
2209	III King and Archb. jointly. As last but without M ; (a) early lettering, trefoil stops; *mm.* lis, tun and lis/lis	35	110
2210	— — (b) ornate lettering, rosette stops; *mm.* tun, lis in combinations.....	30	100
2211	— — (c) — saltire or no stops; *mm.* 123, 123 & 30/123	30	100
2212	*York,* Royal mint. (a) Double-arched crown, lis on breast (rarely omitted). R. Lozenge panel in centre; *mm.* lis...	40	125
2213	— — (b) Similar, but unarched crown, tressure broken, *mm.* lis.	35	110

		F	*VF*
		£	£
2214	— Archb. Savage. (a) Double-arched crown, keys at neck, no tressure; ornate lettering; *mm.* martlet	30	110
2215	— — (b) Similar, but fleured tressure, small square lettering; *mm.* martlet	35	110
2216	— — (c) As last, but tall thin lettering; *mm.* martlet	35	110
2217	— As last but no keys; *mm.* martlet	45	135

2221   2226

		F	*VF*
2218	**Penny.** Old type. London; *mm.* 40/-	150	457
2219	— — — crosses by bust, mm. small cross (obv.)	175	500
2220	— *Canterbury,* Archb. Morton. Open crown, *mm.* tun/- R. M in centre .	200	525
2221	— — King and Archb. jointly, arched crown; *mm.* tun, tun/-	60	175
2222	— *Durham,* Bp. Sherwood. S on breast. R. D in centre; *mm.* 7a/-	50	150
2223	— *York,* Archb. Rotherham. With or without cross on breast, *mm.* 33/-, T and cross or key at neck. R. h in centre	35	125
2224	— — — T and trefoil at neck. R. Quatrefoil in centre and two extra pellets; *mm.* 39/-	35	125
2225	'Sovereign' type. *London.* Early lettering, no stops, no pillars to throne; no *mm.*	90	275
2226	— — — single pillar on king's right side, trefoil stops; no *mm.* or 31/-..	40	120
2227	— — Ornate letters, rosette stops, single pillar; *mm.* lis (can be muled with above)	50	135
2228	— — saltire stops or none, two pillars; *mm.* none, -/30	40	120
2229	— — Similar, but small square lettering; no *mm.*	40	120
2230	— — Similar, but lettering as profile groats two double pillars; *mm.* 21, 53, none (sometimes on one side only)	35	110

2231   2233   2235

		F	*VF*
2231	— *Durham,* Bp. Sherwood. Crozier to r. of king, throne with one pillar. R. D and S beside shield	35	110
2232	— — Throne with two pillars, no crozier. R. As last	40	125
2233	— — Bp. Fox. Throne with one pillar. R. Mitre above shield, RD or DR at sides, no *mm.*	30	90
2234	— — Similar, but two pillars	35	95

	F £	VF £
2235 *York,* Archb. Rotherham. Keys below shield; early lettering, trefoil stops, no pillars to throne, no *mm.*	30	90
2236 — — single pillar	30	90
2237 — — — ornate lettering, rosette or no stops,	30	90
2238 — — two pillars sometimes with crosses between legs of throne	30	90

2239   2244A   2245

	F £	VF £
2239 **Halfpenny,** *London.* I. Open crown; *mm.* 40, 42	35	120
2240 — — trefoils at neck; no *mm.,* rose	40	125
2241 — — crosses at neck; *mm.* rose, cross fitchée	35	120
2242 — II. Double arched crown; *mm.* cinquefoil, none	30	80
2243 — — saltires at neck; no *mm.*	30	80
2244 — IIIa. Crown with single arch, ornate lettering; no *mm.,* pansy	25	70
2244A — IIIb. Similar but with rosette stops; *mm.* none, rose, lis	30	90
2245 — IIIc. Much smaller portrait; *mm.* pheon, lis, none	25	70
2246 *Canterbury,* Archb. Morton. I. Open crown, crosses by neck; R. M in centre	65	200
2247 — — II. Similar, but arched crown, saltires by bust; *mm.* profile eye (82)	60	175
2247A — — — no marks at neck	50	165
2248 — III. King and Archb. Arched crown; *mm.* lis, none	40	110

2249   2250

	F £	VF £
2249 *York,* Archb. Savage. Arched crown, key below bust to l or r. *mm.* martlet	45	135
2250 **Farthing,** *London.* hЄNRIC DI GRA RЄX (A), arched crown	275	850

*No.s 2239-49 have *mm.* on *obv.* only.

Profile issue

	F £	VF £
2251 Testoon (ls.). Type as groat. hЄNRIC (VS); *mm.* lis	11000	20000
2252 — hЄNRIC VII; *mm.* lis	11500	21000

2253

	F £	VF £
2253 — hЄNRIC SЄPTIM; *mm.* lis	12000	22500

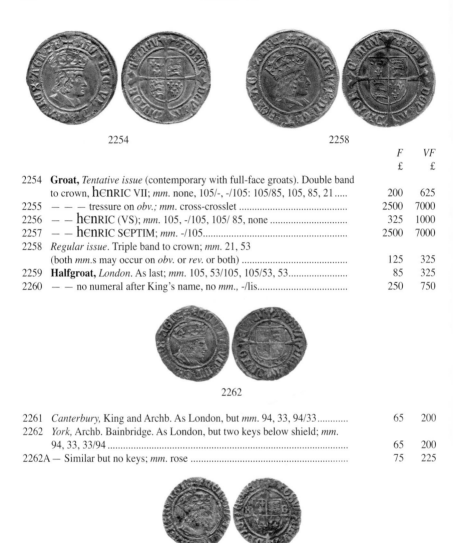

2254   2258

		F £	VF £
2254	**Groat,** *Tentative issue* (contemporary with full-face groats). Double band to crown, hЄnRIC VII; *mm.* none, 105/-, -/105: 105/85, 105, 85, 21	200	625
2255	— — — tressure on *obv.; mm.* cross-crosslet	2500	7000
2256	— — hЄnRIC (VS); *mm.* 105, -/105, 105/ 85, none	325	1000
2257	— — hЄnRIC SЄPTIM; *mm.* -/105..	2500	7000
2258	*Regular issue.* Triple band to crown; *mm.* 21, 53 (both *mm.*s may occur on *obv.* or *rev.* or both)	125	325
2259	**Halfgroat,** *London.* As last; *mm.* 105, 53/105, 105/53, 53......................	85	325
2260	— — no numeral after King's name, no *mm.*, -/lis...................................	250	750

2262

2261	*Canterbury,* King and Archb. As London, but *mm.* 94, 33, 94/33	65	200
2262	*York,* Archb. Bainbridge. As London, but two keys below shield; *mm.* 94, 33, 33/94	65	200
2262A	— Similar but no keys; *mm.* rose	75	225

2263

2263	— — XB beside shield; *mm.* rose/martlet..	200	575
2263A	— — Similar but two keys below shield *mm.* rose(?)/martlet	225	625

Henry VIII is held in ill-regard by numismatists as being the author of the debasement of England's gold and silver coinage; but there were also other important numismatic innovations during his reign. For the first sixteen years the coinage closely followed the pattern of the previous issues, even to the extent of retaining the portrait of Henry VII on the larger silver coins.

In 1526, in an effort to prevent the drain of gold to continental Europe, the value of English gold was increased by 10%, the sovereign to 22s. 0d. and the angel to 7s. 4d., and a new coin valued at 4s. 6d.—the Crown of the Rose—was introduced as a competitor to the French *écu au soleil*. The new crown was not a success and within a few months it was replaced by the Crown of the Double Rose valued at 5s but made of gold of only 22 carat fineness, the first time gold had been minted below the standard 23c. At the same time the sovereign was again revalued to 22s. 6d. and the angel to 7s. 6d., with a new coin, the George Noble, valued at 6s. 8d. (one-third pound).

The royal cyphers on some of the gold crowns and half-crowns combine the initial of Henry with those of his queens: Katherine of Aragon, Anne Boleyn and Jane Seymour. The architect of this coinage reform was the chancellor, Cardinal Thomas Wolsey, who besides his other changes had minted at York a groat bearing his initials and cardinal's hat in addition to the other denominations normally authorized for the ecclesiastical mints.

When open debasement of the coinage began in 1544 to help finance Henry's wars, the right to coin of the archbishops of Canterbury and York and of the bishop of Durham was not confirmed. Instead, a second royal mint was opened in the Tower as in subsequent years were six others, at Southwark, York, Canterbury, Bristol, Dublin and Durham House in the Strand. Gold, which fell to 23c. in 1544, 22c. in 1545, and 20c. in 1546 was much less debased than silver which declined to 9oz 2dwt. in 1544, 6oz 2dwt. in 1545 and 4oz 2dwt. in 1546. At this last standard the blanched silver surface of the coins soon wore away to reveal the copper alloy beneath which earned for Henry the nickname 'Old Coppernose'.

Mintmarks

53	69	70	108	33	94	73	11
105	22	23	30	78	15	24	110
52	72a	44	8	65a	114	121	90
36	106	56	S	E	116	135

1509-26	Pheon (53)		1509-14	Martlet (94, *York*)
	Castle (69)		1509-23	Radiant star (22, *Durham & York*)
	Castle with H (70, gold)		1513-18	Crowned T (135, *Tournai*)
	Portcullis crowned (108)		1514-26	Star (23, *York & Durham*)
	Rose (33, *Canterbury*)			Pansy (30, *York*)
	Martlet (94, *Canterbury*)			Escallop (78, *York*)
	Pomegranate (73, but broader, *Cant.*)			Voided cross (15, *York*)
	Cross fitchée (11, *Cant.*)		1523-26	Spur rowel (24, *Durham*)
	Lis (105, *Canterbury, Durham*)			

1526-44	Rose (33)		1526-32	Cross patONCE (8, *Cant.*)

1526-44 Rose (33)
         Lis (105)
         Sunburst 110)
         Arrow (52)
         Pheon (53)
         Lis (106)
         Star (23, *Durham*)
1526-9 Crescent (72a, *Durham*)
         Trefoil (44 variety,
         Durham)
         Flower of eight petals and
         circle centre (*Durham*)
1526-30 Cross (7a, sometimes
         slightly voided, *York*)
         Acorn (65a, *York*)

1526-32 Cross patonce (8, *Cant.*)
         T (114, *Canterbury*)
         Uncertain mark (121,
         Canterbury)
1529-44 Radiant star (22, *Durham*)
1530-44 Key (90, *York*)
1533-44 Catherine wheel (36,
         Canterbury)
1544-7 Lis (105 and 106)
         Pellet in annulet (56)
         S (Southwark)
         Є or E (Southwark)
1546-7 WS monogram (116, *Bristol*)

GOLD

First coinage, 1509-26

2265

	F	VF
	£	£

2264 **Sovereign** (20s.). Similar to last sov. of Hen. VII; *mm.* 108 .... 7500 18500

2264A **Ryal** (10s.) King in ship holding sword and shield. R. Similar to 1950,
mm.-/108 .... *Extremely rare*

2265 **Angel** (6s. 8d.). As Hen. VIII, but hЄNRIC? VIII DI GRA RЄX, etc.; *mm.*
53, 69, 70, 70/69, 108, R. May omit h and rose, or rose only; *mm.* 69, 108   550 1250

2266 **Half-angel.** Similar (sometimes without VIII), *mm.* 69, 70, 108/33, 108   475 1100

Second coinage, 1526-44

2267

2267 **Sovereign** (22s. 6d.). As 2264, R. single or double tressure *mm.* 110, 105,
105/52 .... 6500 16500

2268 **Angel** (7s. 6d.). As 2265, hЄNRIC VIII D(I) G(RA) R(ЄX) etc,; *mm.*
110, 105 .... 725 2000

	F	VF
	£	£
2269 **Half-angel.** Similar; *mm.* lis...	750	2250

2270

2272

2270 **George-noble** (6s. 8d.). As illustration; *mm.* rose	6250	18500
2270A— Similar, but more modern ship with three masts, without initials hR. R. St. George brandishing sword behind head.	6750	20000
2271 **Half-George-noble.** Similar to 2270 *mm* rose, lis...............................	5500	15000
2272 **Crown of the rose** (4s. 6d., 23 c. 3 ¹/₂ gr.). As illustration; *mm.* rose, two legend varieties	3750	12500
2273 **Crown of the double-rose** (5s., 22 c). Double-rose crowned, hK (Henry and Katherine of Aragon) both crowned in field. R. Shield crowned; *mm.* rose	500	1100

2274

2285

2274 — hK both sides; *mm.* rose/lis, lis, arrow	475	1050
2275* — hK/hA or hA/hK; *mm.* arrow	900	2750
2276* — hR/hK or hI/hR; *mm.* arrow	700	1750
2277 — hA (Anne Boleyn); *mm.* arrow	975	3000
2278 — hA/hR; *mm.* arrow	900	2750
2279 — hI (Jane Seymour); *mm.* arrow	550	1250
2280* — hK/hI; *mm.* arrow	750	2000
2281 — hR/hI; *mm.* arrow..	725	1850
2282 — hR (Rex); *mm.* arrow...	550	1200
2283 — — *mm.* pheon	750	2000
2284 **Halfcrown**. Similar but king's name henric 8 on *rev.,* no initials; *mm.* rose	850	2500
2285 — hK uncrowned on *obv.; mm.* rose	475	1050
2286 — hK uncrowned both sides; *mm.* rose/lis, lis, arrow	475	1050
2287 — hI uncrowned both sides; *mm.* arrow	550	1350
2288 — hR uncrowned both sides; hIB RCX; *mm.* pheon	600	1500

*The hK initials may on later coins refer to Katherine Howard (Henry's fifth wife).

Third coinage, 1544-7

2291

		F £	*VF* £
2289	**Sovereign,** I (20s., Wt. 200 gr., 23 c.). As illustration but king with larger face and larger design; *mm.* lis..	16500	57500
2290	II (20s., wt. 200 or 192 grs., 23, 22 or 20 ct.). *Tower.* As illustration; *mm.* lis, pellet in annulet/lis	4000	10000
2291	— *Southwark.* Similar; *mm.* S, Є/S..	3750	9500
2292	— — Similar but Є below shield; *mm.* S/Є..	4250	10000
2293	— *Bristol.* As London but *mm.* WS/-...	5750	15000

2294

2294	**Half-sovereign** (wt. 100 or 96 gr.), *Tower.* As illus.; *mm.* lis, pellet in annulet..	750	2000
2295	— Similar, but with annulet on inner circle (either or both sides)........	800	2250
2296	*Southwark.* Mm. S	750	2000
2297	— Є below shield; *mm.* S, Є, S/Є, Є/S, (known without sceptre; *mm.* S)	700	1850
2298	*Bristol.* Lombardic lettering; *mm.* WS, WS/-.......................................	1250	3500
2299	**Angel** (8s., 23 c). Annulet by angel's head and on ship, hЄnRIC' 8; *mm.* lis	525	1250
2300	— Similar, but annulet one side only or none......................................	550	1350
2301	**Half-angel.** Annulet on ship; *mm.* lis...	500	1200
2302	— No annulet on ship; *mm.* lis..	525	1250

2303   2304

2303	— Three annulets on ship; *mm.* lis..	575	1350
2304	**Quarter-angel** Angel wears armour; *mm.* lis	500	1250

		F	VF
		£	£
2304A	— Angel wears tunic; *mm*. lis	525	1250
2305	**Crown**, *London*. Similar to 2283, but hɛnRIC' 8 ; Lombardic lettering;		
	mm . 56	575	1350
2306	— without RVTILAnS; *mm*. 56	600	1450
2307	— — — with annulet on inner circle	600	1450
2307A	— King's name omitted. DEI GRA both sides, *mm*. 56	675	1750
2308	— *Southwark*. As 2306; *mm*. S, ɛ, E/S, ɛ/-, E/ɛ	625	4500
2309	*Bristol.* hɛnRIC VIII. ROSA etc. R. D G, etc.; *mm*.-/WS	575	1350
2310	— Similar but hɛnRIC(VS) 8 R. DɛI) G(RA); *mm*. -/WS, WS	600	1400
2311	**Halfcrown**, *London*. Similar to 2288; *mm*. 56, 56/-	450	950
2312	— — with annulet on inner circle *mm*. 56	450	1000
2313	*Southwark*. As 2311; *mm*. S	475	1050
2314	— *O*. hɛnRIC 8 ROSA SINɛ SPIn. R. DɛI GRA, etc.; *mm*. ɛ	475	1050
2315	*Bristol*. *O*. RVTILAnS, etc. R. hɛnRIC 8; *mm*. WS/-	575	1350
	For other gold coins in Henry's name see page 221-2.		

SILVER

First coinage, 1509-26

| 2316 | 2322 |

2316	**Groat**. Portrait of Hen. VII. *London mm*. 53, 69, 108, 108 over 135 ..	125	375
2317	— *Tournai; mm*. crowned T. R. CIVITAS TORnACɛn*	525	1500
2318	**Halfgroat**. Portrait of Hen. VII. London; *mm*. 108, 108/-	125	425
2319	— *Canterbury*, Archb. Warham. POSVI *rev*.; *mm*. rose	135	450
2320	— — — WA above shield; *mm*. martlet	90	250
2321	— — — WA beside shield; *mm*. cross fitchee	90	250
2322	— — CIVITAS CAnTOR *rev.*, similar; *mm*. 73, 105, 11/105	70	200
2323	— *York*, POSVI *rev.*, Archb. Bainbridge (1508-14). Keys below shield;		
	mm. martlet	65	200
2324	— — — XB beside shield no keys; *mm*. martlet	80	225
2325	— — — Archb. Wolsey (1514-30). Keys and cardinal's hat below shield;		
	mm. 94, 22	175	525
2326	— — CIVITAS ɛBORACI *rev*. Similar; *mm*. 22, 23, 30, 78, 15, 15/78	65	175
2327	— — As last with TW beside shield; *mm*. voided cross	110	325
2327A	— *Tournai*. As 2317	575	1500

*Other non-portrait groats and half-groats exist of this mint, captured during an invasion of France
in 1513. (Restored to France in 1518.)

| | 2328 | 2334 | 2336 |

		F	VF
		£	£
2328	**Penny,** 'Sovereign' type, *London; mm.* 69, 108 /-, 108/108	50	125
2329	— *Canterbury.* WA above shield; *mm.* martlet	85	250
2330	— — — WA beside shield; *mm.* 73/-...	65	175
2331	— *Durham,* Bp. Ruthall (1509-23). TD above shield; *mm.* lis	35	90
2332	— — — TD beside shield; above or below horizontal line *mm.* lis, radiant star	35	90
2333	— — Bp. Wolsey (1523-9). DW beside shield, cardinal's hat below; *mm.* spur rowel	125	375
2334	**Halfpenny.** Facing bust, hЄnRIC DI GRA RЄX (AGL). *London; mm.* 69, 108/-........	20	75
2335	— *Canterbury.* WA beside bust; *mm.* 73/-, 11	50	150
2335A	— *York.* Key below bust, *mm.* star, escallop	70	200
2336	**Farthing.** *mm.* 108/-, hЄnRIC DI GRA RЄX, portcullis. R. CIVITAS LOnDON, rose in centre of long cross	225	600

Second coinage, 1526-44

| | 2337 | 2337D | 2337E |

		F	VF
2337	**Groat.** His own young portrait. *London;* Laker bust A, large renaissance-style bust, crown arch breaking inner circle. Roman/Roman lettering, roses in cross-ends; *mm.* rose	425	1350
2337A	— — Roman/Lombardic lettering, saltires in cross-ends; *mm.* rose....	225	750
2337B	— — Lombardic/Lombardic lettering, roses in cross-ends; *mm.* rose	275	900
2337C	— — Lombardic/Lombardic lettering, saltires in cross-ends; *mm.* rose	135	450
2337D	— Laker bust B, smaller face with pointed nose, crown arch does not break inner circle. Lombardic lettering; *mm.* rose..............................	90	325
2337E	— Laker bust D, larger squarer face with roman nose, fluffy hair, crown arch does not break inner circle. Lombardic lettering; *mm.* 33, 105, 110, 52, 53 (sometimes muled)	75	250
2338	— — with Irish title HIB; reads hЄnRIC 8; *mm.* 53, 105, 53/105, 105/53,	275	700
2339	— *York,* Archb. Wolsey. TW beside shield, cardinal's hat below; *mm.* voided cross, acorn, muled (both ways)...	90	325
2340	— — — omits TW; *mm.* voided cross	300	850

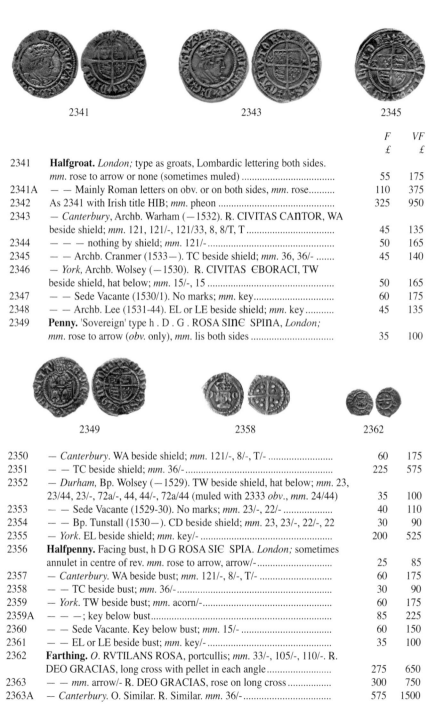

	2341	2343	2345

		F	VF
		£	£
2341	**Halfgroat.** *London;* type as groats, Lombardic lettering both sides. mm. rose to arrow or none (sometimes muled)	55	175
2341A	— — Mainly Roman letters on obv. or on both sides, *mm.* rose	110	375
2342	As 2341 with Irish title HIB; *mm.* pheon	325	950
2343	— *Canterbury,* Archb. Warham (—1532). R. CIVITAS CAПTOR, WA beside shield; *mm.* 121, 121/-, 121/33, 8, 8/T, T	45	135
2344	— — — nothing by shield; *mm.* 121/-	50	165
2345	— — Archb. Cranmer (1533—). TC beside shield; *mm.* 36, 36/-	45	140
2346	— *York,* Archb. Wolsey (—1530). R. CIVITAS ЄBORACI, TW beside shield, hat below; *mm.* 15/-, 15	50	165
2347	— — Sede Vacante (1530/1). No marks; *mm.* key	60	175
2348	— — Archb. Lee (1531-44). EL or LE beside shield; *mm.* key	45	135
2349	**Penny.** 'Sovereign' type h . D . G . ROSA SIПЄ SPIПA, *London;* *mm.* rose to arrow (*obv.* only), *mm.* lis both sides	35	100

	2349	2358	2362

2350	— *Canterbury.* WA beside shield; *mm.* 121/-, 8/-, T/-	60	175
2351	— — TC beside shield; *mm.* 36/-	225	575
2352	— *Durham,* Bp. Wolsey (—1529). TW beside shield, hat below; *mm.* 23, 23/44, 23/-, 72a/-, 44, 44/-, 72a/44 (muled with 2333 *obv.*, *mm.* 24/44)	35	100
2353	— — Sede Vacante (1529-30). No marks; *mm.* 23/-, 22/-	40	110
2354	— — Bp. Tunstall (1530—). CD beside shield; *mm.* 23, 23/-, 22/-, 22	30	90
2355	— *York.* EL beside shield; *mm.* key/-	200	525
2356	**Halfpenny.** Facing bust, h D G ROSA SIЄ SPIA. *London;* sometimes annulet in centre of rev. *mm.* rose to arrow, arrow/-	25	85
2357	— *Canterbury.* WA beside bust; *mm.* 121/-, 8/-, T/-	60	175
2358	— — TC beside bust; *mm.* 36/-	30	90
2359	— *York.* TW beside bust; *mm.* acorn/-	60	175
2359A	— — —; key below bust	85	225
2360	— — Sede Vacante. Key below bust; *mm.* 15/-	60	150
2361	— — EL or LE beside bust; *mm.* key/-	35	100
2362	**Farthing.** *O.* RVTILANS ROSA, portcullis; *mm.* 33/-, 105/-, 110/-. R. DEO GRACIAS, long cross with pellet in each angle	275	650
2363	— — *mm.* arrow/- R. DEO GRACIAS, rose on long cross	300	750
2363A	— *Canterbury.* O. Similar. R. Similar. *mm.* 36/-	575	1500

2364

		F	VF
		£	£

Third coinage, 1544-7 (Silver progressively debased. 9oz (2dwt), 6oz (2dwt) 4oz (2dwt)).

2364	**Testoon.** *Tower.* hЄnRIC'. VIII, etc. R. Crowned rose between crowned h and R.POSVI, etc.; *mm.* lis, lis and 56, lis/two lis	850	3500
2365	— hЄnRIC 8, *mm.* 105 and 56, 105/56, 105 and 56/56, 56	725	2500
2366	— — annulet on inner circle of rev. or both sides; *mm.* pellet in annulet	750	2750

2367

| 2367 | — *Southwark.* As 2365. R. CIVITAS LOnDON; *mm.* S, Є, S/Є, Є/S | 750 | 2750 |
| 2368 | — *Bristol. mm.*-/WS monogram. (Tower or local dies.) | 800 | 3000 |

2370 Bust 1   2374 Bust 2

2369	**Groat.** *Tower.* As ill. above, busts 1, 2, 3; *mm.* lis/-, lis	100	350
2369A	Bust 1, R. As second coinage; i.e. saltires in forks; *mm.* lis	125	425
2370	Bust 2 or 3 annulet on inner circle, both sides or rev. only	110	375
2371	*Southwark.* As 2367, busts 1, 2, 3, 4; no *mm.* or lis/-; S or S and Є or Є in forks	100	375
2372	*Bristol. Mm.*-/WS monogram, Bristol bust and Tower bust 2 or 3	110	400
2373	*Canterbury.* Busts 1, 2, (2 var); no *mm.*, or lis/–	100	375
2374	*York.* Busts 1 var., 2, 3, no *mm.*	100	375
2375	**Halfgroat.** *Tower.* As 2365, bust 1; *mm.* lis, none	65	225
2376	*Southwark.* As 2367, bust 1; no *mm.*; S or Є and S in forks	100	325

2377	*Bristol. Mm.-/WS* monogram	75	275
2378	*Canterbury.* Bust 1; no *mm.*..	45	175
2379	*York.* Bust 1; no *mm.*...	60	200
2380	**Penny.** *Tower.* Facing bust; no *mm.* or lis/-	45	135
2381	*Southwark.* Facing bust; *mm.* S/-, Є/-, -/Є..	85	275
2382	*Bristol.* Facing bust; no *mm.* (Tower dies or local but truncated at neck)	50	165

2384   2388A

2383	*Canterbury.* Facing bust; no *mm.*	45	135
2384	*York.* Facing bust; no *mm.*	45	135
2385	**Halfpenny.** *Tower.* Facing bust; pellet in annulet in *rev.* centre,		
	no *mm.* or lis/-..	55	175
2386	*Bristol.* Facing bust; no *mm.*..	60	200
2387	*Canterbury.* Facing bust; no *mm.*, (some read H 8).............................	40	125
2388	*York.* Facing bust; no *mm.*	35	110
2388A	**Farthing** *obv.* Rose. R. Cross and pellets	575	1500

These coins were struck during the reign of Edward VI but bear the name and portrait of Henry VIII, except in the case of the half-sovereigns which bear the youthful head of Edward.

Mintmarks

56	105	52	K	E	116

66	115	33	122	t	94

GOLD

		F	VF
		£	£
2389	**Sovereign** (20 c), *London.* As no. 2290, but Roman lettering; *mm.* lis	4750	13500
2390	— *Bristol.* Similar but *mm.* WS	6000	16500

2391

2393

2391	**Half-sovereign.** As 2294, but with youthful portrait with sceptre. *Tower; mm.* 52, 105, 94 (various combinations)	650	1650
2391A	— Similar but no sceptre; *mm.* 52, 52/56	675	1750
2392	— — — K below shield; *mm.*-/K, none,. E/-	675	1750
2393	— — — grapple below shield; *mm.* 122, none, 122/-, -/122.	700	1800
2394	— *Southwark. Mm.* E, E/-, -/E, Є /E. Usually Є or E (sometimes retrograde) below shield (sceptre omitted; *mm.* -/E)	650	1650
2394A	— — — R. As 2296; *mm.*-/S	750	2000

2395

		F	VF
		£	£
2395	**Crown.** Similar to 2305. *London; mm.* 52, 52/-, -/K, 122, 94, ...	575	1350
2396	— Similar but transposed legends without numeral; *mm.* -/arrow.......	600	1500
2396A	— As 2395, but omitting RVTILANS; *mm.* arrow	600	1500
2396B	Similar, but RVTILANS both sides; *mm.* arrow................................	675	1750
2397	— *Southwark.* Similar to 2396; *mm.* E...................................	650	1700
2398	— — King's name on *obv.*; *mm.* E/-, -/E................................	600	1600
2399	**Halfcrown.** Similar to 2311. *London; mm.* 52, K/-, 122/-, 94, -/52.....	525	1250
2399A	As last but E over h on *rev.*, *mm.* 56/52................................	700	1750
2399B	As 2399 but RVTILANS etc. on both sides, *mm.* arrow	600	1500
2400	— *Southwark. mm.* E, E/-, -/E...	525	1250

SILVER

AR (4oz .333)

2401	**Testoon.** *Tower.* As 2365 with lozenge stops one side; -/56, 56...........	1500	6500

2403 Bust 4   2403 Bust 6

Some of the Bristol testoons, groats and halfgroats with WS monogram were struck after the death of Henry VIII but cannot easily be distinguished from those struck during his reign.

2403	**Groat.** *Tower.* Busts 4, 5, 6 (and, rarely, 2). R. POSVI, etc.; *mm.* 105-94 and none (frequently muled)	95	325
2404	— *Southwark.* Busts 4, 5, 6. R. CIVITAS LONDON; no *mm.* -/E; lis/-, -/lis, K/E; roses or crescents or S and Є in forks, or rarely annulets...	90	300
2405	— *Durham House.* Bust 6. R. REDDE CVIQVE QVOD SVVM EST; *mm.* bow	175	575
2406	— *Bristol. mm.* WS on *rev.* Bristol bust B, Tower bust 2 and 3	100	350
2407	— — *mm.* TC on *rev.* Similar, Bristol bust B............................	110	400
2408	— *Canterbury.* Busts 5, 6; no *mm.* or rose/-............................	90	300
2409	— *York.* Busts 4, 5, 6; no *mm.* or lis/-, -/lis	90	300

		F £	VF £
2410	**Halfgroat.** Bust 1. *Tower.* POSVI, etc.; *mm.* 52, 52/-, 52/K , -/K, 52/122, 122, -/122..........	60	225
2411	— *Southwark.* CIVITAS LONDON; *mm.* E, -/E, none, 52/E, K/E......	55	200
2412	— *Durham House.* R. REDD, etc.; *mm.* bow, -/bow............	300	950
2413	— *Bristol. Mm.* WS on *rev.*	60	225
2414	— — *mm.* TC on *rev.*........	65	250
2415	— *Canterbury.* No *mm.* or t/-, -/t,........	50	175

2416

| 2416 | — *York.* No *mm.*, bust 1 and three quarter facing .... | 50 | 185 |

2417    2421

2417	**Penny.** *Tower.* CIVITAS LONDON. Facing bust; *mm.* 52/-, -/52, -/K, 122/-, -/122, none	40	125
2418	— — three-quarter bust; no *mm.*........	45	135
2419	— *Southwark.* As 2417; *mm.* E, -/E	45	135
2420	— *Durham House.* As groat but shorter legend; *mm.* -/bow	275	800
2421	— *Bristol.* Facing busts, as 2382 but showing more body, no *mm.*	75	200
2422	— *Canterbury.* Similar to 2417	40	125
2423	— — three-quarters facing bust; no *mm.*	45	135
2424	— *York.* Facing bust; no *mm.*	40	125
2425	— — three-quarters facing bust; no *mm.*	45	140

2426    2428

2426	**Halfpenny.** *Tower.* 52?, none	35	110
2427	— *Canterbury.* No *mm.*, sometimes reads H8........	40	120
2428	— *York.* No *mm.*	40	110

Coinage in his own name

The 4 oz. 2.5dwt coins of Henry VIII and those issued under Edward in 1547 and 1548 caused much disquiet, yet at the same time government was prevented by continuing financial necessity from abandoning debasement. A stratagem was devised which entailed increasing the fineness of silver coins, thereby making them appear sound, while at the same time reducing their weight in proportion so that in practice they contained no more silver than hitherto. The first issue, ordered on 24 January 1549, at 8 oz.2 dwt. fine produced a shilling which, at 60 gr., was so light that it was rapidly discredited and had to be replaced in April by another at 6 oz. 2 dwt. Weighing 80 gr., these later shillings proved acceptable.

Between April and August 1551 the issue of silver coins was the worst ever – 3 oz. 2dwt. fine at 72s per lb. before retrenchment came in August, first by a 50% devaluation of base silver coin and then by the issue of a fine standard at 11oz. 1dwt. 'out of the fire'. This was the equivalent of 11oz.3dwt. commixture, and means that since sterling was only 11oz. 2dwt., this issue, which contained four new denominations – the crown, halfcrown, sixpence and threepence – was in effect the finest ever issued under the Tudors.

Some base 'pence' were struck in parallel with the fine silver, but at the devalued rate, they and the corresponding 'halfpence' were used as halfpence and farthings respectively.

The first dates on English coinage appear in this reign, first as Roman numerals and then on the fine issue crowns and halfcrowns of 1551-3, in Arabic numerals.

Mintmarks

| 66 | 52 | 35 | 115 | E | 53 | 122 |

| t | T | 111 | Y | 126 | 94 | 91A |

| 92 | 105 | y | 97 | 123 | 78 | 26 |

1547-8	Arrow (52)		
	E (Southwark)		
1548-50	Bow (66, *Durham House*)	1550	Martlet (94)
1549	Arrow (52)	1550	Leopard's head (91A)
	Grapple (122)	1550-1	Lion (92)
	Rose (35, *Canterbury*)		Lis (105, *Southwark*)
	TC monogram (115, *Bristol*)		Rose (33)
	Pheon (53)	1551	Y or y (117, *Southwark*)
	t or T (*Canterbury*)		Ostrich's head (97, gold only)
1549-50	Swan (111)	1551-3	Tun (123)
	Roman Y (*Southwark*)		Escallop (78)
1549-50	6 (126 gold only)	1552-3	Pierced mullet (26, *York*)

GOLD

First period, Apr. 1547-Jan. 1549

2430

		F £	VF £
2429	**Half-sovereign** (20 c). As 2391, but reading EDWARD 6. Tower; *mm.* arrow	1850	6000
2430	— *Southwark* (Sometimes with E or Є below shield); *mm.* E	1650	5250
2431	**Crown.** RVTILANS, etc., crowned rose between ER both crowned. R. EDWARD 6, etc., crowned shield between ER both crowned; *mm.* arrow, E over arrow/-	2250	7000
2431A	— *Obv.* as last. R. As 2305, *mm.* 52/56	1650	5000
2432	**Halfcrown.** Similar to 2431, but initials not crowned; *mm.* arrow	1500	4500

Second period, Jan. 1549-Apr. 1550

2433

		F £	VF £
2433	**Sovereign** (22 ct). As illustration; *mm.* arrow, –/arrow, Y,	3750	10000
2434	**Half-sovereign.** Uncrowned bust. *London.* TIMOR etc., MDXLIX on *obv. mm.* arrow	2750	8500

2435

		F £	VF £
2435	— — SCVTVM, etc., as illustration; *mm.* arrow, **6,** Y	1350	3750

	F £	VF £
2436 — *Durham House*. Uncrowned, 1/2 length bust with **MDXLVIII** at end of *obv.* legend; *mm.* bow; SCVTVM etc.	4500	12500
2437 — Normal, uncrowned bust. LVCERNA, etc., on *obv.; mm.* bow	4250	12000

2438   2441

2438 — Crowned bust. *London*. EDWARD VI, etc. R. SCVTVM, etc.; *mm.* 52, 122, 111/52, 111, Y, 94..	1250	3500
2439 — *Durham House*. Crowned, half-length bust; *mm.* bow	4500	12500
2440 — — King's name on *obv.* and *rev.; mm.* bow (mule of 2439/37)...........	4750	13500
2441 **Crown.** Uncrowned bust, as 2435; *mm.* 6, Y, 52/-, Y/-	1350	4000
2442 — Crowned bust, as 2438; *mm.* 52, 122, 111, Y (usually *obv.* only)........	1250	3500
2443 **Halfcrown.** Uncrowned bust; R. As 2441, *mm.* arrow, Y, Y/-, 52/-	1350	3750
2444 — Crowned bust, as illus. above; *mm.* 52, 52/111, 111, 122, Y, Y/-	1100	3250
2445 — Similar, but king's name on *rev., mm.* 52, 122.....................................	1250	3500

Third period, 1550-3

2446 **'Fine' sovereign** (30s.). King on throne; *mm.* 97, 123	20000	57500

2444   2448

2447 **Double sovereign.** From the same dies, *mm.* 97	47500	175000
2448 **Angel** (10s.). As illustration; *mm.* 97, 123..	6250	16500
2449 **Half-angel.** Similar, *mm.* 97...	7250	22500

2450

		F £	VF £
2450	**Sovereign**. (=20s.). Half-length figure of king r., crowned and holding sword and orb. R. Crowned shield with supporters; *mm*. y, tun	3250	8000

2451

2451	**Half-sovereign**. As illustration above; *mm*. y, tun	1250	3500
2452	**Crown**. Similar, but *rev*. SCVTVM etc., *mm*. y, tun	1350	3750
2453	**Halfcrown**. Similar, *mm*. tun, y	1450	4000

*Small denominations often occur creased or straightened.

SILVER

First period, Apr. 1547-Jan. 1549

2455

2454	**Groat**. Crowned bust r. *Tower*. R. Shield over cross, POSVI, etc.; *mm*. arrow	750	2250
2455	— As last, but EDOARD 6, *mm*. arrow	825	2500
2456	*Southwark. Obv.* as 2454. R. CIVITAS LONDON; *mm*.-/E or none, sometimes S in forks	750	2250
2457	**Halfgroat**. *Tower. Obv.* as 2454; *mm*. arrow	475	1350
2458	*Southwark*. As 2456; *mm*. arrow, E on reverse only	450	1150

2459

		F	VF
		£	£
2459	*Canterbury.* Similar. No *mm.*, reads EDOARD or EDWARD (rare)	325	950
2460	**Penny.** *Tower.* As halfgroat, but E.D.G. etc. R. CIVITAS LONDON; *mm.* arrow	300	950
2461	*Southwark.* As last, but *mm.* -/E..	325	1000
2462	*Bristol.* Similar, but reads ED6DG or E6DG no *mm.*...............................	275	950
2463	**Halfpenny.** *Tower. O.* As 2460, *mm.* E (?). R. Cross and pellets	275	825
2464	*Bristol.* Similar, no *mm.* but reads E6DG or EDG....................................	300	875

Second period, Jan. 1549-Apr. 1550

At all mints except Bristol, the earliest shillings of 1549 were issued at only 60 grains but of 8 oz. 2 dwt standard. This weight and size were soon increased to 80 grains, (S.2466 onwards), but the fineness was reduced to 6 oz. 2 dwt so the silver content remained the same. Dies, mm G were prepared for a coinage of 80gr shillings at York, but were not used. Coins from the *mm* are found suitably overmarked, from other mints, S.2466-8. The shilling bust types are set out in *J. Bispham 'The Base Silver Shillings of Edward VI; BNJ 1985.*

Bust 1   2465A   Bust 2

60 gr; 8oz. 2 dwt.

2465	**Shilling.** *Tower.* Broad bust with large crown. *Obv.* TIMOR etc. MDXLIX. R. Small, oval garnished shield dividing ER. EDWARD VI etc., *mm.* 52, no *mm*, Bust 1; *mm*, –/52, Bust 2	225	850
2465A	*Southwark.* As last, Bust 1, *mm.* Y, EY/Y	200	800
2465B	*Canterbury.* As last, Bust 1, *mm.* -/rose..	250	1000

2465C

| 2465C | *Durham House.* Bust with elaborate tunic and collar TIMOR etc. MDXLIX. R. Oval shield, very heavily garnished in different style. EDWARD VI etc., *mm.* bow (2469) .... | 250 | 900 |

80 gr; 6oz. 2 dwt.

Bust 3   Bust 4

Bust 5   2466C   2468

2472

	F	VF
	£	£

2466	*Tower.* Tall, narrow bust with small crown. *Obv.* EDWARD VI etc. MDXLIX or MDL. ℞. As 2465 but TIMOR etc., Busts 3, 4 and 5, *mm.* 52-91a (frequently muled)	110	475
2466A	— *Obv.* as last, MDXLIX. ℞. Heavily garnished shield, Durham House style, Bust 3 *mm.* grapple	325	1350
2466B	*Southwark.* As 2466, Busts 3, 4 and 5 *mm.* Y, Y/swan	110	450
2466C	— — — Bust 3; ℞. as 2466A. *mm.* Y	325	1350
2467	*Bristol. Obv.* similar to 2466, Bust 3 or local die ℞. Shield with heavy curved garniture or as 2466, *mm.* TC, or rose over G	675	2500
2468	*Canterbury.* As 2466, Bust 3 and 4 *mm.* T, T/t, t/T, t	150	650
2470	*Durham House.* Bust as 2465C. INIMICOS etc., no date. ℞. EDWARD etc.	140	700
2472	— Bust similar to 2466. EDWARD VI etc. ℞. INIMICOS etc.	110	525
2472A	— As last but legends transposed	175	900
2472B	*Tower.* Elegant bust with extremely thin neck. Bust 6, ℞. As 2466, *mm.* martlet	165	750
2472C	*Southwark.* As last, Bust 6, *mm.* Y	135	600

For coins of Edward VI countermarked, see p. 240

Third period, 1550-3

Very base issue (1551) 3oz. 2 dwt.

2473 Bust 6   2474   2476

		F	VF
		£	£
2473	**Shilling**, *Tower*. As 2472B. MDL or MDLI, *mm*. lion, rose, lion/rose	135	550
2473A	*Southwark*. As last, *mm*. lis/Y, Y/lis, lis	125	525
2474	**Base Penny**. *London. O*. Rose. R. Shield; *mm*. escallop (*obv*.)	50	175
2475	— — *York. Mm*. mullet (*obv*.) as illustration	45	160
2476	**Base Halfpenny**. As penny, but single rose	135	525

* The base penny and halfpenny were used as halfpenny and farthing respectively.

Fine silver issue, (1551-3) 11oz. 3 dwt.

2478

2478	**Crown**. King on horseback with date below horse. R. Shield on cross; *mm*. y. 1551; tun, 1551-3 (1553, wire line inner circle may be missing) .	850	2350

2479

2479	**Halfcrown**. Walking horse with plume; *mm*. y, 1551	675	1650
2480	Galloping horse without plume; *mm*. tun, 1551-3	750	1750

2482

2483

		F	VF
		£	£
2481	Large walking horse without plume; *mm.* tun, 1553	1250	3500
2482	**Shilling**. Facing bust, rose l., value XII r. *mm.* y, tun (several bust varieties)	90	375
2483	**Sixpence**. *London*. Similar, as illustration; *mm.* y/-, -/y, y, tun (bust varieties)	110	475
2484	*York*. As last, but CIVITAS ЄBORACI; *mm.* mullet	175	750

2485

2486

2485	**Threepence**. *London*. As sixpence, but III; *mm.* tun	150	675
2486	*York*. As 2484, but III by bust	325	1250

2487

2487A

2487	**Penny**. 'Sovereign' type; *mm.* tun	900	3250
2487A	**Farthing**. *O*. Portcullis, R Cross and Pellets	850	2500

Mary brought English coins back to the sterling standard and struck all her gold coins at the traditional fineness of 0.995. The mintmarks usually appear at the end of the first or second word of the legends.

Pomegranate   Halved rose and castle

GOLD

2488

	F	VF
	£	£

2488   **'Fine' Sovereign** (30s.). Queen enthroned. R. Shield on rose, MDLIII, MDLIIII and undated, *mm.* pomegranate, half-rose (or mule)   3750   11000

2489

2490

2489   **Ryal** (15s.). As illus, MDLIII. R. As 1950 but A DNO etc. *mm.* pomegranate/-   13500   47500

2490   **Angel** (10s.). Class I, annulet stops; *mm.* pomegranate   1350   3500

2490A — Class II, pellet stops, *mm.* pomegranate (often muled with class I reverse)   1450   3750

2490B — Class III, pellet stops, large Roman letters, *mm.* half-rose and castle .   1500   4000

2491   **Half-angel**. Similar; *mm.* pomegranate, pomegranate/-   2750   7500

SILVER

2492

		F £	VF £
2492	**Groat**. Crowned bust l. R. VERITAS, etc.; *mm*. pomegranate,		
	pomegranate/-	120	350
2493	**Halfgroat**. Similar...	675	1850
2494	**Penny**. Similar, but M. D. G. ROSA, etc.	575	1750

2495

2495	— As last. R. CIVITAS LONDON; no *mm*...	575	1750
2495A	— Base penny. Similar to 2474 but M.D.G. etc. .... *All late 19th cent. fabrications*		

The groats and smaller silver coins of this period have Mary's portrait only, but the shillings and sixpences show the bust of the queen's husband, Philip of Spain.

Mintmarks

Lis (105

Half-rose and castle

GOLD

2496A

		F	VF
		£	£
2496	**Angel**. As illustration; wire line inner circles, calm sea, *mm*. lis	2750	7500
2496A	— — New-style, large wings, wire line i.c.	2850	8000
2496B	— — As above but beaded i.c.	3000	8500
2497	**Half-angel**. Similar to 2496	5250	15000

SILVER

2500

2498	**Shilling**. Busts face-to-face, full titles, undated, no *mm*.	350	1350
2499	— — — also without mark of value	375	1500
2500	— — 1554	350	1350
2501	— English titles only 1554, 1555	375	1450
2501A	— — undated..	425	1650
2502	— — without mark of value, 1554, 1555 (rare)...................................	400	1600
2503	— — date below bust, 1554, 1555	1500	4500
2504	— — As last, but without ANG., 1555................................	1650	5000

2505   2506

		F	VF
		£	£
2505	**Sixpence**. Similar. Full titles, 1554 (and undated?)	325	1350
2506	— English titles only, 1555 (no *mm.*, rare), 1557 (*mm.* lis, rounder garnishing)	350	1500
2506A	— As last but heavy beaded i.c. on obv. 1555. (Irish 4d. obv. mule)	375	1600
2507	— — date below bust, 1554, 1557 (very rare)	675	2000

2508

		F	VF
2508	**Groat**. Crowned bust of Mary 1. R. POSVIMVS etc. (several legend vars.);		
	mm. lis..	125	400
2509	**Halfgroat**. Similar, but POSVIM, *mm.* lis	375	975

2510A

		F	VF
2510	**Penny**. Similar to 2495, but P. Z. M. etc.; *mm.* lis	450	1350
2510A	**Base penny**. Similar to 2495A, but P. Z. M . etc.; *mm.* halved rose and		
	castle or castle/–, (used as a halfpenny)..	65	200

Elizabeth's coinage is particularly interesting on account of the large number of different denominations issued. 'Crown' gold coins were again issued as well as the 'fine' gold denominations. In 1560 the base shillings of Edward VI's second and third coinages were called in and countermarked for recirculation at reduced values. Smaller debased coins were also devalued but not countermarked. The old debased groat became a three halfpence and other coins in proportion. The normal silver coinage was initially struck at 0.916 fineness as in the previous reign but between 1560 and 1577 and after 1582 the old sterling standard of 0.925 was restored. Between 1578 and 1582 the standard was slightly reduced and the weights were reduced by 1/32nd in 1601. Gold was similarly reduced slightly in quality 1578-82, and there was a slight weight reduction in 1601.

To help alleviate the shortage of small change, and to avoid the expense of minting an impossibly small silver farthing, a threefarthing piece was introduced to provide change if a penny was tendered for a farthing purchase. The sixpence, threepence, threehalfpence and threefarthings were marked with a rose behind the queen's head to distinguish them from the shilling, groat, half-groat and penny.

Coins of exceedingly fine workmanship were produced in a screw press introduced by Eloye Mestrelle, a French moneyer, in 1561. With parts of the machinery powered by a horse-drawn mill, the coins produced came to be known as 'mill money'. Despite the superior quality of the coins produced, the machinery was slow and inefficient compared to striking by hand. Mestrelle's dismissal was engineered in 1572 and six years later he was hanged for counterfeiting.

Mintmarks

1ST ISSUE	2ND ISSUE				3RD & 4TH ISSUES		
106	21	94	23	53	33	107	92
			74	71	77	65b	27

5TH ISSUE				6TH ISSUE			
7	14	113	60	54	79	72b	86

7TH ISSUE					
1	2	124	123	90	57	0

First Issue

1558-60	Lis (106)		Lis (105, milled)	1584-6	Escallop (79)
Second Issue		1569-71	Castle (71)	1587-9	Crescent (72b)
1560-1	Cross crosslet (21)	1572-3	Ermine (77)	1590-2	Hand (86)
	Martlet (94)	1573-4	Acorn (65b)	1592-5	Tun (123)
Third & Fourth Issue		1573-8	Eglantine (27)	1594-6	Woolpack (124)
1560-6	Star (23, milled)	Fifth Issue		1595-8	Key (90)
1561-5	Pheon (53)	1578-9	Greek cross (7)	1598-1600	Anchor (57)
1565	Rose (33)	1580-1	Latin cross (14)	1600	0
1566	Portcullis (107)	1582	Sword (113)	Seventh Issue	
1566-7	Lion (92)	Sixth Issue		1601-2	1
1567-70	Coronet (74)	1582-3	Bell (60)	1602	2
		1582-4	A (54)		

N.B. *The dates for* mms *sometimes overlap. This is a result of using up old dies, onto which the new mark was punched.*

Hammered Coinage

GOLD

First to Fourth issues, 1559-78. ('Fine' gold of 0.994. 'Crown' gold of 0 .916 fineness. Sovereigns of 240 gr.). Mintmarks; lis to eglantine.

		F £	VF £
2511	**'Fine' Sovereign** (30 s.) Queen enthroned, tressure broken by throne, reads Z not ET, no chains to portcullis. R. Arms on rose; *mm.* lis............	5250	13500

2512

| 2512 | — — Similar but ET, chains on portcullis; *mm.* crosslet .... | 3500 | 9500 |

2513

2513	**Angel**. St. Michael. R. Ship. Wire line inner circles; *mm.* lis...................	1050	3000
2513A	— Similar, but beaded i.c. on *obv.*, *mm.* lis	950	2500
2514	— — Similar, but beaded inner circles; ship to r.; *mm.* 106, 21, 74, 27,..	850	2000
2515	— — — Similar, but ship to l.; *mm.* 77-27	875	2250
2516	**Half Angel**. As 2513, wire line inner circles; *mm.* lis	1500	4500
2516A	— As last, but beaded i.c.s, legend ends. Z.HIB	950	2500
2517	— As 2514, beaded inner circles; *mm.* 106, 21, 74, 77-27.......................	675	1650
2518	**Quarter Angel**. Similar; *mm.* 74, 77-27..	625	1500
2519	**Half Pound** (10 s.) Young crowned bust l. R. Arms. Wire line inner circles; *mm.* lis	2500	7500

2520

		F	VF
		£	£
2520	— Similar, but beaded inner circles; *mm*. 21, 33-107	1100	2750
2520A	— — Smaller bust; *mm*. lion	1350	3500
2520B	— — Broad bust, ear visible; *mm*. 92, 74, 71	1100	2750
2521	**Crown**. As 2519; *mm*. lis	2000	6000
2522	— Similar to 2520; *mm*. 21, 33-107	750	2250
2522A	— Similar to 2520B; *mm*. 74, 71, 92	800	2350
2523	**Half Crown**. As 2519; *mm*. lis	1500	4500
2524	— Similar to 2520; *mm*. 21, 33-107 (2 busts)	700	1750
2524A	— Similar to 2520B; *mm*. 107-71	750	1850

Fifth Issue, 1578-82 (`Fine' gold only of 0.992). *Mms* Greek cross, Latin cross and sword.

2525	**Angel**. As 2514; *mm*. 7, 14, 113	750	1850
2526	**Half Angel**. As 2517; *mm*. 7, 14, 113	675	1650
2527	— Similar, but without E and rose above ship; *mm*. latin cross	750	1850
2528	**Quarter Angel**. As last; *mm*. 7, 14, 113	625	1500

Sixth Issue, 1583-1600 (`Fine' gold of 0.995, `crown' gold of 0.916; pound of 174.5 grs. wt.). Mintmarks: bell to **O**.

2529

2529	**Sovereign** (30 s:). As 2512, but tressure not normally broken by back of throne; *mm*. 54-123	3250	8500

2530

| | *F* | *VF* |
| | £ | £ |

2530　**Ryal** (15 s.). Queen in ship. R. Similar to 1950; *mm.* 54-86 (*rev.* only) .. 　8500　22500

2531

| 2531 | **Angel**. As 2514; *mm.* 60-123, 90-**O** .... | 850 | 2000 |
| 2532 | **Half Angel**. As 2517; *mm.* 60-86, 90-57 .... | 700 | 1750 |

2535

2533	**Quarter Angel**. As 2518; *mm.* 60-123, 90-57/–	625	1500
2534	**Pound** (20 s.). Old bust l., with elaborate dress and profusion of hair; *mm.*, lion and tun/tun, 123-**O**	1850	5000
2535	**Half Pound**. Similar; *mm.* tun..	1750	4500
2535A	— Similar but smaller bust with less hair; *mm.* 123-**O**	1650	4250

2536

| 2536 | **Crown**. Similar to 2534; *mm.* 123-90. **O** .... | 1250 | 3500 |
| 2537 | **Half Crown**. Similar; *mm.* -/123, 123-0, **O** .... | 850 | 2250 |

Seventh Issue, 1601-3 ('Fine' gold of 0.994, 'crown' gold of 0.916; Pound of 172 gr.). Mintmarks: **1** and **2**

		F	VF
		£	£
2538	**Angel**. As 2531; *mm.* **1, 2**	975	2500
2539	**Pound**. As 2534; *mm.* **1, 2**	1850	5250
2540	**Half Pound**. As 2535A; *mm.* **1, 2**	2000	5750
2541	**Crown**. As 2536; *mm.* **1, 2**	1650	4500
2542	**Half Crown**. As 2537; *mm.* **1, 2**	1500	3750

Milled Coinage, 1561-70

2543

2543	**Half Pound**. Crowned bust l.; *mm.* star, lis	2000	5750
2544	**Crown**. Similar; *mm.* star, lis	1650	5000
2545	**Half Crown**. Similar; *mm.* star, lis	2250	6250

For further details on both AV and AR milled coinage, *see* D. G. Borden *'An introduction to the milled coinage of Elizabeth I'*. BNJ 1983

SILVER

Countermarked Edward VI base shillings (1560)

2546   2547

	Fair £	F £
2546 **Fourpence-halfpenny**. Edward VI 2nd period 6oz and 8oz shillings	850	2500
cmkd on obv. with a portcullis; *mm*. 66, –/33, 52, t, 111, Y and 122		
2547 **Twopence-farthing**. Edward VI 3rd period 3 oz. shillings	1100	3500
countermarked on obverse with a seated greyhound; *mm*. 92. 105, 35 and 87		
N.B. *Occasionally the wrong countermark was used*		

First Issue, 1559-60 (.916 fine, shillings of 96 grs.)

2549   2551A

1A   1B   1D   2A   2B

	F £	VF £
2548 **Shilling**. Without rose or date. ELIZABET(H), wire line inner circles, pearls on bodice, busts 1A, and 1B; *mm*. lis.	400	1750
2549 — Similar, ELIZABETH, wire line and beaded inner circles, busts 1A, 1D, 2A and 2B; *mm*. lis...	175	675

			F	VF
1F	1E 2550 only	1G 2551A only	£	£

			F	VF
2550	**Groat**. Without rose or date, wire line or no inner circles (busts 1F and 1E; *mm*. lis		135	575
2551	— Similar, wire line and beaded inner circles, bust 1F *mm*. lis		75	250
2551A—	— Small bust 1G and shield (from halfgroat punches); *mm*. lis		85	325

2552

2552	**Halfgroat**. Without rose or date, wire line inner circles; *mm*. lis	125	525
2553	**Penny**. Without rose or date, wire line inner circles; *mm*. lis	150	675
2554	— Similar but dated 1558 on *obv*.; *mm*. lis	350	1350
2554A—	Similar to 2553, but wire line and beaded innter circles.; *mm*. lis	325	1200

Second Issue, 1560-1 (0.925 fineness, shilling of 96 gr.)

2555   2559

3A   3B   3C   3J

2555	**Shilling**. Without rose or date, beaded inner circles. ET instead of Z busts 3A, 3B, 3C and 3J; *mm*. 21, 94	125	425
2555A—	large bust with pearls on bodice as 2548; *mm*. 21, bust 1A, 94, bust 1B	150	650
2556	**Groat**. Without rose or date, bust as 2551; *mm*. 21, 94	75	250
2557	**Halfgroat**. Without rose or date; *mm*. 21, 94	35	125
2558	**Penny**. Without rose or date (three bust varieties); *mm*. 21, 94	30	85

Third and Fourth Issues, 1561-77 (Same fineness and weight as last)

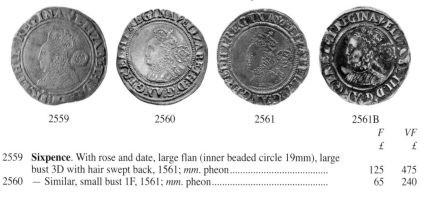

2559   2560   2561   2561B

		F	VF
		£	£
2559	**Sixpence**. With rose and date, large flan (inner beaded circle 19mm), large bust 3D with hair swept back, 1561; *mm.* pheon	125	475
2560	— Similar, small bust 1F, 1561; *mm.* pheon	65	240

3D 2559 only   1F 2560   3E 2561B only

2562   4B 2562

2561	— Smaller flan (inner beaded circle 17.5mm). Small bust 1F, 1561-6; *mm.* 53-107	50	200
2561B	— Similar, very large bust 3E, 1563-5; *mm.* pheon	100	425
2562	— Intermediate bust 4B, ear shows, 1566-73; *mm.* 92-77	50	200
2562A	— Similar, without date; *mm.* lion, coronet, ermine	275	900

2563   5A 2563

2563	— Larger bust 5A, 1573-7; *mm.* 77-27	50	185

		F	VF
		£	£
2564	**Threepence**. With rose and date 1561, large flan (inner circle 15mm.); *mm.* pheon	40	150
2565	— smaller flan (inner circle 14mm.). Regular bust, 1561-7; *mm.* 53-92 .	35	135
2566	— taller bust, ear shows, 1567-77; *mm.* 74-27	35	135
2566A	— Similar, without rose, 1568; *mm.* coronet	175	600

2567   2571

2567	**Halfgroat**. Without rose or date; *mm.* 107-71	45	175
2568	**Threehalfpence**. With rose and date 1561, large flan (inner circle 12.5mm.)		
	mm. pheon	40	135
2569	— — Smaller flan (inner circle 10.5-11.5mm.); 1561-2, 1564-78; *mm.* 53-27	35	125
2570	**Penny**. Without rose or date; *mm.* 33-71, 65b, 27	30	90
2571	**Threefarthings**. With rose and date 1561-2, 1564, 1567, 1568, 1572-7;		
	mm. 53, 74, 77-27	60	185

Fifth Issue, 1578-82 (0.921 fineness, "shilling" of 95.6 gr.)

2572   2573

2572	**Sixpence**. As 2563, 1578-82; *mm.* 7-113	50	185
2573	**Threepence**. As 2566, 1578-82; *mm.* 7-113	35	125
2574	**Threehalfpence**. As 2569, 1578-9, 1581-2; *mm.* 7-113	35	125
2575	**Penny**. As 2570; *mm.* 7-113	30	90
2576	**Threefarthings**. As 2571, 1578-9, 1581-2; *mm.* 7-113	70	200

Sixth Issue, 1582-1600 (0.925 fineness, shilling of 96 gr.)

2577

2577	**Shilling**. Without rose or date, ELIZAB; ear concealed, busts 3B and 6A *mm.*		
	60-72b, ear shows. bust 6B *mm.* 79-**0** (mules occur)	100	350

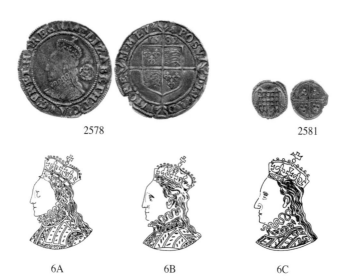

2578   2581

6A   6B   6C

	F £	VF £
2578 **Sixpence**. As 2572, ELIZABETH, 1582, 1583 *mm*. bell	55	200
2578A — Similar, ELIZAB, 1582-1589; *mm*. 60-72b..	50	185
2578B — Similar, but bust 6C 1589-1600, *mm*. 72b-**0**....................................	50	185
2579 **Halfgroat**. Without rose or date, two pellets behind bust. R. CIVITAS LONDON; *mm*. 60-**0** (*mm*. bell sometimes without pellets or with ··/II).	30	80
2580 **Penny**. Without rose or date. R. CIVITAS LONDON; *mm*. 60-**0**; 90-**0** on obv only	30	85
2581 **Halfpenny**. Portcullis. R. Cross and pellets; *mm*. none, 54-**0**	30	80

Seventh Issue, 1601-2 (0.925 fineness, shilling of 92.9 gr.)

2582

2582 **Crown**. As illustration, *mm*. **1**	1350	3250
2582A – Similar, *mm*. **2**	2250	6250

2583   2588

	F	VF
	£	£
2583 **Halfcrown**. As illustration, *mm*. **1**	975	2500
2583A – Similar, *mm*. **2**	2500	7500
2584 **Shilling**. As 2577; bust 6B *mm*. **1, 2**	125	375
2585 **Sixpence**. As 2578B, 1601-2; *mm*. **1, 2**	55	200
2586 **Halfgroat**. As 2579, *mm*. **1, 2**	30	85
2587 **Penny**. As 2580, *mm*. **1, 2**	30	90
2588 **Halfpenny**. As 2581, *mm*. **1, 2**	30	85

Milled coinage

	F	VF
2589 **Shilling**. Without rose or date; *mm*. star. Plain dress, large size (over 31 *mm*.)	675	2000
2590 — decorated dress, large size	375	1100
2591 — — intermediate size (30-31 *mm*.)	250	725
2592 — — small size (under 30 *mm*.)	225	675

2593   2594

2593 **Sixpence**. Small bust, large rose. R. Cross fourchee, 1561 *mm*. star	100	350
2594 Tall narrow bust with plain dress, large rose, 1561-2; *mm*. star	100	350

2595   2596

2595 — similar, but decorated dress, 1562	100	350
2596 Large broad bust, elaborately decorated dress, small rose, 1562; *mm*. star	95	325
2597 — — cross pattée on *rev*., 1562, 64 *mm*. star	110	375

2599

		F	VF
		£	£
2598	— similar, pellet border, 1562-4..	115	385
2598A	Bust with low ruff, raised rim, 1564, 1566 (both overdates)....................	125	425
2599	Small bust, 1567-8, R. As 2593; *mm.* lis	90	300

2600   2601

2600	Large crude bust breaking legend; 1570, *mm.* lis; 1571/0, *mm.* castle (over lis)..	250	900
2601	**Groat**. As illustration...	125	450
2602	**Threepence**. With rose, small bust with plain dress, 1561	135	475
2603	Tall narrow decorated bust with medium rose, 1562............................	110	350
2604	Broad bust with very small rose, 1562	125	400
2605	Cross pattee on *rev.*, 1563, 1564/3...	200	650

2606

2606	**Halfgroat**. As groat	135	525
2607	**Threefarthings**. E . D . G . ROSA, etc., with rose. R. CIVITAS LONDON, shield with 1563 above	1750	5250

Portcullis money

Trade coins of 8, 4, 2, and 1 Testerns were coined at the Tower Mint in 1600/1 for the first voyage of the incorporated 'Company of Merchants of London Trading into the East Indies'. The coins bear the royal arms on the obverse and a portcullis on the reverse and have the *mm*. **O**. They were struck to the weights of the equivalent Spanish silver 8, 4, 2 and 1 reales.

2607A

		F £	VF £
2607A	Eight testerns	2750	7500

2607B

2607B	Four testerns	1500	4250

2607C

2607D

2607C	Two testerns	1150	3000
2607D	One testern	950	2500

THE HOUSE OF STUART, THE COMMONWEALTH, AND THE HOUSE OF ORANGE, 1603-1714

JAMES I, 1603-25

With the accession of James VI of Scotland to the English throne, the royal titles and coat of arms are altered on the coinage; on the latter the Scottish rampant lion and the Irish harp now appear in the second and third quarters. In 1604 the weight of the gold pound was reduced and the new coin became known as the 'Unite'. Fine gold of 0·979 and crown gold of 0·916 fineness were both issued, and a gold four-shilling piece was struck 1604-19. In 1612 all the gold coins had their values raised by 10%; but in 1619 the Unite was replaced by a new, lighter 20s. piece, the 'Laurel', and a lighter rose-ryal, spur-ryal and angel were minted.

In 1613 the king granted Lord Harington a licence to coin farthings of copper as a result of repeated public demands for a low value coinage; this was later taken over by the Duke of Lennox. Towards the end of the reign coins made from silver sent to the mint from the Welsh mines had the Prince of Wales's plumes inserted over the royal arms.

Mintmarks

125	105	33	79	84	74	90

60	25	71	45	32	123	132

72b	7a	16	24	125	105	46

First coinage
1603-4   Thistle (125)
1604-5   Lis (105)

Second coinage
1604-5   Lis (105)
1605-6   Rose (33)
1606-7   Escallop (79)
1607   Grapes (84)
1607-9   Coronet (74)

1609-10   Key (90)
1610-11   Bell (60)
1611-12   Mullet (25)
1612-13   Tower (71)
1613   Trefoil (45)
1613-15   Cinquefoil (32)
1615-16   Tun (123)
1616-17   Book on lectern (132)

1617-18   Crescent (72b, gold)

1618-19   Plain cross (7a)
1619   Saltire cross (16, gold)

Third coinage
1619-20   Spur rowel (24)
1620-1   Rose (33)
1621-3   Thistle (125)
1623-4   Lis (105)
1624   Trefoil (46)

GOLD

First coinage, 1603-4 (Obverse legend reads D' . G' . ANG : SCO : etc.)

		F	VF
		£	£
2608	**Sovereign** (20s.). King crowned r., half-length, first bust with plain armour. R. EXVRGAT, etc.; *mm.* thistle	1500	5250
2609	— second bust with decorated armour; *mm.* thistle, lis	1600	5500

| 2610 | 2611 |

2610	**Half-sovereign**. Crowned bust r. R. EXVRGAT, etc.; *mm.* thistle	2500	9000
2611	**Crown**. Similar. R. TVEATVR, etc.; *mm.* 125, 105/125	1350	4000
2612	**Halfcrown**. Similar; *mm.* thistle, lis	675	1750

N.B. *The Quarter-Angel of this coinage is considered to be a pattern (possibly a later strike), although coin weights are known.*

Second coinage, 1604-19 (Obverse legend reads D' G' MAG : BRIT : etc.)

2613

| 2613 | **Rose-ryal** (30s., 33s. from 1612). King enthroned. R. Shield on rose; *mm.* 33-90, 25-132 | 2000 | 5250 |

2614

		F	*VF*
		£	£
2614	**Spur ryal** (15s., 16s. 6d. from 1612). King in ship; *mm.* 33, 79, 74, 25-32, 132	3500	9500
2615	**Angel** (10s., 11s. from 1612). Old type but larger shield; *mm.* 33-74, 60-16	900	2250
2616	— — pierced for use as touch-piece	575	1250
2617	**Half-angel** (5s., 5s. 6d. from 1612). Similar; *mm.* 71-132, 7a, 16	1500	4750
2618	**Unite** (20s., 22s. from 1612). Half-length second bust r. R. FACIAM etc.; *mm.* lis or rose	575	1350

2619

2619	— fourth bust; *mm.* rose to cinquefoil	475	1150
2620	— fifth bust; *mm.* cinquefoil to saltire	450	1050
2621	**Double-crown.** Third bust r. R. HENRICVS, etc.; *mm.* lis or rose	325	800

2623

2622	Fourth bust; *mm.* rose to bell	300	750
2623	Fifth bust; *mm.* key, mullet to saltire	275	750

		F	*VF*
		£	£
2624	**Britain crown**. First bust r.; *mm.* lis to coronet	225	550
2625	Third bust; *mm.* key to cinquefoil	225	550
2626	Fifth bust; *mm.* cinquefoil to saltire..	200	500

2624    2627

2627	**Thistle crown** (4s.). As illus.; *mm.* lis to plain cross	200	525
2628	— IR on only one side or absent both sides; *mm.* 79, 74, 71-123	210	550
2629	**Halfcrown**. I' D' G' ROSA SINE SPINA. First bust; *mm.* lis to key	185	400
2630	Third bust; *mm.* key to trefoil, trefoil/tower...	185	400
2631	Fifth bust; *mm.* cinquefoil to plain cross	175	375

Third coinage, 1619-25

2632	**Rose-ryal** (30s.; 196.5 grs.). King enthroned. R. XXX above shield; lis, lion and rose emblems around; *mm.* 24, 125, 105	2250	5750
2633	Similar but plain back to throne; *mm.* trefoil...	2500	6000

2634

2634	**Spur-ryal** (15s.). As illus. R. Somewhat like 2614, but lis are also crowned. *mm.* 24-125, 46	3250	9250

2635

2635	**Angel** (10s.) of new type; *mm.* 24-46..	1350	4000
2636	— pierced for use as touch-piece..	650	1500

2637

		F	VF
		£	£
2637	**Laurel** (20s.; 140.5 gr.). First (large) laur, bust l.; *mm.* 24, 24/-	750	2000
2638	Second, medium, square headed bust, `SS' tie ends; *mm.* 24, 33	650	1350
2638A	Third, small rounded head, ties wider apart; *mm.* 33, 125	575	1250
2638B	Fourth head, very small ties; *mm.* 105, 46	575	1250
2638C	Fourth head variety, tie ends form a bracket to value; *mm.* lis	625	1300
2639	Fifth, small rather crude bust; *mm.* trefoil	1850	6000

2641A   2642A

2640	**Half-laurel**. First bust; *mm.* spur rowel	525	1250
2645A	— First bust variety		
2641	— As 2638A; *mm.* rose	525	1250
2641A	— As 2638B; *mm.* 33-46, 105/-	400	850
2642	**Quarter-laurel**. Bust with two loose tie ends; *mm.* 24-105	225	475
2642A	Bust as 2638C; *mm.* 105, 46, 105/46	225	475
2642B	As last but beaded, i.c. on *rev.* or both sides; *mm.* 105, 46	235	525

Rev. mm. on ¹/₂ and ¹/₄ laurels normally follows REGNA.

SILVER

2644

		F	VF
		£	£

First coinage, 1603-4

| 2643 | **Crown**. King on horseback. R. EXVRGAT, etc., shield; *mm.* thistle, lis. | 1000 | 3250 |
| 2644 | **Halfcrown**. Similar .... | 1250 | 4000 |

2645   2646

2645	**Shilling**. First bust, square-cut beard. R. EXVRGAT, etc.; *mm.* thistle ...	110	450
2645A	— transitional bust, nape of neck shows above broad collar, crown similar to first bust, shoulder armour as second bust, *mm.* thistle	175	750
2646	— Second bust, beard appears to merge with collar; *mm.* thistle, lis	75	250
2647	**Sixpence**. First bust; 1603; *mm.* thistle	85	375

2648   2649   2650

2648	Second bust; 1603-4; *mm.* thistle, lis	45	200
2649	**Halfgroat**. First bust, II behind head; *mm.* thistle, lis	35	110
2650	**Penny**. First bust I behind head; *mm.* thistle	65	250
2650A	— Second bust; *mm.* thistle, lis	25	75

2651

| 2651 | **Halfpenny**. As illustration; *mm.* thistle, lis .... | 20 | 70 |

Second coinage, 1604-19

2652

		F	*VF*
		£	£
2652	**Crown**. King on horseback. R. QVAE DEVS, etc. *rev.* stops; *mm.* 105-84	850	2500
2653	**Halfcrown**. Similar; *mm.* 105-79	1250	3500
2654	**Shilling**. Third bust, beard cut square and stands out (*cf.* illus. 2657); *mm.* lis, rose	70	225
2655	— Fourth bust, armour plainer (*cf.* 2658); *mm.* 33-74, 90 over 74, or 60 over 74	75	250

2656

| 2656 | — Fifth bust, similar, but hair longer; single-arched crown, *mm.* 74; higher double-arched crown, *mm.* 74 (rare), 90-7a... | 75 | 250 |

2657   2658

2657	**Sixpence**. Third bust; 1604-6; *mm.* lis, rose, escallop..............................	45	185
2658	— Fourth bust; 1605-16; *mm.* rose to book, 90/60, 25/60......................	50	220
2658A	— Fifth bust, 1618; *mm.* plain cross..	675	2000
2659	**Halfgroat**. As illus. but larger crown on *obv.*; *mm.* lis to coronet............	20	50

2660

	F	VF
	£	£
2660 — — Similar, but smaller crown on *obv.*; *mm.* coronet to plain cross......	20	50
2660A As before, but TVEATVR legend both sides; *mm.* plain cross over book	30	100
2661 **Penny**. As halfgroat but no crowns; *mm.* 105-32,7a and none, -/84, 32/-	15	50
2662 — As before but TVEATVR legend both sides; *mm.* mullet....................	30	90
2663 **Halfpenny**. As illus.; *mm.* 105- 25, 32; all *mms* on *rev.* only	15	45

Third coinage, 1619-25

2664 **Crown**. As 2652, with plain or grass ground line, colon stops on *obv.*, no stops on *rev.*; *mm.* 33-46..	750	1800

2665

2665 — — plume over shield; *mm.* 125-46	900	2500

2667

2666 **Halfcrown**. As 2664 with plain or grass ground line; all have bird-headed harp; *mm.* 33-46..	275	750
2666A — — Similar but no ground line; *mm.* rose	575	1750

2668

		F	VF
		£	£
2667	— — Plume over shield; groundline *mm.* 125-46	375	1250
2668	**Shilling**. Sixth (large) bust, hair longer and very curly; *mm.* 24-46	90	325
2669	— — plume over shield; *mm.* 125-46	185	650

	2670		2672		2673	

2670	**Sixpence**. Sixth bust; 1621-4; *mm.* 33-46; 1621/0, *mm.* rose	60	225
2671	**Halfgroat**. As 2660 but no stops on *rev.*; *mm.* 24-46 and none, 105 and 46, 46/- *mm.* 24 with *rev.* stops known	20	50
2671A	Similar but no inner circles; *mm.* lis, trefoil over lis	20	60
2672	**Penny**. As illus.; *mm.* 24, 105, two pellets, none, trefoil,	15	50
2672A	— Similar but without inner circles on one or both sides; *mm.* lis, two pellets	15	50
2673	**Halfpenny**. As 2663, but no *mm.*	15	45

COPPER

For further details see C. Wilson Peck, *English Copper, Tin and Bronze Coins in the British Museum, 1558-1958.*

	2674		2675		2676	

| 2674 | **Farthing**. 'Harington', small size. 1a, (originally tinned surface). Mintmark on or below cushion of crown. *mm:* A, B, C, D, F, S, Ermine, Millrind, Pellet, :< | 50 | 100 |
| 2675 | — — 1b, (occasionally tinned surface). Mintmark replaces central jewel on circlet of crown. *mm:* Trefoil, Crescent, Mullet or crown unmodified | 35 | 70 |

	F	VF
	£	£

2676   — 2, normal size, mintmark on reverse only; *mm*. Cinquefoil, Cross
saltire, Lis, Martlet, Mullet, Trefoil   20   40

2677   'Lennox'. 3a; mintmark on reverse only; *mm*. Bell, Tower   25   50

2678   2679   2680

2678   — 3b; *mm*. mintmark both sides; *mm:* Flower, Fusil.............................   8   20

2679   — — 3c; mintmark on obverse only; *mm*. Annulet, Bell, Coronet,
Crescent, Cross flory fitchée, Cross patée fourchée, Dagger, Eagle's
head, Fusil, Grapes, Key, Lion passant, Mascle, Quatrefoil,
Rose (double), Star, Star (pierced), Thistlehead, Trefoil, Triangle,
Triangle (pellet below), Tun, Woolpack   8   20

2680   — — 3d; las 3c but with larger crowns; *mm:* A, Dagger, Fusil,
Lion rampant, Lis (three), Mascle, Stirrip, Trefoil, Triangle, Tun.........   8   20

2681   — 4; oval flan, legend starts at bottom left; *mm:* Cross patée. Originally
issued for use in Ireland.   60   120

Numismatically, this reign is one of the most interesting. Some outstanding machine-made coins were produced by Nicholas Briot, a French die-sinker, but they could not be struck at sufficient speed to supplant hand-hammering methods, and the weights often had to be adjusted by blank filing. In 1637 a branch mint was set up at Aberystwyth to coin silver extracted from the Welsh mines and dies supplied from Tower Mint. After the king's final breach with Parliament the parliamentary government continued to issue coins at London with Charles's name and portrait until the king's trial and execution. The coinage of copper farthings continued to be manufactured privately under licences held first by the Duchess of Richmond and, lastly, by Lord Maltravers. Parliament took control of the Token House in 1643, and production ceased the following year.

During the Civil War coins were struck at a number of towns to supply coinage for those areas of the country under Royalist control. Many of these coins have an abbreviated form of the 'Declaration' made at Wellington, Shropshire, Sept., 1642, in which Charles promised to uphold the Protestant Religion, the Laws of England and the Liberty of Parliament. Amongst the more spectacular pieces are the gold triple unites and the silver pounds and half-pounds struck at Shrewsbury and Oxford, and the emergency coins, some made from odd-shaped pieces of silver plate during the sieges of Newark, Scarborough, Carlisle and Pontefract.

Mintmarks

105	10	96	71	57	88	101	35

87	107	60	70	123	57	119a	23

119b	98	112	81	120	109

Tower Mint under Charles I

1625	Lis (105)	1633-4	Portcullis (107)
1625-6	Cross Calvary (10)	1634-5	Bell (60)
1626-7	Negro's head (96)	1635-6	Crown (75)
1627-8	Castle (71)	1636-8	Tun (123)
1628-9	Anchor (57)	1638-9	Anchor (57)
1629-30	Heart (88)	1639-40	Triangle (119a)
1630-1	Plume (101)	1640-1	Star (23)
1631-2	Rose (35)	1641-3	Triangle in circle
1632-3	Harp (87)		(119b)

Tower Mint under Parliament

1643-4	P in brackets (98)
1644-5	R in brackets (112)
1645	Eye (81)
1645-6	Sun (120)
1646-8	Sceptre (109)

Mint mark no. 57 maybe upright, inverted, or horizontal to left or right.

59	B	58*var*	58

Briot's Mint

1631-2	Flower and B (59)	1638-9	Anchor (57)
1632	**B**		Anchor and B (58)
			(B upright or on side)
			Anchor and Mullet (58v)

61	104	35	92	103	6	65b	71
89	91*var*	131	84	94*var*	64	93	34
102	67	127	128	129	25	83	100
	134	71	A	B	75		

Provincial Mints

1638-42	Book (61, *Aberystwyth*)
1642	Plume (104, *Shrewsbury*)
	Pellets or pellet (*Shrewsbury*)
1642-3	Rose (35, *Truro*)
	Bugle (134, *Truro*)
1642-4	Lion (92, *York*)
1642-6	Plume (103, *Oxford*)
	Pellet or pellets (*Oxford*)
	Lis (105, *Oxford*)
1643	Cross pattee (6, *Bristol*)
	Acorn (65b, *Bristol*)
	Castle (71, *Worcester* or *Shrewsbury*)
	Helmet (89, *Worcester* and *Shrewsbury*)
1643-4	Leopard's head (91 *var. Worcester*)
	Two lions (131, *Worcester*)
	Lis (105, *Worcs.* or *Shrews.*)
	Bunch of grapes (84, *Worcs.* or *Shrews.*)
	Bird (94 var., *Worcs.* or *Shrews.*)

1643-4	Boar's head (64 *Worcs.* or *Shrews.*)
	Lion rampant (93, *Worcs.* or *Shrews.*)
	Rosette (34, *Worcs.* or *Shrews.*)
1643-5	Plume (102, *Bristol*)
	Br. (67, *Bristol*)
	Pellets (*Bristol*)
	Rose (35, *Exeter*)
	Rosette (34, *Oxford*)
1643-6	Floriated cross (127, *Oxford*)
1644	Cross pattee (6, *Oxford*)
	Lozenge (128, *Oxford*)
	Billet (129, *Oxford*)
	Mullet (25, *Oxford*)
1644-5	Gerb (83, *Chester*)
	Pear (100, *Worcester*)
	Lis (105, *Hereford?*)
	Castle (71, *Exeter*)
1645-6	Plume (102, *Ashby, Bridgnorth*)
1645	A (*Ashby*)
1646	B (*Bridgnorth*)
1648-9	Crown (75, *Aberystwyth Furnace*)

GOLD

Tower mint, under the King (1625-42), and under Parliament (1642-9)

Tower Gold

For bust varieties on Tower Mint Gold see H. Schneider BNJ 1955-61
Numbers in brackets following each entry refer to numbers employed in previous editions of this catalogue

		F	VF
		£	£
2682	**Angel**. St. Michael slaying dragon, no mark of value. R. Three masted ship, royal arms on mainsail; mm. lis, cross calvary..	2500	8000
2682A	— — — pierced for use as touch-piece (2683)..	850	2500
2683	— X in field to right of St. Michael; m.m. negro's head, castle, anchor, heart, castle and negro's head/castle, anchor and castle/anchor (2684)	2250	7000
2683A	— — — pierced for use as touch-piece (2685)	750	2000
2684	— X in field to left of St. Michael; mm. negro's head, heart, rose, harp, portcullis, bell, crown, tun, anchor, triangle, star, triangle-in-circle (2686)	2000	6000

2684A

2684A	— — — pierced for use as touch-piece (2687)..	700	1850
2685	**Unite**. Group A, first bust, in coronation robes, bust 1, high double-arched crown. R. Square-topped shield, plain or elaborate garnishing; mm. lis (2688, 2688A)..	625	1500
2686	— — bust 1a, flatter single-arched crown; mm. lis, cross calvary (2689, 2689A)	625	1500

2687

2687	Group B, second bust, in ruff, armour and mantle. R. Square-topped shield; m.m. cross calvary, negro's head, castle, anchor, heart (2690)	575	1400
2688	— — more elongated bust, usually dividing legend, mm. anchor, heart, plume (2690A)..	575	1400
2689	— — — anchor below bust; mm. (2691)	1350	4000
2689A	Group B/C mule. R. Oval shield with CR at sides; mm. plume (2691A)	750	2000
2690	Group C, third bust, shorter with heavier armour. R. Oval shield with CR at sides; mm. plume, rose (2692)	625	1500
2691	Group D, fourth bust, with falling lace collar, bust 4, large bust with jewelled crown.R. Oval shield with CR at sides; mm. harp, portcullis (2693)	575	1400
2692	— — bust 5, smaller bust, unjewelled crown; mm. portcullis, bell, crown, tun, anchor, triangle, star (2693A)	525	1350

	F	VF
	£	£

2693 — — — (under Parliament); mm. (P), (P)/- (2710) 800 2000

2694 Group F, sixth 'Briot's' bust, with stellate lace collar. R. Oval shield with
CR at sides, mm. triangle, star, triangle-in-circle (2694)......................... 600 1500

2695 — — (under Parliament); mm. (P), (R) (2711) 900 2250

2696

2696 Group G, (under Parliament), seventh bust, smaller collar; mm. eye, sun, sceptre
(2712) 975 2500

2697

2697 **Double-crown**. Group A, first bust, in coronation robes, bust 1, high double-
arched crown, both arches jewelled. R. Square-topped shield; mm. lis (2696) 625 1800

2698 — — bust 1a, flatter crown, outer arch only jewelled; m.m. lis, cross calvary
(2696A).. 400 975

2699

2699 Group B, second bust, in ruff, armour and mantle, bust 2. R. Square-topped
shield; mm. cross calvary, negro's head, castle, anchor (2697)................ 325 825

2700 — — busts 3-4, more elongated bust, usually dividing legend; mm.
anchor, heart, plume (2697A) 325 850

2701 Group C, third bust, bust 5. R. Oval shield with CR at sides; mm. plume, rose
(2698)... 375 950

2702 Group D, fourth bust, with falling lace collar, bust 6, large bust with jewelled
crown. R. Oval shield with CR at sides; mm. harp, crown (2699).......... 350 900

2703 — — bust 7, smaller head, inner or both arches of crown unjewelled; mm. harp,
portcullis, bell, crown, tun, anchor (2699A-C)...................................... 325 850

	F	*VF*
	£	£

2703A— — — Group Da, (under Parliament), re-cut Group D bust punches;
m.m. eye (2713).. 750 | 2000

2704 Group E, fifth bust, 'Aberystwyth' bust, bust 8, double-arched crown. ℞. Oval
shield with CR at sides; m.m. anchor (2700).. 650 | 1750

2705 — — bust 9, smaller 'Aberystwyth' bust, single-arched crown; m.m. anchor,
triangle (2700A)... 600 | 1500

2705A— — — Group Ea, (under Parliament), re-cut bust 9; m.m. sun, sceptre (2714) 650 | 1750

2706 Group F, sixth 'Briot's' bust, with stellate lace collar, bust 10. ℞. Oval shield
with CR at sides; mm. triangle, star, triangle-in-circle (2701) .... 425 | 1000

2707 — — (under Parliament); mm. (P), (R) (2715) .... 525 | 1350

2708 Group H, (under Parliament), bust 11, dumpy crude bust, single flat-arched
crown; mm. sun (2716).. 850 | 2500

2710   2715

2709 **Crown**. Group A, first bust, in coronation robes, bust 1 var, tall narrow bust,
double-arched crown. ℞. Square-topped shield; mm. lis (2703) .... 225 | 550

2710 — bust 1, broader, less angular bust; m.m. lis, cross calvary (2703A) .... 250 | 625

2711 Group B, second bust, in ruff, armour and mantle, bust 2. ℞. Square-topped
shield; mm. cross calvary, negro's head, castle (2704)............................ 225 | 500

2712 — — bust 3, narrower; more elongated bust; m.m. anchor, heart, plume
(2704A) .... 200 | 475

2713 — — — anchor below bust; mm. anchor (2704B)................................... 650 | 1500

2713A Group B/C mule. ℞. Oval shield with CR at sides; mm. plume, rose (2705) 225 | 525

2714 Group C, third bust, bust 4. ℞. Oval shield with CR at sides; mm. plume
(2706) .... 350 | 850

2715 Group D, fourth bust, with falling lace collar, busts 5, 7. ℞. Oval shield
with CR at sides; m.m. harp, -/harp, portcullis, portcullis/bell, bell, crown,
tun, anchor, triangle, star/triangle, star, triangle-in-circle (2707)............. 200 | 450

2716 — — (under Parliament), bust 5, jewelled crown; m.m. (P), (R), eye, sun
(2717)... 300 | 675

2716A— — (under Parliament), bust 6, unjewelled crown; m.m. eye, sun, sceptre
(2717A)... 300 | 700

2717 Group E, fifth bust, small 'Aberystwyth' bust, bust 8. ℞. Oval shield
with CR at sides; mm. anchor (2708) .... 450 | 1250

2721C — Group F, sixth 'Briot's' bust, bust 9, only known as Briot/hammered
mule (see 2721C below)... 1250 | 3500

	F	VF
	£	£

Nicholas Briot's coinage, 1631-2

2718 **Angel**. Type somewhat as Tower but smaller and neater; *mm*. -/B 3000 9000

2719

2719 **Unite**. As illustration. R. FLORENT etc.; *mm*. flower and B/B............... 2500 7250
2720 **Double-crown**. Similar but X. R. CVLTORES, etc. *mm*. flower and B/B 1650 4500
2720A Similar but King's crown unjewelled: *mm*. flower and B/B, B 1650 4500
2721 **Crown**. Similar; *mm*. B 2500 7500

Briot's Hammered issue, 1638-9

2721A **Unite**. Briot's (sixth) bust, large lace collar. R. FLORENT etc., Briot's
square-topped shield dividing crowned C R; *mm*. anchor....................... 3500 12000
2721B **Double-crown**. Briot's bust, similar. R. CVLTORES etc., square-topped
shield dividing crowned C R; *mm*. anchor 2000 5750
2721C **Crown**. Briot's bust, similar. R. CVLTORES etc., oval shield dividing
crowned C R (a Briot hammered issue/Tower mule); *mm*. anchor........... 1250 3500

Provincial issues, 1638-49

Chester mint, 1644

2722 **Unite**. As Tower. Somewhat like a crude Tower sixth bust. R. Crowned,
oval shield, crowned CR, *mm*. plume...................................... 17500 65000

Shrewsbury mint, 1642 (See also 2749)

2723 **Triple unite**, 1642. Half-length figure l holding sword and olive-branch;
mm.: R. EXVRGAT, etc., around RELIG PROT, etc., in two wavy lines.
III and three plumes above, date below 37500 135000

Oxford mint, 1642-6

2724 **Triple unite**. As last, but *mm*. plume, tall narrow bust, 1642 .... 7500 19500
2725 Similar, but 'Declaration' on continuous scroll, 1642-3............................ 8500 22500
2725A Large bust of fine style. King holds short olive branch; *mm*. small lis 27500 90000
2726 As last, but taller bust, with scarf behind shoulder, 1643, *mm*. plume 8250 21000

2727

		F	VF
		£	£
2727	Similar, but without scarf, longer olive branch, 1643	7500	19500
2728	Similar, but OXON below 1643, rosette stops	12500	35000
2729	Smaller size, olive branch varies, bust size varies, 1644 OXON	8250	21500
2730	— Obv. as 2729, 1644 / OX	8500	22500
2731	**Unite**. Tall thin bust. R. 'Declaration' in two wavy lines, 1642; *no mm*...	1850	5500
2732	— R. 'Declaration' in three lines on continuous scroll, 1642-3	1850	5750
2733	Tall, well-proportioned bust. R. Similar, 1643, no *mm*.	2000	6500
2734	Shorter bust, king's elbow not visible. R. Similar, 1643; *mm*. plume/-....	1750	5250

2735

2735	Similar but longer olive branch curving to l. 1644 / OX; *mm*. plume	1750	5250
2735A	Similar, but dumpy bust breaking lower i.c., small flan	1850	5500
2736	Tall bust to edge of coin. R. Similar, 1643	2750	9500
2737	As 2734. R. 'Declaration' in three straight lines, 1644 / OX....................	2600	8500
2738	Similar to 2734, but smaller size; small bust, low olive branch. 1645	2500	7500
2739	— R. Single plume above 'Declaration', 1645-6 / OX; *mm*. plume,		
	rosette, none..	2250	7000
2740	**Half-unite**. 'Declaration' in three straight lines, 1642	2000	5250
2741	'Declaration' on scroll; *mm*. plume; 1642-3	1850	5000

2742

		F	VF
		£	£
2742	Bust to bottom of coin, 1643; Oxford plumes	1650	3750
2743	— 1644 / OX. Three Shrewsbury plumes (neater work).........................	1850	5000

Bristol mint, 1643-5

2744	**Unite**. Somewhat as 2734; Two busts known. *mm*. Br. or Br/ plumelet.;		
	1645	16500	52500
2745	**Half-unite**. Similar 1645	9500	30000

Truro mint, 1642–3

2745A	**Half-Unite**. Crowned bust l. (similar to Tower 4th bust). R.		
	CVLT, etc., crowned shield	9500	30000

Exeter mint, 1643–5

2746	**Unite**. *obv*. sim. to early Oxford bust. R. FLORENT, etc., crowned oval		
	shield between crowned CR, *mm*. rose...	18500	67500
2747	— R. CVLTORES, etc., similar but no CR	17500	65000

Worcester mint, 1643-4

2748	**Unite**. Crude bust R. FLORENT, etc., double annulet stops, crowned oval		
	shield, lion's paws on either side of garniture, no *mm*.............................	16500	60000

Salopia (Shrewsbury) mint, 1644

| 2749 | **Unite**. *Obv*. bust in armour. R. Cr. shield, crowned CR. *mm*. lis/- .... | 17000 | 62500 |

Colchester besieged, 1648

2750	**Ten Shillings** Gateway of castle between CR; below OBS COL 16 S/X 48.		
	Uniface – now considered a later concoction		

Pontefract besieged, 1648-9. After the death of Charles I, in the name of Charles II

2751	**Unite**. DVM : SPIRO : SPERO around CR crowned. CAROLVS :		
	SECVMDVS : 16 48, castle, OBS on l., PC above.	47500	175000
2752	**Unite**. CAROL : II, etc., around HANC : DEVS, etc. R. POST : MORTEM,		
	etc.,around castle. *Octagonal*...	45000	160000

SILVER

Tower mint, under the King (1625-42), and under Parliament (1642-9)

2753	**Crown**. Group I, first horseman, type 1a, king on horseback left, horse		
	caparisoned with plume on head and crupper. R. Square-topped shield over		
	long cross fourchee; *mm*. lis, cross calvary	650	1750
2754	— — 1b. R. Plume above shield, no cross fourchee; *mm*. lis, cross		
	calvary, castle..	950	2750
2755	Group II, second horseman, type 2a, smaller horse, plume on head only,		
	cross on housing. R. Oval shield over cross fourchee, CR above; *mm*. harp	625	1650
2756	— — 2b1. R. Plume between CR above shield, no cross fourchee; *mm*.		
	plume, rose...	750	2000
2757	— — 2b2. R. Plume between CR, cross fourchee; *mm*. harp	850	2250

2758

		F £	*VF* £
2758	Group III, third horseman, type 3a, horse without caparisons, sword upright. R. Oval shield without CR; mm. bell, crown, tun, anchor, triangle, star..	625	1600
2759	— — 3b. R. Plume above shield; mm. portcullis, crown, tun................	725	1850
2760	'Briot's' horseman with groundline, lozenge stops on obverse; mm. triangle in circle	3250	8500
2761	Group IV, (under Parliament), fourth horseman, type 4, foreshortened horse R. Oval shield; mm. (P), (R), eye, sun (2838)	675	1850
2762	Group V, (under Parliament), fifth horseman, type 5, tall spirited horse; mm. sun (2839)	800	2500

2763

2763	**Halfcrown.** Group I, first horseman, type 1a1, horse caparisoned with plume on head and crupper, rose on housings, ground-line. R. Square-topped shield over long cross fourchee; mm. lis (2761)	275	1050
2764	— — 1a2. No rose on housings, no ground-line; mm. lis, cross calvary (2762)	200	650
2765	— — — ground-line; mm. lis (2762A)...	350	1000
2766	— — 1a3. No rose on housings, no ground-line. R. No long cross, heavy or light garnishing to shield; mm. cross calvary*, negro's head, castle (2763-2763B)	175	525
2767	— — — 1b. R. Plume above shield, heavy or light garnishing; mm. lis, cross calvary*, negro's head, castle, anchor (2765, 2765A)..............................	675	1750
2768	Group II, second horseman, type 2/1b, plume on horse's head only, rose on housings. R. Plume over shield; mm. heart, plume (2766)	1250	3000
2769	— — 2a. Smaller horse, cross on housings. R. Oval shield with CR above (CR divided by rose (very rare), lis over rose (rare), or lis); mm. plume, rose, plume/rose (2767)	100	325
2770	— — — 2b. R. Plume between CR above shield; mm. plume, rose (2768)	225	675

2771

		F £	VF £
2771	— — 2c. R. Oval draped shield with CR at sides; mm. harp, portcullis, portcullis/harp (2769)	100	275
2772	— — — 2d. R. Plume above shield; mm. harp (2770)	1250	3000

2776   2779

2773	Group III, third horseman, type 3a1, no caparisons on horse, scarf flying from king's waist. R. Oval garnished shield; mm. bell, bell/crown, crown, tun, triangle (2771)	70	200
2774	— — — 3b. R. Plume above shield; mm. portcullis, bell, crown, tun (2772)	150	525
2775	— — 3a2. King wears cloak flying from shoulder. R. Oval garnished shield; mm. tun, anchor, triangle, star, triangle-in-circle (2773)..........................	65	185
2776	— — — — rough ground under horse; mm. triangle, star (2774)..........	65	185
2777	— — horseman of finer style, short busy tail, cloak like arrowhead behind shoulder, no ground below; mm. triangle, star (2773 var.)......................	100	350
2778	— — 3a3, (under Parliament), no ground, cruder workmanship; mm. (P), (R), eye, sun (2840)	50	175
2779	Group IV, fourth horseman, type 4, foreshortened horse. R. Oval garnished shield; mm. star, triangle in circle (2775)	50	175
2779A	— — (under Parliament); mm. (P) (2841)	135	475
2780	Group V, (under Parliament), fifth horseman, type 5, tall spirited horse. R. Oval garnished shield; mm. sun, sceptre (2842).................................	80	225

* Light weight half crowns (204 grains) exist of No. 2766, mm. cross calvary

2781   2782

	F	VF
	£	£

2781 **Shilling.** Group A, first bust, type 1, in coronation robes, bust 1, high double-arched crown, both arches jewelled. R. Square-topped shield over cross fourchee (Sharp A1/1); mm. lis (2776) .... | 110 | 400

2782 — — bust 2, larger crown, outer arch only jewelled (Sharp A2/1-2); mm. lis*, cross calvary* (2776A, 2777).. | 100 | 375

2783 — — — 1b1. R. Plume above shield, no cross fourchee (Sharp A2/3); mm. lis, cross calvary (2778).. | 675 | 2000

2784 Group B, second bust, type 1a, in ruff, armour and mantle. R. Square-topped shield over cross fourchee (Sharp B1-5/1); mm. cross calvary*, negro's head, castle (2779, 2780).. | 90 | 350

2785 — — 1b2. R. Plume above shield, no cross fourchee (Sharp B1-5/2); mm. cross calvary*, negro's head, castle, anchor, heart, plume (2781, 2781A) | 175 | 675

2786 — — 1b3. R. Plume above shield, cross fourchee (Sharp B2/3); mm. negro's head (2782) .... | 1750 | 4500

2787 Group C, third bust, type 2a, with more visible armour. R. Oval garnished shield with CR above (Sharp C1/1, C2/1-3); mm. plume, rose (2783) .... | 75 | 250

2788 — — 2b. R. Plume above shield (Sharp C1/4, C2/4-6, C3/5); mm. plume, rose (2784).. | 150 | 650

2789 Group D, fourth bust, type 3.1, with falling lace collar, inner circles. R. Garnished oval shield with CR at sides (Sharp D1-6/1); mm. harp, portcullis (2785).. | 60 | 240

2790 — — — 3.2. R. Plume above shield (Sharp D1- 3/2); mm. harp (2786) | 675 | 2000

2794

2791 — — 3a, no inner circles. R. Round garnished shield, no CR (Sharp E1/1-2, E2/1-2; E3/2); mm. bell, crown, tun (2787) .... | 40 | 175

2792 — — — rare bust varieties, no inner circles: (a) large crude bust (Sharp E4/2); mm. tun; (b) neat 'Aberystwyth' bust (Sharp E5/2); mm. tun (2787 var.) | 90 | 350

2793 — — 3b. R. Plume above shield (Sharp E1-2/3); mm. bell, crown, tun (2788) | 100 | 375

2794 Group E, fifth "Aberystwyth" bust, type 4.2, double-arched crown, small or large XII. R. Square-topped shield over cross moline (Sharp F1/1); mm. tun, anchor (2791).. | 60 | 250

		F	VF
		£	£
2795	— — 4.1, larger bust, single-arched crown, small or large XII (Sharp F2/1); mm. tun, anchor (2789)	75	325
2796	— — 4.3, smaller bust, single-arched crown, large XII (Sharp F3/1-2); mm. tun, anchor, triangle (2792)	40	175

2797   2800

| 2797 | — — 4.1var., larger bust with rounded shoulder, large XII (Sharp F5/1-2); mm. anchor, triangle (2790) .... | 45 | 200 |
| 2798 | — — rare bust varieties : (a) small 'Aberystwyth' bust, double-arched crown (Sharp F4/1); mm. anchor (to right); (b) small 'Briot's' bust, with stellate lace collar, single-arched crown (Sharp F6/1-2); mm. triangle; (c) small 'Aberystwyth' bust, single-arched crown (Sharp F7/2); mm. triangle-in-circle (2790 var.) .... | 125 | 450 |

2803   2804

2799	Group F, sixth large 'Briot's' bust, type 4.4, with stellate lace collar, double-arched crown. R. Square-topped shield over cross moline (Sharp G 1/1-2); mm. triangle, star, triangle-in-circle (2793)	35	140
2800	— — — (under Parliament) (Sharp G1-2/2); mm. (P), (R), eye, sun (2843)	40	150
2801	— — 4.4 var., (under Parliament), small thin bust, 'nick' below truncation (Sharp G3/2); mm. sun (2843A)	250	750
2802	Group G, (under Parliament), seventh bust, type 4.5, tall coarse narrow bust. R. Square-topped shield over cross moline (Sharp H1/1); mm. sun, sceptre (2844)	60	250
2803	— — 4.6, shorter slim better proportioned bust (Sharp H2/2); mm. sceptre (2845)	50	225
2804	— — — short broad bust (Sharp H3/2); mm. sceptre (2845A)	75	325

* Light weight shillings (81.75 grains) exist of No. 2782, mm. lis, cross calvary
over lis; No. 2784, mm. cross calvary; and No. 2785 mm. cross calvary
See Sharp BNJ 1977 for bust varieties.

		F £	VF £
2805	**Sixpence.** Group A, first bust, in coronation robes, type 1, small bust, double-arched crown. R. Square-topped shield over cross fourchee, date above; 1625, mm. lis (2794)	90	350
2806	— — broader bust, larger crown; 1625, mm. lis, cross calvary*; 1626, mm. cross calvary* (2794, 2794A)	100	375
2807	Group B, second bust (several varieties), type 1a1, in ruff, armour and mantle. R. Square-topped shield over cross fourchee, date above; 1625, mm. cross calvary; 1626, mm. cross calvary*, negro's head; 1627, mm. negro's head, castle; 1628, mm. castle, anchor; 1629, mm. anchor, heart (2795, 2795A)	110	400
2808	— — 1a2. R. No cross fourchee; 1630, mm. heart, plume (2796)	225	750

2810   2811

		F £	VF £
2809	Group C, third bust, type 2a. R. Oval garnished shield with CR above; mm. plume, rose (2797)	75	275
2810	— — 2b. R. Plume above shield; mm. plume, rose, plume/rose (2798)	110	450
2811	Group D, fourth bust, type 3, with falling lace collar, inner circles, (medium, large and small bust). R. Oval garnished shield with CR at sides; mm. harp, portcullis (2799)	50	175
2812	— — — omits C R by shield; mm. portcullis (2799A)	125	450
2813	— — 3a, no inner circles (type 3/3a mules exist); mm. bell, crown, tun (2800)	45	175

2814   2819

		F £	VF £
2814	Group E, fifth 'Aberystwyth' bust, type 4.1, double-arched crown, small or large VI. R. Square-topped shield over cross moline; mm. tun, anchor (2801, 2802)	60	225
2815	— — — R. Lyre cross-ends; mm. tun (2801A)	85	350
2816	— — 4.2, single-arched crown; mm. tun, anchor, triangle (2803, 2804)	40	165
2817	Group F, sixth 'Briot's' bust, type 4.3, with stellate lace collar. R. Square-topped shield over cross moline; mm. triangle, star, triangle-in-circle (2805)	50	200
2818	— — (under Parliament); mm. (P), (R) (2846)	85	275
2819	Group G, (under Parliament), late 'Aberystwyth' bust with riveted shoulder, type 4.4. R. Square-topped shield over cross moline; mm. (P), (R), eye, sun, sceptre (2847)	75	250
2820	— — 4.5, squat bust of crude style; mm. eye, sun (over eye) (2848)	135	450
2821	— — 4.5 var., small 3a type bust, double-arched crown, inner circle both sides; mm. sun (over eye) (2848A)	250	750

* *Light weight sixpences (40.85 grains) exist of No. 2806, 1625, mm. cross calvary, 1626, mm. cross calvary; and No. 2807, 1626, mm. cross calvary*

2822   2824   2832

		F	VF
		£	£

2822	**Halfgroat**. Group A, without bust, crowned rose each side, type 1, inner circles on one or both sides;mm. lis, lis/-, cross calvary, castle, none (2806)	25	85
2823	— — 1a, without inner circles; mm. negro's head, castle, anchor, heart, plume (2807)	25	85
2824	Group B, second bust, type 2a, in ruff and mantle. R. Oval shield; mm. plume, rose (2808)	25	90
2825	— — 2b. R. plume above shield; mm. plume, plume/-, rose (2809)	35	150
2826	Group C, third bust, more armour, crown breaks inner circle; mm. plume, rose (2809A)	25	90
2827	— — R. Plume above shield; mm. plume (2809B)	35	150
2828	Group D, fourth bust, type 3.1, no inner circles. R. Oval shield dividing C R; mm. harp, portcullis crown (2810)	20	60
2829	— — — — 3.2-4, inner circle on one or both sides; mm. harp, portcullis, ../harp (2811-13)	20	60
2830	— — — — 3.5-6. R. Oval shield, no C R, no inner circle or obv. only; mm. harp, portcullis (2814-15)	25	65
2831	— — 3a1. R. Rounder shield, no inner circles; mm. bell, crown, tun, anchor, triangle (2816)	20	60
2832	— — 3a2-3, inner circles on obverse or both sides; mm. anchor, triangle, star, triangle-in-anchor (2817-18)	25	70
2833	— — — (under Parliament), type 3a3, inner circles both sides; mm. (P)/triangle-in-circle, (P), (R), eye, sun, sceptre (2849)	20	65
2834	Group E, fifth 'Aberystwyth' bust, types 3a4-5, no inner circles or on reverse only; mm. anchor (2819-20)	40	110
2835	— — 3a6, very small bust (from penny puncheon), no inner circles; mm. anchor (2821)	50	135
2836	Group G, (under Parliament), seventh bust, type 3a7, older bust with pointed beard; mm. eye, sun, sceptre (2850)	20	65
2837	**Penny**. Group A, without bust, rose each side, type 1, inner circles; mm. lis, negro's head, one or two pellets (2822)	20	60
2838	— — 1a, no inner circles; mm. lis, anchor, one or two pellets (2823)	20	60
2839	— — 1b, inner circle on reverse; mm. negro's head/two pellets (2824).	40	100
2840	Group B, second bust, type 2, in ruff and mantle. R. Oval shield, inner circles; mm. plume, plume/rose, rose (2825)	30	80
2841	— — 2.1, no inner circles; mm. plume, rose (2826)	30	80
2842	Group C, third bust, type 2a1, more armour visible, no inner circles; mm. plume, plume/rose, rose (2827)	25	70
2843	— — 2a2-4, inner circles on obverse, both sides or reverse; mm. plume, rose (2828-30)	25	70

2845   2851

		F £	VF £
2844	Group D, fourth bust, type 3.1, with falling lace collar. R. CR by shield, no inner circles; mm. harp, one or two pellets (2831)	20	45
2845	— — — 3.2, no C R by shield, no inner circles; mm. harp, portcullis, pellets, none (2832)	20	45
2846	— — — — 3.3-4, inner circles on obverse or reverse; mm. harp, two pellets (2833-34)	20	50
2847	— — 3a1, shield almost round with scroll garniture, no inner circles; mm. bell, triangle, one to four pellets, none (2835)	20	50
2848	— — 3a1 var., inner circle on one or both sides; mm. triangle/two pellets (2835A)	25	60
2849	Group E, fifth 'Aberystwyth' bust, type 3a3, inner circle on obverse or none; mm. triangle, anchor, one or two pellets, none (2836)	20	50
2850	Group G, (under Parliament), seventh bust, type 3a2, older bust, inner circle on obverse only; mm. one or two pellets (2851)	25	75
2851	**Halfpenny**. Rose each side, no legend or mm (2837)	15	45

Nicholas Briot's coinage, 1631-9, First milled issue, 1631-2

2852	**Crown**. King on horseback. R. Crowned shield between CR crowned; *mm.* flower and B / B	900	2250

2853

2853	**Halfcrown**. Similar	475	1350
2854	**Shilling**. Briot's early bust with falling lace collar. R. Square-topped shield over long cross fourchee; R. Legend starts at top or bottom (extr. rare) *mm.* flower and B/B, B	375	950

2855

2855	**Sixpence**. Similar, but VI behind bust; *mm.* flower and B/B, flower and B/-	175	450

2856 2856A

		F	VF
		£	£

2856 **Halfgroat**. Briot's bust, B below, II behind. R. IVSTITIA, etc., square-
topped shield over long cross fourchee 45 135

2856A Pattern halfgroat. Uncrowned bust in ruff r. R. crowned, interlocked Cs.
(North 2687). (Included because of its relatively regular appearance.) ... 45 135

2857 **Penny**. Similar, but I behind bust, B below bust; position of legend may vary 60 175

Second milled issue, 1638-9

2859

2858 **Halfcrown**. As 2853, but *mm.* anchor and B... 450 1000

2859 **Shilling**. Briot's late bust, the falling lace collar is plain with broad lace
border, no scarf. R. As 2854 but cross only to inner circle; *mm.* anchor and
B, anchor or muled 175 475

2860 **Sixpence**. Similar, but VI; *mm.* anchor, anchor and mullet/anchor.......... 80 250
The last two often exhibit flan reduction marks.

Briot's hammered issue, 1638-9

2861 **Halfcrown**. King on Briot's style horse with ground line. R. Square-topped
shield; *mm.* anchor, triangle over anchor. Also muled with Tower *rev*..... 750 2000

2862 **Shilling**. Briot's first hammered issue, Sim. to 2859; R. Square-topped
shield over short cross fleury, contraction stops on *obv.,* pellet stops
rev. mm. anchor 750 2250

2862A — Briot's second hammered issue. As 2862 but lozenge stops both sides.
mm. anchor, triangle over anchor or triangle 325 850

2862B Tower, Group E, obv. type 4.1 var. (S.2797) above R. as Briot's 1st or 2nd
hammered issue; mm. Δ over anchor.. 275 800

2862C Tower, Group F, obv. type 4.4 (S.2799 above) R. as Briot's 2nd hammered
issue; mm Δ/Δ over anchor. 225 750

Provincial and Civil War issues, 1638-49

York mint, 1643-4. *Mm*. lion

2863	**Halfcrown**. 1. Ground-line below horse. R. Square-topped shield between CR	675	2000
2864	— 2. — R. Oval shield as Tower 3a, groundline grass or dotted	575	1750

		F £	VF £
2865	— 3. No ground-line. R. Similar	525	1650
2866	— 4. As last, but EBOR below horse with head held low. Base metal, often very base (*These pieces are contemporary forgeries*)	85	225
2867	— 5. Tall horse, mane in front of chest, EBOR below. R. Crowned square-topped shield between CR, floral spray in legend	350	925

2868

| 2868 | — 6. As last, but shield is oval, garnished (*rev.* detail variations)............ | 300 | 825 |
| 2869 | — 7. Similar, but horse's tail shows between legs. R. Shield as last, but with lion's skin garniture, no CR or floral spray .... | 275 | 750 |

2870

2870	**Shilling**. 1. Bust in scalloped lace collar similar to 3[1]. R. EBOR above square-topped shield over cross fleury...	225	675
2871	— 2. Similar, but bust in plain armour, mantle; coarse work	250	750
2872	— 3. Similar R. EBOR below oval shield	250	750
2873	— 4. — Similar, but crowned oval shield (*obv.* finer style).....................	225	600
2874	— 5. — As last, but lion's skin garniture	225	600
2875	**Sixpence**. *Obv.* Sim. to 2870. Crowned oval shield	300	850

| 2876 | | 2877 |

| 2876 | — — Crowned CR at sides .... | 275 | 700 |
| 2877 | **Threepence**. As type 1 shilling, but III behind bust. R. As 2870............. | 50 | 150 |

F	*VF*
£	£

Aberystwyth mint, 1638/9-42. *Mm.* book.
Plume 1=with coronet and band. Plume 2=with coronet only

2879

2878 **Halfcrown**. Horseman similar to 2773, but plume 2 behind. R. Oval
garnished shield with large plume above. *Obv.* plume 2, *rev.* plume 1..... 825 3000
2879 — Similar to 2774, plume 1 behind King, ground below horse. *Obv.* squat
plume 1, *rev.* plume 1 .... 875 3500
2880 As 2773 but more spirited horse, no ground. FRAN ET HIB, plume 2/1 750 2750

2881

2881 **Shilling**. Bust with large square lace collar, plume 2 before, small XII. R.
As Tower 3b.. 475 1350
2882 — inner circle on *rev.* 425 1250
2883 As 2881, but large plume 1 or 2, large XII, inner circles, large or 425 1250
small shield

2884

2884 As last, but small narrow head, square lace collar, large or square plume 525 1500
2885 Small Briot style face, small crown, plume 2, large shield 575 1750
2885A **Sixpence**. *Obv.* as Tower bust 3a, plume before. R. as 2889; inner circles
both sides, *mm.* book (*obv.* only).. 475 1250

2886

		F £	*VF* £
2886	Somewhat as 2881, but double-arched crown, small VI; no inner circles	325	925
2887	Similar to 2886, but single arched crown, plume 2, inner circle *obv*. Large VI	350	950
2888	Similar, but with inner circles both sides..	350	950
2889	— — *Rev.* with small squat-shaped plume above, sometimes no *rev. mm.*	325	925
2890	Bust as the first Oxford sixpence; with crown cutting inner circle	475	1250

2891   2894

2891	**Groat**. Large bust, lace collar, no armour on shoulder. Crown breaks or touches inner circle. R. Shield, plume 1 or 2...	55	165
2892	— Similar, armour on shoulder, shorter collar. R. Similar	60	175
2893	— Smaller, neater bust well within circle. R. Similar	55	165
2894	**Threepence**. Small bust, plume 2 before. R. Shield, plume 1 or 2 above, *obv.* legend variations	45	140
2895	— Similar, but crown cuts i.c. squat pl. on *obv*., R. Pl. 2, *obv.* legend variations	45	150
2900	**Halfgroat**. Bust as Tower type 3. R. Large plume. No inner circles, *mm.* pellet/book,book	45	150
2900A	Bust as 2886. R. As last, no inner circle	50	175

2901   2903   2907

2901	Bust with round lace collar; single arch crown, inner circles, colon stops	45	150
2902	After Briot's bust, square lace collar: inner circles.................................	45	150
2903	**Penny**. As 2901; CARO; no inner circles	65	200
2904	As 2901; CARO; inner circles..	60	175
2905	As last but reads CAROLVS; inner circles..	70	225

		F	VF
		£	£
2906	*Obv.* similar to 2890, tall narrow bust, crown touches inner circle	75	250
2907	**Halfpenny**. No legend. *O*. Rose. R. Plume	150	500

Aberystwyth-Furnace mint, 1648/9. *Mm.* crown

2908	**Halfcrown**. King on horseback. R. Sim. to 2878	1750	5000
2909	**Shilling**. Aberystwyth type, but *mm.* crown	2000	6500
2910	**Sixpence**. Similar	850	2500

2911   2913

2911	**Groat**. Similar	225	525
2912	**Threepence**. Similar	200	500
2913	**Halfgroat**. Similar. R. Large plume	300	750
2914	**Penny**. Similar	675	1750

Uncertain mint (? Hereford) 1644-5

2915

2915	**Halfcrown**. As illustration, dated 1645 or undated	2250	6750
2915A	— Scarf with long sash ends. CH (Chirk castle?) below horse. R. Oval shield 1644	2750	8500
2915B	— R. Crowned oval shield, lion paws	2500	7500

Shrewsbury mint, 1642. Plume without band used as *mm.* or in field.

2917	**Pound**. King on horseback, plume behind, from the puncheon of Tower grp. 3 crowns. R. Declaration between two straight lines, XX and three Shrewsbury plumes above, 1642 below; *mm.* pellets, pellets/-	2250	5750
2918	Similar, but Shrewsbury horse walking over pile of arms; no *mm.*, pellets	2000	5250
2919	As last, but cannon amongst arms and only single plume and XX above Declaration, no *mm.*	2500	6250
2920	**Half-pound**. As 2917, but X; *mm.* pellets	1650	4000
2921	Similar, but only two plumes on *rev.*; *mm.*, pellets	2000	5750
2922	Shrewsbury horseman with ground-line, three plumes on *rev.*; *mm.*, none, pellets/-	1450	3250
2923	— with cannon and arms or arms below horse; *mm.* pellets/-	1500	3500
2924	— no cannon in arms, no plume in *obv.* field; *mm.* plume/pellets, plume/-	1200	2500

2925 **Crown**. Aberystwyth horseman from the puncheon of a Tower halfcrown
no ground line   8500   35000

2926

	F	VF
	£	£
2926 Shrewsbury horseman with ground-line; *mm.* -/pellets, pellets/-, none ...	900	2750
2927 **Halfcrown**. *O*. From Aberystwyth die; (S2880); *mm.* book. R. Single plume		
above Declaration, 1642	1750	6500
2928 Sim. to Aberystwyth die, fat plume behind. R. Three plumes above		
Declaration; *mm.* pellets, pellets/-	675	1850
2929 Shrewsbury horseman, no ground line. R. As 2927, single plume, no *mm.*	725	2000
2929A — — R. As 2933	675	1850

2930

2930 — R. 2: plume; 6, above Declaration	1250	4500
2931 — with ground-line. R. Similar	1350	5000
2932 — — R. As 2927, single plume	725	2000
2933 — — R. Three plumes above Declaration; *mm.* none or pellets	575	1750
2933A — — R. Aberystwyth die, plume over shield; *mm.* -/book......................	1650	6000
2934 As 2933 but no plume behind king; *mm.* plume/pellets	525	1500
2935 **Shilling**. *O*. From Aberystwyth die; S2885 *mm.* book. R. Declaration type	1250	3250
2936 *O*. From Shrewsbury die. R. Similar	2000	6000

Oxford mint, 1642-6. *Mm.* usually plume with band, except on the smaller denominations when it is lis or pellets. There were so many dies used at this mint that we can give only a selection of the more easily identifiable varieties.

For many years Oxford Halfcrowns and Shillings have been catalogued according to Morrieson obverse die varieties. In many cases, these are very small and difficult to identify. We have, therefore, simplified the obverse classification and used the available space to expand the listing of the more interesting reverse varieties.

2938

		F £	VF £
2937	**Pound.** Large horseman over arms, no exergual line, fine workmanship. R. Three Shrewsbury plumes and XX above Declaration, 1642 below; *mm.* plume/pellets	2850	8000
2938	— Similar, but three Oxford plumes, 1643; *mm.* as last	2750	7500
2939	Shrewsbury horseman trampling on arms, exergual line. R. As last, 1642	2250	5750
2940	— — cannon amongst arms, 1642-3; *mm.* similar	2100	5250
2941	— as last but exergue is chequered, 1642; *mm.* similar	2500	6500
2942	Briot's horseman, 1643; *mm.* similar	3250	9000
2943	*O.* As 2937. R. Declaration in cartouche, single large plume above, 1644 OX below	6750	18500
2944	**Half-pound.** Shrewsbury horseman over arms, Oxford plume behind. R. Shrewsbury die, 1642; mm. plume/-	1350	3000
2945	— R. Three Oxford plumes above, 1642; mm. plume/-	1250	2800
2945A	— — 1643; *mm.* plume/-	1275	2850
2946	**Crown.** Shrewsbury die with groundline. R. Three Oxford plumes, 1642; no mm.	950	2400
2946A	— — 1643; no *mm.*	950	2400
2947	Oxford horseman, grass below. R. Three Oxford plumes, 1643; *mm.* plume/-	1350	3750

2948

		F £	*VF* £

2948 Rawlins' crown. King riding over a view of the city. R. Floral scrolls
above and below Declaration, date in script, 1644 OXON; *mm.*
floriated cross/- *(Electrotypes and copies of this coin are common)* 13500 45000
2949 **Halfcrown.** *O.* Shrewsbury die with groundline, plume behind. R.
Oxford die, declaration in two lines, three Oxford plumes above,
1642 below; no *mm.* 575 1750
2950 — no plume behind. R. as last, 1642; *mm.* plume/- 475 1350
2951 Shrewsbury horseman with groundline, Oxford plume behind. R.
Shrewsbury die, 1642; *mm.* plume/- 475 1350
2952 — R. Three Oxford plumes, 1642; *mm.* plume/- 300 850
2953 — — without groundline, 1642; *mm.* plume/- 300 850

2954

2954 Oxford horseman without groundline, 1643; *mm.* plume/- 275 825
2954A — — R. Shrewsbury die, 1642; *mm.* plume/- or no *mm.* 475 1350
2955 — with groundline. R. Three Oxford plumes, 1643; *mm.* plume/- 275 825
2956 Briot horseman, grassy, rocky or uneven ground. R. Three Oxford plumes,
1643; *mm.* plume/-, plume & rosette/- 275 800
2957 — — 1643 OX; *mm.* plume/rosette, rosette 300 850

2961   2965A

		F	VF
		£	£
2958	— — 1644 OX; *mm.* plume/-	300	850
2958A	— — lozenges by OX, 1644 OX; *mm.* plume/-	325	875
2959	— — 1645 OX; *mm.* plume/-, plume/rosette	300	850
2959A	— — pellets by date, 1645 OX; *mm.* plume/-	350	950
2960	— — 1646 OX; *mm.* plume/-	325	900
2961	— — pellets or annulets by plumes and date, 1646 OX; *mm.* plume/- ...	375	950
2962	— R. Large central plume and two Oxford plumes, 1643; *mm.* plume/-	325	875
2963	— — 1643 OX; *mm.* plume/-, rosette/-, plume & rosette/rosette, plume & rosette/-	300	850
2964	— — rosettes by OX, 1643 OX; *mm.* rosette/-, plume & rosette/-	325	900
2965	— — plain, pellets or lozenges by plumes and/or OX, 1644 OX; *mm.* plume/- plume/rosette, rosette	275	750
2965A	— — date in script, 1644 OX; *mm.* plume/-	325	850
2966	— — rosettes by plumes and date, 1644 OX; *mm.* plume & rosette/rosette	400	1050
2967	— — small plumes by date, 1644 OX; *mm.* plume & rosette/-, rosette ..	475	1350
2968	— R. Large central plume and two small Shrewsbury plumes, lozenges in field, date in script, 1644 OX; *mm.* plume/rosette	475	1350
2969	— — small plumes by date, pellets by OX, 1644 OX; *mm.* plume/-	525	1500
2970	**Shilling.** *O.* Shrewsbury die. R. Declaration in three lines, three Oxford plumes above, 1642; *mm.* plume/-	850	2500

2971

2971	Oxford bust (small). R. Three Oxford plumes, 1642; *mm.* Oxford plume/-,	350	1050
2972	Oxford bust (small or large). R. Three Oxford plumes, 1643; *mm.* Oxford plume/-, Oxford plume/rosette	325	1000
2972A	— — pellets by date, 1644; *mm.* plume/-	375	1100
2972B	— — 1644 OX; mm. plume/rosette	375	1100
2973	— R. Oxford and two Shrewsbury plumes, lozenges by date, 1644 OX; *mm.* plume/-	425	1250
2974	— R. Three Shrewsbury plumes, 1643; *mm.* plume/-	350	1100

	F	VF
	£	£

2975 Fine Oxford bust. R. Three Oxford plumes, lozenges in field, 1644
OX; *mm.* Shrewsbury plume/- 325 1050

2975A — — large date in script, 1644 OX; *mm.* plume/- 400 1250

2976 — 1645 OX; *mm.* plume/- 950 2750

2976A — R. Oxford and two Shrewsbury plumes, 1644 OX; *mm.* plume/- 400 1250

2977 — R. Three Shrewsbury plumes, 1644 OX; *mm.* plume/- 350 1100

2978 — — annulets or pellets at date, 1646; *mm.* plume/floriated cross,
plume/- 375 1250

2979

2979 Rawlins' die. Fine bust with R. on truncation. R. Three Oxford plumes,
rosettes or lozenges by plumes, lozenges by date, 1644 OX; *mm.*
Shrewsbury plume/rosette, Shrewsbury plume/- 675 2000

2979A — — pellets by date, no OX, 1644; *mm.* plume/- 750 2200

2979B — R. Oxford and two Shrewsbury plumes, 1644 OX; *mm.* plume/- 850 2500

2980A

2980 **Sixpence.** O. Aberystwyth die R. Three Oxford plumes, 1642; *mm.* book/- 375 950

2980A — — 1643; *mm.* book/- 350 900

2981 — R. Three Shrewsbury plumes, 1643; *mm.* book/- 325 850

2982 — R. Shrewsbury plume and two lis, 1644 OX (groat rev. die); *mm.* book/- 675 1500

2983 **Groat.** O. Aberystwyth die. R. Shrewsbury plume and two lis, 1644 OX;
mm. book/- 175 575

2984 — R. Three Shrewsbury plumes, 1644 OX; mm. book/- 225 675

2985

2985 Oxford bust within inner circle. R. As 2983, 1644 OX; mm. floriated cross/- 135 425

		F	*VF*
		£	£
2985A	— R. Three Shrewsbury plumes, 1644 OX; *mm.* floriated cross/-...........	225	650
2985B	— R. Single plume, 2 scrolls and OX monogram over Decl, 1645; *mm.* floriated cross/-	225	675
2986	Large bust to top of coin. R. As 2983, 1644 OX; *mm.* lis/-	250	750
2987	Large bust to bottom of coin. R. As 2983, 1644 OX; no *mm.*	225	675
2988	— R. Single plume, 2 scrolls and OX monogram over Decl, 1645; no *mm.*	150	475
2989	Rawlins' die, no inner circle, R on shoulder. R. As 2983, 1644 OX; no *mm.*	250	750

2990

2990	— R. Single plume, Declaration in cartouche, 1645; no *mm.*	225	650
2991	— — 1646/5; no mm.	200	625
2992	**Threepence.** *O.* Aberystwyth die. R. Three lis over Declaration, 1644 OX; *mm.* book/-	150	450
2993	Rawlins; die, R below shoulder. R. Aberystwyth die, oval shield; *mm.* lis/book	150	450
2994	— R. Three lis over Declaration, 1644; *mm.* lis/-	110	285

2994   3000

2995	Crown breaks inner circle, no R. R. Three lis, 1646/4; *mm.* lis/-	110	285
2996	**Halfgroat.** Small bust, beaded or wireline inner circle. R. Large plume in field; *mm.* mullet/lis, lis, -/lis, plain cross/-, plain cross/lis	110	300
2997	— R. Three lis over Delcration, 1644 OX; *mm.* lis	125	325
2998	**Penny.** *O.* Aberystwyth die, CARO. R. Small plume in field; *mm.* book/-	135	425
2999	Aberystwyth die, CAROLVS; R. Large plume; *mm.* book/-	150	450
3000	Rawlins' die, CARO. R. Small plume; *mm.* lis/mullet, lis/-	250	750
3001	Broad bust, CAROL. R. Small plume; *mm.* lis	250	750
3002	— R. Three lis over Declaration, 1644; *mm.* lis	750	1750

Bristol mint, 1643-5. *Mm.* usually plume or Br., except on small denominations

3003	**Halfcrown.** *O.* Oxford die with or without ground-line. R. Declaration, three Bristol plumes above, 1643 below, *mm.* plume/- or plume/cross....	525	1350
3004	— Obv. as above. R as above, but *mm.* Br. 1643....................................	575	1500
3005	King wears unusual flat crown, *obv. mm.* acorn? between four pellets. R. As 3003, 1643..	525	1350
3006	— Obv. as above. R as 3004, *mm.* Br., 1643-4......................................	475	1100
3007	Shrewsbury plume behind king. R. As last...	375	900
3008	— Obv. as above. R as 3004 but Br below date instead of as *mm* . 1644	400	950

3009

		F	VF
		£	£
3009	— Obv. as 3007 but Br below horse. R as above but 1644-5	375	900
3010	— Obv. as above. R as 3004, *mm*. Br. and Br. below date, 1644-5	400	1000
3011	**Shilling**. *O*. Oxford die. R. Declaration, 1643, 3 crude plumes above, no *mm*.	475	1350

3012   3014

3012	— — R Similar, but *mm*. Br., 1643-4, less crude plumes	425	1100
3013	—Obv. Coarse bust. R. As 3011, no *mm*., 1643	625	1750
3014	— — Coarse bust, R. as 3012, *mm*. Br, but 1644	475	1350

3016A   3017

3015	Obv. Bust of good style, plumelet before face. R. As 3012 *mm*. Br. but 1644-5	400	1000
3016	— — R.as 3012, 1644, but Br below date instead of *mm*.	400	1000
3016A	— — R as 3012, 1644 but plume and plumelet either side	375	950
3017	—Obv. Taller bust with high crown, no plumelets before, *mm*. Br. on its side. R		
	As 3016 Br.below 1644-5	450	1250
3018	—Obv. As 3017 but no *mm*. R as above but *mm*. Br., no Br below 1644-5	450	1250
3018A	— — R as above but plume and plumelets, 1645	475	1350
3019	**Sixpence**. Small bust, nothing before. R. Declaration surrounded by		
	CHRISTO etc., 1643; *mm*. ./Br.	525	1500

3020

		F	VF
		£	£
3020	Fine style bust. Plumelet before face, 1644; *mm*. ./Br. (on its side)	300	850
3021	**Groat**. Bust l. R. Declaration, 1644	225	575
3022	— Plumelet before face, 1644	200	525
3023	— Br. below date, 1644	200	525
3023A	— Similar, but larger bust and more spread plume before. Mm. pellet/Br; nothing below 1644	225	575

3024   3026   3027

3024	**Threepence**. *O*. As 2992. Aberystwyth die; *mm*. book. R. Declaration, 1644	175	475
3025	Bristol die, plume before face, no *mm*., 1644	250	700
3026	**Halfgroat**. Br. in place of date below Declaration	250	700
3027	**Penny**. Similar bust, I behind. R. Large plume with bands	325	850

This penny may belong to the late declaration issue. It has the same reverse plume punch as 3044.

Late 'Declaration' issues, 1645-6

After Bristol surrendered on 11 September 1645, many of the Royalist garrison returned unsearched to Oxford and the Bristol moneyers appear to have continued work, using altered Bristol dies and others of similar type bearing the marks A, B and plume. Ashby de la Zouch was reinforced from Oxford in September 1645 and, following its fall on 28 February 1645/6, Royalist forces marched to Bridgnorth-on-Severn, holding out until 26 April 1646. Mr Boon suggested (cf. SCBI 33, p. xli) that Ashby and Bridgnorth are plausible mint sites and the most likely candidates for the A and B marked issues, if these do indeed represent fixed mint locations.

Ashby de la Zouch mint (?), 1645

3028	**Halfcrown**. Horseman of Bristol type, A below. R. Altered Bristol die. A (over Br) below date, 1645; *mm*. plume/A (over Br)	2500	7500
3029	- - R. A below date (new die), 1645; *mm*. plume/A	2500	7500
3030	- - R. Nothing below date 1645; *mm*. plume/A...	2250	6250
3031	**Shilling**. Crowned bust left. R. Declaration type, A below date, 1645; mm. plume/A	950	2750

3032

		F	VF
		£	£

3032   - plumelet before face, 1645; *mm.* plume/A 1050   3250

3033   **Sixpence.** Bust of Bristol style, plumelet before face. R. Declaration type, 1645; *mm.* A (on its side)/- 850   2250

3034   **Groat.** Similar, plumelet before face, 1645; *mm.* A (on its side)/- 750   2000

3035   **Threepence.** Similar, plumelet before face. R. Single plumelet above Declaration, 1645; no *mm.* 575   1500

Bridgnorth-on-Severn mint (?), 1646

3036   **Halfcrown.** Horseman of Bristol type, A below (same die as 3028-30). R. Scroll above Declaration, B below, 1646; *mm.* plume/A 2500   7500

3036A- - R. Nothing below date, 1646; *mm.* plume/- 1850   5250

3037

3037   - plumelet (over A) below horse (same die as 3028-30 recut). R. Nothing below date, 1646; *mm.* plume, plume/- 1250   3500

3038   - - plumelet below date, 1646; *mm.* plume 1250   3500

3039   **Shilling.** Crowned bust left, plumelet before face (same die as 3032). R. Scroll above Declaration, 1646; *mm.* plume/plumelet 575   1500

3039A- Bristol obverse die, nothing before face. R. Scroll above Declaration, 1646; *mm.* Br/- 650   1750

3040   - - plume before face (altered die of 3039A), 1646; *mm.* plumelet (over Br)/- 575   1500

3041

		F	VF
		£	£
3041	**Sixpence.** Crowned bust left, plume before face. R. Scroll above Declaration, 1646; *mm*. B/-	250	625
3042	**Groat.** Similar, plumelet before face, 1646; *mm*. plumelet, plumelet/-	225	525
3043	**Threepence.** Similar, plumelet before face. R. Single plume above Declaration, 1646; *mm*. plumelet/-	200	450
3044	**Halfgroat.** Crowned bust left, II behind. R. Large plume with bands dividing date, 1646; no *mm*.	425	975

Truro mint, 1642-3. *Mm*. rose except where stated

3045	**Crown.** King on horseback, head in profile, sash flies out in two ends. R. CHRISTO, etc., round garnished shield	375	900
3046	**Halfcrown.** King on walking horse, groundline below, R. Oblong shield, CR above, *mm*. bugle/–	2250	6000
3047	Galloping horse, king holds baton. R. Oblong shield, CR at sides	2000	6000

3045   3048

3048	Walking horse, king holds sword. R. Similar	900	2650
3049	— R. Similar, but CR above	950	2850
3050	Galloping horse, king holds sword. R. Similar, but CR at sides	1250	3500
3051	— R. Similar, but CR above	1350	3750
3052	Trotting horse. R. Similar, but CR at sides	750	2250
3053	**Shilling.** Small bust of good style. R. Oblong shield	2500	7500

Exeter mint, 1643-6. Undated or dated 1644-5 *Mm*. rose except where stated

| 3054 | **Half-pound.** King on horseback, face towards viewer, sash in large bow. R. CHRISTO, etc., round garnished shield. Struck from crown dies of 3055 on a thick flan | 3250 | 9000 |
| 3055 | **Crown.** King on horseback, sash in large bow. R. Round garnished shield | 425 | 900 |

		F	VF
		£	£
3056	— Shield garnished with twelve even scrolls	475	1200
3057	As 3055, R Date divided by *mm*. 16 rose 44	475	1250
3058	— R Date to l. of *mm*. 1644	425	900
3059	— *mm*: rose/Ex, 1645	475	1250
3060	King's sash flies out in two ends; *mm*. castle/rose, 1645	525	1450
3061	— *mm*. castle/Ex, 1645	425	950
3062	— *mm*. castle, 1645	400	875
3063	**Halfcrown**. King on horseback, sash tied in bow. R. Oblong shield CR at sides	675	1750
3064	— R. Round shield with eight even scrolls	350	925

3065

| 3065 | — R. Round shield with five short and two long scrolls | 325 | 825 |
| 3066 | — R. Oval shield with angular garnish of triple lines | 800 | 2000 |

3067

3067	Briot's horseman with lumpy ground. R. As 3064	450	1100
3068	— R. As 3065	375	950
3069	— R. As 3066	800	2000
3070	— R. As 3065, date to l. of *mm*. 1644	525	1350

3071

| 3071 | King on spirited horse galloping over arms. R. Oval garnished shield, 1642 in cartouche below | 5250 | 13500 |

		F £	*VF* £
3072	— R̟. As 3070, date to 1. of *mm.* 1644-5	5250	15000
3073	— R̟. *mm.* castle, 1645	5750	16500
3074	Short portly king, leaning backwards on ill-proportioned horse, 1644, 16 rose 44	975	3000
3075	Horse with twisted tail, sash flies out in two ends R̟. As 3064	525	1400

3076

3076	— R̟. As 3070, date divided by *mm.* 16 rose 44, or date to 1. of *mm.* 1644-5	475	1350
3077	— R̟. *mm.* castle, 1645	575	1500
3078	— R̟. *mm.* Ex, 1645	575	1500
3079	— R̟. Declaration type; *mm.* Ex. 1644-5	2250	7500
3080	— R̟. Similar, Ex also below declaration, 1644	2000	7000
3081	**Shilling.** Large Oxford style bust. R̟. Round shield with eight even scrolls	950	2750
3082	— R̟. Oval shield with CR at sides	950	2750
3083	Normal bust with lank hair. R̟. As 3081	675	1750
3083A	— R̟. As 3082	750	2000
3084	— R̟. Round shield with six scrolls	475	1150

3085

3085	— R̟. Similar, date 1644, 45 to left of rose *mm.* 16 rose 44 (rare), 1644 to right of rose (very rare)...................................	450	1050
3086	— R̟. Declaration type, 1645	1250	3500

3087A

3087	**Sixpence.** Similar to 3085, large bust and letters 1644 rose	275	800
3087A	— Smaller bust and letters from punches used on 3088, small or large VI, 16 rose 44	300	850

	F	*VF*
	£	£
3088 **Groat**. Somewhat similar but 1644 at beginning of *obv*. legend..............	135	325

3089 3090 3092		
3089 **Threepence**. Similar. R. Square shield, 1644 above......................	110	275
3090 **Halfgroat**. Similar, but II. R. Oval shield, 1644	250	600
3091 — R. Large rose, 1644..	275	650
3092 **Penny**. As last but I behind head..	350	950

Worcester mint 1643-4

3093 **Halfcrown**. King on horseback l., W below; *mm.* two lions. R. Declaration type 1644 altered from 1643 Bristol die; *mm.* pellets..............................	1250	3500
3094 — R. Square-topped shield; *mm.* helmet, castle......................................	850	2250
3095 — R. Oval shield; *mm.* helmet	900	2500

3096

3096 Similar but grass indicated; *mm.* castle. R. Square-topped shield; *mm.* helmet or pellets...	800	2100
3097 — R. Oval draped shield, lis or lions in legend..	825	2250
3098 — R. Oval shield CR at sides, roses in legend	825	2250
3099 — R. FLORENT etc., oval garnished shield with lion's paws each side .	900	2500
3100 Tall king, no W or *mm.* R. Oval shield, lis, roses, lions or stars in legend	825	2250
3101 — R. Square-topped shield; *mm.* helmet..	900	2500
3102 — R. FLORENT, etc., oval shield; no *mm.*...	950	2650
3103 Briot type horse, sword slopes forward, ground-line. R. Oval shield, roses in legend; *mm.* 91v, 105, none (combinations)...	900	2500
3104 — Similar, but CR at sides, 91v/-..	900	2500
3105 Dumpy, portly king, crude horse. R. As 3100; *mm.* 91v, 105, none	950	2650

3106

		F £	VF £
3106	Thin king and horse. R. Oval shield, stars in legend; *mm.* 91v, none......	825	2250

Worcester or Salopia (Shrewsbury) 1643-4

3107	**Shilling**. Bust of king l., adequately rendered. R. Square-topped shield; *mm.* castle	1500	5250
3108	— R. CR above shield; *mm.* helmet and lion	1500	5250
3109	— R. Oval shield; *mm.* lion, pear	1350	5000
3110	— Bust a somewhat crude copy of last (two varieties); *mm.* bird, lis. R. Square-topped shield with lion's paws above and at sides; *mm.* boar's head, helmet..	1500	5500

3108

3111	— — CR above	1750	6000
3112	— R. Oval shield, lis in legend; *mm.* lis...	1350	4500
3113	— R. Round shield; *mm.* lis, 3 lis..	1350	4500
3114	Bust r.; *mm.* pear/-, pear/lis. R. draped oval shield with or without CR. (Halfcrown reverse dies)..	2000	6500
3115	**Sixpence**. As 3110; *mm.* castle, castle/boar's hd	1750	4500

3116

3117

3116	**Groat**. As 3112; *mm.* lis/helmet, rose/helmet...	675	1500
3117	**Threepence**. Similar; *mm.* lis...	375	750
3118	**Halfgroat**. Similar; *mm.* lis (*O.*) various (*R.*)	625	1250

	F £	VF £

Salopia (Shrewsbury) mint, 1644

3119 **Halfcrown**. King on horseback l. SA below; *mm*. lis. R. (*mm*. lis, helmet,
        lion rampant, none). Cr. oval shield; CHRISTO etc. *mm*. helmet .... | 4500 | 12500 |

3120 — R. FLORENT, etc., crowned oval shield, no *mm*. .... | 4500 | 12500 |

3121 — SA erased or replaced by large pellet or cannon ball; *mm*. lis in legend,
        helmet. R. As 3119.. | 1850 | 5750 |

3122 Tall horse with mane blown forward, nothing below; *mm*. lis. R.
        Large round shield with crude garniture; *mm*. helmet............................ | 975 | 2750 |

3123 — R. Uncrowned square-topped shield with lion's paw above and at sides;
        mm. helmet.. | 1200 | 3250 |

3124 — R. Small crowned oval shield; *mm*. various .... | 975 | 2750 |

3125

3125 — R. As 3120	1100	3000
3126 Finer work with little or no mane before horse. R. Cr. round or oval shield	1250	3250
3127 Grass beneath horse. R. Similar; *mm*. lis or rose	1500	4250
3128 Ground below horse. R. As 3120...	1850	5750

Hartlebury Castle (Worcs.) mint, 1646

3129

3129 **Halfcrown**. O. *Mm*. pear. R. HC (Hartlebury Castle) in garniture below
        shield; *mm*. three pears .... | 1500 | 4000 |

Chester mint, 1644

3130

		F	VF
		£	£
3130	**Halfcrown**. As illus. R. Oval shield; *mm*. three gerbs and sword............	975	2750
3131	— Similar, but without plume or CHST; R. Cr. oval shield with lion skin; *mm*. prostrate gerb; -/cinquefoil, -/⁞	1050	3000
3132	— R. Crowned square-topped shield with CR at sides both crowned *rev*.; *mm*. cinquefoil (these dies were later crudely recut)	1350	5250
3133	As 3130, but without plume or CHST. R. Declaration type, 1644 *rev*.; *mm*. plume	1250	4750
3133A	**Shilling**. Bust l. R. Oval garnished shield; *mm*. ∴ (obv. only)	1250	4250
3133B	— R. Square-topped shield; *mm*. as last...	1250	4250
3133C	— R . Shield over long cross..	1250	4250
3134	**Threepence**. R. Square-topped shield; *mm*.-/ prostrate gerb	950	3000

Welsh Marches mint? 1644

3135

3135	**Halfcrown**. Crude horseman, l. R. Declaration of Bristol style divided by a dotted line, 3 plumes above, 1644 below	950	3000

Carlisle besieged, 1644-5

3137   3139

		F £	VF £
3136	**Three shillings**. Large crown above C R between rosettes III. S below. rev. OBS . CARL / . 1645, rosette below	7000	17500
3137	Similar but :- OBS :/-: CARL :./.1645, rosette above and below	6250	15000
3138	**Shilling**. Large crown above C R between trefoil of pellets, XII below. rev. as 3137	4750	11500
3139	R. Legend and date in two lines	5250	12000

Note. (3136-39) Round or Octagonal pieces exist.

Newark besieged, several times 1645-6, surrendered May 1646

3140   3144

		F	VF
3140	**Halfcrown**. Large crown between CR ; below, XXX. rev. OBS / NEWARK / 1645	800	1850
3140A	— Similar 1646	750	1750
3141	**Shilling**. Similar but crude flat shaped crown, NEWARKE, 1645	850	2250
3142	Similar but normal arched crown, 1645	725	1600
3143	— NEWARK, 1645 or 1646	700	1500
3144	**Ninepence**. As halfcrown but IX, 1645 or 1646	650	1300
3145	— NEWARKE, 1645	675	1350

3146

		F	VF
		£	£

3146 **Sixpence**. As halfcrown but VI, 1646 800   1650

Pontefract besieged, June 1648-March 1648-9
3147 **Two shillings** (lozenge shaped). DVM : SPIRO : SPERO around CR
crowned. R. Castle surrounded by OBS, PC, sword and 1648................. 5750   16500

3148

3148 **Shilling** (lozenge shaped, octagonal or round). Similar........................... 2000   5250
3149 — Similar but XII on r. dividing PC 1750   5000
After the death of Charles I (30 Jan. 1648/9), in the name of Charles II

3150

3150 **Shilling** (octagonal). *O.* As last. R. CAROLVS : SECVИDVS : 1648, castle
gateway with flag dividing PC, OBS on l., cannon protrudes on r. 2000   5250
3151 CAROL : II : etc., around HANC : DE / VS : DEDIT 1648. R. POST :
MORTEM : PATRIS : PRO : FILIO around gateway etc. as last 2250   5750

Scarborough besieged, July 1644-July 1645

3156

3165

3169

		VF
Type I. Large Castle with gateway to left, SC and value Vs below		
3152	**Crown.** (various weights)	45000
Type II. Small Castle with gateway, no SC, value punched on flan		
3153	**Five shillings and eightpence.**	25000
3154	**Crown.** Similar	37500
3155	**Three shillings.** Similar	18500
3156	**Two shillings and tenpence.** Similar	17500
3157	**Two shillings and sevenpence.** Similar	17500
3158	**Halfcrown.** Similar	25000
3159	**Two shillings and fourpence.** Similar	17500
3161	**One shilling and ninepence.** *Struck from a different punch, possibly of later manufacture.*	
3162	**One shilling and sixpence.** Similar to 3159	15000
3163	**One shilling and fourpence.** Similar	15000
3164	**One shilling and threepence.** Similar	15000
3165	**Shilling.** Similar	20000
3166	**Sixpence.** Similar	16500
3167	**Groat.** Similar	14500

		VF

Type III. Castle gateway with two turrets, value punched below

3168	**Two shillings and twopence**	10500
3169	**Two shillings.** Castle punched twice	10500
3170	**One shilling and sixpence.** Similar to 3168	9500
3171	**One shilling and fourpence.** Similar	9500
3172	**One shilling and threepence.** Similar	9500
3173	**One shilling and twopence.** Similar	8250
3174	**One shilling and one penny.** Similar	8250
3175	**Shilling.** Similar	12500
3176	**Elevenpence.** Similar	7500
3177	**Tenpence.** Similar	7500
3178	**Ninepence.** Similar	7500
3178A	**Eightpence.** Similar	7250
3179	**Sevenpence.** Similar	7250
3180	**Sixpence.** Similar	10000

COPPER

For further details see C. Wilson Peck, *English Copper, Tin and Bronze Coins in the British Museum, 1558-1958.*

3181

3183

	F	*VF*
	£	£

3181   **Royal farthing.** 'Richmond' 1a, colon stops, CARO over IACO; *mm.* on *obv.* only; *mm:* Coronet, Crescent with mullet, Dagger, Mascle 15   30

3182   — — 1b. CARA; (Contemporary forgeries manufactured from official punches. Usually F for E in REX) *mm.* on *obv.* only; *mm:* Annulet, Coronet, Cross patée fourchée, Dagger, Fusil, Key, Mascle, Trefoil, Tun 100   200

3183   — — 1c. CARO; *mm.* on *obv.* only; *mm:* A, A with pellet, Annulet, Annulet with pellet within, Bell, Book, Cinquefoil, Crescent (large and small), Cross (pellets in angles), Cross calvary, Cross patée, Cross patée fitchée, Cross patonce, Cross patonce in saltire, Cross saltire, Dagger, Ermine, Estoile, Estoile (pierced), Eye, Fish hook, Fleece, Fusil, Fusils (two), Gauntlet, Grapes, Halberd, Harp, Heart, Horseshoe, Leaf, Lion passant, Lis (large), Lis (demi), Lis (three), Martlet, Mascle with pellet within, Nautilus, Rose (single), Shield, Spearhead, Tower, Trefoil, Woolpack, Woolpack over annulet. 10   24

3184   3185

	·F £	VF £
3184 — — 1d, apostrophe stops, eagle-headed harp, *mm.* on *obv.* only; *mm:* Crescent (large), Lion rampant, Rose (double), Trefoil	10	24
3185 — 1e. Beaded harp, *mm* Rose (double) on *obv.* only	10	24
3186 — 1f. Scroll-fronted harp, 5 jewels on circlet *mm* Rose (double) on *obv.* only	15	35
3187 — 1g. Scroll-fronted harp, 7 jewels on circlet *mm* Rose (double) on *obv.* only	10	24

3187A

3187A— 1g on uncut square flan	150	300
— Longer strips of two to nine farthings also exist	*Extremely Rare*	

3188   3190

3188 Transitional issue 2, double-arched crowns *mm* on *obv.* only; *mm:* Harp, Quatrefoil	20	50
3189 'Maltravers' 3a; inner circles *mm.* on *obv.* only; *mm:* Bell, Rose (double) Woolpack	30	75
3190 — 3b. *mm.* both sides; *mm:* Bell, Cross patée, Lis (large), Lis (small), Martlet, Rose (double), Woolpack	10	24

3191   3192

3191 — 3c. Different *mm.* on each side; *mm:* Bell/Cross patée fitchée, Cross patée fitchée/Bell, Harp/Bell, Harp/Billet, Harp/Woolpack, Lis/Portcullis Martlet/Bell, Woolpack/Portcullis, Woolpack/Rose (double)	10	24
3192 'Richmond' oval. 4a. CARO over IACO; legend starts at bottom left, *mm:* Cross patée on both sides	45	90
3193 — 4a, *mm.* Cross patée on *obv.* only	45	90

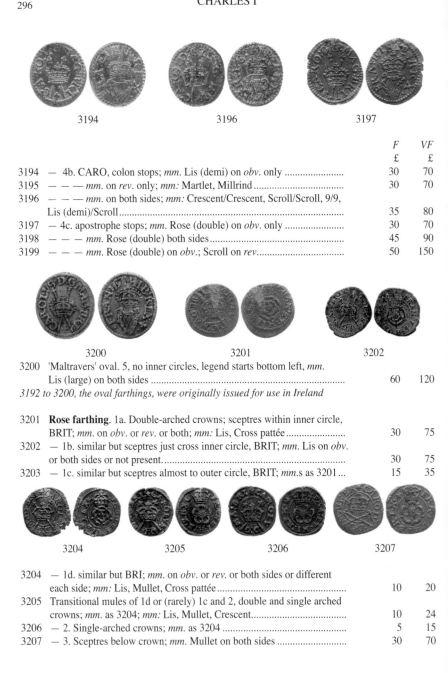

			3194	3196	3197

		F	*VF*
		£	£
3194	— 4b. CARO, colon stops; *mm.* Lis (demi) on *obv.* only	30	70
3195	— — — *mm.* on *rev.* only; *mm:* Martlet, Millrind	30	70
3196	— — — *mm.* on both sides; *mm:* Crescent/Crescent, Scroll/Scroll, 9/9, Lis (demi)/Scroll...	35	80
3197	— 4c. apostrophe stops; *mm.* Rose (double) on *obv.* only	30	70
3198	— — — *mm.* Rose (double) both sides..	45	90
3199	— — — *mm.* Rose (double) on *obv.*; Scroll on *rev.*...............................	50	150

3200	3201	3202

| 3200 | 'Maltravers' oval. 5, no inner circles, legend starts bottom left, *mm.* Lis (large) on both sides .... | 60 | 120 |

3192 to 3200, the oval farthings, were originally issued for use in Ireland

3201	**Rose farthing**. 1a. Double-arched crowns; sceptres within inner circle, BRIT; *mm.* on *obv.* or *rev.* or both; *mm:* Lis, Cross pattée	30	75
3202	— 1b. similar but sceptres just cross inner circle, BRIT; *mm.* Lis on *obv.* or both sides or not present...	30	75
3203	— 1c. similar but sceptres almost to outer circle, BRIT; *mm.*s as 3201 ...	15	35

3204	3205	3206	3207

3204	— 1d. similar but BRI; *mm.* on *obv.* or *rev.* or both sides or different each side; *mm:* Lis, Mullet, Cross pattée	10	20
3205	Transitional mules of 1d or (rarely) 1c and 2, double and single arched crowns; *mm.* as 3204; *mm:* Lis, Mullet, Crescent.....................................	10	24
3206	— 2. Single-arched crowns; *mm.* as 3204	5	15
3207	— 3. Sceptres below crown; *mm.* Mullet on both sides	30	70

The coins struck during the Commonwealth have inscriptions in English instead of Latin which was considered to savour too much of popery. St. George's cross and the Irish harp take the place of the royal arms. The silver halfpenny was issued for the last time. Coins with *mm.* anchor were struck during the protectorship of Richard Cromwell.

Mintmarks

1649-57 Sun 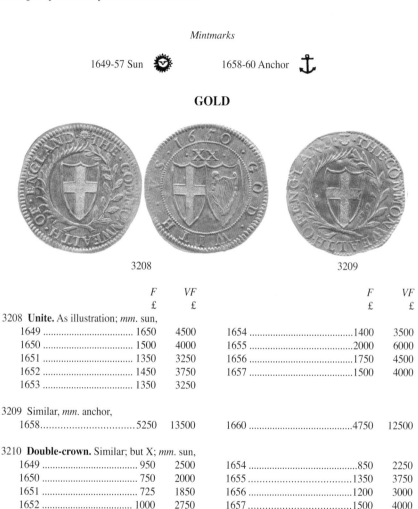   1658-60 Anchor

GOLD

	3208			3209	

	F	*VF*		*F*	*VF*
	£	£		£	£
3208 Unite. As illustration; *mm.* sun,					
1649	1650	4500	1654	1400	3500
1650	1500	4000	1655	2000	6000
1651	1350	3250	1656	1750	4500
1652	1450	3750	1657	1500	4000
1653	1350	3250			
3209 Similar, *mm.* anchor,					
1658	5250	13500	1660	4750	12500
3210 Double-crown. Similar; but X; *mm.* sun,					
1649	950	2500	1654	850	2250
1650	750	2000	1655	1350	3750
1651	725	1850	1656	1200	3000
1652	1000	2750	1657	1500	4000
1653	725	1850			
3211 Similar, *mm.* anchor, 1660				2500	7000

3212

	F £	VF £		F £	VF £
3212 Crown. Similar, but V; *mm.* sun,					
1649	725	2000	1654	750	1850
1650	675	1750	1655	1250	3250
1651	700	1800	1656	1050	3000
1652	675	1750	1657	1050	3000
1653	675	1750			
3213 Similar *mm.* anchor,					
1658	1750	4750	1660	1850	5500

3215

SILVER

	F £	VF £		F £	VF £
3214 Crown. Same type; *mm.* sun,					
1649	2000	6500	1653	725	1650
1651	1350	3250	1654	825	1850
1652	800	1750	1656	800	1750
3215 Halfcrown. Similar; *mm.* sun,					
1649	425	1250	1654	250	725
1651	275	750	1655	725	2500
1652	275	750	1656	225	525
1653	225	525	1657	1350	3500
3216 Similar, *mm.* anchor					
1658	950	2250	1660	950	2250
1659	2250	6500			

3217 rev   3218 obv

	F	VF		F	VF
	£	£		£	£

3217 **Shilling.** Similar; *mm.* sun,

1649	225	575	1654	150	400
1651	150	400	1655	275	750
1652	150	400	1656	150	400
1653	140	375	1657	425	1000

3218 Similar, *mm.* anchor

1658	575	1500	1660	575	1500
1659	1750	5000			

3219

3219 **Sixpence.** Similar; *mm.* sun,

1649	135	425	1654	130	375
1651	125	350	1655	325	925
1652	130	375	1656	130	375
1653	125	350	1657	325	925

3220 Similar; *mm.* anchor,

1658	475	1250	1660	475	1250
1659	900	2250			

3221   3222

3221 **Halfgroat**. 30   90
3222 **Penny**. Similar, but I above shields 25   75

3223

3223 **Halfpenny**. 20   60

Oliver Cromwell, 'the Great Emancipator' was born on 25th April 1599 in Huntingdon. He married Elizabeth Bourchier in August 1620 and had nine children seven of whom survived infancy. The Protectorate was established on 16th December 1653, with work on the production of portrait coins authorised in 1655. Although often referred to as patterns, there is in fact nothing to suggest that the portrait coins of Oliver Cromwell were not intended for circulation. Authorised in 1656, the first full production came in 1657 and was followed by a second more plentiful one before Cromwell's death on 3rd September 1658. All coins were machine made, struck from dies by Thomas Simon in the presses of the Frenchman, Pierre Blondeau. Later, some of Simon's puncheons were sold in the Low Countries and an imitation Crown was made there. Other Dutch dies were prepared and some found their way back to the Mint, where in 1738 it was decided to strike a set of Cromwell's coins. Shillings and Sixpences were struck from the Dutch dies, and Crowns from new dies prepared by John Tanner. Thomas Simon who was born in 1618, later died in the Great Plague of 1665. Oliver was succeeded as Lord Protector by his son Richard for whom no coins were struck.

GOLD

	F £	VF £	EF £
3224 **Fifty shillings**. Laur. head l. R. Crowned Shield of the Protectorate, die axis ↑↓ 1656.	12500	27500	65000

Inscribed edge PROTECTOR · LITERIS · LITERÆ · NUMMIS · CORONA · ET · SALUS

3225
1656 gold Broad

	F	VF	EF
3225 **Broad.** of Twenty Shillings. Laur. head l. R. Crowned Shield of the Protectorate, but grained edge die axis ↑↓ 1656.	3250	5500	11000

SILVER

3226
1658 Crown 8 over 7 - Die flawed drapery

		F	VF	EF
3226	**Crown.** Dr. bust l. R. Crowned shield, 1658/7. Inscribed edge ↑↓	1500	2250	4500
3226A	**Crown.** Dutch copy, similar with A𝖵G legend 1658	1750	3000	7000
3226B	**Crown.** Tanner's copy (struck 1738) dated 1658	1750	3000	7000

	F	*VF*	*EF*
	£	£	£

3227 **Halfcrown.** Dr. bust l. R. Crowned shield 1656 HI type
legend die axis ↑↓ 2000 3750 7500

3227A
1658 Halfcrown with HIB obverse legend

3227A Halfcrown. Similar,1658 HIB type legend die axis ↑↓ 900 1650 3250

3228
1658 Shilling

3228 **Shilling.** Dr. bust l. R. Crowned shield, grained edge, 1658 die
axis↑↓ 500 1100 2500

3229 **Sixpence.** Similar 1658 die axis↑↓ .... *Extremely rare*

COPPER

3230 **Farthing.** Dr. bust l. R. CHARITIE AND CHANGE, shield ↑↓.. 3000 6500 —
There are also other reverse types for this coin.

For the first two years after the Restoration the same denominations, apart from the silver crown, were struck as were issued during the Commonwealth although the threepence and fourpence were soon added. Then, early in 1663, the ancient hand hammering process was finally superceded by the machinery of Blondeau.

For the emergency issues struck in the name of Charles II in 1648/9, see the siege pieces of Pontefract listed under Charles I, nos. 3150-1.

Hammered coinage, 1660-2

Mintmark: Crown.

GOLD

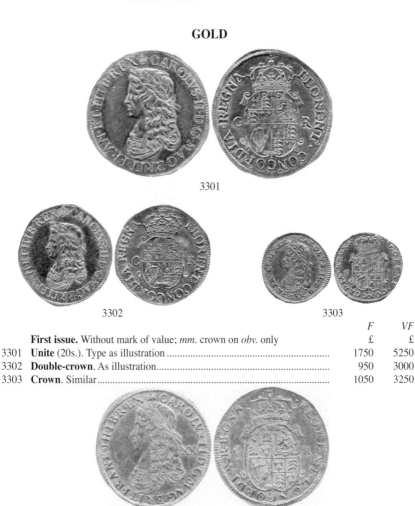

3301

3302   3303

		F	*VF*
	First issue. Without mark of value; *mm.* crown on *obv.* only	£	£
3301	**Unite** (20s.). Type as illustration	1750	5250
3302	**Double-crown**. As illustration	950	3000
3303	**Crown**. Similar	1050	3250

3304

	Second issue. With mark of value; *mm.* crown on *obv.* only		
3304	**Unite**. Type as illustration	1250	3250
3305	**Double-crown**. As illustration	850	2500
3306	**Crown**. Similar	950	3000

SILVER

3307

		F £	*VF* £

First issue. Without inner circles or mark of value; *mm*. crown on *obv*. only

| 3307 | **Halfcrown.** Crowned bust, as 3308 .... | 900 | 3250 |

3308

3309

3308	**Shilling**. Similar	375	1250
3309	**Sixpence**. Similar	275	900
3310	**Twopence**. Similar	35	110
3311	**Penny**. Similar...	35	100
3312	As last, but without mintmark	45	125

3313

3316

Second issue. Without inner circles, but with mark of value; *mm*. crown on *obv*. only

3313	**Halfcrown.** Crowned bust...	850	3000
3314	**Shilling**. Similar	475	1350
3315	**Sixpence**. Similar	1250	3500
3316	**Twopence**. Similar, but mm. on obv. only	75	275

		F	VF
		£	£
3317	Similar, but mm. both sides (machine made)	25	70
3318	Bust to edge of coin, legend starts at bottom l. (machine made, single arch crown)..	20	60
3319	**Penny**. As 3317	25	75
3320	As 3318 (single arch crown)...	20	60

3321   3226

Third issue. With inner circles and mark of value; *mm.* crown on both sides

		F	VF
3321	**Halfcrown**. Crowned bust to i.c. (and rarely to edge of coin)	225	750
3322	**Shilling**. Similar, rarely *mm.* crown on *obv.* only	150	450
3323	**Sixpence**. Similar	135	425
3324	**Fourpence**. Similar	30	85
3325	**Threepence**. Similar...	25	70
3326	**Twopence**. Similar	20	55
3327	**Penny**. Similar..	20	50

Grading of Early and Later Milled Coinage

Milled coinage refers to coins that are struck by dies worked in a mechanical coining press. The early period is defined from the time of the successful installation of Peter Blondeau's hand powered machinery at the mint, initiated to strike the first portrait coins of Oliver Cromwell in 1656. The early period continuing until the advent of Matthew Boulton's steam powered presses from 1790. The coinage of this early period is therefore cruder in it's execution than the latter. When pricing coins of the early peiod, we only attribute grades as high as extremely fine, and as high as uncirculated for the latter period. Most coins that occur of the early period in superior grades than those stated, in particular copper coins retaining full original lustre, will command considerably higher prices, due to their rarity. We suggest the following definitions for grades of preservation:

Milled Coinage Conditions

Proof A very carefully struck coin from specially prepared dies, to give a superior definition to the design, with mirror-like fields. Occurs occasionally in the Early Milled Coinage, more frequently in the latter period. Some issues struck to a matt finish for Edward VII.

FDC *Fleur-de-coin*. Absolutely flawless, untouched, without wear, scratches, marks or hairlines. Generally applied to proofs.

UNC *Uncirculated*. A coin in as new condition as issued by the Mint, retaining full lustre or brilliance but, owing to modern mass-production methods of manufacture and storage, not necessarily perfect.

EF *Extremely Fine*. A coin that exhibits very little sign of circulation, with only minimal marks or faint wear, which are only evident upon very close scrutiny.

VF *Very Fine*. A coin that exhibits some wear on the raised surfaces of the design, but really has only had limited circulation.

F *Fine*. A coin that exhibits considerable wear to the raised surfaces of the design, either through circulation, or damage perhaps due to faulty striking

Fair *Fair*. A coin that exhibits wear, with the main features still distinguishable, and the legends, date and inscriptions still readable.

Poor *Poor*. A coin that exhibits considerable wear, certainly with milled coinage of no value to a collector unless it is an extremely rare date or variety.

Examples of Condition Grading

Early Milled

Gold A̸V   Silver A̸R   Copper Æ

Extremely Fine

Gold Aᵥ

Silver Åᴿ

Copper Æ

Very Fine

Fine

George III
fifth bust Guinea

James II
Second bust Crown

George II
old head Halfpenny

Later Milled

Gold Aᵥ

Silver Åᴿ

Copper Æ

Uncirculated

Gold Æ	Silver Æ	Copper Æ

Extremely Fine

Very Fine

Fine

Victoria
Jubilee head Half-Sovereign

George IV
laureate bust Crown

Victoria
Young head Farthing

Charles II was born at St James Palace on 29th May 1630. He spent a long exile in France and returned after the fall of the Protectorate in 1660. The Restoration commenced and he married Catherine of Braganza, but he bore no legitimate successor. Charles II died on 6th February 1685.

Early in 1663, the ancient hand hammering process was finally superceded by the machinery of Blondeau. John and Joseph Roettier, two brothers, engraved the dies with a safeguard against clipping, the larger coins were made with the edge inscribed DECVS ET TVTAMEN and the regnal year. The medium-sized coins were given a grained edge.

The new gold coins were current for 100s., 40s., 20s. and 10s., and they came to be called 'Guineas' as the gold from which some of them were made was imported from Guinea by the Africa Company (whose badge was the Elephant and Castle). It was not until some years later that the Guinea increased in value to 21s. and more. The Africa Co. badge is also found on some silver and so is the plume symbol indicating silver from the Welsh mines. The four smallest silver denominations, though known today as 'Maundy Money', were actually issued for general circulation: at this period the silver penny was probably the only coin distributed at the Royal Maundy ceremonies. Though never part of the original agreement, smaller coins were eventually also struck by machinery.

A good regal copper coinage was issued for the first time in 1672, but later in the reign, farthings were struck in tin (with a copper plug) in order to help the Cornish tin industry.

Engravers and designers: John Roettier (1631-1700), Thomas Simon (1618-1665)

GOLD

3328
1672 First bust type Five-Guineas

Milled coinage

	F £	VF £	EF £		F £	VF £	EF £

3328   Five Guineas. First laur. bust r., pointed trun., regnal year on edge in words, die axis ↑↓
(e.g. 1669=VICESIMO PRIMO), R. Crowned cruciform shields, sceptres in angles

1668 VICESIMO 1650	4500	10500	1671 – TERTIO 1750	4750	11000
1668 V. PRIMO 2250	6250	13000	1672 – QVARTO 1650	4500	10500
1669 – PRIMO........ 1600	4250	10000	1673 – QVINTO........ 1600	4250	10000
1670 – SECVNDO.. 1500	4000	9750	1674 – SEXTO 1750	4750	12000
1670 – Similar proof *FDC* —	—	57500			

3328A Five Guineas. First bust. Similar hair of different style. Shorter ties

1675 V. SEPTIMO.. 1650	4500	10500	1677 – NONO 1600	4250	9750
1676 – SEPTIMO ... 1600	4500	10500	1678/7 – TRICESIMO.. 1650	4500	10500
1676 – OCTAVO..... 1700	4650	11000			

3329   Five Guineas. First bust with elephant below, similar die axis ↑↓

1668 VICESIMO ... 1500	4000	9500	1675 V. SEPTIMO..... 1900	5000	12000
1669 – PRIMO........ 2000	5250	12500	1677/5 – NONO	*Extremely rare*	

3330

1676 Five-Guineas with elephant and castle provenance mark

	F	VF	EF		F	VF	EF
	£	£	£		£	£	£

3330 **Five Guineas.** First bust with elephant and castle below, similar die axis ↑↓

1675 – SEPTIMO	*Extremely rare*		1677 – NONO 1850	5000	11000
1676 – OCTAVO..... 1800	4750	10500	1678/7– TRICESIMO.. 1850	5000	11000

3331 **Five Guineas.** Second laur. bust r., rounded trun. similar die axis ↑↓

1678/7 TRICESIMO. 1650	4750	10000	1682 T. QVARTO......1500	4000	9500
1679 – PRIMO........ 1500	4000	9500	1683 – QVINTO........1500	4000	9500
1680 – SECVNDO.. 1650	4750	10000	1683/2 –QVINTO.......1650	4750	10000
1681 – TERTIO....... 1650	4750	10000	1684 – SEXTO 1500	4000	9500

3332 **Five Guineas.** Second laur. bust r., with elephant and castle below, similar die axis ↑↓

1680 T. SECVNDO 2000	5250	–	1683 T. QVINTO.......1750	5000	11000
1681 – TERTIO....... 1750	5000	11000	1684 – SEXTO 1600	4250	9750
1682 – QVARTO..... 1650	4500	10000			

3333

1664 First bust type Two Guineas

3333 **Two Guineas.** First laur. bust r., pointed trun. ℞. Crowned cruciform shields, sceptres in angles, die axis ↑↓

1664 900	2750	6500	1671 1050	3750	8500
1665	*Extremely rare*		1673	*Extremely rare*	
1669	*Extremely rare*				

3334

1664 Two Guineas with elephant only below

3334 **Two Guineas.** First bust with elephant below, similar die axis ↑↓

1664...875 2400 5750

3335
1675 Two Guineas - second bust   3339
1663 Guinea first bust, elephant below

	F	VF	EF		F	VF	EF
	£	£	£		£	£	£

3335 Two Guineas. Second laur. bust r., rounded trun, similar die axis ↑↓

1675	1000	2750	6250	1680	1200	3250	6750
1676	975	2650	6000	1681	975	2650	6000
1677	975	2650	6000	1682	975	2650	6000
1678/7	950	2500	5750	1683	975	2650	6000
1679	975	2650	6000	1684	1000	2750	6250

Overstruck dates are listed only if commoner than the normal date or if no normal date is known.

3336 Two Guineas. Second bust with elephant and castle below, similar die axis ↑↓

1676	1100	2850	6750	1682	1100	2850	6750
1677		*Extremely rare*		1683	1200	3000	7250
1678	1100	2850	6750	1684	1100	2850	7000

3337 Two Guineas. Second bust with elephant only below, die axis ↑↓ 1678 ...   *Extremely rare*

3337A Broad of 20s. Laur. and dr. bust r. R. Crowned shield of arms (approx. 3400 issued),
die axis ↑↓ 1662 . 1050   2250   4500

3338 Guinea. First laur. bust r., R. Crowned cruciform shields, die axis
↑↓ 1663 1050   3250   9000

3339 Guinea. First bust with elephant below, similar die axis ↑↓ 1663 800   2650   7000

3340 Guinea. Second laur. bust r.,similar die axis ↑↓ 1664 725   2400   6500

3341
1664 Guinea second bust elephant below   3342
1666 Guinea - third bust

3341 Guinea. Second bust with elephant below, similar die axis ↑↓ 1664 .. 1750   5000   12500

3342 Guinea. Third laur. bust r. similar die axis ↑↓

1664	625	2200	5500	1669	575	2000	5250
1665	575	2000	5250	1670	575	2000	5250
1666	575	2000	5250	1671	575	2000	5250
1667	575	2000	5250	1672	625	2250	5750
1668	550	1850	5000	1673	625	2250	5750

3343 Guinea. Third laur. bust r., with elephant below, similar die axis ↑↓

1664	700	2450	6500	1668		*Extremely rare*	
1665	700	2450	6500				

3344
Fourth bust

3345
Fourth bust - elephant and castle below

	F	VF	EF		F	VF	EF
	£	£	£		£	£	£

3344 Guinea. Fourth laur. bust r., rounded trun. similar die axis ↑↓

1672	525	1650	4750	1679	425	1500	4000
1673	475	1600	4500	1679 ' O' over ' o' on it's side		*Extremely rare*	
1674	475	1600	4500	1680	450	1500	4250
1675	475	1600	4500	1681	475	1600	4500
1675 CRAOLVS error	1500	—	—	1682	475	1600	4500
1676	450	1500	4250	1682 rev.@90° axis	600	1750	5250
1677	450	1500	4250	1683	450	1500	4250
1677 GRATIR error		*Extremely rare*		1684	475	1600	4500
1678	450	1500	4250				

3345 Guinea. Fourth laur. bust r., with elephant and castle below, similar die axis ↑↓

1674		*Extremely rare*		1679	550	1850	5750
1675	525	1750	5750	1680	550	1850	5750
1676	500	1700	5500	1681	550	1850	5750
1677	500	1700	5500	1682	550	1850	5750
1677	2250	—	—	1683	525	1700	5500
1678	525	1700	5500	1684	600	1900	6000

3346 Guinea. — — with elephant below bust, similar die axis ↑↓

1677/5		*Extremely rare*		1678		*Extremely rare*	

3347
1669 Half-Guinea, first bust

3348
1684 Half-Guinea, second bust

3347 Half-Guinea. First laur. bust r., pointed trun.R. Crowned cruciform shields, sceptres in angles die axis ↑↓

1669	325	950	3750	1671	375	1000	4000
1670	300	900	3250	1672	350	975	3750

3348 Half-Guinea. Second laur. bust r., rounded trun. similar die axis ↑↓

1672	325	950	3500	1678/7	325	950	3500
1673	325	950	3750	1679	325	925	3500
1674	350	975	4000	1680	325	950	3500
1675	325	950	3750	1681	325	950	3750
1676	300	900	3250	1682	325	950	3500
1676/4	325	950	3500	1683	325	925	3500
1677	325	950	3500	1684	300	900	3250
1678	325	950	3750				

	F	VF	EF		F	VF	EF
	£	£	£		£	£	£

3349 Half-Guinea. Second bust with elephant and castle below, similar die axis ↑↓

1676	375	1200	4250	1681	375	1200	4250
1677	350	1100	4000	1682	350	1100	4000
1678/7	350	1100	4000	1683		*Extremely rare*	
1680	375	1200	4250	1684	350	1100	4000

SILVER

3350
1662 Crown, first type, rose below bust

3350 Crown. First dr. bust r., rose below, R. Crowned cruciform shields, interlinked C's in angles
edge undated, die axis ↑↓ 1662 175   650   3750

3350A Crown. — — Similar, die axis ↑↑ 1662 225   750   —

3350B Crown. — striped cloak to drapery, 1662 similar die axis ↑↓ 250   850   —

3350C Crown. — — II of legend at 12 o'clock, similar die axis ↑↓ 1662 .. 1500   —   —

3351 Crown. — — edge dated, similar die axis ↑↓ 1662 175   700   3750

3352 Crown. — no rose, edge dated, similar die axis ↑↓ 1662 200   750   4000

3353 Crown. — — edge not dated, similar die axis ↑↓ 1662 200   750   4000

3354 Crown. — — legend re-arranged shields altered, 1663, similar regnal year on edge in
Roman figures ANNO REGNI XV die axis ↑↓ 185   700   3750

     1663 no stops on reverse 225   750   3750

3354A

	F	VF	EF		F	VF	EF
	£	£	£		£	£	£

3354A Pattern 'Petition' Crown, 1663 by Thomas Simon. Laur. Bust r. of fine style in high relief, *Simon* below, edge inscription of Simon's 'petition': THOMAS SIMON. MOST. HVMBLY. PRAYS. YOVR MAJESTY etc., etc. .... — 50000 180000

3354B Pattern 'Reddite' Crown, 1663, by Thomas Simon, struck from the same dies, edge inscription: REDDITE. QVAE. CESARIS etc., etc. .... — 45000 165000

3355 Crown. Second dr. bust r., regnal year on edge in Roman figures (e.g. 1664 = XVI), die axis ↑↓

1664 edge XVI 185	550	3500	1665 XVII 700 2250	—
1664 Proof *FDC* £20000			1666 XVIII.................... 200 575	3500
1665 XVI....................... *Extremely rare*			1666 XVIII RE·X 275 875	3750
1665/4 XVII 700	2250	—	1667 XVIII.................. 2500 .... —	—

3356 Crown. Second bust elephant below, similar, die axis ↑↓

1666 XVIII 575	2250	9000	1666 XVIII RE·X 675	2500	—

3357
1668 Crown - second bust

3357 Crown. Second bust, similar Regnal year on edge in words (e.g. 1667= DECIMO NONO) die axis ↑↓

1667 D. NONO 175	575	3500	1669 V· PRIMO............. 250	950	—
1667 — AN.· REG.· . 175	575	3500	1669/8 V· PRIMO.......... 325	1000	—
1668 VICESIMO 165	550	3250	1670 V. SECVNDO 175	550	3350
1668 — error edge			1670/69 V. SECVND...... 185	650	3500
inverted..................... 325	—	—	1671 V· TERTIO 165	550	3250
1668/7 VICESIMO 185	575	3500	1671 — T/R in ET 350	1150	—
1668/5 VICESIMO	*Extremely rare*		1671 — ET over FR 375	1250	—

3358
Third bust Crown

	F £	VF £	EF £		F £	VF £	EF £
3358 Crown. Third dr. bust r. R.Similar die axis ↑↓							
1671 V. TERTIO	150	525	3250	1675 — EGNI error 575		1850	—
1671 V. QVARTO.......475		1250	—	1676 V. OCTAVO 150		525	3250
1672 V. QVARTO.....	150	525	3250	1676 OCCTAVO 175		575	3250
1673 V. QVARTO		*Extremely rare*		1677 V. NONO...............175		600	3500
1673 V. QVINTO	150	525	3250	1677/6 V. NONO 175		600	3500
1673 B/R in BR	200	750	—	1678/7 TRICESIMO......200		675	—
1673/2 V. QVINTO ...	175	575	3500	1679 T. PRIMO..............150		525	3250
1674 V. SEXTO..............		*Extremely rare*		1680/79 T. SECVNDO.......175		600	3500
1675/3 V. SEPTIMO .	475	1650	—	1680 T. SECVNDO 175		600	3500
1675 — ..							

3359
Fourth bust Crown

3359 Crown. Fourth dr. bust r. R.Similar die axis ↑↓							
1679 T. PRIMO.........	150	525	3000	1682/1 T. QVARTO 150		525	3000
1679 HIBR·EX	350	975	—	1682 T. QVARTO...........250		725	4000
1680 T. SECVNDO...	150	525	3000	1682/1 QVRRTO error.....225		675	3500
1680/79 T. SECVNDO ..225		675	3500	1683 T. QVINTO 300		800	4500
1681 T. TERTIO........	150	550	3250	1684 T. SEXTO..............275		750	4000
3360 Crown.— elephant and castle below bust, die axis ↑↓ 1681 T. TERTIO.........	2750	6500	—				

3361 - First bust Halfcrown

3362 - Second bust Halfcrown

	F	VF	EF		F	VF	EF
	£	£	£		£	£	£

3361 **Halfcrown.** First dr. bust r. R. Crowned cruciform shields, interlinked C's in angles, regnal year on edge in Roman figures die axis ↑↓

1663 XV	110	650	3000
1663 XV V/S in CAROLVS	175	750	3250
1663 XV A/T in GRATIA	175	750	3250
1663 XV no stops on obverse	225	850	3500

3362 **Halfcrown.** Second dr. bust r., similar die axis ↑↓ 1664 XVI 225 1000 4500

3363 **Halfcrown.** Third dr. bust r., similar die axis ↑↓ 1666/4 XVIII .... 850 3000 —

3364 - Third bust, elephant below Halfcrown

3364 **Halfcrown.** Third bust elephant below, die axis ↑↓ 1666 XVIII .... 750 2250 —

3365 - 1670 Halfcrown, third bust

3365 **Halfcrown.** Third dr. bust r. regnal date on edge in words (eg. 1667=DECIMO NONO) ↑↓

1667/4 D. NONO	3000	—	—	1670 V. SECVNDO	90	475	2250
1668/4 VICESIMO	275	1250	—	1670 – MRG for MAG	225	850	—
1669/4 V. PRIMO	225	850	—	1670 V/S CAROLVS	150	625	—
1669 V. PRIMO	350	1500	—	1670 E/R in ET	150	625	—
1669 — R/I in PRIMO	350	1500	—				

3366
1671 Halfcrown third bust variety

| | *F* | *VF* | *EF* | | *F* | *VF* | *EF* |
| | £ | £ | £ | | £ | £ | £ |

3366 Halfcrown. Third bust variety r. R. Similar die axis ↑↓

1671 V. TERTIO 90	475	2250	1672 V. TERTIO .... *Extremely rare*
1671 A/R in MAG 150	625	—	1672 V. QVARTO ...... 90 ..... 4752 250
1671/0 V. TERTIO 135	575	2500	

3367
Fourth bust Halfcrown

3367 Halfcrown. Fourth dr. bust r. R. Similar die axis ↑↓

1672 V. QVARTO 90	425	2250	1678 TRICESIMO 150	575	—
1673 V. QVINTO 90	425	2250	1679 T. PRIMO 90	400	2000
1673 — A/R in FRA 150	575	—	1679 — DECNS error 175	575	—
1673 — B/R in BR 150	575	—	1679 — DNCVS error 150	525	—
1673 — FR/M in FRA .. 150	575	—	1679 — PRICESIMO 135	475	2350
1674 V. SEXTO 110	475	2350	1680 T. SECVNDO 100	425	2000
1674/3 V. SEXTO 225	675	—	1680 T. SECVNCIO error 125	475	2250
1675 V. SEPTIMO 110	475	2350	1681 T. TERTIO 110	450	2250
1675 — Retrograde 1 125	550	2400	1681/0 — 250	750	—
1676 V. OCTAVO 90	400	2000	1682 T. QVARTO 100	425	2000
1676 R/T in BR 225	675	—	1682/79 T. QVARTO 225	675	—
1676 — Retrograde 1 100	425	2250	1683 T. QVINTO 90	400	2000
1676 F/H in FRA 150	575	—	1684/3 T. SEXTO 225	675	—
1677 F/H in FRA 150	575	—			
1677 V. NONO 90	400	2000			

3369 - Plume in centre

	F £	VF £	EF £

3368 Halfcrown. Fourth bust plume below, R. Similar die axis ↑↓
1673 V. QVINTO ....4500 12500 — 1683 T. QVINTO .... 5500 15000 —
3369 Halfcrown. — plume below bust and in centre of *rev.*, die axis ↑↓
1673 V. QVINTO .... 6500 17500 —

3370 - Elephant and Castle below bust

3370 Halfcrown. — elephant and castle below bust, die axis ↑↓ 1681 T. TERTIO ... 2250 7500 22500

SHILLINGS

First bust   First bust variety   Second bust   Third bust

First bust   First bust var.   First bust and   Second bust
first bust variety   single top leaf

3371 - First bust

	F	*VF*	*EF*		*F*	*VF*	*EF*
	£	£	£		£	£	£

3371 Shilling. First dr. bust r.R. Crowned cruciform shields interlinked C's in angles edge milled,

1663 die axis ↑↑ (en medaille)	125	475	—
1663 die axis ↑↓ as usual	90	325	1250
1663 GARTIA error, die axis ↑↓	675	—	—
1663 Transposed shields of Scotland and Ireland, die axis ↑↓	250	750	—
1663 A over G in FRA, die axis ↑↓	375	—	—

3372   3374

3372 Shilling. First bust variety r. similar die axis ↑↓

1663	90	325	1250	1668	475	1750	—
1666		*Extremely rare*		1669/6		*Extremely rare*	

3373 Shilling. First bust variety r. elephant below bust, die axis ↑↓ 1666.. 400   1350   4500

3374 Shilling. Guinea head, elephant below bust, die axis ↑↓ 1666 1500   4000   —

3375 - Second bust shilling

3375 Shilling. Second dr. bust r. similar die axis ↑↓

1666	1500	4000	—	1676	90	375	1350
1668	75	325	1250	1676/5	125	475	1600
1668/7	110	450	1500	1677	110	450	1500
1669		*Extremely rare*		1678	125	475	1600
1670	125	475	1600	1678/7	135	525	1750
1671	125	475	1600	1679	110	450	1500
1672	125	475	1600	1679/7	135	525	1750
1673	125	475	1600	1680	850	2250	—
1673/2	135	525	1750	1681	150	625	1850
1674	135	525	1750	1681/0	175	650	2000
1674/3	125	475	1600	1682/1	850	2250	—
1675	175	650	2000	1683	850	2250	—
1675/4	175	650	2000				

3376 - Plume both sides shilling of 1671

	F £	VF £	EF £		F £	VF £	EF £

3376 Shilling. Second Bust — plume below bust and in centre of *rev.* similar die axis ↑↓

1671	250	800	2600	1676	300	1000	3000
1673	275	900	2750	1679	250	800	2600
1674	250	800	2600	1680	525	1750	4500
1675	275	900	2750	1680/79	525	1750	4500

3378
1679 Shilling - plume on obverse only

3377 Shilling. — Plume *rev.* only, similar die axis ↑↓ 1674 575   1850   4750
3378 Shilling. — Plume *obv.* only similar die axis ↑↓
1677 625   2000   5000   1679 525   1750   4500
3379 Shilling. — elephant and castle below bust, die axis ↑↓ 1681/0 2250   —   —

3380   3381
Third bust Shilling   1684 Shilling - fourth bust

3380 Shilling. Third dr. (large) bust r. similar die axis ↑↓
1674 350   1250   3750   1675/3 275   950   3000
1675 300   1000   3250
3381 Shilling. Fourth dr. (large) bust r., older features, similar die axis ↑↓
1683 175   575   1500   1684 175   575   1500

3382
1677 Sixpence

	F £	VF £	EF £		F £	VF £	EF £

3382 Sixpence. Dr. bust r. R. Crowned cruciform shields, interlinked C's in angles die axis ↑↓

	F	VF	EF		F	VF	EF
1674	50	225	650	1679	65	265	750
1675	55	240	675	1680	65	265	750
1675/4	60	250	700	1681	50	225	650
1676	70	275	800	1682	75	300	850
1676/5	70	275	800	1682/1	65	265	750
1677	50	225	650	1683	50	225	650
1678/7	60	250	700	1684	55	240	675

3383
Undated Fourpence

3384 -
1678 Fourpence

3383 Fourpence. Undated. Crowned dr. bust l. to edge of coin, value
behind. R. Shield, die axis ↑↓ 20   50   130

3384 Fourpence. Dated. Dr. bust r. R. Crowned four interlinked Cs quartered emblems die axis ↑↓

	F	VF	EF		F	VF	EF
1670	18	35	110	1678	10	30	90
1671	10	35	100	1678/6	10	30	100
1672/1	10	30	90	1678/7	10	30	100
1673	10	30	90	1679	10	30	90
1674	10	30	90	1680	10	30	90
1674/4 sideways	12	35	150	1681	10	30	90
1674 7 over 6	10	35	100	1681 B/R in HIB	12	35	150
1675	10	30	90	1681/0	10	30	100
1675/4	10	35	100	1682	10	30	90
1676	10	30	90	1682/1	10	30	100
1676 7 over 6	10	35	100	1683	10	30	90
1676/5	10	35	100	1684	10	30	100
1677	10	30	90	1684/3	10	30	90

3386 - 1678 Threepence

	F	VF	EF		F	VF	EF
	£	£	£		£	£	£

3385 Threepence. Undated. As 3383, die axis ↑↓ 10 35 110

3386 Threepence. Dated. Dr. bust r. R. Crowned three interlinked C's, die axis ↑↓

1670 10	25	85	1678 10	20	75		
1671 10	20	75	1678 on 4d flan 10	20	90		
1671 GRѦTIA 15	35	150	1679 10	20	75		
1671 GRѦTIA 10	25	100	1679 O/A in CAROLVS 12	35	150		
1672/1 10	20	75	1680 10	20	75		
1673 10	20	75	1681 10	20	75		
1674 10	20	75	1681/0 10	25	85		
1675 10	25	85	1682 10	20	75		
1676 10	20	75	1682/1 10	25	85		
1676/5 10	25	85	1683 10	20	75		
1676 ERA for FRA 10	35	160	1684 10	20	75		
1677 8	25	85	1684/3 10	25	85		

3387 Twopence. Undated. As 3383 (double arch crown) die axis ↑↓ 8 25 75

3388 - 1678 Twopence   3390 - 1678 Penny

3388 Twopence. Dated. Dr. bust r. R. Crowned pair of linked C's, die axis ↑↓

1668 die axis ↑↑ 10	25	85	1678/6 10	25	80		
1670 8	20	70	1679 8	20	70		
1671 8	20	70	1679 HIB over FRA... 10	35	150		
1672/1 8	20	70	1680 8	20	70		
1672/1 GRѦTIA 10	35	165	1680/79 10	25	85		
1673 10	25	80	1681 8	20	70		
1674 8	20	70	1682/1 10	25	80		
1675 8	20	70	1682/1 ERA for FRA . 10	35	150		
1676 8	20	70	1683 8	20	70		
1677 10	25	80	1683/2 10	25	80		
1678 8	25	75	1684 10	25	80		

3389 Penny. Undated. As 3383 (double arch crown) die axis ↑↓ 8 30 110

	F £	VF £	EF £		F £	VF £	EF £

3390 Penny. Dated. Dr. bust r. R. Crowned C die axis ↑↓

Date	F £	VF £	EF £	Date	F £	VF £	EF £
1670	10	25	100	1678 RATIA error	10	35	150
1671	10	25	100	1678	10	30	120
1672/1	10	25	100	1679	10	30	120
1673	10	25	100	1680	10	25	100
1674	10	25	100	1680 on 2d flan		*Extremely rare*	
1674 ꓱRATIA error	12	35	150	1681	10	35	145
1675	10	25	100	1682	10	30	110
1675 ꓱRATIA error	12	35	150	1682/1	10	35	145
1676	10	30	120	1682 ERA for FRA	10	35	150
1676 ꓱRATIA error	12	35	175	1683/1	10	25	100
1677	10	25	100	1684	10	30	120
1677 ꓱRATIA error	12	35	175	1684/3	10	35	145

3391 Maundy Set. Undated. The four coins.. 95   350   700

3392 Maundy Set. Dated. The four denominations. Uniform dates

Date	F £	VF £	EF £	Date	F £	VF £	EF £
1670	80	225	600	1678	80	280	700
1671	70	190	600	1679	70	200	650
1672	80	200	650	1680	70	190	625
1673	70	190	600	1681	80	280	700
1674	70	190	600	1682	70	200	650
1675	80	200	650	1683	70	190	600
1676	80	200	650	1684	70	200	650
1677	80	200	650				

COPPER AND TIN

3393 - 1675 Halfpenny

	F	VF	EF		F	VF	EF
	£	£	£		£	£	£

3393 Copper **Halfpenny** Cuir. bust l. R. Britannia seated l. date in ex., die axis ↑↓

1672	55	300	1200	1673 no rev. stop	80	450	—
1672 CRAOLVS error		*Extremely rare*		1675	55	300	1200
1673	40	275	1100	1675 no stops on obv.	80	400	—
1673 CRAOLVS error	175	—	—	1675/3	150	550	—
1673 no stops on obv.		*Extremely rare*					

3394
1672 Farthing

3394 Copper **Farthing.** Cuir. bust l. R. Britannia sealed l. date in ex., die axis ↑↓

1672	40	225	675	1673 BRITINNIA error	200	—	—
1672 Rev.				1673 no stops on obv.	150	—	—
loose drapery	50	300	800	1673 no rev. stop	150	—	—
1672 no stops on obv.	60	300	900	1674	50	250	750
1672 RO/OL on obv.	80	400	—	1675	40	225	700
1672 die axis ↑↑	60	300	900	1675 no stop after			
1673	45	225	700	CAROLVS	150	—	—
1673 CAROLA error	120	450	—	1679	50	250	750
1673 O/sideways O	70	300	1000	1679 no rev. stop	60	300	1000

3395 - Tin Farthing

Prices for tin coinage based on corrosion free examples, and in the top grades with some lustre

3395 Tin **Farthing.** Somewhat similar, but with copper plug, edge inscribed NUMMORVM FAMVLVS, and date on edge only die axis ↑↓

1684	various varieties of edge	50	225	750	3000
1685				*Extremely rare*

James II, brother of Charles II, was born on 14th October 1633, he married Anne Hyde with whom he produced 8 children. He lost control of his reign when the loyalist Tories moved against him over his many Catholic appointments. Parliament invited his protestant daughter Mary with husband William of Orange to be joint rulers. James II abdicated and died in exile in France.

During this reign the dies continued to be engraved by John Roettier (1631-1700), the only major difference in the silver coinage being the ommission of the interlinked C's in the angles of the shields on the reverses. The only provenance marked silver coin of this reign is the extremely rare plume on reverse 1685 Shilling. The elephant and castle provenance mark continues to appear on some of the gold coins of this reign. Tin halfpence and farthings provided the only base metal coinage during this short reign. All genuine tin coins of this period have a copper plug.

GOLD

	F	VF	EF		F	VF	EF
	£	£	£		£	£	£

3396 Five Guineas. First laur. bust l., R. Crowned cruciform shields sceptres misplaced in angles smaller crowns date on edge in words (e.g. 1686 = SECVNDO)
die axis ↑↓ 1686 SECVNDO 1850   5250   13500

3397 Five Guineas. First laur bust l. R. similar bust sceptres normal. die axis ↑↓
1687 TERTIO 1750   5000   12500   1688 QVARTO 1750   5000   12500

3397A
1687 Five Guineas, second bust

3397A Five Guineas. Second laur. bust l. R. similar die axis ↑↓
1687 TERTIO 1650   4500   1200   1688 QVARTO 1650   4500   11000

3398
1687 Five Guineas, first bust, elephant and castle below

3398 Five Guineas. First laur. bust l. Elephant and castle below R. Similar die axis ↑↓
1687 TERTIO 1750   4750   12000   1688 QVARTO 1750   4750   12500

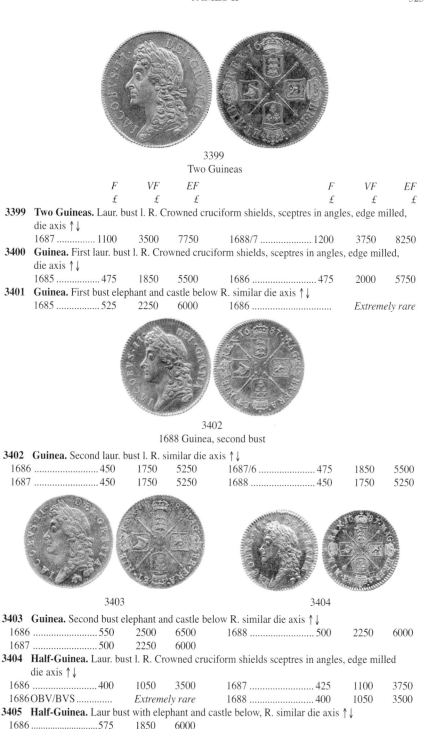

3399
Two Guineas

	F	VF	EF			F	VF	EF
	£	£	£			£	£	£

3399 **Two Guineas.** Laur. bust l. R. Crowned cruciform shields, sceptres in angles, edge milled, die axis ↑↓

| 1687 | 1100 | 3500 | 7750 | 1688/7 | 1200 | 3750 | 8250 |

3400 **Guinea.** First laur. bust l. R. Crowned cruciform shields, sceptres in angles, edge milled, die axis ↑↓

| 1685 | 475 | 1850 | 5500 | 1686 | 475 | 2000 | 5750 |

3401 **Guinea.** First bust elephant and castle below R. similar die axis ↑↓

| 1685 | 525 | 2250 | 6000 | 1686 | | *Extremely rare* | |

3402
1688 Guinea, second bust

3402 **Guinea.** Second laur. bust l. R. similar die axis ↑↓

| 1686 | 450 | 1750 | 5250 | 1687/6 | 475 | 1850 | 5500 |
| 1687 | 450 | 1750 | 5250 | 1688 | 450 | 1750 | 5250 |

| 3403 | | | | | 3404 | | | |

3403 **Guinea.** Second bust elephant and castle below R. similar die axis ↑↓

| 1686 | 550 | 2500 | 6500 | 1688 | 500 | 2250 | 6000 |
| 1687 | 500 | 2250 | 6000 | | | | |

3404 **Half-Guinea.** Laur. bust l. R. Crowned cruciform shields sceptres in angles, edge milled die axis ↑↓

| 1686 | 400 | 1050 | 3500 | 1687 | 425 | 1100 | 3750 |
| 1686 OBV/BVS | | *Extremely rare* | | 1688 | 400 | 1050 | 3500 |

3405 **Half-Guinea.** Laur bust with elephant and castle below, R. similar die axis ↑↓

| 1686 | 575 | 1850 | 6000 |

SILVER

3406
1686 Crown, first bust

	F	VF	EF		F	VF	EF
	£	£	£		£	£	£

3406 Crown. First dr. bust, l. regnal year on edge in words (e.g. 1686 = SECVNDO) die axis ↑↓

1686 SECVNDO 225   800   4250

1686 — No stops on obverse... 250   900   4500

3407
1687 Crown, second bust

3407 Crown. Second dr. bust l. R. Crowned cruciform shields edge inscribed in raised letters die axis ↑↓

1687 TERTIO........... 175	525	2250	1688/7 QVARTO 225	800	3200
1688 QVARTO......... 225	750	3000			

| | 3408 | | | | 1st bust | | 2nd bust |
| 1686 Halfcrown, first bust | | | | | Halfcrown hair ties | | |

	F	VF	EF		F	VF	EF
	£	£	£		£	£	£

3408 Halfcrown. First laur and dr. bust, l. regnal year on edge in words
(e.g. 1685 = PRIMO) die axis ↑↓

1685 PRIMO.............160	550	2500		1686 TERTIO.............185	575	2600
1686 SECVNDO.........160	550	2500		1687 TERTIO.............160	525	2500
1686/5 —.....................200	700	2650		1687/6 —....................200	750	2650
1686 TERTIO V over S or B				1687 — 6 over 8.........275	850	—
in JACOBVS......175	575	2600		1687 A/R in GRATIA .225	750	—

3409 Halfcrown. Second laur and dr. bust l. R. Crowned cruciform shields
edge inscribed in raised letters die axis ↑↓

1687 TERTIO.............175	575	2600		1688 QVARTO............135	525	2500

3410
1687 Shilling

3410 Shilling. Laur and Dr. bust l. R. Crowned cruciform shields die axis ↑↓

1685 130	450	1350		1686 G/A in MAG 160	500	1500
1685 no stops on rev......160	575	1600		1687 160	500	1500
1686 130	425	1350		1687/6 130	450	1350
1686/5..........................180	650	1750		1687 G/A in MAG 180	525	1500
1686 V/S in JACOBVS .160	500	1500		1688 170	575	1600
				1688/7 160	525	1500

3411 Shilling. Similar, plume in centre of *rev.,* die axis ↑↓ 1685 ....Fair £5750

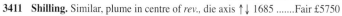

3412
1686 Sixpence, early shileds, indented tops

3412 Sixpence. Laur and dr. bust l. R. Early type crowned cruciform shields die axis ↑↓

1686 95	375	850		1687/6 110	450	950
1687 110	450	950				

3413
1687 Sixpence, later shields

	F £	VF £	EF £		F £	VF £	EF £

3413 Sixpence. Similar R. Late type shields die axis ↑↓

| 1687 | 100 | 400 | 900 | 1687 Later/early shields | 125 | 475 | 950 |
| 1687/6 | 125 | 475 | 950 | 1688 | 110 | 425 | 900 |

3414	3415	3416	3417
Fourpence	Threepence	Twopence	Penny

3414 Fourpence. Laur. head l. R. IIII Crowned die axis ↑↓

1686	15	30	100	1688	12	30	100
1686 Date over crown	15	30	110	1688 1 over 8	20	55	150
1687/6	12	25	90	1688/7	12	30	100
1687 8 over 7	15	30	110				

3415 Threepence. Laur. head l. R. III Crowned die axis-↑↓

1685	10	30	100	1687	12	35	110
1685 Groat flan	30	80	150	1687/6	10	30	100
1686	10	30	100	1688	10	30	100
1686 4d obv. die	15	35	120	1688/7	12	35	110

3416 Twopence. Laur. head l. R. II Crowned die axis ↑↓

1686	12	25	90	1687 ERA for FRA	20	45	140
1686 IΛCOBVS	15	35	100	1688	12	30	90
1687	12	25	90	1688/7	12	30	100

3417 Penny. Laur. head l. R. I Crowned die axis ↑↓

1685	15	30	100	1687/8	18	35	110
1686	15	30	100	1688	15	30	100
1687	15	30	100	1688/7	15	30	100
1687/6	15	30	100				

3418 Maundy Set. As last four. Uniform dates

| 1686 | 90 | 300 | 700 | 1688 | 90 | 300 | 700 |
| 1687 | 90 | 300 | 700 | | | | |

TIN

3419 Tin Halfpenny

	Fair	F	VF	EF
	£	£	£	£

Prices for tin coinage based on corrosion free examples, and in the top grades with some lustre

3419   Halfpenny. Laur. and dr. bust r. R. Britannia seated l. date on edge die axis ↑↓

1685 various varieties of edge	85	200	650	3250
1686	95	225	700	3750
1687	75	200	650	3250

3420
Cuirassed bust Tin Farthing

3420   Farthing. Laur. and Cuir. bust r. R. Britannia seated l. date on edge die axis ↑↓

1684			Extremely rare	
1685 various varieties of edge	60	175	600	2500
1686 two varieties of edge	75	200	650	2750
1687			Extremely rare	

3421   Farthing. Dr. bust r.; date on edge, 1687 various varieties of edge ↑↓

	90	225	750	3250

Mary Stuart was born on 30 April 1662, and married William of Orange as part of Charles II's foreign policy. She eventually became William's loyal servant but bore him no children. The Bill and the Claim of Rights were both passed in 1689 and forbade the Royal and Prerogative rights of Monarchs. Mary died from smallpox on 28 December 1694.

Due to the poor state of the silver coinage, much of it worn hammered coin, the Guinea, which was valued at 21s. 6d. at the beginning of the reign, circulated for as much as 30s. by 1694. The elephant and elephant and castle provenance marks continue on some gold coin. The tin Halfpennies and Farthings were replaced by copper coins in 1694. The rampant Lion of Nassau is now placed as an inescutcheon on the centre of the royal arms. The WM monogram appears in the angles of the silver coins of this reign.

Engravers and designers: George Bower (d.1689), Henry Harris (d.1704), John Roettier (1631-1700), James Roettier (1663-1698), Norbert Roettier (b.1665)

GOLD

3422
Five Guineas

	F	VF	EF		F	VF	EF
	£	£	£		£	£	£

3422 Five Guineas. Conjoined busts r. regnal year on edge in words (e.g. 1691 = TERTIO) ↑↓

	F	VF	EF		F	VF	EF
1691 TERTIO	1600	4250	9750	1693 QVINTO	1600	4250	9750
1692 QVARTO	1600	4500	10000	1694/2 SEXTO	1800	4500	11000
1692 QVINTO	2250	6500	—	1694 SEXTO	1700	4250	10500

3423
Elephant and castle below busts

3423 Five Guineas. Conjoined busts, elephant and castle below, R. Crowned shield of arms die axis ↑↓

	F	VF	EF		F	VF	EF
1691 TERTIO	1700	4250	10500	1694/2 SEXTO	1900	4750	12500
1692 QVARTO	1700	4250	10500	1694 SEXTO	1750	4500	12000
1693 QVINTO	1800	4500	11000				

3424
1694 Two Guineas

	F	VF	EF		F	VF	EF
	£	£	£		£	£	£

3424 Two Guineas. Conjoined busts r. R. Crowned shield of arms, Lion of Nassau at centre
die axis ↑↓

1693	900	2750	6500	1694/3	900	2750	6500

3425 Two Guineas. Conjoined busts, elephant and castle below, R. similar die axis ↑↓

1691		*Extremely rare*		1694/3	1050	3000	7500
1693	1250	3250	8000				

3426
1689 Guinea

3427
1689 Elephant and castle below busts

3426 Guinea. Conjoined busts r. R. Crowned shield of arms Lion of Nassau at centre die axis ↑↓

1689	450	1750	5000	1692	525	2000	5500
1690	525	2000	5500	1693	525	2000	5500
1690 GVLIFLMVS	575	2200	6000	1694	500	1850	5250
1691	525	2000	5500	1694/3	525	2000	5500

3427 Guinea. Conjoined busts elephant and castle below R. Similar die axis ↑↓

1689	475	1900	5500	1693	700	2250	6500
1690	700	2250	6500	1694	525	2100	5750
1691	500	2000	5750	1694/3	550	2250	6250
1692	525	2100	5750				

3428 Guinea. Conjoined busts elephant only below, R. Similar die axis ↑↓

1692	575	2250	6500	1693	625	2400	6750

Overstruck dates are listed only if commoner than the normal date or if no normal date is known.

3429   3430
1689 Half-Guniea, first busts, first shield   1690 Half-Guinea, second busts, second shield

	F	VF	EF		F	VF	EF
	£	£	£		£	£	£

3429 Half-Guinea. First busts r. R. First Crowned shield of arms die axis ↑↓

| 1689 | 450 | 1100 | 3750 |

3430 Half-Guinea. Second busts r. R. Second Crowned shield of arms die axis ↑↓

1690	475	1200	3850	1693		*Extremely rare*	
1691	475	1200	3850	1693/2	525	1350	4250
1692	500	1200	3850	1694	475	1100	3750

3431 Half-Guinea. Second busts elephant and castle below, R. Second shield of arms die axis ↑↓

| 1691 | 475 | 1200 | 3850 | 1692 | 475 | 1200 | 3850 |

3432 Half-Guinea. Second busts elephant only below, R. Second shield of arms die axis ↑↓

| 1692 | 675 | 2000 | 6000 |

SILVER

3433
Crown

3433 Crown. Conjoined busts r. regnal year on edge in words (e.g. 1691 = TERTIO) die axis ↑↓

1691 TERTIO	400	1250	3500	1692 QVARTO	400	1250	3500
1691 I/E in legend	450	1350	—	1692/ℤ QVARTO	400	1350	3750
1691 TERTTIO	425	1350	—	1692/ℤ QVINTO	400	1250	3500

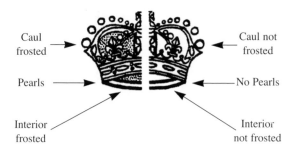

Caul frosted →

← Caul not frosted

Pearls →

← No Pearls

Interior frosted

Interior not frosted

3434
1689 Halfcrown - first reverse

3435
1689 Halfcrown - second reverse

	F £	VF £	EF £		F £	VF £	EF £

3434 Halfcrown. First busts, r. R. First crowned shield, 1689 PRIMO R. Crown with caul and interior frosted, with pearls edge inscribed die axis ↑↓ 85 325 1500

1689— 2nd L/M in GVLIELMVS 90 350 1600

1689 — 1st V/A in GVLIELMVS, only caul frosted 90 350 1600

1689 — — interior also frosted, no pearls.................90 350 1600

1689 Caul only frosted, pearls.................85 325 1500

1689 — no pearls 90 350 1600

1689 No frosting, pearls.................85 325 1500

1689 No stops on obverse 150 475 1750

1689 FRA for FR.................125 625 2000

3435 Halfcrown. First busts r. R. Second crowned shield die axis ↑↓

1689 PRIMO R. Caul . 85 325 1500 and interior frosted with pearls	1689 no frosting, pearls......85 325 1500
1689 — — no pearls 90 350 1600	1689 no frosting, no pearls.......................85 325 1500
1689 Caul only frosted pearls 85 325 1500	1690 SECVNDO —.......145 450 1750
1689 interior frosted, ... no pearls............. 90 350 1600	1690 — GRETIA error.....175 575 2000
1689 Caul only frosted, no pearls................ 90 350 1600	1690 TERTIO.................145 450 1800

3436

Halfcrown, second busts, third reverse

	F	VF	EF		F	VF	EF
	£	£	£		£	£	£

3436 Halfcrown. Second busts r. ℞. Crowned cruciform shields, WM monogram in angles
die axis ↑↓

	F	VF	EF		F	VF	EF
1691 TERTIO	110	425	1850	1692 QVINTO	200	750	—
1692 QVARTO	110	425	1850	1693 QVINTO	100	375	1750
1692 R/G in REGINA also				1693 3/inverted 3	125	475	2000
showing H/B in HI	150	475	2000	1693 inverted 3	175	625	2250

3437
Shilling

3438
Sixpence

3437 Shilling. Conjoined busts r. ℞. Crowned cruciform shields, WM monogram in angles die axis ↑↓

	F	VF	EF		F	VF	EF
1692	135	450	1500	1693 9/0	175	575	1650
1692 inverted 1	175	575	1650	1693	135	450	1500
1692 RE/ET on R	200	625	—				

3438 Sixpence. Conjoined busts r. ℞. Crowned cruciform shields, WM monogram in angles die axis ↑↓

	F	VF	EF		F	VF	EF
1693	110	350	850	1694	110	375	950
1693 inverted 3	150	500	1250				

3439
Groat, first busts

3439 Fourpence. First busts, r. no tie to wreath. ℞. Crowned 4 die axis ↑↓

	F	VF	EF		F	VF	EF
1689 GV below bust	15	30	100	1690	15	35	110
1689 G below bust	15	30	100	1690 6 over 5	15	40	120
1689 stop befor G	15	30	110	1691	15	40	130
1689 berries in wreath	15	30	110	1691/0	15	35	115
1689 GVLEELMVS	55	175	—	1694	15	40	130

3440
Groat, Second busts

	F	VF	EF		F	VF	EF
	£	£	£		£	£	£

3440 Fourpence. Second busts r. tie to wreath. R. Crowned 4 die axis ↑↓

	F	VF	EF		F	VF	EF
1692	15	40	110	1693/2	15	40	120
1692/1	15	40	120	1694	12	40	120
1692 MAR•IA		*Extremely rare*		1694 small lettering	15	40	120
1693	15	40	120				

3441 Threepence. First busts, r. no tie to wreath. R. Crowned 3 die axis ↑↓

	F	VF	EF		F	VF	EF
1689	10	25	90	1690 6 over 5	15	30	100
1689 No stops on rev.	15	35	110	1690 Large lettering	15	30	100
1689 LMV over MVS	15	35	110	1690 9 over 6	15	30	100
1689 Hyphen stops on rev.	15	30	100	1691	30	90	200
1690	15	30	100				

3442 Threepence. Second busts, r. tie to wreath R. Crowned 3 die axis ↑↓

	F	VF	EF		F	VF	EF
1691	15	35	120	1693 GV below bust	15	35	110
1692 G below bust	15	35	120	1694 G below bust	15	35	110
1692 GV below bust	15	35	120	1694 — MARIΛ error	18	45	150
1692 GVL below bust	15	35	120	1694 GV below bust	15	35	110
1693 G below bust	15	35	110	1694 GVL below bust	15	35	110
1693/2 G below bust	15	35	110				

3443 Twopence. Conjoined busts r. R. Crowned 2 die axis ↑↓

	F	VF	EF		F	VF	EF
1689	10	25	90	1694/3	12	35	110
1691	10	25	90	1694/3 no stop after DG	12	35	110
1692	10	30	100	1694 MARLA error	25	55	250
1693	10	30	100	1694 HI for HIB	12	35	110
1693/2	12	35	110	1694 GVLI below bust	12	35	110
1693 GV below bust	12	35	110	1694 GVL below bust	12	35	110
1694	12	35	110				

3444 - Penny   3445 - Legend intruded

3444 Penny. Legend continuous over busts, R. Crowned 1 die axis ↑↓

	F	VF	EF		F	VF	EF
1689	125	300	650	1689 MΛRIΛ	150	300	650
1689 GVIELMVS error	200	400	900				

3445 Penny. Legend broken by busts, R. Crowned 1 die axis ↑↓

	F	VF	EF		F	VF	EF
1690	18	45	150	1694 date spread	15	40	120
1691/0	15	40	120	1694 no stops on obv.	15	45	140
1692	18	45	150	1694 HI for HIB	22	55	190
1692/1	18	45	160	1694 — 9/6	18	45	140
1693	15	40	125				

3446 - Maundy Set

	F £	VF £	EF £		F £	VF £	EF £
3446 Maundy Set. The four denominations. Uniform dates							
1689	250	600	1100	1693	150	300	850
1691	110	225	750	1694	110	225	750
1692	150	300	850				

TIN AND COPPER

3447
Tin Halfpenny first busts

	Fair £	F £	VF £	EF £
Prices for tin coinage based on corrosion free examples, and in the top grades with some lustre				
3447 Tin Halfpenny. Small dr. busts r.; date on edge ↑↓ 1689	850	1650	—	—
— — — obv. with star stops 1689			*Extremely rare*	

3448
Tin Halfpenny cuirassed busts

	Fair	F	VF	EF
3448 Tin Halfpenny. — Large cuir. busts r.; R. Britannia seated L. date only on edge, die axis ↑↓				
1690 various edge varieties	75	175	650	2750
3449 Tin Halfpenny. Similar date in ex. and on edge die axis ↑↓				
1691 various edge varieties	60	150	600	2250
1691 in ex. 1692 on edge			*Extremely rare*	
1692	60	150	600	2250
3450 Tin Farthing. Small dr. busts r. R. Britannia seated l. die axis ↑↓				
1689	250	650	2000	—
1689, in ex. 1690 on edge			*Extremely rare*	

3451
Tin Farthing

	Fair	*F* £	*VF* £	*EF* £
3451 Tin **Farthing.** Large cuir. busts r. R. Britannia seated l. die axis ↑↓				
1690, in ex. 1689 on edge			*Extremely rare*	
1690 various edge varieties 50		150	575	2500
1691 various edge varieties 50		150	575	2500
1692 65		175	625	2500

3452
1694 Halfpenny

3452 Copper **Halfpenny,** Conjoined busts r. R. Britannia die axis ↑↓			
1694	70	225	900
1694 GVLIEMVS error	200	550	–
1694 MVRIΛ error..	250	600	–
1694 MΛRIΛ error	150	475	–
1694 BRITΛNNI/Λ	175	500	–
1694 no rev. stop	150	475	–
1694 GVLEELMVS	250	575	–

3453
1694 Farthing

3453 Copper **Farthing,** Conjoined busts r. R. Britannia die axis ↑↓			
1694	65	225	850
1694 MΛRIΛ error..	180	450	–
1694 no stop after MΛRIΛ..	110	375	–
1694 — BRITΛNNIΛ	125	375	–
1694 no stop on rev.	110	325	–
1694 no stop on obv.	110	325	–
1694 GVLIELMS, BRITΛNNIΛ errors	225	475	–
1694 BRITΛNNIΛ	140	425	–
1694 Broad heavier flan 25.5mm..	200	450	–

William of Orange was born on 4th November 1650. He married Mary Stuart under Charles II's foreign policy and was invited to England by Parliament, where he proceeded to supress the Jacobite rebellion. The Bank of England was founded during this reign, and William ruled alone and without issue after Mary's death until his own demise on 8th March 1702 following a serious fall from his horse.

In 1696 a great re-coinage was undertaken to replace the hammered silver that made up most of the coinage in circulation, much of it being clipped and badly worn. Branch mints were set up at Bristol, Chester, Exeter, Norwich and York to help with the re-coinage. For a short time before they were finally demonetized, unclipped hammered coins were allowed to circulate freely provided they were officially pierced in the centre. Silver coins with roses between the coats of arms were made from silver obtained from the West of England mines. The elephant and castle provenance mark continues on some guineas and half-guineas.

Engravers and designers: Samuel Bull (d.c.1720), John Croker (1670-1740), Henry Harris (d.1704), John Roettier (1663-1698).

GOLD

3454
1699 Five Guineas, first bust

	F	VF	EF		F	VF	EF
	£	£	£		£	£	£

3454 Five Guineas. First laur. bust r. regnal year on edge in words (e.g. 1699 = UNDECIMO) ↑↓
1699 UNDECIMO.. 1550   4250   10500   1700 DVODECIMO 1650   4500   11000

3455
Elephant and castle below first bust

3455 Five Guineas. First bust elephant and castle below, 1699 UNDECIMO 1750   4750   13000

3456
1701 Five Guineas 'Fine Work'

	F	VF	EF			F	VF	EF
	£	£	£			£	£	£

3456 **Five Guineas.** Second laur. bust r. ('fine work'), R. Crowned cruciform shields Plain or ornamental sceptres DECIMO TERTIO die axis ↑↓ 1701...1500 4250 10500

3457
'Fine work' Two Guineas

3457 **Two Guineas.** ('fine work'), Laur. bust r. similar die axis ↑↓ 1701 ....1000 2750 6250

3458
1695 Guinea, first bust

3458 **Guinea.** First laur. bust r. R. Crowned cruciform shields, sceptres in angles die axis ↑↓
1695 ....350 1350 4250   1697 ....400 1500 4750
1696 ....400 1500 4750
3459 **Guinea.** First bust elephant and castle below R. Similar die axis ↑↓
1695 ....475 1850 5500   1696 ....*Extremely rare*

3460
Second bust

3463
Ornamental sceptres

	F	VF	EF			F	VF	EF
	£	£	£			£	£	£

3460 **Guinea.** Second laur. bust r. R. Similar with human-headed harp in Irish arms. die axis ↑↓

1697	375	1450	4500	1699	375	1500	4500
1698	350	1350	4250	1700	350	1350	4250

3461 **Guinea.** Second bust elephant and castle below. R. Similar die axis ↑↓

1697	750	3000	—	1699		*Extremely rare*	
1698	475	1850	5500	1700	725	3000	—

3462 **Guinea.** Second laur. bust. r. R. Similar with Human headed harp. Large lettering and
large date, die axis ↑↓ 1698.. 350   1500   4500

3463 **Guinea.** — R. Narrow crowns, plain or ornamented sceptres, axis ↑↓ 1701........325   1350   4250

3464 **Guinea.** Second bust elephant and castle below, die axis ↑↓ 1701 .... *Extremely rare*

3465 **Guinea.** Third laur. bust r. ('fine work'), R. Similar die axis ↑↓1701........475   2250   6500

3466
1695 Half-Guniea, early harp

3468
Later harp

3466 **Half-Guinea.** Laur. bust r. R. With early harp, die axis ↑↓ 1695 200   750   2100

3467 **Half-Guinea.** Laur. bust elephant and castle below. R. With early harp, die axis ↑↓

1695	350	1250	3750	1696	275	1000	3250

3468 **Half-Guinea.** Laur. bust r. R. Crowned cruciform shields, sceptres in angles with late harp, die axis ↑↓

1697	350	1250	3750	1700	225	850	2500
1698	200	750	2100	1701	200	800	2250
1699		*Extremely rare*					

3469 **Half-Guinea.** Laur. bust elephant and castle below, die axis ↑↓ 1698 300   1200   3750

SILVER

3470

Crown - first bust - round collar

	F	VF	EF		F	VF	EF
	£	£	£		£	£	£

3470 Crown. First dr. bust, r. R.First harp, regnal year on edge in words (e.g. 1696 = OCTAVO) ↑↓

1695 SEPTIMO........... 80	275	1450	1696 G/D IN GRA... 175	475	—
1695 OCTAVO............ 80	275	1450	1696 — no stops 275	625	—
1695 TVTA·EN error	*Extremely rare*		1696/5 175	475	—
1695 plain edge proof *FDC* £6750			1696 GEI for DEI 300	750	—
1696 OCTAVO............ 70	275	1350	1696 — no stops 375	850	—
1696 No stops on			1696 plain edge proof *FDC* £6750		
obverse...............250	575	—			

3471

1696 Crown, second bust - hair across breast

3471 Crown. Second dr. bust r. R. Second harp (hair across breast), 1696 (two varieties) die axis ↑↓
OCTAVO .... *Each unique*

3472
Third bust, straight breastplate

	F	*VF*	*EF*
	£	£	£

3472 Crown. Third dr. bust, r. R. First harp, die axis ↑↓ 1696 OCTAVO 75   275   1400
    1696 TRICESIMO ....   *Extremely rare*
    1696 plain edge proof ....   *FDC* £6500
3473 Crown. Similar, R. Second harp, die axis ↑↓ 1697 NONO 1250   3500   14500

3474
1700 Crown, third bust variety

3474 Crown. Third bust variety r. R. Third harp, ↑↓ 1700 DVODECIMO 90   300   1500
    1700 DECIMO. TERTIO... 90   325   1600
3475 Halfcrown. First bust r. R. Small shields, 1696 die axis ↑↓ OCTAVO 50   225   1000
    — — 1696 DECⱯS error 70   250   1100
3476 Halfcrown. B (*Bristol*) below First bust, die axis ↑↓ 1696 OCTAVO....... 75   275   1250
    — 1696 B Similar proof *FDC* £12000

3477	3478
Chester Mint	Exeter Mint

3477 Halfcrown. C (*Chester*) below first bust, die axis ↑↓ 1696 OCTAVO 125   475   1650
3478 Halfcrown. E (*Exeter*) below first bust, die axis ↑↓ 1696 OCTAVO 125   475   1650

		F	VF	EF
		£	£	£

3479 **Halfcrown.** N (*Norwich*) below first bust, die axis ↑↓ 1696 OCTAVO .. 110   425   1500
3480 **Halfcrown.** y (*York*) below first bust, die axis ↑↓ 1696 OCTAVO 120   450   1600

3480
1696 Halfcrown - York Mint

3481
1696 Halfcrown, large shield
reverse with early harp

3481 **Halfcrown.** First bust r. Ŗ. Large shield, early harp,
  die axis ↑↓ 1696 OCTAVO.. 50   225   1000
  1696 Proof plain edge .... −   −   8500
3482 **Halfcrown.** — B (*Bristol*) below bust, die axis ↑↓ 1696 OCTAVO 70   275   1250
3483 **Halfcrown.** — C (*Chester*) below bust, die axis ↑↓ 1696 OCTAVO 125   475   1650
3484 **Halfcrown.** — E (*Exeter*) below bust, die axis ↑↓ 1696 OCTAVO............110   425   1500
3485 **Halfcrown.** — N (*Norwich*) below bust, die axis ↑↓ 1696 OCTAVO..........175   750   −
3486 **Halfcrown.** — y (*York*) below bust, die axis ↑↓ 1696 OCTAVO 100   375   1350
  — — die axis ↑↓ 1696 y (*York*), Scots Arms at date............................   *Extremely rare*
  — die axis ↑↓ y over E 1696 175   750   −

3487
Large shields, ordinary harp

	F	VF	EF		F	VF	EF
	£	£	£		£	£	£

3487 **Halfcrown.** First bust r. Ŗ. Large shields, ordinary harp die axis ↑↓
  1696 OCTAVO 125   475   1600   1697 G/A in MAG...........350   −   −
  1697 NONO 50   200   850   1697/6 — 135   475   1600
  1697 — GRR for GRA.............. *Extremely rare*   1697 Proof plain edge *FDC* £8000
3488 **Halfcrown.** — B (*Bristol*) below first bust, die axis ↑↓ 1697 NONO........ 75   300   1200
  1697 proof on thick flan *FDC*...   *Extremely rare*
  1697 — no stops on reverse 125   475   1500

3489
Chester Mint Halfcrown, large shields

	F	VF	EF		F	VF	EF
	£	£	£		£	£	£

3489   Halfcrown. — C *(Chester)* below first bust, similar die axis ↑↓

1696 OCTAVO 125	475	1500	1697 NONO 100	425	1400

3490
Exeter Mint Halfcrown, large shields

3490   Halfcrown. — E *(Exeter)* below first bust, similar die axis ↑↓

1696 OCTAVO 90	400	1350	1697 NONO 65	250	950
1696 NONO 375	—	—	1697 E over C or B		
1697 OCTAVO 375	—	—	under bust 175	575	—

3491
Norwich Mint Halfcrown, large shields

3491   Halfcrown. — N *(Norwich)* below first bust, similar die axis ↑↓

1696 OCTAVO 325	750	—	1697 NONO 100	400	1350
1697 OCTAVO 325	750	—	1697 — Scots Arms at date	*Fair* £750	

3492   Halfcrown. — — y *(York)* below first bust, similar die axis ↑↓

1697 NONO 65	250	950	1697 OCTAVO 275	—	—

3493   Halfcrown. Second dr. bust r. (hair across breast), die axis ↑↓ 1696 OCTAVO   *Unique*

3494
1700 Halfcrown, modified large shields

	F	VF	EF		F	VF	EF
	£	£	£		£	£	£

3494 Halfcrown. First dr. bust R. Modified large shields die axis ↑↓

	F	VF	EF		F	VF	EF
1698 OCTAVO	375	—	—	1699 — Lion of			
1698 DECIMO	45	180	750	Nassau inverted	475	1250	—
1698/7 —	350	850	—	1700 DVODECIMO	60	225	850
1698 UNDECIMO	325	750	—	1700 D. TERTIO	65	250	900
1699 UNDECIMO	100	425	1350	1700 — DECⱯS error	65	250	900
1699 — Inverted A's for				1701 D. TERTIO	60	225	900
V's on edge	125	475	—	1701 — no stops			
1699 — Scots Arms at				on reverse	90	375	1200
date	675	—	—				

3495
1701 Halfcrown, elephant and castle below bust

3495 Halfcrown. – elephant and castle below bust, die axis ↑↓

		F	VF	EF
1701 D. TERTIO		2250	3750	—

3496
1701 Halfcrown, plumes on reverse

3496 Halfcrown. – R. Plumes in angles, die axis ↑↓ 1701 D. TERTIO 175   575   1750

SHILLINGS

First bust

Third bust

Third bust variety

3497
First bust

3498
Bristol Mint

3499
1696 Chester Mint Shilling

	F £	VF £	EF £		F £	VF £	EF £
3497 Shilling. First dr. bust r. R. Crowned cruciform shields edge milled die axis ↑↓							
1695 35	125	525		1696-1669 error date.........750	—	—
1696 30	110	425		1697 30	90	375
1696 no stops on reverse....90	275	750		1697 E/A in DEI 275	750	—
1696 MAB for MAG				1697 GRI for GRA error...375	—	—
error 475	—	—		1697 Arms of Scot/Ireland		
1696 GVLIEMVS				transposed 575	—	—
error 475	—	—		1697 Irish Arms at date 675	—	—
1696 GVLIELMVꟼS............				1697 no stops on reverse 90	275	750
error 150	475	—		1697 GVLELMVS error...475	—	—
1696 GꟼLIELMVS............				1697 GVLIELMVꟼS error		
error 175	525	—		error 200	575	—
1696 GVLELMVS 475	—	—		1697 L/M in legend...........225	650	—
1696 2nd L over M.......225	650	—				
3498 Shilling. Similar B (*Bristol*) below bust die axis ↑↓						
1696 50	175	650		1697 60	185	675
3499 Shilling. Similar C (*Chester*) below bust die axis ↑↓						
1696 75	225	750		1696 thick flan proof *FDC...*	*Extremely rare*	
1696 R/V in GRA..........125	375	1250		1697 75	225	750

3500

	F	VF	EF			F	VF	EF
	£	£	£			£	£	£

3500 Shilling. Similar E (*Exeter*) below bust die axis ↑↓

1696 75   225   750   1697 75   225   750

1697 E over N ....   *Extremely rare*

3501 Shilling. Similar N (*Norwich*) below bust die axis ↑↓

1696 75   225   750   1697 65   200   700

1697 no stops on obv.......   *Extremely rare*

3502 Shilling. Similar y (*York*) below bust die axis ↑↓

1696 50   175   675   1697 Arms of Scotland/Ireland

1697 65   200   700   transposed 750   —   —

1697 Arms of France/Ireland

transposed.....................750   —   —

3503 Shilling. Similar Y (*York*) below bust die axis ↑↓

1696 80   250   850   1697 90   275   900

1697 Y over ⅄.................   *Extremely rare*

3504 Shilling. Second dr. bust r. (hair across breast), similar die axis ↑↓ 1696   *Unique*

3505
Third bust

3507
Chester Mint

3505 Shilling. Third dr. bust r., similar die axis ↑↓ 1697......................................40   135   450

3506 Shilling. Similar B (*Bristol*) below bust, die axis ↑↓ 1697 75   240   825

3507 Shilling. Similar C (*Chester*) below bust die axis ↑↓

1696 125   375   1100   1697 no stops on reverse.....75   225   750

1697 50   175   675   1697 Arms of Scotland

1697 FR.A error 90   275   900   at date ....   *Extremely rare*

3508 Shilling. Similar E (*Exeter*) below bust, die axis ↑↓

1696...........................1500   —   —   1697 80   250   850

3509 Shilling. Similar N (*Norwich*) below bust, die axis ↑↓ 1697 80   250   850

3510 Shilling. Similar y (*York*) below bust die axis ↑↓

1696 ....   *Extremely rare*   1697 65   200   700

3511 Shilling. Third bust variety r. similar die axis ↑↓

1697 G⅄LIELMVS 1698 50   175   675

      error 175   525   —   1698 plain edge proof *FDC* £2500

1697 30.......................125   425

1697 GVLIELM⅄S

      error 175   525   —

	F	VF	EF		F	VF	EF
	£	£	£		£	£	£

3512 Shilling. Similar B (*Bristol*) below bust, die axis ↑↓ 1697 80   225   850

3513 Shilling. Similar C (*Chester*) below bust, die axis ↑↓ 1697 125   375   1100

3514 Shilling. Similar R. Plumes in angles, die axis ↑↓ 1698 175   525   1350

Third bust   Fourth bust   Fifth bust

3515   3516
Fourth bust   Fifth bust

3515 Shilling Fourth dr. bust ('flaming hair') r. similar die axis ↑↓

1698 125   425   1250   1699 110   400   1200

1698 No stops on reverse .. *Extremely rare*   1699 plain edge proof *FDC* £4000

1698 plain edge proof *FDC* £4250

3516 Shilling. Fifth dr. bust (hair high) r. similar die axis ↑↓

1699 90   275   900   1700 Tall O's no stops

1700 30   100   350   on reverse 50   150   450

1700 Circular small 1701 70   200   675

O's in date 40   125   375   1701 DEI/GRA 250   —   —

1700 no stop after DEI.... 175   —   —

3517
1701 Shilling, plumes on reverse

3517 Shilling. Similar R. Plumes in angles die axis ↑↓

1699 125   425   1250   1701 125   425   1250

3518
1699 Shilling, roses on reverse

3520
First bust Sixpence, French arms at date

	F £	VF £	EF £		F £	VF £	EF £
3518 **Shilling.** Similar R. Roses in angles, die axis ↑↓ 1699					150	475	1500
3519 **Shilling.** Similar plume below bust, die axis ↑↓ 1700					1350	3750	—

SIXPENCES

First bust   Third bust   Early harp. large crown.   Later harp, small crown.

3520 Sixpence. First dr. bust r. R. Crowned cruciform shields, edge milled early harp die axis ↑↓

1695	30	75	250	1696 Scots Arms			
1696	25	65	175	at date	300	—	—
1696 Heavy flan	500	—	—	1696/5	40	95	350
1696 French Arms				1696 no stops on			
at date	325	—	—	obverse	45	110	375
1696 GVLIELMⱯS	40	90	325	1696 DFI for DEI	175	—	—

3521 Sixpence. Similar B *(Bristol)* below bust, die axis ↑↓ 1696	30	75	275
— — 1696 B over E	45	100	375
3522 Sixpence. Similar C *(Chester)* below bust, die axis ↑↓ 1696	35	90	325

3523

3525
1696 York Mint sixpence,
early harp, first bust

3523 Sixpence. Similar E *(Exeter)* below bust, die axis ↑↓ 1696	40	100	375
3524 Sixpence. Similar N *(Norwich)* below bust, die axis ↑↓ 1696	40	100	375
3525 Sixpence. Similar y *(York)* below bust, die axis ↑↓ 1696	30	85	300

		F £	VF £	EF £		F £	VF £	EF £
3526	**Sixpence.** Similar Y *(York)* below bust, die axis ↑↓ 1696	35	90	325				
	— — — 1696 no stops on obverse	70	175	475				
3527	**Sixpence.** Similar R. Later harp, large crowns, die axis ↑↓ 1696	65	165	450				
	— — — 1696 no stops on obverse	100	275	—				
3528	**Sixpence.** — — — B *(Bristol)* below bust, similar die axis ↑↓							
	1696	75	175	475	1697	50	125	400
	1696 no stops on obv.	90	225	525				
3529	**Sixpence.** — — — C *(Chester)* below bust, similar die axis ↑↓ 1697	90	225	525				
3530	**Sixpence.** — — — E *(Exeter)* below bust, similar die axis ↑↓ 1697	50	125	400				
3531	**Sixpence.** — — R. small crowns, similar die axis ↑↓							
	1696	65	165	450	1697 Arms of France/Ireland			
	1697	25	70	250	transposed	325	—	—
	1697 GVLIELMⱯS	65	175	—				

3532
Bristol Mint Sixpence, small crowns

		F £	VF £	EF £		F £	VF £	EF £
3532	**Sixpence.** — — — B *(Bristol)* below bust, similar die axis ↑↓							
	1696	70	175	475	1697	30	75	275
	1696 no stops on O.	90	225	525	1697 B over E	45	110	375
3533	**Sixpence.** — — — C *(Chester)* below bust, similar die axis ↑↓							
	1696	90	250	575	1697 Irish shield			
	1697	35	90	325	at date	300	—	—
					1697 Plain edge	125	325	750
3534	**Sixpence.** — — — E *(Exeter)* below bust, similar die axis ↑↓							
	1697	40	100	375	1697 E over B	90	275	—
3535	**Sixpence.** — — — N *(Norwich)* below bust, similar die axis ↑↓							
	1696	70	175	475	1697	35	90	325
	1697 GVLIEMVS	150	375	—				
3536	**Sixpence.** — — — y *(York)* below bust, similar die axis ↑↓							
	1697	40	100	375	1697 Irish shield at date	275	—	—

3537
Second bust Sixpence

3538
Sixpence, third bust,
later harp, large crowns

	F	VF	EF		F	VF	EF
	£	£	£		£	£	£

3537 Sixpence. Second dr. bust r. R. Similar die axis ↑↓

1696	250	650	1650	1696 GVLELMVS...	325	750	1500
1697 GVLIELMⱯS..	160	450	1250	1697	110	350	1100
1697 G/I in GRA	160	450	1250	1697 GR/DE in GRA	175	450	1250
1697 GVLIEMVS	225	575	1350				

3537A Sixpence. Third dr. bust, r. early harp, large crowns. E *(Exeter)* below
bust, 1696... 850   —   —

3537B Sixpence. — — — Y *(York)* below bust, similar die axis ↑↓ 1696 750   —   —

3538 Sixpence. Third dr. bust, r., R. Later harp, large crowns, similar die axis ↑↓

1697 GVLIEIMVS	35	85	275	1699	90	250	600
1697	25	70	225	1700	30	75	275
1697 GⱯLIELMVS	40	90	300	1701	45	100	350
1698	35	85	275				

3539 Sixpence. — — B *(Bristol)* below bust, similar die axis ↑↓

1697	50	125	400	1697 IRA for FRA....	100	275	—

3540
Chester Mint Sixpence, third bust

3540 Sixpence. — — C *(Chester)* below bust, similar die axis ↑↓ 1697	90	225	525				
3541 Sixpence. — — E *(Exeter)* below bust, similar die axis ↑↓ 1697	95	250	575				

3542 Sixpence. Third dr. bust, r. R. Small crowns, similar die axis ↑↓

1697	35	85	275	1697 G/D in GRA	95	250	—
1697 D/F in DEI	95	250	—				

3543 Sixpence. — — C *(Chester)* below bust, similar die axis ↑↓ 1697	65	175	450
3544 Sixpence. — — E *(Exeter)* below bust, similar die axis ↑↓ 1697	70	175	475

3545
York Mint Sixpence - Y provenance mark

3547
Sixpence, roses on reverse

	F	VF	EF		F	VF	EF
	£	£	£		£	£	£

3545 Sixpence.— — Y *(York)* below bust, similar die axis ↑↓ 1697 .... 65 — 175 — 450

3546 Sixpence.— — R. Plumes in angles, similar die axis ↑↓

1698 .... 50 — 125 — 400 — 1699 .... 50 — 125 — 400

3547 Sixpence.— R. Roses in angles, similar die axis ↑↓

1699 .... 60 — 150 — 525 — 1699 GΛLIELMVS . 125 — 275 — —

3548
1700 Sixpence, plume below bust

3549
1699 Groat or Fourpence

3548 Sixpence.— plume below bust, R. Similar die axis ↑↓ 1700............ 1350 — — — —

3549 Fourpence. Laur. and dr. bust r. R. 4 Crowned die axis ↑↓

1697 .... — *Unique* — 1700 .... 15 — 30 — 110

1698 .... 18 — 35 — 150 — 1701 .... 18 — 35 — 125

1699 .... 15 — 30 — 110 — 1702 .... 15 — 30 — 100

3550 Threepence. Laur. and dr. bust r. R. 3 Crowned die axis ↑↓

1698 .... 15 — 30 — 100 — 1701 GBA for GRA ... 18 — 40 — 140

1699 .... 15 — 35 — 110 — 1701 small lettering ... 15 — 30 — 100

1700 .... 15 — 30 — 100 — 1701 large lettering .... 15 — 35 — 100

3551 Twopence. Laur. and dr. bust r. R. Crown to edge of coin, large figure 2 die axis ↑↓

1698 .... 18 — 45 — 120

3551A Twopence. Laur. and dr. bust r. R Crown within inner circle of legend, smaller figure 2, die axis ↑↓

1698 .... 12 — 35 — 100 — 1700 .... 12 — 30 — 90

1699 .... 12 — 30 — 90 — 1701 .... 12 — 30 — 90

3552 Penny. Laur. and dr. bust r. R. 1 Crowned die axis ↑↓

1698 .... 15 — 30 — 100 — 1699 .... 15 — 35 — 100

1698 IRA for FRA error 18 — 40 — 110 — 1700 .... 15 — 35 — 100

1698 HI.BREX error... 18 — 40 — 110 — 1701 .... 15 — 35 — 100

3553 - 1701 Maundy Set

	F £	VF £	EF £		F £	VF £	EF £
3553 Maundy Set. The four denominations. Uniform dates							
1698 85	250	700		1700 100	250	750	
1699 100	275	750		1701 85	250	700	

COPPER

3554 - Halfpenny

3554 Halfpenny. First issue. Laur. and cuir. bust r. ℞. Britannia with r. hand raised die axis ↑↓

	F	VF	EF		F	VF	EF
1695 45	175	900		1697 30	150	750
1695 BRITANNIΛ error 200	—	—		1697 all stops omitted 225	—	—
1695 no stop on rev. 65	250	—		1697 I/E in TERTIVS 225	—	—
1695 no stops on obv...... 65	250	—		1697 GVLILMVS,		
1696 30	150	800		no rev. stop 300	—	—
1696 GVLIEMVS,				1697 no stop		
no rev. stop 300	—	—		after TERTIVS 50	250	—
1696 TERTVS error.......275	—	—		1698 45	175	900

3555 Halfpenny. Second issue. Laur. and cuir. bust r. ℞. Britannia Date in legend die axis ↑↓

	F	VF	EF		F	VF	EF
1698 Stop after date 35	160	900		1699 GVLIEMVS error 225	—	—
1699 no stop after date 30	140	800		1699 BRITAN IA error.......225	—	—
1699 BRITANNIΛ error 225	—	—				

3556 Halfpenny. Third issue. Laur. and cuir. bust r. ℞. Britannia with r. hand on knee die axis ↑↓

	F	VF	EF		F	VF	EF
1699 30	150	800		1700 BRITANNIΛ error ... 40	150	800
1699 stop after date....... 225	—	—		1700 — no stop after 45	175	850
1699 BRITANNIΛ error .. 95	350	—		1700 BRIVANNIA error ..... *Extremely rare*		
1699 GVLILEMVS error ...275	—	—		1700 GVLIELMS 95	325	—
1699 TERTVS error...... 275	—	—		1700 GVLIEEMVS 60	200	950
1699 — no rev. stop...... 150	—	—		1700 TER TIVS 45	175	900
1699 no stops on obv. 85	350	—		1700 I/V in TERTIVS 225	—	—
1699 no stop after..............				1701 35	140	800
GVLIELMVS 85	300	—		1701 BRITANNIΛ 50	200	850
1700 30	140	800		1701 — no stops on obv. 225	—	—
1700 no stops on obv. 95	325	—		1701 — inverted A's		
1700 no stop after				for V's 60	225	900
GVLIELMVS 95	325	—				

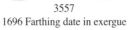

	3557				3558		
1696 Farthing date in exergue				1699 Farthing date in legend			

	F	VF	EF		F	VF	EF
	£	£	£		£	£	£

3557 Farthing. First issue Laur. and cuir. bust r. R. Britannia l. die axis ↑↓

1695 40	200	800	1698 200	575	—
1695 GVLIELMV error 200	—	—	1698 B/G on rev. 325	—	—
1696 35	175	750	1699 35	200	750
1697 30	150	700	1699 GVLILEMVS•..... 175	400	—
1697 GVLIELMS error......250	—	—	1700 30	125	700
1697 TERTIV error........ 250	—	—	1700 RRITANNIA........ 225	—	—

3558 Farthing. Second issue. Laur. and cuir. bust r. R. Britannia date at end of legend die axis ↑↓

1698 Stop after date 45	225	850	1699 — No stop before or after *Extremely rare*
1699 no stop after date.... 50	250	900	1699 BRITANNIA........ 225	—	—
1699 no stop after...............			1699 BRITANNIA........ 225	—	—
GVLIELMVS 125	—	—

Anne, the second daughter of James II, was born on 6th February 1665 and as a protestant succeeded to the throne on William III's death. Anne married Prince George of Denmark and produced 17 children, sadly none surviving to succeed to the throne. Anne died on 1st August 1714.

The Act of Union of 1707, which effected the unification of the ancient kingdoms of England and Scotland into a single realm, resulted in a change in the royal arms—on the Post-Union coinage the English lions and Scottish lion are emblazoned per pale on the top and bottom shields. After the Union the rose in the centre of the reverse of the gold coins is replaced by the Garter star.

Following a successful Anglo-Dutch expedition against Spain, bullion seized in Vigo Bay was sent to be minted into coin, and the coins made from this metal had the word VIGO placed below the Queen's bust. The elephant and castle provenance mark continues on some guineas in the Post-Union period.

Engravers and designers: Samuel Bull (d.c1720), Joseph Cave (d.c1760), James Clerk, John Croker (1670-1741), Godfrey Kneller (1646-1723)

GOLD

3560
1705 Pre-Union Five Guineas

Before Union with Scotland. The shields on the reverse are Pre-Union type.

	F	VF	EF		F	VF	EF
	£	£	£		£	£	£

3560 Five Guineas. Dr. bust l, regnal year on edge in words (e.g. 1705 = QVARTO) die axis ↑↓

1705 QVARTO	2000	5250	13500	1706 QVINTO	2000	5250	13500

3561 Five Guineas. Similar VIGO below bust, die axis ↑↓ 1703 (Three varieties)

SECVNDO 17500 52500 125000

3562
1705 Pre-Union Guinea

3563
1703 VIGO Guinea

3562 Guinea. Dr. bust l. R. Crowned cruciform shields sceptres in angles die axis ↑↓

1702 525	2000	5000	1706 575	2250	5250
1702 proof *FDC*	*Extremely rare*		1707 575	2250	5250
1705 575	2250	5250			

3563 Guinea. Similar with VIGO below bust, die axis ↑↓ 1703 .... 6500 17500 32500

3564
Pre-Union Half-Guinea

3565
VIGO Half-Guinea

	F £	VF £	EF £			F £	VF £	EF £

3564 Half-Guinea. Dr bust l. R. Crowned cruciform shields sceptres in angles die axis ↑↓

1702 ....600 1750 5000   1705 ....575 1650 4750

3565 Half-Guinea. Similar with VIGO below bust, 1703...............................3500 8500 17500

3566
1706 Post-Union Five Guineas

After Union with Scotland. The shields on the reverse are changed to Post-Union type die axis ↑↓

3566 Five Guineas. Dr. bust l., regnal year on edge in words 1706 QVINTO 1750 4500 11000

3567
1709 - Narrow shields

3568
1711 - Broad shields

3567 Five Guineas. Similar R. Narrower shields, tall narrow crowns, larger rev. lettering, die axis ↑↓

1709 OCTAVO 1800 4750 12000

3568 Five Guineas. New bust l. R. Broader shields edge inscribed die axis ↑↓

1711 DECIMO .... 1800 4750 12000   1714/3 D. TERTIO....... 1850 5000 12500

1713 DVODECIMO 1850 5000 12500   1714 D. TERTIO.......... 1850 5000 13000

3569
1713 Two Guineas

	F	VF	EF		F	VF	EF
	£	£	£		£	£	£

3569 Two Guineas. Dr. bust l.R. Crowned cruciform shields sceptres in angles edge milled die axis ↑↓

1709	850	2400	6000	1713	850	2400	6000
1711	800	2250	5750	1714/3	900	2500	6250

3570 Guinea. First dr. bust l. R. Crowned cruciform shields sceptres in angles edge milled die axis↑↓

1707	475	1650	4250	1708	500	1750	4500

3571   3574
1708 Guinea, first bust, elephant and castle below   1713 Guinea, third bust

3571 Guinea. First dr. bust l. elephant and castle below, R. Similar die axis ↑↓

1707	575	2250	5500	1708		*Extremely rare*	

3572 Guinea. Second dr. bust l. R. Similar die axis ↑↓

1707	450	1500	4000	1709	400	1350	3500
1708	400	1350	3500				

3573 Guinea. Second bust elephant and castle below R. Similar die axis ↑↓

1708	575	2250	5500	1709	525	2000	5250

3574 Guinea. Third dr. bust l. R. Similar die axis ↑↓

1710	375	1200	2750	1713	325	1000	2250
1711	375	1200	2750	1714	350	1100	2500
1712	375	1200	2750	1714 GRATIΛ	325	1000	2250
1713/1	350	1100	1100				

3575 - 1710 Half-Guinea

3575 Half-Guinea. Dr. bust l. R. Crowned cruciform shields, sceptres in angles, edge milled die axis ↑↓

1707	300	750	2250	1711	275	725	2100
1708	325	800	2500	1712	300	750	2250
1709	300	750	2250	1713	275	700	2000
1710	275	700	2000	1714	275	700	2000

SILVER

3576
1703 VIGO Crown

	F	VF	EF		F	VF	EF
	£	£	£		£	£	£

Before Union with Scotland. The shields on the reverse are Pre-Union type.

3576 Crown. VIGO below dr. bust, l., regnal year on edge in words (e.g. 1703 = TERTIO) die axis↑↓

1703 TERTIO 300 1000 3250

3577
1705 Crown, plumes on reverse

3578
1707 Pre-Union crown, roses and plumes

3577 Crown. Dr bust l. ℞. Plumes in angles, die axis ↑↓ 1705 QVINTO ..425 1400 4750

3578 Crown. ℞. Similar Crowned cruciform shields Roses and plumes in angles die axis ↑↓

1706 QVINTO .... 200 700 1850 1707 SEXTO............ 160 475 1800

3579
1703 Halfcrown, plain below bust

3579 Halfcrown . Dr. bust l. ℞. Similar Regnal year on edge in words die axis ↑↓

1703 TERTIO 575 2250 8500

3580
1703 VIGO Halfcrown

	F	VF	EF		F	VF	EF
	£	£	£		£	£	£

3580 Halfcrown. Similar VIGO below bust, die axis ↑↓ 1703 TERTIO 125   400   1500

3581
Halfcrown, plumes on reverse

3581 Halfcrown. Dr. bust l. R. Plumes in angles, similar die axis ↑↓
1704 TERTIO 140   575   2400   1705 QVINTO 140   550   2250

3582   3583
Halfcrown, Pre-Union,   Shilling
roses and plumes

3582 Halfcrown. Dr. bust l. R. Roses and plumes in angles, similar die axis ↑↓
1706 QVINTO 100   350   1350   1707 SEXTO.............. 95   300   1250

First bust   Second bust
3583 Shilling. First dr. bust l. R. Similar die axis ↑↓1702 75   225   675

	F	VF	EF			F	VF	EF
	£	£	£			£	£	£

3584 **Shilling.** Similar R. Plumes in angles, die axis ↑↓ 1702 75   275   800

3585 **Shilling.** First dr. bust VIGO below , die axis ↑↓

1702 70   200   600   1702 :ANNA.................. 125   375   975

3586
1703 VIGO Shilling

3587
'Plain' Shilling

3586 **Shilling.** Second dr. bust, l. VIGO below R. Similar, die axis ↑↓ 1703 60   200   575

3587 **Shilling.** Similar R. Crowned cruciform shields, angles plain, die axis ↑↓

1704 275   950   —   1705 100   425   1100

3588 **Shilling.** Second dr. bust l. R. Plumes in angles die axis ↑↓

1704 90   375   975   1705 90   300   850

3589 **Shilling.** Second dr. bust l. R. Roses and plumes in angles die axis ↑↓

1705 90   300   850   1707 125   375   975

3590 **Sixpence.** Dr. bust l. VIGO below dr. bust, l. die axis ↑↓ 1703.................. 35   100   350

3591 **Sixpence.** Dr bust l., R. Angles plain, die axis ↑↓ 1705 60   175   475

3592 **Sixpence.** Similar R. Early shields, plumes in angles, die axis ↑↓ 1705........ 45   135   400

3593
1705 Plumes Sixpence

Early Shield

Late Shield

3593 **Sixpence.** Similar R. Late shields, plumes in angles, die axis ↑↓1705.......... 50   150   450

3594 **Sixpence.** Similar R. Crowned cruciform shields Roses and plumes in angles die axis ↑↓

1705 50   150   450   1707 45   135   425

3595
Groat or fourpence, first bust

3595 **Fourpence.** First dr. bust l. small face, curls at back of head point downwards.

R Small crown above the figure 4 die axis ↑↓

1703 15   30   90   1704 10   25   80

3595C
Groat or Fourpence, second bust

	F	VF	EF		F	VF	EF
	£	£	£		£	£	£

3595A Fourpence. Second dr. bust l. larger face, curls at back of head point upwards die axis ↑↓

1705	15	35	90	1709	10	25	75
1706	10	25	75	1710	10	25	75
1708	10	25	75				

3595B –Fourpence. Similar R Large crown with pearls on arch, larger serifs on the figure 4 die axis ↑↓

| 1710 | 10 | 25 | 75 | 1713 | 10 | 25 | 80 |

3595C Fourpence. Second dr. bust l., but with re-engraved hair R. Crowned 4 die axis ↑↓

| 1710 | 10 | 25 | 75 | 1713 | 10 | 25 | 80 |

3596 Threepence. First dr. bust l., broader, tie riband pointing outwards. R. Crowned 3 die axis ↑↓

| 1703 7 above crown | 15 | 35 | 100 | 1703 7 not above crown | 15 | 35 | 100 |

3596A Threepence. Second dr. bust l., taller and narrow, tie riband pointing inwards die axis ↑↓

| 1704 | 10 | 30 | 90 | 1706 | 10 | 25 | 75 |
| 1705 | 10 | 30 | 90 | | | | |

3596B
Threepence, third bust

3596B Threepence. Third larger more finely engraved dr. bust l. R. Crowned 3, die axis ↑↓

1707	10	25	75	1710	10	25	75
1708	10	25	85	1713	10	25	75
1708/7	10	25	75	1713 mule with 4d obv.			
1709	10	25	75	die	15	35	130

3597 Twopence. First dr. bust l., as fourpence, R. Crown to edge of coin, small figure 2 die axis ↑↓

1703	12	30	85	1705	10	25	70
1704	10	25	65	1706	10	25	75
1704 No stops on obv.	12	30	85	1707	10	25	75

3597A Twopence. Second dr. bust l., as fourpence, R Crown within inner circle of legend, large figure 2 die axis ↑↓

| 1708 | 10 | 25 | 65 | 1710 | 10 | 25 | 65 |
| 1709 | 10 | 30 | 75 | 1713 | 10 | 25 | 65 |

3598 Penny. Dr. bust l. R. Crowned 1 die axis ↑↓

1703	15	35	100	1709	12	30	85
1705	12	30	85	1710	15	35	100
1706	12	30	85	1713/0	15	30	100
1708	15	35	100				

3599
1713 Maundy Set

	F £	VF £	EF £		F £	VF £	EF £
3599 Maundy Set. The four denominations. Uniform dates							
1703 80		175	700	1709 80		175	600
1705 80		175	700	1710 85		200	700
1706 70		150	600	1713 75		175	625
1708 85		200	700				

After Union with Scotland

The shields on the reverse are changed to the Post-Union types. The Edinburgh coins have been included here as they are now coins of Great Britain.

3600 **Crown.** Second dr. bust, l. E (Edinburgh) below, R. Crowned
cruciform shields regnal year on edge in words, die axis ↑↓
(e.g. 1708 = SEPTIMO)

1707 SEXTO 110	425	1350	1708/7 SEPTIMO 135	500	1500
1708 SEPTIMO.........125	475	1450			

3601
Crown, second bust, plain reverse

3601 **Crown.** Second dr. bust l. R. Crowned cruciform shields, angles plain die axis ↑↓

1707 SEPTIMO 135	475	1450	1708 SEPTIMO 150	500	1500

3602 **Crown.** Similar R. Plumes in angles, die axis ↑↓

1708 SEPTIMO 140	500	1500	1708 — BR for BRI....... *Extremely rare*

3603

1713 Crown, third bust, roses and plumes

	F £	VF £	EF £		F £	VF £	EF £

3603 Crown. Third dr. bust. l. R. Roses and plumes, 1713 DVODECIMO 135   450   1400

3604

1708 Halfcrown, Post-Union

3604 Halfcrown. Dr. bust R. Plain, regnal year on edge in words (e.g. 1709 = OCTAVO), die axis ↑↓

1707 SEPTIMO 65	250	950	1709 OCTAVO 65	250	950
1707 no stops on reverse .. 110	450	—	1713 DVODECIMO 65	250	950
1708 SEPTIMO 70	275	1050			

3605

3605 Halfcrown. Dr. bust E below R. Crowned cruciform shields die axis ↑↓

1707 SEXTO 65	250	900	1708 SEPTIMO 70	275	1000
1707 SEPTIMO 225	—	—	1709 OCTAVO 175	675	—

3606
1708 Halfcrown, plumes on reverse

3607
1714 Halfcrown, roses and plumes

	F	VF	EF		F	VF	EF
	£	£	£		£	£	£
3606 Halfcrown. Similar R. Plumes in angles, die axis ↑↓ 1708 SEPTIMO	75	300	1200				
3607 Halfcrown. Similar R. Roses and plumes in angles die axis ↑↓							
1710 NONO 70		275	1050	1714 D. TERTIO............. 70		275	950
1712 UNDECIMO 65		250	900	1714/3 D. TERTIO........ 100		375	1250
1713 DVODECIMO 65		250	900				

3608
1707 Edinburgh Mint Shilling, second bust

3609
1708 E* Shilling

3608 Shilling. Second dr. bust, l. E *(Edinburgh)* below, R. Crowned cruciform shields die axis ↑↓

1707 85		275	850	1707 Plain edge proof *FDC* £4000			
1707 no stops on		—	—	1708 135		450	1250
reverse.............. 275							

3609 Shilling. Similar E* *(Edinburgh)* below bust die axis ↑↓

| 1707 .... 110 | | 350 | 1000 | 1708/7 .... 275 | | — | — |
| 1708 .... 100 | | 325 | 950 | 1708 no rays to garter star...... *Extremely rare* | | | |

3609A Shilling. Similar E* *(Edinburgh)* local dies die axis ↑↓

| 1707 .... 200 | | 600 | — | 1708 .... 225 | | 675 | — |

Third bust   Fourth bust

3610
Shilling, third bust

3611
Shilling, plumes on reverse

	F	VF	EF		F	VF	EF
	£	£	£		£	£	£
3610 Shilling Third dr. bust. l. R. Crowned cruciform shields, angles Plain, die axis ↑↓							
1707	35	110	375	1709	35	100	350
1708	30	95	325	1711	95	275	875
3611 Shilling. Third dr. bust. l. R. Plumes in angles die axis ↑↓							
1707	100	300	900	1708	90	275	850
3612 Shilling. Third dr. bust. E below R. angles plain die axis ↑↓							
1707	75	225	700	1708/7	125	375	1000
1708	80	250	800				
3613 Shilling. Second dr. bust l. R. Roses and plumes, die axis ↑↓ 1708	125	375	975

3614
1708 Shilling, roses and plumes

3614 Shilling. Third dr. bust l. R. Crowned cruciform shields Roses and plumes die axis ↑↓

1708	80	250	800	1710	75	225	750

3615	3620	3623
Edinburgh bust – E* Shilling	Edinburgh Mint Sixpence	1707 Sixpence, plumes on reverse

	F	VF	EF		F	VF	EF
	£	£	£		£	£	£

3615 Shilling. 'Edinburgh' bust, E* below, R. Crowned cruciform shields die axis ↑↓

| 1707 | 375 | — | — | 1709 | 90 | 275 | 800 |
| 1708 | 95 | 300 | 850 | | | | |

3616 Shilling. — E below, R. Similar die axis ↑↓ 1709 ... 300 ... 950 ... —

3617 Shilling. Fourth dr. bust. l. R. Roses and plumes die axis ↑↓

1710	80	250	750	1713/2	80	250	750
1710 plain edge proof *FDC*		*Extremely rare*		1714	60	175	525
1712	60	175	525	1714/3	85	275	750

3618 Shilling. Similar, R. angles plain, die axis ↑↓

| 1711 | 30 | 90 | 325 | 1711 plain edge proof *FDC* | | *Extremely rare* | |

3619 Sixpence. Normal dr. bust. l. R. angles plain die axis ↑↓

1707	35	100	350	1711	25	75	225
1707 BR. FRA error		*Extremely rare*		1711 Large Lis	30	85	250
1708	40	110	375				

3620 Sixpence. Normal dr. bust E *(Edinburgh)* below R. Similar die axis ↑↓

| 1707 | 45 | 135 | 400 | 1708/7 | 65 | 185 | 525 |
| 1707 Proof FDC £2750 | | | | 1708 | 60 | 175 | 475 |

3621 Sixpence. Normal dr. bust E* *(Edinburgh)* below, R. Similar die axis ↑↓

| 1708 | 60 | 175 | 475 | 1708/7 | 65 | 185 | 525 |

3622 Sixpence. 'Edinburgh' bust, l. E* below, R. Similar die axis ↑↓ 1708 .. 60 ... 175 ... 475

3623 Sixpence. Normal dr. bust. l. R. Plumes in angles die axis ↑↓

| 1707 | 45 | 135 | 400 | 1708 | 50 | 150 | 450 |

3624 Sixpence. Similar R. Roses and plumes in angles, die axis ↑↓ 1710 ... 50 ... 150 ... 450

COPPER

3625
1714 Farthing

3625 Farthing. Dr. bust l. R. Britannia 1714 pattern only, die axis ↑↓ .... 250 ... 500 ... 950

GEORGE I, 1714-27

George I was born on 28th May 1660 son of Ernest, Elector of Hanover and Sophia grandaughter of James I, and inherited the English Throne on a technicality, Parliament considered him a better alternative than James Edward Stuart – Anne's half-brother. He was however, thoroughly German, did not want to learn English and spent over half his reign in Germany. He brought two mistresses with him to England while his wife ironically languished in a German prison on a charge of adultery. His reign created a government that could run independently of the King. The office of Prime Minister was created in 1721. He also kept England out of war for his entire reign, and he died on 11 June 1727.

The coins of the first of the Hanoverian kings have the arms of the Duchy of Brunswick and Luneberg on one of the four shields, the object in the centre of the shield being the Crown of Charlemagne. The King's German titles also appear, in abbreviated form, and name him 'Duke of Brunswick and Luneberg. Arch-treasurer of the Holy Roman Empire, and Elector', and on the Guinea of 1714, 'Prince Elector'. A Quarter-Guinea was struck for the first time in 1718, but it was of an inconvenient size, and the issue was discontinued. The elephant and castle provenance mark continues on some guineas and half-guineas, but today are rarely seen.

Silver coined from bullion supplied to the mint by the South Sea Company in 1723 shows the Company's initials S.S.C.; similarly Welsh Copper Company bullion has the letters W.C.C. below the King's bust; and plumes and an interlinked CC in the reverse angles. Roses and plumes together on the reverse indicate silver supplied by the Company for Smelting Pit Coale and Sea Coale.

Engravers and Designers: Samuel Bull (d.c.1720), John Croker (1670-1741), John Rudulf Ochs Snr, (1673-c.1748), Norbert Roettier (b.1665)

Prime Minister: Sir Robert Walpole (1676 – 1745) –Whig, 1721-42

GOLD

3626
1717 Five Guineas

	F	VF	EF		F	VF	EF
	£	£	£		£	£	£

3626 Five Guineas. Laur. head r. regnal year on edge in words (e.g. 1717 = TERTIO) die axis↑↓

	F	VF	EF		F	VF	EF
1716 SECVNDO	1850	5000	15000	1720 SEXTO	2250	6000	17000
1717 TERTIO	2000	5500	16000	1726 D. TERTIO....	1850	5000	15000

3627
Two Guineas

	F £	VF £	EF £		F £	VF £	EF £

3627 Two Guineas. Laur. head r. R. Crowned cruciform shields, sceptres in angles, edge milled, die axis ↑↓

1717	750	1850	5250	1720/17	800	2000	5500
1720	750	1850	5250	1726	725	1850	5000

3628	3630	3631
1714 'Prince Elector' Guinea	Third bust	Fourth bust

3628 Guinea. First laur. head r. R. Legend ends ET PR . EL (Prince Elector), die axis ↑↓

1714		900	2250	5500

3629 Guinea. Second laur. head, r. tie with two ends, R. Crowned cruciform shields, sceptres in angles normal legend ↑↓ 1715 .... 525 1350 3500

3630 Guinea. Third laur. head, r. no hair below truncation R. Similar die axis ↑↓

1715	450	1250	3000	1716	475	1350	3250

3631 Guinea. Fourth laur. head, r. tie with loop at one end R. Similar die axis ↑↓

1716	350	1050	2750	1720	375	1100	2850
1717	400	1200	3000	1721	400	1200	3000
1718		*Extremely rare*		1722	350	1100	2850
1718/7		*Extremely rare*		1722/0	425	1200	3000
1719	350	1100	2850	1723	375	1100	2850
1719/6		*Extremely rare*					

3632 Guinea. Fourth Laur. head, elephant and castle below R. Similar die axis ↑↓

1721		*Extremely rare*	1722		*Extremely rare*

3633
Guinea, fifth bust

	F	VF	EF		F	VF	EF
	£	£	£		£	£	£

3633 Guinea. Fifth (older) laur. head, r. tie with two ends R. Similar die axis ↑↓

1723	350	1000	2750	1726	325	950	2500
1724	350	1000	2750	1727	425	1200	3250
1725	350	1000	2750				

3634 Guinea. Fifth laur. head, elephant and castle below, die axis ↑↓ 1726 ...... 1100 3250 8500

3635 Half-Guinea. First laur. head r. R. Crowned cruciform shields, sceptres in angles die axis ↑↓

1715	375	850	2500	1721	*Extremely rare*		
1717	225	450	1600	1722	225	450	1600
1718	200	425	1500	1722/0	250	475	1700
1718/7	250	450	1600	1723	325	675	2250
1719	200	450	1600	1724	350	675	2250
1720	250	500	1750				

3636 Half-Guinea. First laur. head elephant and castle below, die axis ↑↓ 1721   *Extremely rare*

3637   3638
Half-Guinea, second bust   Quarter Guinea

3637 Half-Guinea. Second (older) laur. head r. R. Crowned cruciform shields, sceptres in angles die axis ↑↓

1725	200	400	1400	1727	200	425	1500
1726	200	425	1500				

3638 Quarter-Guinea. Laur. head R. Similar die axis ↑↓ 1718 ...... 125 200 500

SILVER

3639A - 1726 Crown - small roses and plumes

	F	VF	EF		F	VF	EF
	£	£	£		£	£	£

3639 Crown. Laur and dr. bust r. ℞. Roses and plumes in angles, regnal year on edge in words
(e.g. 1716 = SECVNDO) die axis ↑↓

1716 SECVNDO 325	900	3250	1720/18 SEXTO 325	1050	3500
1718/6 QUINTO 350	1000	3750			

3639A Crown. Similar ℞. small roses and plumes in angles

1720 SEXTO 375	950	4000	1726 D. TERTIO 325	1000	3500

3640 .... Crown. Similar ℞. SSC (South Sea Company) in angles, die axis ↑↓

1723 DECIMO 325	850	3250

3641 - 1715 Pattern Halfcrown

3641 Halfcrown. Laur and dr. bust r. ℞. Angles plain (pattern only), die axis ↑↓ 1715 *FDC* £6000

3642 - Halfcrown, roses and plumes

3642 Halfcrown. — ℞. Roses and plumes in angles, regnal year on edge in words
(e.g. 1717 = TIRTIO)

1715 SECVNDO 200	575	2500	1717 TIRTIO 200	575	2500
1715 Edge wording out...			1720/17 SEXTO 160	575	2500
of order 275	850	3000	1720 SEXTO 225	750	2750
1715 Plain edge 375	1250	—			

3643
1723 SSC Halfcrown

	F	VF	EF		F	VF	EF
	£	£	£		£	£	£

3643 Halfcrown. Similar R̦. SSC in angles, die axis ↑↓1723 DECIMO 150   500   2000

3644
1726 Halfcrown small roses and plumes

3644 Halfcrown. — R. Small roses and plumes, die axis ↑↓ 1726 D.TERTIO ...2750   5250   12500

3645
Shilling, roses and plumes

3646
1721 Shilling, plain reverse

3645 Shilling. First laur. and dr. bust. r. R. Roses and plumes in angles, die axis ↑↓

1715	50	160	650	1721	95	300	950
1716	90	275	900	1721/0	60	175	700
1717	60	175	700	1721/19	95	300	950
1718	50	150	600	1721/18 plumes and			
1719	90	275	900	roses error	300	900	—
1720	65	200	750	1722	60	175	700
1720/18	125	375	1250	1723	75	225	800

3646 Shilling. First laur. and dr. bust r. R. angles plain (i.e. no marks either side) die axis ↑↓

1720	30	100	450	1721	95	300	950
1720 large O	40	125	500				

	3647				3649		
	1723 SSC Shilling, first bust				1727 Shilling, second bust		
	F	VF	EF		F	VF	EF
	£	£	£		£	£	£

3647 Shilling. First laur. and dr. bust r. R. SSC in angles, die axis ↑↓

1723	20	75	225	1723 C/SS in 3rd			
1723 French Arms at				quarter	30	90	375
date	90	250	850				

3648 Shilling. Second dr. bust, r. bow to tie. R. Similar, die axis ↑↓ 1723 ... 40   110   475

3649 Shilling. Similar R. Roses and plumes in angles die axis ↑↓

1723	70	200	750	1726	475	1500	—
1724	70	200	750	1727	450	1350	—
1725	70	200	750	1727 no stops on rev.	400	1250	—
1725 no stops on obv.	75	210	775				

3650
1726 WCC Shilling

3650 Shilling. Second laur. and dr. bust r. W.C.C. (Welsh Copper Company) below bust die axis ↑↓

1723	375	1150	4000	1725	425	1250	4250
1724	375	1150	4000	1726	425	1250	4250

3651 Sixpence. Laur. and dr. bust r. R. Roses and plumes in angles, die axis ↑↓

1717	60	175	500	1720/17	60	175	500
1717 Plain edge		*Extremely rare*					

	3652	3653
	1723 SSC Sixpence	1726 Sixpence, small roses and plumes

3652 Sixpence. Laur. and dr. bust r. R. SSC in angles, die axis ↑↓

1723	25	70	250	1723 larger lettering...	30	80	275

3653 Sixpence. Similar R. Small roses and plumes, die axis ↑↓ 1726 60   175   500

	F £	VF £	EF £		F £	VF £	EF £
3654 **Fourpence.** Laur. and dr. bust r. R. Crowned 4, die axis ↑↓							
1717	10	30	100	1723	10	30	100
1721	10	30	100	1727	15	35	110
3655 **Threepence.** Laur. and dr. bust r, R. Crowned 3, die axis ↑↓							
1717	10	35	90	1723	10	30	100
1721	12	35	100	1727 small lettering	10	30	100
3656 **Twopence.** Laur. and dr. bust r. R. Crowned 2, die axis ↑↓							
1717	8	25	60	1726	8	20	55
1721	8	20	55	1727 small lettering	10	25	65
1723	10	30	75				
3657 **Penny.** Laur. and dr. bust r. R. Crowned 1, die axis ↑↓							
1716	8	25	60	1723	8	25	60
1718	8	25	60	1725	8	25	60
1720	8	25	60	1726	10	30	65
1720 HIPEX error	15	65	120	1727 BRI·FR	15	45	85

3658

3658 **Maundy Set.** As last four. Uniform dates

	F £	VF £	EF £		F £	VF £	EF £
1723	90	225	800	1727	90	200	700

COPPER

3659

3659 **Halfpenny.** 'Dump' issue obv. legend continuous over bust, plain edge, die axis ↑↓

	F £	VF £	EF £		F £	VF £	EF £
1717	35	200	650	1718 no stops on obv.	150	450	—
1717 no stops on obv.	95	475	—	1719	650	—	—
1718	30	175	600	1719 grained edge	900	—	—
1718 R/B on rev.	50	200	750				

3660   3660A

	F £	VF £	EF £		F £	VF £	EF £

3660 Halfpenny. Second issue, second obverse, plain left shoulder strap, less hair to the right of tie knot, R. Britannia plain edge, die axis ↑↓

	F	VF	EF		F	VF	EF
1719	40	175	725	1722	30	130	575
1719 grained edge	900	–	–	1722 Ɐ for V on obv.	100	450	–
1720	30	150	700	1723	30	130	625
1721	30	125	625	1723 Thin Flan	*Extremely rare*		
1721 stop after date	40	160	675	1723 no stop on rev.	100	475	–
1721/0	40	160	675	1724	30	130	550

3660A Halfpenny. Second issue, second obverse, ornate shoulder straps, die axis ↑↓

	F	VF	EF
1719	40	160	750

3661   3662

3661 Farthing. 'Dump' issue, Similar die axis ↑↓

	F	VF	EF		
1717	200	575	1000	1718	*Unique*

3662 Farthing. Second issue laur. and cuir. bust r. R. Britannia, date in ex. die axis ↑↓

	F	VF	EF		F	VF	EF
1719 small letters	60	275	650	1720 obv. large letters	75	325	–
1719 no stop on rev.	65	325	–	1721	25	100	500
1719 large lettering on obv.	30	125	525	1721/0	40	140	550
1719 — no stops on obv.	70	375	–	1721 stop after date	35	140	525
1719 — no stops on rev.	85	400	–	1722	30	120	525
1719 last A/I on rev.	75	325	–	1722 obv. large letters	40	175	600
1720	30	125	500	1723 R/≈ in REX	95	300	725
1720 milled edge	150	450	1000	1723	30	140	500
				1724	30	140	525

George II was born on 30 October 1683 and was raised in Hanover, but upon his succession to the throne as George I's only child, he adapted himself to English society. His passions were the military, music and his wife – Caroline of Anspach, though he despised his eldest son Frederick as his own father despised him. George declared war on Spain in 1739 and he was the last King to have personally led his troops at the battle of Dettingen on 17 June 1743. Upon his death on 25 October 1760 the throne passed to his grandson George as Frederick had already died.

Silver was coined only spasmodically by the Mint during this reign; and no copper was struck after 1754. Gold coins made from bullion supplied by the East India Company bear the Company's E.I.C. initials. Some of the treasure seized by Admiral Anson during his circumnavigation of the globe, 1740-4, and by other privateers, was made into coin, which had the word LIMA below the king's bust to celebrate the expedition's successful harassment of the Spanish Colonies in the New World. Hammered gold was finally demonetized in 1733.

Engravers and designers: John Croker (1670-1741), John Rudolf Ochs Snr (1673-1748) and jnr (1704-88), Johann Sigismund Tanner (c.1706-75)

Prime Ministers: Sir Robert Walpole (1676-1745) Whig, 1721-43; Spencer Compton (1673-1743) Whig 1742-3; Henry Pelham (c.1695-1754) Whig 1743-54; William Cavendish (1720-1764) Whig 1756-7; Thomas Pelham-Holles (1693-1768) Whig 1754-6; 1757-62.

GOLD

3663A
1741 Five Guineas - revised shield

	F £	VF £	EF £		F £	VF £	EF £
3663 Five Guineas. Young laur. head l. ℞. Crowned shield of arms, die axis ↑↓ regnal year							
on edge in words (e.g. 1729 = TERTIO)				1729 TERTIO	1550	4000	11000
1729 Plain edge proof *FDC* £37500							
3663A Five Guineas. Similar ℞. Revised shield garnish die axis ↑↓							
1731 QVARTO	2000	4750	13500	1738 DVODECIMO	1600	4000	11000
1731 QVARTO proof *FDC* £40000				1741/38 D. QVARTO	1550	3750	10000
1735 NONO	2000	4750	13500	1741 D. QVARTO	1450	3500	9500
3664 Five Guineas. Young laur. head, E.I.C. (East India Company) below, die axis ↑↓							
1729 TERTIO					1400	3250	9000

3665

1746 LIMA Five Guineas

	F	VF	EF		F	VF	EF
	£	£	£		£	£	£
3665 Five Guineas. Old laur. head, l. LIMA below, ↑↓1746 D. NONO ..	1450	3500	9250				
3666 Five Guineas. Old laur. head plain below, R. Crowned shield, edge inscribed die axis ↑↓							
1748 V. SECVNDO	1450	3500	9500	1753 V. SEXTO	1450	3750	10000
3667 Two Guineas. Young laur. head l. R Crowned shield with rounded arches, die axis ↑↓							
1733 Proof *FDC*.£20000				1734/3 975	2250	5000	

3667A

1735 Two Guineas - new reverse

3667A Two Guineas. − R. Crown with pointed arches, new type of shield garnishing die axis ↑↓

1735 550   1200   3000

3667B Two Guineas. Repositioned legend on obverse R. Similar

1738*.........................450   850   2100   1739 450   900   2200

3668

1740 Two Guineas - Intermediate head

3668 Two Guineas. Intermediate laur. head l. R. Crowned shield of arms die axis ↑↓

1739*.........................450   850   2100   1740 450   900   2200

1740/39.....................475   925   2250

3669 Two Guineas. Old laur. head l. R. Crowned shield of arms die axis ↑↓ ..

1748 500   1050   2750   1753 550   1200   3000

Beware recent forgeries.

Overstruck dates are listed only if commoner than normal date or if no normal date is known.

	F	VF	EF		F	VF	EF
	£	£	£		£	£	£

3670 Guinea. First young laur. head, l. small lettering, die axis ↑↓ 1727 ... 450 1500 4000

3671

3676

1727 Guinea - small reverse shield

3671 Guinea. Similar larger lettering, smaller shield, die axis ↑↓

1727 .... 450 1500 4000 1728 .... 475 1600 4250

3672 Guinea. Second (narrower) young laur. head l. die axis ↑↓

1729 Proof *FDC* £8500 1731 .... 375 1250 3250

1730 .... 400 1350 3500 1732 .... 400 1350 3500

3673 Guinea. Second young laur. head, E.I.C. below R. Crowned shield of arms die axis ↑↓

1729 .... 525 1750 5000 1732 .... 475 1600 4500

1731 .... 500 1650 4750

3674 Guinea. Second young laur. head l. larger lettering R. Crowned shield of arms die axis ↑↓

1732 .... 400 1250 2850 1736 .... 375 1200 2750

1733 .... 350 1100 2500 1737 .... 400 1250 2850

1734 .... 375 1150 2650 1738 .... 400 1250 2850

1735 .... 375 1200 2750

3675 Guinea. – – E.I.C. below, die axis ↑↓ 1732 .... 475 1600 4500

3676 Guinea. Intermediate laur. head l. r. Crowned shield of arms die axis ↑↓

1739 .... 350 1100 2500 1741/39 .... 575 1750 5000

1740 .... 400 1200 2750 1743 .... 575 1750 5000

3677 Guinea. Similar E.I.C. below, R. Similar die axis ↑↓ 1739 .... 525 1650 4500

3678 Guinea. Similar larger lettering on *obv.*, GEORGIUS die axis ↑↓

1745 .... 375 1250 3000

3678A

1746 Guinea - GEORGIVS legend

3679

LIMA Guinea

3678A Guinea. Similar as last but reads GEORGIVS die axis ↑↓

1746 .... 400 1350 3250

3679 Guinea. Intermediate laur. head LIMA below, die axis ↑↓ 1745 .... 975 2750 6500

3680
Old head Guinea

	F	VF	EF		F	VF	EF
	£	£	£		£	£	£

3680 Guinea. Old laur. head l. R. Crowned shield of arms die axis ↑↓

1747	325	800	2250	1753	325	800	2250
1748	325	800	2250	1755	325	800	2250
1749	325	800	2250	1756	300	750	2000
1750	325	800	2250	1758	275	700	1650
1751	300	750	2000	1759	250	675	1600
1752	300	750	2000	1760	275	700	1650

3681 Half-Guinea. Young laur. head. l. R First shield of arms, die axis ↑↓

1728	300	700	2250	1729	375	850	2750

1728 Proof *FDC* £6000

3681A
1731 Half-Guinea - modified shield

3681A Half-Guinea. Young laur. head l. R. Modified garnished shield die axis ↑↓

1730	375	850	2750	1736	300	700	2250
1731	275	675	2250	1737	375	850	2750
1732	300	700	2250	1738	275	650	2000
1734	275	675	2250	1739	275	675	2250

3682 Half-Guinea. Young laur. head l. E.I.C. below R. Similar die axis ↑↓

1729	425	950	3500	1732		*Extremely rare*	
1730	625	1500	4750	1739		*Extremely rare*	
1731		*Extremely rare*					

3683A
Half-guinea - GEORGIVS legend

3683 Half-Guinea. Intermediate laur. head l. R. Similar die axis ↑↓

1740	275	675	2250	1745	275	675	2250
1743		*Extremely rare*					

3683A Half-Guinea. Similar, but reads GEORGIVS, die axis ↑↓ 1746 .... 225 | 525 | 1650

	3684			3685		
	LIMA Half-Guinea			Half-Guinea, old head		

	F	VF	EF		F	VF	EF
	£	£	£		£	£	£

3684 Half-Guinea. Intermediate laur. head LIMA below, die axis ↑↓ 1745 .. 825   2500   5500

3685 Half-Guinea. Old laur. head l. R. Similar die axis ↑↓

	F	VF	EF		F	VF	EF
1747	225	550	1650	1753	210	475	1450
1748	225	550	1650	1755	220	450	1350
1749	250	600	1750	1756	200	425	1250
1750	225	550	1650	1758	225	525	1500
1751	225	525	1600	1759	190	400	1250
1751/0	250	550	1650	1759/8	210	475	1400
1752	210	475	1450	1760	200	425	1250

SILVER

3686
Crown, young head

3686 Crown. Young laur. and dr. bust. l. R. Crowned cruciform shields Roses and plumes
in angles, regnal year on edge in words (e.g. 1736 = NONO), die axis ↑↓

1732 SEXTO	190	650	2000	1735 OCTAVO	190	625	1850
1732 Proof, plain edge *FDC* £5250				1736 NONO	190	625	1900
1734 SEPTIMO	225	675	2000				

3687

3687 Crown. Similar R. Roses in angles die axis ↑↓

1739 DVODECIMO	160	600	1850	1741 D. QVARTO	145	575	1850

3688
Crown, old head

	F	VF	EF		F	VF	EF
	£	£	£		£	£	£

3688 Crown. Old laur. and dr. bust l. R. Crowned cruciform shields Roses in angles, die axis ↑↓
1743 D. SEPTIMO 140 575 1700

3689 Crown. — LIMA below, die axis ↑↓ 1746 D. NONO............................ 140 525 1850

3690
Plain reverse

3691
1731 Pattern Halfcrown

3690 Crown. Old laur. and dr. bust l. R. angles Plain (i.e. no marks either side) die axis ↑↓
1746 Proof only, VICESIMO *FDC* £3750
1750 V. QVARTO ...... 175 600 2000 1751 V. QVARTO 175 625 2250

3691 Halfcrown. Young dr. bust l. R. angles plain (pattern only), 1731 *FDC* £4500

<table>
<tr><td>3692</td><td>3693</td></tr>
<tr><td>1736 Halfcrown, roses and plumes</td><td>1741 Halfcrown, roses on reverse</td></tr>
</table>

	F	VF	EF		F	VF	EF
	£	£	£		£	£	£

3692 Halfcrown. Young laur. and dr. bust l. R. Roses and plumes, regnal year on edge in words
(e.g. 1732 = SEXTO), die axis ↑↓

1731 QVINTO	80	325	1050	1735 OCTAVO	90	400	1300
1732 SEXTO	80	325	1050	1736 NONO	90	400	1300
1734 SEPTIMO	90	400	1300				

3693 Halfcrown. Young laur. and dr. bust l. R. Roses in angles die axis ↑↓

1739 DVODECIMO	70	250	950	1741 Large *obv.* letters	85	325	1050
1741 D. QVARTO	70	275	975	1741/39 D. QVARTO	90	350	1100

3694 Halfcrown. Old dr. bust. l. GEORGIUS R. Roses in angles die axis ↑↓

1743 D. SEPTIMO	65	225	875	1745/3 D. NONO	75	250	950
1745 D. NONO	65	225	875				

3695 Halfcrown. Old laur. and dr. bust LIMA below die axis ↑↓

1745 D. NONO	60	160	575	1745/3	70	175	675

3695A Halfcrown. Old laur. and dr. bust as last but reads GEORGIVS die axis ↑↓

1746 D. NONO	55	125	550	1746/5 D. NONO	65	150	625

<table>
<tr><td>3696</td><td>3697</td></tr>
<tr><td>Halfcrown</td><td>1731 Plumes Shilling</td></tr>
</table>

3696 Halfcrown. Old laur. and dr. bust l. R. Plain angles die axis ↑↓
1746 proof only VICESIMO *FDC* £1500

1750 V. QVARTO	90	425	1400	1751 V. QVARTO	100	450	1500

3697 Shilling. Young laur. dr. bust. l. R. Plumes in angles, die axis ↑↓

1727	65	275	975	1731	70	300	1100

3698

Shilling, young bust, small letters

3699

Young bust Shilling, large letters

	F £	VF £	EF £		F £	VF £	EF £

3698 Shilling. Young laur. and dr. bust l. R. Roses and plumes in angles, die axis ↑↓

1727	40	175	675	1731	40	185	700
1728	45	225	800	1732	45	200	750
1729	45	225	800				

3699 Shilling. Similar larger lettering. R. Roses and plumes in angles die axis ↑↓

1734	35	175	650	1736/5	40	200	750
1735	40	185	700	1737	35	175	650
1736	35	175	650				

3700

Shilling, plain reverse

3701

Shilling, roses reverse

3700 Shilling. Young laur. and dr. bust l. R. Plain, die axis ↑↓ 1728 100   350   1000

3701 Shilling. Young laur. and dr. bust l. R. Roses in angles die axis ↑↓

1739	30	135	500	1741	30	135	500
1739/7	100	350	1000	1741/39	100	350	950
1739 smaller garter star	75	250	750				

3702

Shilling, old bust, roses

3703

LIMA Shilling

3702 Shilling. Old laur. and dr. bust, l. R. Roses in angles die axis ↑↓

1743	25	90	425	1745/3	45	135	575
1743/1	45	135	575	1747	30	100	450
1745	30	100	450				

3703 Shilling. Old laur. and dr. bust LIMA below die axis ↑↓

1745	25	90	400	1746/5	75	225	750
1746	75	225	750				

3704
1758 Shilling

	F	VF	EF			F	VF	EF
	£	£	£			£	£	£

3704 Shilling. Old laur. and dr. bust R. plain angles die axis ↑↓

1746 Proof only *FDC* £1200				1750 Wide O 45	150	575
1750 35	125	500		1751 75	225	750
1750/6........................45	150	575		1758 20	60	150

3705	3706	3707
1728 Sixpence, young bust	1728 Sixpence, plumes on reverse	1728 Sixpence, roses and plumes

3705 Sixpence. Young laur. and dr. bust. l. R. Angles plain, die axis ↑↓ 1728 .. 40   110   375
1728 Proof *FDC* £2500

3706 Sixpence. Similar R. Plumes in angles die axis ↑↓ 1728..................... 40   125   375

3707 Sixpence. Young laur. and dr. bust l. R. Roses and plumes in angles die axis ↑↓

1728 25	100	325	1735 30	150	350
1731 25	100	325	1735/4 45	135	400
1732 25	100	325	1736 35	125	375
1734 30	110	350			

3708	3709
Sixpence, roses	Sixpence, old bust, roses

3708 Sixpence. Young laur. and dr. bust l., R. Roses in angles, die axis ↑↓

1739 30	95	325	1741 30	100	325
1739 O/R in legend.....40	125	400			

3709 Sixpence. Old laur. and dr. bust. l. R. Roses in angles die axis ↑↓

1743 20	70	225	1745/3 25	85	275
1745 25	70	250			

	F £	VF £	EF £		F £	VF £	EF £

3710 Sixpence. Old laur. and dr. bust LIMA below bust R. angle plain die axis ↑↓
1745 .... 25　70　250

3710A Sixpence. Similar as last but reads GEORGIVS die axis ↑↓
1746 .... 15　60　200　1746/5 .... 35　100　375

3711
Proof Sixpence

3711 Sixpence. Old laur. and dr. bust l. R. angles plain die axis ↑↓
1746 *proof only FDC* £800

1750 25	75	275	1758 10	30	90
1751 30	90	350	1758 ÐEI error 25	65	175
1757 10	30	90	1758/7 20	50	150

3712 Fourpence. Young laur. and dr. bust l. R. Small dome-shaped crown without pearls on arch, figure 4
1729 .... 10　25　70　1731 .... 8　25　70

3712A Fourpence. Similar R.Double arched crown with pearls, large figure 4, die axis ↑↓

1732 10	25	70	1740 10	25	70
1735 10	25	70	1743 10	25	70
1737 10	25	70	1743/0 15	65	140
1739 10	25	70	1746 8	20	60
			1760 10	25	65

3713 Threepence. Young laur. and dr. bust l. R. Crowned 3, pearls on arch, die axis ↑↓
1729 .... 10　25　70

3713A Threepence. Similar R. Ornate arch die axis ↑↓
1731 Smaller lettering　10　25　65　1731 .... 8　25　65

3713B Threepence. Similar R. Double arched crown with pearls, die axis ↑↓

1732 10	25	65	1743 Large lettering.....8	20	60
1732 with stop over head. 10	30	75	1743 Small lettering.....8	20	60
1735 10	25	65	1743 — stop over head 10	25	65
1737 8	20	60	1746 8	20	60
1739 8	20	60	1746/3 10	25	65
1740 8	20	60	1760 8	20	60

3714 Twopence. Young laur. and dr. bust l. R. Small crown and figure 2, die axis ↑↓
1729 ....5　20　50　1731 .... 4　20　50

3714A Twopence. Young laur. and dr. bust l. R. Large crown and figure 2 die axis ↑↓

1732 5	20	45	1743/0 5	20	50
1735 5	20	45	1746 5	20	45
1737 5	20	45	1756 5	20	45
1739 5	20	50	1759 5	20	45
1740 8	25	60	1760 5	20	45
1743 5	20	45			

3715 Penny. Young laur. and dr. bust l. head. R. Date over small crown and figure 1, die axis ↑↓
1729 ....8　25　55　1731 .... 6　20　50

	F	VF	EF		F	VF	EF
	£	£	£		£	£	£

3715A Penny. Young laur. and dr. bust l. R. Large crown dividing date die axis ↑↓

	F	VF	EF		F	VF	EF
1732 6	20	50		1753/2 6	25	55
1735 8	25	60		1753 5	20	50
1737 8	25	55		1754 5	20	50
1739 6	20	50		1755 5	20	50
1740 6	20	50		1756 5	20	50
1743 6	20	50		1757 5	20	50
1746 6	20	50		1757 GRATIA:............6	30	65
1746/3 8	25	55		1758 5	20	50
1750 5	20	50		1759 5	20	50
1752 5	20	50		1760 6	25	55
1752/0 8	25	55				

3716

3716 Maundy Set. The four denominations. Uniform dates

	F	VF	EF		F	VF	EF
1729 70	175	475		1739 60	160	425
1731 70	175	475		1740 60	160	425
1732 60	160	425		1743 70	175	475
1735 60	160	425		1746 60	160	425
1737 60	160	425		1760 80	220	475

COPPER

3717

3717 Halfpenny. Young laur. and cuir. bust l. R. Britannia, date in ex. die axis ↑↓

	F	VF	EF		F	VF	EF
1729 15	80	350		1733 12	70	300
1729 rev. no stop 20	90	375		1734 12	70	300
1730 12	80	325		1734 R/O on obv 20	120	375
1730 GEOGIVS error . 20	125	425		1734/3 30	175	—
1730 stop after date 20	90	350		1734 no stops on obv. 30	175	—
1730 no stop after				1735 12	70	300
REX 25	130	425		1736 15	90	325
1731 12	70	325		1736/0 20	110	375
1731 rev. no stop 20	120	400		1737 15	85	325
1732 12	80	325		1738 10	65	300
1732 rev. no stop 20	120	400		1738 V/S on obv 20	120	375
				1739 12	65	300

	F	VF	EF		F	VF	EF
	£	£	£		£	£	£

3718   Halfpenny. Old laur. and cuir. bust l., GEORGIUS R. Britannia, date in ex. die axis ↑↓

1740	10	70	275	1743	10	70	275
1742	10	70	275	1744	10	70	275
1742/0	20	110	350	1745	10	70	275

3719
1746 Halfpenny

3719   Halfpenny. Old laur. and cuir. bust l. GEORGIVS, R. Britannia, date in ex. die axis ↑↓

1746	10	55	275	1751	10	55	275
1747	10	60	300	1752	10	55	275
1748	10	60	300	1753	10	55	275
1749	10	60	275	1754	10	60	300
1750	10	60	300				

3720

3720   Farthing. Young laur. and cuir. bust l. R. Britannia, date in ex. die axis ↑↓

1730	12	60	275	1735 3 over 5	20	110	350
1731	12	60	275	1736	12	60	275
1732	15	65	300	1736 triple tie ribands	30	110	350
1732/1	20	90	325	1737 small date	10	55	250
1733	12	60	275	1737 large date	10	55	250
1734	15	65	300	1739	10	55	250
1734 no stop on obv.	30	100	325	1739/5	—	80	250
1735	10	55	250				

3721   Farthing. Old laur. and cuir. bust. GEORGIUS R. Britannia, date in ex. die axis ↑↓

1741	15	70	250	1744	10	55	225

3722   Farthing. Similar R. Britannia, date in ex. die axis ↑↓

1746	8	55	200	1750	15	65	225
1746 V over U		*Extremely rare*		1754	5	35	110
1749	15	65	225	1754/0	25	110	250

George III, grandson of George II was born on 4 June 1738. He married Charlotte of Mecklenburg and they had nine sons and six daughters. The French Revolution and the American War of Independence both happened in his long reign, the longest yet of any King. The naval battle of Trafalgar and the Battle of Waterloo also took place during his reign. Later in his reign, he was affected by what seems to be the mental disease porphyria, and the future George IV was appointed as regent. George III died at Windsor Castle on 29 January 1820.

During the second half of the 18th century very little silver or copper was minted. In 1797 Matthew Boulton's 'cartwheels', the first copper Pennies and Twopences, demonstrated the improvement gleaned from the application of steam power to the coining press.

During the Napoleonic Wars bank notes came into general use when the issue of Guineas was stopped between 1799 and 1813, but gold 7s. pieces, Third-Guineas; were minted to relieve the shortage of smaller money. As an emergency measure Spanish 'Dollars' were put into circulation for a short period after being countermarked, and in 1804 Spanish Eight Reales were overstruck and issued as Bank of England Dollars.

The transition to a 'token' silver coinage began in 1811 when the Bank of England had 3s and 1s. 6d. tokens made for general circulation. Private issues of token money in the years 1788-95 and 1811-15 helped to alleviate the shortage of regal coinage. A change over to a gold standard and a regular 'token' silver coinage came in 1816 when the Mint, which was moved from its old quarters in the Tower of London to a new site on Tower Hill, began a complete re-coinage. The Guinea was replaced by a 20s. Sovereign, and silver coins were made which had an intrinsic value lower than their face value. The St. George design used on the Sovereign and Crown was the work of Benedetto Pistrucci.

Engravers and Designers:– Conrad Heinrich Kuchler (c.1740-1810), Nathaniel Marchant (1739-1816), John Rudulf Ochs Jnr. (1704-88), Lewis Pingo (1743-1830), Thomas Pingo (d.1776) Benedetto Pistrucci (1784-1855), Johann Sigismond Tanner (c.1706-75), Thomas Wyon (1792-1817), William Wyon (1795-1851), Richard Yeo (d.1779).

GOLD

Early Coinages

3723
1770 Pattern Five Guineas

3723 Five Guineas. Pattern only, young long haired bust r. R. crowned shield of
arms, die axis ↑↑ (en medaille)
1770 *FDC* £100,000   1773 *FDC* £90,000
3723A Five Guineas. Pattern only, young bust right, hair extends under bust similar
1777 *FDC* £80,000

3724
1768 Pattern Two Guineas

3724A
1777 Pattern Two Guineas

3724 Two Guineas. Pattern only, young long haired bust r. R. crowned shield of arms, die axis ↑↑
(en medaille)

1768 *FDC* £24,000   1773 *FDC* £22,000

3724A Two Guineas. Pattern only, young bust right, hair extends under bust similar

1777 *FDC* £22,000

There are six different bust varieties for 3723 and 3724, for further details see Rasmussen & Wilson

3725
1761 Guinea first head, two leaf wreath

3726
1763 Guinea second head

	F	VF	EF		F	VF	EF
	£	£	£		£	£	£
3725 Guinea. First laur. head r., 1761 (varieties with two or three leaves at top of wreath). R. Crowned shield of arms die axis ↑↓ 1000					2850	5250
3726 Guinea. Second laur. head r. R. Crowned shield of arms die axis ↑↓						
1763 950	2400	5000	1764 900	2200	4750

	3727	3728		3729
	Guinea, third head	Guinea, fourth head		Guinea, fifth head, 'spade' type

	F	VF	EF		F	VF	EF
	£	£	£		£	£	£

3727 Guinea. Third laur. head r. R. Crowned shield of arms die axis ↑↓

	F	VF	EF		F	VF	EF
1765	200	425	950	1770	300	525	1100
1766	200	400	925	1771	250	450	975
1767	350	600	1350	1772	225	425	950
1768	225	425	975	1773	175	375	900
1769	275	475	1000	1773 7 over 1	300	850	—

3728 Guinea. Fourth laur. head r. R. Crowned shield of arms die axis ↑↓

	F	VF	EF		F	VF	EF
1774	150	350	700	1781	185	425	850
1774 Proof *FDC* £4000				1782	165	375	725
1775	140	325	675	1783	200	450	950
1776	150	350	700	1784	175	400	800
1777	175	400	800	1785	135	325	675
1778	250	550	1250	1786	165	375	725
1779	175	400	800				

3729 Guinea. Fifth laur. head r. R. 'Spade'-shaped shield, die axis ↑↑

	F	VF	EF		F	VF	EF
1787	130	300	650	1794	140	325	675
1787 Proof *FDC* £2750				1795	150	350	700
1788	140	325	675	1796	180	400	850
1789	150	350	700	1797	180	400	850
1790	150	350	700	1798*	130	275	600
1791	135	300	650	1798/7	200	450	950
1792	150	350	700	1799	175	375	900
1793	140	325	675	*Beware counterfeits*			

	3730		3731
	1813 Guinea "Military type"		Half-Guinea, first head

3730 Guinea. Sixth laur. head. r. R. Shield in Garter, known as the Military guinea, die axis ↑↑

1813	500	1250	2250

3731 Half-Guinea. First laur. head r. R. Crowned shield of arms die axis ↑↓

	F	VF	EF		F	VF	EF
1762	425	1250	3000	1763	550	1650	3750

3732   3733
1764 Half-Guinea, second head   Half-Guinea, third head

	F	VF	EF		F	VF	EF
	£	£	£		£	£	£

3732 Half-Guinea. Second laur. head r. R. Crowned shield of arms die axis ↑↓

1764	140	375	850	1772		*Extremely rare*	
1765	450	950	—	1773	225	575	1250
1766	150	425	1000	1774	275	625	1550
1768	175	475	1000	1775	325	750	1900
1769	175	475	1050				

3734   3735
Half-Guinea, fourth head   Half-Guinea, fifth head

3733 Half-Guinea Third laur. head (less fine style) r. R. Crowned shield of arms die axis ↑↓

1774		*Extremely rare*		1775	775	1850	4000

3734 Half-Guinea Fourth laur. head r. R. Crowned shield of arms die axis ↑↓

1775	110	275	550	1781	165	400	750
1775 Proof *FDC* £3750				1783	425	1250	—
1776	140	325	625	1784	150	375	700
1777	125	300	600	1785	140	325	625
1778	150	375	700	1786	110	275	550
1779	150	375	700				

3735 Half-Guinea Fifth laur. head. r. R. 'Spade' shaped shield, date below, die axis ↑↑

1787	95	200	425	1794	145	350	600
1787 Proof *FDC* £2000				1795	150	375	675
1788	110	250	500	1796	120	275	525
1789	150	375	675	1797	110	250	500
1790	140	325	575	1798	125	300	550
1791	140	325	575	1798/7	200	350	675
1792	500	1550	—	1800	250	675	—
1793	110	250	500				

3736
Half-Guinea, sixth head

3736 Half-Guinea Sixth laur. head. r. R. Shield in Garter, date below die axis ↑↑

1801	75	150	325	1803	80	165	350
1802	80	165	350				

	3737			3738			3739	
1813 Half-Guinea, seventh head				Third-Guinea, first type			Third-Guinea, second reverse	

	F	VF	EF		F	VF	EF
	£	£	£		£	£	£

3737 Half-Guinea Seventh laur. head. r. with short hair. R. Shield in garter, date below die axis ↑↑

1804	75	150	325	1809	90	165	400
1805		*Extremely rare*		1810	90	165	400
1806	120	225	500	1811	160	350	750
1808	100	180	425	1813	100	250	525

3738 Third-Guinea. First laur. head r. R. Crown, date in legend, die axis ↑↑

1797	60	120	325	1799	65	150	350
1798	60	120	325	1800	60	120	325

3739 Third-Guinea. First laur. head r. R. Similar but date below crown, die axis ↑↑

1801	60	120	325	1803	60	120	325
1802	60	120	325				

3740

1804 Third Guinea, second head

3740 Third-Guinea. Second laur. head r. with short hair, R. Similar, die axis ↑↑

1804	65	110	300	1810	65	110	300
1806	70	125	325	1811	225	500	1100
1808	70	125	325	1813	125	300	700
1809	70	125	325				

3741 Quarter-Guinea. Laur. head r. R. Crowned shield die axis ↑↓ 1762 90   275   450

For gold of the 'new coinage', 1817-20, see page 391.

SILVER

3742

1763 Northumberland shilling

3742 Shilling. Young laur. and dr. bust, r. known as the 'Northumberland' shilling, die axis ↑↓

1763 300   600   1200

3743 Shilling. Older laur. and dr. bust, R. No semée of hearts in Hanoverian shield, die axis ↑↑

1787 20   40   100

1787 Proof *FDC* .... *Extremely rare*

1787 plain edge proof *FDC* .... *Extremely rare*

	F £	VF £	EF £		F £	VF £	EF £
3744 Shilling. — No stop over head, die axis ↑↑ 1787	30	60	150				

3745

	F £	VF £	EF £
3745 Shilling. — No stops at date, die axis ↑↑ 1787	40	90	225
3745AShilling. — No stops on *obv.*, die axis ↑↑ 1787	250	675	1500
3746 Shilling. — R. With semée of hearts, die axis ↑↑ 1787	20	40	100
1787 1/1 retrograde	40	110	300
1787 plain edge proof *FDC*			*Extremely rare*

Hanoverian Arms

No semée of hearts   With semée of hearts

3747 - 1798 Shilling

3747 Shilling. No stop over head, 1798: known as the 'Dorrien and Magens' shilling *UNC* £16,000

3748 Sixpence. Laur. and dr. bust r. R. Without semée of hearts, die axis ↑↑

1787	15	35	85	1787 Proof *FDC*		*Extremely rare*	

3749 Sixpence. Similar R. With semée of hearts, die axis ↑↑ 1787 15   35   85

3749

3750

1787 Sixpence, with hearts

3750 Fourpence. Young laur. and dr. bust r. R. Crowned 4, die axis ↑↓

1763	5	15	40	1772/0	5	20	40
1763 Proof *FDC of highest rarity*				1776	5	18	40
1765	200	400	800	1780	5	18	40
1766	5	20	40	1784	5	20	40
1770	5	20	40	1786	6	25	50
1772	5	20	40				

3751	3753	3755

	F	VF	EF		F	VF	EF
	£	£	£		£	£	£

3751 Fourpence. Older laur. and dr. bust. R. Thin 4 ('Wire Money'), die axis ↑↑

1792 10	35	75				

3752 Fourpence. Older laur. and dr. bust r. R. Normal Crowned 4, die axis ↑↑

1795 5	18	45	1800 5	18	40

3753 Threepence. Young laur. dr. bust r. R. Crowned 3, die axis ↑↓

1762 5	12	35	1772 small III..............6	18	40
1763 5	12	35	1772 very large III 6	18	40
1763 Proof *FDC of highest rarity*			1780 6	18	40
1765 150	300	700	1784 8	20	45
1766 8	20	40	1786 6	18	40
1770 8	20	40			

3754 Threepence. Older laur. dr. bust. r. R. Thin 3 ('Wire Money'), die axis ↑↑

1792 10	35	75			

3755 Threepence. Older laur. and dr. bust r. R. Normal Crowned 3, die axis ↑↑

1795 8	18	40	1800 8	18	40

3756 Twopence. Young laur. and dr. bust r. R. Crowned 2, die axis ↑↓

1763 6	25	40	1776 4	18	35
1763 Proof *FDC of highest rarity*			1780 4	18	35
1765 100	250	600	1784 4	18	35
1766 4	18	35	1786 3	15	35
1772 4	18	35	1786 large obv. lettering . 3	15	35
1772 second 7/6 5	20	40			

3756

3757 Twopence. Older laur. and dr. bust. r. R. Thin 2 ('Wire Money'), die axis ↑↑

1792 10	30		75		

3758 Twopence. Older laur. and dr. bust r. R. Normal Crowned 2, die axis ↑↑

1795 3	15	35	1800 3	15	35

3759 Penny. Young laur. and dr. bust r. R. Crowned 1, die axis ↑↓

1763 5	20	40	1779 4	18	40
1763 Proof *FDC of highest rarity*			1780 5	20	45
1766 4	18	40	1781 3	12	30
1770 3	12	30	1784 3	12	30
1772 4	18	40	1786 3	12	30
1776 4	18	40			

3760 Penny. Older laur. and dr. bust. r. R. Thin 1 ('Wire Money'), die axis ↑↑

1792 8	30	65			

	F	VF	EF		F	VF	EF
	£	£	£		£	£	£

3761 Penny. Older laur. and dr. bust r. ℞. Normal Crowned 1, die axis ↑↑

1795	3	12	35	1800	3	12	35

3762 Maundy Set. Young laur. and dr. bust. r. Uniform dates

1763	50	150	350	1780	50	150	350
1763 Proof set *FDC*		*Extremely rare*		1784	50	150	350
1766	50	150	350	1786	50	150	350
1772	50	150	350				

3763 Maundy Set. — Older laur. and dr. bust. r. ℞. Thin numerals ('Wire Money'),

1792	115	275	600

3764 Maundy Set. Older laur. and dr. bust r. ℞. Normal numerals. Uniform dates

1795	40	140	300	1800	35	125	275

Emergency Issue, die axis ↑↑

3765 Dollar. Pillar type (current for 4s 9d). Spanish American 8 Reales, oval countermark with head of George III.

Mexico City Mint — m̥	500	1000	2250
Bolivia, Potosi Mint – PTS monogram	750	1900	—
Peru, Lima Mint – LIMÆ monogram	750	1650	—

3765A

Portrait type Dollar with oval countermark

3765A Dollar. Portrait type, oval countermark.

Mexico City Mint — m̥	120	350	750
Bolivia, Potosi Mint — PTS monogram	200	650	—
Chile, Santiago Mint — s̥	575	1600	—
Guatemala Mint — NG	500	1450	—
Spain, Madrid Mint	300	800	1850
Spain, Seville Mint	325	650	1700
Peru, Lima Mint — LIMÆ monogram	175	475	1000

3765B Dollar. — Oval countermark on French Ecu .... *Extremely rare*

3765C Dollar. — Oval countermark on USA Dollar............................ *Of highest rarity*

3766
Portrait Dollar with octagonal countermark

	F	VF	EF
	£	£	£
3766 Dollar octagonal countermarks with head of George III			
Mexico City Mint — m̥ 225		650	1150
Bolivia, Potosi Mint — PTS monogram 700		—	—
Guatamala Mint — NG 875		1850	—
Peru, Lima Mint — LIME monogram.................................. 350		700	1600
Spain, Madrid Mint.. 525		1100	—
Spain, Seville Mint 550		1300	—
3766A Dollar. — Octagonal countermark on French Ecu...........................		*Of highest rarity*	
3766B Dollar. — Octagonal countermark on USA Dollar		*Extremely rare*	

3767
Half-Dollar with oval countermark

		F	VF	EF
3767 Half-Dollar. With similar oval countermark. Mints of Potosi,				
Santiago, Madrid & Seville ....*from*		135	350	650
3767A Half Dollar. With Octagonal countermark. Similar ....*from*		375	800	—

Bank of England Issue

3768

	F	VF	EF
	£	£	£

3768 Dollar. (current for 5s.). laur. and dr. bust of king. r. ℞.
    Britannia seated l., several varieties occur, die axis ↑↑

	F	VF	EF
1804 O. Top leaf to left side of E, R. Upright K to left of shield	130	275	575
1804 — —no stops in CHK on truncation	165	350	625
1804 O. Top leaf to centre of E R. Similar	130	275	575
1804 — —no stop after REX	150	325	600
1804 —R. K inverted to left of shield	190	400	675
1804 —R. K inverted and incuse	190	400	675
1804 O. Top leaf to right side of E, R. normal K	140	300	600
1804 —R. K inverted to left of shield	190	400	675
1804 Proof striking of all varieties above *FDC from* £1000			

These dollars were re-struck from Spanish-American 8-Reales until at least 1811. Dollars that show dates and Mint marks of original coin are worth rather more.

3769   3770
1811 Three Shillings, first bust   Three Shillings, second head

3769 Three Shillings. Dr and laur. bust in armour r. ℞. BANK / TOKEN /
    3 SHILL. / date (in oak wreath), die axis ↑↑

1811	25	60	175	1812 Proof *FDC* £600		
1811 Proof *FDC* £500				1812 Proof in gold *FDC*		*Extremely rare*
1812	25	70	200	1812 Proof in platinum *FDC*		*Extremely rare*

3770 Three Shillings. — Laureate head r. Top leaf between I/G ℞. As before but wreath of oak
    and olive, die axis ↑↑

1812	25	60	175	1815	25	70	200
1813	25	70	200	1816	275	650	1450
1814	25	70	200				

3771   3772
Eighteenpence, first bust   Eighteenpence, second head

	F	VF	EF		F	VF	EF
	£	£	£		£	£	£

3771 Eighteenpence. Dr. and laur. bust r. in armour ℞ BANK/TOKEN/Is. 6D./date (in oak wreath) ↑↑

1811	15	35	120	1812	15	35	130

1811 Proof *FDC* £450

3772 Eighteenpence. Laureate head r. die axis ↑↑

1812	15	35	120	1813 Platinum proof *FDC* £12500			
1812 Proof *FDC* £400				1814	15	40	140
1812 Platinum proof *FDC* £12500				1815	15	40	140
1812 Proof R. Small letters *FDC* £1700				1816	15	40	140
1813	15	40	140				

3773
1812 Pattern Ninepence, 9D type

3773 Ninepence. Similar, Laur. head 1812, ℞. 9D type (pattern only) die axis ↑↑ *FDC* £1100

3773A Ninepence. — — 1812, ℞. 9 pence type (pattern only) die axis ↑↑ FDC   *Extremely rare*

COPPER

First Issue — Tower Mint, London

3774   3775

REV.C, leaves point between A and N

	F	VF	EF		F	VF	EF
	£	£	£		£	£	£

3774 Halfpenny. Laur. and Cuir. bust r. R. Britannia l. date in ex., die axis ↑↓

	F	VF	EF		F	VF	EF
1770	12	50	225	spear blade	10	45	250
1770 Proof die axis ↑↑ *FDC* £1200				1772 no incuse			
1770 Proof in silver *FDC*	*Extremely rare*			hair coil	10	45	225
1770 no stop on rev.	20	65	250	1772 — no stop on rev.	20	65	250
1771	10	45	250	1773	10	45	225
1771 no stop on rev.	20	65	250	1773 no stop after			
1771 ball below				REX	18	60	250
spear blade	10	45	250	1773 no stop on rev.	20	65	250
1772 incuse hair coil				1774 different obv.			
on rev.	10	45	250	profile	18	75	275
1772 GEORIVS error	35	90	325	1775 —	10	55	225

3775 Farthing. Laur. and cuir. bust r. R. Britannia l. date in ex., die axis ↑↓

	F	VF	EF		F	VF	EF
1771 REV A. leaf to r.	20	65	250	1773 no stop after REX	25	75	250
1771 REV B. leaf to N	20	65	250	1774	12	45	185
1771 REV C.	20	65	250	1775	12	45	185
1771 1st 7/1	30	175	475	1775 struck en			
1773	10	40	185	medaille ↑↑	25	75	250
1773 no stop on rev.	15	50	200	1775 GEORG Ⅴ Ⅰ	35	200	600

Second Issue— Soho Mint. Birmingham 'Cartwheel' coinage, die axis ↑↓

3776

	V	F	EF	UNC
3776 Twopence. Legends incuse on raised rim, 1797	40	140	375	1200

1797 Copper proof *FDC* £800   1797 Gold proof *FDC* £15000

1797 Bronzed proof *FDC* £750   1797 Gilt copper *FDC* £1250

1797 Silver proof *FDC* £4000

3777

	VF	EF	UNC		F	VF	EF	UNC
	£	£	£		£	£	£	£

3777 Penny. 1797. Similar, 10 leaves in wreath on obv. .... 10 | 55 | 275 | 1000
1797 11 leaves in wreath on obv. .... 15 | 75 | 325 | 1250
1797 Gilt copper proof *FDC* £950
1797 Copper proof *FDC* £650
1797 Bronzed proof *FDC* £600
1797 Silver proof *FDC* £3250
1797 Gold proof *FDC* £12500

Halfpence and Farthings of this issue are patterns.

Third Issue—Soho Mint, Birmingham, die axis ↑↓

3778   3779

3778 Halfpenny. Laur. and dr. bust r., R. Britannia l. date below

1799 Ship on rev. with				1799 Ship with			
5 incuse gunports	10	60	150	plain hull	15	75	180
1799 Ship with 6				1799 — raised line			
relief gunports	12	65	160	on hull	15	75	180
1799 Ship with 9 relief				1799 Copper proof *FDC* £325			
gunports	15	75	180	1799 Bronzed proof *FDC* £275			
				1799 Gilt copper proof *FDC* £450			

3779 Farthing. Laur. and dr. bust r. date below R. Britannia l.

1799 Obv. with 3 berries				1799 Obv. with 4 berries			
in wreath	8	50	125	in wreath	8	50	125
1799 Copper *FDC* £250.				1799 Gold proof *FDC* £7500			
1799 Bronzed proof *FDC* £225				1799 Silver proof *FDC* £2750			
1799 Copper gilt proof *FDC* £375							

Fourth Issue—Soho Mint, Birmingham, die axis ↑↓

3780

	VF £	EF £	UNC £		VF £	EF £	UNC £

3780 Penny. Shorter haired, laur. and dr. bust r. date below. R. Britannia l. date below

1806 incuse hair curl ..				1807 10	70	300
by tie knot 10	60	275	1807 Copper proof *FDC* £475
1806 no incuse hair curl 15	75	300	1807 Bronzed proof *FDC* £425
1806 Copper proof *FDC* £325			1807 Gilt copper proof *FDC* £1200
1806 Bronzed proof *FDC* £325			1807 Silver proof *FDC* £3500
1806 Gilt copper proof *FDC* £500			1807 Gold proof *FDC* ... *Extremely rare*
1806 Silver proof *FDC* £3500			1807 Platinum proof *FDC Extremely rare*
			1808 Proof *FDC Unique*

3781   3782

3781 Halfpenny. Shorter haired laur. and dr. bust r. date below, R. Britannia l.

1806 rev. no berries....... 6	35	150	1807 8	40	165
1806 rev. 3 berries....... 10	60	175	1807 Copper proof *FDC* £300
1806 Copper proof *FDC* £275			1807 Bronzed proof *FDC* £275
1806 Bronzed proof *FDC* £250			1807 Gilt copper *FDC* £400
1806 Gilt proof *FDC* £375			1807 Silver proof *FDC* £2500
1806 Silver proof *FDC* £2750			1807 Gold proof *FDC*.... *Extremely rare*

3782 Farthing. Shorter haired laur. and dr. bust r. date below, R. Britannia l.

1806 K. on tr. 6	70	125	1807 8	45	150
1806 incuse dot on tr .. 35	100	300	1807 Copper proof *FDC* £275
1806 Copper proof *FDC* £250			1807 Bronzed proof *FDC* £250
1806 Bronzed proof *FDC* £225			1807 Gilt copper proof *FDC* £400
1806 Gilt copper proof *FDC* £375			1807 Silver proof *FDC* £3000
1806 Silver proof *FDC* £2500			1807 Gold proof *FDC*.... *Extremely rare*
1806 Gold proof *FDC*..... *Extremely rare*

Last or new coinage, 1816-20

The year 1816 is a landmark in the history of our coinage. For some years at the beginning of the 19th century Mint production was virtually confined to small gold denominations, regular full production being resumed only after the Mint had been moved from the Tower of London to a new site on Tower Hill. Steam powered minting machinery made by Boulton and Watt replaced the old hand-operated presses and these produced coins which were technically much superior to the older milled coins.

In 1816 for the first time British silver coins were produced with an intrinsic value somewhat below their face value, the first official token coinage. The old Guinea was replaced by a Sovereign of twenty shillings in 1817, the standard of 22 carat (0.916) fineness still being retained.

Mint Master or Engraver's and/or designer's initials:

B.P. (Benedetto Pistrucci 1784-1855)   WWP (William Wellesley Pole)

GOLD

3783

3783 Five Pounds. 1820 LX (Pattern only) laur. head r. date below R. St George and dragon, edge inscribed die axis ↑↓ *FDC*£70000

1820 Similar plain edge proof *FDC* £85000

3784

3784 Two Pounds. 1820 LX (Pattern only) laur. head r. date below R. St George and dragon, edge inscribed die axis ↑↓ *FDC* £17500

1820 Similar plain edge proof *FDC Extremely rare*

3785

3785A

	F	VF	EF	UNC		F	VF	EF	UNC
	£	£	£	£		£	£	£	£

3785 Sovereign. laur. head r. coarse hair, legend type A (Descending colon after BRITANNIAR, no space between REX and F:D:). R. St. George and dragon, die axis ↑↓

1817 275	450	1050	1650	1818 450	875	1850	2600
1817 Proof *FDC* £6750				1819 22500	45000	85000	—

	F	*VF*	*EF*	*UNC*			*F*	*VF*	*EF*	*UNC*
	£	£	£	£			£	£	£	£

3785A Sovereign. Similar legend type B (Ascending colon after BRITANNIAR, space between REX and F:D:) ↑↓
1818 450   875   1850   2600   1818 Proof *FDC* £8500

3785B Sovereign. laur head r. hair with tighter curls, legend type A. (as above) R. Similar die axis ↑↓
1818 ....   *Extremely rare*

3785C
Large date, open 2 variety

3785C Sovereign. Similar legend type B. (as above) die axis ↑↓

1818	*Extremely rare*	1820 large date open				
1820 Roman I.............	*Extremely rare*	2 close to 8 ..275	475	1100	1650
1820 Small O, closed		1820 short date 2			
2 thin date 325 650 1200 1850		nearly closed ..325	600	1200	—
1820 Proof *FDC* £7000		1820 closed 2 350	700	1750	—
1820 Slender date Proof *FDC* £9000		1820 spread 18 and 20			
		short date	*Extremely rare*		

3786
1817 Half-Sovereign

3786 Half-Sovereign. laur head r. date below R. Crowned shield, edge milled die axis ↑↓

1817 90	200	325	550	1818 Proof *FDC* £4500			
1817 Proof *FDC* £3750				1818 130	275	450	700
1818/7.................... 275	550	1400	—	1820 100	225	400	650

SILVER

3787
1818 George III Crown

	F	VF	EF	UNC		F	VF	EF	UNC
	£	£	£	£		£	£	£	£

3787 Crown. Laur. head r. ℞. Pistrucci's St. George and dragon within Garter edge inscribed, die axis ↑↓

		F	VF	EF	UNC
1818, edge LVIII		35	75	280	650
1818	LVIII error edge inscription	*Extremely rare*			
1818	LVIII Proof *FDC*	*Extremely rare*			
1818	LIX	35	75	280	650
1818	LIX TUTΛMEN error	50	200	—	—
1819	LIX	30	65	260	600
1819	LIX no stops on edge	45	100	425	900
1819	LIX ℞. Thicker ruled garter	75	225	500	—
1819/8	LIX	50	175	500	—
1819	LX	40	80	300	700
1819	LX no stop after TUTAMEN	50	175	475	—
1820	LX	35	75	280	650
1820	LX ℞. S/T in SOIT	75	225	360	—
1820/19	LX	75	225	500	—

3788
1817 Halfcrown, large bust

3788 Halfcrown. Large laur. bust or 'bull' head r. date below ℞. Crowned garter and shield die axis ↑↑

1816	30	65	250	400		1817 E/R in DEI	*Extremely rare*
1816 Proof *FDC* £2000						1817 S/I in PENSE	*Extremely rare*
1816 Plain edge proof *FDC* £2000						1817 Proof *FDC* £2000	
1817	30	65	250	400		1817 Plain edge proof *FDC* £2250	
1817 D/T in DEI	45	175	575	—			

3789

1817 Halfcrown, small head

	F	VF	EF	UNC		F	VF	EF	UNC
	£	£	£	£		£	£	£	£

3789 Halfcrown. Small laur. head r. date below, R. Crowned garter and shield die axis ↑↑

	F	VF	EF	UNC		F	VF	EF	UNC
1817 30	60	200	425		1818 Proof *FDC* £2500				
1817 Proof *FDC* £2000					1819 Proof *FDC* £2250				
1817 Plain edge proof *FDC* £2000					1819 30	60	275	450	
1817 Reversed s's in garter	*Extremely rare*				1819/8		*Extremely rare*		
1818 Reversed s's in garter	*Extremely rare*				1820 40	85	325	550	
1818 35	70	275	500		1820 Proof *FDC* £2500				
					1820 Plain edge proof *FDC* £2000				

3790

1819 Shilling

3790 Shilling. laur head r. date below R. Crowned Shield in Garter edge milled, die axis ↑↑

	F	VF	EF	UNC		F	VF	EF	UNC
1816 10	15	45	95		1818 30	60	180	300	
1816 Proof *FDC* £500					1818 High 8 35	80	175	375	
1816 Plain edge proof *FDC* £500					1819/8 20	40	100	250	
1816 Proof in gold *FDC*	*Extremely rare*				1819 10	20	55	135	
1817 10	18	50	100		1820 10	20	55	135	
1817 RRITT flaw ...15	25	100	—		1820 I/S in HONI...40	80	225	475	
1817 Plain edge proof *FDC* £400					1820 Proof *FDC* £450				
1817 GEOE error..100	225	500	—						

3791
1817 Sixpence

	F	VF	EF	UNC		F	VF	EF	UNC
	£	£	£	£		£	£	£	£

3791 Sixpence. laur head r. date below R. Crowned Shield in Garter edge milled, die axis ↑↑

	F	VF	EF	UNC		F	VF	EF	UNC
1816	6	12	35	75	1819/8	12	25	50	95
1816 Proof plain edge *FDC* £500					1819	10	20	45	85
1816 Proof in gold *FDC* *Extremely rare*					1819 small 8	10	20	45	85
1817	8	15	40	80	1820	10	20	45	85
1817 Proof plain edge *FDC* £500					1820 inverted 1	75	275	450	—
1817 Proof milled edge *FDC* £950					1820 I/S in HONI	75	275	425	—
1818	10	20	45	85	1820 obv. no colons	100	375	550	—
1818 Proof milled edge *FDC* £900					1820 Proof *FDC* £900				

3792

3792 Maundy Set. (4d., 3d., 2d. and 1d.) laur. head, date below die axis ↑↑

		F	VF	EF	UNC			F	VF	EF	UNC
1817		65	160	400		1820		65	160	400	
1818		65	160	400							

			F	VF	EF	UNC
3793	— **Fourpence.** 1817, 1818, 1820	...*from*			15	45
3794	— **Threepence.** 1817, 1818, 1820	...*from*			15	45
3795	— **Twopence.** 1817, 1818, 1820	...*from*			10	35
3796	— **Penny.** 1817, 1818, 1820	...*from*			10	30

George IV, eldest son of George III, was born on 12 August 1762 and was almost a complete opposite to his father. He was very extravagant and lived in the height of luxury. He especially influenced fashion of the time which became known as the 'Regency' style. He had numerous mistresses, and had an arranged marriage with Caroline of Brunswick. She later moved to Italy with their only daughter, but returned to claim her place as Queen upon George's accession. George banned her from ever being crowned, and he died without ever conceiving a son on 26 June 1830, when his younger brother William ascended the throne.

The Mint resumed the coinage of copper farthings in 1821, and pennies and halfpennies in 1825. A gold Two Pound piece was first issued for general circulation in 1823. A full cased proof set of the new bare head coinage was issued in limited quantities in 1826.

Engraver's and/or designer's initials on the coins:
B. P. (Benedetto Pistrucci)   W.W. P. (William Wellesley Pole) – Master of the Mint
J. B. M. (Jean Baptiste Merlen)

Engravers and Designers:– Francis Legett Chantrey (1781-1842) Jean Baptiste Merlen (1769-c.1850) Benedetto Pistrucci (1784-1855) William Wyon (1795-1851)
Prime Ministers:– Earl of Liverpool, (1770-1828) Tory, 1812-27; George Canning, (1770-1827) Tory, 1827; Viscount Goderich, (1782-1859), Tory 1827-8; Duke of Wellington, (1769-1852), Tory, 1828-30.

GOLD

3797

3797 Five Pounds. 1826 Bare head l. date below R. Crowned shield and mantle, inscribed edge, die axis ↑↓   Proof *FDC* £12500
1826 Piedfort proof *FDC* .... *Extremely rare*

3798

	VF	EF	UNC
	£	£	£

3798 Two Pounds. 1823 Proof *FDC* £5000
1823 Proof no JBM below truncation *FDC* .... *Extremely rare*
1823 Large bare head. l. R. St. George, inscribed edge ↑↓ .... 700 | 1350 | 2250

3799

3799 Two Pounds. Bare head l. date below R. Crowned shield and mantle inscribed edge
die axis ↑↓

1824 Proof *FDC*	*Extremely rare*	1826. Piedfort proof *FDC* *Extremely rare*
1825 Proof plain edge *FDC* £6500		1826. Proof *FDC* £4500

3801
Sovereign, second type

	F	VF	EF	UNC		F	VF	EF	UNC
	£	£	£	£		£	£	£	£

3800   Sovereign. Laur. head. l. R. St. George and dragon date in ex., die axis ↑↓

	F	VF	EF	UNC		F	VF	EF	UNC
1821	250	450	1100	1700	1823	500	1650	4000	—
1821 Proof *FDC* £3750					1824	325	500	1250	1900
1822*	300	475	1200	1850	1825	375	1200	3250	—

Beware counterfeits.

3801   Sovereign. Bare head. date below l. R. Crowned shield, die axis ↑↓

	F	VF	EF	UNC		F	VF	EF	UNC
1825	250	450	975	1550	1828	3000	6250	13500	—
1825 Proof *FDC* £3750					1829	300	525	1100	1750
1825 Plain edge proof *FDC* £3750					1830	300	525	1100	1750
1826	250	450	975	1550	1830 struck 'en				
1826 Proof *FDC* £2750					medaille'	1000	2000	—	—
1827*	275	500	1000	1650					

Beware counterfeits

3803
Half-Sovereign, second reverse

3802 Half-Sovereign. Laur. head. l. R. Ornately garnished Crowned shield. die axis ↑↓

1821	425	1100	2250	3500
1821 Proof *FDC* £3750				

3803 Half-Sovereign. Laur. head l. R. Plain Crowned shield die axis ↑↓

	F	VF	EF	UNC		F	VF	EF	UNC
1823	85	225	450	750	1825	70	160	400	650
1824	80	200	425	650					

3804

1825 Half Sovereign, bare head

	F	VF	EF	UNC		F	VF	EF	UNC
	£	£	£	£		£	£	£	£

3804 Half-Sovereign. Bare head. date below l. R. Crowned garnished shield die axis ↑↓

1826	80	160	375	700	1827	80	160	400	700
1826 Proof *FDC* £1300					1828	80	160	400	700

3804A Half-Sovereign. Similar with extra tuft of hair to l. ear, much heavier border, die axis ↑↓

1826	70	130	325	600	1827	70	120	325	600
1826 Proof *FDC* £1250					1828	75	140	350	650

SILVER

3805

1821 Laureate bust Crown

3805 Crown. Laur. head. l. R. St. George, date in exergue, B.P. to upper right, WWP under lance, die axis ↑↓

1821, edge	SECUNDO	50	185	800	2000
1821	SECUNDO WWP inverted under lance	60	300	1000	2500
1821	SECUNDO Proof *FDC* £3450				
1821	SECUNDO Proof in copper *FDC* £3250				
1821	TERTIO Proof *FDC* £4000				
1822	SECUNDO	65	250	900	2250
1822	TERTIO	50	200	850	2000

3806

1826 Proof Crown, bare head

3806 Crown. Bare head. l. R. Shield with crest inscribed edge, die axis ↑↓

1825 Proof *FDC* £7250	1826 Proof *FDC* £4750

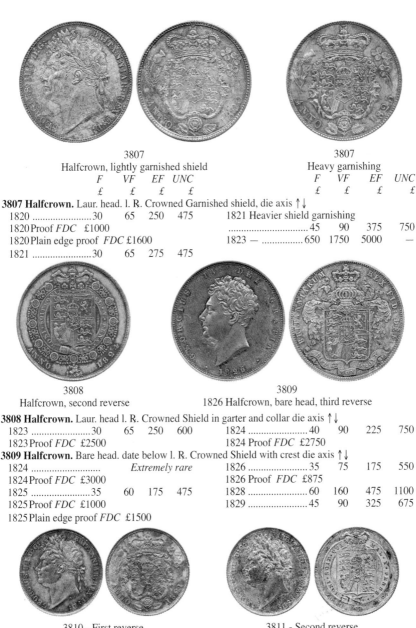

	3807					3807		
Halfcrown, lightly garnished shield					Heavy garnishing			
	F	VF	EF	UNC		F	VF	EF	UNC
	£	£	£	£		£	£	£	£

3807 Halfcrown. Laur. head. l. R. Crowned Garnished shield, die axis ↑↓

1820	30	65	250	475	1821 Heavier shield garnishing			
1820 Proof *FDC* £1000						45	90	375	750
1820 Plain edge proof *FDC* £1600					1823 —	650	1750	5000	—
1821	30	65	275	475				

3808
Halfcrown, second reverse

3809
1826 Halfcrown, bare head, third reverse

3808 Halfcrown. Laur. head l. R. Crowned Shield in garter and collar die axis ↑↓

1823	30	65	250	600	1824	40	90	225	750
1823 Proof *FDC* £2500					1824 Proof *FDC* £2750				

3809 Halfcrown. Bare head. date below l. R. Crowned Shield with crest die axis ↑↓

1824		*Extremely rare*			1826	35	75	175	550
1824 Proof *FDC* £3000					1826 Proof *FDC* £875				
1825	35	60	175	475	1828	60	160	475	1100
1825 Proof *FDC* £1000					1829	45	90	325	675
1825 Plain edge proof *FDC* £1500									

3810 - First reverse

3811 - Second reverse

3810 Shilling. Laur. head. l. R. Crowned garnished shield, die axis ↑↓

1821						10	40	140	350
1821 Proof *FDC* £850									

3811 Shilling. Laur. head l. R. Crowned shield in Garter die axis ↑↓

1823	50	100	275	650	1825	18	50	200	450
1823 Proof *FDC* £2250					1825 Proof *FDC* £2250				
1824	10	40	165	400	1825/3		*Extremely rare*		
1824 Proof *FDC* £2250									

3812 - Third reverse

	F	VF	EF	UNC		F	VF	EF	UNC
	£	£	£	£		£	£	£	£

3812 Shilling. Bare head l. date below R. Lion on crown die axis ↑↓

1825 10	40	110	300	1826/2		*Extremely rare*	
1825 Roman I		*Extremely rare*		1827 40	95	325	650
1825 Proof *FDC* £750				1829 30	60	225	550
1826 8	30	90	250	1829 Proof *FDC* £2250			
1826 Proof *FDC* £425							

3813 - First reverse   3814 - Second reverse   3815 -Third reverse

3813 Sixpence. Laur. head. l. R. Crowned Garnished shield, die axis ↑↓

| 1821 ....10 | 25 | 95 | 300 | 1821 BBITANNIAR 75 | 250 | 700 | — |
| 1821 Proof *FDC* £550 | | | | | | | |

3814 Sixpence. Laur. head l. R. Crowned Shield in Garter die axis ↑↓

1824 10	25	95	300	1825 Proof *FDC* £1000			
1824 Proof *FDC* £1000				1826 40	95	250	600
1825 10	25	95	300	1826 Proof *FDC* £1350			

3815 Sixpence. Bare head. l. with or without tuft of hair to l. of ear date below R. Lion on crown die axis ↑↓

1826 10	25	95	300	1828 10	45	175	400
1826 Proof *FDC* £325				1829 10	25	95	325
1827 35	95	275	600	1829 Proof *FDC* £1100			

3816

	EF	FDC		EF	FDC
	£	£		£	£

3816 Maundy Set. (4d., 3d., 2d. and 1d.) laur head l. die axis ↑↓

1822	145	320	1827	120	275
1822 Proof set *FDC*	*Extremely rare*		1828	120	275
1823	120	275	1828 Proof set *FDC*	*Extremely rare*	
1824	145	320	1829	120	275
1825	120	275	1830	120	275
1826	120	275			

3817	**Maundy Fourpence.** 1822-30 ....*from*	15	35
3818	**— Threepence.** small head, 1822	30	55
3819	**— Threepence.** normal head, 1823-30 ....*from*	14	30
3820	**— Twopence.** 1822-30 ....*from*	12	25
3821	**— Penny.** 1822-30 ....*from*	10	20

COPPER

3822

	F £	VF £	EF £	UNC £		F £	VF £	EF £	UNC £

First Issue, 1821-6

3822 Farthing. Laur. and dr. bust l. R. Britannia r. date in ex. die axis ↑↓

1821 2	10	60	120	1823 — I for 1 in date... 25	85	275	—
1822 leaf ribs incuse 2	10	55	100	1825 — 2	10	60	110
1822 — inv. A's legend . 25	95	275	—	1825 — D/U in DEI..........20	75	250	—
1822 leaf ribs raised....... 2	10	55	110	1825 leaf ribs raised 4	15	65	130
1822 Proof *FDC* £650				1825 gold proof *FDC*........		*Extremely rare*	
1822 Proof die axis ↑↑ *FDC* £800				1826 — 5	15	70	150
1823 — 3	12	65	120	1826 R/E in GRATIA.... 20	75	250	—

3823

Second issue, 1825-30

3823 Penny. Laur. head. l. R. Britannia, with shield bearing saltire of arms die axis ↑↑

1825 12	40	200	475	1826-Proof *FDC* .. 450			
1825 Proof *FDC* £1150				1826 thick line on			
1826 plain saltire				saltire............. 15	60	250	575
on rev..................... 10	40	175	475	1826-Proof *FDC* £400			
1826-Proof *FDC* £400				1827 plain saltire .. 160	550	1950	—
1826 thin line on							
saltire 10	45	225	475				

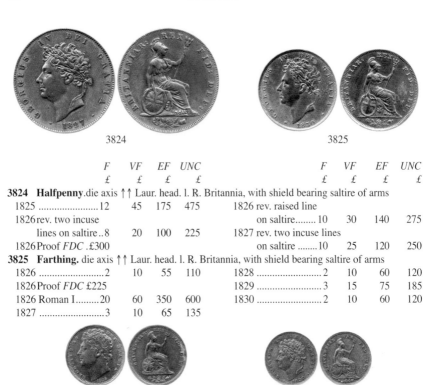

3824   3825

	F	VF	EF	UNC			F	VF	EF	UNC
	£	£	£	£			£	£	£	£

3824 Halfpenny. die axis ↑↑ Laur. head. l. R. Britannia, with shield bearing saltire of arms

1825 12	45	175	475	1826 rev. raised line			
				on saltire........ 10	30	140	275
1826 rev. two incuse				1827 rev. two incuse lines			
lines on saltire ..8	20	100	225	on saltire 10	25	120	250
1826 Proof *FDC* .£300							

3825 Farthing. die axis ↑↑ Laur. head. l. R. Britannia, with shield bearing saltire of arms

1826 2	10	55	110	1828 2	10	60	120
1826 Proof *FDC* £225				1829 3	15	75	185
1826 Roman I.........20	60	350	600	1830 2	10	60	120
1827 3	10	65	135				

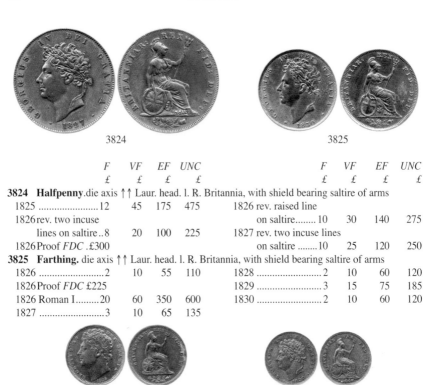

3826   3827

3826 Half-Farthing. (for use in Ceylon). Laur. head. l. date below R.Britannia die axis ↑↑

1828 rev. helmet intrudes				1830 rev. helmet to			
legend.............10	25	100	250	base of legend 25	75	250	—
1828 rev. helmet to base				1830 rev. helmet intrudes			
of legend 10	25	110	300	legend............10	25	110	300

3827 Third-Farthing. (for use in Malta). Laur. head. l. date below R.Britannia die axis ↑↑

1827	15	65	175
1827 Proof *FDC* £400			

Copper coins graded in this catalogue as UNC have full mint lustre.

PS1 Proof Set, new issue, 1826. Five pounds to Farthing (11 coins) *FDC* £28500
PS1A — — Similar, including Maundy Set (15 coins) *FDC* £30000

William IV was born on 21 August 1765, and ascended the throne on his elder brother's death. From c.1791-1811 while Duke of Clarence, he was cohabiting with the actress Dorothea Jordan (1762-1816) who bore him ten illegitimate children. After the death of George IV's daughter, William was forced into a legitimate marriage with Adelaide of Saxe-Coburg and Meinigen. She bore him two daughters who both died in childhood. His reign was most notable for the introduction of the Reform bill and abolition of slavery. William was the last King of Hanover, and died on 20 June 1837 when the throne passed to his niece Victoria.

In order to prevent confusion between the Sixpence and Half-Sovereign the size of the latter was reduced in 1834, although the weight remained the same. The smaller gold piece was not acceptable to the public and in the following year it was made to the normal size. In 1836 the silver Groat was again issued for general circulation: it is the only British silver coin which has a seated Britannia as the type and was revised upon the suggestion of Mr Joseph Hume thus rendering the nickname "Joey". Crowns were not struck during this reign for general circulation; but proofs or patterns of this denomination were made and are greatly sought after. Silver Threepences and Three-Halfpence were minted for use in the Colonies.

Engraver's and/or designer's initials on the coins:
W. W. (William Wyon)
Engravers and Designers:– Francis Legett Chantry (1781-1842) Jean Baptiste Merlen (1769-c.1850) William Wyon (1795-1851).
Prime Ministers:– Earl Grey, (1764-1845), Whig, 1830-34; William Lamb, Viscount Melbourne (1779-1848) Whig, 1834, 1835-41; Sir Robert Peel, (1788-1850), Tory, 1834-5.

GOLD

3828
1831 Proof Two Pounds

3828 Two Pounds. bare head r. R. crowned shield and mantle, date below, edge plain. die axis ↑↓
1831 (proof only)... *FDC* £5500

	F	VF	EF	UNC		F	VF	EF	UNC
	£	£	£	£		£	£	£	£

3829 Sovereign. First bust. r. top of ear narrow and rounded, nose to 2nd N of BRITANNIAR, fine obv. beading. R. Crowned shield. Die axis ↑↓

	F	VF	EF	UNC		F	VF	EF	UNC
1831	375	675	1600	2500	1832	300	575	1250	1900
					1832Proof *FDC* £5500				

3829B
Second bust with broad ear top

	F	VF	EF	UNC			F	VF	EF	UNC
	£	£	£	£			£	£	£	£

3829A Sovereign. Similar, WW without stops die axis ↑↓

1831 650   1250   2750   4250

3829B Sovereign. Second bust. r. top of ear broad and flat, nose to 2nd I in BRITANNIAR,
    coarser obv. beading.↑↓

1830 plain edge proof *FDC* £6500   1836 300   500   1250   1750
1831 4000   8000   —   —   1836 N ofANNO struck in shield
1831 Proof plain edge *FDC* £2750   in shield....... 3500   8500 15000   —
1832* 275   500   1200   1750   1837 350   650   1500   2250
1833 350   650   1500   2250   1837 Tailed 8........ 400   800   1600   —
1835 350   650   1550   2250

* Beware of counterfeits

3830
Proof Half-sovereign

3831
Large size Half-Sovereign

3830   Half-Sovereign. Small size, bare head r.R. Crowned shield and mantle. die axis ↑↓
    1831 Proof plain edge *FDC* £2000   1834 135   275   750   1250
    1831 Proof milled edge *FDC* £4000

3831   Half-Sovereign. Large size, bare head r.R. Crowned shield and mantle.die axis ↑↓
    1835 135   275   650   1000   1837 135   300   700   1100
    1836 160   325   725   1100

3832
Half-Sovereign - Sixpence obverse die

3832 Half-Sovereign. *Obv.* struck from Sixpence. die in error, 1836...... 1200   2500   4500   —

SILVER

3833

	F	VF	EF	UNC		F	VF	EF	UNC
	£	£	£	£		£	£	£	£

3833 Crown. R. Shield on mantle, 1831 Proof only W.W. on trun. struck ↑↓ .... *FDC* £10000

1831 Proof struck in gold *FDC* £85000

1831 Bare head r. W. WYON on trun. struck ↑↑ en medaille (medal die axis) *FDC* £12500

1831 Bare head r. similar die axis ↑↓ *FDC* £13000

1834 Bare head r. W.W. on trun. struck die axis ↑↓ .... *FDC* £18000

WW script

WW block

3834

3834 Halfcrown. Bare head. WW in script on trun. R. Shield on mantle, die axis ↑↓

						F	VF	EF	UNC
1831 Plain edge proof *FDC* £1150					1835	40	110	400	850
1831 Milled edge proof *FDC* £1850					1836/5	50	110	575	950
1834	30	70	275	575	1836	30	65	275	575
1834 Plain edge proof *FDC* £2850					1836 Proof *FDC* £2200				
1834 Milled edge proof *FDC* £1450					1837	45	135	450	925

3834A

3834A Halfcrown. Bare head r. block WW on trun. R. Similar. die axis ↑↓

1831 Proof *FDC* £1200

1834 50   160   550   1100

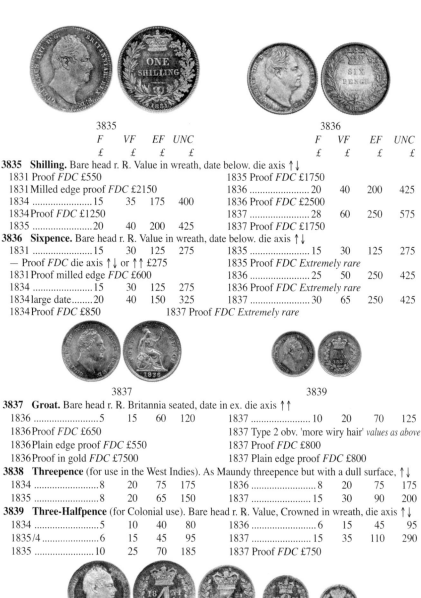

3835

3836

	F	VF	EF	UNC		F	VF	EF	UNC
	£	£	£	£		£	£	£	£

3835 Shilling. Bare head r. R. Value in wreath, date below. die axis ↑↓

1831 Proof *FDC* £550					1835 Proof *FDC* £1750				
1831 Milled edge proof *FDC* £2150					1836	20	40	200	425
1834	15	35	175	400	1836 Proof *FDC* £2500				
1834 Proof *FDC* £1250					1837	28	60	250	575
1835	20	40	200	425	1837 Proof *FDC* £1750				

3836 Sixpence. Bare head r. R. Value in wreath, date below. die axis ↑↓

1831	15	30	125	275	1835	15	30	125	275
— Proof *FDC* die axis ↑↓ or ↑↑ £275					1835 Proof *FDC Extremely rare*				
1831 Proof milled edge *FDC* £600					1836	25	50	250	425
1834	15	30	125	275	1836 Proof *FDC Extremely rare*				
1834 large date	20	40	150	325	1837	30	65	250	425
1834 Proof *FDC* £850					1837 Proof *FDC Extremely rare*				

3837

3839

3837 Groat. Bare head r. R. Britannia seated, date in ex. die axis ↑↑

1836	5	15	60	120	1837	10	20	70	125
1836 Proof *FDC* £650					1837 Type 2 obv. 'more wiry hair' *values as above*				
1836 Plain edge proof *FDC* £550					1837 Proof *FDC* £800				
1836 Proof in gold *FDC* £7500					1837 Plain edge proof *FDC* £800				

3838 Threepence (for use in the West Indies). As Maundy threepence but with a dull surface, ↑↓

1834	8	20	75	175	1836	8	20	75	175
1835	8	20	65	150	1837	15	30	90	200

3839 Three-Halfpence (for Colonial use). Bare head r. R. Value, Crowned in wreath, die axis ↑↓

1834	5	10	40	80	1836	6	15	45	95
1835/4	6	15	45	95	1837	15	35	110	290
1835	10	25	70	185	1837 Proof *FDC* £750				

3840

	EF	FDC		EF	FDC
	£	£		£	£

3840 Maundy Set (4d., 3d., 2d. and 1d.). Bare head r. Die axis ↑↓

1831	140	350	1834	110	300
— Proof *FDC* £425			1835	110	300
1831 Proof struck in gold *FDC* £14500			1836	140	350
1832	120	325	1837	140	350
1833	110	300			

	EF	FDC
	£	£
3841 — **Fourpence,** 1831-7 ....*from*	12	30
3842 — **Threepence,** 1831-7 ....*from*	20	40
3843 — **Twopence,** 1831-7 ....*from*	10	25
3844 — **Penny,** 1831-7 ....*from*	10	20

COPPER

3845

	F	VF	EF	UNC		F	VF	EF	UNC
	£	£	£	£		£	£	£	£

3845 Penny. Bare head r. No initials on trun. date below. R. Britannia r. die axis ↑↑

1831 18	55	300	750	1834 20	60	350	750
1831 Proof *FDC* ↑↓ £450				1837 45	110	475	1500
1831 Proof *FDC* ↑↑ £500							

3846 Penny. Bare head r. date below. incuse initials on trun. R. Britannia r. die axis ↑↑

1831 W.W on trun	*Extremely rare*	1831 .W.W on trun. 30	85	350	750

3847

3848

3847 Halfpenny. Bare head r. date below. R. Britannia r. die axis ↑↑

1831 12	25	100	275	1834 12	25	110	275
1831 Proof *FDC* ↑↓ £300				1837 10	20	95	250
1831 Proof *FDC* ↑↑ £400							

3848 Farthing. Bare head r. date below. R. Britannia r. die axis ↑↑

1831 rev. incuse line				1835 die axis ↑↓ 5	20	95	185
on saltire 2	10	60	120	1835 die axis ↑↑ 2	10	60	120
1831 Proof *FDC* ↑↓ £275				1835 rev. incuse line			
1831 Proof *FDC* ↑↑ £325				on saltire..........2	10	60	120
1834 incuse saltire 2	10	60	120	1836 rev. raised line			
1834 rev. raised line				on saltire..........2	10	60	120
on saltire 2	10	60	120	1837 — 2	10	60	120

3849

	F	VF	EF	UNC
	£	£	£	£

3849 Half-Farthing (for use in Ceylon). Bare head r. date below. R. Britannia r. die axis ↑↑

1837 50   160   325   —

3850

3850 Third-Farthing (for use in Malta). Bare head r. date below. R. Britannia r. die axis ↑↑

1835 5   15   80   225

1835 Proof *FDC* £450

Copper coins graded in this catalogue as UNC have full mint lustre

PS2 Proof set. Coronation, 1831. Two pounds to farthing (14 coins). *FDC* £23500

Victoria was born on 24 May 1819, and enjoyed the longest reign of any Monarch so far. She marrried the German, Prince Albert with whom she enjoyed 17 years of Marriage. Upon Albert's death she became the 'Widow of Windsor' descending into a 25 year period of mourning. She skillfully avoided conflict with other European powers, and produced connections with many Royal houses all over Europe. The Great Exhibition of 1851 was a sign of the power of the largest Empire in the world. Victoria died on 22 January 1901 at the age of 81.

In 1849, as a first step towards decimalization, a silver Florin (^{1}/10 th pound) was introduced, but the coins of 1849 omitted the usual *Dei Gratia* and these so-called 'Godless' Florins were replaced in 1851 by the 'Gothic' issue. The Halfcrown was temporarily discontinued but was minted again from 1874 onwards. Between 1863 and 1880 reverse dies of the gold and silver coins were numbered in the course of Mint experiments into the wear of dies. The exception was the Florin where the die number is on the obverse below the bust.

The gold and silver coins were redesigned for the Queen's Golden Jubilee in 1887. The Double-Florin which was then issued was abandoned after only four years; the Jubilee Sixpence of 1887, known as the 'withdrawn' type, was changed to avoid confusion with the Half-Sovereign. Gold and silver were again redesigned in 1893 with an older portrait of the Queen, but the 'old head' was not used on the bronze coinage until 1895. The heavy copper Penny had been replaced by the lighter bronze 'bun' Penny in 1860. In 1874-6 and 1881-2 some of the bronze was made by Heaton in Birmingham, and these have a letter H below the date. From 1897 Farthings were issued with a dark surface.

Early Sovereigns had a shield-type reverse, but Pistrucci's St. George design was used again from 1871. In order to increase the output of gold coinage, branches of the Royal Mint were set up in Australia at Sydney and Melbourne and, later, at Perth for coining gold of imperial type.

Engraver's and/or designer's initials on the coins:

W. W. (William Wyon 1795-1851) T. B. (Thomas Brock 1847-1922)
L. C. W. (Leonard Charles Wyon 1826-91) B. P. (Benedetto Pistrucci, 1784-1855)
J. E. B. (Joseph Edgar Boehm 1834-90)

Engravers and Designers: George William De Saulle, (1862-1903) William Dyce (1806-64), Jean Baptiste Merlen (1769-c.1850) Edward Poynter (1836-1919)

GOLD

Young Head Coinage, 1838-87

3851
1839 Five Pounds - DIRIGIT reverse

3851 Five Pounds. 1839. Young filleted bust l. plain rear fillet R. 'Una and the lion' (proof only)
DIRIGIT legend, inscribed edge, die axis ↑↑   *FDC* £28,500
  – 1839 Similar – DIRIGIT legend, struck on thick flan   *FDC* £36,500
  – 1839 Similar – DIRIGIT legend, plain edge die axis ↑↑   *FDC* £28,000
  – 1839 –13 leaves to rear fillet, R. DIRIGE legend–proof   *FDC* £27,500
  – 1839 Similar – DIRIGE legend edge letters off-centre   *FDC* £28,500
  – 1839 Similar – DIRIGE legend edge plain proof   *FDC* £28,500
  – 1839 –9 leaves to rear fillet, DIRIGE legend   *FDC* £27,500
  – 1839 Similar – DIRIGE legend edge plain   *FDC* £31,500
  – 1839 Similar – DIRIGE legend edge letters off-centre   *FDC* £28,500
  – 1839 Similar – DIRIGIT legend edge plain proof   *FDC* £31,500

3852
Sovereign - first young head

3852C
Second large head

	F £	VF £	EF £	UNC £		F £	VF £	EF £	UNC £

3852 Sovereign. First (small) young head. l. date below. R. First shield. London mint, die axis ↑↓

1838	425	800	1650	2950
1838 Proof *FDC*		*Extremely rare*		
1838 Plain edge proof *FDC* £5000				
1839	625	1100	2000	3750
1839 die axis ↑↓ Proof *FDC* £3500				
1839 die axis ↑↑ Proof *FDC* £3750				
1839 Milled edge proof *FDC* £7500				
1841	1750	2650	7500	—
1842	100	150	350	600
1842 Open 2	500	1000	—	
1843	100	150	350	600
1843 Roman I	550	1000	—	—
1843/2	175	325	800	1850
1844 large 44	100	150	350	600
1844 small 44	160	275	700	1400
1844 4/ƥ		*Extremely rare*		
1845 4/ƥ		*Extremely rare*		
1845	100	140	325	550
1845 Roman I	550	1100	—	—
1846	100	140	325	550
1846 4/ƥ		*Extremely rare*		
1846 Roman I	550	1100	—	—
1847	100	140	325	550
1847 Roman I		*Extremely rare*		
1848	450	1100	3500	—

3852A Sovereign. Similar R similar but leaves of the wreath arranged differently with tops of leaves closer to crown.

| 1838 | | | 2500 | 4750 | — | — |

3852B Sovereign. Similar narrower shield. Considerably modified floral emblems, different leaf arrangement ↑↓

| 1843 | | | 2750 | 5250 | — | — |

3852C Sovereign. Second (large) head. l. W W still in relief. date below R. Shield with repositioned legend die axis ↑↓

1848	BV	110	280	500
1849	BV	110	280	500
1849 Roman I	450	900	1650	—
1850	BV	125	325	625
1850 Roman I	500	1000	—	—
1851	BV	110	225	400
1852 Roman I	500	1000	1500	—
1852	BV	110	225	400
1853	BV	110	225	400
1853 F over E in DEF	450	950	—	—
1854	140	300	850	—
1855	120	225	425	—
1872	BV	110	190	375

3852D	3852E
WW Incuse	Extra line in ribbon - Ansell

	F	VF	EF	UNC			F	VF	EF	UNC
	£	£	£	£			£	£	£	£

3852D Sovereign. Similar — WW incuse on trun. die axis ↑↓

	F	VF	EF	UNC		F	VF	EF	UNC
1853	110	200	450	—	1860 DEI GRΛ ....Extremely rare			
— Proof *FDC* £7000					1860 ....BV	110	225	450
1854 .... BV	110	220	425		1860 large 0............ 90	110	250	550
1855 .... BV	110	220	425		1861 ....BV	110	220	400
1856 .... BV	110	220	425		1861 Roman I....... 225	475	1100	—
1857 .... BV	110	220	425		1862 Roman I....... 250	600	—	—
1858 ....BV	110	250	450		1862 wide date ......BV	110	220	400
1858 8/7 700	—	—	—		1862 R/Яin VICTORIA............. Extremely rare
1859 .... BV	110	200	400		1862 F/Ɐ in DEF narrow date........Extremely rare
1860 O over C in obv. leg. ....Extremely rare					1863 ....BV	110	220	400
1860 Roman I....... 500	1000	—	—		1863 Roman I (1/1) 250	600	—	—
1860 ⱯICTORIA................... Extremely rare								

3852E Sovereign. Similar — As 3852D 'Ansell' ribbon. Additional raised line on the lower part of the ribbon ↑↓

1859 ....475 1150 3750 —

3852F Sovereign. Similar — As 3852D with die number 827 on trun. die axis ↑↓

1863 ....2600 4750 — —

3853
Die number location

3853 Sovereign. Similar As 3852D R. die number in space below wreath, above floral emblem, die axis ↑↓

1863 ....BV	110	200	350	1866/5 DIE 17 only..... 95	200	400	950
1864 ....BV	110	175	325	1868 .... BV	110	200	350
1865 ....BV	110	200	375	1869 .... BV	110	175	325
1866 ....BV	110	175	325	1870 .... BV	110	250	450

3853A Sovereign. Similar — As 3853 with die number 827 on trun. R. die number is always no. 22 die axis ↑↓

1863 ....2500 4500 — —

3853B Sovereign. Similar — WW in relief on trun. R. die number below wreath, above floral emblem die axis ↑↓

1870 ....BV	110	200	375	1873 .... BV	110	200	325
1871 ....BV	100	150	300	1874 1200	2500	5250	—
1872 ....BV	100	150	300				

	3854					3855		
	Melbourne Mint mark					Sydney Mint mark		
	F	VF	EF	UNC		F	VF	EF	UNC
	£	£	£	£		£	£	£	£

3854 Sovereign Second (large) head. l. WW in relief date below R. M below wreath for Melbourne Mint, Australia ↑↓

	F	VF	EF	UNC			F	VF	EF	UNC
1872 M................. BV	100	175	600		1883 M................. 100	220	500	1500
1872/1 M............... 125	275	750	2000		1884 M.................BV	100	150	475
1874 M................. BV	100	165	1000		1885 M.................BV	100	150	475
1880 M................. 325	700	1800	3750		1886 M................. 750	2450	3750	6450
1881 M................. BV	100	180	1250		1887 M................. 375	750	2350	4250
1882 M................. BV	100	145	600					

3855 Sovereign. Similar — As 3854 R. with S below wreath for Sydney Mint, Australia die axis ↑↓

		VF	EF	UNC				VF	EF	UNC
1871 S .... BV	100	150	550		1880 S ..... VICTORIA		*Extremely rare*	
1872 S .... BV	100	175	800		1881 S ....BV	110	175	650
1873 S .... BV	100	180	700		1882 S ....BV	100	150	475
1875 S .... BV	100	180	700		1883 S ....BV	100	150	475
1877 S .... BV	100	140	475		1884 S ....BV	100	140	475
1878 S .... BV	100	140	475		1885 S ....BV	100	140	475
1879 S .... BV	100	140	475		1886 S ....BV	100	140	475
1880 S .... BV	100	160	650		1887 S ....BV	100	200	700

3855A Sovereign. Second (large) head WW incuse on trun. date below R. with S below wreath for Sydney Mint die axis ↑↓

1871 S 95	120	175	600

3856A
Horse with long tail
Small BP in exergue

3856 Sovereign. First young head. l. WW buried in narrow trun. R. St. George. London mint. Horse with short tail. Large BP and date in ex. die axis ↑↓

1871..BV	100	140	300
1871 Proof milled edge *FDC* £9500			
1871 Plain edge proof *FDC* £5000			

3856A Sovereign. — — As 3856 R. Horse with long tail. Small BP and date in ex.die axis ↑↓

1871...................... BV	100	140	250		1876 ....BV	100	140	250
1871 Proof *FDC* plain edge £6500					1878 ....BV	100	140	250
1872...................... BV	100	140	275		1879 200	500	1450	—
1873...................... BV	100	140	250		1880 ....BV	100	140	250
1874...................... BV	100	140	275					

3856B Sovereign. — — As 3856 R. Horse with short tail, small BP and date in ex.die axis ↑↓

1880...................... BV	100	140	250		1884 ....BV	100	130	250
1880 8/7 .... BV	110	175	350		1885 ....BV	100	150	275

	F	VF	EF	UNC		F	VF	EF	UNC
	£	£	£	£		£	£	£	£

3856C Sovereign. — — As 3856 R. Horse with short tail, date but no BP in ex.die axis ↑↓

1880 Second 8/7...BV 110 175 325

3856D Sovereign. Second head. l. WW complete, on broad trun. R.
    Horse with long tail, small BP and date in ex.die axis ↑↓

1880 8/7 ....BV 120 160 325

1880...BV 100 140 275

3856E Sovereign. — — As 3856D R. Horse with short tail. Date but no BP in ex. die axis ↑↓

1880...BV 100 140 275

3856F Sovereign. — — As 3856E R. Horse with short tail, small BP and date in ex. die axis ↑↓

1880.....................BV 110 160 325   1885 ....BV 100 150 300

1884.....................BV 100 130 300

3857
Melbourne Mint
WW buried in truncation

3857 Sovereign. — — First head. l. WW buried in trun. M below head for Melbourne Mint,
    Australia. R. Horse with long tail, small BP and date in ex. die axis ↑↓

1872 M..................110	185	625	2500	1877 M..................BV	100	175	475
1873 M..................BV	100	175	850	1878 M..................BV	100	175	475
1874 M..................BV	100	175	850	1879 M..................BV	95	140	475
1875 M..................BV	95	145	650	1880 M..................BV	100	145	475
1876 M..................BV	95	140	550	1881 M..................BV	100	145	475

3857A Sovereign. — — As 3857 R. horse with short tail, date but no BP in ex die axis ↑↓

1881 M..................BV	95	140	550	1884 M..................BV	110	275	—
1882 M..................BV	95	140	550				

3857B Soveriegn. First head l. WW buried in trun. M below head for Melbourne Mint, Australia R.
    Horse with short tail, small BP and date in ex. die axis ↑↓

1879 M......................	*Extremely rare*			1883 M..................BV	100	140	475
1880 M......................	*Extremely rare*			1884 M..................BV	100	140	425
1882 M..................BV	100	150	475	1885 M..................BV	100	140	450

3857C Sovereign. — — Second head. l. WW complete on broad truncation. R. Horse with short tail, small BP in ex.

1882 M..................BV	100	150	475	1885 M..................BV	100	140	450
1883 M..................BV	100	140	475	1886 M..................BV	100	140	425
1884 M..................BV	100	140	425	1887 M..................BV	100	160	475

3858 Sovereign First head. l. WW buried in narrow trun. S below head for Sydney Mint, Australia,
    R. Horse with short tail, large BP and date in ex. die axis ↑↓

1871 S ....BV 150 600 1600

3858A Sovereign. — — As 3858 R. Horse with long tail, small BP and date in ex. die axis ↑↓

1871 S ....BV	120	450	1250	1875 S ....BV	125	220	800
1872 S ....BV	120	180	900	1876 S ....BV	125	220	650
1873 S ....BV	100	240	950	1879 S ....BV	140	900	2500
1874 S ....BV	125	220	1000	1880 S ....BV	100	175	550

3858B Sovereign. — — As 3858 R. Horse with short tail, date but no BP in ex. die axis ↑↓

1880 S ....BV	100	160	550	1881 S ....BV	100	150	500

3859　　　　　　　　　　3859A
Type A1　　　　　　　　Type A2

	F	VF	EF	UNC		F	VF	EF	UNC
	£	£	£	£		£	£	£	£

3858C Sovereign. Second head. l. WW complete on broad trun. R.
Horse with long tail, small BP and date in ex. die axis ↑↓

| 1880 S | | | | | | BV | 100 | 160 | 550 |

3858D Sovereign. — — As 3858C R. Horse with short tail, date but no BP in ex. die axis ↑↓

| 1881 S | | 75 | 110 | 650 | 1882 S | BV | 95 | 130 | 350 |

3858E Sovereign. — — As 3858D R. Horse with short tail small BP and date in ex. die axis ↑↓

1882 S	BV	95	130	350	1885 S	BV	95	130	475
1883 S	BV	110	175	900	1886 S	BV	95	130	475
1884 S	BV	95	130	500	1887 S	BV	95	130	475

3859 Half-Sovereign. Type A1. First (smallest) young head. date below l. R. First shield, die axis ↑↓

1838	75	125	350	800	1849	50	100	300	550
1839 die axis ↑↓ or ↑↑ Proof only *FDC* £1950					1850	125	300	1000	—
1839 Milled edge proof *FDC* Extremely rare					1851	50	90	250	450
1841	80	125	400	950	1852	65	110	275	550
1842	50	100	300	600	1853	50	90	225	450
1843	70	145	400	750	1853 Proof small date *FDC* £4000				
1844	65	110	350	650	1853 Proof large date *FDC* £6000				
1845	135	400	1250	—	1855	45	80	275	550
1846	65	110	325	650	1856	45	80	225	450
1847	65	110	325	650	1856/5	85	140	325	650
1848 Close date	65	110	325	650	1857	65	95	275	550
1848/7	115	200	450	900	1858	65	95	275	550
1848 Wide date	80	145	400	750					

3859A Half-Sovereign. Type A2, Second (larger) young head. date below. R. First shield die axis ↑↓

1858	55	80	225	450	1861	55	80	225	450
1859	55	80	225	450	1862	325	1000	3750	—
1860	55	80	225	450	1863	55	80	225	450

3860　　　　　　3860D　　　　　　3860E　　　　　　3860F
Die number　　　Type A3　　　　　Type A4　　　　　Type A5
location

3860 Half-Sovereign. Type A2, second head, date below R. die number below shield, die axis ↑↓

1863	65	100	325	650	1867	55	80	225	425
1864	55	80	225	425	1869	55	80	225	425
1865	55	80	225	425	1870	55	80	225	400
1866	55	80	225	425	1871	55	80	225	400

	F	VF	EF	UNC		F	VF	EF	UNC
	£	£	£	£		£	£	£	£

3860A Half-Sovereign. Second head, date below R. Re-engraved shield legend and rosettes closer to border, coarse boarder teeth both sides, with die number below shield die axis ↑↓

| 1870 | 100 | 250 | 750 | — | 1871 | 100 | 250 | 750 | — |

3860B Half-Sovereign. Second head, date below R. As last but with normal border teeth and no die number below shield die axis ↑↓

| 1871 | | | | | | 200 | 425 | 1000 | — |

3860C Half-Sovereign. Second head, date below obv. with repositioned legend, nose now points to T in VICTORIA. R. Similar to last but with die number below shield die axis ↑↓

| 1871 | 125 | 275 | 800 | — | 1872 | 100 | 225 | 675 | — |

3860D Half-Sovereign. Type A3, Third (larger still) young head l, date below. R. As 3860A, with die number below shield die axis ↑↓

1872	45	80	225	400	1875	45	75	225	350
1873	45	80	225	400	1876	45	75	225	350
1874	45	85	225	400	1877	45	75	225	350

3860E
Half Sovereign

3861
Type A5

3860E Half-Sovereign. Type A4. Fourth young head l. hair ribbon now narrow, date below. R. As last with die number below shield die axis ↑↓

| 1876 | 55 | 75 | 175 | 350 | 1878 | 55 | 75 | 175 | 350 |
| 1877 | 55 | 75 | 175 | 350 | 1879 | 60 | 100 | 325 | 600 |

3860F Half-Sovereign. Type A5. Fifth young head l. in very low relief, date below. R. As last with die number below shield die axis ↑↓

| 1880 | | | | | | 60 | 95 | 325 | 600 |

3861 Half-Sovereign. Fifth head, date below. R. Cross on crown buried in border. Legend and rosettes very close to heavy border, no die number below shield die axis ↑↓

1880	55	85	200	400	1885	55	75	175	300
1883	55	75	175	300	1885/3	80	140	300	650
1884	55	75	175	300					

3862 Half-Sovereign. Type A2, Second (larger) young head l. nose points between T and O. Date below R. First crowned shield cross clear of border with S below shield for Sydney Mint, Australia, die axis ↑↓

| 1871 S | | | | | | 55 | 100 | 600 | 2150 |

3862A Half-Sovereign. Similar obv. with repositioned legend, nose now points to T in VICTORIA. Date below R Re-engraved shield cross touches border, S below shield die axis ↑↓

| 1872 S | | | | | | 55 | 100 | 600 | 2150 |

3862B Half-Sovereign. Type A3. Third (larger still) young head l. I of DEI points to rear fillet. Date below R. As last die axis ↑↓

| 1875 S | | | | | | 55 | 100 | 600 | 2150 |

3862C Half-Sovereign. Type A4. Fourth young head l. front hair fillet now narrow. R. As last, die axis ↑↓

| 1879 S | | | | | | 55 | 110 | 525 | 2150 |

3862D Half-Sovereign. Type A5. Fifth young head l. in low relief wider tr. no front ear lobe. Date below R as last. die axis ↑↓

| 1882 S | 140 | 475 | 2650 | 6850 | 1883 S | 55 | 110 | 500 | 3000 |

3862E Half-Sovereign. Fifth head, date below R. Cross on crown buried in border. Legend and rosettes very close to heavy border, S below shield die axis ↑↓

1880 S	55	120	650	2500	1883 S	55	110	500	2750
1881 S	55	135	800	2750	1886 S	55	120	800	2200
1882 S	120	475	2500	6500	1887 S	55	120	650	1800

* Beware recent forgeries

	F	VF	EF	UNC			F	VF	EF	UNC
	£	£	£	£			£	£	£	£

3863 Half-Sovereign. Type A3. Third (larger still) young head l. Date below R. Re-engraved shield with M below shield for Melbourne Mint, Australia die axis ↑↓

	F	VF	EF	UNC			F	VF	EF	UNC
1873 M	45	120	650	2350		1877 M	45	110	580	2150

3863A Half-Sovereign. Type A4, fourth young head l. hair ribbon now narrow. R. As last die axis ↑↓

1877 M	45	110	600	2150		1882 M	45	110	500	1650

3863B Half-Sovereign. Type A5. Fifth young head l. in low relief. Date below R. As last die axis ↑↓

1881 M	70	150	1250	3650		1885 M	140	350	1850	5150
1882 M	45	110	500	1650		1886 M	75	175	1350	3650
1884 M	55	220	1350	3850		1887 M	100	275	1850	5150

Jubilee Coinage, 1887-93, die axis ↑↑

3864

1887 Five Pounds

3864* Five Pounds. Jubilee bust l. R. St. George date in ex. 1887 450   675   850   1200
— Proof *FDC* £2750
— Proof no B.P. in exergue £3250

3864A* Five Pounds. Jubilee bust l. R. St George, S on ground for Sydney Mint, Australia 1887 S
Extremely rare

3865* Two Pounds. Jubilee bust l. R. St George die axis ↑↑ 1887 250   325   450   650
1887 Proof *FDC* £1000
1887 Proof no BP in exergue FDC .... *Extremely rare*

3865A* Two Pounds. R. St George, S on ground for Sydney Mint, Australia ↑↑ 1887S.... *Extremely rare*

3866* Sovereign. Normal JEB (angled J) designer's initials fully on trun. R. St. George. die axis ↑↑
1887............................. 110   185   1888 .... BV   130   200

3866A Sovereign. Similar with tiny JEB (hooked J) designer's initials at base of truncation die axis ↑↑
1887... *Extremely rare*

3688B

1887 Sovereign

3866B Sovereign. Similar repositioned legend. G: of D:G: now closer to crown. Normal JEB (angled J)
designer's initials at base of trun. ↑↑

1887 Proof *FDC* £800   1890 .... BV   125   200
1888.................................BV   125   200   1891 .... *Extremely rare*
1889.................................BV   125   200

* Beware recent forgeries

	VF £	EF £	UNC £		VF £	EF £	UNC £

3866C Sovereign. Similar obv. as last. ℞. Horse with longer tail die axis ↑↑
1891....................................BV   125   200   1892 ....   BV   125   200

3867
Melbourne Mint

3867 Sovereign. Similar with small spread JEB (angled J)designer's initials fully on trun. ℞. M on
ground for Melbourne Mint, Australia, die axis ↑↑
1887M...   BV   100   180
3867A Sovereign. Similar with normal JEB designer's initials on trun. die axis ↑↑
1887M...   BV   100   180
1888M...   *Extremely rare*
1889M...   *Extremely rare*
1890M...   *Extremely rare*
3867B Sovereign. Similar repositioned legend. G: of D: G: now closer to crown. Normal JEB (angled J)
initials at base of trun. die axis ↑↑
1887M.......................   110   175   1889M.......................   BV   100   175
1888M.......................   110   185   1890M.......................   BV   120   180
3867C Sovereign. Similar obv. as last. ℞. Horse with longer tail die axis ↑↑
1891M.......................   110   175   1893M.......................   BV   125   200
1892M.......................   85   150
3868 Sovereign. Similar with normal JEB (hooked J) initials in arc on trun. ℞. S on ground for
Sydney Mint, Australia die axis ↑↑
1887S   150   275   1250
1887S Proof ....   *Extremely rare*
3868A Sovereign. Similar with small spread JEB designer's initials straight on trun.(hooked J) die
axis ↑↑
1887S ....   *Extremely rare*
1888S ....   BV   100   175
1889S ....   *Extremely rare*
3868B Sovereign. Similar repositioned legend. G: of D:G: now closer to crown. Normal JEB (angled J)
initials on trun. die axis ↑↑
1888S   110   180   1890S ....   BV   110   180
1889S   100   160
3868C Sovereign. Similar obv. as last. ℞. Horse with longer tail die axis ↑↑
1891S   110   180   1893S ....   BV   125   195
1892S   100   160

          3869   3869C

                                      Plain trun., higher shield

	VF	EF	UNC		F	VF	EF	UNC
	£	£	£		£	£	£	£

3869 Half-Sovereign. Similar obv. normal JEB designer's initials. on trun. R. High shield die axis ↑↑

1887... 65   120   1890 120   225   —

— Proof *FDC* £400

3869A Half-Sovereign. Similar small close JEB intitials. on trun. R. High shield die axis ↑↑

1887............................ 120   225   —

3869B Half-Sovereign. Similar normal JEB initials. on trun. R. Lower shield, date therefore spread apart, complete cross at top, die axis ↑↑

1890............................ 120   225   —   1892 120   225   —

3869C Half-Sovereign. Similar no JEB initials on trun. R. High Shield die axis ↑↑

1887............................ 120   225   —   1891 120   225   —

1890............................ BV   60   95   1892 120   225   —

3869D Half-Sovereign. Jubilee bust 1. R. Lower shield, date therefore spread apart die axis ↑↑

1890............................ BV   60   95   1892 .... BV   60   95

1891............................ BV   75   110   1893 .... BV   85   120

                                   3870

3870 Half-Sovereign. Similar small very spread JEB initials on trun. R. High shield, M below for Melbourne Mint, Australia, die axis ↑↑

1887M..BV   75   225   800

3870A Half-Sovereign. Similar small close JEB initials on trun. R. As last die axis ↑↑

1887M..BV   75   225   800

3870B Half-Sovereign. Similar normal JEB initials on trun. R. Lower shield, date therefore spread part die axis ↑↑

1893M..BV   120   450   1650

3871 Half-Sovereign. Similar small very spread JEB initials on trun. (hooked J) R. High shield S below for Sydney Mint, Australia ↑↑

1887S ....BV   75   225   825

3871A Half-Sovereign. Similar small close JEB initials on trun. R As last. die axis ↑↑

1887S ....BV   75   225   825

3871B Half-Sovereign. Jubilee bust 1. Normal JEB initials on trun. R. Lower shield, date therefore spread apart, S below for Sydney Mint, Australia die axis ↑↑

1889S 55   125   450   1650

3871C Half-Sovereign. Jubilee bust 1. Normal JEB initials on trun. R. High shield, S below for Sydney Mint, Australia die axis ↑↑

1891S 55   125   450   1650

3871D Half-Sovereign. Jubilee bust 1. No JEB initials on trun. R. As last die axis ↑↑

1891S 55   125   450   1650

Old Head coinage, 1893-1901, die axis ↑↑

3872
1893 Five Pounds

	F	VF	EF	UNC
	£	£	£	£

3872* Five Pounds. Old veiled bust 1. R. St. George and dragon, date and BP in ex.

1893 .... 500 850 1350 2000
1893 Proof *FDC* £3500

3873
1893 Two Pounds

3874
1893 Sovereign

3873* Two Pounds. Old veiled bust 1. R. St. George and dragon, date and BP in ex. die axis ↑↑

1893 .... 250 375 600 900
1893 Proof *FDC* £1200

	EF	UNC		EF	UNC
	£	£		£	£

3874 Sovereign. Old veiled bust 1. R. St. George, London Mint die axis ↑↑

1893 110	175	1898 100	140
1893 Proof *FDC* £950		1899 100	140
1894 100	150	1900 100	140
1895 100	150	1901 100	150
1896 100	150		

3875 Sovereign. Similar R. St. George. M on ground for Melbourne Mint, Australia die axis ↑↑

1893 M 110	240	1898 M 100	140
1894 M 100	140	1899 M 100	140
1895 M 100	160	1900 M 100	140
1896 M 100	140	1901 M 100	140
1897 M 100	140		

* Beware recent forgeries

3876
Perth Mint mark

	F	VF	EF	UNC		F	VF	EF	UNC
	£	£	£	£		£	£	£	£

3876 Sovereign. Similar — P on ground for Perth Mint, Australia die axis ↑↑

1899 P	BV	150	350	1150	1901 P			100	150
1900 P			95	150					

3877 Sovereign. Similar — S on ground for Sydney Mint, Australia die axis ↑↑

1893 S			100	140	1898 S			100	160
1894 S			100	140	1899 S			BV	140
1895 S			100	140	1900 S			100	140
1896 S			110	160	1901 S			100	140
1897 S			100	140					

3878
1893 Half -Sovereign

3878 Half-Sovereign. Old veiled bust 1.R. St. George. Date in ex. London Mint die axis ↑↑

1893			55	100	1897			55	100
— Proof *FDC* £475					1898			55	100
1894			55	100	1899			55	100
1895			55	100	1900			55	100
1896			50	100	1901			55	100

3879 Half-Sovereign. Similar — M on ground for Melbourne Mint, Australia die axis ↑↑

1893 M		*Extremely rare*			1899 M	50	100	325	1400
1896 M	50	100	325	1350	1900 M	55	110	325	1400

3880 Half-Sovereign. Similar — P on ground for Perth Mint, Australia die axis ↑↑

1899 P		Proof only *unique*			1900 P	75	135	415	1850

3881 Half-Sovereign. Similar — S on ground for Sydney Mint, Australia die axis ↑↑

1893 S	50	85	250	1000	1900 S	50	75	215	1000
1897 S	50	85	225	1000					

SILVER

Young head coinage, die axis ↑↓

3882
1844 Crown

	F	VF	EF	UNC		F	VF	EF	UNC
	£	£	£	£		£	£	£	£

3882 Crown. Young head. l. R. Crowned shield, regnal year on edge in Roman figures (eg 1847 = XI)

1839 Proof only *FDC* £4750

	F	VF	EF	UNC
1844 Star stops VIII	50	135	925	2500
1844 Cinquefoil stops VIII	50	135	925	2500
1844 Mistruck edge lettering	80	275	1250	–
1845 Star stops VIII	50	135	925	2500
1845 Cinquefoil stops VIII	50	135	925	2500
1847 XI	60	200	1100	2950

3883
1847 Gothic Crown

3883*Crown. 'Gothic' type, bust l. R. Crowned cruciform Shields, emblems in angles. inscribed edge, mdcccxlvii=1847 Undecimo on edge die axis ↑↓ 450   800   1350   2750

1847 Septimo on edge of highest rarity.　　　1847 Proof, Plain edge die axis ↑↑ *FDC* £3500

1847 Proof in gold plain edge *FDC* of highest rarity　　1847 Proof in white metal plain edge *FDC* £6000

3884 Crown. Similar mdcccliii=1853. Septimo on edge die axis ↑↑ Proof *FDC* £6750

1853 plain edge proof *FDC* £8750

3885 Halfcrown. Type A^1. Young head l. with one ornate and one plain fillet binding hair. WW in relief on trun. R. Crowned shield of arms, edge milled. Die axis ↑↓

1839 Milled edge Proof *FDC* Extremely rare　　　1839 Proof plain edge *FDC* £1500

3886 Halfcrown. Type A^2 Similar, but two ornate fillets binding hair.die axis ↑↓

1839 Proof only *FDC* £2750

3886A Halfcrown. Type A$^{2/3}$ Similar, Two plain fillets, WW relief, die axis ↑↓ plain edge

1839 Proof *FDC* £3750

*Beware of recent forgeries.

	F	VF	EF	UNC		F	VF	EF	UNC
	£	£	£	£		£	£	£	£

3887 Halfcrown. Type A³. Similar two plain fillets. WW incuse on trun. die axis ↑↓

1839	...625	2200	4500	—	1839 Milled edge Proof *FDC* £2250				
1839 Plain edge Proof *FDC* £3000					1840	...30	100	525	1000

3888 Halfcrown. Type A⁴. Similar but no initials on trun. die axis ↑↓

1841	...475	875	2450	3500	1849 large date	...45	140	575	1200
1842	...40	90	475	950	1849/7		*Extremely rare*		
1843	...90	225	650	1250	1849 small date	...80	200	600	1200
1844	...35	75	400	800	1850	...40	125	550	1100
1844 not in edge collar		*Extremely rare*			1850 Proof *FDC Extremely rare*				
1845	...40	70	400	800	1853 Proof *FDC* £1750				
1845 5/3		*Extremely rare*			1862 Proof *FDC Extremely rare*				
1846	...40	75	400	800	1862 Plain edge Proof *FDC* £4750				
1848/6	...100	200	700	1750	1864 Proof *FDC* £5000				
1848/7		*Extremely rare*			1864 Plain edge Proof *FDC* £4750				
1848	...75	300	1100	2250					

3889
Type A5 Halfcrown

3890
1849 'Godless' Florin

3889 Halfcrown. Similar Type A⁵. As last but design of inferior workmanship R. Crowned shield die axis ↑↓

1874	...20	40	150	400	1881	...18	40	150	400
1874 Proof *FDC* £3750					1881 Proof *FDC* £3250				
1875	...20	40	150	400	1881 Plain edge proof *FDC* £3750				
1875 Proof *FDC* £3750					1882	...20	45	175	425
1876	...20	45	175	425	1883	...15	40	150	400
1876/5	...30	55	315	650	1883 Plain edge proof *FDC* £3750				
1877	...20	40	150	400	1884	...15	40	150	400
1878	...25	40	150	400	1885	...15	40	150	400
1878 Proof *FDC* £3250					1885 Proof *FDC* £3000				
1879	...25	45	220	500	1886	...15	40	150	400
1879 Proof *FDC* £3750					1886 Plain edge proof *FDC* £3750				
1880	...18	40	150	400	1887	...20	50	175	400
1880 Proof *FDC* £3750					1887 Proof *FDC* £3250				

3890 Florin. 'Godless' type A (i.e. without D.G.), WW behind bust within linear circle, die axis ↑↓

1848 Plain edge (Pattern) *FDC* £950					1849 WW obliterated	35	75	235	425
1848 Milled edge ↑↑ or ↑↓ Proof *FDC* £2250					1849	...20	40	150	275

3891 Florin. 'Gothic' type B¹. Reads brit:, WW below bust, date at end of obverse legend in gothic numerals (1851 to 1863) Crowned cruciform Shields, emblems in angles, edge milled. die axis ↑↓

mdcccli Proof only *FDC* £8000					mdccclvii Proof *FDC* £2500				
mdccclii	...18	40	150	350	mdccclviii	...20	45	150	375
mdccclii Proof *FDC* £2000					mdccclviii Proof *FDC* £2500				
mdccclii, ii/i	...20	50	175	425	mdccclix	...20	45	150	375
mdcccliii	...18	40	150	350	mdccclx	...25	50	175	400
mdcccliii Proof *FDC* £1750					mdccclxii	...125	325	750	1650
mdcccliv	...400	950	3000	—	mdccclxii Plain edge Proof *FDC* £3500				
mdccclv	...25	75	200	450	mdccclxiii	...475	1000	2000	3250
mdccclvi	...25	75	200	450	mdccclxiii Plain edge Proof *FDC* £4000				
mdccclvii	20	45	150	375					

3891 3893

1853 Florin Type B1

	F	VF	EF	UNC		F	VF	EF	UNC
	£	£	£	£		£	£	£	£

3892 Florin. Type B[2]. Similar as last but die number below bust (1864 to 1867) die axis ↑↓

mdccclxiv	20	45	175	425	mdccclxv	40	100	285	525
mdccclxiv heavy flan	250	500	1000	1850	mdccclxvi	35	75	235	450
mdccclxiv heavy flan Proof		*FDC* £3000			mdccclxvii	30	70	235	450

3893 Florin. Type B[3]. Similar reads britt:, die number below bust (1868 to 1879) die axis

mdccclxvii Proof *FDC* £2750					mdccclxxiii	20	50	175	350
mdccclxviii	30	85	265	575	mdccclxxiii Proof *FDC* £2600				
mdccclxix	25	75	265	525	mdccclxxiv	25	55	200	425
mdccclxix Proof *FDC* £2850					mdccclxxiv iv/iii	35	75	265	525
mdccclxx	20	50	185	425	mdccclxxv	25	50	175	400
mdccclxx Proof *FDC* £2850					mdccclxxvi	20	45	150	375
mdccclxxi	20	50	185	425	mdccclxxvii	25	50	175	425
mdccclxxi Proof *FDC* £2350					mdccclxxix			*Extremely rare*	
mdccclxxii	18	40	125	325					

3894 Florin. Type B[4]. Similar as last but with border of 48 arcs and no WW below bust die axis ↑↓
1877 mdccclxxvii .... *Extremely rare*

3895 Florin. Type B[5]. Similar but border of 42 arcs (1867, 1877 and 1878) die axis ↑↓

| mdccclxvii | ......£2750 | | | | mdccclxxviii | 20 | 45 | 150 | 350 |
| mdccclxxvii | 25 | 55 | 200 | 475 | mdccclxxviii Proof *FDC* | | *Extremely rare* | | |

3896 Florin. Type B[5/6]. Similar as last but no die number below bust (1877, 1879) die axis ↑↓

| mdccclxxvii | 100 | 225 | 475 | 950 | mdccclxxix | 100 | 225 | 475 | 950 |

3897 Florin. Type B[6]. Similar reads britt:, WW; Border of 48 arcs (1879) die axis ↑↓
mdccclxxix 20 45 150 375

3898 Florin. Type B[7]. Similar as last but no WW, Border of 38 arcs (1879) die axis ↑↓
mdccclxxix 20 45 150 375
mdccclxxix Proof *FDC* £3000

3899 Florin. Type B[3/8]. Similar as next but younger portrait (1880) die axis ↑↓
mdccclxxx .... *Extremely rare*

3900 Florin. Type B[8]. Similar but border of 34 arcs (1880 to 1887) die axis ↑↓

mdccclxxx	18	40	150	350	mdccclxxxiii Proof *FDC* £2350				
mdccclxxx Proof *FDC*£2350					mdccclxxxiv	18	40	125	300
mdccclxxxi	18	40	125	350	mdccclxxxv	20	45	150	325
mdccclxxxi Proof *FDC* £2350					mdccclxxxv Proof *FDC* £2350				
mdccclxxxi/xxri	30	75	200	450	mdccclxxxvi	18	35	125	325
mdccclxxxiii	18	40	125	350	mdccclxxxvi Proof *FDC* £2600				

3901 Florin. Type B[9]. Similar but border of 46 arcs die axis ↑↓
1887 mdccclxxxvii 30 60 250 475
mdccclxxxvii Proof *FDC* .... *Extremely rare*

3902 Shilling. Type A[1]. First head l., WW on trun.R. crowned mark of value within wreath, date
below, die axis ↑↓

| 1838 | 18 | 35 | 165 | 350 | 1839 | 35 | 75 | 275 | 550 |
| 1838 Proof *FDC* £1850 | | | | | 1839 Proof *FDC* £950 | | | | |

3903 Shilling Type A[2]. Second head, l. WW on trun. (proof only), 1839 die axis ↑↑ *FDC* £500

3904
Type A3 Shilling

	F	VF	EF	UNC		F	VF	EF	UNC
	£	£	£	£		£	£	£	£

3904 Shilling Type A³. Second head, l. no initials on trun. R. Similar die axis ↑↓

1839	20	45	135	300	1852	12	20	100	225
1839 Proof plain edge *FDC* £525					1853	12	20	90	225
1839 Proof milled edge *FDC Extremely rare*					1853 Proof *FDC* £475				
1840	25	70	190	350	1854	90	300	750	1750
1840 Proof *FDC* £2500					1854/1	160	575	1750	—
1841	60	65	175	400	1855	12	20	90	225
1842	20	40	115	250	1856	12	20	90	225
1842 Proof *FDC* £2500					1857	12	20	90	225
1843	25	60	175	400	1857 REG F: Ɔ:error	125	350	950	—
1844	20	35	115	250	1858	12	20	90	225
1845	20	35	125	300	1859	12	20	90	225
1846	20	35	115	250	1859 Proof *FDC* £2750				
1848 over 6	65	150	575	950	1860	15	25	135	300
1849	25	45	140	325	1861	15	25	135	300
1850	275	900	2000	—	1861 D/B in FD		*Extremely rare*		
1850/49	275	1000	2250	—	1862	40	60	190	375
1851	50	110	350	800	1863	60	120	300	650
1851 Proof *FDC* £3000					1863/1	90	200	550	—

3905 Shilling Type A⁴. Similar as last, R. Die number above date die axis ↑↑

1864	15	30	90	225	1866 BBITANNIAR.	50	175	500	—
1865	15	30	90	225	1867	15	30	100	225
1866	15	30	90	225					

3906 Shilling Type A⁵. Third head, l. R. Similar no die number above date die axis ↑↓

1867 Proof £2250					1879	200	400	900	1500
1867 Proof plain edge £2750									

3906A   Die number location
Type A6 Shilling   above date

3906A Shilling Type A⁶. Third head, l. R. Similar die number above date die axis ↑↓

1867	125	300	900	—	1874	10	20	90	225
1868	10	25	90	225	1875	10	20	90	225
1869	20	35	125	250	1876	15	30	100	250
1870	20	35	125	250	1877	10	20	90	225
1871	10	20	90	225	1878	20	40	150	300
1871 Plain edge proof *FDC* £2350					1878 Proof *FDC* £2350				
1871 Milled edge proof *FDC* £2150					1879		*Extremely rare*		
1872	10	20	90	225	1879 Proof *FDC* £2350				
1873	10	20	90	225					

	F	VF	EF	UNC		F	VF	EF	UNC
	£	£	£	£		£	£	£	£

3907 Shilling Type A[7]. Fourth head, l. R. Similar no die number above date die axis ↑↓

| 1879 | 10 | 20 | 90 | 200 |
| 1879 Proof *FDC* £2350 |
| 1880 | 10 | 20 | 80 | 175 |
| 1880 Proof plain edge £2150 |
| 1880 Proof milled edge £1650 |
| 1881 | 10 | 20 | 80 | 175 |
| 1881 Proof plain edge £2750 |
| 1881 Proof milled edge £1850 |
| 1882 | 15 | 40 | 125 | 250 |
| 1883 | 10 | 20 | 80 | 175 |

| 1883 plain edge Proof *FDC* £3750 |
| 1884 | 10 | 20 | 80 | 175 |
| 1884 Proof *FDC* £2150 |
| 1885 | 10 | 15 | 70 | 150 |
| 1885 Proof *FDC* £2150 |
| 1886 | 10 | 15 | 70 | 150 |
| 1886 Proof *FDC* £2150 |
| 1887 | 15 | 30 | 100 | 250 |
| 1887 Proof *FDC* £1850 |

3907A Shilling. Type A7. Fourth head, R. Similar die number above date die axis ↑↓

| 1878 | 10 | 20 | 80 | 175 | 1879 | 15 | 40 | 125 | 250 |

3908
Type A1 Sixpence

3908 Sixpence. Type A[1]. First head l. R. Crowned mark of value within wreath, date below die axis ↑↓

| 1838 | 10 | 20 | 80 | 200 |
| 1838 Proof *FDC* £950 |
| 1839 | 10 | 20 | 80 | 200 |
| 1839 Proof *FDC* £400 |
1840	10	20	80	225
1841	12	25	85	250
1842	10	20	80	225
1843	10	20	80	225
1844 Small 44	10	20	75	210
1844 Large 44	15	30	90	250
1845	10	20	80	225
1846	10	20	75	210
1848	30	85	325	775
1848/6 or 7	40	100	375	825
1850	10	20	80	225
1850/3	15	30	115	300
1851	10	20	80	225

| 1852 | 8 | 20 | 75 | 175 |
| 1853 | 7 | 20 | 75 | 150 |
| 1853 Proof *FDC* £450 |
1854	100	250	550	1250
1855	8	18	75	210
1855/3	12	25	85	250
1855 Proof *FDC*		*Extremely rare*
1856	8	18	80	225
1857	8	18	80	225
1858	8	18	80	225
1858 Proof *FDC*		*Extremely rare*
1859	7	14	75	225
1859/8	10	20	80	225
1860	10	20	80	225
1862	60	150	350	850
1863	50	90	225	650
1866		*Extremely rare*

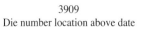

3909
Die number location above date

3912
Type 'A5' Sixpence

3909 Sixpence. Type A[2]. First head, R. Similar die number above date die axis ↑↓

| 1864 | 8 | 15 | 75 | 215 | 1866 | 8 | 15 | 75 | 215 |
| 1865 | 9 | 18 | 85 | 250 |

	F	VF	EF	UNC		F	VF	EF	UNC
	£	£	£	£		£	£	£	£

3910 Sixpence. Type A^3. Second head, l. R. Similar die number above date die axis ↑↓

	F	VF	EF	UNC		F	VF	EF	UNC
1867	10	18	80	250	1873	7	12	60	210
1867 Proof *FDC* £1350					1874	7	12	60	210
1868	10	18	80	250	1875	7	12	60	210
1869	10	20	110	300	1876	10	18	85	275
1869 Proof *FDC* £1600					1877	7	12	60	210
1870	10	20	110	300	1878	7	12	60	210
1870 plain edge Proof *FDC* £1600					1878 DRITANNIAR.	50	125	500	—
1871	8	15	65	215	1878 Proof *FDC* £1350				
1871 plain edge Proof *FDC* £1350					1878/7	35	100	450	—
1872	7	15	65	215	1879	10	18	85	275

3911 Sixpence. Type A^4. Second head, l. R. Similar No die number die axis ↑↓

	F	VF	EF	UNC		F	VF	EF	UNC
1871	8	16	75	225	1879 milled edge Proof *FDC* £1350				
1871 Proof *FDC* £1250					1879 plain edge Proof *FDC* £1600				
1877	7	15	65	210	1880	8	16	75	215
1879	7	15	65	210					

3912 Sixpence. Type A^5. Third head l. R. Similar die axis ↑↓

	F	VF	EF	UNC		F	VF	EF	UNC
1880	6	10	50	125	1883 plain edge Proof *FDC* *Extremely rare*				
1880 Proof *FDC* £1500					1884	6	10	45	110
1881	6	10	45	110	1885	6	10	45	110
1881 plain edge Proof *FDC* *Extremely rare*					1885 Proof *FDC* £1350				
1881 milled edge Proof *FDC* *Extremely rare*					1886	6	10	45	110
1882	10	30	80	250	1886 Proof *FDC* £1350				
1883	6	10	45	110	1887	6	12	40	100
1883 Small R legend	15	35	95	275	1887 Proof *FDC* £850				

3913 Groat (4d.). Young head l.R. Britannia seated r. date in ex, edge milled, die axis ↑↓

	F	VF	EF	UNC		F	VF	EF	UNC
1837 Proof only *FDC* of highest rarity					1846	6	14	45	120
1838	4	10	40	110	1847/6 (or 8)	25	80	375	—
1838 plain edge Proof *FDC* £750					1848/6	10	30	75	150
1838/∞	6	20	50	165	1848	3	12	40	110
1839	5	12	40	110	1848/7	10	28	90	250
1839 die axis ↑↑ Proof *FDC* £300					1849	5	12	40	110
1839 die axis ↑↓ Proof *FDC* £375					1849/8	7	14	45	120
1840	5	12	40	110	1851	20	70	200	525
1840 small round o	8	18	45	135	1852	35	100	275	625
1841	6	14	50	120	1853	40	120	325	725
1842	6	14	45	120	1853 Proof *FDC* milled edge £475				
1842 Proof *FDC* £700					1853 Proof *FDC* plain edge *Extremely rare*				
1842/1	8	18	50	165	1854	5	12	35	95
1843	6	14	45	120	1855	5	12	35	95
1843 4 over 5	10	22	55	175	1857 Proof only *FDC* £1100				
1844	6	14	45	120	1862 Proof only *FDC*. *Extremely rare*				
1845	6	14	45	120					

	F	VF	EF	UNC		F	VF	EF	UNC
	£	£	£	£		£	£	£	£

3914 Threepence. Type A^1. First bust, young head, high relief, ear fully visible. Dei axis ↑↓
R Crowned 3; as Maundy threepence but with a less prooflike surface.

	F	VF	EF	UNC		F	VF	EF	UNC
1838*...................... 10	25	60	125		1851 10	18	60	135
1838 BRITANNIAB ...		*Extremely rare*			1851 5 over 8 18	40	110	—
1839*...................... 10	30	75	175		1852* 60	175	500	—
1839 Proof (see Maundy)					1853 18	40	85	200
1840*...................... 10	28	70	150		1854 10	18	60	125
1841*...................... 10	30	75	175		1855 10	30	75	175
1842*...................... 10	30	75	175		1856 10	18	55	120
1843*...................... 10	25	60	125		1857 10	30	75	175
1844*...................... 10	30	75	175		1858 10	18	55	120
1845.......................... 8	15	45	100		1858 BRITANNIAB ..		*Extremely rare*	
1846...................... 15	25	85	200		1858/6 18	35	110	—
1847*...................... 50	150	350	750		1858/5 15	30	90	—
1848*...................... 40	125	325	700		1859 10	18	55	120
1849...................... 10	30	75	175		1860 10	30	75	175
1850.......................... 8	15	50	90		1861 10	18	55	120

*Issued for Colonial use only.

3914A	3914C
Type A2	Type A4

3914A Threepence. Type A^2. First bust variety, slightly older portrait with aquiline nose ↑↓

	F	VF	EF	UNC		F	VF	EF	UNC
1859.......................... 8	15	55	110		1865 8	18	75	150
1860.......................... 8	15	55	110		1866 8	15	55	110
1861.......................... 8	15	55	110		1867 8	15	55	110
1862...................... 15	25	55	110		1868 8	15	55	110
1863...................... 18	35	75	150		1868 RRITANNIAR ..		*Extremely rare*	
1864.......................... 8	15	55	110					

3914B Threepence. Type A^3. Second Bust, slightly larger, lower relief, mouth fuller,
nose more pronounced, rounded truncation die axis ↑↓

	F	VF	EF	UNC
1867.. 8	25	75	150

3914C Threepence. Type A^4. Obv. as last. R. Tie ribbon further from tooth border, cross on
crown nearer to tooth border die axis ↑↓

	F	VF	EF	UNC		F	VF	EF	UNC
1866		*Extremely rare*			1874 5	12	40	70
1867.......................... 8	30	75	150		1875 5	12	40	70
1868.......................... 8	30	75	150		1876 5	12	40	70
1869...................... 15	30	85	175		1877 6	15	50	80
1870.......................... 6	18	60	100		1878 6	15	50	80
1871.......................... 8	20	65	125		1879 6	15	50	80
1872.......................... 8	20	65	125		1879 Proof *FDC*........		*Extremely rare*	
1873.......................... 4	10	40	70		1884 4	8	35	60

3914D Threepence. Type A^5. Third bust, older features, mouth closed, hair strands
leading from 'bun' vary, die axis ↑↓

	F	VF	EF	UNC		F	VF	EF	UNC
1880.......................... 4	10	45	75		1885 3	6	30	60
1881.......................... 3	6	30	60		1885 Proof *FDC*........		*Extremely rare*	
1882.......................... 5	10	55	110		1886 3	6	30	60
1883.......................... 3	6	30	60		1887 4	10	45	75

3914E Twopence. Young head 1. R Date divided by a crowned 2 within a wreath, die axis ↑↓

	F	VF	EF	UNC		F	VF	EF	UNC
1838.......................... 3	7	20	50		1848 5	10	25	60

3915 - Three-Halfpence

	F	VF	EF	UNC		F	VF	EF	UNC
	£	£	£	£		£	£	£	£

3915 Three-Halfpence. (for Colonial use).Young head 1. R̥. Crowned value and date, die axis ↑↓

	F	VF	EF	UNC		F	VF	EF	UNC
1838	5	12	35	75	1843 Proof *FDC*		*Extremely rare*		
1838 Proof *FDC* £500.					1843/34	8	20	80	175
1839	4	10	30	70	1843/34 Proof *FDC*		*Extremely rare*		
1840	8	22	75	150	1860	6	18	60	125
1841	5	14	40	90	1862	6	18	60	125
1842	5	14	40	90	1862 Proof *FDC* £650				
1843	4	6	25	65	1870 Proof only £650				

3916 - 1880 Maundy Set

3916 Maundy Set. (4d., 3d., 2d. and 1.) Young head 1., die axis ↑↓

1838	125	275		1864		110	225
1838 Proof *FDC* £1000				1865		110	225
1838 Proof in gold *FDC* £15000				1866		100	220
1839	120	250		1867		100	220
1839 Proof die axis ↑↑ *FDC* £400				1867 Proof set *FDC* £600		
1840	135	300		1868		100	220
1841	140	325		1869		110	250
1842	120	250		1870		100	200
1843	120	250		1871		85	175
1844	130	300		1871 Proof set *FDC* £600		
1845	110	240		1872		85	175
1846	150	400		1873		85	175
1847	130	325		1874		85	175
1848	140	300		1875		85	175
1849	140	300		1876		85	175
1850	100	275		1877		85	175
1851	100	250		1878		95	200
1852	110	275		1878 Proof set *FDC* £600		
1853	135	300		1879		85	175
1853 Proof *FDC* £500				1880		85	175
1854	110	250		1881		85	175
1855	110	250		1881 Proof set *FDC* £600		
1856	110	225		1882		85	175
1857	110	225		1882 Proof set *FDC* £600		
1858	100	200		1883		85	175
1859	100	200		1884		85	175
1860	100	200		1885		85	175
1861	110	225		1886		85	175
1862	110	225		1887		95	200
1863	110	225					

			F	VF	EF	UNC
3917 — **Fourpence**, 1838-87		*from*			10	25
3918 — **Threepence**, 1838-87		*from*			15	40
3919 — **Twopence**, 1838-87		*from*			8	20
3920 — **Penny**, 1838-87		*from*			7	15

Maundy Sets in good quality original cases are worth approximately £15 more than the prices quoted.

Jubilee Coinage 1887-93, die axis ↑↑

3921
1887 Crown

	F	VF	EF	UNC		F	VF	EF	UNC
	£	£	£	£		£	£	£	£

3921 Crown. Jubilee bust l. R. St. George and dragon,date in ex, edge milled, die axis ↑↑

	F	VF	EF	UNC		F	VF	EF	UNC
1887......................... 15	25	60	140		1889..................... 15	25	70	200
1887 Proof *FDC* £500					1890..................... 15	30	95	225
1888 narrow date..... 20	35	95	225		1891..................... 15	40	120	300
1888 wide date 60	175	475	—		1892..................... 20	45	150	350

3922 Double-Florin (4s.).Jubilee bust l. R. (As Florin) Crowned cruciform shields. Septre in angles. Roman I in date, die axis ↑↑

		F	VF	EF	UNC
1887.. 12			20	45	100

1887 Proof *FDC* £350

3923	3924
1887 Double-Florin	1887 Halfcrown
Arabic 1 in date	

3923 Double-Florin Jubilee bust l. R. Similar but Arabic 1 in date, die axis ↑↑

	F	VF	EF	UNC		F	VF	EF	UNC
1887....................... 12	20	45	90		1889 12	20	55	110
1887 Proof *FDC* £275					1889 inverted 1 for I in			
1888....................... 12	20	60	130		VICTORIA.... 25	60	175	385
1888 inverted 1 for I in					1890 12	20	60	120
VICTORIA...... 25	60	175	385					

3924 Halfcrown. Jubilee bust l. R. Crowned shield in garter and collar, die axis ↑↑

	F	VF	EF	UNC		F	VF	EF	UNC
1887......................... 7	12	25	60		1890....................... 10	20	60	150
1887 Proof *FDC* £150					1891....................... 10	20	65	160
1888....................... 10	15	45	130		1892....................... 10	20	75	175
1889....................... 10	20	45	130					

3925
Florin

	F	VF	EF	UNC		F	VF	EF	UNC
	£	£	£	£		£	£	£	£

3925 Florin. Jubilee bust 1. R. Crowned cruciform shields, sceptres in angles, die axis ↑↑

1887........................... 5	10	20	55		1890........................ 10	30	100	325
1887 Proof *FDC* £120					1891........................ 25	65	175	450
1888 obverse die of 1887 . 10	30	75	150		1892........................ 25	65	175	525
1888........................... 7	15	35	85		1892 Proof *FDC* £2000			
1889........................... 8	25	50	125					

3926
small head Shilling

3926 Shilling. Small Jubilee head. R. Crowned shield in Garter, die axis ↑↑

1887...........................3	8	14	30		1888/7 5	10	25	75
1887 Proof *FDC* £90					1889 35	90	300	485

3927 Shilling. Large Jubilee head. R. Similar as before, die axis ↑↑

1889...........................5	9	30	80		1891 5	15	40	90
1889 Proof *FDC* £900					1891 Proof *FDC* £1500			
1890...........................5	10	35	85		1892 5	15	40	90

3928
1887 'withdrawn type' Sixpence

3928 Sixpence. JEB designer's initials below trun. R. Shield in Garter (withdrawn type), die axis ↑↑

1887...........................2	6	12	25		1887 JEB on trun. .. 15	45	100	215
1887 Proof *FDC* £80					1887 R/V in			
					VICTORIA.... 10	35	80	185

3929
Sixpence

3930
1888 Groat

	F	VF	EF	UNC		F	VF	EF	UNC
	£	£	£	£		£	£	£	£

3929 Sixpence. R. Jubilee bust 1. Crowned, value in wreath, die axis ↑↑

	F	VF	EF	UNC		F	VF	EF	UNC
1887.............................2	6	12	30	1890 4	10	20	65
1887 Proof *FDC* £650				1890 Proof *FDC*.........	*Extremely rare*		
1888.............................4	10	20	60	1891 6	15	25	70
1888 Proof *FDC* £1250				1892 8	20	30	90
1889.............................4	10	20	60	1893 300	700	2350	—

3930 Groat (for use in British Guiana). Jubilee Bust 1. R. Britannia seated r. date in axis, die axis ↑↑

1888 Proof *FDC* £775				1888 10	25	50	110

3931 Threepence. As Maundy but less prooflike surface, die axis ↑↑

1887.......................... —	1	5	12	1890 1	3	10	20
1887 Proof *FDC* £50				1891 2	4	12	25
1888.............................2	5	15	30	1892 2	5	15	30
1889.............................1	3	10	20	1893 15	40	100	250

3932
1888 Maundy Set

	EF	FDC		EF	FDC
	£	£		£	£

3932 Maundy Set. (4d., 3d., 2d. and 1d.) Jubilee bust 1.die axis ↑↑

1888..90	140	1890	90	140
1888 Proof set *FDC* .... *Extremely rare*	1891	90	140
1889..90	140	1892	90	140
3933 — Fourpence, 1888-92 ....*from*	10	20
3934 — Threepence, 1888-92 ....*from*	15	25
3935 — Twopence, 1888-92 ....*from*	8	15
3936 — Penny, 1888-92 ....*from*	8	15

Maundy Sets in the original undamaged cases are worth approximately £15 more than the prices quoted.

Old Head Coinage 1893-1901, die axis ↑↑

3937
1893 Old Head Crown

	F	VF	EF	UNC
	£	£	£	£

3937 Crown. Old veiled bust l. R. St. George. date in ex. Regnal date on edge, die axis ↑↑

	F	VF	EF	UNC
1893 edge LVI	15	30	150	325
1893 Proof *FDC* £600				
1893 LVII	25	75	275	550
1894 LVII	15	40	190	475
1894 LVIII	15	40	190	475
1895 LVIII	15	35	165	425
1895 LIX	15	35	150	400
1896 LIX	20	65	275	550
1896 LX	15	35	165	425
1897 LX	15	35	140	375
1897 LXI	15	35	140	375
1898 LXI	25	70	275	550
1898 LXII	15	40	165	450
1899 LXII	15	40	150	425
1899 LXIII	15	40	185	475
1900 LXIII	15	40	150	425
1900 LXIV	15	40	150	400

3938
Halfcrown

	F	VF	EF	UNC		F	VF	EF	UNC
	£	£	£	£		£	£	£	£

3938 Halfcrown. Old veiled bust l. R. Shield in collar, edge milled, die axis ↑↑

	F	VF	EF	UNC		F	VF	EF	UNC
1893	8	15	40	90	1897	8	15	45	110
1893 Proof *FDC* £190					1898	10	18	55	125
1894	10	20	80	185	1899	10	16	45	110
1895	9	18	65	150	1900	10	16	50	120
1896	9	18	65	150	1901	10	16	45	100

3938A Small reverse design with long border teeth

	F	VF	EF	UNC
1896	12	25	95	240

3939
Old Head Florin

	F	VF	EF	UNC		F	VF	EF	UNC
	£	£	£	£		£	£	£	£

3939 Florin. Old veiled bust l. R. Three shields within garter, die axis ↑↑

	F	VF	EF	UNC		F	VF	EF	UNC
1893	7	15	40	80	1897	6	12	40	90
1893 Proof *FDC* £140					1898	6	15	45	110
1894	10	20	60	160	1899	6	12	45	100
1895	7	18	55	135	1900	6	12	40	80
1896	7	15	45	135	1901	6	12	40	85

3940A
1901 Shilling

3941
1897 Sixpence

3940 Shilling. Old veiled bust l. R. Three shields within Garter, small rose, die axis ↑↑

	F	VF	EF	UNC		F	VF	EF	UNC
1893	5	10	25	65	1894	7	15	35	95
1893 small lettering	5	10	25	65	1895	10	20	50	120
1893 Proof *FDC* £95...					1896	8	15	35	95

3940A Shilling. Old veiled bust l. R. Second reverse, larger rose, die axis ↑↑

	F	VF	EF	UNC		F	VF	EF	UNC
1895	5	10	30	75	1899	5	10	30	75
1896	5	10	25	70	1900	5	10	30	70
1897	5	10	25	70	1901	5	10	25	70
1898	5	10	25	70					

3941 Sixpence. Old veiled bust l. R. Value in wreath, die axis ↑↑

	F	VF	EF	UNC		F	VF	EF	UNC
1893	5	8	18	50	1897	6	10	20	50
1893 Proof *FDC* £65					1898	6	10	20	55
1894	8	12	25	75	1899	6	10	20	55
1895	6	10	20	60	1900	6	10	20	50
1896	6	10	20	55	1901	5	8	15	45

3942 Threepence. Old veiled bust l. R. Crowned 3. As Maundy but less prooflike surface, die axis ↑↑

	F	VF	EF	UNC		F	VF	EF	UNC
1893	1	2	7	35	1897	1	2	6	18
1893 Proof *FDC* £40					1898	1	2	7	22
1894	1	3	10	35	1899	1	2	7	22
1895	1	3	10	25	1900	1	2	5	15
1896	1	2	10	25	1901	1	2	6	18

3943
1899 Maundy Set

	EF	FDC			EF	FDC
	£	£			£	£

3943 Maundy Set. (4d., 3d., 2d. and 1d.) Old veiled bust l., die axis ↑↑

	EF	FDC		EF	FDC
1893.......................	70	100	1897	75	100
1893 Proof from 1893 proof set FDC £85			1898	75	100
1894.......................	75	110	1899	80	110
1895.......................	75	100	1900	80	110
1896.......................	75	100	1901	75	100

			EF	FDC
3944 — Fourpence. 1893-1901 ....*from*			6	12
3945 — Threepence. 1893-1901 ....*from*			12	22
3946 — Twopence. 1893-1901 ....*from*			6	12
3947 — Penny. 1893-1901..*from*			6	18

Maundy Sets in the original undamaged cases are worth approximately £10 more than the prices quoted.

COPPER AND BRONZE

Young Head Copper Coinage, 1838-60, die axis ↑↑

3948
Penny
Rev. with ornamental trident prongs (OT)

	F	VF	EF	UNC		F	VF	EF	UNC
	£	£	£	£		£	£	£	£

3948 Penny. Young head l. date below R. Britannia seated r.

	F	VF	EF	UNC		F	VF	EF	UNC
1839 Bronzed proof *FDC* £1100					1845 OT	15	30	150	450
1841 Rev. OT 5	10	80	300		1846 OT	10	20	110	350
1841 Proof *FDC* £1250					1846 OT colon close .				
1841 Silver Proof *FDC* £3500					to DEF...........	15	25	125	400
1841 OT. no colon					1847 — — 8	15	90	250
after REG 5	10	80	450		1847 OT DEF—:......8	15	90	250
1843 OT. —..............65	275	1250	2950		1848/7 OT 5	15	85	225
1843 OT REG: 35	140	1000	2500		1848 OT 5	15	90	225
1844 OT 10	15	85	225		1848/6 OT 20	75	400	—
1844 Proof *FDC* £1500					1849 OT 160	425	1600	2450

	F	VF	EF	UNC		F	VF	EF	UNC
	£	£	£	£		£	£	£	£
1851 OT	10	20	110	425	1856 Proof *FDC* £1250				
1851 OT DEF:........	10	20	110	350	1856 OT DEF—:......	70	225	625	1550
1853 OT DEF—:......	5	12	75	180	1857 OT DEF—:......	8	15	85	210
1853 Proof *FDC* £550					1857 PT DEF:	5	10	75	225
1853 Plain trident, (PT)					1858 OT DEF—:......	5	10	75	175
DEF:	10	20	95	325	1858/7 — —	5	10	80	200
1854 PT	5	12	75	180	1858/3	25	75	400	—
1854/3 PT	12	25	110	350	1858 no ww on trun	5	15	85	225
1854 OT DEF—:......	8	15	80	210	1859	5	10	75	210
1855 OT —	5	12	75	180	1859 Proof *FDC* £2000				
1855 PT DEF:	5	12	75	180	1860/59	200	650	2250	4000
1856 PT DEF:	65	175	450	1300					

3949

1845 Halfpenny

3949 Halfpenny. Young head l. date below R. Britannia seated r., die axis ↑↑   1853 Rev. incuse dots

	F	VF	EF	UNC		F	VF	EF	UNC
1838............................	5	12	45	130	1852 Rev. normal shield ...	8	18	55	160
1839 Bronzed proof FDC £300					1853 dots on shield........	3	8	30	105
1841	4	10	40	120	1853 — Proof FDC £225				
1841 — Proof FDC £800					1853/2 —	15	35	105	285
1841 Silver proof FDC		*Extremely rare*			1854 —	3	8	30	105
1843	25	45	115	385	1855 —	3	8	30	105
1844	6	15	50	140	1856 —	5	15	55	150
1845	65	150	675	—	1857 —	4	10	40	110
1846	8	18	55	150	1857 Rev. normal				
1847	8	18	55	150	shield	4	10	40	110
1848	20	50	120	275	1858 —	5	10	45	130
1848/7	12	30	85	200	1858/7 —	5	10	45	130
1851	5	15	50	140	1858/6 —	5	10	45	130
1851 Rev. incuse dots ..					1859 —	5	10	45	130
on shield.............	5	15	50	140	1859/8 —	10	20	75	225
1852 Similar...............	8	18	55	160	1860 —	750	2000	4500	—

Overstruck dates are listed only if commoner than normal date, or if no normal date is known.

*These 1860 large copper pieces are not to be confused with the smaller and commoner bronze issue with date on reverse (nos. 3954, 3956 and 3958).

3950
1849 Farthing

	F	VF	EF	UNC		F	VF	EF	UNC
	£	£	£	£		£	£	£	£

3950 Farthing. Young head l. date below R. Britannia seated r. die axis ↑↑

	F	VF	EF	UNC		F	VF	EF	UNC
1838 WW raised on trun.	5	10	40	110	1850 5/4	10	30	85	260
1839	4	8	40	95	1851	10	20	65	175
1839 Bronzed Proof *FDC* £275					1851 D/Ↄ in DEI	75	175	400	650
1839 Silver Proof *FDC*		*Extremely rare*			1852	10	20	65	175
1839 Copper Proof *FDC* £400					1853	5	10	45	110
1840	4	8	40	95	1853 WW incuse				
1841	4	8	40	95	on trun	10	30	95	285
1841 Proof *FDC*		*Extremely rare*			1853 Proof *FDC* £400				
1842	15	35	115	285	1854	5	10	40	90
1843/2	10	30	85	235	1855	5	10	50	120
1843	4	8	40	100	1855 WW raised	8	15	55	130
1843 I for 1 in date	50	275	650	1300	1856 WW incuse	8	20	60	175
1844	65	140	650	1300	1856 R/E in				
1845	8	10	45	110	VICTORIA	15	40	150	300
1846	8	15	60	150	1857	5	10	45	110
1847	5	10	45	110	1858	5	10	40	110
1848	5	10	45	110	1859	10	20	65	175
1849	40	75	295	—	1860	825	2000	4500	
1850	5	10	45	110	1864 IWW on truncation		*Extremely rare*		

3951	3952	3953
Half-Farthing	Third-Farthing	Quarter-Farthing

3951 Half-Farthing. Young head l. R. Crowned Value and date, die axis ↑↑

	F	VF	EF	UNC		F	VF	EF	UNC
1839	5	10	40	110	1852	4	10	45	105
1839 Bronzed proof *FDC* £350					1853	5	15	50	145
1842	5	10	40	110	1853 Proof *FDC* £350				
1843		5	30	80	1854	8	25	90	225
1844		3	25	70	1856	8	25	90	225
1844 E/N in REGINA	10	20	75	210	1856 Large date	50	110	275	625
1847	4	8	30	95	1868 Proof *FDC* £450				
1851 5/0	10	20	85	195	1868 Cupro nickel Proof *FDC* £600				
1851	5	10	45	105					

3952 Third-Farthing (for use in Malta). Young head l. date below R. Britannia seated r. die axis ↑↑

	F	VF	EF	UNC		F	VF	EF	UNC
1844	20	35	95	235	1844 RE for REG	30	65	325	725

3953 Quarter-Farthing (for use in Ceylon). Young head l. R. Crowned Value and date, die axis ↑↑

	F	VF	EF	UNC		F	VF	EF	UNC
1839	10	18	45	110	1853	10	20	55	130
1851	10	20	50	130	1853 Proof *FDC* £700				
1852	10	18	45	110	1868 Proof *FDC* £500				
1852 Proof *FDC* £500					1868 Cupro-nickel Proof *FDC* £600				

Copper coins graded in this catalogue as UNC have full mint lustre.

Bronze Coinage, "Bun Head" Issue, 1860-95, die axis ↑↑

When studying an example of the bronze coinage, if the minutiae of the variety is not evident due to wear from circulation, then the coin will not be of any individual significance. Proofs exist of most years and are generally extremely rare for all denominations.

3954 The Bronze Penny. The bronze coinage is the most complicated of the milled series from the point of view of the large number of different varieties of obverse and reverse and their combinations. Below are set out good illustrations with explanations of all the varieties. The obverse and reverse types listed below reflect those as listed originally by C W Peck in his British Museum Catalogue of Copper, Tin and Bronze Coinage 1558-1958, and later in "the Bronze Coinage of the United Kingdom" by Michael J Freeman which gives much fuller and detailed explanations of the types. Reference can also be compared to "The British Bronze Penny" by Michael Gouby.

OBVERSES

Obverse 1 (1860) - laureate and draped bust facing left, hair tied in bun, wreath of 15 leaves and 4 berries, L C WYON raised on base of bust, beaded border and thin linear circle.

Obverse 1* (1860) - laureate and draped bust facing left, hair tied in bun, more bulging lowered eye with more rounded forehead, wreath of 15 leaves and 4 berries, which are weaker in part, L C WYON raised on base of bust, beaded border and thin linear circle.

Obverse 2 (1860-62) - laureate and draped bust facing left, hair tied in bun, wreath of 15 leaves and 4 berries, L C WYON raised lower on base of bust and clear of border, toothed border and thin linear circle both sides.

Obverse 3 (1860-61) - laureate and draped bust facing left, hair tied in bun, complete rose to drapery, wreath of 15 leaves and 4 berries, two leaves have incuse outlines, L C WYON raised on base of bust nearly touches border, toothed border and thin linear circle both sides.

OBVERSES *(continued)*

Obverse 4 (1860-61) - laureate and draped
bust facing left, hair tied in bun, finer hair
strands at nape of neck, wreath of 15 leaves
and 4 berries, two leaves have incuse outlines,
L C WYON below bust, nearly touches border,
toothed border of shorter teeth, and thin linear
circle both sides.

Obverse 5 (1860-61) - laureate and draped
bust facing left, hair tied in bun, finer hair
strands at nape of neck, wreath of 15 leaves
and 4 berries, leaf veins incuse, two leaves
have incuse outlines, no signature below bust,
toothed border and thin linear circle both sides.

Obverse 6 (1860-74) - laureate and draped
bust facing left, hair tied in bun, finer hair
strands at nape of neck, wreath of 16 leaves,
leaf veins raised, no signature, toothed border
and thin linear circle both sides.

Obverse 7 (1874) - laureate and draped bust
facing left, hair tied in bun, finer hair strands
at nape of neck, wreath of 17 leaves, leaf veins
raised, 6 berries, no signature, toothed border
and thin linear circle both sides.

OBVERSES *(continued)*

Obverse 8 (1874-79) - laureate and draped bust facing left, hair tied in bun, with close thicker ties to ribbons, wreath of 17 leaves, leaf veins raised, 6 berries, no signature, toothed border and thin linear circle both side.

Obverse 9 (1879-81) - laureate and draped bust facing left, hair tied in bun, with close thicker ties, wreath of 17 leaves, double leaf veins incuse, 6 berries, no signature, toothed border and thin linear circle both side.

Obverse 10 (1880-81) - laureate and draped bust facing left, hair tied in bun, with close thicker ties, wreath of 15 leaves, leaf veins raised and recessed, 4 berries, no signature, toothed border and thin linear circle both side.

Obverse 11 (1881-83) - laureate and draped bust facing left, more hooked nose, hair tied in bun, with close thicker ties, nose more hooked, wreath of 15 leaves, leaf veins raised, 4 berries, no signature, toothed border and thin linear circle both sides, weak circle on obverse.

OBVERSES *(continued)*

Obverse 12 (1881-94) - laureate and draped bust facing left, hair tied in bun, with close thicker ties, no curls at nape of neck, nose more hooked, wreath of 15 leaves, leaf veins raised, 4 berries, no signature, toothed border, more numerous teeth, and thin linear circle both sides, weak on obverse, larger lettering.

Obverse 13 (1889) - laureate and draped bust facing left, hair tied in bun, with close thicker ties, no curls at nape of neck, nose more hooked, wreath of 14 leaves, leaf veins raised, no signature, toothed border and thin linear circle both sides, larger lettering.

REVERSES

Reverse A (1860) - Britannia seated right on rocks with shield and trident, crosses on shield outlined with double raised lines, L.C.W. incuse below shield, date below in exergue, lighthouse with 4 windows to left, ship sailing to right, beaded border and linear circle.

Reverse B (1860) - Britannia with one incuse hemline, seated right on rocks with shield and trident, crosses on shield outlined with treble incuse lines, L.C.W. incuse below shield, date below in exergue, lighthouse with 4 windows to left, ship sailing to right, beaded border and linear circle.

REVERSES (*continued*)

Reverse C (1860) - Britannia seated right on rocks with shield and trident, crosses on shield outlined with wider spaced thinner double raised lines, thumb touches St. George Cross, L.C.W. incuse below shield, date below in exergue, lighthouse with 4 windows to left, rocks touch linear circle, ship sailing to right, beaded border and linear circle.

Reverse D (1860-61) - Britannia seated right on rocks with shield and trident, crosses on shield outlined with wider spaced thinner double raised lines, thumb touches St. George Cross, L.C.W. incuse below shield, date below in exergue, lighthouse with 4 windows to left, rocks touch linear circle, ship sailing to right, toothed border.

Reverse E (1860) - Britannia seated right on rocks with thick rimmed shield and trident, crosses on shield outlined with wider spaced thinner double raised lines, thumb touches St. George Cross, L.C.W. incuse below foot, date below in exergue, lighthouse with sharper masonry to left, rocks touch linear circle, ship sailing to right, toothed border.

Reverse F (1861) - Britannia seated right on rocks with thick rimmed shield and trident, incuse lines on breastplate, crosses on shield outlined with wider spaced thinner double raised lines, thumb touches St. George Cross, no L.C.W. extra rocks, date below in exergue, lighthouse with rounded top and sharp masonry, three horizontal lines between masonry and top, rocks touch linear circle, ship sailing to right, toothed border.

REVERSES *(continued)*

Reverse G (1861-75) - Britannia seated right on rocks with convex shield and trident, no signature, date below in exergue, bell-topped lighthouse to left, lamp area depicted with five vertical lines, no rocks to left, sea crosses linear circle, ship sailing to right, toothed border.

Reverse H (1874-75, 1877) - Britannia seated right on rocks, smaller head, thinner neck, with convex shield and trident, no signature, narrow date below in exergue, tall thin lighthouse to left with 6 windows, lamp area of four vertical lines, close date numerals, tiny rock to left, sea touches linear circle, ship sailing to right, toothed border.

Reverse I (1874) - Britannia seated right on rocks with convex shield and trident, thick trident shaft, no signature, narrow date below in exergue, thicker lighthouse to left with 4 windows, lamp area of four vertical lines, close date numerals, tiny rock to left, sea touches linear circle, ship sailing to right, toothed border.

Reverse J (1875-81) - larger Britannia seated right on rocks with shield and trident, left leg more visible, wider date below in deeper exergue, lighthouse to left, ship sailing to right, sea does not meet linear circle either side, toothed border.

REVERSES (*continued*)

Reverse K (1876, 1879) - Britannia with larger head seated right on rocks with convex shield and trident, thicker helmet, no signature, narrow date and in exergue, tall thin lighthouse to left, tiny rock to left, sea touches linear circle, ship sailing to right, toothed border.

Reverse L (1880) - Britannia seated right on rocks with shield and trident, extra feather to helmet plume, trident with three rings above hand, date below in exergue, lighthouse with cluster of rocks to left, ship sailing to right, toothed border.

Reverse M (1881-82) - larger Britannia seated right on rocks with shield and trident, flatter shield heraldically coloured, date and H below in exergue, lighthouse to left with faint masonry, ship sailing to right, sea does not meet linear circle, toothed border.

Reverse N (1881-94) - thinner Britannia seated right on rocks with shield and thinner trident, helmet plume ends in a single strand, shield heraldically coloured with different thickness crosses, date in exergue, thinner lighthouse to left, ship sailing to right, sea meets linear circle, toothed border with more teeth.

Reverse O (1882 - proof only) – larger Britannia seated right on rocks withshield and trident, flatter shield heraldically coloured, date and H in exergue, lighthouse to left with faint masonry, ship sailing to right, sea meets linear circle, toothed border with more teeth.

3954
Penny

	F	£	£	£		£	£	£	£
		£	£	£		£	£	£	£

3954 Penny. Laur. bust l. R. Britannia seated r. date in ex. lighthouse l. ship to r., die axis ↑↑

	F	£	£	£		£	£	£	£
1860 obv 1, rev A 75		140	400	1100	1866 obv 6, rev G 5		15	75	325
1860 obv 1, rev B 20		45	150	650	1867 obv 6, rev G 8		30	150	650
1860 obv 1*, rev A 150		450	900	1650	1868 obv 6, rev G 15		35	160	725
1860 obv 1, rev C 65		125	425	1300	1869 obv 6, rev G 90		350	950	2500
1860 obv 1*, rev C 120		425	800	1400	1870 obv 6, rev G 12		25	125	475
1860 obv 1, rev D 425		800	1650	2800	1871 obv 6, rev G 40		110	450	1100
1860 obv 2, rev A 425		800	1650	2800	1872 obv 6, rev G 5		15	65	300
1860 obv 2, rev D 5		15	50	250	1873 obv 6, rev G 5		15	65	300
1860 — heavy flan ...... —		—	—	1500	1874 obv 6, rev G 5		15	90	475
1860 N/Z in ONE, 2+D 75		250	450	850	1874 obv 7, rev G 10		35	100	375
1860 obv 3, rev D 5		15	60	250	1874 obv 8, rev G 25		55	150	625
1860 obv 3, rev E 150		350	650	1300	1874 obv 8 rev H 20		50	120	575
1860 obv 4, rev D 2		10	60	300	1874 obv 6, rev H 30		80	300	650
1860 obv 5, rev D 10		45	150	500	1874 obv 7, rev H 10		35	100	375
1860 obv 6, rev D 35		125	325	750	1875 obv 8, rev G 20		60	180	450
1861 obv 2, rev D 75		175	350	900	1875 obv 8, rev H 3		10	50	275
1861 obv 2, rev F 120		250	700	1250	1875 obv 8, rev J 5		15	65	300
1861 obv 2, rev G 30		110	285	700	1877 obv 8, rev J 2		10	60	275
1861 obv 3, rev D 275		550	1100	1900	1877 obv 8, rev H 1000		—	—	—
1861 obv 4, rev D 3		15	65	300	1878 obv 8, rev J 3		15	80	475
1861 — — heavy flan. —		—	—	1500	1879 obv 8, rev J 10		20	105	525
1861 obv 4, rev F 125		325	800	1900	1879 obv 9, rev J 2		7	50	200
1861 obv 4, rev G 40		175	400	1100	1879 obv 9, rev K 30		95	285	900
1861 obv 5, rev D 2		10	60	275	1880 obv 9, rev J 3		15	100	375
1861 obv 5, rev F 500		—	—	—	1880 obv 9, rev L 3		15	100	375
1861 obv 5, rev G 125		350	850	1650	1881 obv 9, rev J 4		15	80	475
1861 obv 6, rev D 2		10	60	250	1881 obv 10, rev J 30		95	285	700
1861 — — — 6 over 8 500		1250	—	—	1881 obv 11, rev J 60		150	400	900
1861 obv 6, rev F 180		500	1000	—	1882* obv 11, rev N .. 750		1450	—	—
1861 obv 6, rev G 2		10	60	275	1883 obv 12, rev N 3		10	60	250
1861 — 8 over 6 450		1000	—	—	1883 obv11, rev N 3		10	60	250
1862 obv 2, rev G 500		1200	1950	2500	1884 obv 12, rev N 2		8	50	175
1862 obv 6, rev G 2		10	60	250	1885 obv 12, rev N 2		8	50	175
1862 — 8 over 6 450		1000	—	—	1886 obv 12, rev N 2		10	50	200
1862 — Halfpenny					1887 obv 12, rev N 2		8	50	175
numerals 600		1750	—	—	1888 obv 12, rev N 2		10	50	200
1863 obv 6, rev G 2		10	60	250	1889 obv 13, rev N 2		8	45	175
1863 Die number below ..950		1850	—	—	1889 obv 12, rev N 4		15	70	350
1863 slender 3 800		—	—	—	1890 obv 12, rev N 2		8	45	175
1864 Upper serif 20		95	500	1750	1891 obv 12, rev N 2		7	40	150
1864 Crosslet 4 25		125	600	1900	1892 obv 12, rev N 2		8	45	175
1865 obv 6, rev G 8		20	125	525	1893 obv 12, rev N 2		8	45	175
1865/3 obv 6, rev G 40		125	375	1000	1894 obv 12, rev N 3		15	65	250

* not to be confused with Heaton Mint

3955
H Mint mark location

	F	VF	EF	UNC		F	VF	EF	UNC
	£	£	£	£		£	£	£	£

3955 Penny. Similar R. Britannia, H Mint mark below date – (struck by Ralph Heaton & Sons, Birmingham)

	F	VF	EF	UNC		F	VF	EF	UNC
1874 H obv 6, rev G......5	20	80	325		1876 H obv 8, rev J........10	30	120	425
1874 H obv 6, rev H....10	30	120	425		1881 H obv 11, rev M.....3	15	60	300
1874 H obv 7, rev G....10	30	100	375		1881 H obv 9, rev M 400	950	1850	—
1874 H obv 7, rev H......5	20	80	325		1882 H obv12,rev M ...10	25	90	475
1874 H obv 7, rev I...150	450	1400	—		1882 H obv 12, rev N 2	10	50	200
1875 H obv 8, rev J.....35	100	675	—		1882/1 H obv 11, rev M.....10	25	80	475
1876 H obv 8, rev K......2	15	65	260					

3956
1860 Halfpenny Beaded border

1860 Beaded border 1	5	45	150		1861 — R. no hemline			
1860 no tie to wreath ...5	15	75	275		to drapery 3	12	65	250
1860 Toothed border ...2	10	55	200		1861 — R. door on ...			
1860 round top light house	15	75	275		lighthouse........1	5	45	150
1860 5 berries in					1861 HALP error . 150	380	—	—
wreath.................4	12	65	250		1861 6 over 8 150	400	—	—
1860 — 15 leaves,					1862 1	4	40	125
4 berries..............3	10	60	175		1862 Die letter to left of lighthouse			
1860 — rounded					A................400	900	1250	2000
lighthouse...........4	12	65	250		B................600	1250	—	—
1860 — Double incuse .					C................600	1250	—	—
leaf veins 5	15	75	275		1863 small 3.............2	6	60	200
1860 — 16 leaves					1863 large 3.............2	6	60	200
wreath...............10	30	110	375		1864 2	10	65	250
1860 TB/BBmule	*Extremely rare*				1865 3	15	75	325
1861 5 berries in					1865/3......................40	100	285	725
wreath...............10	30	100	325		1866 2	10	65	250
1861 15 leaves in					1867 3	15	75	325
wreath................6	20	75	275		1868 2	10	70	275
1861 — R. no hemline .					1869 20	65	275	750
to drapery 10	30	100	325		1870 2	8	60	200
1861 — R. Door on					1871 20	75	275	750
lighthouse...........5	15	75	275		1872 2	7	55	175
1861 4 leaves double					1873 2	10	65	250
incuse veins........2	10	55	175		1873 R. hemline to			
1861 16 leaves wreath ..5	15	75	275		drapery 2	10	65	250
1861 — R. LCW incuse					1874 5	25	120	425
on rock 10	30	100	325		1874 narrow date ...15	50	275	650

	F	VF	EF	UNC		F	VF	EF	UNC
	£	£	£	£		£	£	£	£
1874 older features......5	25	120	425		1885 1	4	45	150
1875............................1	6	55	175		1886 1	4	45	150
1877	1	6	55	175		1887 1	4	45	150
1878............................5	20	100	375		1888 1	4	45	150
1878 wide date 75	150	350	750		1889 1	4	45	150
1879............................1	5	45	150		1889/8 20	40	140	375
1880............................2	7	55	175		1890 1	4	40	125
1881............................2	7	55	175		1891 1	4	40	125
1883............................1	7	55	175		1892 1	6	55	175
1883 rose for brooch obv.	*Extremely rare*				1893 1	4	45	150
1884............................1	4	45	150		1894 1	7	55	175

3957 Halfpenny. Similar R. Britannia, H Mint mark below date (struck by Ralph Heaton & Sons, Birmingham)

	F	VF	EF	UNC		F	VF	EF	UNC
1874 H..........................1	5	55	175		1881 H..........................1	5	55	175
1875 H..........................2	6	60	200		1882 H..........................1	5	55	175
1876 H..........................1	5	55	175					

3958
1860 Farthing

3960
1868 Third-Farthing

3958 Farthing. Laur bust l. R. Britannia seated r. date in ex. lighthouse l. ship to r. die axis ↑↑

	F	VF	EF	UNC		F	VF	EF	UNC
1860 Beaded border	3	25	85		1875 small date 10	25	95	325
1860 Toothed border	5	30	100		1875 —older features..8	20	85	275
1860 — 5 berries.............	3	28	95		1877 Proof only £5750			
1860 TB/BB mule 100	250	500	—		1878	2	20	75
1861 5 berries.................	3	28	95		1879 large 9...............	5	25	95
1861 4 berries.................	4	30	100		1879 normal 9	2	20	80
1862...............................	3	30	95		1880	3	30	100
1862 large 8.................50	125	275	—		1881	2	20	85
1863...........................20	45	175	425		1883 2	10	40	120
1864 4 no serif	5	35	110		1884	1	15	50
1864 4 with serif	8	40	120		1885	1	15	50
1865...............................	3	28	95		1886	1	15	50
1865/2	10	35	140		1887	2	25	80
1866...............................	3	25	95		1888	2	20	75
1867...............................	4	30	105		1890	2	20	75
1868...............................	4	30	105		1891	1	15	65
1869...............................	10	40	140		1892 2	10	40	120
1872...............................	3	28	95		1893	1	15	65
1873...............................	2	28	95		1894	2	18	75
1875 large date 5	10	40	145		1895 10	20	65	170

Bronze coins graded in this catalogue as UNC have full mint lustre

	F	VF	EF	UNC		F	VF	EF	UNC
	£	£	£	£		£	£	£	£

3959 Farthing. Similar R. Britannia. H Mint mark below date (struck by Ralph Heaton & Sons, Birmingham)

	F	VF	EF	UNC		F	VF	EF	UNC
1874 H older features....	5	10	35	110	1876 H large 6........	10	30	75	170
1874 H, Ʊ over sideways					1876 H normal 6.....	5	10	40	120
Ʊ on obv..............	100	250	550	—	1881 H....................	2	5	25	85
1875 H younger features .	75	200	375	750	1882 H....................	2	5	25	85
1875 H older features......		2	15	75					

3960 Third-Farthing (for use in Malta). Laur. head l. R. Crowned date and Value die axis ↑↑

	F	VF	EF	UNC		F	VF	EF	UNC
1866............................	1	3	18	60	1881	2	4	20	70
1868............................	1	3	18	60	1884	1	3	18	60
1876............................	2	4	20	70	1885	1	3	18	60
1878............................	1	3	18	60					

Old Head Issue, 1885-1901, die axis ↑↑

Proofs exist of most years and are generally extremely rare for all denominations

3961
1897 Penny

	VF	EF	UNC		VF	EF	UNC
	£	£	£		£	£	£

3961 Penny. Old veiled bust l. R. Britannia seated r. date in ex., die axis ↑↑

	VF	EF	UNC		VF	EF	UNC
1895............................	2	16	65	1898	4	20	70
1896............................	2	15	55	1899	2	16	60
1897............................	2	15	55	1900	3	12	45
1897 O'NE flawed	75	400	1200	1901	1	10	25

3961 'Normal Tide'
Horizon is level with folds in robe

3961A 'Low Tide'
Horizon is level with hem line of robe

		VF	EF	UNC
3961A Penny. Similar As last but 'Low tide' and 'P' 2mm from trident, 1895.		50	200	650
3961B Penny. Similar, higher tide level above two folds of robe, 1897..........		60	250	750

3962 Halfpenny. Old veiled bust l. R. Britannia seated r. date in ex., die axis ↑↑

	VF	EF	UNC		VF	EF	UNC
1895............................	2	10	45	1898	2	10	45
1896............................	2	8	40	1899	2	8	40
1897............................	2	8	40	1900	2	8	35
1897 Higher tide level.	5	12	45	1901	2	5	25

	VF £	EF £	UNC £		VF £	EF £	UNC £

3963 Farthing. Old veiled bust l. R. Britannia seated r. date in ex. Bright finish, die axis ↑↑

	VF	EF	UNC		VF	EF	UNC
1895	2	5	25	1897	2	5	30
1896	2	5	25				

3962
Old Head Halfpenny

3964
Old Head Farthing

3964 Farthing. Similar Dark finish, die axis ↑↑

	VF	EF	UNC		VF	EF	UNC
1897	2	5	20	1899	2	5	20
1897 Higher tide level.	5	10	30	1900	2	5	20
1898	2	5	20	1901		2	15

Proof Sets

PS3 Young head, **1839.** 'Una and the Lion' Five Pounds, and Sovereign to Farthing
(15 coins) .... *FDC*   £38500

PS4 — **1853.** Sovereign to Half-Farthing, including Gothic type Crown
(16 coins) .... *FDC*   £34500

PS5 Jubilee head. Golden Jubilee, **1887.** Five pounds to Threepence (11 coins). *FDC*   £7750

PS6 — — **1887.** Crown to Threepence (7 coins) .... *FDC*   £1550

PS7 Old head, **1893.** Five Pounds to Threepence (10 coins) .... *FDC*   £9250

PS8 — — **1893.** Crown to Threepence (6 coins) .... *FDC*   £1800

EDWARD VII, 1901-10

'Edward the Peacemaker' was born on 9 November 1841, and married Princess Alexandra of Denmark. He indulged himself in every decadent luxury, while his wife tried to ignore his extra-marital activities. Edward travelled extensively and was crucial in negotiating alliances with Russia and France. Edward VII died on 6 May 1910.

Five Pound pieces, Two Pound pieces and Crowns were only issued in 1902. A branch of the Royal Mint was opened in Canada at Ottawa and coined Sovereigns of imperial type from 1908.

Unlike the coins in most other proof sets, the proofs issued for the Coronation in 1902 have a matt surface in place of the more usual brilliant finish.

Designer's initials: De S. (G. W. De Saulles 1862-1903)
B. P. (Benedetto Pistrucci, d. 1855)

Engravers and Designers: WHJ Blakemore, George William De Saulles (1862-1903), Benedetto Pistrucci (1784-1855)

Prime Ministers:– Earl of Salisbury (1830-1903), Conservative 1895-1902, Arthur James Balfour (1848-1930), Conservative 1902-5, Sir Henry Campbell-Bannerman (1836-1908), Liberal 1905-8, Herbert Henry Asquith (1852-1928), Liberal 1908-16

GOLD

Die axis: ↑↑

3966 - Matt Proof Five Pounds 1902

	EF	UNC		F	VF	EF	UNC
	£	£		£	£	£	£

3965   Five Pounds. Bare head r. R. St. George and dragon, date in ex.

| | | | | 1902 | 450 | 650 | 800 | 1000 |

3966   Five Pounds. Similar Proof. 1902. *Matt surface FDC* £950

3966A   Five Pounds. Similar Proof 1902S. S on ground for Sydney Mint, Australia   *Extremely rare*

3967
1902 Two Pounds

3969
1902 Sovereign

3967   Two Pounds. Bare head r. R. St George and dragon, date in ex.

| | | | | 1902 | 200 | 300 | 450 | 600 |

3968   Two Pounds. Similar Proof. 1902. *Matt surface FDC* £475

3968A   Two Pounds. Similar Proof 1902S. S on ground for Sydney Mint, Australia   *Extremely rare*

3969   Sovereign. Bare head r. R . St. George and dragon, date in ex. London mint, die axis ↑↑

1902 Matt proof *FDC* £200				1906		BV	100	145
1902		BV	100	145	1907		BV	100	145
1903		BV	100	145	1908		BV	100	145
1904		BV	100	145	1909		BV	100	145
1905		BV	100	145	1910		BV	100	145

3970 Sovereign. Similar R. C on ground for Ottawa Mint, Canada

1908 C (Satin proof only) *FDC* £2750		1910 C		95	130	250
1909 C		140	275			

	UNC £		UNC £

3971 Sovereign. Similar R. St. George M on ground for Melbourne Mint, Australia, die axis ↑↑

1902 M	120	1907 M	130
1903 M	120	1908 M	130
1904 M	120	1909 M	130
1905 M	120	1910 M	130
1906 M	120		

3972 Sovereign. Similar R. P on ground for Perth Mint, Australia die axis ↑↑

1902 P	110	1907 P	120
1903 P	120	1908 P	120
1904 P	120	1909 P	120
1905 P	120	1910 P	120
1906 P	120		

3973 Sovereign. Similar R. S on ground for Sydney Mint, Australia die axis ↑↑

1902 S	110	1906 S	120
1902 S Proof	*Extremely rare*	1907 S	120
1903 S	120	1908 S	120
1904 S	135	1909 S	120
1905 S	120	1910 S	120

3974A
1902 Half-Sovereign, no BP in exergue

	F £	VF £	EF £	UNC £		F £	VF £	EF £	UNC £

3974 A Half-Sovereign. Bare head r. R. St. George. London Mint no BP in exergue, die axis ↑↑

1902 Matt proof *FDC* £120									
1902	BV	50	75		1903		BV	50	75
					1904		BV	50	75

3974 B Half-Sovereign. R. Similar with BP in exergue

1904	BV	50	75	1909	BV	50	75
1905	BV	50	75	1910	BV	50	75
1906	BV	50	75				
1907	BV	50	75				
1908	BV	50	75				

3975 Half-Sovereign. Similar R. M on ground for Melbourne Mint, Australia, die axis ↑↑

1906 M	50	100	350	1300	1908 M		BV	75	375
1907 M	BV	60	90	375	1909 M		50	100	425

3976 A Half-Sovereign. — P on ground for Perth Mint, Australia R. no BP in exergue, die axis ↑↑

1904 P	65	165	580	1250

3976 B Half-Sovereign. Similar R. P on ground for Perth Mint, Australia R. with BP in exergue, die axis ↑↑

1904 P	65	165	580	1250	1909 P	60	150	415	1250
1908 P	65	165	500	1575					

3977 A Half-Sovereign. Similar R. S on ground for Sydney Mint, Australia R. No BP in exergue, die axis ↑↑

1902 S	50	95	325	1903 S		BV	100	425
1902 S Proof	*Extremely rare*							

3977 B Half-Sovereign. — S on ground for Sydney Mint, Australia R. with BP in exergue, die axis ↑↑

1906 S	BV	75	300	1910 S	BV	60	150
1908 S	BV	60	150				

SILVER

3978
1902 Crown

	F	VF	EF	UNC
	£	£	£	£

3978 Crown. Bare head r. R̟. St. George and dragon date in ex. die axis ↑↑

1902..50   85   140   225

3979 Crown. Similar Matt proof *FDC* £185

3980
1904 Halfcrown

3981
Florin

	F	VF	EF	UNC
	£	£	£	£

3980 Halfcrown. Bare head r. R̟. Crowned Shield in Garter, die axis ↑↑

1902	15	35	70	140		1906	15	45	200	600
1902 Matt proof *FDC* £125						1907	15	45	200	600
1903	100	375	1200	2250		1908	20	50	325	850
1904	50	200	475	1200		1909	15	45	275	700
1905*	250	650	2000	4000		1910	15	35	175	500

3981 Florin. Bare head r. R̟. Britannia standing on ship's bow die axis ↑↑

1902	8	20	50	85		1906	10	25	100	325
1902 Matt proof *FDC* £75						1907	10	35	120	350
1903	10	25	100	325		1908	15	45	200	525
1904	12	35	120	350		1909	15	45	180	475
1905	55	135	450	1000		1910	10	20	85	275

Beware of recent forgeries.

3982
1902 Shilling

3983
1902 Sixpence

	F	VF	EF	UNC			F	VF	EF	UNC
	£	£	£	£			£	£	£	£

3982 Shilling. Bare head r. ℞. Lion rampant on crown die axis ↑↑

1902	5	15	40	65	1906	5	10	50	150
1902 Matt proof *FDC* £70					1907	5	10	55	175
1903	8	20	120	325	1908	10	25	125	400
1904	8	15	100	260	1909	10	25	125	400
1905	65	200	750	2000	1910	3	10	45	95

3983 Sixpence. Bare head r. ℞. Value in wreath die axis ↑↑

1902	5	10	30	50	1906	4	10	30	80
1902 Matt proof *FDC* £60					1907	5	10	35	85
1903	4	10	30	80	1908	5	12	40	90
1904	6	25	60	150	1909	4	10	35	85
1905	5	20	50	120	1910	3	5	25	55

3984 Threepence. As Maundy but dull finish die axis ↑↑

1902	3	8	15		1906	2	7	35	75
1902 Matt proof *FDC* £18					1907	1	7	25	45
1903	1	7	25	45	1908	1	2	10	25
1904	3	10	35	75	1909	1	7	25	45
1905	2	7	25	65	1910		1	10	30

3985
1903 Maundy Set

	EF	FDC		EF	FDC
	£	£		£	£

3985 Maundy Set (4d., 3d., 2d. and 1d.) Bare head r. die axis ↑↑

1902		65	90	1906	65	80
1902 Matt proof *FDC* £70				1907	65	80
1903		65	80	1908	65	80
1904		65	80	1909	75	110
1905		65	80	1910	75	110

	EF	FDC
	£	£

3986 — **Fourpence.** 1902-10 ....*from* 6 12
3987 — **Threepence.** 1902-10 ....*from* 6 15
3988 — **Twopence.** 1902-10 ....*from* 6 10
3989 — **Penny.** 1902-10 ....*from* 7 12

Maundy sets in the original undamaged cases are worth approximately £15 more than the prices quoted.

3990
1902 Penny

3990 Normal Tide'   3990A 'Low Tide'

	VF	EF	UNC		F	VF	EF	UNC
	£	£	£		£	£	£	£

3990 Penny. Bare head r. ℞. Britannia seated r. date in ex. die axis ↑↑

1902....................................1	8	45	1906....................................3	15	65
1903 Normal 3 2	12	55	1907....................................4	20	75
1903 Open 3....................60	300	—	1908....................................3	15	65
1904....................................5	35	100	1909....................................4	20	75
1905....................................4	30	90	1910....................................2	12	55

3990A Penny. Similar ℞. As last but 'Low tide', 1902 5   20   90   185

3991
Halfpenny

	VF	EF	UNC		F	VF	EF	UNC
	£	£	£		£	£	£	£

3991 Halfpenny. Bare head r. R. Britannia seated r. date in ex. die axis ↑↑

	VF	EF	UNC		F	VF	EF	UNC
1902	1	7	25	1908	1	10	45
1903	2	10	40	1909	2	12	55
1904	2	15	70	1910	2	10	45
1905	2	12	55				
1906	2	12	50				
1907	1	10	45				

3991A Halfpenny. Similar R. As last but 'Low tide', 1902 10   30   100   275

3992
Farthing

3993
1902 Third-Farthing

3992 Farthing. Bare head r. R. Britannia seated r. date in ex. Dark finish die axis ↑↑

	VF	EF	UNC		F	VF	EF	UNC
1902	—	5	20	1907	1	5	20
1903	1	5	20	1908	1	5	20
1904	2	8	25	1909	1	5	20
1905	1	5	20	1910	2	10	30
1906	1	5	20				

3993 Third-Farthing (for use in Malta) Bare head r. R. Crowned date and value die axis ↑↑.
1902 10   35
No proofs of the bronze coins were issued in 1902

Proof Sets
PS9   Coronation, **1902**. Five Pounds to Maundy Penny, matt surface, (13 coins) *FDC*   £2500
PS10 — 1902. Sovereign to Maundy Penny, matt surface, (11 coins)................... *FDC*   £975

George V, the second son of Edward VII, was born on 3 June 1865 and married Mary of Teck who bore him five sons and a daughter. He was King through World War I and visited the front on several occasions. He suffered a fall breaking his pelvis on one of these visits, an injury that would pain him for the rest of his life. He watched the Empire divide; Ireland, Canada, Australia, New Zealand and India all went through changes. He died on 20th January 1936 only months after his Silver Jubilee.

Paper money issued by the Treasury during the First World War replaced gold for internal use after 1915 but the branch mints in Australia and South Africa (the main Commonwealth gold producing countries) continued striking Sovereigns until 1930-2. Owing to the steep rise in the price of silver in 1919/20 the issue of standard (.925) silver was discontinued and coins of .500 silver were minted.

In 1912, 1918 and 1919 some Pennies were made under contract by private mints in Birmingham. In 1918, as Half-Sovereigns were no longer being minted, Farthings were again issued with the ordinary bright bronze finish. Crown pieces had not been issued for general circulation but they were struck in small numbers about Christmas time for people to give as presents in the years 1927-36, and in 1935 a special commemorative Crown was issued in celebration of the Silver Jubilee.

As George V died on 20 January, it is likely that all coins dated 1936 were struck during the reign of Edward VIII.

Engravers and Designers:– George Kuger Gray (1880-1943), Bertram MacKennal (1863-1931), Benedetto Pistrucci (1784-1855) Percy Metcalfe (1895-1970)

Prime Ministers:– Herbert Henry Asquith (1852-1928), Liberal 1908-16, David Lloyd George, (1863-1945) Liberal 1916-22, Andrew Bonar Law (1858-1923), Conservative, 1922-3, Stanley Baldwin, (1867-1947) Conservative, 1923, 1924-1, 1935-7, James Ramsey MacDonald, (1866-1937) Labour 1924-7, 1929-35

Designer's initials:

B. M. (Bertram Mackennal)	P. M. (Percy Metcalfe)
K. G. (G. Kruger Gray)	B. P. (Benedetto Pistrucci; d. 1855)

Die axis: ↑↑

GOLD

FDC
£

3994 Five Pounds.* Bare head l. R. St. George and dragon, date in ex., 1911 (Proof only).....2100
3995 Two Pounds.* Bare head l. R. St. George and dragon, date in ex., 1911 (Proof only).......850

3996

	VF	EF	UNC		VF	EF	UNC
	£	£	£		£	£	£

3996 Sovereign. Bare head l. R. St. George and dragon. London Mint die axis: ↑↑

	VF	EF	UNC		VF	EF	UNC
1911.........................BV		95	130	1914........................BV		95	130
1911 Proof *FDC* £500				1915........................BV		95	130
1911 Matt Proof *FDC of highest rarity*				1916........................BV		95	145
1912........................BV		95	130	1917*....................2200		5250	—
1913........................BV		95	130	1925........................BV		95	130

*Forgeries exist of these and of most other dates and mints.

	F	VF	EF	UNC			F	VF	EF	UNC
	£	£	£	£			£	£	£	£

3997 Sovereign. Bare head l. R̩. St George, C on ground for the Ottawa Mint, Canada die axis: ↑↑

1911 C	BV	120	175	1917 C	BV	120	175
1913 C	125	625	—	1918 C	BV	120	175
1914 C	175	375	—	1919 C	BV	120	175
1916 C*	3250	7500	—				

* Beware of recent forgeries

3997
Canada 'c' Mint mark

3998 Sovereign. Similar R. I on ground for Bombay Mint, India 1918 110
3999 Sovereign. Similar R. M on ground for Melbourne Mint, Australia die axis: ↑↑

1911 M			100	1920 M	750	1750	2250	3150
1912 M			100	1921 M	2000	3500	5500	7500
1913 M			100	1922 M	1500	2750	4250	6000
1914 M			100	1923 M				100
1915 M			100	1924 M				100
1916 M			100	1925 M				100
1917 M			100	1926 M				100
1918 M			100	1928 M	500	850	500	2000
1919 M			95	125				

4000 Sovereign. Similar small bare head l. die axis: ↑↑

1929 M	500	900	1400	1850	1931 M	110	200	250	375
1930 M		100	130	175					

4000
1930 M Sovereign, small head

4001
Perth Mint Sovereign

4001 Sovereign. Similar R. P on ground for Perth Mint, Australia die axis: ↑↑

1911 P				100	1920 P				100
1912 P				100	1921 P				100
1913 P				100	1922 P				100
1914 P				100	1923 P				100
1915 P				100	1924 P	BV	100	125	160
1916 P				100	1925 P	100	150	200	275
1917 P				100	1926 P	400	800	1200	1450
1918 P				100	1927 P	BV	180	275	400
1919 P				100	1928 P	BV	110	150	165

	VF	*EF*	*UNC*			*F*	*VF*	*EF*	*UNC*
	£	£	£			£	£	£	£

4002 Sovereign. Similar — small bare head l. die axis: ↑↑

1929 P	100	1931 P	100
1930 P	100		

4003 Sovereign. Similar R. S on ground for Sydney Mint, Australia die axis: ↑↑

1911 S	100	1919 S				100
1912 S	100	1920 S .... —	—	—	200000
1913 S	100	1921 S 400	650	1000	1600
1914 S	100	1922 S 3100	5000	7300	9150
1915 S	100	1923 S 2500	4000	6500	7650
1916 S	100	1924 S 325	575	850	1250
1917 S	100	1925 S			85
1918 S	100	1926 S 4100	7750	11500	13000

4004 Sovereign. Similar R. SA on ground for Pretoria Mint, South Africa die axis: ↑↑

1923 SA.....................900	1750	3500	1926 SA	95
1923 SA Proof *FDC* £475			1927 SA	95
1924 SA...................1500	3000	—	1928 SA	95
1925 SA	95			

4005 Sovereign. Similar — small head die axis: ↑↑

1929 SA	95	1931 SA	95
1930 SA	95	1932 SA	95

4003
1921 Sydney 's' Sovereign

4006
1914 Half-sovereign

4006 Half-Sovereign. Bare head l. R. St. George and dragon date in ex. London Mint die axis: ↑↑

1911.................................BV	50	75	1913....................................	50	75
1911 Proof *FDC* £275			1914....................................	50	75
1911 Matt Proof *FDC of highest rarity*			1915....................................	50	75
1912.................................BV	50	75			

4007 Half-Sovereign. Similar R. M on ground for Melbourne Mint, Australia die axis: ↑↑

1915 M ....BV	55	90

4008 Half-Sovereign. Similar R. P on ground for Perth Mint, Australia die axis: ↑↑

1911 P............................55	100	125	1918 P 125	250	500	825
1915 P 55	85	750				

4009 Half-Sovereign. Similar R. S on ground for Sydney Mint, Australia die axis: ↑↑

1911 S 55	75	90	1915 S ....BV	55	70
1912 S 50	60	80	1916 S ....BV	55	70
1914 S ....BV	55	80			

4010 Half-Sovereign. Similar R. SA on ground for Pretoria Mint, South Africa die axis: ↑↑

1923 SA Proof *FDC* £275			1926 SA.........................BV	50	70
1925 SA.........................BV	50	70			

SILVER

First Coinage. Sterling silver (.925 fine)

4011
1911 Halfcrown

	F £	VF £	EF £	UNC £		F £	VF £	EF £	UNC £

4011 Halfcrown. Bare head l. R. Crowned shield in Garter die axis: ↑↑

	F	VF	EF	UNC		F	VF	EF	UNC
1911	5	18	40	140	1915	4	10	25	60
1911 Proof *FDC* £110					1916	4	10	25	60
1912	6	25	55	160	1917	5	15	40	85
1913	8	30	65	180	1918	4	10	25	60
1914	4	10	25	70	1919	5	15	40	85

4012   4013
1912 Florin   1911 Proof

4012 Florin. Bare head l. R. Crowned Cruciform shields sceptres in angles die axis: ↑↑

	F	VF	EF	UNC		F	VF	EF	UNC
1911	5	10	35	85	1916	4	10	25	60
1911 Proof *FDC* £85					1917	6	12	30	75
1912	5	15	45	100	1918	4	10	25	60
1913	8	25	65	140	1919	6	12	30	75
1914	4	10	25	65					
1915	6	20	40	120					

4013 Shilling. Bare head l. R. Lion rampant on crown, within circle die axis: ↑↑

	F	VF	EF	UNC		F	VF	EF	UNC
					1915		4	20	45
1911	2	8	20	45	1916		4	20	45
1911 Proof *FDC* £60					1917		5	25	70
1912	4	12	30	65	1918		4	20	45
1913	8	15	55	125	1919	4	10	30	60
1914	3	10	25	50					

4014
1911 Sixpence

	F £	VF £	EF £	UNC £		F £	VF £	EF £	UNC £

4014 Sixpence. Bare head l. R. Lion rampent on crown, within circle die axis: ↑↑

1911.......................2	8	15	35		1916.......................2	8	15	35
1911 Proof *FDC* £45					1917.......................5	15	40	95
1912.......................4	10	25	50		1918.......................2	8	15	35
1913.......................5	12	30	55		1919.......................4	10	20	45
1914.......................2	8	15	35		1920.......................4	10	25	50
1915.......................2	8	15	45					

4015 Threepence. As Maundy but dull finish die axis: ↑↑

1911..............................1	5	15		1916..............................1	3	10
1911 Proof *FDC* £35				1917..............................1	3	10
1912..............................1	5	15		1918..............................1	3	10
1913..............................1	5	15		1919..............................1	3	10
1914..............................1	5	15		1920..............................1	5	15
1915..............................1	5	20				

4016
1915 Maundy Set

	EF £	FDC £		EF £	FDC £

4016 Maundy Set (4d., 3d., 2d. and 1d.) die axis: ↑↑

1911..............................	65	100	1916..............................	65	100
1911 Proof *FDC* £80			1917..............................	65	100
1912..............................	65	100	1918..............................	65	100
1913..............................	65	100	1919..............................	65	100
1914..............................	65	100	1920..............................	65	100
1915..............................	65	100			

4017 — Fourpence. 1911-20 ....*from*	8	15
4018 — Threepence. 1911-20 ....*from*	10	18
4019 — Twopence. 1911-20 ....*from*	7	12
4020 — Penny. 1911-20...*from*	8	15

Second Coinage. Debased silver (.500 fine). Types as before.

	F	VF	EF	UNC		F	VF	EF	UNC
	£	£	£	£		£	£	£	£

4021 Halfcrown. Deeply engraved. Bare head l. R. Crowned shield in garter die axis: ↑↑

| 1920 | 4 | 8 | 35 | 110 | | | | | |

4021A — recut shallow portrait

1920	6	12	45	120	1924 Specimen Finish			*Extremely rare*	
1921	5	10	30	90	1925	20	50	200	500
1922	4	8	35	100	1926	5	15	50	120
1923	3	5	15	45	1926 No colon				
1924	5	10	35	80	after OMN	15	35	110	225

4022 Florin. Deeply engraved. Bare head l. R. Crowned cruciform shields, sceptres in angles die axis: ↑↑

| 1920 | 3 | 8 | 30 | 85 | | | | | |

4022A — recut shallow portrait

1920	5	12	40	95	1924	4	10	40	80
1921	3	8	30	65	1924 Specimen Finish			*Extremely rare*	
1922	3	6	25	55	1925	25	45	125	300
1922 Proof in gold *FDC of highest rarity*					1926	3	10	40	80
1923	2	5	20	50					

4023 Shilling. Deeply engraved. Bare head l. R. Lion rampant on crown within circle die axis: ↑↑

| 1920 | 3 | 6 | 25 | 50 | 1921 nose to S | 15 | 30 | 60 | 150 |

4023A — recut shallow portrait

1920	5	15	40	100	1924	3	8	30	55
1921 nose to SV	5	15	40	100	1925	5	10	45	100
1922	3	6	25	50	1926	3	6	20	50
1923	2	5	20	45					

4024 Sixpence. Bare head l. R. Lion rampant on crown within circle die axis: ↑↑

1920	2	4	15	40	1924	2	4	12	30
1921	2	4	15	40	1924 Specimen Finish			*Extremely rare*	
1922	2	5	15	40	1924 Proof in gold *FDC of highest rarity*				
1923	3	6	20	55	1925	2	4	15	35

4025
George V Sixpence

4026
Threepence

4025 Sixpence. Similar new beading and broader rim die axis: ↑↑

| 1925 | 2 | 4 | 12 | 30 | 1926 | 2 | 4 | 15 | 30 |

4026 Threepence. Bare head l. R. Crowned 3 die axis: ↑↑

1920		1	3	15	1924 Proof in gold *FDC of highest rarity*				
1921		1	3	15	1925	—	2	14	40
1922		1	15	50	1926	1	5	30	65
1924 Specimen Finish			*Extremely rare*						

			EF	FDC				EF	FDC
			£	£				£	£

4027 Maundy Set. (4d., 3d., 2d. and 1d.) die axis: ↑↑

1921			65	100	1925			65	100
1922			65	100	1926			65	100
1923			65	100	1927			65	100
1924			65	100					

			EF	FDC
4028 — **Fourpence.** 1921-7			*from*	10	15
4029 — **Threepence.** 1921-7			*from*	10	18
4030 — **Twopence.** 1921-7			*from*	7	12
4031 — **Penny.** 1921-7			*from*	8	15

2nd coinage
BM more central on tr.

3rd coinage
Modified Effigy
BM to right of tr.

Third Coinage. As before but modified effigy, with details of head more clearly defined. The BM on truncation is nearer to the back of the neck and without stops; beading is more pronounced.

	F £	VF £	EF £	UNC £		F £	VF £	EF £	UNC £
4032 Halfcrown. Modified effigy l. R. Crowned Shield in Garter die axis: ↑↑									
1926	5	15	60	140	1927	4	7	25	45
					1927 Proof in gold *FDC of highest rarity*				
4033 Shilling. Modified effigy l. R. Lion rampant on crown, within circle die axis: ↑↑									
1926	2	4	18	35	1927	2	6	25	45
4034 Sixpence. Modified effigy l. R. Lion rampant on crown, within circle die axis: ↑↑									
1926		3	10	25	1927	2	4	15	30
4035 Threepence. Modified effigy l. R. Crowned 3 die axis: ↑↑									
1926							1	8	30

Fourth Coinage. New types, 1927-36

4036
1927 'Wreath' Crown

4036 Crown. Modified Bare head l. R. Crown and date in wreath die axis: ↑↑

1927 –15,030 struck Proof only *FDC* £210				1931 –4056 struck ... 90	160	275	450
1927 Matt Proof *FDC of highest rarity*				1932 –2395 struck . 125	225	450	650
1928 –9034 struck ... 85	140	225	400	1933 –7132 struck ... 85	140	230	400
1929 –4994 struck ... 85	150	250	425	1934 –932 struck ... 850	1600	2650	3900
1930 -4847 struck 85	150	250	425	1936 –2473 struck . 125	225	450	650

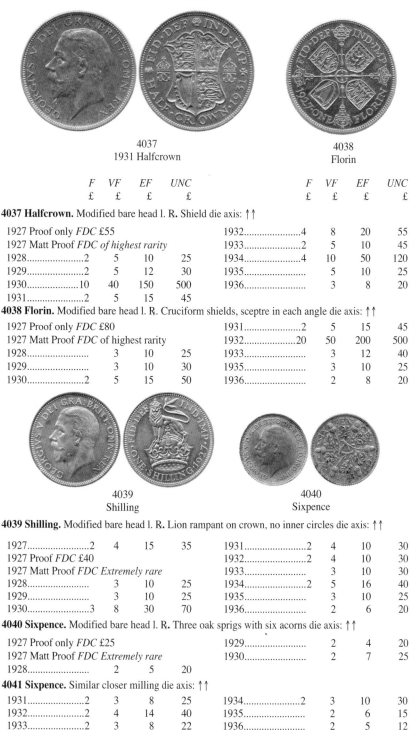

4037
1931 Halfcrown

4038
Florin

	F £	VF £	EF £	UNC £		F £	VF £	EF £	UNC £

4037 Halfcrown. Modified bare head l. R. Shield die axis: ↑↑

1927 Proof only *FDC* £55					1932	4	8	20	55
1927 Matt Proof *FDC of highest rarity*					1933	2	5	10	45
1928	2	5	10	25	1934	4	10	50	120
1929	2	5	12	30	1935		5	10	25
1930	10	40	150	500	1936		3	8	20
1931	2	5	15	45					

4038 Florin. Modified bare head l. R. Cruciform shields, sceptre in each angle die axis: ↑↑

1927 Proof only *FDC* £80					1931	2	5	15	45
1927 Matt Proof *FDC* of highest rarity					1932	20	50	200	500
1928		3	10	25	1933		3	12	40
1929		3	10	30	1935		3	10	25
1930	2	5	15	50	1936		2	8	20

4039
Shilling

4040
Sixpence

4039 Shilling. Modified bare head l. R. Lion rampant on crown, no inner circles die axis: ↑↑

1927	2	4	15	35	1931	2	4	10	30
1927 Proof *FDC* £40					1932	2	4	10	30
1927 Matt Proof *FDC Extremely rare*					1933		3	10	30
1928		3	10	25	1934	2	5	16	40
1929		3	10	25	1935		3	10	25
1930	3	8	30	70	1936		2	6	20

4040 Sixpence. Modified bare head l. R. Three oak sprigs with six acorns die axis: ↑↑

1927 Proof only *FDC* £25					1929		2	4	20
1927 Matt Proof *FDC Extremely rare*					1930		2	7	25
1928		2	5	20					

4041 Sixpence. Similar closer milling die axis: ↑↑

1931	2	3	8	25	1934	2	3	10	30
1932	2	4	14	40	1935		2	6	15
1933	2	3	8	22	1936		2	5	12

BRONZE

4042	4043
Threepence	George V Maundy Set

	F	VF	EF	UNC		F	VF	EF	UNC
	£	£	£	£		£	£	£	£

4042 Threepence. Modified Bare head l. R. Three oak sprigs with three acorns die axis: ↑↑

1927 Proof only *FDC* £75					1932			1	10
1927 Matt Proof *FDC of highest rarity*					1933			1	10
1928	1	3	14	40	1934			1	10
1930	1	3	14	40	1935			1	10
1931			1	10	1936			1	7

			EF	FDC				EF	FDC
			£	£				£	£

4043 Maundy Set. As earlier sets die axis: ↑↑

1928	70	100	1933	70	110
1929	70	100	1934	70	110
1930	70	100	1935	70	110
1931	70	100	1936	70	110
1932	70	100			

The 1936 Maundy was distributed by King Edward VIII

4044 — Fourpence. 1928-36	*from*	10	15
4045 — Threepence. 1928-36	*from*	10	15
4046 — Twopence. 1928-36	*from*	10	15
4047 — Penny. 1928-36	*from*	12	18

Silver Jubilee Commemorative issue, die axis: ↑↑

4048
1935 'Jubilee' Crown

	VF	EF	UNC
	£	£	£
4048 Crown. 1935. R. St. George, incuse lettering on edge –714,769 struck ..	10	15	25
1935 — error edge		*Extremely rare*	
4049 Crown. Similar Specimen striking issued in box			55
4050 Crown. Similar raised lettering on edge 2,500 struck. Proof (.925 Æ) *FDC* £400			
— error edge inscription Proof *FDC* £1500			
— Proof in gold –28 struck £20000			

BRONZE

KN Mint mark location
as above – 4053

4052
1912 H Penny

	F	VF	EF	UNC		F	VF	EF	UNC
	£	£	£	£		£	£	£	£

4051 Penny. Bare head l. R. Britannia seated right die axis: ↑↑

	F	VF	EF	UNC		F	VF	EF	UNC
1911		2	10	40	1919		3	15	45
1912		3	18	50	1920		3	15	45
1913		4	18	50	1921		3	15	45
1914		3	15	45	1922		5	25	75
1915		3	18	50	1922 Rev. of 1927	1500	4000	—	
1916		3	15	45	1922 Specimen finish..		*Extremely rare*		
1917		3	15	45	1926		6	30	90
1918		3	15	45					

4052 Penny. Bare head l. R. Britannia, H (Heaton Mint, Birmingham, Ltd.) to l. of date die axis: ↑↑

	F	VF	EF	UNC		F	VF	EF	UNC
1912 H		10	80	225	1919 H		15	220	700
1918 H		20	200	500					

4053 Penny. Bare head l. R. Britannia KN (King's Norton Metal Co.) to l. of date die axis: ↑↑

	F	VF	EF	UNC		F	VF	EF	UNC
1918 KN	3	40	275	850	1919 KN	5	60	650	1750

4054 Penny. Modified effigy l. R. Britannia Seated r. shorter index finger date in ex. die axis: ↑↑

	F	VF	EF	UNC		F	VF	EF	UNC
1926	20	125	750	1750	1927		2	10	35

4055 Penny. Small bare head l. R. Britannia Seated r. date in ex. die axis: ↑↑

	F	VF	EF	UNC		F	VF	EF	UNC
1928		2	10	25	1933		—	—	55000
1929		2	10	35	1934		4	20	50
1930		3	15	45	1935		1	5	20
1931		3	15	40	1936		0.50	4	15
1932		5	25	100					

4056 Halfpenny. Bare head l. R. Britannia Seated r. date in ex. die axis: ↑↑

	F	VF	EF	UNC		F	VF	EF	UNC
1911			5	30	1919			6	35
1912			6	35	1920			6	35
1913			6	35	1921			6	35
1914			6	40	1922			10	50
1915			6	45	1923			6	35
1916			6	45	1924			6	35
1917			6	35	1924 Specimen finish..		*Extremely rare*		
1918			6	35	1925			6	35

4057 Halfpenny. Modified effigy l. R. Britannia Seated r. date in ex. die axis: ↑↑

	F	VF	EF	UNC		F	VF	EF	UNC
1925			10	50	1927			6	30
1926			6	35					

4056	4058
Halfpenny	Small head

	EF £	UNC £		EF £	UNC £

4058 Halfpenny. Small bare head l. R. Britannia Seated r. date in ex. die axis: ↑↑

1928	5	25	1933	5	25
1929	5	25	1934	8	30
1930	5	25	1935	5	25
1931	5	25	1936	4	20
1932	5	25			

4059	4062
Farthing	Third-Farthing

4059 Farthing. Bare head l. R. Britannia Seated r. date in ex. Dark finish die axis: ↑↑

1911	3	12	1915	4	15
1912	2	10	1916	2	10
1913	2	10	1917	1	10
1914	2	10	1918	9	25

4060 Farthing. Similar Bright finish, die axis: ↑↑ 1918-25 .... 1 10
4061 Farthing. Modified effigy l. R. Britannia Seated r. date in ex. die axis: ↑↑

1926	1	8	1932	1	8
1927	1	8	1933	1	8
1928	1	8	1934	2	10
1929	1	8	1935	5	25
1930	1	8	1936	1	8
1931	1	8			

4062 Third-Farthing (for use in Malta). Bare head l. R. Crowned date and Value die axis: ↑↑
1913 .... 12 30

Proof Sets

PS11 Coronation, **1911.** Five pounds to Maundy Penny (12 coins) .... *FDC* £4000
PS12 — **1911.** Sovereign to Maundy Penny (10 coins) .... *FDC* £1250
PS13 — **1911.** Half crown to Maundy Penny (8 coins) .... *FDC* £550
PS14 New type, **1927.** Wreath type Crown to Threepence (6 coins) .... *FDC* £480

Succeeded his father on 20 January 1936. Abdicated 10 December.

Edward VIII was born 23 June 1894, and was very popular as Prince of Wales. He ruled only for a short time before announcing his intended marriage to the American divorcee Wallis Simpson; a potential religious and political scandal. Edward was not a traditionalist, as evidenced on the proposed coinage, where he insisted against all advice on having his effigy face the same way as his father's, instead of opposite. He abdicated in favour of his brother, and became Edward, Duke of Windsor, marrying Mrs Simpson in France, where they lived in exile. He governed the Bahamas from 1940-45 and died on 28 May 1972.

No coins of Edward VIII were issued for currency within the United Kingdom bearing his name and portrait. The Mint had commenced work on a new coinage prior to the Abdication, and various patterns were made. No Proof Sets were issued for sale and only a small number of sets were struck.

Coins bearing Edward's name, but not his portrait, were issued for the colonial territories of British East Africa, British West Africa, Fiji and New Guinea. The projected U.K. coins were to include a Shilling of essentially `Scottish' type and a nickel brass Threepence with twelve sides which might supplement and possibly supersede the inconveniently small silver Threepence.

Engravers and Designers:– George Kruger Gray (1880-1943), Thomas Humphrey Paget (1893-1974), Benedicto Pistucci (1784-1855) Frances Madge Kitchener, Percy Metcalfe (1895-1970), H Wilson Parker (1896-1980)

Designer's initials: H. P. (T. Humphrey Paget)   B.P. (Benedetto Pistrucci, d. 1855)
                    K. G. (G. Kruger Gray)   M. K. (Madge Kitchener)
                    W. P. (H. Wilson Parker)

Prime Minister:– Stanley Baldwin (1867-1947), Conservative 1935-7

Die axis ↑↑

GOLD

4063
Edward VIII Proof Five Pounds

4063 Proof Set

Gold, Five Pounds, Two Pounds and Sovereign, 1937 .... *not issued*

Silver Crown, Halfcrown, Florin, Scottish shilling, sixpence and threepence, 1937   *not issued*

	UNC £
Five Pounds, Bare head l. R St George and dragon, date in ex	275000
Two Pounds, Bare head l. R St George and dragon, date in ex	120000
Sovereign, Bare head l. R. St George and dragon date in ex	150000
Crown, Bare head l. R. Crowned Shield of arms and supporters	85000
Halfcrown, Bare head l. R. Quartered Standard of arms	45000
Florin, Bare head l. R. Crowned rose and emblems	32500
Shilling, Bare head l. R. Lion seated facing on crown	22500
Sixpence, Bare head l. R. Six interlinked rings	17500
Threepence, Bare head l. R. three interlinked rings	15000

4064A

4064A Nickel brass. **Threepence,** 1937 Bare head l. R. Thrift plant below	35000
Bronze. **Penny,** 1937	40000
Halfpenny, 1937	15000
Farthing, 1937	15000

Pattern

Edward VIII Brass Threepence

4064B Nickel brass dodecagonal **Threepence,** 1937. Bare head l. R. Thrift plant of more
naturalistic style than the modified proof coin. A small number of these coins were
produced for experimental purposes and a few did get into circulation ..   32000

George VI was born on 14 December 1895 and never expected to be King. He suffered ill-health through much of his life and had a stammer. He married Elizabeth Bowes Lyon and together they became very popular especially through the ravages of World War II, when Buckingham Palace was bombed. The war took its toll on George, and ever a heavy smoker he succumbed to lung cancer on 6th February 1952. Elizabeth, known after his death as 'Queen Elizabeth the Queen Mother', lived on to the age of 101 dying on 30 March 2002.

Though they were at first issued concurrently, the twelve-sided nickel-brass Threepence superseded the small silver Threepence in 1942. Those dated 1943-4 were not issued for circulation in the U.K. In addition to the usual English 'lion' Shilling, a Shilling of Scottish type was issued concurrently. This depicts the Scottish lion and crown flanked by the shield of St. Andrew and a thistle. In 1947, as silver was needed to repay the bullion lent by the U.S.A. during the war, silver coins were replaced by coins of the same type and weight made of cupro-nickel. In 1949, after India had attained independence, the title IND:IMP (Indiae Imperator) was dropped from the coinage. Commemorative Crown pieces were issued for the Coronation and the 1951 Festival of Britain.

Engravers and Designers:– Frances Madge Kitchener, George Kruger Gray (1880-1943), Percy Metcalfe (1895-1970) Thomas Humphrey Paget (1893-1974), H Wilson Parker (1896-1980), Benedetto Pistrucci (1784-1855)

Designer's initials: K. G. (G. Kruger Gray)   B. P. (Benedetto Pistrucci, d. 1855)
                         H. P. (T. Humphrey Paget)   W. P. (Wilson Parker)

Prime Ministers:– Stanley Baldwin, (1867-1947) Conservative, 1935-37, Arthur Neville Chamberlain, (1869-1940) National 1937-40, Sir Winston Leonard Spencer Churchill,(1874-1965) National 1940-45. 1951-55 Conservative, Clement Richard Attlee, (1883-1967) Labour 1945-51

Die axis ↑↑

GOLD

4074
1937 Proof Five Pounds

4076
1937 Proof Sovereign

FDC
£

4074 Five Pounds. Bare head l. R. St. George, 1937. Proof plain edge only (5001 struck)..   850
4074-4077 Proof Struck to Matt finish *FDC of highest rarity*
4075 Two Pounds. Similar, 1937. Proof plain edge only (5001 struck)   450
4076 Sovereign. Similar, 1937. Proof plain edge only (5001 struck)   1350
4077 Half-Sovereign. Similar, 1937. Proof plain edge only (5001 struck)   350

SILVER

First coinage. Silver, .500 fine, with title IND:IMP

4078
1937 Crown

	VF £	EF £	UNC £
4078 Crown. Coronation commemorative, 1937. R. Arms and supporters	10	20	30

4079 Crown. Similar 1937 Proof *FDC* £50
        Similar 1937 Frosted 'VIP' Proof £400
        — 1937 Matt Proof *FDC of highest rarity*

4080
Halfcrown

4081
1937 Florin

	EF £	UNC £		EF £	UNC £

4080 Halfcrown. Bare head l. R. Shield die axis: ↑↑

	EF	UNC		EF	UNC
1937	4	15	1941	5	15
1937 Proof *FDC* £20			1942	3	10
1937 Matt Proof *FDC of highest rarity*			1943	5	15
1938	8	35	1944	3	10
1939	5	15	1945	3	10
1940	5	15	1946	3	10

4081 Florin. Bare head l. R. Crowned rose, etc. die axis: ↑↑

	EF	UNC		EF	UNC
1937	3	10	1941	4	12
1937 Proof *FDC* £15			1942	2	8
1937 Matt Proof *FDC of highest rarity*			1943	3	12
1938	8	30	1944	3	10
1939	4	12	1945	2	7
1940	4	12	1946	2	7

4082
1942 'English' Shilling

4083
1945 'Scottish' Shilling

4082 Shilling. 'English' reverse. Bare head l. R. Lion rampant on large crown die axis: ↑↑

	EF	UNC		EF	UNC
1937	3	12	1941	3	12
1937 Proof *FDC* £15			1942	2	10
1937 Matt Proof *FDC of highest rarity*			1943	2	10
1938	8	30	1944	2	10
1939	3	12	1945	1	6
1940	3	12	1946	1	6

	EF	UNC		VF	EF	UNC
	£	£		£	£	£

4083 Shilling. 'Scottish' reverse. Bare head l. R. Lion seated facing on crown die axis: ↑↑

1937..............................	1	8	1941..............................		4	15
1937 Proof *FDC* £15			1942..............................		2	10
1937 Matt Proof *FDC of highest rarity*			1943..............................		2	10
1938..............................	8	25	1944..............................		2	12
1939..............................	3	12	1945..............................		1	6
1940..............................	3	12	1946..............................		1	6

4084
1945 Sixpence

4085
1944 Threepence

4084 Sixpence. Bare head l. R. GRI crowned die axis: ↑↑

1937..............................	1	6	1941..............................	2	10
1937 Proof *FDC* £10			1942..............................	1	8
1937 Matt Proof *FDC of highest rarity*			1943..............................	1	8
1938..............................	6	15	1944..............................	1	8
1939..............................	2	10	1945..............................	1	8
1940..............................	2	10	1946..............................	1	5

4085 Threepence. Bare head l. R. Shield on rose die axis: ↑↑

1937..............................	1	6	1941..............................		4	15
1937 Proof *FDC* £12			1942*...........................5	15	40
1937 Matt Proof *FDC of highest rarity*			1943*...........................5	20	50
1938..............................	1	8	1944*.........................10	30	80
1939..............................	6	15	1945*..........................	*Extremely rare*
1940..............................	3	10	** issued for Colonial use only*

4086
1937 Maundy Set

	FDC		FDC
	£		£

4086 Maundy Set. Silver, .500 fine. Uniform dates die axis: ↑↑

1937..................................	75	1941..	110
1937 Proof *FDC* £75		1942..	110
1937 Matt Proof *FDC of highest rarity*		1943..	110
1938..................................	110	1944..	110
1939..................................	110	1945..	110
1940..................................	110	1946..	110

	FDC		*FDC*
	£		£

4087 — **Fourpence.** 1937-46 .... *from*			12
4088 — **Threepence.** 1937-46 .... *from*			12
4089 — **Twopence.** 1937-46 .... *from*			12
4090 — **Penny.** 1937-46 .... *from*			18

Second coinage. Silver, .925 fine, with title IND:IMP (Maundy only)
4091 Maundy Set (4d., 3d., 2d. and 1d.). Uniform dates die axis: ↑↑

1947	110	1948	110

4092 — **Fourpence,** 1947-8			12
4093 — **Threepence,** 1947-8			12
4094 — **Twopence,** 1947-8			12
4095 — **Penny,** 1947-8			18

Third coinage. Silver, .925 fine, but omitting IND:IMP. (Maundy only)
4096 Maundy Set (4d., 3d., 2d. and 1d.). Uniform dates die axis: ↑↑

1949	110	1951	120
1950	110	1952	125
1951 Matt Proof *FDC Extremely rare*		1952 Proof in copper *FDC Extremely rare*	

The 1952 Maundy was distributed by Queen Elizabeth II.

4097 — **Fourpence,** 1949-52 .... *from*			12
4098 — **Threepence,** 1949-52 .... *from*			12
4099 — **Twopence,** 1949-52 .... *from*			12
4100 — **Penny,** 1949-52 .... *from*			18

CUPRO-NICKEL

Second coinage. Types as first (silver) coinage, IND:IMP.

	EF	*UNC*		*EF*	*UNC*
	£	£		£	£
4101 Halfcrown. Bare head l. R. Shield die axis: ↑↑					
1947	1	8	1948	1	6
4102 Florin. Bare head l. R. Crowned rose die axis: ↑↑					
1947	1	8	1948	1	8
4103 Shilling. 'English' reverse. Bare head l. die axis: ↑↑					
1947	1	8	1948 1		8
4104 Shilling. 'Scottish' reverse. Bare head l. die axis: ↑↑					
1947	1	8	1948 1		8
4105 Sixpence. Bare head l. R. GRI crowned die axis: ↑↑					
1947		6	1948		5

Third coinage. Types as before but title IND:IMP. omitted

4106
1949 Halfcrown

	VF	EF	UNC		VF	EF	UNC
	£	£	£		£	£	£

4106 Halfcrown. Bare head l. R. Shield die axis: ↑↑

1949..............................		3	15	1951 Proof *FDC* £25			
1950..............................		5	20	1951 Matt Proof *FDC of highest rarity*			
1950 Proof *FDC* £20				1952..................................			*Unique*
1950 Matt Proof *FDC of highest rarity*				1952 Proof *FDC* £25000			
1951..............................	1	8	25				

4107 Florin. Bare head l. R. Crowned rose die axis: ↑↑

1949..............................		5	20	1951		8	25
1950..............................		5	15	1951 Proof *FDC* £25			
1950 Proof *FDC* £15				1951 Matt Proof *FDC of highest rarity*			
1950 Matt Proof *FDC of highest rarity*							

4108 Shilling. 'English' reverse. Bare head l. die axis: ↑↑

1949..............................		5	20	1951..............................		6	20
1950..............................		5	15	1951 Proof *FDC* £15			
1950 Proof *FDC* £15				1951 Matt Proof *FDC Extremely rare*			

4109 Shilling. 'Scottish' reverse. Bare head l. die axis: ↑↑

1949..............................		5	20	1951..............................		6	20
1950..............................		5	15	1951 Proof *FDC* £15			
1950 Proof *FDC* £15				1951 Matt Proof *FDC Extremely rare*			
1950 Matt Proof *FDC Extremely rare*							

4110
1952 Sixpence

4110 Sixpence. Bare head l. R. Crowned cypher die axis: ↑↑

1949..............................	1	8		1951..............................		5	12
1950..............................	1	8		1951 Proof *FDC* £12			
1950 Proof *FDC* £10				1951 Matt Proof *FDC Extremely rare*			
1950 Matt Proof *FDC Extremely rare*				1952...................... 5	5	30	95

Festival of Britain issue die axis: ↑↑

4111
Festival of Britain Crown

	EF £	UNC £
4111 Crown. Bare head l. R. St. George and dragon, date in ex, 1951. *Proof-like*	5	12

    Similar — 1951 Frosted 'VIP' Proof £350

    Similar — 1951 Matt Proof *FDC of highest rarity*

    Similar — 1951 Plain edge Proof *FDC* £1000

NICKEL BRASS

First issue, with title IND:IMP.

4112
1937 Brass Threepence

4113
Second issue obverse

	VF £	EF £	UNC £		VF £	EF £	UNC £
4112 Threepence (dodecagonal). Bare head l. R. Thrift plant die axis: ↑↑							
1937		2	8	1942		2	7
1937 Proof *FDC* £15				1943		2	8
1937 Matt Proof *FDC of highest rarity*				1944		2	10
1938		6	20	1945		5	15
1939		10	40	1946	20	140	475
1940		6	20	1948		10	50
1941		3	10				

Second issue, omitting IND:IMP.

4113 Threepence. Bare head l. R. Similar die axis: ↑↑

	VF £	EF £	UNC £		VF £	EF £	UNC £
1949	20	125	425	1951	3	25	125
1950	20	100		1951 Proof *FDC* £40			
1950 Proof *FDC* £35				1951 Matt Proof *FDC of highest rarity*			
1950 Matt Proof *FDC of highest rarity*				1952		5	15

BRONZE

First issue, with title IND:IMP.

4114
1938 Penny

	EF £	UNC £		EF £	UNC £

4114 Penny. Bare head l. R. Britannia Seated r. date in ex die axis: ↑↑

	EF £	UNC £		EF £	UNC £
1937...................		6	1944 —..................	6	25
1937 Proof *FDC* £15			1945 —..................	5	20
1938........................	1	10	1946 —..................	2	8
1939........................	4	15	1947 —...................		6
1940........................	10	40	1948 —...................		6
1940 Double exergue line	4	12	1946 ONE' die flaw 60		—

4115	4116
1937 Halfpenny	1943 Farthing

4115 Halfpenny. Bare head l. R. Ship sailing l. date below die axis: ↑↑

	EF £	UNC £		EF £	UNC £
1937...		6	1943...		6
1937 Proof *FDC* £10			1944...		6
1938........................	1	10	1945........................	1	8
1939........................	3	15	1946........................	2	15
1940........................	3	15	1947........................	1	8
1941..		8	1948........................	1	8
1942..		6			

4116 Farthing. Bare head l. R. Wren l. date above die axis: ↑↑

	EF £	UNC £		EF £	UNC £
1937...		4	1943...		4
1937 Proof *FDC* £10			1944...		4
1938........................		10	1945...		4
1939........................		4	1946...		4
1940........................		4	1947...		4
1941........................		4	1948...		4
1942........................		4			

	VF £	EF £	UNC £		VF £	EF £	UNC £

4117 Penny. Bare head l. R. Britannia Seated r. date in ex. die axis: ↑↑

1949...................................			6	1951....................... 10		35	60
1950......................6		18	60	1951 Proof *FDC* £40			
1950 Proof *FDC* £25				1952 Proof only.....			*Unique*

4118
Second issue Halfpenny

4119
Second issue Farthing

4118 Halfpenny. Bare head l. R. Ship Sailing l. date below die axis: ↑↑

1949..............................	4	14	1951..............................	5	20
1950..............................	3	10	1951 Proof *FDC* £12		
1950 Proof *FDC* £10			1952..............................	1	8

4119 Farthing. Bare head l. R. Wren l. date above die axis: ↑↑

1949..	5	1951..		6
1950..	5	1951 Proof *FDC* £12		
1950 Proof *FDC* £10		1952..		5

The coins dated 1952 were issued during the reign of Elizabeth II.

Proof Sets

PS15 Coronation, **1937.** Five pounds to Half-sovereign (4 coins)........................ *FDC*		£3000
PS16 — 1937. Crown to Farthing, including Maundy Set (15 coins).................. *FDC*		£285
PS17 Mid-Century, **1950.** Halfcrown to Farthing (9 coins) .... *FDC*		£100
PS18 Festival of Britain, **1951.** Crown to Farthing (10 coins) .... *FDC*		£125

Elizabeth II was born on 21 April 1926. Our current Monarch has lived a long and glorious reign celebrating her Golden Jubilee in 2002. She married Philip a distant cousin in 1947 and has four children, Charles, Anne, Andrew and Edward. Significantly she is the first Monarch to pay taxes and her coinage has been an interesting one with the change to decimal coinage and the numerous bust changes since 1953.

The earliest coins of this reign have the title BRITT:OMN, but in 1954 this was omitted from the Queen's titles owing to the changing status of so many Commonwealth territories. The minting of 'English' and 'Scottish' shillings was continued. A Coronation commemorative crown was issued in 1953, another crown was struck on the occasion of the 1960 British Exhibition in New York and a third was issued in honour of Sir Winston Churchill in 1965. A very small number of proof gold coins were struck in 1953 for the national museum collections, but between 1957 and 1968 gold sovereigns were minted again in quantity for sale in the international bullion market and to counteract the activities of counterfeiters.

Owing to inflation the farthing had now become practically valueless; production of these coins ceased after 1956 and the coins were demonetized at the end of 1960. In 1965 it was decided to change to a decimal system of coinage in the year 1971. As part of the transition to decimal coinage the halfpenny was demonetized in August 1969 and the halfcrown in January 1970. (See also introduction to Decimal Coinage.

Prime Ministers:-

Winston Churchill, Conservative, 1951-55
Sir Anthony Eden, Conservative, 1955-57
Harold Macmillan, Conservative, 1957-63
Sir Alec Douglas-Home, Conservative, 1963-64
Harold Wilson, Labour, 1964-70
Edward Heath, Conservative, 1970-74
Harold Wilson, Labour, 1974-76
James Callaghan, Labour, 1976-79
Margaret Thatcher, Conservative, 1979-90
John Major, Conservative, 1990-97
Tony Blair, Labour, 1997-2007
Gordon Brown, Labour, 2007-

Designer's initials:

A. V. (Avril Vaughan)
B. P. (Benedetto Pistrucci, 1784-1855)
B. R. (Bruce Rushin)
C.D. (Clive Duncan)
C. T. (Cecil Thomas)
D. C. (David Cornell)
E. F. (Edgar Fuller)
G. L. (Gilbert Ledward)
I. R. B. (Ian Rank-Broadley)
J. B. (James Butler)
J. M. (Jeffrey Matthews)
J. M. M. (John Mills)
M. B. (Matthew Bonaccorsi)

M. G. (Mary Gillick)
M. M. D. (Mary Milner Dickens)
M. N. (Michael Noakes)
M. R. (Michael Rizzello)
N. S. (Norman Sillman)
P. N. (Philip Nathan)
R. D. (Ron Dutton)
R. D. M. (Raphael David Maklouf)
R. E. (Robert Elderton)
r. e. (Robert Evans)
R. L. (Robert Lowe)
T. N. (Timothy Noad)
W. G. (William Gardner)
W. P. (Wilson Parker 1896-1980)

Other designers whose initials do not appear on the coins:

Christopher Ironside (1913-
Arnold Machin (1911-99)
David Wynne
Professor Richard Guyatt
Eric Sewell

Oscar Nemon
Leslie Durbin
Derek Gorringe
Bernard Sindall
Tom Phillips
Edwina Ellis
David Gentleman

PRE-DECIMAL ISSUES
Die axis ↑↑
GOLD

First coinage, with title BRITT.OMN, 1953. *Proof only*..................	*of the highest rarity*
4120 Five Pounds. Young laur. head r. R. St. George........................	250000
4121 Two Pounds. Young laur. head r. R. St. George........................	120000
4122 Sovereign. Young laur. head r. R. St. George............................	150000
4123 Half-Sovereign. Young laur. head r. R. St. George..................	75000

Second issue, BRITT.OMN omitted

4125
1958 Sovereign

	EF £	UNC £
4124 Sovereign. Young laur head r. R. St. George, fine graining on edge		
1957...BV		85
1957 Proof *FDC* £4500		

	UNC £		UNC £
4125 Sovereign. Similar, but coarser graining on edge			
1958......................................	85	1963 Proof *FDC* £5750	
1958 Proof *FDC* £4500		1964......................................	85
1959......................................	95	1965......................................	85
1959 Proof *FDC* £4500		1966......................................	85
1962......................................	90	1967......................................	85
1963......................................	90	1968......................................	85

SILVER

The Queen's Maundy are now the only coins struck regularly in silver.
The location of the Maundy ceremony is given for each year.

First issue, with title BRITT:OMN:

4126
Maundy Set

	FDC £		FDC £
4126 Maundy Set (4d., 3d., 2d. and 1d.), 1953. *St Paul's Cathedral*			575
1953 Proof struck in gold *FDC* £13000			
1953 Proof struck in nickel bronze *FDC Extremely rare*			
1953 Matt Proof *FDC Extremely rare*			
4127 — Fourpence. 1953			100
4128 — Threepence. 1953..			100
4129 — Twopence. 1953...			100
4130 — Penny. 1953			200

Second issue, with BRITT:OMN: omitted

4131 Maundy Set (4d., 3d., 2d. and 1d.). Uniform dates

1954 *Westminster*	95	1956 *Westminster*	95
1955 *Southwark*	95	1957 *St. Albans*	95

	FDC		*FDC*
	£		£
1958 *Westminster*	95	1965 Canterbury.................................	95
1959 *Windsor*	95	1966 Westminster.............................	95
1960 *Westminster*	95	1967 Durham	95
1961 *Rochester*....................................	95	1968 Westminster.............................	95
1962 *Westminster*	95	1969 Selby	95
1963 *Chelmsford*................................	95	1970 Westminster.............................	95
1964 Westminster...............................	95		

4132 — Fourpence. 1954-70...*from* 12
4133 — Threepence. 1954-70..*from* 12
4134 — Twopence. 1954-70..*from* 12
4135 — Penny. 1954-70...*from* 18

CUPRO-NICKEL

First issue, 1953, with title BRITT.OMN.

4136
1953 Coronation Crown

	EF	UNC	*PROOF* FDC
	£	£	£
4136 Crown. Queen on horseback. R. Crown in centre of emblematical cross, shield of Arms in each angle, 1953	4	8	30

Similar 1953 Frosted 'VIP' proof £550
Similar 1953 Matt Proof *FDC of highest rarity*

4137
1953 Halfcrown

4138
1953 Florin

| **4137 Halfcrown.** with title BRITT:OMN: Young laur. head r. R. Arms, 1953.. | 5 | 15 |
| **4138 Florin.** Young laur. head r. R. Double rose, 1953..................................... | 4 | 10 |

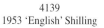

4139	4140	4141
1953 'English' Shilling	'Scottish' reverse	1953 Sixpence

	Proof
UNC	FDC
£	£

4139 Shilling. 'English' reverse. Young laur. head r. R. Three lions, 1953 .... 2 | 8

4140 Shilling. '— 'Scottish' reverse. Young laur. head r. R. Lion rampant in shield, 1953 | 2 | 8

4141 Sixpence. Young laur. head r. R. Interlaced rose, thistle, shamrock and leek, 1953 1 | 6

4142 Set of 9 uncirculated cu-ni, ni-br and Æ coins (2/6 to 1/4d.)
in Royal Mint plastic envelope .... | 20

Second issue, similar types but omitting BRITT.OMN.

4143	4144
1960 Crown	1965 Churchill Crown

	EF	UNC
	£	£

4143 Crown, 1960. Young laur. head r. R. As 4136 .... 5 | 10

— — Similar, from polished dies (New York Exhibition issue) .... 10 | 25

— — 'VIP' *Proof,* frosted design *FDC* £400

4144 Crown, Churchill commemorative, 1965. As illustration. R. Bust of Sir Winston
Churchill r. .... | 2

— — Similar, "Satin-Finish". VIP *Specimen* .... | 850

	EF	UNC		EF	UNC		EF	UNC
	£	£		£	£		£	£

4145 Halfcrown. Young laur. head r. R. As 4137

1954	8	35	1960		10	1965		4
1955		10	1961		4	1966		2
1956		15	1961 Polished die..		10	1967		2
1957		5	1962		4	1970 Proof *FDC* £5		
1958	8	30	1963		4			
1959	8	35	1964		6			

4146
1957 Florin

	EF	UNC		UNC
	£	£		£

4146 Florin. Young laur. head r. R. As 4138

1954	8	40	1962	4
1955		10	1963	3
1956		10	1964	3
1957	8	40	1965	3
1958	6	35	1966	2
1959	8	40	1967	2
1960		10	1970 Proof *FDC* £5	
1961		10		

4147 Shilling. 'English' reverse. Young laur. head r. R. As 4139

1954		5	1961	2
1955		5	1962	1
1956		10	1963	1
1957		4	1964	1
1958	8	40	1965	1
1959		4	1966	1
1960		4	1970 Proof *FDC* £3	

4148 Shilling. 'Scottish' reverse. Young laur. head r. R. As 4140

1954		5	1961	8
1955		6	1962	4
1956		10	1963	1
1957	5	25	1964	1
1958		3	1965	1
1959	10	60	1966	1
1960		4	1970 Proof *FDC* £2	

4149 Sixpence. Young laur. head r. R. As 4141

1954		6		
1955		3	1962	1.50
			1963	1.50
1956		4	1964	1.50
1957		3	1965	1
1958		8	1966	1
1959		2	1967	1
1960		5	1970 Proof *FDC* £3	
1961		5		

NICKEL BRASS

First issue, with title BRITT.OMN.

4152	4153
1953 Brass Threepence	Second issue

	UNC		UNC
	£		£

4152 Threepence (dodecagonal). Young laur. head r. ℞. Crowned portcullis, 1953 4
— Proof *FDC* £10

Second issue (omitting BRIT.OMN)
4153 Threepence Similar type

1954	6	1962	1
1955	8	1963	1
1956	8	1964	1
1957	5	1965	1
1958	12	1966	0.50
1959	5	1967	0.50
1960	4	1970 Proof *FDC* £3	
1961	2		

BRONZE

First issue, with title BRITT.OMN.

4154	4155	4156
1953 Penny	1953 Halfpenny	1953 Farthing
		Proof

	VF	EF	UNC	FDC
	£	£	£	£

4154 Penny. Young laur. head r. ℞. Britannia (only issued with Royal Mint set in
plastic envelope), 1953 Beaded border 1   3   10   20
1953 Toothed border .... *Extremely rare*
4155 Halfpenny. Young laur. head r. ℞. Ship, 1953 3   10
4156 Farthing. Young laur. head r. ℞. Wren, 1953 2   8

Second issue, omitting BRITT.OMN.
4157 Penny. Young laur. head r. ℞. Britannia (1954-60 *not issued*)

1954	Unique	1965	0.50
1961	2	1966	0.50
1962	1	1967	0.25
1963	1	1970 Proof *FDC* £4	
1964	0.50		

	UNC £		UNC £

4158 Halfpenny. Young laur. head r. R. Ship (1961 *not issued*)

1954	7	1960	1
1954 larger border teeth	9	1962	1
1955	5	1963	1
1956	6	1964	1
1957	3	1965	1
1957 calm sea	30	1966	0.50
1958	2	1967	0.50
1959	1	1970 Proof *FDC* £3	

4159
Second issue

4159 Farthing. Young laur. head r. R. Wren

	EF £		UNC £
1954	4	1956	EF 3 / UNC 6
1955	4		

Proof Sets

PS19 Coronation, **1953.** Crown to Farthing (10 coins)	*FDC*	90
PS20 'Last Sterling', **1970.** Halfcrown to Halfpenny plus medallion	*FDC*	20

PRE-DECIMAL PROOF SETS

All prices quoted assume coins are in their original case. Issued by the Royal Mint in official case from 1887 onwards, but earlier sets were issued privately by the engraver. All pieces have a superior finish to that of the current coins.

	No. of coins	FDC £
PS1 **George IV, 1826.** New issue, Five Pounds to Farthing	(11)	28500
PS1A — — Similar to above, including Maundy Set	(15)	30000
PS2 **William IV, 1831.** Coronation, Two Pounds to Farthing	(14)	23500
PS3 **Victoria, 1839.** Young head. "Una and the Lion" Five Pounds and Sovereign to Farthing	(15)	38500
PS4 — **1853.** Sovereign to Half-Farthing, including Gothic type Crown	(16)	34500
PS5 — **1887.** Jubilee bust for Golden Jubilee, Five Pounds to Threepence	(11)	7750
PS6 — **1887.** Silver Crown to Threepence	(7)	1550
PS7 — **1893.** Old bust, Five Pounds to Threepence	(10)	9250
PS8 — **1893.** Silver Crown to Threepence	(6)	1800
PS9 **Edward VII, 1902.** Coronation, Five Pounds to Maundy Penny. Matt finish to surfaces	(13)	2500
PS10 — **1902.** Sovereign to Maundy Penny. Matt finish	(11)	975
PS11 **George V, 1911.** Coronation, Five Pounds to Maundy Penny	(12)	4000
PS12 — **1911.** Sovereign to Maundy Penny	(10)	1250
PS13 — **1911.** Silver Halfcrown to Maundy Penny	(8)	550
PS14 — **1927.** New Coinage. Wreath type Crown to Threepence	(6)	480
PS15 **George VI, 1937.** Coronation. Five Pounds to Half-Sovereign	(4)	2900
PS16 — **1937.** Coronation. Crown to Farthing, including Maundy Set	(15)	295
PS17 — **1950.** Mid-Century, Halfcrown to Farthing	(9)	100
PS18 — **1951.** Festival of Britain, Crown to Farthing	(10)	125
PS19 **Elizabeth II, 1953.** Coronation. Crown to Farthing	(10)	90
PS20 — **1970.** "Last Sterling" set. Halfcrown to Halfpenny plus medallion	(8)	20

A decision to adopt decimal currency was announced in March 1966 following the recommendation of the Halsbury Committee of Enquiry which had been appointed in 1961. The date for the introduction of the new system was 15 February 1971 and it was evident that the Royal Mint facilities which had been located on Tower Hill for more than 150 years would be unable to strike the significant quantities of coins required on that site. The Government therefore decided to build a new mint at Llantrisant in South Wales.

The new system provided for three smaller bronze coins and very large numbers were struck and stock piled for D-Day but the five and ten new pence denominations with the same specifications as the former shilling and florin were introduced in 1968. A further change was the introduction in 1969 of a 50 new pence coin to replace the ten shilling banknote.

In 1982 and 1983 two more new coins were introduced; the 20 pence which helped to reduce demand for five and ten pence pieces, and the first circulating non-precious metal £1 coin which replaced the bank note of the same value.

Increasing raw material costs, and inflation also play a part in the development of a modern coinage system and a smaller 50 pence was introduced in the autumn of 1997, following the reduced size 5 and 10 pence coins in 1990 and 1992 respectively. A bimetallic circulating £2 was also introduced in 1997.

For the collector, many of these changes have been accompanied by special issues often in limited editions struck in precious metal. A variety of designs can now be seen on the £2, £1 and 50 pence coins that circulate, and this has surely added to the interest of collectors and the general public.

In addition crown size pieces which have a face value of £5 seem now to be a regular feature along with commemorative £2 and 50 pence issues in the Royal Mint's range of products.

The major change in the coinage in 1998 was the new, and fourth, portrait of H. M. The Queen. Designed by Ian Rank-Broadley, a whole new series started which has stimulated interest among collectors everywhere.

GOLD

4201

4201 Five pounds. As illustration

1980 Proof *FDC** £550	1982 Proof *FDC** £600
1981 Proof *FDC* (Issued: 5,400)** £550	1984 Proof *FDC* (Issued: 905) £550

4202 As 4201 but, 'U' in a circle to left of date

1984 (Issued: 15,104) *Unc* £500

4203 Two pounds

1980 Proof *FDC** £250	1983 Proof *FDC* (Issued: 12,500)** £250
1982 Proof *FDC** £280	

* *Coins marked thus were originally issued in Royal Mint Sets.*
** *Numbers include coins sold in sets.*

4204

4204 Sovereign. As illustration

1974 .... Unc £100	— Proof *FDC* (Issued: 81,200) £140
1976 .... Unc £100	1981 .... Unc £100
1976 VIP Proof *FDC* ..... *Extremely rare*	— Proof *FDC* (Issued: 32,960) £150
1978 .... Unc £100	1982 .... Unc £100
1979 .... Unc £100	— Proof *FDC* (Issued: 20,000) £150
— Proof *FDC* (Issued: 50,000) £140	1983 Proof *FDC* (Issued: 21,250)** £180
1980 .... Unc £100	1984 Proof *FDC* (Issued: 12,880) £180

4205 Half-sovereign

1980 Proof *FDC* (Issued: 76.700) £80	1983 Proof *FDC* (Issued: 19,710)** £100
1982 .... Unc £60	1984 Proof *FDC* (Issued: 12,410) £100
— Proof *FDC* (Issued: 19,090) £80	

SILVER

	FDC		FDC
	£		£

4211 Maundy Set (4p, 3p, 2p and 1p). Uniform dates. Types as 4131

	FDC		FDC
1971 *Tewkesbury Abbey*..........	95	1991 *Westminster Abbey*............	95
1972 *York Minster*...................	95	1992 *Chester Cathedral*.............	95
1973 *Westminster Abbey*.........	95	1993 *Wells Cathedral*	95
1974 *Salisbury Cathedral*.......	95	1994 *Truro Cathedral*	95
1975 *Peterborough Cathedral*	95	1995 *Coventry Cathedral*	100
1976 *Hereford Cathedral*........	95	1996 *Norwich Cathedral*	100
1977 *Westminster Abbey*.........	95	1997 *Bradford Cathedral*	100
1978 *Carlisle Cathedral*	95	1998 *Portsmouth Cathedral*	100
1979 *Winchester Cathedral*	95	1999 *Bristol Cathedral*	100
1980 *Worcester Cathedral*	95	2000 *Lincoln Cathedral*.............	100
1981 *Westminster Abbey*.........	95	2001 *Westminster Abbey*............	100
1982 *St. David's Cathedral*.....	95	2002 *Canterbury Cathedral*.......	125
1983 *Exeter Cathedral*...........	95	2002 *Proof in gold from set*	
1984 *Southwell Minster*	95	*(see PCGS1)*	1000
1985 *Ripon Cathedral*	95	2003 *Gloucester Cathedral*	125
1986 *Chichester Cathedral*.....	95	2004 *Liverpool Cathedral*	125
1987 *Ely Cathedral*.................	95	2005 *Wakefield Cathedral*	125
1988 *Lichfield Cathedral*........	95	2006 *Guildford Cathedral*	125
1989 *Birmingham Cathedral* ..	95	2007 *Manchester Cathedral*	125
1990 *Newcastle Cathedral*......	95		

4212 — **fourpence,** 1971-2006...*from*	20
4213 — **threepence,** 1971-2006 ....*from*	20
4214 — **twopence,** 1971-2006 ....*from*	20
4215 — **penny,** 1971-2006 ....*from*	25

The place of distribution is shown after each date.

*Coins marked thus were originally issued in Royal Mint sets

** numbers include coins sold in sets

NICKEL-BRASS

4221   4222

UNC
£

4221 **One pound** (Royal Arms design). Edge "DECUS ET TUTAMEN" (Reverse design: Eric Sewell)

1983 5

— Specimen in presentation folder (Issued: 484,900) 5

— Proof *FDC** £5   — Proof piedfort in silver *FDC* (Issued: 10,000) £125

— Proof in silver *FDC* (Issued: 50,000) £35

4222 **One pound** (Scottish design). Edge "NEMO ME IMPUNE LACESSIT" (Reverse design: Leslie Durbin)

1984 5

— Specimen in presentation folder (Issued: 27,960) 5

— Proof *FDC** £5   — Proof piedfort in silver *FDC* (Issued: 15,000) £55

— Proof in silver *FDC* (Issued: 44,855) £26

CUPRO-NICKEL

4223   4224

	UNC		UNC		UNC
	£		£		£

4223 **Fifty new pence** (seven-sided). R. Britannia r.

1969	2	1976......................	2	1979	2
1970	4	— Proof *FDC** £2		— Proof *FDC** £3	
1971 Proof *FDC** £4		1977......................	2	1980	2
1972 Proof *FDC** £5		— Proof *FDC** £2		— Proof *FDC** £2	
1974 Proof *FDC** £3		1978......................	2	1981	2
1975 Proof *FDC** £3		— Proof *FDC** £3		— Proof *FDC** £2	

4224 Accession to European Economic Community. R. Clasped hands, (Reverse design: David Wynne)

1973 .... 1.50

—Proof *FDC*** £3

4224A — .... Design as 4224 above, but struck in very small numbers in silver on thicker blank. Sometimes referred to as a piedfort but not twice the weight of the regular cupro-nickel currency issue. The pieces were presented to EEC Finance Ministers, and possibly senior officials on the occasion of the United Kingdom joining the European Economic Community. 2500

* *Coins marked thus were originally issued in Royal Mint sets as shown on page .*

** *Issued as an individual proof coin and in the year set shown on page .*

4225

	UNC £		UNC £		UNC £

4225 Fifty pence. 'New' omitted. As illustration

1982 2   1983......................... 2   1984* 3
— Proof *FDC** £2   — Proof *FDC** £2   — Proof *FDC** £2

4226

4226 Twenty-five pence. Silver Wedding Commemorative (Reverse design: Arnold Machin)

1972 2
— Proof *FDC** (in 1972 Set, See PS22) £6
— Silver proof in case *FDC* (Issued: 100,000) £30

4227

	UNC £

4227 Twenty-five pence Silver Jubilee Commemorative (Obverse and reverse design: Arnold Machin)

1977 .... 1.50
— Specimen in presentation folder 2
— Proof *FDC** (in 1977 Set, See PS27) £5
— Silver proof in case *FDC* (Issued: 377,000) £22

* Coins marked thus were originally issued in Royal Mint sets

4228

4228 **Twenty-Five pence** Queen Mother 80th Birthday Commemorative (Reverse design: Richard Guyatt)

1980 2

— Specimen in presentation folder 3

— Silver proof in case *FDC* (Issued: 83,672) £40

4229

4229 **Twenty-five pence.** Royal Wedding Commemorative (Reverse design: Philip Nathan)

1981 2

— Specimen in presentation folder 3

— Silver proof in case *FDC* (Issued: 218,142) £35

4230

	UNC £		UNC £		UNC £

4230 **Twenty (20) pence.** R crowned rose

1982	0.40	1983	0.40	1984	0.40

— Proof *FDC** £2   — Proof *FDC** £1   — Proof *FDC** £1

— Proof piedfort in silver *FDC* (Issued: 10,000) £50

* Coins marked thus were originally issued in Royal Mint sets

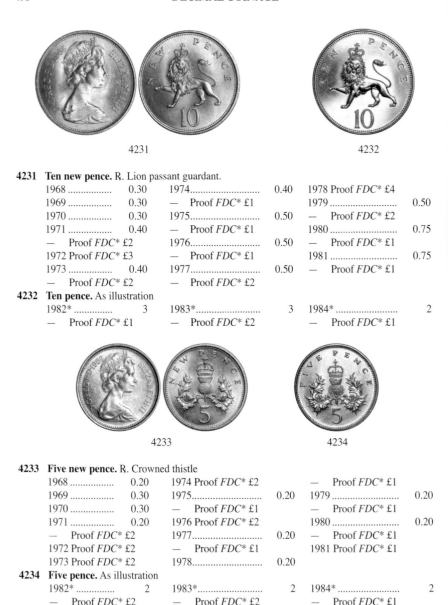

4231

4232

4231 **Ten new pence.** ℞. Lion passant guardant.

1968	0.30	1974	0.40	1978 Proof *FDC** £4	
1969	0.30	— Proof *FDC** £1		1979	0.50
1970	0.30	1975	0.50	— Proof *FDC** £2	
1971	0.40	— Proof *FDC** £1		1980	0.75
— Proof *FDC** £2		1976	0.50	— Proof *FDC** £1	
1972 Proof *FDC** £3		— Proof *FDC** £1		1981	0.75
1973	0.40	1977	0.50	— Proof *FDC** £1	
— Proof *FDC** £2		— Proof *FDC** £2			

4232 **Ten pence.** As illustration

1982*	3	1983*	3	1984*	2
— Proof *FDC** £1		— Proof *FDC** £2		— Proof *FDC** £1	

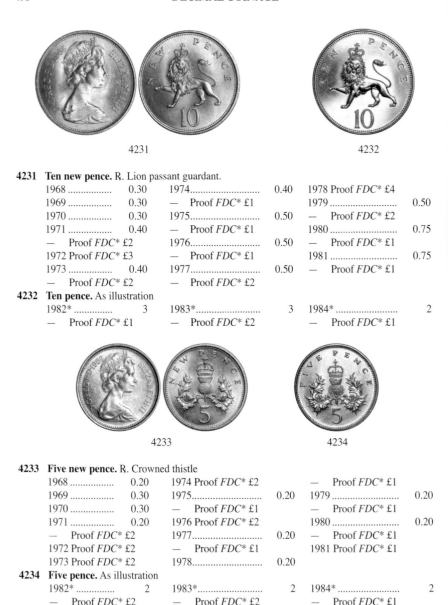

4233

4234

4233 **Five new pence.** ℞. Crowned thistle

1968	0.20	1974 Proof *FDC** £2		— Proof *FDC** £1	
1969	0.30	1975	0.20	1979	0.20
1970	0.30	— Proof *FDC** £1		— Proof *FDC** £1	
1971	0.20	1976 Proof *FDC** £2		1980	0.20
— Proof *FDC** £2		1977	0.20	— Proof *FDC** £1	
1972 Proof *FDC** £2		— Proof *FDC** £1		1981 Proof *FDC** £1	
1973 Proof *FDC** £2		1978	0.20		

4234 **Five pence.** As illustration

1982*	2	1983*	2	1984*	2
— Proof *FDC** £2		— Proof *FDC** £2		— Proof *FDC** £1	

* Coins marked thus were originally issued in Royal Mint sets.

BRONZE

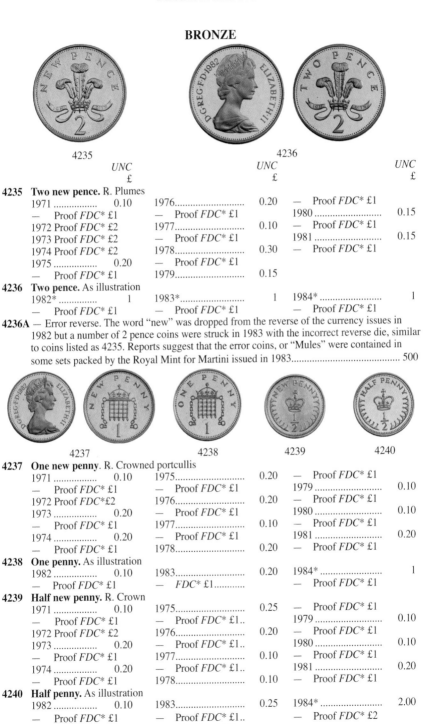

4235

4236

	UNC £		UNC £		UNC £

4235 Two new pence. R. Plumes

1971	0.10	1976	0.20	— Proof FDC* £1	
— Proof FDC* £1		— Proof FDC* £1		1980	0.15
1972 Proof FDC* £2		1977	0.10	— Proof FDC* £1	
1973 Proof FDC* £2		— Proof FDC* £1		1981	0.15
1974 Proof FDC* £2		1978	0.30	— Proof FDC* £1	
1975	0.20	— Proof FDC* £1			
— Proof FDC* £1		1979	0.15		

4236 Two pence. As illustration

| 1982* | 1 | 1983* | 1 | 1984* | 1 |
| — Proof FDC* £1 | | — Proof FDC* £1 | | — Proof FDC* £1 | |

4236A — Error reverse. The word "new" was dropped from the reverse of the currency issues in 1982 but a number of 2 pence coins were struck in 1983 with the incorrect reverse die, similar to coins listed as 4235. Reports suggest that the error coins, or "Mules" were contained in some sets packed by the Royal Mint for Martini issued in 1983.. 500

4237

4238

4239

4240

4237 One new penny. R. Crowned portcullis

1971	0.10	1975	0.20	— Proof FDC* £1	
— Proof FDC* £1		— Proof FDC* £1		1979	0.10
1972 Proof FDC* £2		1976	0.20	— Proof FDC* £1	
1973	0.20	— Proof FDC* £1		1980	0.10
— Proof FDC* £1		1977	0.10	— Proof FDC* £1	
1974	0.20	— Proof FDC* £1		1981	0.20
— Proof FDC* £1		1978	0.20	— Proof FDC* £1	

4238 One penny. As illustration

| 1982 | 0.10 | 1983 | 0.20 | 1984* | 1 |
| — Proof FDC* £1 | | — FDC* £1 | | — Proof FDC* £1 | |

4239 Half new penny. R. Crown

1971	0.10	1975	0.25	— Proof FDC* £1	
— Proof FDC* £1		— Proof FDC* £1..		1979	0.10
1972 Proof FDC* £2		1976	0.20	— Proof FDC* £1	
1973	0.20	— Proof FDC* £1..		1980	0.10
— Proof FDC* £1		1977	0.10	— Proof FDC* £1	
1974	0.20	— Proof FDC* £1..		1981	0.20
— Proof FDC* £1		1978	0.10	— Proof FDC* £1	

4240 Half penny. As illustration

| 1982 | 0.10 | 1983 | 0.25 | 1984* | 2.00 |
| — Proof FDC* £1 | | — Proof FDC* £1.. | | — Proof FDC* £2 | |

* Coins marked thus were originally issued in Royal Mint sets.

The new effigy was designed by Raphael David Maklouf, FRSA. It is the third portrait of the Queen to be used on UK coinage, the previous change of portrait being in 1968 with the introduction of decimal coins. The designer's initials R.D.M. appear on the truncation. There is no portrait change on the Maundy coins (see 4211-4215).

GOLD

4251   4253

4251 Five pounds. R. St. George
1985 Proof *FDC* (Issued: 281) £600
1990 Proof *FDC** £600   1993 Proof *FDC** £650   1996 Proof *FDC** £650
1991 Proof *FDC** £600   1994 Proof *FDC** £650   1997 Proof *FDC** £650
1992 Proof *FDC** £650   1995 Proof *FDC** £650

4252 Five pounds R. St George, 'U' in a circle to left of date.

	UNC		UNC
1985 (Issued: 13,626)	£500	1993 (Issued: 906)	£550
1986 (Issued: 7,723)	£500	1994 (Issued: 1,000)	£550
1990 (Issued: 1,226)	£550	1995 (Issued: 1,000)	£550
1991 (Issued: 976)	£550	1996 (Issued: 901)	£550
1992 (Issued: 797)	£550	1997 (Issued: 802)	£550

4253 Five pounds Uncouped portrait of Queen Elizabeth II. As illustration. R. St. George, 'U' in a circle to left of date.
1987 (Issued: 5,694) £550   1988 (Issued: 3,315) £550

4254 Five pounds 500th Anniversary of Sovereign. (Designs: Bernald Sindall) As illustration 4277
1989 (Issued: 2,937) £650   — — Proof *FDC** £800

4261 Two pounds. R. St. George
1985 Proof *FDC** £250   1991 Proof *FDC* (Issued: 620) £300
1987 Proof *FDC* (Issued: 1,801) £250   1992 Proof *FDC* (Issued: 476) £300
1988 Proof *FDC* (Issued: 1,551) £250   1993 Proof *FDC* (Issued: 414) £300
1990 Proof *FDC* (Issued: 716) £300   1996 Proof *FDC* £300

4262 Two pounds 500th Anniversary of Sovereign. As illustration 4277
1989 Proof *FDC* (Issued: 2,000) £450

The 1986 £2, 1994 £2 and two types of 1995 £2 commemorative coins in gold previously listed as 4262, 4264, 4265 & 4266 respectively are now shown in the section commencing 4311 with their respective types in other metals.

4271 Sovereign. R. St. George
1985 Proof *FDC* (Issued: 11,393) £225   1992 Proof *FDC* (Issued: 4,772) £280
1986 Proof *FDC* (Issued: 5,079) £225   1993 Proof *FDC* (Issued: 4,349) £325
1987 Proof *FDC* (Issued: 9,979) £225   1994 Proof *FDC* (Issued: 4,998) £280
1988 Proof *FDC* (Issued: 7,670) £225   1995 Proof *FDC* (Issued: 7,500) £280
1990 Proof *FDC* (Issued: 4,767) £280   1996 Proof *FDC* (Issued: 7,500) £280
1991 Proof *FDC* (Issued: 4,713) £280   1997 Proof *FDC* (Issued: 7,500) £280

* *Coins marked thus were originally issued in Royal Mint sets. Where numbers of coins issued or the Edition limit is quoted, these refer to individual coins. Additional coins were included in sets which are listed in the appropriate section.*

4272 Sovereign. 500th Anniversary of Sovereign. As illustration 4277
1989 Proof *FDC* (Issued: 10,535) £750

4277

4276 Half-sovereign. R. St. George

1985 Proof *FDC* (Issued: 9,951) £125	1992 Proof *FDC* (Issued: 3,783) £150
1986 Proof *FDC* (Issued: 4,575) £125	1993 Proof *FDC* (Issued: 2,910) £150
1987 Proof *FDC* (Issued: 8,187) £125	1994 Proof *FDC* (Issued: 5,000) £150
1988 Proof *FDC* (Issued: 7,074) £125	1995 Proof *FDC* (Issued: 4,900) £150
1990 Proof *FDC* (Issued: 4,231) £150	1996 Proof *FDC* (Issued: 5,730) £150
1991 Proof *FDC* (Issued: 3,588) £150	1997 Proof *FDC* (Issued: 7,500) £150

4277 Half-sovereign 500th Anniversary of Sovereign. As illustration 4277
1989 Proof *FDC* (Issued: 8,888) £250

4281

	UNC		*UNC*

4281 Britannia. One hundred pounds. (1oz of fine gold) R. Britannia standing. (Reverse design :
Philip Nathan)

1987	£400	1989	£400
— Proof *FDC* (Issued: 2,485) £500		— Proof *FDC* (Issued: 338) £500	
1988	£400		
— Proof *FDC* (Issued: 626) £500			

4282 Britannia. One hundred pounds. (1oz of fine gold alloyed with silver) R. Britannia standing.

1990	£450	1994	£450
— Proof *FDC* (Issued: 262) £550		— Proof *FDC** £500	
1991	£450	1995	£450
— Proof *FDC* (Issued: 143) £550		— Proof *FDC** £500	
1992	£450	1996	£450
— Proof *FDC** £550		— Proof *FDC** £500	
1993	£450		
— Proof *FDC** £500			

Where numbers of coins are quoted, these refer to individual coins. Additional coins were included in sets which are listed in the appropriate section.

* Coins marked thus were originally issued in Royal Mint sets.

4283

4283 Britannia. One Hundred pounds. (1 oz of fine gold, alloyed with silver) R. Standing figure of Britannia in horse drawn chariot. 10th Anniversary of Britannia issue. (Reverse design: Philip Nathan)

1997 .... £500   1997 Proof *FDC* (Issued: 164) £700

4286

4286 Britannia. Fifty pounds. (1/2oz of fine gold). R. Britannia standing.
1987 .... £225   1989 .... £225
— Proof *FDC* (Issued: 2,486) £250   — Proof *FDC** £250
1988 .... £225
— Proof *FDC** £250

4287 Britannia. Fifty pounds. (1/2oz of fine gold, alloyed with Silver)
R. Britannia standing.
1990 .... £225   1994 .... £250
— Proof *FDC** £300   — Proof *FDC** £300
1991 .... £225   1995 .... £250
— Proof *FDC** £300   — Proof *FDC** £300
1992 .... £250   1996 .... £250
— Proof *FDC** £300   — Proof *FDC** £300
1993 .... £250
— Proof *FDC** £300

4288

4288 Britannia. Fifty pounds. (1/2 oz fine gold, alloyed with silver) R. Standing figure of Britannia in horse drawn chariot 10th Anniversary of Britannia issue
1997 Proof *FDC** £350

* *Coins marked thus were originally issued in Royal Mint sets*

4291

4291 **Britannia. Twenty five pounds.** (1/4oz of fine gold). R. Britannia standing.

1987	£100	1989	£80
— Proof *FDC* (Issued: 3,500) £100		— Proof *FDC** £100	
1988	£100		
— Proof *FDC** £100			

4292 **Britannia. Twenty five pounds.** (1/4oz of fine gold alloyed with silver).
R. Britannia standing.

1990	£120	1994	£120
— Proof *FDC** £150		— Proof *FDC** £150	
1991	£120	1995	£120
— Proof *FDC** £150		— Proof *FDC** £150	
1992	£120	1996	£120
— Proof *FDC** £150		— Proof *FDC** £150	
1993	£150		
— Proof *FDC** £150			

4293   4296

4293 **Britannia. Twenty five pounds.** (1/4 oz fine gold, alloyed with silver) R. Standing figure of Britannia in horse drawn chariot. 10th Anniversary of Britannia issue
1997 Proof *FDC* (Issued: 923) £200

4296 **Britannia. Ten pounds.** (1/10oz of fine gold). R. Britannia standing.

1987	£50	1989	£50
— Proof *FDC* (Issued: 3,500) £70		— Proof *FDC* (Issued: 1,609) £70	
1988	£50		
— Proof *FDC* (Issued: 2,694) £70			

4297 **Britannia. Ten pounds.** (1/10oz of fine gold alloyed with silver). R. Britannia standing.

1990	£60	1994	£80
— Proof *FDC* (Issued: 1,571) £80		— Proof *FDC* (Issued: 994) £80	
1991	£60	1995	£60
— Proof *FDC* (Issued: 954) £80		— Proof *FDC* (Issued: 1,500) £80	
1992	£80	1996	£60
— Proof *FDC* (Issued: 1,000) £80		— Proof *FDC* (Issued: 2,379) £80	
1993	£60		
— Proof *FDC* (Issued: 997) £80			

* Coins marked thus were originally issued in Royal Mint sets.

4298

4298 **Britannia. Ten pounds.** (1/10 oz fine gold, alloyed with silver) R. Standing figure of
Britannia in horse drawn chariot. 10th Anniversary of Britannia issue
1997 Proof *FDC* (Issued: 1,821) £100

SILVER

4300

4300 **Britannia. Two pounds.** (1 oz fine silver) R. Standing figure of Britannia in horse drawn
chariot. 10th Anniversary of Britannia issue. (Reverse design: Philip Nathan)
1997 Proof *FDC* (Issued: 4,173) £65

4300A **Britannia. One pound.** (1/2 oz of fine silver) R. Standing figure of Britannia in horse drawn
chariot. 10th Anniversary of Britannia issue (see 4300)
1997 Proof *FDC** £25

4300B **Britannia. Fifty pence.** (1/4 oz of fine silver) R. Standing figure of Britannia in horse drawn
chariot. 10th Anniversary of Britannnia issue (see 4300)
1997 Proof *FDC** £20

4300C **Britannia. Twenty pence.** (1/4 oz of fine silver) R. Standing figure of Britannia in horse
drawn chariot. 10th Anniversary of Britannia issue (see 4300)
1997 Proof *FDC* (Issued: 8,686) £15

* Coins marked thus were originally issued in Royal Mint Sets.

CUPRO-NICKEL

4301

UNC
£

4301 Five pounds (crown). Queen Mother 90th birthday commemorative.(Reverse design: Leslie
Durbin)
1990 8
— Specimen in presentation folder (Issued: 45,250) 10
— Proof in silver *FDC* (Issued: 56,102) £50
— Proof in gold *FDC* (Issued: 2,500) £650

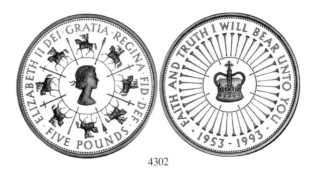

4302

4302 Five pounds (crown). 40th Anniversary of the Coronation. (Obverse design: Raphael
Maklouf, reverse design: Robert Elderton)
1993 7
— Specimen in presentation folder 9
— Proof *FDC* (in 1993 set, see PS51)* £9
— Proof in silver *FDC* (Issued: 58,877) £35
— Proof in gold *FDC* (Issued: 2,500) £650

* Coins marked thus were originally issued in Royal Mint Sets.

4303

UNC
£

4303 Five pounds (crown). 70th Birthday of Queen Elizabeth II. R. The Queen's personal flag, the
Royal Standard, the Union Flag, two pennants bearing the dates '1926' and '1996' all against
a backdrop of Windsor Castle. Edge: VIVAT REGINA ELIZABETHA. (Reverse design: Avril
Vaughan)

1996 7

— Specimen in presentation folder (issued: 73,311)... 9

— Proof *FDC* (in 1996 set, See PS57) * £12

— Proof in silver *FDC* (Issued: 39,336) £50

— Proof in gold *FDC* (Issued: 2,127) £650

4304

4304 Five pounds (crown). Golden Wedding of Queen Elizabeth II and Prince Philip. Conjoint
portraits of The Queen and Prince Philip. R. Royal Arms and Arms of Prince Philip
surmounted by St. Edward's crown which divides the dates 1947 and 1997 20 November,
and an anchor below with the denomination. (Obverse design: Philip Nathan, reverse design:
Leslie Durbin)

1997 7

— Specimen in presentation folder 9

— Proof *FDC* (in 1997 set, See PS59)* £12

— Proof in silver *FDC* (Issued: 33,689) £55

— Proof in gold *FDC* (Issued: 2,574) £750

* Coins marked thus were originally issued in Royal Mint Sets.

NICKEL-BRASS

4311

UNC
£

UNC
£

4311 **Two pounds.** R. St. Andrew's cross surmounted by a thistle of Scotland. Edge XIII "COMMONWEALTH GAMES SCOTLAND" (Reverse design: Norman Sillman)
1986 5
— Specimen in presentation folder   5   — Proof in silver *FDC* (Issued: 59,779) £35
— .500 silver (Issued: 58,881)   15   — Proof in gold *FDC* (Issued: 3,277) £300
— Proof *FDC** £6

4312   4313   4314

UNC
£

UNC
£

4312 **Two pounds** 300th Anniversary of Bill of Rights. R Cypher of William and Mary, House of Commons mace and St. Edward's crown. (Reverse design: John Lobban)
1989   4   — Proof in silver *FDC* (Issued: 25,000) £30
— Specimen in presentation folder   5   — Proof piedfort in silver *FDC** £60
— Proof *FDC** £10

4313 **Two pounds** 300th Anniversary of Claim of Right (Scotland). R. As 4312, but with crown of Scotland. (Reverse design: John Lobban)
1989   12   — Proof in silver *FDC* (Issued: 24,852) £30
— Specimen in presentation folder   15   — Proof piedfort in silver *FDC** £60
— Proof *FDC** £10

4314 **Two pounds** 300th Anniversary of the Bank of England. R: Bank's original Corporate Seal, with Crown & Cyphers of William III & Mary II. Edge "SIC VOS NON VOBIS". (Reverse design: Leslie Durbin)
1994   5   — Proof piedfort in silver *FDC* (Issued: 9,569) £60
— Specimen in presentation folder   5   — Proof in gold *FDC* (Issued: 1,000) £450
— Proof *FDC** £6 ....   — gold error. Obverse as 4251 (Included in
— Proof in silver *FDC* (Issued: 27, 957) £30   above) £1250

* *Coins marked thus were originally issued in Royal Mint Sets.*

4315   4316

UNC
£

4315   Two pounds 50th Anniversary of the End of World War II. ℞: A Dove of Peace.
Edge "1945 IN PEACE GOODWILL 1995". (Reverse design: John Mills)
1995 5
— Specimen in presentation folder 5
— Proof *FDC* *£6 ....   — Proof piedfort in silver *FDC* (Edition: 10,000) £60
— Proof in silver *FDC* (Issued: 35,751) £30 — Proof in gold *FDC* (Issued: 2,500) £350

4316   Two pounds 50th Anniversary of the Establishment of the United Nations. ℞: 50th
Anniversary symbol and an array of flags. Edge "NATIONS UNITED FOR PEACE"
1945-1995". (Reverse design: Michael Rizzello)
1995 5
— Specimen in presentation folder 7
— Proof in silver *FDC* (Edition: 175,000) £30   — Proof in gold *FDC* (Edition: 17,500) £350
— Proof piedfort in silver *FDC* (Edition: 10,000) £60

4317

4317   Two pounds European Football Championships. ℞: A stylised representation of a football.
Edge: "TENTH EUROPEAN CHAMPIONSHIP". (Reverse design: John Mills)
1996 6
— Specimen in presentation folder 6
— Proof *FDC** £6 ....   — Proof piedfort in silver *FDC* (Issued: 7,634) £65
— Proof in silver *FDC* (Issued: 25,163) £35 — Proof in gold *FDC* (Issued: 2,098) £350

* Coins marked thus were originally issued in Royal Mint sets.

4318

UNC
£

4318 **Two pounds** Bimetallic currency issue. R. Four concentric circles representing the Iron Age, 18th century industrial development, silicon chip, and Internet. Edge: "STANDING ON THE SHOULDERS OF GIANTS". (Reverse design: Bruce Ruskin)

1997 4

— Specimen in presentation folder 6

— Proof *FDC** £6

— Proof in silver FDC (Issued: 29,910) £32

— Proof piedfort in silver *FDC* (Issued: 10,000) £60

— Proof in gold *FDC* (Issued: 2,482) £350

4331   4332

4331 **One pound** (Welsh design). Edge "PLEIDIOL WYF I'M GWLAD". (Reverse design: Leslie Durbin)

1985 4

— Specimen in presentation folder (Issued: 24,850) 4

— Proof *FDC** £5

— Proof in silver *FDC* (Issued: 50,000) £26

— Proof piedfort in silver *FDC* (Issued: 15,000) £60

1990 5

— Proof *FDC** £6

— Proof in silver *FDC* (Issued: 23,277) £28

4332 **One pound** (Northern Irish design). Edge "DECUS ET TUTAMEN". (Reverse design: Leslie Durbin)

1986 5

— Specimen in presentatioon folder (Issued: 19,908) 5

— Proof *FDC** £4

— Proof in silver *FDC* (Issued: 37, 958) £26

— Proof piedfort in silver *FDC* (Issued: 15,000) £60

1991 5

— Proof *FDC** £6

— Proof in silver *FDC* (Issued: 22,922) £28

* Coins marked thus were originally issued in Royal Mint sets.

4333   4334

	UNC £		UNC £

4333 One pound (English design). Edge "DECUS ET TUTAMEN". (Reverse design: Leslie Durbin)

1987 4
— Specimen in presentation folder (Issued: 72,607) 4
— Proof *FDC** £6
— Proof in silver *FDC* (Issued: 50,000) £26
— Proof piedfort in silver *FDC* (Issued: 15,000) £60
1992 5
— Proof *FDC** £6
— Proof in silver *FDC* (Issued: 13,065) £30

4334 One pound (Royal Shield). Edge "DECUS ET TUTAMEN". (Reverse design: Derek Gorringe)

1988 5
— Specimen in presentation folder (Issued: 29,550) 5
— Proof *FDC** £6
— Proof in silver *FDC* (Issued: 50,000) £35
— Proof piedfort in silver *FDC* (Issued: 10,000) £60

4335 One pound (Scottish design). Edge "NEMO ME IMPUNE LACESSIT" (Illus. as 4222)

1989 5   — Proof in silver *FDC* (Issued: 22,275) £26
— Proof *FDC** £6   — Proof piedfort in silver *FDC* (Issued: 10,000) £60

4336 One pound (Royal Arms design). Edge "DECUS ET TUTAMEN" (Illus. as 4221)

1993 5   — Proof in silver *FDC* (Issued: 16,526) £30
— Proof *FDC** £6   — Proof piedfort in silver *FDC* (Issued: 12,500) £60

4337   4338   4339   4340

4337 One pound (Scottish design). R: Lion rampant within a double tressure. Edge "NEMO ME I MPUNE LACESSIT". (Reverse design: Norman Sillman)

1994 4   — Proof in silver *FDC* (Issued: 25,000) £30
— Specimen in presentation folder 5   — Proof piedfort in silver *FDC* (Issued: 11,722) £60
— Proof *FDC** £6

* Coins marked thus were originally issued in Royal Mint sets.

4338 One pound (Welsh design). R. Heraldic dragon Edge "PLEIDIOL WYF I'M GWLAD".
(Reverse design: Norman Sillman)
1995   4
— Specimen in presentation folder, English version £5
— Specimen in presentation folder, Welsh version £8
— Proof *FDC** £5
— Proof in silver *FDC* (Issued: 27,445) £28
— Proof in piedfort in silver *FDC* (Issued: 8,458) £60

4339 One pound (Northern Irish design). R. A Celtic cross incorporating a pimpernel at its centre.
Edge "DECUS ET TUTAMEN". (Reverse design: Norman Sillman)
1996   4   — Proof in silver *FDC* (Issued: 25,000) £28
— Specimen in presentation folder   6   — Proof piedfort in silver *FDC* (Issued: 10,000) £50
— Proof *FDC** £6

4340 One pound (English design) R. Three lions. Edge: "DECUS ET TUTAMEN". (Reverse
design: Norman Sillman)
1997   4
— Specimen in presentation folder (Issued 56,996) £5
— Proof *FDC** £5
— Proof in silver *FDC* (Issued: 20,137) £28
— Proof piedfort in silver *FDC* (Issued: 10,000) £50

* *Coins marked thus were originally issued in Royal Mint sets.*

CUPRO-NICKEL

4351

UNC   *UNC*
£   £

4351 **Fifty pence.** R. Britannia r. (4341)

1985	6	— Proof *FDC** £3....		1995*	3	
— Proof *FDC** £3		1990*	4	— Proof *FDC** £4		
1986*	3	— Proof *FDC** £5....		1996*	3	
— Proof *FDC** £3		1991*	4	— Proof *FDC** £4		
1987*	3	— Proof *FDC** £5....		— Proof in silver *FDC** £20		
— Proof *FDC** £3		1992*	4	1997	3	
1988*	3	— Proof *FDC** £5....		— Proof *FDC** £4		
— Proof *FDC** £4		1993*	4	— Proof in silver *FDC** £24		
1989*	4	— Proof *FDC** £4				

4352

4352 **Fifty pence** Presidency of the Council of European Community Ministers and completion of the Single Market. R Conference table top and twelve stars. (Reverse design: Mary Milner Dickens)

1992-1993 10   — Proof piedfort in silver *FDC* (Issued: 10,993) £45
— Proof *FDC** £10 ....   — Proof in gold *FDC* (Issued: 1,864) £450
— Proof in silver *FDC** (Issued: 26,890) £24

4352A — Specimen in presentation folder with 1992 date 4351 15

4353

4353 **Fifty pence** 50th Anniversary of the Normandy Landings on D-Day. R: Allied Invasion Force. (Reverse design: John Mills)

1994 2   — Proof in silver *FDC* (Issued: 40,000) £30
— Specimen in presentation folder   3   — Proof piedfort in silver *FDC* (Issued: 10,000) £50
— Proof *FDC** £5   — Proof in gold *FDC* (Issued: 1,877) £500

* *Coins marked thus were originally issued in Royal Mint sets.*

UNC
£

4354 **Fifty pence** R. Britannia: diam 27.3mm
1997 1   — Proof in silver *FDC* (Issued: 1,632) £27
— Proof *FDC** £4   — Proof piedfort in silver *FDC* (Issued: 7,192) £46

4361

	UNC £		UNC £		UNC £

4361 **Twenty pence.** R. Crowned double rose

1985		— Proof *FDC** £3.....		1994	
— Proof *FDC** £2		1990...........................		— Proof *FDC** £3	
1986*	1	— Proof *FDC** £3.....		1995	
— Proof *FDC** £2		1991...........................		— Proof *FDC** £3	
1987		— Proof *FDC** £3.....		1996	
— Proof *FDC** £2		1992...........................		— Proof *FDC** £3	
1988		— Proof *FDC** £3.....		— Proof in silver *FDC** £15	
— Proof *FDC** £3		1993...........................		1997	
1989		— Proof *FDC** £3.....		— Proof *FDC** £3	

4366

4366 **Ten pence.** R. Lion passant guardant

1985*	3	1988*.........................	3	1991*	4
— Proof *FDC* * £2		— Proof *FDC** £3....		— Proof *FDC** £3	
1986*	2	1989*.........................	4	1992*	3
— Proof *FDC** £2		— Proof *FDC** £3.....		— Proof *FDC** £4	
1987*	3	1990*.........................	4	— Proof in silver *FDC** £14	
— Proof *FDC** £3		— Proof *FDC** £3			

* *Coins marked thus were originally issued in Royal Mint sets.*

4367

4367 Ten pence R Lion passant guardant: diam. 24.5mm

1992 ....   1995.....................
— Proof *FDC** £3 ....   — Proof *FDC** £2
— Proof in silver *FDC** £14 .   1996.....................
— Proof piedfort in silver *FDC** (Issued: 14,167) £25   — Proof *FDC** £2
1993* ....   — Proof in silver *FDC** £15
— Proof *FDC** £2 ....   1997.....................
1994* ....   — Proof *FDC** £2
— Proof *FDC** £2 ....

4371   4372

		UNC				*UNC*
		£				£

4371 Five pence. R. Crowned thistle

1985*   1   — Proof *FDC** £2....   1990*   2
— Proof *FDC** £1   1988..........................   — Proof *FDC** £3
1986*   1   — Proof *FDC** £2....   — Proof in silver *FDC** £12
— Proof *FDC** £1   1989..........................
1987 ....   — Proof *FDC** £2

4372 Five pence. R. Crowned thistle: diam 18mm

1990 ....   1992 ....   — Proof *FDC** £2
— Proof *FDC** £2   — Proof *FDC** £2....   1996 ....
— Proof in silver *FDC** £12   1993*.........................   — Proof *FDC** £2
— Proof piedfort in silver   — Proof *FDC** £2....   — Proof in silver *FDC** £15
FDC (Issued: 20,000) £25 1994..........................   1997 ....
1991 ....   — Proof *FDC** £2....   — Proof *FDC** £2
— Proof *FDC** £2   1995..........................

* *Coins marked thus were originally issued in Royal Mint sets.*

BRONZE

4376   4381

4376 Two pence. R. Plumes

1985	1988	1991 ....
— Proof *FDC** £1	— Proof *FDC** £1....	— Proof *FDC** £1
1986	1989	1992* ....
— Proof *FDC** £1	— Proof *FDC** £1....	— Proof *FDC** £1
1987	1990	
— Proof *FDC** £1	— Proof *FDC** £1	

4381 One penny. R. Portcullis with chains

1985	1988	1991 ....
— Proof *FDC** £1	— Proof *FDC** £1....	— Proof *FDC** £1
1986	1989	1992* ....
— Proof *FDC** £1	— Proof *FDC** £1....	— Proof *FDC** £1
1987	1990	
— Proof *FDC** £1	— Proof *FDC** £1	

COPPER PLATED STEEL

4386 Two pence R. Plumes

1992	— Proof *FDC** £1....	— Proof *FDC** £1
1993	1995	— Proof in silver *FDC** £15
— Proof *FDC** £1	— Proof *FDC** £1....	1997 ....
1994	1996	— Proof *FDC** £1

4391 One penny R. Portcullis with chains

1992	— Proof *FDC** £1....	— Proof *FDC** £1
1993	1995	— Proof in silver *FDC** £15
— Proof *FDC** £1	— Proof *FDC** £1....	1997 ....
1994	1996	— Proof *FDC** £1

* Coins marked thus were originally issued in Royal Mint sets.

GOLD

4400

4400　Five pounds. R. St.George
1998 Proof *FDC** £650
1999 Proof *FDC** £650
2000 Bullion type £500
— 　Proof *FDC** £650
2001 Proof *FDC** £650
2003 Proof *FDC** £650
— 　Unc (Issued: 812) £550

2004 Proof *FDC** £650
— 　Unc (Issued : 1,000) £550
2006 Proof *FDC** £750
— 　Unc £725
2007 Proof *FDC** £650
— 　Unc £780

4401　　　　　　　　　　　　4402

4401　Five pounds. R. Shield, as illustration. (Reverse design: Timothy Noad)
　　　2002 Proof *FDC** £700　　　Unc (Issued: 1,370) £600
4402　Five pounds. R. St.George. (Reverse design: Timothy Noad)
　　　2005 Proof *FDC** £700　　　Unc (Issued: 936) £600
4410　Five pounds. R. St. George, 'U' in a circle to left of date
　　　1998 (Issued: 825) £550　　　2000 (Issued: 994) £550
　　　1999 (Issued: 970) £550　　　2001 (Issued: 1,000) £550
4420　Two pounds. R. St. George
　　　1998 Proof *FDC** £300　　　2003 Proof *FDC** £300　　　2006 Proof *FDC** £300
　　　2000 Proof *FDC** £300　　　2004 Proof *FDC** £300　　　2007 Proof *FDC** £300
4421　Two pounds. R. Shield (see 4401)
　　　2002 Proof *FDC** £350
4422　Two pounds. R. St.George (see 4402)
　　　2005 Proof *FDC** £350

* *Coins marked thus were originally issued in Royal Mint sets.*

4430 Sovereign. R. St.George
1998 Proof *FDC* (Issued: 10,000)£280
1999 Proof *FDC* (Issued: 10,000) £350
2000 Bullion type £115
— Proof *FDC* (Issued: 9,909) £225
2001 Bullion type £115
— Proof *FDC* (Issued: 8,915) £225
2003 Bullion type £115
— Proof *FDC* (Issued: 12,433) £225

2004 Bullion type £115
— Proof *FDC* (Issued: 10,175) £225
2006 Bullion type......................£110
— Proof *FDC* (Edition: 15,000) £180
2007 Bullion type (Edition: 75,000) £120
— Proof *FDC* (Edition: 10,000) £180

4431 Sovereign. R. Shield (see 4401)
2002 (issued: 80,499.............. £125
- Proof *FDC* (Edition: 12,500) £280

4432 Sovereign. R. St.George (see 4402)
2005 Bullion type........ ..... £125
- Proof *FDC* (Edition 12,500) £250

4440 Half sovereign. R. St.George
1998 Proof *FDC* (Issued: 6,147) £150
1999 Proof *FDC* (Issued: 7,500) £200
2000 Bullion type £65
— Proof *FDC* (Issued: 7,458) £125
2001 Bullion type £65
— Proof *FDC* (Issued: 4,596) £125
2003 Bullion type £65
— Proof *FDC* (Issued: 4,868) £125

2004 Bullion type £65
— Proof *FDC* (Issued: 4,446) £125
2006 Bullion type £58
— Proof *FDC* (Edition: 5,000) £97
2007 Bullion type (Edition: 75,000) £63
— Proof *FDC* (Edition: 5,000) £98

4441 Half Sovereign. R. Shield (see 4401)
2002 (issued: 62,540) £75
- Proof *FDC* (Issued: 10,000) £175

4442 Half sovereign. R. St.George (see 4402)
2005 Bullion type.............. £75
- Proof *FDC* (Issued: 5,011) £125

4450   4451

4450 Britannia. One Hundred pounds. (1oz fine gold alloyed with silver) R. Standing figure of Britannia.
(Reverse design : Philip Nathan)
1998 Proof *FDC* £550
1999 .... £450
1999 Proof *FDC* £550
2000 .... £450
2000 Proof *FDC* £550

2002 Proof *FDC* £550
2004 ....£450
2004 Proof *FDC* £550
2006 Proof *FDC* £550

4451 Britannia. One Hundred pounds. (1oz fine gold alloyed with silver) R. Helmeted figure of
Britannia holding a trident and a shield with a lion in the background. (Reverse design : Philip
Nathan)
2001............................£500   2001 Proof *FDC* £600

* Coins marked thus were originally issued in Royal Mint sets.

4452   4453

4452 Britannia. One Hundred pounds. (1oz fine gold alloyed with silver) R. Helmeted figure of
Britannia with stylised waves. (Reverse design: Philip Nathan)
2003 ....£500   2003 Proof *FDC** £600

4453 Britannia. One Hundred pounds. (1oz fine gold alloyed with silver) R. Seated figure of
Britannia facing left. (Reverse design: Philip Nathan)
2005 Proof *FDC* * £600

4454

4454 Britannia. One Hundred pounds. (1 oz fine gold alloyed with silver) R. Seated figure
of Britannia facing right holding a trident in her right hand and a sprig of olive in the
left hand with a lion at her feet (Reverse design : Christopher Le Brun)
2007 ....£500   2007 Proof FDC * £675

4460

4460 Britannia. Fifty pounds. (1/2 oz fine gold alloyed with silver) R. Standing figure of Britannia
1998 Proof *FDC** £300   2000 Proof *FDC** £300
1999......................£225   2002 Proof *FDC* * £300
1999 Proof *FDC** £300   2004 Proof *FDC* * £300
2000......................£225   2006 Proof *FDC** £300

4461 Britannia. Fifty pounds. (1/2 oz fine gold alloyed with silver) R. Helmeted figure of Britannia
holding a trident and a shield with a lion in the background (see 4451)
2001 ....£250   2001 Proof *FDC** £350

* *Coins marked thus were originally issued in Royal Mint sets.*

4462 Britannia. Fifty pounds. (1/2 oz fine gold alloyed with silver) R. Helmeted figure of Britannia with stylised waves (see 4452)
2003........................£250   2003 Proof *FDC** £300

4463 Britannia. Fifty pounds. (1/2 oz fine gold alloyed with silver) R. Seated figure of Britannia facing left
2005 Proof *FDC* * £300

4464 Britannia. Fifty pounds. (1/2 oz fine gold alloyed with silver) R. Seated figure of Britannia facing right holding a trident in her right hand and a sprig of olive in the left hand with a lion at her feet (see 4454)
2007..................... £275   2007 Proof *FDC* * £350

4470   4480

4470 Britannia. Twenty five pounds. (1/4 oz fine gold alloyed with silver) R. Standing figure of Britannia

1998 Proof *FDC* (Issued: 560) £150	2000 Proof *FDC* (Issued: 500) £150
1999...............................£120	2002 Proof *FDC* (Issued: 750) £150
1999 Proof *FDC* (Issued: 1,000) £150	2004 Proof *FDC* (Issued: 750) £150
2000...............................£120	2006 Proof *FDC* (Edition: 1,000) £165

4471 Britannia. Twenty five pounds. (1/4 oz fine gold alloyed with silver) R. Helmeted figure of Britannia holding a trident and a shield with a lion in the background (see 4451)
2001........................ ....£150   2001 Proof *FDC* (Issued: 500) £180

4472 Britannia. Twenty five pounds. (1/4 oz fine gold alloyed with silver) R. Helmeted figure of Britannia with stylised waves (see 4452)
2003 Proof *FDC* (Issued: 609) £160

4473 Britannia. Twenty five pounds. (1/4 oz fine gold alloyed with silver) R. Seated figure of Britannia facing left
2005 Proof *FDC* (Issued: 750) £180

4474 Britannia. Twenty five pounds. (1/4 oz fine gold alloyed with silver) R. Seated figure of Britannia   facing right holding a trident in her right hand and a sprig of olive in the left hand with a lion at her feet (see 4454)
2007...............................£150   2007 Proof *FDC* (Edition: 750) £175

4480 Britannia. Ten pounds. (1/10 oz fine gold alloyed with silver) R. Standing figure of Britannia

1998 Proof *FDC* (Issued: 392) £80	2002 ....£60
1999...............................£60	2002 Proof *FDC* (Issued: 1,500) £80
1999 Proof *FDC* (Issued: 1,058) £80	2004 Proof *FDC* (Issued: 929) £80
2000...............................£60	2006 Proof *FDC* (Edition: 1,500) £90
2000 Proof *FDC* (Issued: 659) £80	

4481 Britannia. Ten pounds. (1/10 oz fine gold alloyed with silver) R. Helmeted figure of Britannia holding a trident and a shield with a lion in the background (see 4451)
2001........................ ....£70   2001 Proof *FDC* (Issued: 1,557) £100

4482 Britannia. Ten pounds. (1/10 oz fine gold alloyed with silver) R. Helmeted figure of Britannia with stylised waves (see 4452)
2003 ....£60   2003 Proof *FDC* (Issued: 1,382) £80

4483 Britannia. Ten pounds. (1/10 oz fine gold alloyed with silver) R. Seated figure of Britannia facing left
2005 Proof *FDC* (issued: 1,225) £80

4484 Britannia. Ten pounds. (1/10 oz fine gold alloyed with silver) R. Seated figure of Britannia facing right holding a trident in her right hand and a sprig of olive in the left hand with a lion at her feet (see 4454)
2007 ....£70   2007 Proof *FDC* (Edition: 1,500) £95

* Coins marked thus were originally issued in Royal Mint sets.

SILVER

4500

4500 **Britannia. Two pounds.** (1 oz of fine silver) R. Standing figure of Britannia
1998 (Issued: 88,909) £18   2004 (Edition: 100,000) £18
— Proof *FDC* (Issued: 2,168) £65   — Proof *FDC* (Issued: 2,174) £40
2000 (Issued: 81,301) £18   2006 (Edition 100,000) £15
2002 (Issued: 36,543) £18   — Proof *FDC* (Edition: 2,500) £48

4500A Britannia. Two pounds. (1 oz of fine silver) R. Standing figure of Britannia
2006 - Proof *FDC** with selected gold plating of obverse and reverse £55

4501 **Britannia. Two pounds.** (1 oz of fine silver) R. Standing figure of Britannia in
horse drawn chariot (Illus. as 4300)
1999 (Issued: 69,394) £18

4501A Britannia. Two pounds. (1 oz of fine silver) R. Standing figure of Britannia in
horse drawn chariot
2006 - Proof *FDC** with selected gold plating of obverse and reverse £55

4502 **Britannia. Two pounds.** (1 oz of fine silver) R. Helmeted figure of Britannia holding a
trident and a shield with a lion in the background (see 4451)
2001 (Issued: 44,816) £18   — Proof *FDC* (Issued: 3,047) £45

4502A Britannia. Two pounds. (1 oz of fine silver) R. Helmeted figure of Britannia holding a
trident and a shield with a lion in the background
2006 - Proof *FDC** with selected gold plating of obverse and reverse £55

4503

4503 **Britannia. Two pounds.** (1oz fine silver) R. Helmeted figure of Britannia with stylised waves
2003 (Issued: 73,271) £18   — Proof *FDC* (Issued: 2,016) £37

4503A Britannia. Two pounds. (1oz fine silver) R. Helmeted figure of Britannia with stylised waves
2006 - Proof *FDC** with selected gold plating of obverse and reverse £55

* Coins marked thus were originally issued in Royal Mint sets.

4504   4505

4504 **Britannia. Two pounds.** (1 oz of fine silver) R. Seated figure of Britannia facing left
2005 (Edition: 100,000) £18
Proof *FDC* (Issued: 1,539) £43

4504A **Britannia. Two pounds.** (1 oz of fine silver) R. Seated figure of Britannia facing left
2006 - Proof *FDC** with selected gold plating of obverse and reverse £55

4505 **Britannia. Two pounds.** (1 oz of fine silver) R. Seated figure of Britannia facing right
holding a trident in her right hand and a sprig of olive in the left hand with a lion at her
feet (Reverse design : Christopher Le Brun)
2007 (Edition: 100,000) £17   Proof *FDC* (Edition: 2,500) £48

4510 **Britannia. One pound.** (1/2 oz of fine silver) obv. as 4500 but reads "1 POUND" R.
Standing figure of Britannia
1998 — Proof *FDC** £25

4511 **Britannia. One pound.** (1/2 oz of fine silver) R. Helmeted figure of Britannia holding a
trident and a shield with a lion in the background (see 4451)
2001 — Proof *FDC** £25

4512 **Britannia. One pound.** (1/2 oz fine silver) R. Helmeted figure of Britannia with stylised
wave (see 4503)
2003 — Proof *FDC** £25

4513 **Britannia. One pound.** (1/2 oz of fine silver) R. Seated figure of Britannia facing left
2005 – Proof *FDC**

4514 **Britannia. One pound.** (1/2 oz of fine silver) R. Seated figure of Britannia facing right
holding a trident in her right hand and a sprig of olive in the left hand with a lion at her
feet (See 4505)
2007 Proof FDC * £30

4520 **Britannia. Fifty pence.** (1/4 oz of fine silver) R. Standing figure of Britannia
1998 — Proof *FDC** £20

* Coins marked thus were originally issued in Royal Mint sets.

4521 **Britannia. Fifty pence.** (1/4 oz of fine silver) R. Helmeted figure of Britannia holding a
trident and a shield with a lion in the background (see 4451)
2001 — Proof *FDC** £20

4522 **Britannia. Fifty pence.** (1/4 oz fine silver) R. Helmeted figure of Britannia with stylised
wave (see 4503)
2003 — Proof *FDC** £20

4523 **Britannia. Fifty pence.** (Previously listed as 4514) (1/4 oz of fine silver) R. Seated figure of
Britannia facing left
2005 – Proof *FDC* * £25

4524 Britannia. Fifty pence. (1/4 oz of fine silver) R. Seated figure of Britannia facing right
holding a trident in her right hand and a sprig of olive in the left hand with a lion at her feet
(See 4505)
2007 – Proof *FDC* * £25

4530 Britannia. Twenty pence. (1/10 oz of fine silver) R. Standing figure of Britannia
1998 — Proof *FDC* (Issued: 2,724) £20   2006 ....£15

4531 Britannia. Twenty pence. (1/10 oz of fine silver) R. Helmeted figure of Britannia holding a
trident and a shield with a lion in the background (see 4451)
2001 — Proof *FDC* (Issued: 826) £18

4532 Britannia. Twenty pence. (1/10 oz fine silver) R. Helmeted figure of Britannia with stylised
wave (see 4503)
2003 — Proof *FDC* (Issued: 1,179) £18

4533 Britannia. Twenty pence. (Previously listed as 4515) (1/10 oz of fine silver) R. Seated figure
of Britannia facing left
2005 – Proof *FDC** (Issued: 913) £20

4534 Britannia. Twenty pence. (1/10 oz of fine silver) R. Seated figure of Britannia facing right
holding a trident in her right hand and a sprig of olive in the left hand with a lion at her feet
(See 4505)
2007 – Proof *FDC* (Edition: 2,500) £20

CUPRO-NICKEL

4550

UNC
£

4550 Five pounds (crown). Prince of Wales 50th Birthday. R. Portrait of The Prince of Wales with
the inscriptions 'The Prince's Trust' and 'Helping young people to succeed' on a ribbon at
the base of the portrait with the denomination 'Five Pounds' and the dates 1948 and 1998.
(Reverse design: Michael Noakes/Robert Elderton)
1998 ....   £7
— Specimen in presentation folder £10
— Proof *FDC* (in 1998 set, see PS 61)* £12
— Proof in silver *FDC* (Issued: 13,379) £60
— Proof in gold *FDC* (Issued: 773) £850

---

* *Coins marked thus were originally issued in Royal Mint sets.*

4551

UNC
£

4551   Five pounds (crown). Diana, Princess of Wales Memorial. R. Portrait of Diana, Princess of
Wales with the inscription 'In memory of Diana, Princess of Wales' with the denomination
'Five Pounds' and the dates 1961 and 1997. (Reverse design: David Cornell)
1999 ....   £7
— Specimen in presentation folder £12
— Proof *FDC* (in 1999 set, see PS63)* £12
— Proof in silver *FDC* (Issued: 49,545) £45
— Proof in gold *FDC* (Issued: 7,500) £750

4552   4552A

4552   Five pounds (crown). Millennium commemorative. R. In the centre, on a patterned circle, a
representation of the British Isles with a pair of clock hands emanating from Greenwich, set
at 12 o'clock with the inscription 'Anno Domini' with the denomination 'Five Pounds' and
the dates 1999 and 2000. Reverse design: Jeffrey Matthews)
1999 ....   £7
— Specimen in presentation folder £10
— Proof in silver *FDC* (Issued: 49,057) £36
— Proof in gold *FDC* (Issued: 2,500) £650
2000
— Specimen in presentation folder £18
— Proof *FDC* (in 2000 set, see PS65)* £12
— Proof in gold *FDC* (Issued: 1,487) £650

4552A — 2000 Specimen in presentation folder with Dome mint mark £18
(See illustration above - the mintmark is located within the shaded area at 3 o'clock).

4552B — 2000 Proof in silver *FDC* (Issued: 14,255) £50
(The reverse design is the same as the 1999 issue but with the British Isles coloured with 22
carat gold)

* Coins marked thus were originally issued in Royal Mint sets.

4553

UNC
£

4553 Five pounds (crown). Queen Mother commemorative. ℞ Portrait of the Queen Mother with Inscription "Queen Elizabeth the Queen Mother" and cheering crowds in 19th Century and modern day dress with the Queen Mother's signature below and the denomination 'Five Pounds' and the dates 1900 and 2000. (Reverse design: Ian Rank-Broadley)
2000 .... £7
— Specimen in presentation folder £10
— Proof in silver *FDC* (Issued: 31,316) £40
— Proof piedfort in silver *FDC* (Issued: 14,850) £55
— Proof in gold *FDC* (Issued: 3,000) £750

4554

4554 Five pounds (crown) Victorian anniversary. ℞. A classic portrait of the young Queen Victoria based on the Penny Black postage stamp with a V representing Victoria, and taking the form of railway lines and in the background the iron framework of the Crystal Palace, and the denomination "Five Pounds" and the dates 1901 and 2001. (Reverse design: Mary Milner-Dickens)
2001 .... £7
— Specimen in presentation folder £10
— Proof *FDC* (in 2001 set, see PS68)* £10
— Proof in silver *FDC* (Issued: 19,216) £45
— Proof in gold *FDC* (Issued: 2,098) £650

4554A — Proof in silver *FDC* with "reverse frosting" giving matt appearance.
(Issued: 596 – issued with sovereigns of 1901 and 2001)* £125

4554B — Proof in gold *FDC* with "reverse frosting" giving matt appearance.
(Issued: 733 – issued with four different type sovereigns of Victoria, - Young Head with shield, and St.George reverse, Jubilee Head and Old Head.)* £850

* Coins marked thus were originally issued in Royal Mint sets.

4555

UNC
£

4555 Five pounds. (crown) Golden Jubilee commemorative 2002. O. New portrait of The Queen with the denomination "Five pounds". R. Equestrian portrait of the The Queen with the inscription "Elizabeth II DEI GRA REGINA FID DEF" around the circumference and "AMOR POPULI PRAESIDIUM REG" within, and the date 2002 below separated by the central element of the Royal Arms. (Obverse and reverse designs: Ian Rank-Broadley)

2002 .... £7

— Specimen in presentation folder £10
— Proof *FDC* (in 2002 set, see PS 72)* £10
— Proof in silver *FDC* (Issued: 54,012) £40
— Proof in gold *FDC* (Issued: 3,500) £750

4556

4556 Five pounds, (crown) Queen Mother memorial 2002. R. Three quarter portrait of the Queen Mother within a wreath with the inscription "QUEEN ELIZABETH THE QUEEN MOTHER" and the dates 1900 and 2002, with an edge inscription "STRENGTH, DIGNITY AND LAUGHTER". (Reverse design: Avril Vaughan)

2002.. .... £8

— Specimen in presentation folder £15
— Proof in silver *FDC* (Issued: 16,117) £45
— Proof in gold *FDC* (Issued: 2,086) £650

* Coins marked thus were originally issued in Royal Mint sets.

4557

UNC
£

4557   Five pounds. (crown) Coronation commemorative 2003. O. Profile portrait of The Queen in
linear form facing right with the inscription "Elizabeth II DEI GRA REGINA F D ". R. In
the centre the inscription "GOD SAVE THE QUEEN" surrounded by the inscription
"CORONATION JUBILEE" the denomination "FIVE POUNDS" and the date 2003.
(Obverse and reverse designs: Tom Phillips)
2003... ....   £8
   — Specimen in presentation folder (Issued: 100,481) £10
   — Proof *FDC* (in 2003 set, see PS 78)* £10
   — Proof in silver *FDC* (Issued: 28,758) £40
   — Proof in gold *FDC* (Issued: 1,896) £650

4558

4558   Five pounds. (crown) Centenary of Entende Cordiale 2004. R. In the centre the head and
shoulders of Britannia and her French counterpart Marianne with the inscription "Entende
Cordiale" separated by the dates "1904" and "2004". (Reverse design: David Gentleman)
2004 ....   £5
   — Specimen in presentation folder (Issued: 16,507) £10
   — Proof *FDC* with reverse frosting (Issued: 6,065) £18
   — Proof in silver *FDC* (Issued: 11,295) £40
   — Proof Piedfort in silver *FDC* (Issued: 2,500) £150
   — Proof in gold *FDC* (Issued: 926) £700
   — Proof Piedfort in platinum *FDC* (Issued: 501) £3500

* Coins marked thus were originally issued in Royal Mint sets.

4559 4560

UNC
£

4559 Five pounds. (crown) Two hundredth anniversary of the Battle of Trafalgar 2005. R. In the centre the Royal Navy ships Victory and Temeraine as viewed from the French fleet the dates "1805" and "2005" and "Trafalgar" with the edge inscription "ENGLAND EXPECTS THAT EVERY MAN WILL DO HIS DUTY". (Reverse design: Clive Duncan)
2005.. £7
— Specimen in presentation folder (Issued: 79,868) £10
— Proof *FDC* (in 2005 set, see PS84)* £10
— Proof in silver *FDC* (Issued: 21,448) £40
— Proof piedfort in silver *FDC* (see PSS21)* £75
— Proof in gold *FDC* (Issued: 1,805) £700

4560 Five pounds. (crown) Two hundredth anniversary of the death of Nelson 2005. R. In the centre a portrait of Nelson with the dates "1805" and "2005" and "Horatio Nelson" with the edge inscription "ENGLAND EXPECTS THAT EVERY MAN WILL DO HIS DUTY". (Reverse design: James Butler)
2005.. £7
— Specimen in presentation folder (Issued: 72,498) £10
— Proof *FDC* (in 2005 set, see PS84)* £10
— Proof in silver *FDC* (Issued: 12,852) £40
— Proof piedfort in silver *FDC* (see PSS21)* £75
— Proof in gold *FDC* (Issued: 1,760) £700
— Proof piedfort in platinum *FDC* (Edition: 200) £4000

* Coins marked thus were originally issued in Royal Mint sets.

4561

UNC
£

4561 Five pounds. (crown) 80th Birthday of Her Majesty Queen Elizabeth II. ℞. A fanfare of regal trumpets with the inscription "Vivat Regina" and the dates "1926" and "2006", and the edge inscription "DUTY SERVICE FAITH". (Reverse design: Danuta Solowiej-Wedderburn
2006.. £5
— Specimen in presentation folder £10
— Proof *FDC* (in 2006 set, see PS87)* £10
— Proof in silver *FDC* (Edition: 50,000) £40
— Proof in gold *FDC* (Edition: 2,750) £745
— Proof piedfort in platinum *FDC* (Edition: 250) £4000
4561A— Proof piedfort in silver with selected gold plating *FDC* (Edition: 5,000) £80

4562

4562 Five pounds. (crown) Diamond Wedding Anniversary of Her Majesty Queen Elizabeth II and The Duke of Edinburgh. O. Conjoint portrait of The Queen and Prince Philip. R The Rose window of Westminster Abbey with the inscription "TVEATVR VNITA DEVS", the dates "1947" and "2007", the denomination "FIVE POUNDS", and the edge inscription "MY STRENGTH AND STAY" (Obverse design : Ian Rank-Broadley, reverse design : Emma Noble)
2007.. £5
— Specimen in presentation folder £10
— Proof FDC (in 2007 set, see PS90)* £10
— Proof in silver FDC (Edition: 35,000) £40
— Proof piedfort in silver FDC (Edition: 5,000) £80
— Proof in gold FDC (Edition: 2,500) £775
— Proof piedfort in platinum FDC (Edition: 250) £4,000

* Coins marked thus were originally issued in Royal Mint sets.

NICKEL-BRASS

4570 4571 4572

UNC
£

4570 **Two pounds.** Bimetallic currency issue. R. Four concentric circles, representing the Iron Age, 18th century industrial development, silicon chip and Internet. Edge: "STANDING ON THE SHOULDERS OF GIANT"S

1998 .... £4

— Proof *FDC** £6
— Proof in silver *FDC* (Issued: 19,978) £32
— Proof piedfort in silver *FDC* (Issued: 7,646) £50

1999 .... £4

2000	2001
— Proof *FDC** £6	— Proof *FDC** £6
— Proof in silver *FDC* (in 2000 set, see PSS10)* £30	
2002	2003
— Proof *FDC* (in 2002 set, see PS72)* £6	— Proof *FDC** £6
— Proof in gold *FDC* (in 2002 set, see PGJS1)* £350	
2004	2005
— Proof *FDC* * £6	— Proof *FDC** £6
2006	

— Proof *FDC* * £6
— Proof in silver *FDC* (in 2006 set, see PSS22)*

4571 **Two pounds.** Rugby World Cup. R. In the centre a rugby ball and goal posts surrounded by a stylalised stadium with the denomination 'Two Pounds' and the date 1999. (Reverse design: Ron Dutton)

1999 .... £4

— Specimen in presentation folder £6
— Proof *FDC* (in 1999 set, see PS63)* £6
— Proof in silver *FDC* (Issued: 9,665) £35
— Proof in gold *FDC* (Issued: 311) £400

4571A — Proof piedfort in silver with coloured hologram FDC (Issued: 10,000) £150

4572 **Two pounds.** Marconi commemorative. R. Decorative radio waves emanating from a spark of electricity linking the zeros of the date to represent the generation of the signal that crossed the Atlantic with the date 2001 and the denomination "Two Pounds". Edge: "WIRELESS BRIDGES THE ATLANTIC... MARCONI 1901". (Reverse design: Robert Evans)

2001 .... £4

— Specimen in presentation folder £7
— Proof *FDC* (in 2001 set, see PS68)* £10
— Proof in silver *FDC* (Issued: 11,488) £35
— Proof piedfort in silver *FDC* (Issued: 6,759) £50
— Proof in gold *FDC* (Issued: 1,658) £350

4572A — Proof in silver *FDC*, with reverse frosting. (Issued:4,803 in a 2-coin set with a Canadian $5 Marconi silver proof) £50

* Coins marked thus were originally issued in Royal Mint sets.

4573   4574   4575

UNC
£

4573 Two pounds. Commonwealth Games commemorative. England. R. A moving figure of
an athlete holding a banner, the top of which being divided into lines to symbolise lanes
of a running track or swimming pool with a cameo of the English flag and the inscription
"XVII Commonwealth Games 2002" and the denomination "£2". Edge inscription "SPIRIT
OF FRIENDSHIP. MANCHESTER 2002". (Reverse design: Matthew Bonaccorsi)
2002 .... £5
   — Specimen (in Presentation set, see US24)*£6
   — Proof *FDC* (in set, see PS76)* £8
   — Proof in Silver *FDC* (in set, see PSS12)* £35
   — Proof in gold *FDC* (in set, see PCGS1)* £350
4573A As above but with colour added to the flag and parts of the banner, Proof Piedfort in Silver
FDC (in set, see PSS13)* £60

4574 Two pounds. Commonwealth Games commemorative. R. Northern Ireland. As above but
with a cameo of the Northern Ireland flag. Edge inscription "SPIRIT OF FRIENDSHIP.
MANCHESTER 2002".
2002 .... £5
   — Specimen (in Presentation set, see US24)* £6
   — Proof *FDC* (in set, see PS76)* £8
   — Proof in Silver *FDC* (in set, see PSS12)* £35
   — Proof in gold *FDC* (in set, see PCGS1)* £350
4574A As above but with colour added to the flag and parts of the banner, Proof Piedfort in Silver
FDC (in set, see PSS13)* £60

4575 Two pounds. Commonwealth Games commemorative. R. Scotland. As above but with a cameo
of the Scottish flag. Edge inscription "SPIRIT OF FRIENDSHIP. MANCHESTER 2002".
2002 .... £5
   — Specimen (in Presentation set, see US24)* £6
   — Proof *FDC* (in set, see PS76)* £8
   — Proof in Silver *FDC* (in set, see PSS12)* £35
   — Proof in gold *FDC* (in set, see PCGS1)* £350
4575A As above but with colour added to the flag and parts of the banner, Proof Piedfort in Silver
FDC (in set, see PSS13)* £60

* Coins marked thus were originally issued in Royal Mint sets.

4576   4577   4578

UNC
£

4576 Two pounds. Commonwealth Games commemorative. R. Wales. As above but with a cameo of
the Welsh flag. Edge inscription "SPIRIT OF FRIENDSHIP. MANCHESTER 2002".

2002 ....   £5

— Specimen (in Presentation set, see US24)* £6

— Proof *FDC* (in set, see PS76)* £8

— Proof in Silver *FDC* (in set, see PSS12)* £35

— Proof in gold *FDC* (in set, see PCGS1)* £350

4576A As above but with colour added to the flag and parts of the banner, Proof Piedfort in Silver
FDC (in set, see PSS13)* £60

4577 Two pounds. Discovery of the structure of DNA. England. R. In the centre the spiraling
double helix structure of DNA with the inscription "DNA DOUBLE HELIX" and
the dates 1953 and 2003 separated by the denomination "TWO POUNDS". Edge:
"DEOXYRIBONUCLEIC ACID". (Reverse design: John Mills)

2003 ....   £4

— Specimen in presentation folder (Issued: 41,568) £7

— Proof *FDC* (in set, see PS78)* £8

— Proof in Silver *FDC* (Issued: 11,204) £30

— Proof piedfort in silver *FDC* (Issued: 8,728) £50

— Proof in gold *FDC* (Issued: 1,500) £350

4578 Two pounds. R. In the centre a depiction of Trevithick's Locomotive Penydarren and the
denomination "Two Pounds" surrounded by a cog representing the Industrial Revolution
and the inscription "R.TREVITHICK 1804 INVENTION INDUSTRY PROGRESS 2004"
Patterned Edge. (Reverse design Robert Lowe)

2004 ....   £4

— Specimen in presentation folder (Issued: 56,871) £7

— Brilliant uncirculated in silver (Issued: 1,923) £18

— Proof *FDC* (in 2004 set, see PS81)* £8

— Proof in Silver *FDC* (Issued: 10,233) £30

— Proof piedfort in silver *FDC* (Issued: 5,303) £50

— Proof in gold *FDC* (1,500) £400

* Coins marked thus were originally issued in Royal Mint sets.

4579   4580   4581

UNC
£

4579 Two pounds. 400th Anniversary of the Gunpowder Plot. Ŗ. In the centre in a circular
arrangement the symbols of state the mace, crosier and sword the denomination "Two
Pounds" and the dates "1605 and 2005" with the edge inscription "REMEMBER
REMEMBER THE FIFTH OF NOVEMBER". (Reverse design: Peter Forster)
2005 .... £4
   — Specimen in presentation folder (Issued: 12,044) £7
   — Proof *FDC* (in 2005 set, see PS84)* £8
   — Proof in Silver *FDC* (Issued: 4,394) £30
   — Proof piedfort in silver *FDC* (Issued: 4,585) £50
   — Proof in gold *FDC* (Issued: 914) £400

4580 Two pounds. 60th Anniversary of the end of World War II. Ŗ. In the centre a depiction
of the front of St.Paul's Cathedral in full floodlights with the denomination "Two
Pounds" and the dates "1945 and 2005" with the edge inscription "IN VICTORY
MAGNANIMITY IN PEACE GOODWILL". (Reverse design: Robert Elderton)
2005 .... £4
   — Specimen in presentation folder with medal (Issued: 53,686) £10
   — Proof in Silver *FDC* (Issued: 21,734) £30
   — Proof piedfort in silver *FDC* (Issued: 4,798) £50
   — Proof in gold *FDC* (Issued: 1,578 single coins and 1,346 in sets) £400

4581 Two pounds. 200th Anniversary of the birth of Isambard Brunel. Ŗ. In the centre
a portrait of the engineer with segments of a wheel and bridge in the background
surrounded by links of a heavy chain and the date "2006" and the denomination "Two
pounds", with the edge inscription "1806 - 1859 ISAMBARD KINGDOM BRUNEL
ENGINEER". (Reverse design: Robert Elderton)
2006 .... £4
   — Specimen in presentation folder with **4582** £10
   — Proof *FDC** (in 2006 set, see PS87)* £8
   — Proof in silver *FDC* (Edition: 20,000) £30
   — Proof piedfort in silver *FDC** (see PSS25) £50
   — Proof in gold *FDC* (1,500) £385

* *Coins marked thus were originally issued in Royal Mint sets.*

4582   4583   4584

UNC
£

4582 Two pounds. 200th Anniversary of the birth of Isambard Brunel. R. In the centre a section of
the roof of Paddington Station with "Brunel" below and the date "2006 and the denomination
"Two Pounds", with the edge inscription "SO MANY IRONS IN THE FIRE". (Reverse
design: Rod Kelly)

    2006 .... £4

    — Specimen in presentation folder with **4581** £10
    — Proof *FDC** (in 2006 set, see PS87)* £8
    — Proof in silver *FDC* (Edition: 20,000) £30
    — Proof piedfort in silver *FDC** (see PSS25) £50
    — Proof in gold *FDC* (1,500) £385

4583 Two pounds. Tercentenary of the Act of Union between England and Scotland. R.A design
dividing the coin into four quarters, with a rose and a thistle occupying two of the quarters, and
a portcullis in each of the other two quarters. The whole is overlaid with a linking jigsaw motif
and surrounded by the dates "1707" and "2007" and the denomination "TWO POUNDS", with
an edge inscription "UNITED INTO ONE KINGDOM" (Reverse design : Yvonne Holton)

    2007 .... £4

    — Specimen in presentation folder £8
    — Proof FDC* (in 2007 set, see PS90) £8
    — Proof in Silver *FDC* (Edition: 10,000) £30
    — Proof piedfort in silver *FDC** (Edition: 5,000) £50
    — Proof in gold *FDC* (750) £500

* Coins marked thus were originally issued in Royal Mint sets.

4584 Two pounds. Bicentenary of the Abolition of the Slave Trade in the British Empire.
R. The date "1807" with the "0" depicted as a broken chain link , surrounded by the
inscription "AN ACT FOR THE ABOLITION OF THE SLAVE TRADE", and the date
"2007", with an edge inscription "AM I NOT A MAN, AND A BROTHER" (Reverse
design : David Gentleman)

    2006 .... £4

    — Specimen in presentation folder with £8
    — Proof *FDC** (in 2007 set, see PS90) £8
    — Proof in Silver *FDC* (Edition: 10,000) £30
    — Proof piedfort in silver *FDC** (Edition: 5,000) £50
    — Proof in gold *FDC* (1,000) £425

* Coins marked thus were originally issued in Royal Mint sets.

4590

UNC
£

4590 One pound (Royal Arms design). Edge: "DECUS ET TUTAMEN" (rev. as 4221)
1998* £10
— Proof *FDC** £6
— Proof in silver *FDC* (Issued: 13,863) £30
— Proof piedfort in silver *FDC* (Issued: 7,894) £45
2003 .... £3
— Specimen in presentation folder (Issued: 23,760) £5
— Proof *FDC* (in 2003 set, see PS78)*
— Proof in silver *FDC* (Issued: 15,830) £30
— Proof piedfort in silver *FDC* (Issued: 9,871) £49
4591 One pound. (Scottish lion design). Edge: "NEMO ME IMPUNE LACESSIT" (rev as 4337)
1999 .... £3
— Specimen in presentation folder £5
— Proof *FDC* (in 1999 set, see PS63)* £6
— Proof in silver *FDC* (Issued: 16,328) £30
— Proof piedfort in silver *FDC* (Issued: 9,975) £45
4591A — Proof in silver *FDC*, with reverse frosting, (Issued: 1,994)* £40
4592 One pound. (Welsh design). Edge: "PLEIDIOL WYF I'M GWLAD" (rev. as 4338)
2000... £3
— Proof *FDC* (in 2000 set, see PS65)* £6
— Proof in silver *FDC* (Issued: 15,913) £30
— Proof piedfort in silver *FDC* (Issued: 9,994) £47
4592A — Proof in silver *FDC*, with reverse frosting, (Issued: 1,994)* £50
4593 One pound. (Northern Irish design). Edge: "DECUS ET TUTAMEN" (rev. as 4339)
2001... £3
— Proof *FDC** £6
— Proof in silver *FDC* (Issued: 11,697) £30
— Proof piedfort in silver *FDC* (Issued: 8,464) £49
4593A— Proof in silver *FDC*, with reverse frosting, (Issued: 1,540)* £55
4594 One pound. (English design) Edge: "DECUS ET TUTAMEN" (rev. as 4340)
2002... £3
— Proof *FDC* (in 2002 set, see PS72)* £6
— Proof in silver *FDC* (Issued: 17,693) £30
— Proof piedfort in silver *FDC* (Issued: 6,599) £49
— Proof in gold *FDC* (in 2002 set, see PGJS1)* £350
4594A— Proof in silver *FDC*, with reverse frosting, (Issued: 1,540)* £55

* Coins marked thus were originally issued in Royal Mint sets.

4595   4595B

UNC
£

4595 One pound. Scotland R. In the centre a depiction of the Forth Rail Bridge and the
denomination "One Pound" and a border representing a railway track. Patterned Edge.
(Reverse design: Edwina Ellis)
2004 ....   £3
— Specimen in presentation folder (Issued: 24,014) £5
— Proof *FDC* (in 2004 set, see PS81)* £6
— Proof in silver *FDC* (Issued: 11,470) £27
— Proof piedfort in silver *FDC* (Issued: 7,013) £49
— Proof in gold *FDC* (Issued: 2,618) £400

4595A One pound pattern. Scotland. Design as 4595 above but dated 2003 with plain edge and
hallmark, reading "PATTERN" instead of "ONE POUND"
— Proof in silver *FDC* * £25
— Proof in gold *FDC* * £350

4595B One pound pattern. Scotland. R. Unicorn with the word "Pattern" below with plain
edge and hallmark and dated 2004. (Reverse design: Timothy Noad)
— Proof in silver *FDC* *
— Proof in gold *FDC* * £350

4596   4596B

4596 One pound. Wales. R. Menai Straits Bridge and the denomination "One pound".
(Reverse design: Edwina Ellis)
2005 ....   £3
— Specimen in presentation folder (Issued: 24,802) £6
— Proof *FDC* (in 2004 set, see PS84)* £6
— Proof in silver *FDC* (Issued: 8,371) £28
— Proof piedfort in silver *FDC* (Issued: 6,007 £50
— Proof in gold *FDC* (Issued: 1,195) £400

4596A One pound pattern. Wales. R. Menai Straits Bridge but dated 2003 with plain edge and
hallmark
— Proof in silver *FDC* * £25
— Proof in gold *FDC* * £350

4596B One pound pattern. Wales. R Dragon and the word "Pattern" below with plain edge
and hallmark and dated 2004. (Reverse design: Timothy Noad)
— Proof in silver *FDC* * £25
— Proof in gold *FDC* * £350

* Coins marked thus were originally issued in Royal Mint sets.

4597   4597B

UNC
£

4597 One pound. Northern Ireland. R. In the centre a depiction of MacNeill's Egyptian Arch and the denomination "One Pound" Patterned Edge. (Reverse design: Edwina Ellis)
2006 .... £4
- Specimen in presentation folder £6
- Proof *FDC* (in 2006 set, see PS87)* £8
- Proof in silver *FDC* (Edition: 20,000) £29
- Proof piedfort in silver *FDC* (Edition: 7,500) £50
- Proof in gold *FDC* (Edition: 1,500) £365

4597A One pound pattern. Northern Ireland. R.MacNeill's Egyptian Arch but dated 2003 with plain edge and hallmark
- Proof in silver *FDC* * £25
- Proof in gold *FDC* * £350

4597B One pound pattern. Northern Ireland. R Stag and the word "Pattern" below with plain edge and hallmark and dated 2004. (Reverse design: Timothy Noad)
- Proof in silver *FDC* * £25
- Proof in gold *FDC* * £350

4598   4598A   4598B

4598 One pound. England. R. In the centre a representation of the Gateshead Millennium Bridge with a border of struts and the denomination "One Pound" Patterned Edge. (Reverse design : Edwina Ellis)
2007 .... £4
- Specimen in presentation folder £7
- Proof *FDC** (in 2007 set, see PS90) £8
- Proof in silver *FDC* (Edition: 15,000) £29
- Proof piedfort in silver *FDC* (Edition: 7,500) £50
- Proof in gold *FDC* (Edition: 1,500) £375

4598A One pound pattern. England. R. Millennium Bridge but dated 2003 with plain edge and hallmark
- Proof in silver *FDC* * £25
- Proof in gold *FDC* * £350

4598B One pound pattern. England. R. Lion with the word "Pattern" below with plain edge and hallmark and dated 2004. (Reverse design: Timothy Noad)
- Proof in silver *FDC* * £25
- Proof in gold *FDC* * £350

* Coins marked thus were originally issued in Royal Mint sets.

CUPRO-NICKEL

4610 Fifty pence. R. Britannia. (Illus. as 4351)
1998
— Proof *FDC* (in 1998 set, see PS61)* £3
1999
— Proof *FDC* (in 1999 set, see PS63)* £3
2000
— Proof *FDC* (in 2000 set, see PS65)* £3
— Proof in silver *FDC** £25
2001
— Proof *FDC* (in 2001 set, see PS68)* £3
2002
— Proof *FDC* (in 2002 set, see PS72)* £3
— Proof in gold *FDC* (see PGJS1)* £250

2003
— Proof *FDC* (in 2003 set, see PS78) * £3
2004
— Proof *FDC* (in 2004 set, see PS81) * £3
2005
— Proof *FDC* (in 2005 set, see PS84) * £3
2006
— Proof *FDC* (in 2006 set, see PS87) * £3
— Proof in silver *FDC* (see PSS22) * £25

4611 4612 4613

UNC
£

4611 Fifty pence. R. Celebratory pattern of twelve stars reflecting the European flag with the dates 1973 and 1998 commemorating the 25th Anniversary of the United Kingdom's membership of the European Union and Presidency of the Council of Ministers. (Reverse design: John Mills)
1998 .... £2
— Proof *FDC** £5
— Proof in silver *FDC* (Issued: 8,859) £30
— Proof piedfort in silver *FDC* (Issued: 8,440) £50
— Proof in gold *FDC* (Issued: 1,177) £350

4612 Fifty pence. R. A pair of hands set against a pattern of radiating lines with the words Fiftieth Anniversary and the value 50 pence with the initials NHS. (Reverse design: David Cornell)
1998 .... £2
— Specimen in presentation folder £3
— Proof in silver *FDC* (Issued: 9,032) £30
— Proof piedfort in silver *FDC* (Issued: 5,117) £50
— Proof in gold *FDC* (Issued: 651) £400

4613 Fifty pence. Library commemorative. R. The turning pages of a book above the pediment of a classical library building which contains the inscription "Public Libraries" and the denomination "50 pence" and the dates 1850 and 2000. (Reverse design: Mary Milner Dickens)
2000 .... £2
— Specimen in presentation folder £5
— Proof *FDC** £5
— Proof in silver *FDC* (Issued: 7,634) £25
— Proof piedfort in silver *FDC* (Issued: 5,721) £45
— Proof in gold *FDC* (Issued: 710) £350

* Coins marked thus were originally issued in Royal Mint sets.

4614

UNC
£

4614 Fifty pence. Anniversary of the Suffragette Movement commemorative. R. A standing figure
of a woman holding a banner bearing the initials WSPU with railings in the background and
a poster with the words "GIVE WOMEN THE VOTE" the denomination "50 pence" and the
dates 1903 and 2003. (Reverse design: Mary Milner Dickens)
2003..   £2
— Specimen in presentation folder (Issued: 9,582) £5
— Proof *FDC* (in 2003 set, see PS78)* £5
— Proof in silver *FDC* (Issued: 6,267) £25
— Proof piedfort in silver *FDC* (Issued 6,795) £47
— Proof in gold *FDC* (Issued: 942) £350

4615   4616

4615 Fifty pence. 50th anniversary of the first sub four-minute mile. R. The lower half of a
running athlete with a stop clock showing the time and the denomination "50 pence".
(Reverse design: James Butler)
2004..   £2
— Specimen in presentation folder (Issued: 10,371) £5
— Proof *FDC* (in 2004 set, see PS81)* £5
— Proof in silver *FDC* ((Issued: 4,924)) £26
— Proof piedfort in silver *FDC* ((Issued: 4,054)) £47
— Proof in gold *FDC* ((Issued: 644)) £350

4616 Fifty pence. 250th anniversary of the publication of Samuel Johnson's Dictionary of the
English language. R. An interpretation of the words "Fifty" and "Pence" as they appeared
in Johnson's dictionary together with denomination "50" and "Johnson's Dictionary 1755".
(Reverse design: Tom Phillips)
2005..   £2
— Proof *FDC* (in 2005 set, see PS84)* £5
— Proof in silver *FDC* (Issued: 4,029) £27
— Proof piedfort in silver *FDC* ((Issued: 3,808)) £47
— Proof in gold *FDC* ((Issued: 584)) £350

* Coins marked thus were originally issued in Royal Mint sets.

4617	4618	4619

UNC
£

4617 **Fifty pence.** 150th anniversary of the institution of the Victoria Cross. R. Depicts the obverse and reverse of the Victoria Cross with the initials "VC" and the denomination "Fifty pence". Reverse design: Claire Aldridge)

2006 .... £2

— Specimen in presentation folder with **4618** £7
— Proof *FDC* (in 2006 set, see PS87)* £5
— Proof in silver *FDC* (Edition: 7,500) £27
— Proof piedfort in silver *FDC* (see PSS27)) £50
— Proof in gold *FDC* (Edition: 1,000) £325

4618 **Fifty pence.** 150th anniversary of the institution of the Victoria Cross. R. Depicts a soldier carrying a wounded colleague against a silhouette of the Victoria Cross and the denomination "Fify Pence". Reverse design: Clive Duncan)

2006 .... £2

— Specimen in presentation folder with **4617** £7
— Proof *FDC* (in 2006 set, see PS87)* £5
— Proof in silver *FDC* (Edition: 7,500) £27
— Proof piedfort in silver *FDC* (see PSS27)) £50
— Proof in gold *FDC* (Edition: 1,000) £325

4619 **Fifty pence.** Centenary of the Founding of the Scouting Movement. R. A Fleur-de-lis superimposed over a globe and surrounded by the inscription "BE PREPARED", and the dates "1907" and "2007" and the denomination "Fifty pence" (Reverse design : Kerry Jones)

2006 .... £2

— Specimen in presentation folder £7
— Proof FDC* (in 2007 set, see PS90) £5
— Proof in silver FDC (Edition: 12,500) £27
— Proof piedfort in silver FDC* (Edition; 5,000) £50
— Proof in gold FDC (Edition: 1,250) £345

4630 **Twenty pence.** R. Crowned double rose. (Illus. as 4230) ....

1998	1999	2000
— Proof *FDC** £3	— Proof *FDC** £3	— Proof *FDC** £3
		— Proof in silver *FDC**

2001	2002	
— Proof *FDC** £3	— Proof *FDC** £3	
	— Proof in gold *FDC* (in 2002 set, see PGJS1)* £250	

2003	2004	2005
— Proof *FDC** £3	— Proof *FDC** £3	— Proof *FDC** £3

2006
— Proof *FDC** £3
— Proof in silver *FDC**

4650 Ten pence. R. Lion passant guardant. (Illus. as 4232)

1998*	1999*	2000
— Proof *FDC** £3	— Proof *FDC** £3	— Proof *FDC** £3
		— Proof in silver *FDC**
2001	2002	
— Proof *FDC** £3	— Proof *FDC** £3	
	— Proof in gold *FDC* (in 2002 set, see PGJS1)* £200	
2003	2004	2005
— Proof *FDC** £3	— Proof *FDC** £3	— Proof *FDC** £3
2006		
— Proof *FDC** £3		
— Proof in silver *FDC**		

4670 Five pence. R. Crowned thistle. (Illus. as 4234)

1998	1999	2000
— Proof *FDC** £3	— Proof *FDC** £3	— Proof *FDC** £3
		— - Proof in silver *FDC**
2001	2002	
— Proof *FDC** £3	— Proof *FDC**£3	
	— Proof in gold *FDC* (in 2002 set, see PGJS1)* £140	
2003	2004	2005
— Proof *FDC** £3	— Proof *FDC** £3	— Proof *FDC** £3
2006		
— Proof *FDC** £3		
— Proof in silver *FDC**		

COPPER PLATED STEEL

4690 Two pence. R. Plumes. (Illus. as 4376)

1998	1999	2000
— Proof *FDC** £3	— Proof *FDC** £3	— Proof *FDC** £3
		— Proof in silver *FDC**
2001	2002	
— Proof *FDC** £3	— Proof *FDC** £3	
	— Proof in gold *FDC* (in 2002 set, see PGJS1)* £200	
2003	2004	2005
— Proof *FDC** £3	— Proof *FDC** £3	— Proof *FDC** £3
2006		
— Proof *FDC** £3		
— Proof in silver *FDC**		

BRONZE

4700 Two pence. R. Plumes. (Illus. as 4376)

1998

COPPER PLATED STEEL

4710 One pence. R. Portcullis with chains. (Illus. as 4381)

1998	1999	2000
— Proof *FDC** £3	— Proof *FDC** £3	— Proof *FDC** £3
		— Proof in silver *FDC**
2001	2002	
— Proof *FDC** £3	— Proof *FDC** £3	
	— Proof in gold *FDC* (in 2002 set, see PGJS1)* £150	
2003	2004	2005
— Proof *FDC** £3	— Proof *FDC** £3	— Proof *FDC** £3
2006		
— Proof *FDC** £3		
— Proof in silver *FDC**		

* Coins marked thus were originally issued in Royal Mint sets

The practice of issuing annual sets of coins was started by the Royal Mint in 1970 when a set of the £SD coins was issued as a souvenir prior to Decimalisation. There are now regular issues of brilliant uncirculated coin sets as well as proofs in base metal, and issues in gold and silver. In order to simplify the numbering system, and to allow for the continuation of the various issues in the future, the Prefix letters have been changed. The base metal proof sets will continue the series of numbers from the 1970 set, PS20. Other sets, such as those of uncirculated coins, silver and gold now have their numbering series commencing with number 1 in each case.

In addition to the annual sets of uncirculated and proofs coins sold by the Royal Mint to collectors and dealers, the Mint has produced specially packaged sets and single coins for companies. No details are made available of these issues and therefore no attempt has been made to include them in the listings below. The Mint also sells "Christening" and "Wedding" sets in distinctive packaging but the numbers circulating in the market are relatively modest and of limited appeal after the year of issue.

The Mint has recently offered sets of coins to collectors that consist of coins obtained from the market e.g. silver proofs, crowns and gold sovereigns showing different portraits. Although these are available in limited numbers from the Mint, it has been decided that they do not merit listing in the section devoted to sets.

Uncirculated Sets   £

US01–**1982**	Uncirculated (specimen) set in Royal Mint folder, 50p to ^{1}/2p, new reverse type, including 20 pence (Issued: 205,000)	(7)	9
US02–**1983**	'U.K.' £1 (4221) to ^{1}/2p (Issued: 637,100)	(8)	15
US03–**1984**	'Scottish' £1 (4222) to ^{1}/2p (Issued: 158,820)	(8)	13
US04–**1985**	'Welsh' £1 (4331) to 1p, new portrait of The Queen (Issued: 102,015)	(7)	13
US05–**1986**	Commonwealth Games £2 (4311) plus 'Northern Irish' £1 (4332) to 1p, ((Issued: 167,224)	(8)	14
US06–**1987**	'English' £1 (4333) to 1p, (Issued: 172,425)	(7)	12
US07–**1988**	'Arms' £1 (4334) to 1p, (Issued: 134,067)	(7)	15
US08–**1989**	'Scottish' £1 (4335) to 1p, (Issued: 77,569)	(7)	22
US09–**1989**	Bill of Rights and Claim of Right £2s (4312 and 4313) in Royal Mint folder (Issue: not known)	(2)	15
US10–**1990**	'Welsh' £1 (4331) to 1p plus new 5p, (Issued: 102,606)	(8)	20
US11–**1991**	'Northern Irish' £1 (4332) to 1p, (Issued: 74,975)	(7)	20
US12–**1992**	'English' £1 (4333), 'European Community' 50p (4352) and Britannia 50p, 20p to 1p plus new 10p (Issued: 78,421)	(9)	20
US13–**1993**	'UK' £1 (4336), 'European Community' 50p to 1p ((Issued: 56,945)	(8)	25
US14–**1994**	'Bank' £2 (4314), 'Scottish' £1 (4337) and 'D-Day' 50p (4353) to 1p, (Issued: 177,971)	(8)	15
US15–**1995**	'Peace' £2 (4315) and 'Welsh' £1 (4338) to 1p (Issued: 105, 647)	(8)	15
US16–**1996**	'Football' £2 (4317) and 'Northern Irish' £1 (4339) to 1p (Issued: 86,501)	(8)	15
US17–**1997**	'Bimetallic' £2 (4318), 'English' £1 (4340) to 1p plus new 50p (Issued: 109,557)	(9)	15
US18–**1998**	'Bimetallic' £2 (4570), 'UK' £1 (4590) and 'EU' 50 pence (4611) to 1 pence (Issued: 96,192)	(9)	20
US19–**1998**	'EU' and Britannia 50 pence (4611 and 4610) in Royal Mint folder.	(2)	6
US20–**1999**	'Bimetallic' £2 (4571), 'Scottish' £1 (4591) to 1p (Issued: 136,696)	(8)	15
US21–**2000**	'Bimetallic' £2 (4570), 'Welsh' £1 (4592) to 1p plus 'Library' 50 pence (Issued: 117,750)	(9)	15
US22–**2001**	'Bimetallic' £2 (4570), 'Bimetallic' £2 (4572), 'Irish' £1 (4594) to 1p (Issued: 57,741)	(9)	14
US23–**2002**	'Bimetallic' £2 (4570), 'English' £1 (4594) to 1p (Issued: 60,539).	(8)	14
US24–**2002**	'Bimetallic' £2 (4573, 4574, 4575 and 4576) Commonwealth Games (Issued: 47,895)	(4)	15

542

<table>
<tr><td></td><td></td><td>£</td></tr>
<tr><td>US25–2003</td><td>"Bimetallic" "DNA" £2 (4577), "Bimetallic" £2 (4570), "UK" £1 (4590), "Suffragette" 50 pence (4614) and "Britannia" 50 pence (4610) to 1p. (Issued: 62,741) ....(10)</td><td>14</td></tr>
<tr><td>US26 – 2004</td><td>"Bimetallic" "Penydarren engine" £2 (4578), "Bimetallic" £2 (4570), "Forth Rail Bridge" £1 (4595),"Sub four-minute mile" 50 pence (4615) and "Britannia"50pence(4610) to1p. (Issued: 46,032)....................(10)</td><td>14</td></tr>
<tr><td>US27 – 2004</td><td>"Bimetallic" "Penydarren engine" £2 (4578), "Forth Rail Bridge" £1 (4595),"Sub four-minute mile" 50 pence (4615). (Issued: 14,391) . (3)</td><td>9</td></tr>
<tr><td>US28 – 2005</td><td>"Bimetallic" "Gunpowder Plot" £2 (4579), "Bimetallic" £2 (4570), "Menai Straits Bridge" £1 (4596), "Samuel Johnson's Dictionary" 50 pence (4616) and "Britannia" 50 pence (4610) to 1p. (Issued: 51,776) .... (10)</td><td>15</td></tr>
<tr><td>US29 – 2005</td><td>"Bimetallic" "Gunpowder Plot" £2 (4579), "Menai Straits Bridge" £1 (4596), "Samuel Johnson's Dictionary" 50 pence (4616) .... (3)</td><td>10</td></tr>
<tr><td>US30 – 2005</td><td>"Trafalgar" £5, struck in c/n (4559) and "Nelson" £5 struck in c/n (4560) .... (2)</td><td>19</td></tr>
<tr><td>US31 – 2006</td><td>"Bimetallic" "Isambard Brunel" £2 (4581), "Bimetallic" "Paddington Station" £2 (4582), "MacNeill's Egyptian Arch" £1 (4597),, "Victoria Cross" 50 pence (4617), "Wounded soldier" 50 pence (4618) to 1p .... (10)</td><td>15</td></tr>
<tr><td>US32 – 2006</td><td>"Bimetallic" "Isambard Brunel" £2 (4581), "Bimetallic" "Paddington Station" £2 (4582) .... (2)</td><td>10</td></tr>
<tr><td>US33 – 2006</td><td>"Victoria Cross" 50 pence (4617), "Wounded soldier" 50 pence (4618) .... (2)</td><td>7</td></tr>
<tr><td>US34 – 2007</td><td>"Bimetallic" "Act of Union" £2 (4583), "Bimetallic" "Abolition of Slave Trade" £2 (4584), "Gateshead Millennium Bridge" £1 (4598), "Scouting Movement" 50 pence (4619), to 1p .... (9)</td><td>15</td></tr>
</table>

Proof Sets

<table>
<tr><td>PS21–1971</td><td>Decimal coinage set, 50 new pence ('Britannia' to 1/2 new pence, plus medallion in sealed plastic case with card wrapper (Issued: 350,000) .... (6)</td><td>15</td></tr>
<tr><td>PS22–1972</td><td>Proof 'Silver Wedding' Crown struck in c/n (4226) plus 50p to 1/2p (Issued: 150,000).. (7)</td><td>20</td></tr>
<tr><td>PS23–1973</td><td>'EEC' 50p (4224) plus 10p to 1/2p, (Issued: 100,000) .... (6)</td><td>15</td></tr>
<tr><td>PS24–1974</td><td>Britannia 50p to 1/2p, as 1971 (Issued: 100,000) .... (6)</td><td>12</td></tr>
<tr><td>PS25–1975</td><td>50p to 1/2p (as 1974), (Issued: 100,000) .... (6)</td><td>12</td></tr>
<tr><td>PS26–1976</td><td>50p to 1/2p, as 1975, (Issued: 100,000) .... (6)</td><td>12</td></tr>
<tr><td>PS27–1977</td><td>Proof 'Silver Jubilee' Crown struck in c/n (4227) plus 50p to 1/2p, (Issued: 193,000)... (7)</td><td>12</td></tr>
<tr><td>PS28–1978</td><td>50p to 1/2p, as 1976, (Issued: 86,100) .... (6)</td><td>12</td></tr>
<tr><td>PS29–1979</td><td>50p to 1/2p, as 1978, (Issued: 81,000) .... (6)</td><td>12</td></tr>
<tr><td>PS30–1980</td><td>50p to 1/2p, as 1979, (Issued: 143,000) .... (6)</td><td>15</td></tr>
<tr><td>PS31–1981</td><td>50p to 1/2p, as 1980, (Issued: 100,300) .... (6)</td><td>15</td></tr>
<tr><td>PS32–1982</td><td>50p to 1/2p including 20 pence (Issued: 106,800) .... (7)</td><td>12</td></tr>
<tr><td>PS33–1983</td><td>'U.K.' £1 (4221) to 1/2p in new packaging (Issued: 107,800) .... (8)</td><td>17</td></tr>
<tr><td>PS34–1984</td><td>'Scottish' £1 (4222) to 1/2p, (Issued: 106,520)............................... (8)</td><td>16</td></tr>
<tr><td>PS35–1985</td><td>'Welsh' £1 (4331) to 1/2p, (Issued: 102,015).................................. (7)</td><td>16</td></tr>
<tr><td>PS36–1985</td><td>As last but packed in deluxe red leather case (Included above)....... (7)</td><td>20</td></tr>
<tr><td>PS37–1986</td><td>Commonwealth games £2 (4311) plus 'Northern Irish' £1 (4332) to 1p, (Issued: 104,597).. (8)</td><td>20</td></tr>
<tr><td>PS38–1986</td><td>As last but packed in deluxe red leather case (Included above)....... (8)</td><td>23</td></tr>
<tr><td>PS39–1987</td><td>'English' £1 (4333) to 1p, (Issued: 88,659)................................... (7)</td><td>20</td></tr>
</table>

£

PS40–**1987**	As last but packed in deluxe leather case (Included above)............	(7)	24
PS41–**1988**	'Arms' £1 (4334) to 1p, (Issued: 79,314)..	(7)	25
PS42–**1988**	As last but packed in deluxe leather case (Included above)............	(7)	29
PS43–**1989**	Bill of Rights and Claim of Right £2s (4312 and 4313), 'Scottish' £1 (4335) to 1p, (Issued: 85,704)..	(9)	30
PS44–**1989**	As last but packed in red leather case, (Included above)...............	(9)	35
PS45–**1990**	'Welsh' £1 (4331) to 1p plus new 5p, (Issued: 79,052)...................	(8)	27
PS46–**1990**	As last but packed in red leather case (Included above)...............	(8)	32
PS47–**1991**	'Northern Irish' £1 (4332) to 1p, (Issued: 55,144).........................	(7)	27
PS48–**1991**	As last but packed in red leather case (Included above)...............	(7)	33
PS49–**1992**	'English' £1 (4333), 'European community' 50p (4352) and Britannia 50p, 20p to 1p plus new 10p, (Issued: 44,337).................	(9)	28
PS50–**1992**	As last but packed in red leather case (Issued: 17,989).................	(9)	33
PS51–**1993**	'Coronation Anniversary' £5 struck in c/n (4302), 'U.K.' £1 (4336), 50p to 1p, (Issued: 43,509)...	(8)	30
PS52–**1993**	As last but packed in red leather case (Issued: 22,571).................	(8)	35
PS53–**1994**	'Bank' £2 (4314), 'Scottish' £1 (4337), 'D-Day' 50p (4353) to 1p, (Issued: 44,643)...	(8)	30
PS54–**1994**	As last but packed in red leather case (Issued: 22,078).................	(8)	35
PS55–**1995**	'Peace' £2 (4315), 'Welsh' £1 (4338) to 1p, (Issued: 42,842).........	(8)	32
PS56–**1995**	As last but packed in red leather case (Issued: 17,797).................	(8)	35
PS57–**1996**	Proof '70th Birthday' £5 struck in c/n (4303), 'Football' £2 (4317), 'Northern Irish' £1 (4339) to 1p, (Issued: 46,295)	(9)	32
PS58–**1996**	As last but packed in red leather case (Issued: 21,286).................	(9)	37
PS59–**1997**	Proof 'Golden Wedding' £5 struck in c/n (4304), 'Bimetallic' £2 (4318), 'English' £1 (4340) to 1p plus new 50p (Issued: 48,761)...	(10)	33
PS60–**1997**	As last but packed in red leather case (Issued: 31,987).................	(10)	40
PS61–**1998**	Proof £5 'Prince of Wales 50th Birthday', struck in c/n (4550), 'Bimetallic' £2 (4570), 'UK'. £1 (4590), 'EU' 50 pence (4611) to 1 pence. (Issued: 36,907)...	(10)	33
PS62–**1998**	As last, but packed in red leather case. (Issued: 26,763)...................	(10)	40
PS63–**1999**	Proof £5 'Diana, Princess of Wales', struck in c/n (4551), 'Bimetallic' 'Rugby' £2 (4571), 'Scottish' £1 (4591) to 1p. (Issued: 40,317)...	(9)	34
PS64–**1999**	As last, but packed in red leather case. (Issued: 39,827).................	(9)	40
PS65–**2000**	Proof £5 'Millennium', struck in c/n (4552), 'Bimetallic' £2 (4570), 'Welsh' £1 (4592), 'Library' 50 pence (4613) and 'Britannia' 50 pence (4610) to 1p Standard Set, (Issued: 41,379).................	(10)	£30
PS66–**2000**	As last, but Deluxe set (Issued: 21,573 above)	(10)	£40
PS67–**2000**	As last, but Executive set (Issued: 9,517)	(10)	£70
PS68–**2001**	Proof £5 'Victoria', struck in c/n (4554), 'Bimetallic' £2 (4570), 'Bimetallic' £2 (4572), 'Irish' £1 (4593) to 1p. Standard Set. (Issued: 28,244)...	(10)	34
PS69–**2001**	As last, but Gift Set (Issued: 1,351)	(10)	43
PS70–**2001**	As last, but packed in red leather case (Isssued: 16,022)	(10)	48
PS71–**2001**	As last, but Executive Set (Issued: 3,755).....................................	(10)	60
PS72–**2002**	Proof £5 'Golden Jubilee', struck in c/n (4555), 'Bimetallic' £2 (4570), 'English' £1 (4594) to 1p. Standard set. (Issued: 30,884)...............	(9)	32
PS73–**2002**	As last, but Gift Set (Issued:1,544)	(9)	40
PS74–**2002**	As last, but packed in red leather case (Issued: 23,342).................	(9)	46
PS75–**2002**	As last, but Executive Set (Issued: 5,000).....................................	(9)	70
PS76–**2002**	'Bimetallic' £2 (4573, 4574, 4575 and 4576) Commonwealth Games.. (Issued: 3,358)...	(4)	25

			£
PS77–**2002**	As last, but Display Set (Issued: 673)	(4)	33
PS78–**2003**	Proof £5 "Coronation", struck in c/n (4557), "Bimetallic" "DNA" £2 (4577), "Bimetallic" £2 (4570), "UK" £1 (4590), "Suffragette" 50 pence (4614)and "Britannia" 50 pence (4610) to 1p. Standard set. (Issued: 23,650).................................	(11)	34
PS79–**2003**	As last, but packed in red leather case (Issued: 14,863).................	(11)	47
PS80–**2003**	As last, but Executive Set (Issued: 5,000).................................	(11)	70
PS81–**2004**	"Bimetallic" "Penydarren engine" £2 (4578), "Bimetallic" £2 (4570), "Forth Rail Bridge" £1 (4595), "Sub four-minute mile" 50 pence (4615) and "Britannia" 50 pence (4610) to 1p. Standard set. (Issued: 17,951).................................	(10)	30
PS82–**2004**	As last, but packed in red leather case (Issued: 12,968).................	(10)	40
PS83– **2004**	As last, but Executive Set (Issued: 4,101).................................	(10)	65
PS84– **2005**	Proof £5 "Trafalgar", struck in c/n (4559), Proof £5 "Nelson", struck in c/n (4560) "Bimetallic" "Gunpowder Plot" £2 (4579), "Bimetallic" £2 (4570), "Menai Straits Bridge" £1 (4596),"Samuel Johnson's Dictionary" 50 pence (4616) and "Britannia"50 pence (4610) to 1p. (Issued: 21,374)................	(12)	38
PS85– **2005**	As last, but packed in red leather case (Issued: 14,899).................	(12)	49
PS86– **2005**	As last, but Executive Set (Issued: 4,290).................................	(12)	75
PS87– **2006**	Proof £5 "80th Birthday", struck in c/n (4561), "Bimetallic" Isambard Brunel" £2 (4581), "Bimetallic" "Paddington Station" £2 (4582), "Bimetallic" £2 (4570), "MacNeill's Egyptian Arch" £1 (4597), "Victoria Cross" 50 pence (4617), "Wounded soldier" 50 pence (4618) and "Britannia" 50 pence (4610) to 1p (Edition: 30,000)................	(13)	40
PS88 – **2006**	As last, but packed in red leather case (Edition: 15,000).................	(13)	50
PS89 – **2006**	As last, but Executive Set (Edition: 5,000).................................	(13)	78
PS90 – **2007**	Proof £5 "Diamond Wedding", struck in c/n,"Bimetallic" "Act of Union" £2 (4583), "Bimetallic" "Abolition of Slave Trade" £2 (4584), "Gateshead Millennium Bridge" £1 (4598),"Scouting Movement" 50 pence (4619), and "Britannia" 50p (4610) to 1p (Edition: 30,000)................	(12)	40
PS91 – **2007**	As last, but packed in red leather case (Edition: 15,000).................	(12)	50
PS92 – **2007**	As last, but Executive Set (Edition: 5,000).................................	(12)	78

Silver Sets

PSS01–**1989**	Bill of Rights and Claim of Right £2s (4312 and 4313), Silver piedfort proofs (Issued: 10,000).................................	(2)	85
PSS02–**1989**	As last but Silver proofs (Issue figure not known)................	(2)	60
PSS03–**1990**	2 x 5p Silver proofs (4371 and 4372), (Issued: 35,000)................	(2)	30
PSS04–**1992**	2 x 10p Silver proofs (4366 and 4367), (Not known)................	(2)	34
PSS05–**1996**	25th Anniversary of Decimal Currency (4339, 4351, 4361, 4367, 4372, 4386, 4391) in Silver proof (Edition: 15,000)................	(7)	100
PSS06–**1997**	2 x 50p silver proofs (4351 and 4354) (Issued: 10,304)	(2)	65
PSS07–**1998**	'EU' and 'NHS' Silver proofs (4611 and 4612)................	(2)	50
PSS08–**2000**	'Millennium' £5, 'Bimetallic' £2, 'Welsh' £1, 50p to 1p, and Maundy coins, 4p-1p in silver proof (4552, 4570, 4592, 4610, 4630, 4650, 4670, 4212-4215) (Issued: 13,180)................	(13)	245
PSS09–**2002**	Commonwealth Games 'Bimetallic' £2 (4573, 4574, 4575 and 4576) in silver (Issued: 2,553)................	(4)	140
PSS10–**2002**	As above with the addition of colour and piedfort in silver. (4573A, 4574A, 4575A and 4576A) (Issued: 3,497)................	(4)	240
PSS11–**MD**	£5"Golden Jubilee"(4555) and £5 "Coronation" (4557) silver proofs(2)		69

£

PSS12–**2003**	£5 "Coronation"(4557), £2 "Britannia"(4503), £2 "DNA"(4577), £1 "UK"(4590) and 50 pence "Suffragette" (4614) silver proofs (Edition:) .... (5)	140
PSS13–**2004**	£5 "Entende Cordial" (4558), £2 "Britannia" (4500), £2 "Penydarren" (4578) £1 "Forth Rail Bridge" (4595) and 50 pence "Sub four-minute mile" (4615) silver proofs (Edition:) .... (5)	145
PSS14 – **2004**	"Bimetallic" "Penydarren engine" £2 (4578), "Forth Rail Bridge" £1 (4595),"Sub four-minute mile" 50 pence (4615) Silver piedfort proofs (3)	145
PSS15 – **2005**	"Bimetallic" Gunpowder Plot" £2 (4579), Bimetallic" "World War II" £2 (4580), "Menai Straits Bridge" £1 (4596), "Samuel Johnson's Dictionary" 50 pence Silver piedfort proofs .... (4)	190
PSS16 – **2005**	£5 "Trafalgar" (4559) and £5 "Nelson" (4560) silver piedfort proofs, (Issued: 2,818) .... (2)	135
PSS17 – **2006**	"80th Birthday" £5, "Bimetallic" £2, Northern ireland £1, 50p to 1p and Maundy Coins, 4p - 1p in silver proof (4561, 4570, 4597, 4610, 4630, 4650, 4670, 4212 - 4215 (Edition: 8,000) .... (13)	275
PSS18 – **2006**	"Bimetallic" "Isambard Brunel" £2 (4581) and "Bimetallic" "Paddington Station" £2 (4582) silver proofs (Edition: taken from individual coin limits)... (2)	60
PSS19 – **2006**	As last but silver piedforts (Edition: 5,000)................................ (2)	98
PSS20 – **2006**	"Victoria Cross" 50 pence (4617) and "Wounded soldier" 50 pence (4618) silver proofs (Edition: taken from individual coin limits) (2)	55
PSS21 – **2006**	As last but silver piedforts (Edition: 5,000) .... (2)	98
PSS22 – **2006**	"80th Birthday" £5 (4561), "Bimetallic" Isambard Brunel" £2 (4581) and "Bimetallic" "Paddington Station" £2 (4582), "MacNeill's Egyptian Arch" £1 (4597), "Victoria Cross" 50 pence (4617), "Wounded soldier" 50 pence (4618) silver piedforts (Edition: taken from individual coin limits).. (6)	325
PSS23 – **2007**	"Diamond Wedding" £5, Britannia £2,"Bimetallic" "Act of Union"£2, "Bimetallic" "Abolition of Slavery" £2, "Millennium Bridge" £1 and "Scout Movement"50p in silver proof (4562, 4505, 4583, 4584, 4598 and 4619) (Edition: taken from individual coin limits).................... (6)	196
PSS24 – **2007**	"Diamond Wedding" £5, £2,"Bimetallic" "Act of Union"£2, "Bimetallic" "Abolition of Slavery" £2, "Millennium Bridge" £1 and "Scout Movement"50p in silver piedfort (4562, 4583, 4584, 4598 and 4619) (Edition: taken from individual coin limits .... (5)	250
PSS25 – **MD**	Set of four £1 coins "Forth Rail Bridge" (4595), "Menai Straits Bridge" (4596) "MacNiell's Egyptian Arch" (4597) and "Gateshead Millennium Bridge" (4598) in silver proof (Edition: taken from individual coin limits).. (4)	115
PSS26 – **MD**	As above but in silver piedfort (Edition: 1,400 taken from individual coin limits).. (4)	200

Silver Britannia Sets

PSB01 – **1997**(PSS07)	Britannia proofs, £2 – 20 pence (4300, 4300A, 4300B, 4300C) (Issued: 11,832) .... (4)	105
PSB02 – **1998** (PSS08)	Britannia proofs, £2 – 20 pence (4500, 4510, 4520, 4530) (Issued: 3,044) ....(4)	120
PSB03 – **2001** (PSS11)	Britannia proofs, £2 – 20 pence (4502, 4511, 4521, 4531) (Issued: 4,596) .... (4)	90
PBS04 – **2003** (PSS14)	Britannia proofs, £2 – 20 pence (4503, 4512, 4522, 4532) (Issued: 3,669) .... (4)	90

£

PBS05 – **MD** (PSS15) Britannia set of four different £2 designs, 1999- 2003 (4500, 4501, 4502,
4503) (Edition: 5,000) .... (4) 50
PBS06 – **2005** Britannia proofs, £2 – 20 pence (4504, 4513, 4523, 4533)
(Issued: 2,360) .... (4) 120
PBS07 – **2006** Britannia set of five different £2 designs with selected gold Plating of
obverse and reverse (4500A, 4501A, 4502A, 4503A, 4504A)
(Edition: 3,000) .... (5) 275
PBS08 – **2007** Britannia proofs, £2 - 20 pence, (4505, 4514, 4524 and 4538)
(Edition: 2,500) .... (4) 115

Gold Sovereign Proof Sets
PGS01–**1980** Gold £5 to half-sovereign (4201, 4203-4205) (Issued: 10,000) ...... (4) 100
PGS02–**1981** U.K. Proof coin Commemorative collection. (Consists of £5,
sovereign, 'Royal Wedding' Crown (4229) in silver, plus base
metal proofs 50p to 1/2p), (Not known) .... (9) 750
PGS03–**1982** Gold £5 to half-sovereign (Issued: 2,500) .... (4) 1100
PGS04–**1983** Gold £2, sovereign and half-sovereign, (Not known) .... (3) 500
PGS05–**1984** Gold £5, sovereign and half-sovereign, (Issued: 7,095) .... (3) 825
PGS06–**1985** Gold £5 to half-sovereign (4251, 4261, 4271, 4276) (Issued: 5,849).. (4) 1200
PGS07–**1986** Gold Commonwealth games £2, (4311) sovereign and half-
sovereign (Issued: 12,500) .... (3) 650
PGS08–**1987** Gold £2 (4261), sovereign and half-sovereign (Issued: 12,500) ...... (3) 600
PGS09–**1988** Gold £2 to half-sovereign (Issued: 11,192) .... (3) 600
PGS10–**1989** Sovereign Anniversary Gold £5 to half-sovereign (4254, 4263,
4272, 4277), (Issued: 5,000) .... (4) 2000
PGS11–**1989** Gold £2 to half-sovereign (Issued: 7,936) .... (3) 1200
PGS12–**1990** Gold £5 to half-sovereign (as 1985 issue), (Issued: 1,721) .... (4) 1300
PGS13–**1990** Gold £2 to half-sovereign (as 1988 issue), (Issued: 1,937) .... (3) 500
PGS14–**1991** Gold £5 to half-sovereign (Issued: 1,336) .... (4) 1300
PGS15–**1991** Gold £2 to half-sovereign (Issued: 1,152) .... (3) 500
PGS16–**1992** Gold £5 to half-sovereign (Issued: 1,165) .... (4) 1350
PGS17–**1992** Gold £2 to half-sovereign (Issued: 967) .... (3) 500
PGS18–**1993** Gold £5 to half-sovereign with silver Pistrucci medal in case
(Issued: 1,078) .... (5) 1450
PGS19–**1993** Gold £2 to half-sovereign (Issued: 663) .... (3) 850
PGS20–**1994** Gold £5, £2 (as 4314), sovereign and half-sovereign (Issued: 918) .... (4) 1450
PGS21–**1994** Gold £2, (as 4314), sovereign and half-sovereign (Issued: 1,249)... (3) 850
PGS22–**1995** Gold £5, £2 (as 4315), sovereign and half-sovereign (Issued: 718). (4) 1400
PGS23–**1995** Gold £2 (as 4315), sovereign and half-sovereign (Issued: 1,112).... (3) 750
PGS24–**1996** Gold £5 to half-sovereign (as 1992 issue) (Issued: 742) .... (4) 1350
PGS25–**1996** Gold £2 to half-sovereign (as 1992 issue) (Issued: 868) .... (3) 700
PGS26–**1997** Gold £5, £2 (as 4318), sovereign and half-sovereign
(Issued: 860) .... (4) 1400
PGS27–**1997** Gold £2 (as 4318) to half-sovereign (Issued: 817) .... (3) 750
PGS28–**1998** Gold £5 to half sovereign (4400, 4420, 4430, 4440) (Issued: 789) .... (4) 1350
PGS29–**1998** Gold £2 to half sovereign (4420, 4430, 4440) (Issued: 560) .... (3) 700
PGS30–**1999** Gold £5, £2 (as 4571), sovereign and half sovereign (Issued: 991) ...... (4) 1500
PGS31–**1999** Gold £2 (as 4571), sovereign and half sovereign (Issued: 912) .... (3) 900
PGS32–**2000** Gold £5 to half-sovereign (as 1998 issue) (Issued: 1,000) .... (4) 1250
PGS33–**2000** Gold £2 to half-sovereign (as 1998 issue) (Issued: 1,250) .... (3) 625
PGS34–**2001** Gold £5, £2 (as 4572), sovereign and half sovereign (Issued: 1,000) .. (4) 1300
PGS35–**2001** Gold £2 (as 4572), sovereign and half sovereign (Issued: 891) .... (3) 650
PGS36–**2002** Gold £5 to half sovereign (4401, 4421, 4431, 4441) (Issued: 3,000) . (4) 1450

£

PGS37–**2002**	Gold £2 to half sovereign (4421, 4431, 4441) (Issued: 3,947)	(3)	750
PGS38–**2003**	Gold £5 to half sovereign (as 1998 issue) (Issued: 2,050)	(4)	1250
PGS39–**2003**	Gold £2 (as 4577) sovereign and half sovereign (Issued: 1,737).....	(3)	650
PGS40–**2004**	Gold £5 to half sovereign (as 1998 issue) (Issued: 1,749)	(4)	1250
PGS41–**2004**	Gold £2 (as 4578) sovereign and half sovereign (Issued: 761)........	(3)	725
PGS42–**2005**	Gold £5 to half sovereign (4402, 4422, 4432, 4442 (Issued: 2,161)	(4)	1400
PGS43–**2005**	Gold £2 to half sovereign (4422, 4432, 4442) (Issued: 797........	(3)	700
PGS44–**2006**	Gold £5 to half sovereign (as 1998 issue) (Edition: 1,750).............	(4)	1195
PGS45–**2006**	Gold £2 to half sovereign (as 1998 issue) (Edition: 1,750).............	(3)	580
PGS46–**2007**	Gold £5 to half sovereign (as 1998 issue) (Edition: 1,750)	(4)	1295
PGS47–**2007**	Gold £2 to half sovereign (as 1998 issue) (Edition: 750)	(3)	595
PGS48–**2007**	Gold sovereign and half sovereign (as 1998) (Edition: taken from individual coin limits)	(2)	275

Britannia Proof Sets

PBS01–**1987**	Britannia Gold Proofs £100, £50, £25, £10 (4281, 4286, 4291, 4296), (Issued: 10,000)......	(4)	925
PBS02–**1987**	Britannia Gold Proofs £25, £10 (4291 and 4296) (Issued: 11,100) .	(2)	180
PBS03–**1988**	Britannia Proofs £100–£10 (as 1987 issue) (Issued: 3,505).............	(4)	925
PBS04–**1988**	Britannia Proofs £25, £10 (as 1987 issue) (Issued: 894)...............	(2)	180
PBS05–**1989**	Britannia Proofs £100 – £10 (as 1987) (Issued: 2,268)...................	(4)	925
PBS06–**1989**	Britannia Proofs £25, £10 (as 1987 issue) (Issued: 451)..................	(2)	190
PBS07–**1990**	Britannia Proofs, £100-£10, gold with the addition of silver alloy (4282, 4287, 4292, 4297) (Issued: 527)	(4)	1050
PBS08–**1991**	Britannia Proofs, as PS153 (Issued: 509)......	(4)	1050
PBS09–**1992**	Britannia Proofs, as PS153 (Issued: 500)......	(4)	1050
PBS10–**1993**	Britannia Proofs, as PS153 (Issued: 462)......	(4)	1050
PBS11–**1994**	Britannia Proofs, as PS153 ((Issued: 435)......	(4)	1075
PBS12–**1995**	Britannia Proofs, as PS153 (Issued: 500)......	(4)	1050
PBS13–**1996**	Britannia Proofs, as PS153 (Issued: 483)......	(4)	1050
PBS14–**1997**	Britannia proofs £100, £50, £25, £10 (4283, 4288, 4293, 4298) (Issued: 892)......	(4)	1300
PBS15–**1998**	Britannia proofs £100, £50, £25, £10 (4450, 4460, 4470, 4480) (Issued: 750)......	(4)	1050
PBS16–**1999**	Britannia Proofs, as PS161 (Issued: 740)......	(4)	1050
PBS17–**2000**	Britannia Proofs, as PS161 (Issued: 750)......	(4)	1050
PBS18–**2001**	Britannia Proofs £100, £50, £25, £10 (4451, 4461, 4471, 4481) (Issued: 1,000)......	(4)	1200
PBS19–**2002**	Britannia Proofs, as PBS17 (Issued: 945)	(4)	1050
PBS20–**2003**	Britannia Proofs £100, £50, £25, £10 (4452, 4462, 4472, 4482) (Issued: 1,250)......	(4)	1100
PBS21–**2003**	Britannia Proofs £50, £25, £10 (4462, 4472, 4482) (Issued: 825)...	(3)	525
PBS22–**MD**	Britannia £100 set of four different designs, 1987, 1997, 2001, 2003 (4281,4283,4451,4452) (Edition: 2,500)......	(4)	1800
PBS23–**2004**	Britannia Proofs, as PBS15 (Issued: 973)	(4)	1050
PBS24–**2004**	Britannia Proofs, £50, £25, £10 (4460,4470, 4480) (Issued: 223)...	(3)	525
PBS25–**2005**	Britannia Proofs, £100, £50, £25, £10 (4453, 4463, 4473, 4483) (Issued: 1,439)......	(4)	1125
PBS26–**2005**	Britannia Proofs, £50, £25, £10 (4463, 4473, 4483) (Issued: 417)......	(3)	525
PBS27–**2006**	Britannia Proofs, as PBS15 (Edition: 1,250)	(4)	1145
PBS28–**2007**	Britannia Proofs, £100, £50, £25, £10 (4454, 4464, 4474 and 4484) (Edition: 1,250......	(4)	1195

£

Gold Coin Proof Sets

PCGS1–**2002**	Commonwealth Games 'Bimetallic' £2 (4573, 4574, 4575 and 4576) in gold (Issued: 315)..	(4)	1400
PGJS1–**2002**	'Golden Jubilee' £5, 'Bimetallic' £2, 'English' £1, 50p to 1p and Maundy coins, 4p-1p in gold proof (4555, 4570, 4594, 4610, 4630, 4650, 4670, 4212-4215) (Issued: 2,002)	(13)	3500
PGBNS–**2006**	"Bimetallic" Isambard Brunel" £2 (4581) and "Bimetallic" "Paddington Station" £2 (4582) gold proofs (Edition: taken from individual coin limits)...	(2)	770
PGVCS–**2006**	"Victoria Cross" 50 pence (4617), "Wounded Colleague" 50 pence (4618) gold proof (Edition: taken from individual coin limits)........	(2)	650
PGBS1–**MD**	Set of four £1 coins "Forth Rail Bridge" (4595), "Menai Straits Bridge" (4596) "MacNiell's Egyptian Arch" (4597) and "Gateshead Millennium Bridge" (4598) in gold proof (Edition: 300 sets taken from individual coin limits)...	(4)	1500

Pattern Proof sets

PPS1–**2003**	Silver proof set of £1 designs with plain edge and hallmark (4595A, 4596A, 4597A, 4598A) (Edition: 7,500)	(4)	98
PPS2–**2003**	Gold proof set of £1 designs with plain edge and hallmark (4595A, 4596A, 4597A, 4598A) (Edition: 3,000)	(4)	1300
PPS3–**2004**	Silver proof set of £1 designs with plain edge and hallmark (4595B, 4596B, 4597B, 4598B) (Edition: 5,000).......................	(4)	98
PPS4–**2004**	Gold proof set of £1 designs with plain edge and hallmark (4595B, 4596B, 4597B, 4598B) (Edition: 2,250).......................	(4)	1300

APPENDIX I

A SELECT NUMISMATIC BIBLIOGRAPHY

Listed below is a selection of general books on British numismatics and other works that the specialist collector will need to consult.

General Books:

BROOKE, G. C. *English Coins.* 3rd ed., 1966.

CHALLIS, C. E. (ed.) *A New History of the Royal Mint.* 1992

GRUEBER, H. A. *Handbook of the Coins of Great Britain and Ireland.* Revised 1970

KENYON, R. Ll. *Gold Coins of England.* 1884

NORTH, J. J. *English Hammered Coinage*, Vol. I, c. 650-1272. 1994; Vol. II, 1272-1662. 1991

SUTHERLAND, C. H. V. *English Coinage, 600-1900.* 1972

Specialist Works:

ALLEN, D. *The Origins of Coinage in Britain: A Reappraisal.* Reprint 1978

ALLEN, D. F. *The Coins of the Coritani.* (SCBI no. 3) 1963

ALLEN, D. F. *English Coins in the British Museum: The Cross-and-Crosslets ('Tealby') type of Henry II.* 1951

ARCHIBALD, M. M. and BLUNT, C. E. *British Museum. Anglo-Saxon Coins. Athelstan to the reform of Edgar.* 924-c 973. 1986

ASKEW, G. *The Coinage of Roman Britain.* (1951) Reprinted 1980.

BESLY, E. M. *Coins and Medals of the English Civil War.* 1990

BLACKBURN, M. A. S. *Anglo-Saxon Monetary History.* 1986

BLUNT, C. E. and WHITTON, C. A. *The Coinages of Edward IV and of Henry VI (Restored).*

BLUNT, C. E., STEWART, B.H.I.H. and LYON, C.S.S. *Coinage in Tenth-Century England. From Edward the Elder to Edgar's Reform.* 1989

BRAND, J.D. *The English Coinage 1180-1247: Money, Mints and Exchanges* 1994

BROOKE, G. C. *English Coins in the British Museum: The Norman Kings.* 1916

BROWN, I. D. and DOLLEY, M. *Bibliography of Coin Hoards of Great Britain and Ireland 1500-1967.* 1971

CARSON, R. A. G. *Mints, Dies and Currency. Essays in Memory of Albert Baldwin.* 1971

DE JERSEY, P. *Coinage in Iron Age Armorica.* 1994

DOLLEY, R. H. M. (ed.). *Anglo-Saxon Coins; studies presented to Sir Frank Stenton.* 1964

GRIERSON, P. and BLACKBURN, M. A. S. *Medieval European Coinage, vol. 1, The Early Middle Ages.* 1986

HOBBS, R. *British Iron Age Coins in the British Museum.* 1996

KEARY, C. and GREUBER, H. *English Coins in the British Museum: Anglo-Saxon Series.* 1887, reprinted, 1970, 2 volumes.

LAKER, A. J. *The portrait Groats of Henry VIII.* 1978

LAWRENCE, L. A. *The Coinage of Edward III from 1351.*

LINECAR, H. W. A. *The Crown Pieces of Great Britain and the British Commonwealth.* 1962

— — *English Proof and Pattern Crown-Size Pieces.* 1968

MACK, R. P. *The R. P. Mack Collection, Ancient British, Anglo-Saxon and Norman Coins.* (SCBI no. 20) 1973

MANVILLE, H. E. *Encyclopedia of British Numismatics. Numismatic Guide to British and Irish Periodicals 1731-1991.* 1993

MANVILLE, H. E. and ROBERTSON, T. J. *An Annotated Bibliography of British Numismatic Auction Catalogues from 1710 to the Present.* 1986

MARSH, M. A. *The Gold Half Sovereign.* 2nd Edition, revised 2004

MARSH, M. A. *The Gold Sovereign.* 2nd Edition 1999

MASS, J. P. *The J. P. Mass collection of English Short Cross Coins 1180-1247.* (SCBI 56). 2001

NORTH, J. J. *Edwardian English Silver Coins 1279-1351.* (SCBI 39) 1989

NORTH, J. J. and PRESTON-MORLEY, P. J. *The John G. Brooker Collection: Coins of Charles I.* (SCBI 33) 1984

PECK, C. W. *English Copper, Tin and Bronze Coins in the British Museum, 1558-1958.* 1970

RAYNER, P.A. *The English Silver Coinage from 1649.* 5th ed. 1992

REECE, R. *Coinage in Roman Britain,* 1987.

ROBINSON, Dr. B. *The Royal Maundy.* 1992

RUDING, REV. R. *Annals of the Coinage of Great Britain.* 3rd Edition 1840

SEAR, D. R. *Roman Coins and their Values.* 4th Edition (1999) Reprinted 2000

SEAR, DAVID R. *The History and Coinage of the Roman Imperators 49-27 BC.* 1998

THOMPSON, J. D. A. *Inventory of British Coin Hoards, A.D. 600-1500.* 1956

VAN ARSDELL, R. *Celtic Coinage of Britain.* 1989.

VAN ARSDELL, R. D. *The Coinage of the Dobunni.* 1994

WHITTON, C. A. *The Heavy Coinage of Henry VI.*

WILSON, A. and RASMUSSEN, M. *English Patten, Trial and Proof Coin in Gold, 1547-1968.* 2000

WOODHEAD, P. *English Gold Coins 1257-1603. The Herbert Schneider Collection, vol. 1* (SCBI 47) 1996

— — *English Gold Coins 1603-20th Century. The Herbert Schneider Collection, vol. 2* (SCBI 57) 2002

WREN, C. R. *The Short-cross coinage 1180-1247. Henry II to Henry III. An illustrated Guide to Identification.* 1992

— — *The Voided Long-Cross Coinage 1247-1279. Henry III and Edward I.* 1993

— — *The English Long-Cross Pennies 1279-1489. Edward I-Henry VII.* 1995

For further references to British hammered coinage see *Sylloge of Coins of the British Isles,* a serial publication now comprising 54 volumes cataloguing collections in private hands and institutions. For full list of the 54 volumes published to date in this series, please contact Spink at the address below.

Other authoritative papers are published in the *Numismatic Chronicle, British Numismatic Journal and Spink's Numismatic Circular.* A complete book list is available from Spink & Son Ltd., 69 Southampton Row, Bloomsbury, London WC1B 4ET. Tel: 020 7563 4046 Fax: 020 7563 4068.

APPENDIX II

LATIN OR FOREIGN LEGENDS ON ENGLISH COINS

A DOMINO FACTUM EST ISTUD ET EST MIRABILE IN OCULIS NOSTRIS.
(This is the Lord's doing and it is marvellous in our eyes: *Psalm 118.23.*) First used on
'fine' sovereign of Mary.

AMOR POPULI PRAESIDIUM REGIS. (The love of the people is the King's
protection.) Reverse legend on angels of Charles I.

ANNO REGNI PRIMO, etc. (In the first year of the reign, etc.) Used around the edge of
many of the larger milled denominations.

CHRISTO AUSPICE REGNO. (I reign under the auspice of Christ.) Used extensively in
the reign of Charles I.

CIVIUM INDUSTRIA FLORET CIVITAS. (By the industry of its people the State
flourishes.) On the 1951 Festival Crown of George VI.

CULTORES SUI DEUS PROTEGIT. (God protects His worshippers.) On gold double
crowns and crowns of Charles I.

DECUS ET TUTAMEN. (An ornament and a safeguard: Virgil, *Aenid, v.262.*) This
inscription on the edge of all early large milled silver was suggested by Evelyn, he
having seen it on the vignette in Cardinal Richelieu's Greek Testament, and of course
refers to the device as a means to prevent clipping. This legend also appears on the edge
of U.K. and Northern Ireland one pound coins.

DIEU ET MON DROIT. (God and my right.) On halfcrowns of George IV and later
monarchs

DIRIGE DEUS GRESSUS MEOS. (May the Lord direct my steps.) On the 'Una' Five
pounds of Queen Victoria.

DOMINE NE IN FURORE TUO ARGUAS ME. (O Lord, rebuke me not in Thine anger:
Psalm 6, 1.). First used on the half-florin of Edward III and then on all half-nobles.

D*omi*N*us* D*eus* O*mnipotens* REX. (Lord God, Almighty King.) Viking coins.

DUM SPIRO SPERO. (Whilst I live, I hope.) On the coins struck at Pontefract Castle
during the Civil War after Charles I had been imprisoned.

EXALTABITUR IN GLORIA. (He shall be exalted in glory.) On all quarter-nobles.

EXURGAT DEUS ET DISSIPENTUR INIMICI EIUS. (Let God arise and let His
enemies be scattered: *Psalm* 68, 1.) On the Scottish ducat and early English coins of
James I (VI) and was chosen by the King himself. Also on Charles I, civil war, and
Declaration coins,

FACIAM EOS IN GENTEM UNAM. (I will make them one nation: *Ezekiel, 37, 22.*) On
unites and laurels of James I.

FLORENT CONCORDIA REGNA. (Through concord kingdoms flourish.) On gold unite
of Charles I and broad of Charles II.

HANC DEUS DEDIT. (God has given this, i.e. the crown .) On siege-pieces of Pontefract
struck in the name of Charles II.

HAS NISI PERITURUS MIHI ADIMAT NEMO. (Let no one remove these [letters] from
me under penalty of death.) On the edge of crowns and half-crowns of Cromwell.

HENRICUS ROSAS REGNA JACOBUS. (Henry united the roses, James the kingdoms.)
On English and Scottish gold coins of James I (VI).

HONI SOIT QUI MAL Y PENSE. (Evil to him who evil thinks.) The Motto of the Order
of the Garter, first used on the Hereford (?) halfcrowns of Charles I. It also occurs on
the Garter Star in the centre of the reverse of the silver coins of Charles II, but being so
small it is usually illegible; it is more prominent on the coinage of George III.

ICH DIEN. (I serve.) Aberystwyth Furnace 2d, and Decimal 2p. The motto of The Prince
of Wales.

INIMICOS EJUS INDUAM CONFUSIONE. (As for his enemies I shall clothe them with shame: *Psalm 132, 18.*) On shillings of Edward VI struck at Durham House, Strand.

JESUS AUTEM TRANSIENS PER MEDIUM ILLORUM IBAT. (But Jesus, passing through the midst of them, went His way: *Luke iv. 30.*) The usual reverse legend on English nobles, ryals and hammered sovereigns before James I; also on the very rare Scottish noble of David II of Scotland and the unique Anglo-Gallic noble of Edward the Black Prince.

JUSTITIA THRONUM FIRMAT. (Justice strengthens the throne.) On Charles I half-groats and pennies and Scottish twenty-penny pieces.

LUCERNA PEDIBUS MEIS VERBUM EST. (Thy word is a lamp unto my feet: *Psalm 119, 105.*) Obverse legend on a rare half-sovereign of Edward VI struck at Durham House, Strand.

MIRABILIA FECIT. (He made marvellously.) On the Viking coins of (?) York.

NEMO ME IMPUNE LACESSIT. (No-one provokes me with impunity.) On the 1984 Scottish one pound. Motto of The Order of the Thistle.

NUMMORUM FAMULUS. (The servant of the coinage.) The legend on the edge of the English tin coinage at the end of the seventeenth century.

O CRUX AVE SPES UNICA. (Hail! O Cross, our only hope.) On the reverse of all half-angels.

PAX MISSA PER ORBEM. (Peace sent throughout the world.) The reverse legend of a pattern farthing of Anne.

PAX QUÆRITUR BELLO. (Peace is sought by war.) The reverse legend of the Cromwell broad.

PER CRUCEM TUAM SALVA NOS CHRISTE REDEMPTOR. (By Thy cross, save us, O Christ, our Redeemer.) The normal reverse of English angels.

PLEIDIOL WYF I'M GWLAD. (True am I to my country.) Used on the 1985 Welsh one pound. Taken from the Welsh National Anthem.

POST MORTEM PATRIS PRO FILIO. (After the death of the father for the son.) On siege-pieces struck at Pontefract in 1648 (old style) after the execution of Charles I.

POSUI DEUM ADJUTOREM MEUM. (I have made God my Helper: *comp. Psalm* 54, 4.) Used on many English and Irish silver coins from Edward III until 1603. Altered to POSUIMUS and NOSTRUM on the coins of Philip and Mary.

PROTECTOR LITERIS LITERÆ NUMMIS CORONA ET SALUS. (A protection to the letters [on the face of the coin], the letters [on the edge] are a garland and a safeguard to the coinage.) On the edge of the rare fifty-shilling piece of Cromwell.

QUÆ DEUS CONJUNXIT NEMO SEPARET. (What God hath joined together let no man put asunder: *Matthew 19, 6.*) On the larger silver English and Scottish coins of James I after he succeeded to the English throne.

REDDE CUIQUE QUOD SUUM EST. (Render to each that which is his own.) On a Henry VIII type groat of Edward VI struck by Sir Martin Bowes at Durham House, Strand.

RELIGIO PROTESTANTIVM LEGES ANGLIÆ LIBERTAS PARLIAMENTI. (The religion of the Protestants, the laws of England, the liberty of the Parliament.) This is known as the 'Declaration' and refers to Charles I's declaration to the Privy Council at Wellington, 19 September, 1642; it is found on many of his coins struck at the provincial mints during the Civil War. Usually abbreviated to REL:PROT:LEG: ANG:LIB:PAR:

ROSA SINE SPINA. (A rose without a thorn.) Found on some gold and small coins of Henry VIII and later reigns.

RUTILANS ROSA SINE SPINA. (A dazzling rose without a thorn.) As last but on small gold only.

SCUTUM FIDEI PROTEGET EUM or EAM. (The shield of faith shall protect him, or her.) On much of the gold of Edward VI and Elizabeth.

SIC VOS NON VOBIS (Thus we labour but not for ourselves). 1994 £2 Bank of England.

TALI DICATA SIGNO MENS FLUCTUARI NEQUIT. (Consecrated by such a sign the mind cannot waver: from a hymn by Prudentius written in the fourth century, entitled 'Hymnus ante Somnum'.) Only on the gold 'George noble' of Henry VIII.

TIMOR DOMINI FONS VITÆ. (The fear of the Lord is a fountain of life: *Proverbs, 14, 27.*) On many shillings of Edward VI.

TVAETVR VNITA DEVS. (May God guard these united, i.e. kingdoms.) On many English Scottish and Irish coins of James I.

VERITAS TEMPORIS FILIA. (Truth, the daughter of Time.) On English and Irish coins of Mary Tudor.

Some Royal Titles:

REX ANGL*orum*—King of the English.

REX SAXONIORVM OCCIDENTALIVM —King of the West Saxons.

DEI GRA*tia* REX *ANGLiae* ET FRANC*iae DomiNus HYBerniae ET AQVITaniae*—By the Grace of God, King of England and France, Lord of Ireland and Aquitaine.

D*ei GRAtia Magnae Britanniae, FRanciae ET Hiberniae REX Fidei Defensor BRunsviciensis ET Luneburgen-sis Dux, Sacri Romani Imperii Archi-THesaurarius ET ELector*=By the Grace of God, King of Great Britain, France and Ireland, Defender of the Faith, Duke of Brunswick and Luneburg, High Treasurer and Elector of the Holy Roman Empire.

BRITANNIARUM REX —King of the Britains (i.e. Britain and British territories overseas).

BRITT:OMN:REX:FID:DEF:IND:IMP: —King of all the Britains, Defender of the Faith, Emperor of India.

VIVAT REGINA ELIZABETHA — Long live Queen Elizabeth. On the 1996 £5 Queen's 70th birthday £5 crown.

APPENDIX III

NUMISMATIC CLUBS AND SOCIETIES

Coin News, The Searcher and *Treasure Hunting,* are the major monthly magazines covering numismatics. Spink's *Numismatic Circular* is long established, its first issue appeared in December 1892, and is now published 6 times a year. Many local clubs and societies are affiliated to the British Association of Numismatic Societies, (B.A.N.S) which holds an annual Congress. Details of your nearest numismatic club can be obtained from the Hon. Secretary, Philip Mernick, British Association of Numismatic Societies, c/o General Services, 42 Campbell Road, London E3 4DT email: bans@mernicks.com.

The two principal learned societies are the Royal Numismatic Society, c/o Department of Coins and Medals, the British Museum, Great Russell Street, Bloomsbury, London WC1B 3DG, and the British Numismatic Society, c/o The Secretary, C.R.S. Farthing, c/o Warburg Institute, Woburn Square, London WC1H 0AH Tel: 01329 284 661. Both these societies publish an annual journal.

APPENDIX IV

MINTMARKS AND OTHER SYMBOLS ON ENGLISH COINS

A Mintmark (*mm.*), is a term borrowed from Roman and Greek numismatics where it showed the place of mintage; it was generally used on English coins to show where the legend began (a religious age preferred a cross for the purpose). Later, this mark, since the dating of coins was not usual, had a periodic significance, changing from time to time. Hence it was of a secret or 'privy' nature; other privy marks on a coin might be the code-mark of a particular workshop or workman. Thus a privy mark (including the *mintmark.*) might show when a coin was made, or who made it. In the use of precious metals this knowledge was necessary to guard against fraud and counterfeiting.

Mintmarks are sometimes termed 'initial marks' as they are normally placed at the commencement of the inscription. Some of the symbols chosen were personal badges of the ruling monarch, such as the rose and sun of York, or the boar's head of Richard III, the dragon of Henry Tudor or the thistle of James I; others are heraldic symbols or may allude to the mint master responsible for the coinage, e.g. the *mm.* bow used on the Durham House coins struck under John Bowes and the WS mark of William Sharrington of Bristol.

A table of mintmarks is given on the next page. Where mintmarks appear in the catalogue they are sometimes referred to only by the reference number, in order to save space, i.e. *mm. 28* (=mintmark Sun), *mm.28/74 (=mm.* Sun on obverse, *mm.* Coronet on reverse), *mm. 28/-* (=*mm.* Sun on obverse only).

MINTMARKS AND OTHER SYMBOLS

1	Edward III, Cross 1 (Class B+C).	
2	Edward III, broken Cross 1 (Class D).	
3	Edward III, Cross 2 (Class E)	
4	Edward III, Cross 3 (Class G)	
5	Cross Potent (Edw. III Treaty)	
6	Cross Pattée (Edw. III Post Treaty Rich. III).	
7	(a) Plain of Greek Cross. (b) Cross Moline.	
8	Cross Patonce.	
9	Cross Fleuree.	
10	Cross Calvary (Cross on steps).	
11	Long Cross Fitchée.	
12	Short Cross Fitchée.	
13	Restoration Cross (Hen. VI).	
14	Latin Cross.	
15	Voided Cross (Henry VI).	
16	Saltire Cross.	
17	Cross and 4 pellets.	
18	Pierced Cross.	
19	Pierced Cross & pellet.	
20	Pierced Cross & central pellet.	
21	Cross Crosslet.	
22	Curved Star (rayant).	
23	Star.	
24	Spur Rowel.	
25	Mullet.	
26	Pierced Mullet.	
27	Eglantine.	
28	Sun (Edw. IV).	
29	Mullet (Henry V).	
30	Pansy.	
31	Heraldic Cinquefoil (Edw. IV).	
32	Heraldic Cinquefoil (James I).	
33	Rose (Edw. IV).	
34	Rosette (Edw. IV).	
35	Rose (Chas. I).	
36	Catherine Wheel.	
37	Cross in circle.	
38	Halved Sun (6 rays) & Rose.	
39	Halved Sun (4 rays) & Rose.	
40	Lis-upon-Half-Rose.	
41	Lis-upon-Sun & Rose.	
42	Lis-Rose dimidiated.	
43	Lis-issuant-from-Rose.	
44	Trefoil.	
45	Slipped Trefoil, James I (1).	
46	Slipped Trefoil, James I (2).	
47	Quatrefoil.	
48	Saltire.	
49	Pinecone.	
50	Leaf (-mascle, Hen. VI).	
51	Leaf (-trefoil, Hen. VI).	
52	Arrow.	
53	Pheon.	
54	A.	
55	Annulet.	
56	Annulet-with-pellet.	
57	Anchor.	
58	Anchor & B.	
59	Flower & B.	
60	Bell.	
61	Book.	
62	Boar's Head (early Richard III).	
63	Boar's Head (later Richard III).	
64	Boar's Head, Charles I.	
65	Acorn (a) Hen. VIII (b) Elizabeth.	
66	Bow.	
67	Br. (Bristol, Chas. I).	
68	Cardinal's Hat.	
69	Castle (Henry VIII).	
70	Castle with H.	
71	Castle (Chas. I).	
72	Crescent (a) Henry VIII (b) Elizabeth.	
73	Pomegranate. (Mary; Henry VIII's is broader).	
74	Coronet.	
75	Crown.	
76	Crozier (a) Edw. III (b) Hen. VIII.	
77	Ermine.	
78	Escallop (Hen. VII).	
79	Escallop (James I).	
80	Eye (in legend Edw. IV).	
81	Eye (Parliament).	
82	Radiate Eye (Hen. VII).	
83	Gerb.	
84	Grapes.	
85	Greyhound's Head.	
86	Hand.	
87	Harp.	
88	Heart.	
89	Helmet.	
90	Key.	
91	Leopard's Head.	
91A	Crowned Leopard's Head with collar (Edw. VI).	
92	Lion.	
93	Lion rampant.	
94	Martlet.	
95	Mascle.	
96	Negro's Head.	
97	Ostrich's Head.	
98	P in brackets.	
99	Pall.	
100	Pear.	
101	Plume.	
102	Plume. Aberystwyth and Bristol.	
103	Plume. Oxford.	
104	Plume. Shrewsbury.	
105	Lis.	
106	Lis.	
107	Portcullis.	
108	Portcullis, Crowned.	
109	Sceptre.	
110	Sunburst.	
111	Swan.	
112	R in brackets.	
113	Sword.	
114	T (Henry VIII).	
115	TC monogram.	
116	WS monogram.	
117	y or Y.	
118	Dragon (Henry VII).	
119	(a) Triangle (b) Triangle in Circle.	
120	Sun (Parliament).	
121	Uncertain mark.	
122	Grapple.	
123	Tun.	
124	Woolpack.	
125	Thistle.	
126	Figure 6 (Edw. VI).	
127	Floriated cross.	
128	Lozenge.	
129	Billet.	
130	Plume. Bridgnorth or late declaration	
131	Two lions.	
132	Clasped book.	
133	Cross pomée.	
134	Bugle.	
135	Crowned T (Tournai, Hen VIII)	
136	An incurved pierced cross	

The reign listed after a mintmark indicates that from which the drawing is taken. A similar mm. may have been used in another reign and will be found in the chronological list at the beginning of each reign.

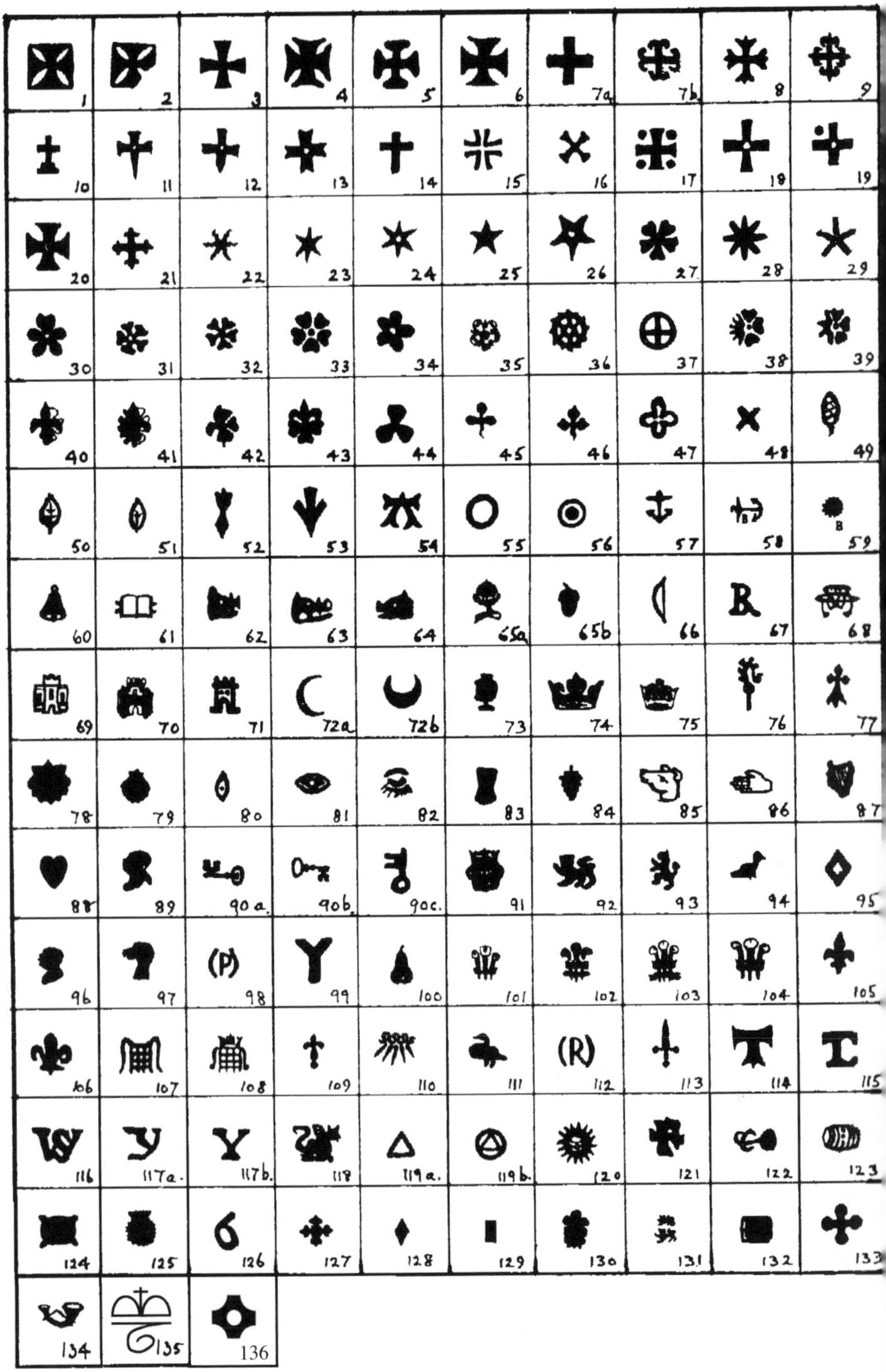
1 2 3 4 5 6 7a 7b 8 9
10 11 12 13 14 15 16 17 18 19
20 21 22 23 24 25 26 27 28 29
30 31 32 33 34 35 36 37 38 39
40 41 42 43 44 45 46 47 48 49
50 51 52 53 54 55 56 57 58 59
60 61 62 63 64 65a 65b 66 67 68
69 70 71 72a 72b 73 74 75 76 77
78 79 80 81 82 83 84 85 86 87
88 89 90a. 90b. 90c. 91 92 93 94 95
96 97 98 99 100 101 102 103 104 105
106 107 108 109 110 111 112 113 114 115
116 117a. 117b. 118 119a. 119b. 120 121 122 123
124 125 126 127 128 129 130 131 132 133
134 135 136